CROSS-REFERENCE INDEX

CROSS-REFERENCE INDEX
A Subject Heading Guide

Thomas V. Atkins, Editor-in-Chief

Editors: Janina Atkins, Marianne Sabados Benedikt,
Edwin V. Erbe, Jr., Louise Rosenberg Fluk, Alan Weiner, Darrow Wood

R.R. BOWKER COMPANY
New York & London, 1974
A Xerox Education Company

XEROX

Published by R. R. Bowker Co. (A Xerox Education Company)
1180 Avenue of the Americas, New York, N.Y. 10036
Copyright © 1974 by Xerox Corporation
Printed and bound in the United States of America

Library of Congress Cataloging in Publication Data
Atkins, Thomas V
Cross-reference index: a subject heading guide.
1. Subject headings.
2. Cross references (Cataloging) I. Title.
Z695.A954   025.3'3   73-23066
ISBN 0-8352-0680-7

Preface

The wealth of information, facts, data, and opinion stored in libraries is, as everyone rightly suspects, tremendous. But, as many researchers have found out, so are the difficulties in retrieving desired information. Using the proper subject heading is of critical importance in effective library research. Subject headings bring together material dealing principally or exclusively with a given subject, whatever the actual terms applied to it by the authors, or whatever terms are applied to it at different times. However, there is no standard set of subject headings used in common by all libraries and all indexes to periodicals and newspapers. There is no single key word which provides open access to all available sources of information on a given subject. *Cross-Reference Index* is a practical guide for library retrieval that will indicate to researchers the most appropriate subject headings in catalogs and indexes.

Whether student or professor, layman or specialist, the researcher faces numerous problems. Sometimes the same subject heading may be used in different catalogs and indexes to cover different material, or significantly different aspects of the same subject. Sometimes the same material will be covered by two, three, or more subject headings, depending on different orientation of the cataloger or indexer. At other times, the same material may be split into exceedingly narrow subject headings in one source, and joined with other related material under one broad subject heading in another source. For, as in every language, the language of library classification responds to terminology introduced by increasing scientific knowledge, and to popular modes of expression—giving new meanings to old words, adding new words and concepts, and dropping old ones. For example, an author may refer to racial pride of the Blacks, but the subject matter may be classified at different times in different sources as Race awareness, Negro race, or Black nationalism. All this makes it necessary for the conscientious researcher not to limit the search to one subject heading but to consult other comparable and related terms, a task that *Cross-Reference Index* simplifies.

Cross-Reference Index lists subject headings drawn from the six sources described below. Each subject heading designates the terms used by each of the six sources, or it directs the reader to the most appropriate heading, as detailed in the section "How to Use This Book."

LC The Library of Congress subject headings[1] are generally used in catalogs of college, university, and research libraries.

SEARS Sears[2] subject headings are generally used in the catalogs of school and public libraries.

RG *The Readers' Guide to Periodical Literature*[3] is an index listing by subject, and often by author and title, periodical articles from a selected list of popular, nontechnical, and a few scholarly magazines in all fields.

NYT The *New York Times Index*,[4] described as a "condensed classified history of the word as recorded daily in the newspaper," is useful for current events and comments, and up-to-date statistical information.

PAIS *Public Affairs Information Service Bulletin*[5] indexes by subject, and sometimes by author, current books, pamphlets, periodical articles, government documents, and other material in the fields of economics and public affairs.

BPI *Business Periodical Index*[6] lists by subject articles from selected periodicals in the fields of accounting, advertising, automation, banking,

[1] U.S. Library of Congress. Subject Cataloging Division. *Subject Headings Used in the Dictionary Catalog of the Library of Congress*, 7th ed., ed. by Marguerite V. Quattlebaum, Washington, 1966. *Library of Congress Subject Headings Supplements 1966–1971 Cumulation.* Berkeley, University of California, September 1972.
[2] Westby, Barbara M. *Sears List of Subject Headings*, 10th ed. N.Y., H. W. Wilson, 1972.
[3] *Readers' Guide to Periodical Literature.* N.Y., H. W. Wilson, Vols 27–31 (March 1967–February 1972).
[4] *New York Times Index.* N.Y., The New York Times. Vols. 1970–1972.
[5] *Bulletin of the Public Affairs Information Service.* N.Y., Public Affairs Information Service. Vols. 1–58 (1915–September 1972).
[6] *Business Periodicals Index.* N.Y., H. W. Wilson. Vols. August 1970–July 1971, August 1971–July 1972.

communication, economics, finance and investments, insurance, labor, management, marketing, public relations, and taxation.

The work in compiling *Cross-Reference Index* was shared by many librarians. In addition to their general contributions in selecting main term subject headings, the following editors were specifically responsible for selecting corresponding, comparable, and related terms in a particular source: Janina Atkins, Lehman College, City University of New York, SEARS; Edwin V. Erbe, Jr., Kean College of New Jersey, NYT; Louise Rosenberg Fluk, Baruch College, City University of New York, RG; Alan Weiner, Baruch College, City University of New York, PAIS; and Darrow Wood, New York City Community College, City University of New York, BPI. Marianne Sabados Benedikt, The City College, City University of New York, was responsible for the coordination of the whole effort, supervision of production of the man-

uscript, as well as assistance in general editing. The idea for the book, as well as the responsibility for the scope and general editing of *Cross-Reference Index* belongs to editor-in-chief Thomas V. Atkins, Baruch College, City University of New York. Work on this volume ended on July 30, 1973.

A word of thanks is due to Lynda Sloan for her helpful advice on preparation of the material and to Bowker editors: David Biesel, R. Cary Bynum, and Patricia Glass Schuman.

This is a first attempt to bring together, in one reference tool, the many variations of subject headings from the most widely used library catalogs and indexes—to be used by both librarians and individual researchers. No book of its kind can be free of errors or omissions. The editors stand ready to acknowledge them and to consider with gratitude any suggestions that might result in the improvement of later editions of *Cross-Reference Index*.

How to Use This Book

Subject headings in *Cross-Reference Index* are arranged alphabetically. Subheadings of a subject and inverted subheadings are alphabetized without regard to punctuation. The subject heading is in the form of (1) a *see* reference, (2) a *use* reference, or (3) a main term entry.

(1) A *see* reference directs the researcher to look under an equivalent main term because the chosen subject heading is not ordinarily used by the six sources examined in compiling *Cross-Reference Index.*

> **APARTHEID.** *See* Segregation

(2) A *use* reference means that the chosen heading is used by one of the six sources and the researcher is directed to one or more main terms which identifies other comparable and related subject headings and indicates their appearance in particular sources.

> **ANTI-SEMITISM.** *Use* Discrimination

(3) A main term entry gives the fullest spectrum of terms in the subject of a researcher's inquiry. Main terms have been chosen for their usefulness, currency, and pertinence to a wide area of research. All subject headings are reproduced as they are found in their respective sources, except for capitalization of words which, for the sake of consistency, has been made uniform in *Cross-Reference Index.*

EXPLANATION OF A MAIN TERM ENTRY

DISCRIMINATION
Scope: General works on social discrimination based on race, religion, sex, social minority status, or other factors. See also headings beginning with Discrimination in . . .
LC   ——; s.a. Civil rights; Human relations; Prejudices and antipathies; Race awareness; Race problems; Segregation; Social problems
SEARS   ——; s.a. Blacks—Segregation; Sex discrimination; Toleration
RG   ——; s.a. Anti-Semitism; Minorities

NYT   ——; s.a. Minorities (ethnic, racial, religious)
PAIS   ——; s.a. Discrimination in education; Prejudice
BPI   RACE DISCRIMINATION; s.a. Discrimination in employment; Discrimination in housing

The scope note indicates, where necessary, the limits of the subject matter. In some cases a main term entry will include a general "see also" reference. This reference applies to headings which may be found in most but not necessarily all of the sources listed. If the researcher is interested in one of these subject headings, he/she should go directly to the source indicated.

In the listing of source material, a dash (——) denotes that the subject heading in the source is the same as the main term heading. A specific "see also" (s.a.) reference gives subject headings for corresponding, comparable, and related material found in that source. The headings are in alphabetical order, rather than in order of importance, and lead to broader and narrower aspects of the main term.

For reasons of space, no attempt was made to duplicate the most obvious s.a. references among the sources. Only subject headings most indicative of the nature of the sources are given. The listings are neither exhaustive nor definitive and the researcher, bearing in mind the flux and rapidity of change in the use of subject headings, is advised to pursue terms not listed under a specific source which may nevertheless appear in that source.

SUBHEADINGS

All the sources frequently use subheadings to help narrow the subject matter. In the example below, Segregation is the subheading.

> DISCRIMINATION; s.a. Blacks—Segregation

The researcher is urged to explore these subheadings to advantage. Some common subheadings are geographical and chronological. Listed below, by form and content, are other possible subheadings frequently found in the cited sources but not generally used in *Cross-Reference Index.*

FORM

Bibliography	Dictionaries and Encyclopedias
Case Studies	Directories
Collections	Handbooks, Manuals, etc.

CONTENT

Commerce and Industry	Politics and Government
Description and Travel	Social Conditions
Economic Conditions	Social Life and Customs
Foreign Relations	Statistics
History	Study and Teaching
Laws and Regulations	

A researcher interested in public housing, for example, could further narrow the search to various aspects of public housing by using the appropriate subheading, e.g., Public housing—Laws and regulations.

OMISSIONS

Cross-Reference Index, in common with other lists of subject headings, usually omits, except as examples, certain popular categories of entries. These include proper names (names of persons, families, places, political units, geographical features, nationalities, national languages and literatures, battles, treaties, tribes, etc.), corporate names (names of societies, institutions, government bodies, etc.), and common names (names of animals, birds, flowers, trees, tools, etc.). All these names, however, may be found to some degree in all sources listed in *Cross-Reference Index.*

A

ABACUS. *Use* Calculating Machines

ABANDONED CHILDREN
LC ——; s.a. Child welfare; Children
SEARS CHILD WELFARE; s.a. Children—Institutional care; Foster home care
RG CRUELTY TO CHILDREN; s.a. Desertion and non-support; Orphans and orphan-asylums
NYT CHILDREN AND YOUTH—ABANDONED CHILDREN; s.a. Children and youth—Child abuse; Orphans and orphanages
PAIS CHILD WELFARE; s.a. Adoption; Foster care
BPI CHILD WELFARE; s.a. Children—Law; Orphans and orphan asylums

ABANDONMENT OF PROPERTY
LC ——; s.a. Abandonment of automobiles; Property
SEARS PROPERTY; s.a. Landlord and tenant; Real estate
RG BUILDINGS, ABANDONED; s.a. Farms, Worn-out; Landlord and tenant
NYT ABANDONED PROPERTY; s.a. Property and investments; Real estate
PAIS ABANDONMENT OF AUTOMOBILES; Buildings, Abandoned
BPI PROPERTY; s.a. Community property; Eminent domain

ABILITY, INFLUENCE OF AGE ON. *Use* Adult Education; Age and Employment; Mind and Body

ABBEYS
See also names of individual abbeys, e.g., Westminster Abbey.
LC ——; s.a. Cathedrals; Convents and nunneries
SEARS ——; s.a. Church architecture; Monasteries
RG ——; s.a. Church architecture; Monasteries
NYT RELIGION AND CHURCHES; s.a. Roman Catholic religious orders
PAIS CONVENTS AND NUNNERIES
BPI CHURCHES; s.a. Cathedrals; subd. *Churches* under names of cities, e.g., Boston—Churches

ABBREVIATIONS
LC ——; s.a. Acronyms; Signs and symbols
SEARS ——; s.a. Ciphers; Shorthand
RG ——; s.a. Acronyms; Symbols
NYT ALPHABETS; s.a. Codes (ciphers); Language and languages

PAIS ——; s.a. Signs and symbols
BPI ——; s.a. Acronyms; Trademarks

ABDUCTION
LC ——; s.a. Criminal law; Kidnapping
SEARS OFFENSES AGAINST THE PERSON; s.a. Criminal law; Hijacking of airplanes
RG KIDNAPPING; s.a. Political crimes and offenses; Ransom
NYT KIDNAPPING; s.a. Children and youth—Crime and criminals; Crime and criminals; Extortion and blackmail
PAIS KIDNAPPING; s.a. Criminal law
BPI KIDNAPPING, POLITICAL; s.a. Crime and criminals; Criminal law

ABILITY
LC ——; s.a. Mental tests; Success; Talented students
SEARS ——; s.a. Leadership; Musical ability, etc.
RG ——; s.a. Executive ability; Learning, Psychology of
NYT Specific fields concerned, e.g., Legal profession; s.a. Education and schools; Mental tests
PAIS ——; s.a. Creative ability; Tests, Mental
BPI ——; s.a. Academic achievement; Creative ability; Success

ABILITY—TESTING
LC ——; s.a. Educational tests and measurements; Mental tests; Prediction of scholastic success
SEARS ——; s.a. Educational tests and measurements; Mental tests
RG APTITUDE TESTS; s.a. Ability tests; Intelligence tests
NYT MENTAL TESTS
PAIS TESTS, ABILITY; s.a. Tests, Educational; Tests, Mental
BPI ABILITY TESTS; s.a. Intelligence; Personality tests; Self-evaluation

ABILITY GROUPING IN EDUCATION. *Use* Educational Psychology; Grading and Marking (Students); Nongraded Schools; Tests, Mental

ABILITY TESTING. *Use* Occupational Aptitude Tests; Personality Tests; Tests, Mental

ABNORMAL CHILDREN. *See* Exceptional Children

ABOLITIONISTS. *Use* Slavery

1

ABORIGINES. *See* Native Races

ABORTION
LC ——; s.a. Birth control; Childbirth; Sex and law
SEARS ——; s.a. Birth control; Illegitmacy
RG ——; s.a. Birth control; Women's liberation movement
NYT ——; s.a. Birth control and planned parenthood; Births
PAIS ——; s.a. Birth control; Sex and law
BPI ——; s.a. Birth control; Family size; Population

ABSENCE FROM SCHOOL. *See* School Attendance

ABSENTEEISM
Scope: Works on absentee ownership.
LC ——; s.a. Agriculture—Economic aspects; Land tenure; Taxation
SEARS REAL ESTATE; s.a. Landlord and tenant; Property
RG PROPERTY; s.a. Farm ownership; Land; Property tax
NYT REAL ESTATE; s.a. Agriculture and agricultural products; Property and investments; Taxation
PAIS REAL PROPERTY; s.a. Farm ownership; Land tenure; Property tax
BPI PROPERTY; s.a. Land; Real property

ABSENTEEISM (Labor)
LC ——; s.a. Labor and laboring classes; Labor supply; Sick leave
SEARS ——; s.a. Labor and laboring classes; Personnel management
RG ABSENTEEISM; s.a. Business and professional women; Labor and laboring classes
NYT LABOR—U.S.—ABSENTEEISM; s.a. Alcoholism; White collar workers
PAIS ——; s.a. Labor; Labor productivity; Sickness
BPI ——; s.a. Sick leave; Work roles

ABSOLUTISM. *See* Despotism

ABSTINENCE. *See* Temperance

ABSTRACT ART. *See* Art, Abstract

ABSTRACTING
LC ——; s.a. Indexing
SEARS INDEXING; s.a. Cataloging; Files and filing
RG INDEXING; s.a. Information services; Subject headings
NYT INDEXES AND INDEXING; s.a. Data processing (information processing) equipment and systems
PAIS ABSTRACTING AND INDEXING SERVICES; s.a. Abstracts; subd. *Abstracts* under specific headings, e.g., Banking—Abstracts
BPI ABSTRACTING AND INDEXING SERVICES; s.a. Indexing; Information storage retrieval systems

ABSTRACTS OF TITLE. *Use* Deeds

ABUSE OF POWER. *See* Despotism

ACADEMIC ACHIEVEMENT
LC ——; s.a. Prediction of scholastic success; Success

SEARS LEARNING AND SCHOLARSHIP; s.a. Culture; Education
RG STUDENT ACHIEVEMENTS; s.a. Performance contracts (education); Prediction of scholastic success; Underachievers
NYT EDUCATION AND SCHOOLS; s.a. Colleges and universities
PAIS ——; s.a. Success; Learning and scholarship
BPI EDUCATION; s.a. Success; Ability

ACADEMIC DEGREES. *See* Degrees, Academic

ACADEMIC FREEDOM
LC TEACHING, FREEDOM OF; s.a. Church and education; Loyalty oaths; Toleration
SEARS ——; s.a. Civil rights; Intellectual freedom; Liberty
RG ——; s.a. Colleges and universities—Political control; Propaganda in the schools
NYT ——; s.a. Colleges—U.S.—Teachers; Teachers and school employees
PAIS ——; s.a. Church and education; Loyalty oaths
BPI TEACHERS; s.a. Education and state; Teaching

ACADEMIC LIBRARIES. *See* Libraries and Librarians

ACADEMIES. *See* Learning and Scholarship

ACCELERATED READING. *See* Reading

ACCELERATORS (Electrons, etc.). *Use* Nuclear Physics

ACCENTS AND ACCENTUATION
LC Subd. *Accents and Accentuation* under specific languages, e.g., German language—Accents and accentuation
SEARS Subd. *Pronunciation* under specific languages, e.g., Spanish language—Pronunciation; s.a. Language and languages; Versification
RG Subd. *Pronunciation* under specific languages, e.g., Portuguese language—Pronunciation
NYT LANGUAGE AND LANGUAGES—[name of language]—ACCENTS AND ACCENTUATION; s.a. Speech
PAIS LANGUAGES; s.a. Speech
BPI SPEECH; s.a. Language and languages—[name of language]

ACCEPTANCES
Scope: Works on trade or bank acceptances as credit instruments.
LC ——; s.a. Bills of exchange; Discount
SEARS BILLS OF EXCHANGE; s.a. Banks and banking; Negotiable instruments
RG NEGOTIABLE INSTRUMENTS; s.a. Charge accounts (retail trade); Debtor and creditor
NYT BANKS AND BANKING; s.a. Commerce; Credit
PAIS ——; s.a. Bills of exchange; Discount
BPI ——; s.a. Banks and banking; Negotiable instruments

ACCIDENT LAW. *Use* Negligence; Occupations, Dangerous; Personal Injuries

ACCIDENTS
See also subd. *Accidents* under subjects, e.g., Firemen—Accidents

LC ——; s.a. Disasters; Medical emergencies
SEARS ——; s.a. Explosions; Fires; Occupations, Dangerous
RG ——; s.a. First aid in illness and injury; Traffic accidents
NYT ACCIDENTS AND SAFETY; s.a. Disasters
PAIS ——; Automobiles—Safety measures
BPI ——; s.a. Accidents, Industrial; Disaster relief; Rescue work

ACCIDENTS, TRAFFIC. *Use* Traffic Accidents

ACCIDENTS AND SAFETY. *Use* Accidents; Disasters; First Aid in Illness and Injury; Mines and Mineral Resources; Negligence; Personal Injuries; Rescue Work; Safety Appliances; Traffic Accidents; Traffic Safety

ACCLIMATIZATION
LC ——; s.a. Animal introduction; Man—Influence of climate
SEARS ADAPTATION (Biology); s.a. Man—Influence of environment; Plant introduction
RG ——; s.a. Altitude, Influence of; Weather—Mental and physiological effects
NYT WEATHER; s.a. Environment
PAIS ENVIRONMENT; s.a. Ecology; Human ecology
BPI WEATHER; s.a. Climate; Ecology; Industry and weather

ACCOMPLICES. *Use* Theft

ACCOUNTABILITY. *See* Liability (Law)

ACCOUNTANTS
See also personal names of accountants and corporate names of accounting firms.
LC ——; s.a. Auditors; Tax consultants
SEARS ——
RG ——; s.a. Tax consultants
NYT ACCOUNTING AND ACCOUNTANTS; s.a. Company reports
PAIS ——; s.a. Negro accountants; Tax consultants
BPI ——; s.a. Accounting; Tax consultants

ACCOUNTING
See also subd. *Accounting* under names of industries, professions, etc., e.g., Corporations—Accounting; Petroleum industry—Accounting
LC ——; s.a. Auditing; Bookkeeping; Double entry bookkeeping; Single entry bookkeeping
SEARS ——; s.a. Auditing; Budget in business; Business arithmetic; Cost accounting
RG ——; s.a. Billing; Controllership; Financial statements; Institutional accounting
NYT ACCOUNTING AND ACCOUNTANTS; s.a. Budgets and budgeting; Company reports
PAIS ——; s.a. Accounts receivable; Auditing; Balance sheets; Cost accounting
BPI ——; s.a. Auditing; Financial statements

ACCOUNTING MACHINES. *Use* Machine Accounting; Office Equipment and Supplies

ACCOUNTS, COLLECTING OF. *See* Collecting of Accounts

ACCOUNTS CURRENT. *Use* Collecting of Accounts

ACCOUNTS RECEIVABLE. *Use* Collecting of Accounts; Debtor and Creditor

ACCREDITATION (Education)
LC ——; s.a. subd. *Accreditation* under types of schools, e.g., High schools—Accreditation
SEARS COLLEGES AND UNIVERSITIES; s.a. Junior colleges; Teachers colleges
RG COLLEGES AND UNIVERSITIES—ACCREDITATION; s.a. Junior colleges—Accreditation; Library schools and education
NYT EDUCATION AND SCHOOLS—U.S.—ACCREDITATION; s.a. Colleges and universities—U.S.—Accreditation
PAIS See subd. *Accreditation* under types of schools, e.g., High schools—Accreditation
BPI COLLEGES AND UNIVERSITIES; s.a. Degrees, Academic; Junior colleges

ACCULTURATION
LC ——; s.a. Assimilation (sociology); Ethnology; Socialization
SEARS ——; s.a. Civilization; East and west; Race problems
RG ——; s.a. Social groups; Social psychology; subd. *Acculturation* under names of groups, e.g., Indians of South America—Acculturation
NYT CULTURE; s.a. Archeology and anthropology; Sociology
PAIS ——; s.a. Assimilation (sociology); Intercultural education
BPI CULTURAL RELATIONS; s.a. Intercultural education; Sociology

ACHIEVEMENT, ACADEMIC. *See* Academic Achievement

ACOUSTICS. *Use* Sound and Sound Recording

ACROBATS AND ACROBATICS. *Use* Gymnastics

ACRONYMS
Scope: Acronyms in general and terms on English acronyms.
LC ——; s.a. Abbreviations; Anonyms and pseudonyms; Code names
SEARS ——; s.a. Abbreviations; Signs and symbols
RG ——; s.a. Abbreviations; Names
NYT CODES (Ciphers)
PAIS ABBREVIATIONS; s.a. Signs and symbols
BPI ——; s.a. Abbreviations; Trademarks

ACT OF STATE. *Use* Rule of Law

ACTING
See also names of actors, e.g., Fonda, Peter.
LC ——; s.a. Drama; Theater
SEARS ——; s.a. Drama in education; Pageants
RG ——; s.a. Gesture; Pantomime
NYT ENTERTAINMENT AND AMUSEMENTS; s.a. amusement names and means, e.g., Theater
PAIS ACTORS; s.a. Theater
BPI ACTORS AND ACTRESSES; s.a. Theater; Theatrical agencies

ACTING AS A PROFESSION. *Use* Moving Pictures as a Profession

ACTIONS AND DEFENSES. *Use* Trials

ACTIVITY SCHOOLS. *See* Educational Planning and Innovations

ACTORS AND ACTRESSES. *Use* Acting; Drama; Entertainers; Motion Pictures as a Profession; Theater

ACTUARIAL SCIENCE. *See* Insurance, Life

ACUPOINT. *See* Chiropractic

ACUPUNCTURE
LC	——; s.a. Counter-irritants; Reflexotherapy
SEARS	MEDICINE; s.a. Theropeutics
RG	——; s.a. Health; Medicine—China (People's Republic)
NYT	——; s.a. Anesthesia and anesthetics; Medicine and health
PAIS	MEDICINE
BPI	——; s.a. Medicine; Physiology

ADAGES. *See* Proverbs; Quotations

ADAPTION (Biology). *Use* Acclimatization; Ecology; Evolution; Genetics

ADAPTIVE CONTROL SYSTEMS. *Use* Automation

ADDING MACHINES. *Use* Machine Accounting; Office Equipment and Supplies

ADDRESSES. *See* Lectures and Lecturing; Speeches, Addresses, etc.

ADDRESSING MACHINES AND DEVICES. *Use* Office Equipment and Supplies

ADHESIVES
LC	——; s.a. Cement; Headings beginning with the word "Adhesive"
SEARS	——; s.a. names of adhesives, e.g., Cement, Glue, etc.
RG	——; s.a. Epoxy adhesives; Glue
NYT	——; s.a. Bandages; Glue
PAIS	ADHESIVES INDUSTRY; s.a. Cement industry
BPI	——; s.a. Resinous products—Adhesives; Sealing (packages)

ADJECTIVE LAW. *See* Procedure (Law)

ADJUSTMENT, SOCIAL. *Use* Mental Hygiene; Social Psychology

ADMINISTRATION. *See* Civil Service; Management; State, The

ADMINISTRATION, PUBLIC. *Use* Public Administration

ADMINISTRATION OF JUSTICE. *See* Justice, Administration of

ADMINISTRATIVE AGENCIES. *Use* Public Administration

ADMINISTRATIVE DISCRETION. *Use* Rule of Law

ADMINISTRATIVE LAW. *Use* Civil Service; Judicial Power; Local Government; Ordinances, Municipal; Public Administration; Rule of Law

ADMINISTRATIVE PROCEDURE. *Use* Procedure (Law)

ADMINISTRATIVE REMEDIES. *Use* Public Administration

ADMISSION OF NON-IMMIGRANTS. *Use* Emigration and Immigration

ADOLESCENCE
LC	——; s.a. Youth
SEARS	——; s.a. Child study; Youth
RG	——; s.a. High school students; Puberty
NYT	CHILDREN AND YOUTH; s.a. Families and family life
PAIS	YOUTH; s.a. Children; Rural youth
BPI	YOUTH; s.a. Children; Students

ADOLESCENT PSYCHIATRY. *Use* Child Psychiatry; Psychiatry

ADOPTION
LC	——; s.a. Abandoned Children; Children, Adopted; Parent and child (law)
SEARS	——; s.a. Child welfare; Foster home care
RG	——; s.a. Children, Adopted; Foster home care
NYT	ADOPTIONS; s.a. Black markets; Orphans and orphanages
PAIS	——; s.a. Foster care; Parent and child (law)
BPI	——; s.a. Foster parents; Orphans and orphan asylums

ADULT EDUCATION
LC	——; s.a. Ability, Influence of age on; Continuing education centers; Education of adults; Education of the aged
SEARS	——; s.a. Education of prisoners; Social group work
RG	——; s.a. Aged—Education; Self culture; University extension
NYT	EDUCATION AND SCHOOLS; s.a. Colleges and universities; Education and schools—[N.Y.C.]—Adult education
PAIS	EDUCATION, ADULT; s.a. Evening and continuation schools; Extension education; Illiteracy
BPI	——; s.a. Education of workers; Occupational training

ADULTERY
LC	——; s.a. Criminal law; Sex crimes
SEARS	DIVORCE; s.a. Domestic relations; Marriage
RG	——; s.a. Marriage and law; Sexual ethics
NYT	——; s.a. Divorce, separations and annulments; Marriages
PAIS	DIVORCE; s.a. Alimony; Marriage—Annulment
BPI	DIVORCE; s.a. Broken homes; Marriage

ADULTHOOD. *Use* Age (Psychology); Growth

ADVENTURE AND ADVENTURES. *Use* Explorers; Voyages and Travels

ADVERTISING
Scope:	Also subd. by topic. e.g., Advertising—Banks and banking, and by type, e.g., Advertising, Classified
LC	——; s.a. Art and industry; Marketing; Propaganda

SEARS ——; s.a. Advertising copy; Commercial art; Mail order business; Propaganda; Radio advertising
RG ——; s.a. Consumption (economics); Publicity; Television advertising
NYT ——; s.a. Market research; Mass communications
PAIS ——; s.a. Legal adversiting; Public relations; Sales promotion
BPI ——; s.a. Advertising—Men exposed to; Editorial advertising (broadcasting); subd. *Advertising* under various subjects, e.g., Airlines—Advertising; Sales management

ADVERTISING, DIRECT-MAIL. *Use* Mail-order Business

ADVERTISING, FRAUDULENT
LC ADVERTISING LAWS; s.a. Trade regulation
SEARS ——
RG ——; s.a. Advertising ethics; Better business bureaus
NYT ADVERTISING—U.S.—MISLEADING AND DECEPTIVE ADVERTISING; s.a. Consumer protection; Frauds and swindling
PAIS ——; s.a. Consumer protection
BPI ——; s.a. Better business bureaus; Television advertising, Fraudulent

ADVERTISING—NEGROES, APPEAL TO. *Use* Negroes and Business

ADVERTISING, NEWSPAPER. *Use* Newspapers

ADVERTISING, OUTDOOR. *Use* Billboards; Posters

ADVERTISING, POLITICAL
LC ——; s.a. Electioneering; Radio in politics; Television in politics
SEARS POLITICS, PRACTICAL; s.a. Campaign literature; Propaganda; Television in politics
RG ——; s.a. Political campaigns; Television in politics
NYT ELECTIONS (U.S.)—ADVERTISING; s.a. Democratic/Republican party—Finances; Elections (U.S.)—Television and radio; Presidential election of [year of election]
PAIS ——; s.a. Radio—Political uses; Television—Political uses
BPI POLITICAL ADVERTISING; s.a. Political campaigns; Radio and politics; Television and politics

ADVERTISING—PRINTING. *Use* Printing Industry

ADVERTISING—PSYCHOLOGICAL ASPECTS. *Use* Marketing Research

ADVERTISING, PUBLIC SERVICE. *Use* Public Relations

ADVERTISING—RESEARCH. *Use* Marketing Research

ADVERTISING, SUBLIMINAL. *Use* Mental Suggestion

ADVERTISING—WOMEN, APPEAL TO. *Use* Woman

ADVERTISING APPROPRIATIONS. *Use* Budget in Business

ADVERTISING ART. *Use* Commercial Art

ADVERTISING COPY
LC ——; s.a. Copy writers
SEARS ——; s.a. Authorship
RG ——; s.a. Authorship; Creative writing
NYT ADVERTISING; s.a. subjects advertised, e.g., Autos
PAIS ——; s.a. Advertising men
BPI ——; s.a. Advertising; Advertising research; Advertising—Themes; Copy writers

ADVERTISING ETHICS. *Use* Advertising, Fraudulent; Business Ethics

ADVERTISING LAWS. *Use* Advertising, Fraudulent

ADVERTISING LAYOUT AND TYPOGRAPHY. *Use* Printing Industry

ADVERTISING RESEARCH. *Use* Marketing Research

ADVOCATES. *See* Lawyers

AERIAL PHOTOGRAPHY
LC AERIAL PHOTOGRAMMETRY; s.a. Photographic surveying; Photography, Aerial
SEARS PHOTOGRAPHY, AERIAL
RG PHOTOGRAPHY, AERIAL; s.a. Mapping, Aerial; Photogrammetry
NYT ——
PAIS PHOTOGRAPHY, AERIAL; s.a. Aerial reconaissance
BPI PHOTOGRAPHY, AERIAL; s.a. Earth—Photographs from space; Moon—Photographs from space

AERIAL RECONAISSANCE. *Use* Aerial Photography; Spies

AERIAL WARFARE. *Use* Air Warfare; War

AERODROMES. *See* Airports

AERODYNAMICS
LC ——; s.a. Aeronautics; Dynamics
SEARS ——; s.a. Aeronuatics; Ground cushion phenomena
RG ——; s.a. Airfoils; Birds—Flight
NYT AERONAUTICS; s.a. Aerospace industries and sciences; Airplanes; Astronautics
PAIS AVIATION; s.a. Air transport; Airplanes
BPI ——; s.a. Turbulence; Wind tunnels

AERONAUTICS
LC ——; s.a. Aerodynamics; Astronautics
SEARS ——; s.a. Flight; Ground cushion phenomena; Helicopters
RG ——; s.a. Airfoils; Balloon ascensions; Birds—Flight; Kites
NYT ——; s.a. Aerospace industries and sciences; Airplanes; Astronautics
PAIS AVIATION; s.a. Air Transport; Airlines
BPI ——; s.a. Aerodynamics; Airplanes; Astronautics; Turbulence; Wind tunnels

AERONAUTICS, COMMERCIAL. *Use* Air Mail Service

AERONAUTICS, COMMERCIAL. *Use* Carriers; Freight and Freightage

AERONAUTICS—CRIMES. *Use* Offenses Against Public Safety

AERONAUTICS—LAWS AND REGULATIONS. *Use* Airspace (International Law)

AERONAUTICS—MEDICAL ASPECTS. *See* Aviation Medicine

AERONAUTICS, MILITARY. *Use* Air Warfare; Armaments; Military Art and Science

AERONAUTICS, MILITARY—STUDY AND TEACH-ING. *Use* Military Service as a Profession

AERONOMY. *See* Atmosphere, Upper

AEROPLANES. *Use* Airplanes

AEROSOLS. *Use* Packaging

AEROSPACE (Law). *See* Airspace (International Law)

AEROSPACE INDUSTRIES
LC ——; s.a. Aeroplane industry and trade; Guided missile industries
SEARS ——; s.a. Airplane industry and trade; Ballistic missiles; Outerspace; Space flight
RG ——; s.a. Airplane industry; Industrial demobilization
NYT AEROSPACE INDUSTRIES AND SCIENCES; s.a. Aeronautics; Astronautics, Communications satellites
PAIS ——; s.a. Airplane industry; Guided missiles
BPI ——; s.a. Avionics industry; Guided missiles industry

AESTHETICS
LC ——; s.a. Art; Philosophy; Value
SEARS ESTHETICS; s.a. Art appreciation; Color
RG ——; s.a. Form (art); Nature (aesthetics)
NYT ART; s.a. Culture; Philosophy
PAIS ESTHETICS; s.a. Art; Communist esthetics
BPI ART; s.a. Art literature; Philosophy

AFFECTION. *See* Love

AFFIDAVITS. *Use* Oaths

AFFORESTATION. *Use* Forests and Forestry; Natural Resources; Trees

AFRICAN LITERATURE. *Use* Black Literature; Literature; Negroes in Literature

AFRO-AMERICAN STUDIES
LC ——; s.a. Negroes—Education; Negroes—History—Study and Teaching
SEARS ——; s.a. Black studies; Blacks—Education
RG ——; s.a. African studies; Negro colleges and universities—Curriculum; Negroes—History—Study and teaching
NYT BLACK STUDIES; s.a. Colleges and universities; Negroes (in U. S.)
PAIS ——; s.a. Negroes—Education
BPI NEGROES—EDUCATION; s.a. Education; Intercultural education

AFRO-AMERICANS. *See* Negroes

AFTER-DINNER SPEECHES. *Use* Speeches, Addresses, etc.

AFTER-IMAGES. *Use* Senses and Sensation

AFTER-LIFE. *See* Heaven

AGE
LC ——; s.a. subd. *Age* under subjects, e.g. Domestic animals—Age; Longevity
SEARS AGED; s.a. Old Age; Youth
RG ——; s.a. Aging, Longevity
NYT AGED AND AGE; s.a. Medicine and health; Nursing homes; Population and vital statistics
PAIS ——; s.a. Longevity; Old age
BPI ——; s.a. Middle age; Old age

AGE (Law)
LC ——; s.a. Age of consent; Capability and disability
SEARS AGE AND EMPLOYMENT; s.a. Marriage; Suffrage
RG AGE; s.a. Marriage; Suffrage
NYT LAW AND LEGISLATION; s.a. Children and youth; Marriages
PAIS AGE OF MAJORITY (Law)
BPI ——; s.a. Age and employment; Child labor

AGE (Psychology)
LC ——; s.a. Adulthood; Childishness; Naturation (psychology)
SEARS OLD AGE; s.a. Middle age
RG ——; s.a. Age and intelligence; Maturity
NYT PSYCHOLOGY AND PSYCHOLOGISTS; s.a. Aged and age
PAIS AGE
BPI AGE; s.a. Psychology

AGE AND AGED. *Use* Geriatrics; Insurance, Social; Invalids; Middle Age; Nursing Homes; Old Age; Old Age Assistance; Old Age Homes; Retirement

AGE AND AGED—MEDICAL CARE. *Use* Old Age Assistance; Medical Care

AGE AND EMPLOYMENT
LC ——; s.a. Ability, Influence of age on; Age (law); Life span—Productive
SEARS ——; s.a. Child labor; Discrimination in employment
RG ——; s.a. Equal pay for equal work; Retirement; Working life, Length of
NYT AGED AND AGE; s.a. Labor—U. S.—Older workers; Labor—U. S.—Youth, Employment of
PAIS ——; s.a. Child labor; Working life, Length of
BPI ——; s.a. Child labor; Lifespan, Productive

AGE AND INTELLIGENCE. *Use* Age (Psychology)

AGE GROUPS. *Use* Conflict of Generations; Demography; Middle Age; Population

AGE OF CONSENT. *Use* Age (Law)

AGE OF MAJORITY. *Use* Age (Law)

AGED, KILLING OF
LC ——; s.a. Euthanasia; Manners and customs
SEARS AGED; s.a. Murder; Old age
RG EUTHANASIA; s.a. Gerontology; Murder

NYT   MERCY DEATH (Euthanasia); s.a. Aged and
       age; Medicine and health
PAIS   OLD AGE
BPI   AGED; s.a. Geriatrics; Old age

AGENCY (Law). *Use* Partnership

AGENTS PROVOCATEURS. *Use* Police; Spies

AGGRESSION (International law). *Use* International
       Offenses; International Relations; War (Inter-
       national law)

AGGRESSIVENESS (Psychology). *Use* Violence

AGNOSTICISM. *Use* Atheism; Belief and Doubt; God;
       Rationalism; Religion; Secularism; Truth

AGRARIAN QUESTION. *See* Land Tenure

AGREEMENTS. *See* Contracts

AGRICULTURAL ADMINISTRATION. *Use* Subsides

AGRICULTURAL ASSISTANCE. *Use* Economic
       Assistance, Foreign; Prices

AGRICULTURAL CHEMICALS. *Use* Chemical In-
       dustries; Fertilizers and Manures; Soils

AGRICULTURAL COLONIES. *Use* Colonization

AGRICULTURAL COOPERATIVE. *Use* Collective
       Farming

AGRICULTURAL CREDIT. *Use* Banks and Banking;
       Credit; Mortgages

AGRICULTURAL EDUCATION. *Use* Vocational
       Education

AGRICULTURAL EQUIPMENT. *Use* Farms and
       Farming

AGRICULTURAL ESTIMATING AND REPORTING.
       Use Crops

AGRICULTURAL EXHIBITIONS. *Use* Fairs

AGRICULTURAL EXPERIMENT STATIONS. *Use*
       Farms and Farming

AGRICULTURAL LABOR. *Use* Migrant Labor;
       Peasantry

AGRICULTURAL MACHINERY INDUSTRY AND
       TRADE. *Use* Machinery—Trade and
       Manufacture

AGRICULTURAL PESTS. *Use* Bacteriology, Agricul-
       tural; Pests; Weeds; Zoology, Economic

AGRICULTURAL PRICE SUPPORTS. *Use* Prices

AGRICULTURAL PROCESSING
Scope: Works on the processing of agricultural products
       in general, see also specific products, e.g., Fruit
       and vegetables.
LC   ———; s.a. Food industry and trade; Fruit pro-
       cessing (canning and preserving)
SEARS FARM PRODUCE; s.a. Food-preservation
RG   FARM PRODUCE; s.a. Canneries; Food industry
NYT   AGRICULTURE AND AGRICULTURAL PRO-
       DUCTS; s.a. Food and grocery trade

PAIS   AGRICULTURAL PRODUCTS; s.a. Commodi-
       ties; Surplus agricultural products
BPI   FARM PRODUCE; s.a. Commodities; Crops

AGRICULTURAL PRODUCTS. *Use* Crops; Farm
       Produce

AGRICULTURE
See also headings beginning with the word *Agricultural*;
       names of agricultural products, e.g., Wheat; and
       types of farming, e.g., Truck farming.
LC   ———; Agriculture and state; Farmers; Food
       industry and trade; Land; Seasonal industries
SEARS ———; s.a. Domestic animals; Farms; Pastures
RG   ———; s.a. Dairying; Tillage
NYT   AGRICULTURE AND AGRICULTURAL PROD-
       UCTS; s.a. Food and grocery trade; Pesticides
       and pests
PAIS   ———; s.a. Collective farming; headings beginning
       with the word *Farm*
BPI   ———; s.a. Crops; Farm produce

AGRICULTURE, COOPERATIVE. *Use* Collective
       Farming; Cooperation; Cooperative Societies;
       Farms and Farming

AGRICULTURE AND STATE. *Use* Agriculture; Indus-
       try and State

AGRONOMY. *See* Agriculture

AID TO DEVELOPING COUNTRIES. *See* Economic
       Assistance, Foreign

AIR—POLLUTION
LC   ———; s.a. Air; Man—influence of nature; Odors;
       Smog; Smoke
SEARS ———; s.a. Noise—Pollution; Smoke prevention
RG   ———; s.a. Plants, Effect of air pollution on;
       subd. *Pollution* under subjects and names of
       cities, e.g., Automobiles—Pollution
NYT   ———; s.a. Atmosphere, Lower; Environ-
       ment; Smoke; Water pollution
PAIS   ———; s.a. Airplanes—Exhaust; Atmosphere;
       Motor vehicles—Exhaust
BPI   ———; s.a. Automobile engines—Exhaust; Fuel—
       Smokeless fuel; Fume control; Incinerators;
       Pollution

AIR—PURIFICATION. *Use* Disinfection and Disin-
       fectants

AIR—PURIFICATION. *Use* Sanitation

AIR BASES. *Use* Airports

AIR CONDITIONING
LC   ———; s.a. Environmental engineering (buildings);
       Ventilation
SEARS ———; s.a. Refrigeration and refrigerating ma-
       chinery; Ventilation
RG   ———; s.a. Air filters; subd. *Air conditioning*
       under subject, e.g., School buildings—Air
       conditioning
NYT   AIR CONDITIONING AND VENTILATING;
       s.a. Fields of use, e.g., Housing—Air conditioning
       and ventilating

AIR CONDITIONING, *cont.*
PAIS   AIR CONDITIONING INDUSTRY; s.a. Office buildings—Air conditioning; Refrigeration industry
BPI   ——; s.a. Building—Heating and cooling aspects; Environmental engineering (buildings)

AIR DEFENSES. *Use* Air Warfare; Radar; United States—Defenses

AIR DEFENSES, CIVIL. *Use* Civil Defense

AIR FILTERS. *Use* Air Conditioning

AIR FREIGHT SERVICE. *Use* Airlines; Freight and Freightage

AIR MAIL SERVICE
LC   ——; s.a. Aeronautics, Commercial; Postal service
SEARS   ——; s.a. Aeronautics, Commercial; Postal service
RG   ——; s.a. Pigeon post; Rocket mail
NYT   POSTAL SERVICE; s.a. Airlines; Letters
PAIS   ——; s.a. Aviation, Commercial; Postal service
BPI   ——; s.a. Postal service, Airlines

AIR NAVIGATION. *See* Aeronautics

AIR RAID SHELTERS. *Use* Civil Defense

AIR SPACE (International law). *See* Airspace (International law)

AIR TRAFFIC CONTROL. *Use* Airspace (International law)

AIR TRANSPORT. *Use* Aerodynamics; Aeronautics; Airlines

AIR TRANSPORT — CRIMES. *Use* Kidnapping; Offenses Against Public Safety

AIR TRAVEL. *Use* Airlines

AIR WARFARE
See also names of wars with subd. *Aerial operations,* e.g., World War, 1939-1945—Aerial operations.
LC   ——; s.a. Bombing, Aerial; Military art and science; Projectiles, Aerial
SEARS   AERONAUTICS, MILITARY; s.a. Air defenses; Atomic warfare; Chemical warfare
RG   AERONAUTICS, MILITARY; s.a. Airplanes, Military; Aviation—Formation flying
NYT   ARMAMENT AND DEFENSE; s.a. Airplanes; U.S. armament and defense
PAIS   AERIAL WARFARE
BPI   AERONAUTICS, MILITARY; s.a. Air defenses; Airplanes, Military

AIRBORNE TROOPS. *Use* Parachuting

AIRCRAFT. *Use* Airplanes

AIRCRAFT CARRIERS. *Use* Naval Art and Science; Sea Power; Warships

AIRCRAFT PRODUCTION. *See* Aerospace Industries

AIRDROMES. *See* Airports

AIRDROP. *Use* Parachuting

AIRFOILS. *Use* Aerodynamics

AIRGLOW. *Use* Atmosphere, Upper

AIRLINES
See also names of specific airlines, e.g., Pilgrim.
LC   AIR LINES; s.a. Aeronautics; Air mail service; Airports; Airways
SEARS   AIR LINES; s.a. Aeronautics, Commercial; Airplanes
RG   ——; s.a. Aeronautics, Commercial; Air travel
NYT   ——; s.a. Airplanes; Transportation
PAIS   AIR TRANSPORT; s.a. Local service air lines
BPI   ——; s.a. Air freight service

AIRLINES—ACCIDENTS AND SAFETY. *Use* Radar

AIRLINES—HIJACKING. *Use* Kidnapping; Offenses Against Public Safety; Sabotage

AIRLINES—HOTEL OPERATIONS. *Use* Hotels, Taverns, etc.

AIRLINES—SUBSIDIES. *Use* Subsidies

AIRPLANE HIJACKING. *Use* Kidnapping; Offenses Against Public Safety; Sabotage

AIRPLANE INDUSTRY. *Use* Aerospace Industries

AIRPLANE INDUSTRY AND TRADE. *Use* Aerospace Industries

AIRPLANES
LC   AEROPLANES; s.a. Aerodynamics; Flying machines; Helicopters; Seaplanes
SEARS   ——; s.a. Balloons; Gliders (aeronautics); Propellers, Aerial
RG   ——; s.a. Air-Ships; Autogiros; Flight; Jet planes; Salvage (airplanes)
NYT   ——; s.a. Aerospace industries and sciences; Airlines; Armament and defense; Gliders
PAIS   ——; s.a. Aviation; Helicopters; Radar
BPI   ——; s.a. Aeronautics; Aerospace industries; Aircraft; Airplanes, Business

AIRPLANES, FREIGHT. *Use* Cargo Handling

AIRPLANES-INTERNATIONAL INCIDENTS. *Use* Airspace (International law)

AIRPLANES, JET. *Use* Jet Planes

AIRPLANES, MILITARY. *Use* Air Warfare

AIRPLANES—PHYSIOLOGICAL ASPECTS OF FLYING. *Use* Aviation Medicine

AIRPLANES, ROCKET-PROPELLED. *Use* Rockets (Aeronautics)

AIRPLANES, SUPERSONIC. *Use* Jet Planes

AIRPORTS
LC   ——; s.a. Access to airports; International airports
SEARS   ——; s.a. Air bases; Heliports
RG   ——; s.a. Seaplane bases; subd. *Airports* under names of cities
NYT   ——; s.a. Airlines; Helicopters—Heliports; subd. *Military Bases* under names of places, e.g., France—Military bases

PAIS   ——; s.a. Airport authorities
BPI   ——; s.a. Airport buildings; Heliports

AIRSHIPS. *Use* Airplanes

AIRSICKNESS. *Use* Aviation Medicine

AIRSPACE (International law)
LC   ——; s.a. Aeronautics—Laws and regulations; Jurisdiction over aircraft; Sovreignty
SEARS   SPACE LAW; s.a. Aeronautics and civilization; International law; Outer space
RG   ——; s.a. Air traffic control; Aviation—Laws and regulations
NYT   AIRPLANES—INTERNATIONAL INCIDENTS; s.a. International relations
PAIS   ——; s.a. Space, Outer; Space law
BPI   AIRSPACE (Law); s.a. Aeronautics—Laws and regulations; Air traffic control—Fee system

AIRWAYS. *Use* Airlines

ALBINOS AND ALBINISM. *Use* Color of Man

ALCHEMY. *Use* Chemistry

ALCOHOL
LC   ——; s.a. Beverages; Distillation; Liquors
SEARS   ——; s.a. Alcoholism; Liquor traffic
RG   ——; s.a. Distilleries; Liquor industry
NYT   ——; s.a. Alcoholism; Liquor
PAIS   ——; s.a. Distilling industry; Liquor industry
BPI   ——; s.a. Alcohol—Physiological effect; Alcoholism

ALCOHOL AND CHILDREN. *Use* Liquor Problem

ALCOHOL AND JEWS. *Use* Liquor Problem

ALCOHOL AND NEGROES. *Use* Liquor Problem

ALCOHOL AND WOMEN. *Use* Liquor Problem

ALCOHOL AND YOUTH. *Use* Liquor Problem

ALCOHOLICS. *Use* Liquor Problem; Temperance

ALCOHOLISM
LC   ——; s.a. Liquor problem; Prohibition; Temperance
SEARS   ——; s.a. Absenteeism (labor); Alcohol—Physiological effect; Temperance
RG   ——; s.a. Alcohol and youth; Liquor problem
NYT   ——; s.a. Alcohol; Labor—U. S.—Absenteeism; Liquor
PAIS   ——; s.a. Liquor problem; Personnel management—Alcohol problem
BPI   ——; s.a. Liquor problem; Personnel management—Liquor problem

ALCOHOLISM AND CRIME. *Use* Crime and Criminals

ALE. *Use* Beer and Brewing Industry

ALGAE
LC   ——; s.a. Agar; Diatoms
SEARS   ——; s.a. Marine plants
RG   ——; s.a. Red tide; Water bloom
NYT   SEAWEED; s.a. Marine biology; Oceans and oceanography

PAIS   SEAWEED INDUSTRY
BPI   ——; s.a. Carrageen; Algae as food

ALGEBRA, ABSTRACT. *Use* Logic, Symbolic and Mathematical

ALGEBRA, BOOLEAN. *Use* Logic, Symbolic and Mathematical

ALIEN LABOR. *Use* Aliens; Citizenship; Contract Labor; Emigration and Immigration; Labor and Laboring Classes; Migrant Labor; Migration of Nations; Native Labor

ALIENATION (Social psychology)
LC   ——; s.a. Social isolation; Social psychology
SEARS   ——; s.a. Human relations; Social psychology
RG   ——; s.a. Morale, National
NYT   PSYCHOLOGY AND PSYCHOLOGISTS; s.a. Children and youth—Behavior and training; Sociology
PAIS   SOCIAL PSYCHOLOGY; s.a. Human relations; Small groups
BPI   ——; s.a. Psychology; Social psychology

ALIENATION OF AFFECTIONS. *Use* Divorce

ALIENS
LC   ——; s.a. Allegiance; Emigration and immigration; Naturalization
SEARS   ——; s.a. Exiles; Immigration and emigration; Refugees
RG   ——; s.a. Alien labor; Citizenship
NYT   IMMIGRATION AND EMIGRATION; s.a. Citizenship; Minorities (ethnic, racial, religious); Refugees
PAIS   ——; s.a. Deportation; Diplomatic protection; Nationality
BPI   ——; s.a. Admission of nonimmigrants; Asylum, Right of; Repatriation

ALIMENTATION. *See* Nutrition

ALIMONY
LC   ——; s.a. Divorce; Separate maintenance
SEARS   DIVORCE; s.a. Desertion and non-support; Marriage
RG   ALIMONY; s.a. Desertion and non-support
NYT   DIVORCE, SEPARATIONS AND ANNULMENTS; s.a. Courts; Marriages
PAIS   ——; s.a. Desertion and non-support; Divorce
BPI   ——; s.a. Desertion and non-support; Divorce

ALLEGIANCE. *Use* Aliens; Loyalty; Patriotism

ALLEGORIES. *Use* Tales

ALLERGY
See also types of allergies, e.g., Hay fever.
LC   ——; s.a. Antihistamines; Immunity
SEARS   ——; s.a. Immunity
RG   ——; s.a. Drug allergy; Food allergy
NYT   ——; s.a. Antihistamines; Medicine and health; Skin
PAIS   RESPIRATORY ORGANS—DISEASES; s.a. Sickness
BPI   ——; s.a. Antihistamines; Medicines, Proprietary

ALLEYS. *See* Streets

ALLIANCES. *Use* Treaties

ALLITERATION. *Use* Versification

ALLOCATIONS, INDUSTRIAL. *See* Priorities, Industrial

ALLOTMENT OF LAND. *Use* Land Tenure

ALLOYS. *Use* Solder and Soldering

ALLUSIONS. *Use* Terms and Phrases

ALMANACS. *Use* Handbooks

ALPHABET
LC ——; s.a. Extinct languages; Phonetic alphabet; Transliteration; Writing
SEARS ——; s.a. Alphabets; Writing
RG ——; s.a. Calligraphy; Lettering
NYT ALPHABETS; s.a. Handwriting; Language and languages
PAIS LANGUAGES; s.a. subd. *Languages* under names of countries
BPI ——; s.a. Alphabets; Lettering

ALTERNATIVE CONVICTIONS. *Use* Judgments

ALTERNATIVE LIFE STYLE. *See* Subculture

ALTITUDE, INFLUENCE OF. *Use* Acclimatization; Man—Influence of Environment

ALTRUISM. *Use* Charity; Social Ethics; Wealth, Ethics of

ALUMINUM
LC ——; s.a. Creep of aluminum; Light metals
SEARS ——; s.a. Aluminum alloys; Alloys
RG ——; s.a. Metals; Plants, Effect of aluminum on
NYT ——; s.a. Containers and packaging; specific fields of use, e.g., Astronautics
PAIS ALUMINUM INDUSTRY; s.a. Bauxite industry
BPI ——; s.a. Aluminum industry; Bauxite

AMATEUR JOURNALISM. *Use* Press

AMATEUR RADIO STATIONS. *Use* Radio, Short Wave; Radio Stations

AMATEUR THEATRICALS. *Use* Theater

AMATEURISM (Sports). *Use* Athletes

AMBASSADORS. *Use* Diplomacy

AMBIGUITY. *Use* Semantics

AMBIVALENCE. *Use* Emotions

AMBULANCES
LC ——; s.a. Accidents; Vehicles
SEARS ACCIDENTS; s.a. Automobiles; First aid
RG ——; s.a. First aid in illness and injury; Hospitals—Emergency services
NYT AMBULANCE SERVICES; s.a. subd. *Ambulance Services* under Medicine and health, e.g., Medicine and health—N.Y.C.—Ambulance services
PAIS AMBULANCE SERVICE; s.a. Accidents; Motor vehicles
BPI ——; s.a. Accidents; Helicopters in medical service

AMBUSHES AND SURPRISES. *Use* Military Art and Science

AMENDMENTS (Parliamentary Practice). *Use* Parliamentary Practice

AMERICA—DISCOVERY AND EXPLORATION. *Use* Discoveries (Geography); Explorers

AMERICA—LITERATURES. *Use* Literature

AMERICAN DRAMA, ENGLISH DRAMA, ETC. *Use* Drama; Theater

AMERICAN LEGION. *Use* Veterans

AMERICAN LITERATURE. *Use* Black Literature; Literature

AMERICAN NEWSPAPERS. *Use* Blacks and the Press

AMERICAN STOCK EXCHANGE. *Use* Wall Street

AMERICAN STUDENTS ABROAD. *Use* Americans in Foreign Countries

AMERICAN STUDIES. *Use* Area Studies

AMERICAN TEACHERS IN FOREIGN COUNTRIES. *Use* Americans in Foreign Countries

AMERICAN TRAVELERS. *See* Americans in Foreign Countries; Travel

AMERICANISM. *Use* Loyalty; Nationalism

AMERICANISM (Catholic controversy). *Use* Catholic Church in the U.S.

AMERICANISMS
Scope: Works dealing with usage of words and idiomatic expressions peculiar to the U.S.
LC ——; s.a. English language in the U.S.; English language—Dialects
SEARS ——; s.a. English language—Dialects; English language
RG AMERICANISMS (Speech); s.a. English language—Dialects; Negro-English dialects; Slang
NYT LANGUAGE AND LANGUAGES—ENGLISH; s.a. Slang
PAIS ENGLISH LANGUAGE
BPI ENGLISH LANGUAGE; s.a. English language—Business English; Words

AMERICANIZATION. *Use* Citizenship

AMERICANS IN FOREIGN COUNTRIES
See also Americans in [name of country], e.g., Americans in Greece.
LC ——; s.a. U.S.—Officials and employees in foreign countries
SEARS ——
RG ——; s.a. American teachers in foreign countries; Travelers
NYT U.S.—AMERICANS ABROAD; s.a. Travel and resorts; U.S.—Foreign service
PAIS ——; s.a. American students abroad; Employment in foreign countries
BPI ——; s.a. U.S.—Armed forces—Europe, Western; Newspapers—Foreign correspondents

AMMUNITION
LC ——; s.a. Armaments; Bombs
SEARS ——; s.a. Explosives; Gunpowder

RG ——; s.a. Cartridges; Explosives
NYT ARMAMENT, DEFENSE AND MILITARY FORCES; s.a. Firearms; U.S. Armament and defense
PAIS ——; s.a. Armaments; Munitions
BPI ——; s.a. Firearms; Munitions; Projectiles

AMNESIA
LC ——; s.a. Aphasia; Memory
SEARS BRAIN—DISEASES; s.a. Memory; Mental illness
RG ——; s.a. Memory; Recall (psychology)
NYT ——; s.a. Memory; Mental health and disorders
PAIS MENTALLY HANDICAPPED; s.a. Mental illness
BPI MENTALLY HANDICAPPED; s.a. Mental illness; Brain—Diseases

AMNESTY
LC ——; s.a. Pardon; Punishment
SEARS PUNISHMENT; s.a. Crime and criminals; Criminal law
RG ——; s.a. Military service, Compulsory—Draft resisters; Political prisoners
NYT AMNESTIES; s.a. Crime and Criminals; Prisons and prisoners; U.S. Armament and defense—Draft
PAIS ——; s.a. Crime and criminals—Punishment; Pardon
BPI PUNISHMENT; s.a. Criminal law; Prisoners

AMORTIZATION. *Use* Loans

AMORTIZATION DEDUCTIONS. *Use* Depreciation

AMPHIBIANS. *Use* Animals

AMPLIFICATION SYSTEMS. *Use* Radio—Apparatus and Supplies

AMPLIFIERS, VACUUM-TUBE. *Use* Radio—Apparatus and Supplies

AMPUTATION. *Use* Surgery

AMPUTEES
LC ——; s.a. Amputation; Physically handicapped
SEARS PHYSICALLY HANDICAPPED; s.a. Handicapped. Orthopedia
RG ——; s.a. Artificial limbs; Handicapped
NYT HANDICAPPED; Limbs; Prosthesis
PAIS DISABLED; Artificial limbs;
BPI ——; s.a. Arms, Artificial; Veterans, Disabled

AMUSEMENT PARKS
See also names of specific amusement parks, e.g., Disneyland
LC ——; s.a. Merry-go-round; Picnic grounds; Railroads, Miniature
SEARS ——; s.a. Parks
RG ——; s.a. Recreation areas; Sideshows
NYT ——; s.a. Entertainment and Amusements; Recreation
PAIS ——
BPI ——; s.a. Amusement industry; Parks

AMUSEMENTS
See also specific types of amusements, e.g., Circus, Puzzles, etc.
LC ——; s.a. Family recreations; Scientific recreation; subd. *Amusements* under city, e.g., Boston —Amusements

SEARS ——; s.a. Entertaining; Indoor games
RG ——; s.a. Games; Hobbies
NYT ENTERTAINMENT AND AMUSEMENTS; s.a. Expositions; Recreation
PAIS AMUSEMENT INDUSTRY; s.a. Performing arts; Recreation
BPI AMUSEMENT INDUSTRY; s.a. Moving picture industry; Night clubs

ANAEMIA. *See* Anemia

ANAESTHESIA. *See* Anesthesia and Anesthetics

ANAESTHETICS. *See* Anesthesia and Anesthetics

ANALGESICS
See also names of individual analgesics, e.g., Aspirin, Morphine, etc.
LC ——; s.a. Analgesia; Anasthetics
SEARS ANESTHETICS; s.a. Materia medica; Pain
RG ——; s.a. Analgesia; Pharmacology
NYT PAIN—RELIEVING DRUGS; s.a. Drugs and drug trade
PAIS DRUGS; s.a. Narcotics; Psychotropic drugs
BPI ——; s.a. Drugs; Medicine, Proprietary

ANALOG COMPUTERS. *See* Computers

ANALYSIS (Mathematics). *See* Mathematics

ANALYSIS OF VARIANCE. *Use* Sampling (Statistics)

ANARCHISM AND ANARCHISTS. *Use* Liberty; Political Crimes and Offenses; Terrorism

ANASTHETICS. *Use* Analgesics

ANATOMY. *Use* Anatomy, Human; Body, Human

ANATOMY, ARTISTIC. *Use* Drawing

ANATOMY, COMPARATIVE. *Use* Evolution

ANATOMY, HUMAN
See also names of parts of the body, e.g., Head, Ears, etc.
LC ——; s.a. Body, Human, Dissection; Somatology
SEARS ANATOMY; s.a. Biology; Medicine
RG ANATOMY; s.a. Body, Human; Physiology
NYT BODY, HUMAN; s.a. Biology and biochemistry
PAIS PHYSIOLOGY
BPI PHYSIOLOGY; s.a. Biology; Medicine

ANCESTOR WORSHIP. *Use* Funeral Rites and Ceremonies; Mythology; Worship

ANCESTRY. *See* Genealogy; Heredity

ANCIENT ART. *See* Art, Ancient

ANECDOTES. *Use* Wit and Humor

ANEMIA
LC ——; s.a. Blood; Hemoglobinopathy
SEARS BLOOD—DISEASES; s.a. Leukemia; Physiology
RG ——; s.a. Blood—Diseases; Leukemia
NYT ——; s.a. Food and grocery trade; Medicine and health
PAIS BLOOD
BPI ——; s.a. Blood—Diseases; Leukemia

ANESTHESIA AND ANESTHETICS
See also names of anesthetics, e.g., Ether.
LC ——; s.a. Analgesia; Analgesics; Geriatric anesthesia; Sedatives
SEARS ——; s.a. Anesthetics; Materia medica; Pain; Surgery
RG ——; s.a. Analgesia; Anesthetics; Operations, surgical; Pharmacology
NYT ——; s.a. Acupuncture; Medicine and health; Sedatives
PAIS SEDATIVES; s.a. Medicine
BPI ——; s.a. Sedatives; Tranquilizing drugs

ANGLES. *Use* Heaven

ANGLO-CATHOLICISM. *Use* Catholic Church; Protestantism

ANIMAL HUSBANDRY. *See* Stock and Stock Breeding

ANIMAL INDUSTRY. *Use* Domestic Animals; Stock and Stock Breeding

ANIMAL INTELLIGENCE. *Use* Learning, Psychology of

ANIMAL INTRODUCTION. *Use* Acclimatization

ANIMAL LORE. *Use* Folklore; Natural History

ANIMAL PARASITES. *See* Parasites

ANIMAL POPULATIONS. *Use* Ecology

ANIMAL PRODUCTS. *Use* Raw Materials

ANIMALS
LC ——; s.a. Amphibians; Vertebrates; Zoo animals; Zoology
SEARS ——; s.a. Desert animals; Domestic animals; Fur-bearing animals
RG ——; s.a. Amphibia; Pets; Wildlife
NYT ——; s.a. Biology and biochemistry; Zoos
PAIS ——; s.a. Names of animals, e.g., Horses; Pets; Predatory animals
BPI ——; s.a. Livestock; Pets; Wildlife, Conservation of; Zoology, Economic

ANIMALS, DOMESTIC. *See* Domestic Animals

ANIMALS, HABITS AND BEHAVIOR OF. *Use* Behavior (Psychology)

ANIMALS, PREDATORY. *Use* Predatory Animals

ANIMALS—PROTECTION. *Use* Wildlife Conservation

ANIMALS—TREATMENT. *Use* Domestic Animals

ANIMALS AS CARRIERS OF INFECTION. *Use* Diseases

ANIMALS IN RELIGION, FOLKLORE, ETC. *Use* Totemism

ANIMAL-WORSHIP. *Use* Totemism

ANNIVERSARIES. *Use* Special Days, Weeks and Months

ANNUAL INCOME GUARANTEE. *See* Guaranteed Annual Income

ANNUALS. *See* Almanacs

ANNUALS (Plants)
LC ——; s.a. Floriculture; Plants, Cultivated
SEARS ——; s.a. Flower gardening; Flowers

RG ——; s.a. Horticulture
NYT PLANTS; s.a. Agriculture and agricultural products; Flowers; Horticulture
PAIS PLANTS
BPI FLOWERS; s. a. Gardening; Plants

ANNUITIES
LC ——; s.a. Investments; Pensions; Survivor's benefits
SEARS ——; s.a. Insurance, Life; Pensions; Retirement
RG ——; s.a. Insurance, Life; subd. *Pensions* under occupation, e.g., College professors and instructors—Pensions
NYT PENSIONS AND RETIREMENT; s.a. Life insurance (for variable annuities); Stocks and bonds
PAIS ——; s.a. Investments; Pensions
BPI ——; s.a. Annuities, variable; Insurance, Life—Equity programs

ANNULMENT OF MARRIAGE. *See* Divorce; Marriage Law

ANNULMENTS. *Use* Alimony

ANONYMS AND PSEUDONYMS
LC ——; s.a. Acronyms; Names, Personal
SEARS PSEUDONYMS
RG PSEUDONYMS; s.a. Names; Names, Personal
NYT NAMES, PERSONAL, s.a. Books and literature; Writing and writers
PAIS AUTHORS
BPI AUTHORS

ANTARCTIC EXPLORATION. *Use* Discoveries (Geography)

ANTARCTIC REGIONS. *Use* Discoveries (Geography)

ANTHEMS, NATIONAL. *See* National Songs

ANTHROPO-GEOGRAPHY
LC ——; s.a. Geopolitics; Human ecology; Man — Influence of climate
SEARS ——; s.a. Geopolitics; Man—Influence of environment; Migration of nations
RG ——; s.a. Geography; Man—Migrations
NYT ARCHEOLOGY AND ANTHROPOLOGY; s.a. Geography; Man; Weather
PAIS ANTHROPOLOGY; s.a. Geography
BPI GEOGRAPHY; s.a. Ecology; Man

ANTHROPOLOGY
See also names of races and tribes, e.g., Semitic race, Cherokee Indians, etc.
LC ——; s.a. Civilization; Ethnology; Mythology; National characteristics; Race psychology
SEARS ——; s.a. Man; Social change; Woman
RG ——; s.a. Evolution; Soceity, Primitive
NYT ARCHEOLOGY AND ANTHROPOLOGY; s.a. Evolution; Race
PAIS ——; s.a. Man; Races of man; Woman
BPI MAN; s.a. Archaeology; Race

ANTHROPOMETRY. *Use* Man

ANTI-AMERICANISM. *Use* Prejudices and Antipathies

ANTIBIOTICS
See also names of specific antibiotics, e.g., Penicillin,
    Streptomycin, etc.
LC   ——; s.a. Plants, Effect of antibiotics on
SEARS ——; s.a. Chemotheraphy
RG   ——; s.a. Bacteria—Resistance and sensitivity;
    Fungi—Resistance and sensitivity
NYT   ——; s.a. Drugs and drug trade
PAIS   ——
BPI   ——; s.a. Drugs; Medicines, Proprietary

ANTI-CLERICALISM. *Use* Secularism

ANTI-COMMUNIST MOVEMENTS. *Use* Communism

ANTIDEPRESSANTS
See also names of specific drugs, e.g., Amphetamines.
LC   ——; s.a. Depression, Mental; Psychopharmaco-
    logy
SEARS DRUGS; s.a. Chemistry, Medical and
    pharmaceutical; Narcotics
RG   ——; s.a. Narcotics; Pharmacology
NYT   STIMULANTS (Drugs); s.a. Drug addiction,
    abuse and traffic; Drugs and drug trade;
    Sedatives
PAIS   DRUGS; s.a. Hallucinogenic drugs; Narcotics
BPI   ——; s.a. Depression, Mental; Drugs

ANTI-DISCRIMINATION LAWS. *See* Race Discimina-
    tion

ANTIGENS AND ANTIBODIES. *Use* Toxins and Anti-
    toxins; Vaccination

ANTIHISTAMINE DRUGS. *Use* Allergy

ANTIMILITARISM. *See* Militarism

ANTIPATHIES. *See* Prejudices and Antipathies

ANTIPATHY. *Use* Emotions

ANTIQUES. *Use* Furniture

ANTIQUITIES
See subd. *Antiquities* under names of countries, e.g.,
    Greece—Antiquities.
LC   ——; s.a. Archaeology; Christian antiquities
SEARS ARCHEOLOGY; s.a. Bible—Antiquities; Classi-
    cal antiquities
RG   ARCHAEOLOGY; s.a. Excavations (archaeology)
NYT   ARCHEOLOGY AND ANTHROPOLOGY; s.a.
    Art; Art objects
PAIS   ——; s.a. Archaeology
BPI   ——; s.a. Antiques

ANTI-SEMITISM. *Use* Discrimination; Jews; Prejudices
    and Antipathies; Race Problems

ANTISEPTICS. *Use* Disinfection and Disinfectants;
    Surgery

ANTISLAVERY. *See* Slavery

ANTITOXINS. *See* Toxins and Antitoxins

ANXIETY
LC   ——; s.a. Defensiveness (psychology); Emotions
SEARS FEAR; s.a. Neuroses; Worry
RG   ——; s.a. Peace of mind; Worry

NYT   MENTAL HEALTH AND DISORDERS; s.a.
    Psychology and psychologists
PAIS   PSYCHOANALYSIS
BPI   ——; s.a. Emotions; Fear

AORTA. *Use* Arteries

APARTHEID. *See* Segregation

APARTMENT HOUSES
LC   ——; s.a. Housing management; Real estate
    management
SEARS ——; s.a. Architecture, Domestic; Housing
RG   ——; s.a. Rent laws; Row houses; Skyscrapers
NYT   HOUSING; s.a. Building; Real estate
PAIS   ——; s.a. Housing management; Landlord and
    tenant
BPI   ——; s.a. Apartment houses, Cooperative;
    Condominium (housing); Real estate manage-
    ment

APES
See also types of apes, e.g., Chimpanzees, Gorillas, etc.
LC   ——; s.a. Apes (in religion, folk-lore, etc.);
    Monkeys
SEARS MONKEYS; s.a. Primates
RG   ——; s.a. Monkeys; Primates
NYT   MONKEYS AND APES; s.a. Animals; Evolution
PAIS   ANIMALS; s.a. Laboratory animals
BPI   ANIMALS

APHASIA. *Use* Amnesia

APHORISMS AND APOTHEGMS. *Use* Proverbs; Quota-
    tions

APOCALYPTIC LITERATURE. *Use* Prophecies

APOPLEXY. *Use* Paralysis

APOSTASY. *Use* Sects

APOSTLES. *Use* Evangelicalism; Saints

APOSTOLIC SUCCESSION. *Use* Papcy

APPAREL. *Use* Boots and Shoes; Clothing and Dress;
    Costume; Fashion; Leather Industry and Trade;
    Men's Clothing; Models, Fashion; Sewing;
    Tailoring

APPARITIONS. *Use* Miracles; Occult Sciences; Psychical
    Research

APPELLATE COURTS. *Use* Courts

APPELLATE PROCEDURE. *Use* Courts; Procedure
    (Law)

APPERCEPTION
LC   ——; s.a. Comprehension; Knowledge, Theory
    of; Perception
SEARS ——; s.a. Attention; Consciousness; Educational
    psychology
RG   PERCEPTION; s.a. Cognition; Human informa-
    tion processing
NYT   PHILOSOPHY; s.a. Brain; Mind; Psychology and
    psychologists
PAIS   KNOWLEDGE, THEORY OF
BPI   PERCEPTION; s.a. Extrasensory perception;
    Knowledge, Theory of

APPLIANCE STORES. *Use* Department Stores

APPLIANCES, ELECTRIC. *See* Household Equipment and Furnishings

APPLICATIONS FOR POSITIONS
LC ———; s.a. Employment references; Resumes (employment); Success
SEARS ———; s.a. Employment agencies; Interviewing
RG ———; s.a. Employment interviewing
NYT LABOR; s.a. Labor—U.S.—Employment Agencies; Labor—U.S.—Unemployment and job market
PAIS ———; s.a. Employment; Job hunting; Recruiting of employees
BPI ———; s.a. Employee outplacement; Employment references

APPLIED ART. *See* Art Industries and Trade

APPLIED MECHANICS. *See* Mechanical Engineering

APPLIED SCIENCE. *See* Technology

APPORTIONMENT (Election law)
LC ———; s.a. Election districts; Representative government and representation
SEARS ———; s.a. Representative government and representation
RG ———; s.a. Gerrymander; Representative government and representation
NYT ELECTIONS (U.S.)—REAPPORTIONMENT; s.a. Elections (U.S.)—Local government; Politics and government (general)
PAIS LEGISLATURES—APPORTIONMENT; s.a. Election districts; Proportional representation
BPI ELECTION DISTRICTS; s.a. Gerrymander; Proportional representation; Representative government and representation

APPRAISAL. *See* Valuation

APPRECIATION OF ART. *See* Aesthetics; Art—Study and Teaching

APPREHENSION. *See* Perception

APPRENTICES
LC ———; s.a. Child labor; Employees, Training of; Learners, Industrial
SEARS ———; s.a. Labor and laboring classes; Technical education
RG ———; s.a. Education, Cooperative; Employees—Taining; Trade schools
NYT LABOR; s.a. Commercial education
PAIS APPRENTICESHIP; s.a. Employees—Training; Manuel labor; Technical education
BPI ———; s.a. Employees, Training of; headings beginning with *Interns*, e.g., Interns (business); Occupational training

APTITUDE TESTS. *Use* Ability—Testing; Occupational Aptitude Tests; Tests, Mental

AQUANAUTS. *Use* Underwater Exploration

AQUARIUMS
LC ———; s.a. Fish—Culture; Water gardens
SEARS ———; s.a. Goldfish; Marine aquariums
RG ———; s.a. Fish culture; Marine biology
NYT AQUARIUMS AND OCEANARIUMS; s.a. Fishing and Fish; Marine biology
PAIS ———; s.a. Fish culture
BPI ———; s.a. Fishes; Pet industries; Pets

AQUARIUMS AND OCEANARIUMS. *Use* Fisheries

AQUATIC SPORTS. *Use* Boats and Boating

AQUEDUCTS. *Use* Water — Supply

ARAB COUNTRIES
See also subd. *Arab countries* under specific headings, e.g., Labor—Arab states.
LC ———; s.a. Mohammedan countries; Near East
SEARS ———; s.a. Arabs; Near East
RG ARAB STATES; s.a. Islam; Jewish-Arab relations; Panarabism
NYT ARAB LEAGUE; s.a. Arabs; Middle East
PAIS ARAB STATES; s.a. Persian Gulf region
BPI ———; s.a. Israeli-Arab war, 1967

ARABIC LITERATURE. *Use* Islam

ARAB-ISRAELI CONFLICT. *See* Jewish-Arab Relations

ARAB-JEWISH RELATIONS. *See* Jewish-Arab Relations

ARABS. *Use* Arab Countries; Jewish-Arab Relations

ARABS IN PALESTINE. *Use* Jewish-Arab Relations

ARBITRAGE. *Use* Foreign Exchange

ARBITRATION, INDUSTRIAL
LC ———; s.a. Collective bargaining; Grievance procedures
SEARS ———; s.a. Labor unions; Strikes and lockouts
RG ———; s.a. Industrial relations; Labor courts
NYT LABOR—U.S.—ARBITRATION, CONCILIATION AND MEDIATION; s.a. labor union names, e.g., International Ladies' Garment Workers' Union (ILGWU)
PAIS ———; s.a. Collective bargaining; Labor disputes
BPI ———; s.a. Industrial relations; Trade unions; Work councils

ARBITRATION, INTERNATIONAL
LC ———; s.a. International courts; Mediation, International
SEARS ———; s.a. Disarmament; Treaties; United Nations
RG ———; s.a. International law; Peace
NYT INTERNATIONAL LAW; s.a. International court of arbitration; International relations; United Nations
PAIS ———; s.a. International court of justice; United Nations
BPI ———; s.a. Disarmament and arms control; International relations

ARBITRATION AND AWARD. *Use* Commercial Law; Justice, Administration of

ARBOCULTURE. *Use* Horticulture

ARCHAEOLOGY
LC ———; s.a. Anthropology; Antiquities; Ethnology
SEARS ARCHEOLOGY; s.a. Architecture, Ancient; Excavations (archeology)

RG ——; s.a. Man, Prehistory; Stone age
NYT ARCHEOLOGY AND ANTHROPOLOGY; s.a. Civilization; Paleontology
PAIS ——; s.a. Anthropology
BPI ——; s.a. Man

ARCHAEOLOGY, SUBMARINE. *Use* Underwater Exploration

ARCHEOLOGY. *Use* Archaeology

ARCHES. *Use* Roofs

ARCHITECTS
LC ——; s.a. Building designers; City planners
SEARS ——; s.a. Architecture as a profession
RG ——; s.a. Architecture as a profession; Negro architects
NYT ARCHITECTURE AND ARCHITECTS; s.a. Building
PAIS ——; s.a. Women as architects
BPI ——; s.a. Architecture; Building; Houses

ARCHITECTURAL DRAWING. *Use* Drawing

ARCHITECTURAL ENGINEERING. *See* Building

ARCHITECTURAL LIGHTING. *See* Lighting

ARCHITECTURAL MODELS. *Use* Models and Model-making

ARCHITECTURAL PERSPECTIVE. *See* Drawing

ARCHITECTURAL RENDERING. *Use* Drawing

ARCHITECTURE
See also names of types of buildings, e.g., Office buildings, Skyscrapers, etc. and styles of architecture, e.g. Architecture, Gothic, Architecture, Spanish, etc.
LC ——; s.a. Architecture, Domestic; Building; Engineering
SEARS ——; s.a. Monuments; Public buildings
RG ——; s.a. City planning; Remodeling (architecture)
NYT ARCHITECTURE AND ARCHITECTS; s.a. Area planning and renewal; Building; Housing
PAIS ——; s.a. Landscape architecture; subd. *Architecture* under specific subjects, e.g., Library Buildings—Architecture
BPI ——; s.a. Building; Space (architecture)

ARCHITECTURE, ANCIENT. *Use* Archaeology

ARCHITECTURE, DOMESTIC. *Use* Apartment Houses

ARCHITECTURE, DOMESTIC. *Use* Suburbs

ARCHITECTURE AND ARCHITECTS. *Use* Architects

ARCHITECTURE AND SOLAR RADIATION. *Use* Sun

ARCHITECTURE AS A PROFESSION. *Use* Architects

ARCHIVES
LC ——; s.a. Charters; Information services; Public records
SEARS ——; s.a. Bibliography; Manuscripts
RG ——; s.a. Documentation; Documents; Historical research; Records, Preservation of

NYT ARCHIVES AND RECORDS; s.a. Libraries and librarians; names of cities, states, etc., for national, state and municipal archives
PAIS ——; s.a. Business records; Government records
BPI ; s.a. Presidential libraries; Records

ARCTIC EXPLORATION. *Use* Discoveries (Geography)

ARCTIC REGIONS. *Use* Earth

AREA PLANNING AND RENEWAL. *Use* Architecture; Building; Cities and Towns; City Planning; Community; Housing; Land; Metropolitan Government; Neighborhood; Public Housing; Reclamation of Land; Regional Planning; Suburbs; Urban Renewal; Urbanization

AREA RESEARCH. *See* Area Studies

AREA STUDIES
LC ——; s.a. Education; Geography—Study and teaching
SEARS ——; s.a. names of specific area studies, e.g., Afro-American studies; Education
RG ——; s.a. African studies; American studies
NYT ——; s.a. area names, e.g., Far East; Language and languages
PAIS ——; s.a. Oriental studies; Slavic studies
BPI EDUCATION; s.a. Colleges and universities; Intellectual education

ARGUMENTATION. *See* Debates and Debating; Logic; Oratory

ARID REGIONS. *Use* Water—Supply; Water Resources Development

ARISTOCRACY
LC ——; s.a. Democracy; Nobility
SEARS ——; s.a. Social classes; Upper classes
RG ——; s.a. Great Britain—Peerage; Upper classes
NYT NOBILITY; s.a. names of nobles, e.g., Elizabeth II, Queen; Society
PAIS SOCIAL STATUS; s.a. Class struggle; Democracy
BPI ELITE (Social sciences); s.a. Groups (sociology); Social classes

ARITHMETIC. *Use* Mathematics

ARMAMENT, DEFENSE AND MILITARY FORCES. *Use* Armed Forces; Arms and Armor; Bombs; Gunnery; Militarism; Military Art and Science; Munitions; Ordnance; Pacifism; Priorities, Industrial; Revolutions

ARMAMENTS
LC ——; s.a. Aeronautics, Military; Armies
SEARS ARMIES; s.a. Industrial mobilization; Munitions
RG ——; s.a. Ammunition; Disarmament; weapons
NYT ARMAMENT, DEFENSE AND MILITARY FORCES; s.a. Arms control and limitation and disarmament; U.S. armament and defense
PAIS ——; s.a. Bombs; Munitions
BPI ——; s.a. Disarmament and arms control; Firearms industry; Ordnance

ARMATURES. *Use* Electric Motors

ARMED FORCES
See also names of countries with appropriate subdivision,
        e.g., Spain—Armed forces; France—Armies, etc.
LC   ——; s.a. Sociology, Military; Soldiers
SEARS   ARMIES; s.a. Navies; Seamen
RG   ——; s.a. Military life; Servicemen
NYT   ARMAMENT, DEFENSE AND MILITARY
        FORCES; s.a. Military art and science; U.S.
        armament and defense
PAIS
BPI   ——; s.a. Disarmament and arms control;
        Servicemen

ARMED SERVICES. *See* Armed Forces

ARMIES. *Use* Armaments; Armed Forces; Militarism;
        Military Art and Science; Soldiers; War

ARMIES, COST OF. *Use* Disarmament; War—Economic
        Aspects

ARMISTICES. *Use* War (International law)

ARMOR. *See* Arms and Armor

ARMORED VESSELS. *Use* Warships

ARMS, ARTIFICIAL. *Use* Amputees; Artificial Organs

ARMS AND ARMOR
LC   ——; s.a. Firearms; Pistols
SEARS   ——; s.a. Ordnance; Rifles
RG   WEAPONS; s.a. Firearms; Munitions
NYT   ARMOR; s.a. Armament, defense and military
        forces; Firearms; Weapons
PAIS   ARMAMENTS; s.a. Bombs; Munitions
BPI   ——; s.a. Munitions; Ordnance

**ARMS CONTROL AND LIMITATION AND DISARMA-
        MENT.** *Use* Armament; Disarmament; Inter-
        national Relations; Nonviolence; Pacifism; Sea
        Power; United States—Defenses; War

ARMY—RECRUITING, ENLISTMENT, ETC. *Use*
        Military Service, Compulsory

ARMY LIFE. *See* Soldiers

ARREST
LC   ——; s.a. Bail; Detention of persons; Preventive
        detention
SEARS   CRIME AND CRMINALS; s.a. Prisons; Punish-
        ment
RG   ——; s.a. Concentration camps; Fugitives from
        justice; Habeas corpus
NYT   CRIME AND CRIMINALS; s.a. Courts; Prisons
        and prisoners
PAIS   ——; s.a. Bail; Detention of persons; Imprison-
        ment
BPI   CRIME AND CRIMINALS; s.a. Criminal investi-
        gation; Criminal law; Criminal registers; Prisoners

ARREST OF JUDGMENT. *Use* Judgments

ARSON
LC   ——; s.a. Criminal law; Liability for fire damages
SEARS   ——; s.a. Criminal law; Offenses against public
        safety
RG   ——; s.a. Fires; Trials (arson)

NYT   ——; s.a. Crime and criminals; Fires
PAIS   ——; s.a. Criminal law; Fires
BPI   ——; s.a. Crime and criminals; Criminal law

ART
Scope: General works on the visual arts (Architecture;
        Painting; Photography; Artistic, Sculpture; etc.);
        See also headings beginning with Art, e.g., Art,
        Ancient.
LC   ——; s.a. Aesthetics; specific subjects, e.g., Love
        in art; Soul in art; Technology in art.
SEARS   ——; s.a. Arts and crafts; Graphic arts; Painting
RG   ——; s.a. Art sales; Auctions; Design; Erotica;
        names of schools of art, e.g., Impressionism (art);
        Nude in art
NYT   ——; s.a. Architecture and Architects; Art
        Objects; Graphic arts; Handicrafts
PAIS   ——; s.a. Forgery of works of art; Graphic arts
        industry; Performing arts
BPI   ——; s.a. Artists; Drawings; Painting

ART, ABSTRACT
LC   ——; s.a. Art, Modern—20th century; Modern-
        ism; Optical art
SEARS   ——; s.a. Kinetic art
RG   ——; s.a. Abstract expressionism; Constructivism
NYT   ART; s.a. Multimedia
PAIS   ART; s.a. Modernism
BPI   ART

ART, AMATEUR. *Use* Recreation

ART, ANCIENT
LC   ——; s.a. Art, Greco-Roman; Seven wonders of
        the world
SEARS   ——; s.a. Art, Primitive; Classical antiquities
RG   ——; s.a. Art, Greek; Sculpture, Ancient
NYT   ARCHEOLOGY AND ATHROPOLOGY; s.a.
        Art; Art objects
PAIS   ART
BPI   ART

ART, APPLIED. *See* Design, Industrial; Engineering
        Design

ART, BYZANTINE. *Use* Art, Medieval

ART, COMMERCIAL. *Use* Art and Industry; Art
        Industries and Trade; Commercial Art

ART, DECORATIVE. *Use* Art Industries and Trade;
        Design; Interior Decoration; Tapestry

ART—EXPERTISING. *Use* Forgery of Works of Art

ART—FRAUDS. *Use* Forgery of Works of Art

ART—GALLERIES AND MUSEUMS. *Use* Museums

ART, GOTHIC. *Use* Art, Medieval

ART, GRAPHIC. *See* Graphic Arts

ART, IMMORAL
LC   ——; s.a. Art and morals; Nude in art; Sex in art:
        Theater—Moral and religious aspects
SEARS   PORNOGRAPHY; s.a. Obscenity (law)
RG   IMMORAL LITERATURE AND PICTURES:
        s.a. Art and morals; Censorship; Obscenity (law)

NYT   ART; s.a. Pornography and obscenity
PAIS   PORNOGRAPHY; s.a. Obscenity
BPI   OBSCENITY; s.a. Arts and society; Moral
       conditions

ART, MEDIEVAL
LC   ——; s.a. Art, Byzantine; Art, Gothic
SEARS ——; s.a. Civilization, Medieval; Illumination of
       books and manuscripts
RG   ——; s.a. Christian art and symbolism; Church
       architecture
NYT   ART; s.a. Art objects
PAIS   ART
BPI   ART; s.a. Illumination of books and manuscripts

ART, MODERN. *Use* Art, Modern—20th Century;
Modernism (Art); Optical Art

ART, MODERN—20TH CENTURY
LC   ——; s.a. Art—History—20th century; Art,
       Abstract; Cubism; Expressionism (art); Modern-
       ism (art); Surrealism
SEARS ART, MODERN; s.a. Art, Modern—19th century;
       Postimpressionism (art)
RG   ART, MODERN; s.a. Abstract expressionism;
       Dadaism; Environment (art); Happenings (Art)
NYT   ART; s.a. Art objects
PAIS   ART
BPI   ART

ART, OPTICAL. *See* Optical Art

ART, ORIENTAL. *Use* Oriental Studies

ART, PRE-COLUMBIAN. *Use* Art, Primitive

ART, PREHISTORIC. *See* Art, Primitive

ART, PRIMITIVE
See also subd. *Antiquity* under names of countries.
LC   ——; s.a. Folk art; Idols and images
SEARS ——; s.a. Cave drawings; Indians of North
       America—Art
RG   ——; s.a. Art, Pre-Columbian; Petroglyphs
NYT   ART; s.a. Archeology and anthropology; Art
       objects
PAIS   ART
BPI   ART

ART—STUDY. *Use* Art—Study and Teaching

ART—STUDY AND TEACHING
LC   ——; s.a. Art in universities and colleges; Art—
       Scholarships, Fellowships, etc.
SEARS ——; s.a. Art—Study, Method of; Art—
       Techniques
RG   ——; s.a. Art education; Design—Study and
       teaching
NYT   ART; s.a. names of art schools, e.g., Art Students
       League
PAIS   ART EDUCATION
BPI   ART; s.a. Art centers; Art libraries

ART—TECHNIQUE. *Use* Graphic Arts

ART—TECHNIQUES. *Use* Art—Study and Teaching

ART ANALYSIS. *See* Art—Study and Teaching

ART AND INDUSTRY
LC   ——; s.a. Art industries and trade; Commercial
       art; Industry in art
SEARS COMMERCIAL ART; s.a. Advertising; Costume
       design; Textile design
RG   ——; s.a. Art, Commercial; Art in factories
NYT   ART; s.a. Advertising; Graphic arts
PAIS   ——
BPI   ——; s.a. Art; Arts and crafts

ART AND MORALS. *Use* Art, Immoral

ART AND RACE
LC   ——; s.a. Ethnopsychology
SEARS RACE AWARENESS; s.a. Black art; Blacks in
       literature and art
RG   ETHNOPSYCHOLOGY; s.a. Art and politics;
       Negroes in art
NYT   ART; s.a. Culture; Minorities (ethnic, racial,
       religious); Race
PAIS   ART
BPI   ARTS AND SOCIETY; s.a. Art; Race

ART AND RELIGION
LC   ——; s.a. Gods in art; Idols and images
SEARS ——; s.a. Art and mythology; Art and society;
       Christian art and symbolism
RG   ——; s.a. Christian art and symbolism; Icons
NYT   ART; s.a. Culture; Religion and churches
PAIS   ART; s.a. Religion
BPI   ARTS AND SOCIETY: s.a. Art; Religion

ART AND SCIENCE
LC   ——; s.a. Biological illustration; Medicine and
       art
SEARS SCIENCE AND THE HUMANITIES
RG   ——; s.a. Art and religion; Art and technology
NYT   ART; s.a. Culture; Science and technology
PAIS   SCIENCE AND THE HUMANITIES
BPI   ARTS AND SOCIETY; s.a. Arts; Society

ART AND STATE
Scope: Works on state encouragement of science,
       literature and art; see Art patronage for works
       on private support of art
LC   ——; s.a. Art commissions; State encouragement
       of science, literature and arts; Theater and state;
       Federal aid to the arts
SEARS ——; s.a. Art, Municipal; Art and society
RG   ——; s.a. Art and society; Capitols; Public
       buildings; State encouragement of science,
       literature and art: The Arts—Finance
NYT   ART; s.a. Culture
PAIS   ——; s.a. Art museums; Art and society;
       Communism and art; U.S. National Council on
       the Arts
BPI   ——; s.a. Art and industry; Arts and society

ART AND TECHNOLOGY. *Use* Art and Science

ART APPRECIATION. *Use* Aesthetics

ART AS A PROFESSION. *Use* Artists

ART CENTERS. *Use* Art—Study and Teaching

ART DESIGNS. *Use* Interior Decoration

ART EDUCATION. *Use* Art—Study and Teaching

ART FORGERIES. *See* Forgery of Works of Art

ART IN THE HOME. *Use* Art Objects

ART IN WAR. *Use* Art and History

ART INDUSTRIES AND TRADE
See also subd. *Art Industries* under names of places, e.g., Poland—Art industries.

LC	——; s.a. Art, Decorative; Commercial art; Industrial arts
SEARS	——; s.a. Arts and crafts; Design
RG	ART, COMMERCIAL; s.a. Advertising art; Decoration and ornament; Design, industrial
NYT	HANDICRAFTS; s.a. Art; Interior decoration
PAIS	ARTS MARKET; s.a. Handicrafts
BPI	ART; s.a. Art and industry; Arts and crafts

ART LITERATURE. *Use* Aesthetics

ART OBJECTS

Scope:	Works about articles of artistic merit. See also classes of art objects and names of particular objects, e.g., Bronzes, Glassware, etc.
LC	——; s.a. Antiquities; Found objects (art); Miniature objects; Relics and reliquaries
SEARS	
RG	——; s.a. Art, Primitive; Art in the home; Collage; Display of antiques, art objects, etc.
NYT	
PAIS	ART; s.a. Pottery industry
BPI	ART; s.a. Arts and crafts

ART THERAPY. *Use* Occupational Therapy

ARTERIES

LC	——; s.a. Blood—Circulation; Veins
SEARS	BLOOD; s.a. Blood—Circulation
RG	——; s.a. Aorta; Arteriosclerosis
NYT	BLOOD VESSELS; s.a. Blood; names of diseases, e.g., Arteriosclerosis; Thrombosis and embolism
PAIS	BLOOD
BPI	BLOOD; s.a. Blood pressure; Cardiovascular system; Heart

ARTICLES OF PARTNERSHIP. *Use* Partnership

ARTIFICIAL FEEDING. *Use* Nutrition

ARTIFICIAL INSEMINATION. *Use* Reproduction

ARTIFICIAL INTELLIGENCE. *Use* Electronic Data Processing

ARTIFICIAL LANGUAGES. *See* Language and Languages

ARTIFICIAL LIGHT GARDENING. *Use* Horticulture

ARTIFICIAL ORGANS
See also names of organs, e.g., Heart.

LC	——; s.a. Prosthesis; Surgery
SEARS	——
RG	[Name of organ], ARTIFICIAL, e.g., Kidneys, Artificial; s.a. Artificial limbs; Prosthesis
NYT	PROSTHESIS; s.a. Handicapped

PAIS	ARTIFICIAL LIMBS; s.a. Transplantation of organs, tissues, etc.
BPI	ARTIFICIAL LIMBS; s.a. Arms, Artificial; Handicapped

ARTIFICIAL RESPIRATION. *Use* First Aid in Illness and Injury

ARTIFICIAL SATELLITES

LC	——; s.a. Artificial satellites in telecommunication; Astronautics in meteorology; Earth stations (satellite communication); Expandable space structures; Radiotelephone; Satellite launching strips; Scientific satellites; Space law; Space stations
SEARS	——; s.a. Meteorological satellites; names of specific satellites or projects, e.g., Telstar project; Space stations; Space vehicles
RG	——; s.a. Communications satellites; Moon; Space stations; Telecommunications
NYT	COMMUNICATIONS SATELLITES; s.a. Communications; Data processing (information processing) equipment and systems; International relations; Space and upper atmosphere—Moon; Space and upper atmosphere—Planets; Television and radio—Communications satellites
PAIS	SATELLITES, ARTIFICIAL; s.a. Communications systems; Satellites, Artificial—Communication uses; Space law
BPI	SATELLITES, ARTIFICIAL; s.a. Biosatellite program; Communications satellites; Satellites; Satellites, Communication; Telecommunication

ARTILLERY. *Use* Gunnery

ARTISANS. *Use* Handicraft

ARTISANS. *Use* Industrial Arts

ARTISTIC PHOTOGRAPHY. *See* Photography, Artistic

ARTISTS
See also names of specific types of artists, e.g., Painters; Musicians, Cartoonists, Illustrators, etc.

LC	——; s.a. Art as a profession; Youth as artists
SEARS	——; s.a. Black artists; Women as artists
RG	—— s.a. Artists colonies; Negro artists
NYT	Names of various art forms, e.g., Art, Dancing, Music, etc.; s.a. Culture
PAIS	——
BPI	——; s.a. Painting

THE ARTS

Scope:	Works on the arts in general, including visual arts, literature, and the performing arts.
LC	——; Art and industry; Art and religion; Art and state; Art and society; Art industries and trade
SEARS	——; s.a. Art; The arts, American
RG	——; s.a. Multiple arts
NYT	ART; s.a. Culture
PAIS	ART; s.a. Literature; Performing arts
BPI	ART; s.a. Artists; Arts and society

ARTS, DECORATIVE. *See* Design; Interior Design

ARTS, FINE. *See* Art; Arts, The

ARTS, GRAPHIC. *See* Graphic Arts

ARTS AND CRAFTS. *Use* Art and Industry; Art Industries and Trade; Handicrafts

ARTS AND CRAFTS MOVEMENT. *Use* Handicraft

THE ARTS AND MORALS. *Use* Moral Conditions

ARTS AND SOCIETY. *Use* Art and Morals; Art and Race; Art and Religion; Art and Science; Art and State; The Arts

ASCETICISM. *Use* Monasticism and Religious Orders

ASSASSINATION
See also subd. *Assassination* under names of victims, e.g., Kennedy, John F.—Assassination.
LC ——; s.a. Regicide; Terrorism
SEARS ——; s.a. Offenses against the person; Political crimes and offenses
RG ——; s.a. Political crimes and offenses
NYT MURDERS AND ATTEMPTED MURDERS; s.a. Capital Punishment; Deaths
PAIS ——; s.a. Crime and criminals; Murder
BPI ——

ASSAULT AND BATTERY
LC ——; s.a. Indecent assault; Offenses against the person
SEARS OFFENSES AGAINST THE PERSON; s.a. Crime and criminals; Criminal law
RG ——; s.a. Offenses against the person; Trials (assault and battery)
NYT ASSAULTS AND DISORDERLY CONDUCT; s.a. Crime and Criminals; Murders and Attempted Murders
PAIS ——; s.a. Murder; Rape; Violence
BPI CRIME AND CRIMINALS, s.a. Police, Self defense

ASSEMBLY, RIGHT OF. *Use* Civil Rights; Liberty; Liberty of Speech; Riots

ASSEMBLY LINE METHODS. *Use* Factory Management; Plant Layout

ASSESSMENT. *Use* Property; Taxation; Valuation

ASSESSMENTS. *Use* Real Property

ASSIGNMENTS. *Use* Transfer (Law)

ASSIMILATION (Sociology). *Use* Acculturation; Emigration and Immigration; Minorities; Social Groups

ASSOCIATION OF IDEAS. *Use* Memory; Thought and Thinking

ASSOCIATIONS. *Use* Trade and Professional Associations

ASTRODYNAMICS. *Use* Space Flight

ASTROLOGY
LC ——; s.a. Medical astrology; Moon—Influence on man
SEARS ——; s.a. Divination; Fortune-telling
RG ——; s.a. Computers—Astrological applications; Occult sciences
NYT ——; s.a. Occult sciences

PAIS OCCULT SCIENCES; s.a. Fortune tellers
BPI ——

ASTRONAUTICAL RESEARCH. *Use* Outer Space

ASTRONAUTICS
LC ——; s.a. Aeronautics; Outer space
SEARS ——; s.a. Aerodynamics; Interplanetary voyages; Manned space flight
RG SPACE FLIGHT; s.a. Aeronautics—History; Ground support systems (space flight); Orbital rendezvous (space flight)
NYT ——; s.a. Aerospace industries and sciences; Communication satellites; Space and upper atmosphere
PAIS ——; s.a. Aviation; Space flight
BPI ——; s.a. Atmosphere upper; Satellites, Artificial; Space flight

ASTRONAUTICS IN METEROLOGY. *Use* Artificial Satellites

ASTRONAUTS. *Use* Space Flight

ASTRONOMICAL PHYSICS. *See* Astrophysics

ASTRONOMY
See also names of stars, sun and planets, e.g., Earth; etc.
LC ——; s.a. Life on other planets; Mechanics, Celestial; Plurality of worlds; Space sciences
SEARS ——; s.a. Galaxies; Planets; Solar system
RG ——; s.a. Constellations; Stars; Universe; Zodiac
NYT SPACE AND UPPER ATMOSPHERE; s.a. names of observatories, e.g., Hayden Planetarium; Telescopes
PAIS ——; s.a. Planetariums; Telescope
BPI ——; s.a. Radio astronomy; Satellites, Artificial Astronomical use

ASTRONOMY, SPHERICAL AND PRACTICAL. *Use* Time

ASTROPHYSICS
LC ——; s.a. Astronomy; Stars—Atmospheres
SEARS ——; s.a. Physics; Stars
RG ——; s.a. Neutron stars; Universe
NYT SPACE AND UPPER ATMOSPHERE; s.a. names of observatories, e.g., Hayden Planetarium; Physics
PAIS ASTRONOMY; s.a. Space research
BPI SPACE RESEARCH

ASYLUM, RIGHT OF
LC ——; s.a. Extradition; Refugees, Political
SEARS REFUGEES, POLITICAL; s.a. Aliens; Immigration and emigration
RG ——; s.a. Emigrés; Political crimes and offenses; Refugees, Political
NYT ——; s.a. country denoting refugee's origin, e.g., Cuba; Refugees
PAIS ——; s.a. Extradition; Refugees, Political
BPI ——; s.a. Extradition; Political defectors

ASYLUMS. *Use* Mental Institutions

ATHEISM
LC ——; s.a. Agnosticism; Rationalism; Theology
SEARS ——; s.a. Deism; God; Skepticism

ATHEISM, *cont.*
RG ——; s.a. Skepticism; Theism
NYT ——; s.a. Religion and churches
PAIS ——; s.a. Churches; Religion
BPI RELIGION; s.a. Church

ATHLETES
See also personal names of athletes, e.g., Mays, Willy.
LC ——; s.a. Athletic ability; Deaf as athletes
SEARS ——; s.a. Black athletes
RG ——; s.a. Amateurism (sports—; types of athletes, e.g. Football players
NYT ATHLETICS; s.a. Sports
PAIS ——; s.a. Negro athletes; Sports
BPI ——; s.a. Advertising—Sports tie-in; Sportsmen

ATHLETIC CLUBS. *Use* Clubs

ATHLETICS
See also names of specific sports, e.g., Baseball; Boxing; Racing; etc.
LC ——; s.a. Football coaching, Soccer coaching, etc; Intramural sports; Moving pictures in sports
SEARS ——; s.a. Coaching; College sports; Gymnastics; Olympic games; School sports
RG ——; s.a. Coaches (athletics); School athletics; Sportsmanship
NYT ——; s.a. Exercise; Physical education and training; Sports
PAIS COLLEGE ATHLETICS; s.a. Physical education; School athletics; Sports
BPI ——; s.a. Athletes; Coaches; Sports

ATLASES. *Use* Cartography

ATMAN. *Use* Soul

ATMOSPHERE
LC ——; s.a. Air; Atmosphere, Upper; Earth sciences
SEARS ——; s.a. Air—Pollution; Meteorology
RG ——; s.a. Meteorology; Winds
NYT ATMOSPHERE, LOWER; s.a. Air; Space and upper atmosphere
PAIS EARTH SCIENCES; s.a. Air pollution; Meteorology
BPI ——; s.a. Air; Earth sciences; Meteorology

ATMOSPHERE, UPPER
LC ——; s.a. Stratosphere; Thermosphere
SEARS ——; s.a. Outer space; Stratosphere
RG ——; s.a. Airglow; Rockets—Meteorological use
NYT SPACE AND UPPER ATMOSPHERE; s.a. Astronautics; Weather—Weather satellites and rockets
PAIS EARTH SCIENCES
BPI ——

ATOMIC BOMB. *Use* Atomic Warfare; Bombs

ATOMIC BOMB SHELTERS. *Use* Civil Defense; Radiation

ATOMIC ENERGY
LC ——; s.a. Atomic bomb; Nuclear excavation; Nuclear physics; Underground nuclear explosions
SEARS ——; s.a. Atomic blasting: Atomic power plants; Nuclear engineering

RG ATOMIC POWER; s.a. Nuclear fusion; Nuclear reactors; Underdeveloped areas—Atomic power
NYT ATOMIC ENERGY AND WEAPONS; s.a. Explosions; Nuclear research; Radiation; U.S. armament and defense
PAIS ATOMIC POWER; s.a. Nuclear fuels; Nuclear fusion
BPI ATOMIC POWER; s.a. Atomic batteries; Electric utilities—Atomic power activities; Nuclear reactions

ATOMIC MASS. *Use* Nuclear Physics

ATOMIC MEDICINE. *Use* Radiation; Radiotherapy

ATOMIC POWER. *Use* Atomic Bomb; Atomic Energy; Atomic Warfare; Force and Energy; Nuclear Reactions

ATOMIC POWER PLANTS. *Use* Electric Power Plants

ATOMIC RESEARCH. *Use* Nuclear Physics

ATOMIC WARFARE
LC ——; s.a. Air warfare; Atomic bomb; Atomic weapons; Atomic weapons—Testing; Ballistic missiles; Nuclear rockets
SEARS ——; s.a. Atomic bombs; Hydrogen bomb; Intercontinental ballistic missiles; Radioactive fallout
RG ——; s.a. Civil defense; Emergency communication systems; Guided missiles
NYT ATOMIC ENERGY AND WEAPONS; s.a. Armament, defense and military forces; NATO; U.S. armament and defense
PAIS ——; s.a. Atomic power; Atomic weapons; Strategic arms limitation talks
BPI ATOMIC WEAPONS; s.a. Atomic bombs; Hydrogen bomb; War

ATOMIC WARFARE AND SOCIETY. *Use* War and Society

ATOMIC WEAPONS AND DISARMAMENT. *Use* Disarmament

ATOMS
LC ——; s.a. Matter—Constitution; Protons
SEARS ——; s.a. Cyclotron; Electrons
RG ——; s.a. Nuclear physics; Quantum theory
NYT ——; s.a. Atomic energy and weapons; names of elements, e.g., Plutonium; Nuclear Research
PAIS See headings beginning with the word Atomic, e.g., Atomic Research
BPI ——; s.a. Neutrons; Protons

ATONEMENT. *Use* Jesus Christ; Sin

ATROCITIES
See also subd. *Atrocities* under names of wars, e.g., European war, 1914–18—Atrocities.
LC ATROCITIES, MILITARY; s.a. Jews—Persecution; Political atrocities
SEARS ——; s.a. Cruelty; Persecution
RG ——; s.a. Cruelty
NYT ——; s.a. Minorities—Nazi policies; Torture; War crimes and criminals

PAIS ——
BPI WAR CRIMES; s.a. subd. *Atrocities* under various subjects, e.g., Vietnam—Atrocities

ATTENTION. *Use* Apperception; Educational Psychology; Memory; Thought and Thinking

ATTITUDE (Psychology)
LC ——; s.a. Behavior (psychology); Emotions; Students—Attitudes
SEARS ——; s.a. Conformity; Public opinion
RG ——; s.a. Attitude change; Value (psychology)
NYT PSYCHOLOGY AND PSYCHOLOGISTS; s.a. Mental health and disorders
PAIS ——; s.a. Attitude change; Employee attitude
BPI ——; s.a. Dogmatism; Job satisfaction

ATTITUDE (Psychology)—TESTING. *Use* Tests, Mental

ATTITUDES. *Use* Public Opinion

ATTORNEYS. *See* Lawyers

ATTORNEYS—GENERAL. *Use* Justice, Administration of

AUCTIONS. *Use* Sales

AUDIO-VISUAL AIDS. *Use* Audio-visual Materials; Instructional Materials Centers

AUDIO-VISUAL EDUCATION
LC ——; s.a. Educational media personnel; Educational technology; Radio in education; Visual education
SEARS ——; s.a. Instructional materials centers; Moving pictures in education; Phonograph records
RG AUDIO-VISUAL INSTRUCTION; s.a. Educational Media personnel; Libraries and audio-visual materials
NYT EDUCATION AND SCHOOLS—U.S.—TEACHING AIDS; s.a. Audio-visual devices; Television and radio—Noncommercial TV and radio
PAIS AUDIO-VISUAL INSTRUCTION; s.a. Teaching machines; Television in education
BPI AUDIO-VISUAL INSTRUCTION; s.a. Instructional materials centers; Teaching machines; Television in education

AUDIO-VISUAL EQUIPMENT. *Use* Audio-visual Materials; Educational Technology; Instructional Materials Centers

AUDIO-VISUAL INSTRUCTION. *Use* Educational Planning and Innovations; Motion pictures in Education; Radio in Education; Teaching

AUDIO-VISUAL LIBRARY SERVICE. *Use* Instructional Materials Centers; Libraries and Librarians

AUDIO-VISUAL MATERIALS
LC ——; s.a. Filmstrips; Lantern slides; Moving pictures; Phonorecords
SEARS ——; s.a. Library education—Audio-visual aids; Motion pictures
RG AUDIO-VISUAL AIDS; s.a. Instructional materials centers; Slides (photography); Teaching machines

NYT AUDIO-VISUAL DEVICES; s.a. Education and schools—U.S.—Teaching Aids
PAIS AUDIO-VISUAL EQUIPMENT; s.a. Filmstrips; Microphotographic equipment; Slides, Photographic
BPI ——; s.a. Filmstrips; Transparencies; Video recordings

AUDIO-VISUAL MATERIALS CENTERS. *Use* Instructional Materials Centers

AUDITING. *Use* Accounting; Tax Accounting and Auditing

AUDITORS. *Use* Accountants

AURORAS. *Use* Magnetism, Terrestrial

AUTARCHY. *Use* Economic Policy

AUTHENTICATION. *Use* Legal Aid

AUTHORITARIANISM. *Use* Despotism; Totalitarianism

AUTHORITY. *Use* Despotism; Management

AUTHORITY (Religion). *Use* Papacy

AUTHORITY, DELEGATION OF. *See* Management

AUTHORS. *Use* Authorship

AUTHORS AND PUBLISHERS. *Use* Contracts; Copyright; Editing; Publishers and Publishing

AUTHORSHIP
Scope: General works treating the means of becoming an author. For specific genre of authorship, see Playwrighting; Television authorship; Sociology—Authorship, etc.
LC ——; s.a. Authors: Fiction—Technique; Drama—Technique; Editing; Precis writing; Style; Literary
SEARS ——; s.a. Authors and publishers; Technical writing
RG ——; s.a. Copyright; Creative writing; Editors and editing; Style, Literary
NYT WRITING AND WRITERS; s.a. Books and literature; names of authors, e.g., Roth, Philip
PAIS AUTHORS; s.a. Press Law; Technical writing
BPI ——; s.a. Authors and publishers; Literary agents; Poets; Report writing

AUTOBIOGRAPHIES. *Use* Biography

AUTOGENIC TRAINING. *Use* Mental Suggestion

AUTOGIROS. *Use* Airplanes

AUTOMATIC CONTROL
LC ——; s.a. Automation; Information theory
SEARS ——; s.a. Cybernetics; Electric controllers
RG ——; s.a. Feedback control systems; Inertial guidance systems
NYT AUTOMATION; s.a. Data processing (information processing) equipment and systems
PAIS AUTOMATION; s.a. Information processing systems
BPI ——; s.a. Automation; Numerical control

AUTOMATIC DATA COLLECTION SYSTEMS. *Use* Information Storage and Retrieval Systems

AUTOMATIC DATA PROCESSING. *See* Electronic Data Processing

AUTOMATIC MACHINERY. *See* Machinery; Machinery in Industry

AUTOMATIC PRODUCTION. *See* Automation

AUTOMATIC SPEECH RECOGNITION. *Use* Voice

AUTOMATION
Scope: Works on industrial applications of automation and its impact on labor.
LC   ———; s.a. Automatic control; Machinery, Automatic
SEARS   ———; s.a. Machinery in industry; Servo-mechanisms
RG   ———; s.a. Adaptive control systems; Computers—Industrial use
NYT   ———; s.a. Data processing (information processing) equipment and systems; Labor
PAIS   ———; s.a. Cybernetics; Systems engineering
BPI   ———; s.a. Electronic data processing; subd. *Automation* under various subjects, e.g., Libraries—Automation

AUTOMATION—ECONOMIC ASPECTS. *Use* Economic History

AUTOMOBILE—U.S.—REPAIR SERVICES. *Use* Mechanical Engineering

AUTOMOBILE ACCIDENTS. *See* Traffic Accidents

AUTOMOBILE DRIVERS—EDUCATION. *Use* Automobiles—Safety Measures

AUTOMOBILE DRIVERS—LIQUOR PROBLEM. *Use* Traffic Accidents

AUTOMOBILE DRIVERS' TESTS. *Use* Traffic Safety

AUTOMOBILE DRIVING. *Use* Traffic Accidents; Traffic Safety

AUTOMOBILE MECHANICS. *Use* Mechanical Engineering

AUTOMOBILE MECHANICS (Persons). *Use* Mechanical Engineering

AUTOMOBILE SEAT BELTS. *Use* Automobiles—Safety Measures; Safety Appliances

AUTOMOBILE THIEVES. *Use* Theft

AUTOMOBILE TOURING. *Use* Travel

AUTOMOBILES
LC   ———; s.a. Automobiles, Racing; Commercial vehicles; Transportation
SEARS   ———; s.a. Buses; Trucks
RG   ———; s.a. Sports cars; Station wagons
NYT   ———; s.a. Traffic (vehicular and pedestrian) and parking; Transportation
PAIS   MOTOR VEHICLES; s.a. Automobile racing; Motor trucks; Taxicabs
BPI   ———; s.a. Automobile engines; Garages

AUTOMOBILES—ABANDONMENT. *See* Abandonment of Property

AUTOMOBILES — ACCIDENTS AND SAFETY. *Use* Automobiles — Safety Measures

AUTOMOBILES, ELECTRIC. *Use* Electric Motors

AUTOMOBILES—LAWS AND REGULATIONS. *Use* Traffic Safety

AUTOMOBILES—POLLUTION CONTROL DEVICES. *Use* Pollution

AUTOMOBILES—ROAD GUIDES. *Use* Maps

AUTOMOBILES—SAFETY MEASURES
LC   ———; s.a. Accidents—Prevention; Automobile seat belts
SEARS   ———; s.a. Automobile drivers—Education; Safety appliances
RG   AUTOMOBILES—SAFETY DEVICES AND MEASURES; s.a. Brakes, Automobile; Safety belts
NYT   AUTOMOBILES—ACCIDENTS AND SAFETY; s.a. Traffic—U.S.—Automobile safety features and defects
PAIS   MOTOR VEHICLES—SAFETY MEASURES; s.a. Accidents—Prevention
BPI   ———; s.a. Automobile seat belts; Automobiles—Bumpers

AUTOMOTIVE VEHICLES. *See* Motor Vehicles

AUTONOMY. *Use* Nationalism; Sovereignty

AUTOPSY
LC   ———; s.a. Death—Causes; Medical jurisprudence
SEARS   MEDICAL JURISPRUDENCE; s.a. Death
RG   ———; s.a. Death—Causes; Medical jurisprudence
NYT   AUTOPSIES; s.a. Deaths; Medicine and health
PAIS   ———; s.a. Medicine, Forensic
BPI   DEATH—CAUSES; s.a. Death; Medicine

AUTOSUGGESTION. *See* Hypnotism; Mental Healing; Mental Suggestion

AVARICE. *Use* Wealth, Ethics of

AVERAGE. *Use* Probabilities

AVIATION. *Use* Flight

AVIATION, COMMERCIAL. *Use* Air Mail Service

AVIATION—MEDICAL ASPECTS. *Use* Aviation Medicine

AVIATION MECHANICS (Persons). *Use* Mechanical Engineering

AVIATION MEDICINE
LC   ———; s.a. Flight—Physiological aspects; Space medicine
SEARS   ———; s.a. Medicine; Space medicine
RG   AVIATION—MEDICAL ASPECTS; s.a. Aviation—Physiological aspects; Motion sickness
NYT   AIRPLANES—PHYSIOLOGICAL ASPECTS OF FLYING; s.a. Airsickness; Medicine and health
PAIS   ———; s.a. Space flight—Physiological aspects
BPI   SPACE FLIGHT—PHYSIOLOGICAL EFFECT; s.a. Medicine; Weightlessness

AVIONICS INDUSTRY. *Use* Aerospace Industries

AVOIDANCE (Psychology). *Use* Emotions

AWARDS. *See* Rewards (Prizes, etc.)

AWARENESS. *Use* Perception; Race Awareness

B

BABY SITTERS. *Use* Child Welfare; Children

BACHELORS. *Use* Celibacy

BACKPACKING
LC ———; s.a. Camping; Pack transportation
SEARS ———; s.a. Camping; Hiking
RG WALKING; s.a. Hitchhiking; Trails
NYT CAMPS AND CAMPING; s.a Hitchhiking; Parks, playgrounds, and other recreation areas; Walking
PAIS CAMPS AND CAMPING
BPI CAMPING; s.a. Leisure; Vacations

BACTERIA
Scope: Works on biological studies of bacteria.
LC ———; s.a. Autolysis; Communicable diseases; Viruses
SEARS BACTERIOLOGY; s.a. Disinfection and disinfectants; Germ theory of disease
RG ———; s.a. Mutation (bacteria); Microorganisms
NYT ———; s.a. Antibiotics; Bacteria and disease names, e.g., Bacilli; Biology and biochemistry
PAIS MEDICINE; s.a. Health
BPI ———; s.a. Bacteriology; Microorganisms; Viruses

BACTERIA—RESISTANCE AND SENSITIVITY. *Use* Antibiotics

BACTERIAL WARFARE. *See* Biological Warfare

BACTERIOLOGY
LC ———; s.a. Germ theory of disease; Microbiology
SEARS ———; s.a. Immunity; Microorganisms; Parasites
RG ———; s.a. Filters and filtration (bacteriology); Toxins and antitoxins
NYT BACTERIA; s.a. Biology and biochemistry; Medicine and health; Microorganisms
PAIS MEDICINE; s.a. Health
BPI ———; s.a. Bacteria; Microorganisms; Viruses

BACTERIOLOGY, AGRICULTURAL
LC ———; s.a. Dairy bacteriology; Nitrification
SEARS ———; s.a. Fruit—Diseases and pests; Soils—Bacteriology
RG BACTERIOLOGY; s.a. Agricultural pests; Bacteria, Photosynthetic
NYT AGRICULTURE AND AGRICULTURAL PRODUCTS; s.a. Bacteria; Food contamination; Pesticides and pests
PAIS PLANTS—DISEASES AND PESTS
BPI BACTERIOLOGY; s.a. Agriculture; Bacteria; Microorganisms

BACKWARD AREAS. *See* Underdeveloped Areas

BACKWARD CHILDREN. *See* Mentally Handicapped Children

BAD DEBTS. *See* Collecting of Accounts

BAHAISM. *Use* Islam

BAIL
LC ———; s.a. Arrest; Criminal procedure
SEARS CRIME AND CRIMINALS; s.a. Justice, Administration of; Prisons; Trials

RG ———; s.a. Habeas corpus; Preventive detention
NYT COURTS; s.a. Crime and criminals
PAIS ———; s.a. Arrest; Criminal procedure
BPI COURTS; s.a. Judges; Justice, Administration of

BAILMENTS. *Use* Property

BAKERY. *Use* Cookery

BAKING
LC ———; s.a. Baked products; Bread; Cookery
SEARS ———; s.a. Cake; Pastry
RG ———; s.a. Dough; names of specific baked goods, e.g., Bread; Ovens
NYT BAKERIES AND BAKED PRODUCTS; s.a. Bread; Food and grocery trade
PAIS BAKING INDUSTRY; s.a. Bread industry
BPI ———; s.a. Baked goods; Bakers and bakeries; Pastry

BALANCE OF NATURE. *See* Ecology

BALANCE OF PAYMENTS
LC ———; s.a. Foreign exchange; International clearing; International finance; International liquidity
SEARS ———; s.a. Foreign exchange; International economic relations
RG ———; s.a. Balance of trade; Eurodollar market
NYT COMMERCE; s.a. Currency; International relations
PAIS ———; s.a. Exchange, Foreign; Money—International aspects
BPI ———; s.a. Balance of trade; Money—International aspects

BALANCE OF POWER. *Use* International Relations

BALANCE OF TRADE. *Use* Balance of Payments; Foreign Trade; Free Trade and Protection; Tariff

BALLADS. *Use* Singing and Songs

BALLET
LC ———; s.a. Choreography; Dancing
SEARS ———; s.a. Pantomimes; Performing arts
RG ———; s.a. Moving pictures—Dance films; Television programs—Dance programs
NYT DANCING; s.a. Entertainment and amusements; Opera; Theater
PAIS DANCING; s.a. Opera; Theater
BPI ———; s.a. Opera; Theater

BALLISTIC MISSILES
LC ———; s.a. Atomic weapons; Intercontinental ballistic missiles; Nuclear rockets
SEARS ———; s.a. Guided missiles; Rockets (aeronautics)
RG GUIDED MISSILES; s.a. Jet propulsion; MIRV
NYT MISSILES; s.a. Aerospace industries and sciences; Atomic energy and weapons; U.S. armament and defense
PAIS GUIDED MISSILES; s.a. Aerospace industries; Guided missile bases

BALLISTICS MISSILES, *cont.*
BPI   GUIDED MISSILES; s.a. Ballistic missile early warning system; Guidance systems (flight); Inertial guidance systems

BALLET MUSIC. *Use* Dance Music

BALLISTICS
LC   ——; s.a. Gunnery; headings beginning with *Ballistic*, e.g., Ballistic missiles
SEARS   SHOOTING; s.a. Ordnance; Projectiles
RG   ——; s.a. Firearms; Projectiles
NYT   MISSILES; s.a. Aerospace industries and sciences; U.S. armament and defense
PAIS   GUIDED MISSILES; s.a. Aerospace industries; Armaments
BPI   ——; s.a. Firearms; Gunnery

BALLOONS
LC   ——; s.a. Aeronautics; Expandable space structures
SEARS   ——; s.a. Aeronautics; Airships
RG   ——; s.a. Aeronautics—History; Balloon ascensions
NYT   ——; s.a. Aeronautics; Astronautics; Weather
PAIS   ——; s.a. Aviation
BPI   ——; s.a. Aeronautics; Airplanes

BALLOT. *Use* Elections; Voting

BALLROOM DANCING. *Use* Dancing

BALLS (Parties). *Use* Entertaining

BANDAGES AND BANDAGING. *Use* Adhesives; First Aid in Illness and Injury

BANDS (Music)
LC   ——; s.a. Conducting; Orchestra
SEARS   ——; s.a. Dance music; Drum majoring; Instrumental music; Jazz music
RG   ——; s.a. Prison bands; Rock groups
NYT   MUSIC; s.a. Culture; Entertainment and amusements
PAIS   ORCHESTRAS; s.a. Industrial relations—Orchestras; Music
BPI   BANDS; s.a. Orchestras; Rock groups

BANK CONSOLIDATIONS AND MERGERS. *Use* Conglomerate Corporations

BANK DEPOSITS. *Use* Banks and Banking

BANK ROBBERS. *Use* Theft

BANK MERGERS. *Use* Banks and Banking, Conglomerate Corporations

BANK LOANS. *Use* Banks and Banking; Loans

BANK INVESTMENTS. *Use* Investments

BANK EMPLOYEES. *Use* Clerks; Office Employees

BANKING
LC   BANKS AND BANKING; s.a. Capital; Economics
SEARS   BANKS AND BANKING; s.a. Bills of exchange; Investments
RG   BANKS AND BANKING; s.a. Foreign exchange; Loans, Bank
NYT   BANKS AND BANKING; s.a. Currency; Property and investments

PAIS   ——; s.a. Checks; Credit
BPI   BANKS AND BANKING; s.a. Savings banks; Trust companies

BANKING—CHECKING ACCOUNTS. *Use* Checks (Banking)

BANKING, INTERNATIONAL. *Use* Finance

BANKING, NATIONAL. *Use* National Banks (U.S.)

BANKING LAW. *Use* National Banks (U.S.); Negotiable Instruments

BANK-NOTES. *Use* Money

BANKRUPTCY
LC   ——; s.a. Business mortality; Finance
SEARS   ——; s.a. Business law; Commercial law; Corporations; Debtor and creditor; Mortgages
RG   ——; s.a. Business failures; Corporations—Reorganization
NYT   BANKRUPTCIES; s.a. Banks and banking; Credit
PAIS   ——; s.a. Business failures; Referees (law)
BPI   ——; s.a. Debtor and creditor; Liquidation

BANKS AND BANKING
LC   ——; s.a. Acceptances; Bank deposits; Bank loans; Bank mergers; Banks and banking, Central; Deposit banking; Liquidity (economics); Mortgage banks; Syndicates (finance)
SEARS   ——; s.a. Agricultural credit; Building and loan associations; Consumer credit; Federal Reserve banks; Interest and usury; Investment trusts; Money; Negotiable instruments; Trust companies
RG   ——; s.a. Checks; Credit; Interest; Loans—Bank
NYT   ——; s.a. Credit Cards; Currency; Savings and loan associations
PAIS   BANKING; s.a. Certificates of deposit; Development banks; Finance; Investment banking; Savings banks
BPI   ——; s.a. Clearing houses; Foreign exchange; Trust companies

BANKS AND BANKING, CENTRAL. *Use* National Banks (U.S.)

BANKS AND BANKING—HISTORY. *Use* Economic History

BANKS AND BANKING, COOPERATIVE. *Use* Cooperative Societies

BANKS AND BANKING, INTERNATIONAL. *Use* International Cooperation; International Finance

BANKS AND BANKING—POLITICAL ACTIVITIES. *Use* Business and Politics

BANQUETS. *See* Dinners and Dining

BAPTISM
LC   ——; s.a. Rites and ceremonies; Sacraments
SEARS   ——; s.a. Rites and ceremonies; Theology
RG   ——; s.a. Rites and ceremonies; Sacraments
NYT   RELIGION AND CHURCHES; s.a. Roman Catholic church
PAIS   RITES AND CEREMONIES; s.a. Churches; Religion
BPI   RELIGION; s.a. Catholic church; Christianity

BAR EXAMINATIONS. *Use* Examinations; Law

BAR MITZVAH. *Use* Jews — Rites and Ceremonies

BARBECUE COOKERY. *Use* Outdoor Life

BARBITURATES
See also names of individual barbituates, e.g., Phenobarbital.
LC ——; s.a. Antispasmodics; Sedatives
SEARS DRUGS
RG ——; s.a. Narcotics; Sedatives
NYT SEDATIVES; s.a. Drug addiction, abuse and traffic; Drugs and drug trade
PAIS ——; s.a. Drugs; Sedatives
BPI ——; s.a. Drugs; Sedatives; Tranquilizing drugs

BARGES. *Use* Waterways

BARRISTERS. *See* Lawyers

BARS AND BARROOMS
LC RESTAURANTS, LUNCH ROOM, ETC.; s.a. Bartenders
SEARS RESTAURANTS, BARS, ETC.
RG ——; s.a. Bars and barrooms—Automation; Liquor traffic
NYT HOTELS, BARS, MOTELS, NIGHT CLUBS, AND RESTAURANTS; s.a. Alcohol; Entertainment and amusements; Liquor
PAIS BARTENDERS
BPI BARS AND BAR ROOMS; s.a. Restaurants, lunchrooms, etc.; Taverns

BARTENDERS. *Use* Bars and Barrooms

BARTER
LC ——; s.a. Commerce; Economics
SEARS COMMERCE; s.a. Currency question; Exchange; Markets
RG ——; s.a. Commerce, Markets
NYT ——; s.a. commodity names, e.g., Cotton; U.S.—Economic conditions and trends (general)
PAIS ——; s.a. Commerce, Foreign; Economics
BPI ——; s.a. Commerce; Money

BASEBALL
LC ——; s.a. College sports; Softball
SEARS ——; s.a. Baseball clubs; Little league baseball
RG ——; s.a. Little leagues; Pitching (baseball)
NYT ——; s.a. Athletics; Softball; Sports
PAIS ——; s.a. College athletics; Sports
BPI ——; s.a. Sports; Stadiums; Strikes—Baseball players

BASES (Chemistry). *Use* Chemistry

BASHFULNESS. *Use* Emotions

BASKET MAKING
LC ——; s.a. Arts and crafts movement; Raffia work
SEARS ——; s.a. Industrial arts education; Weaving
RG ——; s.a. Arts and crafts; Indians of North America—Basket making
NYT BASKETS; s.a. Handicrafts; Weaving
PAIS HANDICRAFTS
BPI HANDICRAFT; s.a. Arts and crafts; Hobbies

BASKETBALL
LC ——; s.a Netball
SEARS ——; s.a. College sports; Games
RG ——; s.a. College athletics; Sports
NYT ——; s.a. Athletics; Sports
PAIS ——; s.a. College athletics; Sports
BPI ——; s.a. Athletics

BASTARDY. *See* Illegitimacy

BATH PREPARATIONS. *Use* Toilet

BATHING. *Use* Baths

BATHING BEACHES. *Use* Beaches

BATHS
LC ——; s.a. Hygiene; Shower-baths; Toilet
SEARS ——; s.a. Hydrotherapy; Physical therapy
RG ——; s.a. Hydrotherapy; Sun baths
NYT BATHING; s.a. Bathrooms; Sanitation
PAIS PUBLIC BATHS
BPI ——; s.a. Baths, Vapor; Bathtubs

BATIK. *Use* Dyes and Dyeing

BATIK INDUSTRY. *Use* Textile Industry and Fabrics

BATS. *Use* Caves

BATTERY (Law). *See* Assault and Battery

BATTERY RADIOS. *See* Radio—Apparatus and Supplies

BATTLES
See also names of battles, e.g., Harlem Heights, Battle of 1776.
LC ——; s.a. Attack and defense (military science); Bombardment; Combat; Military history; Sieges; subd. *Campaigns* and *battles* under names of wars, e.g., U.S.—History—Civil war—Campaigns and battles
SEARS ——; s.a. Military art and science; Naval battles; War
RG ——; s.a. Strategy; War
NYT MILITARY ART AND SCIENCE; s.a. Armament, defense and military forces; U.S. Armament and defense; War and Revolution
PAIS MILITARY ART AND SCIENCE; s.a. Aerial warfare; War—Strategy
BPI MILITARY ART AND SCIENCE; s.a. Strategy; War

BATTLESHIPS. *Use* Warships

BAUXITE AND BAUXITE INDUSTRY. *Use* Aluminum

BAYESIAN STATISTICAL DECISION THEORY. *Use* Decision Making

BAZAARS, CHARITABLE. *Use* Fairs

BEACHES
LC ——; s.a. Bathing beaches; Littoral drift
SEARS SEASHORE; s.a. Erosion; Reclamation of land; Sand dunes
RG ——; s.a. Beach erosion; Coast changes; Shore protection
NYT ——; s.a. Coast erosion; Parks, playgrounds and other recreation areas
PAIS ——; s.a. Shore lines; Shore protection
BPI ——; s.a. Beach erosion; Beaches—Insurance; Seaside resorts

BEADWORK
LC   BEADS; s.a. Glass beads; Rosary
SEARS   ——; s.a. Arts and crafts; Embroidery
RG   ——; s.a. Arts and crafts; Beads
NYT   JEWELS AND JEWELRY; s.a. Art objects
PAIS   JEWELRY BUSINESS; s.a. Handicrafts
BPI   GLASS BEADS; s.a. Arts and crafts; Handicraft; Jewelry

BEANS
LC   ——; s.a. Forage plants; Soybean
SEARS   SOYBEAN; s.a. Cookery; Forage plants
RG   ——; s.a. Cookery—Vegetables; Lima beans
NYT   ——; s.a. Agriculture and agricultural products; Food and grocery trade
PAIS   BEAN INDUSTRY; s.a. Soybean industry
BPI   ——; s.a. Soy sauce; Soybean oil; Soybeans

BEARINGS (Machinery)
Scope: Terms relating to engineering supports, particularly those in machinery, and especially to the moving parts.
LC   ——; s.a. Electric suspension; Tribology
SEARS   ——; s.a. Lubrication and lubricants; Machinery
RG   ——; s.a. Automobiles—Bearings; Machinery industry
NYT   BEARINGS; s.a. Machine tools and dies; Machinery, Industrial equipment and supplies
PAIS   BEARINGS; s.a. Machinery
BPI   ——; s.a. Cars—Bearings; Magnetic suspension

BEAT GENERATION. *Use* Bohemianism

BEATIFICATION. *Use* Canonization

BEATNIKS. *Use* Bohemianism

BEATS. *See* Bohemianism

BEAUTIFICATION OF THE LANDSCAPE. *See* Landscape Protection

BEAUTY. *See* Aesthetics

BEAUTY, PERSONAL
LC   ——; s.a. Hygiene; Toilet
SEARS   ——; s.a. Beauty shops; Costume
RG   ——; s.a. Cosmetics; Grooming, Personal; Make up
NYT   TOILETRY AND COSMETICS; s.a. Body, Human; Medicine and health
PAIS   BEAUTY CULTURE; s.a. Cosmetic industry; Toilet goods industry
BPI   ——; s.a. Hygiene; Skin; Women—Health and hygiene

BE-BOP MUSIC. *See* Jazz Music

BEDS AND BEDDING
LC   ——; s.a. Blankets; Hospital beds; Sheets
SEARS   COVERLETS; s.a. Interior decoration
RG   BEDS; s.a. Bedding; Coverlets; Cribs (beds); Quilts
NYT   BEDDING; s.a. Furniture; Household equipment and furnishings
PAIS   BEDDING INDUSTRY; s.a. Blanket industry; Furniture industry
BPI   BEDS; s.a. Bedding; Mattress industry; Mattresses; Pillows

BEE CULTURE. *Use* Bees

BEEF
LC   ——; s.a. Corned beef; Meat
SEARS   ——; s.a. Cattle; Meat
RG   ——; s.a. Cattle, Beef; Cookery—Meat
NYT   MEAT; s.a. Cattle; Livestock
PAIS   BEEF INDUSTRY; s.a. Cattle industry; Meat industry
BPI   ——; s.a. Cattle; Meat

BEEF INDUSTRY. *Use* Meat Industry and Trade

BEER AND BREWING INDUSTRY
LC   BREWING INDUSTRY; s.a. Ale; Beer; Brewing; Liquor traffic
SEARS   BEER; s.a. Beverages
RG   BEER; s.a. Brewing industries; Cookery—Beer
NYT   ——; s.a. Beverages
PAIS   BREWING INDUSTRY; s.a. Beverage industry
BPI   BEER; s.a. Breweries; Brewing industry

BEES
LC   ——; s.a. Bee hunting; Honeycombs
SEARS   ——; s.a. Honey; Insects
RG   ——; s.a. Bee culture; Beeswax
NYT   ——; s.a. Honey
PAIS   BEE INDUSTRY; s.a. Honey industry
BPI   ——; s.a. Honey; Insects, Injurious and beneficial

BEETS AND BEET SUGAR
LC   ——; s.a. Cookery (beets); Sugar
SEARS   ——; s.a. Sugar
RG   BEETS; s.a. Sugar industry; Vegetables
NYT   BEETS; s.a. Agriculture and agricultural products; Sugar
PAIS   BEETS AND BEET SUGAR INDUSTRY; s.a. Sugar industry
BPI   VEGETABLES; s.a. Crops; Farm produce

BEGGING
LC   ——; s.a. Poor; Vagrancy
SEARS   ——; s.a. Charity; Tramps
RG   BEGGING AND BEGGARS; s.a. Homeless, The; Tramps
NYT   BEGGARS AND BEGGING; s.a. Philanthropy; Vagrancy
PAIS   BEGGARS AND BEGGING; s.a. Tramps; Vagrancy
BPI   POVERTY; s.a. Charities; Food relief

BEHAVIOR. *Use* Character; Conditioned Response; Ethics; Human Relations; Virtues

BEHAVIOR (Psychology)
LC   ——; s.a. Animals, Habits and behavior of; Conditioned response; Displacement (psychology); Human behavior; Social adjustment
SEARS   BEHAVIOR; s.a. Attitude (psychology); Behaviorism (psychology); Conformity; Emotions; Individuality; Neuroses
RG   ——; s.a. Group relations training; Motivation (psychology); Social norm
NYT   PSYCHOLOGY AND PSYCHOLOGISTS; s.a. Brain; Mind

PAIS ———; s.a. Behaviorial sciences; Deviant behavior; Psychology; Society and the individual
BPI ———; s.a. Conformity; Human relations; Influence (psychology)

BEHAVIOR PROBLEMS. *See* Problem Children

BEHAVIOR THERAPY
LC ———; s.a. Group relations training; Psychotherapy; Rational-emotive psychotherapy
SEARS BEHAVIOR; s.a. Behaviorism (psychology); Psychotherapy
RG ———; s.a. Psychotherapy; Social education
NYT MENTAL HEALTH AND DISORDERS; s.a. Psychology and psychologists
PAIS BEHAVIOR (Psychology); s.a. Group behavior; Psychotherapy
BPI BEHAVIOR (Psychology); s.a. Conditioned response; Psychotherapy; Violence

BEHAVIORAL SCIENCES. *Use* Behavior (Psychology); Social Sciences

BELIEF AND DOUBT
Scope: Works treating the subject from the philosophical standpoint; works on religious belief are entered under Faith.
LC ———; s.a. Agnosticism; Knowledge, Theory of
SEARS ———; s.a. Emotions; Rationalism; Truth
RG ———; s.a. Credulity; Skepticism
NYT PHILOSOPHY; s.a. Psychology and psychologists
PAIS KNOWLEDGE, THEORY OF
BPI KNOWLEDGE, THEORY OF; s.a. Ideology; Subjectivity

BELLES-LETTRES. *See* Literature

BELLIGERENCY. *Use* War (International law)

BENEVOLENCE. *See* Charity

BEQUESTS. *See* Inheritance and Succession

BEST SELLERS. *Use* Book Industries and Trade; Books; Publishers and Publishing

BETTER BUSINESS BUREAUS. *Use* Advertising, Fraudulent; Business Ethics; Consumer Protection

BETTING. *Use* Gambling

BEVERAGES
See also names of beverages, e.g. Cocoa; Coffee; Tea, etc.
LC ———; s.a. Bottling; Carbonated beverages
SEARS ———; s.a. Diet; Food; Liquors
RG ———; s.a. Alcoholic beverages; Soft drink industry
NYT ———; s.a. Alcohol; Hotels, bars, motels, night clubs and restaurants; Liquor
PAIS BEVERAGE INDUSTRY; s.a. Bottling industry; Brewing industry; Tea industry
BPI ———; s.a. Bottles; Bottling plants; Canned beverages

BHAKTI YOGA. *See* Yoga

BIBLE
LC ———; s.a. Bible, O.T.; Bible, N.T.
SEARS ———; s.a. History, Ancient; Sacred books

RG ———; s.a. Jews; Prophets
NYT ———; s.a. Archeology and anthropology; Prayers and prayer books
PAIS RELIGIOUS LITERATURE; s.a. Christianity and other religions; Jews
BPI ———; s.a. Christianity; Jews

BIBLE—EVIDENCES, AUTHORITY, ETC. *Use* Miracles

BIBLE—HOMILETICAL USE. *Use* Preaching

BIBLE—PROPHECIES—MESSIAH. *Use* Messiah

BIBLE IN THE SCHOOLS. *See* Religious Education

BIBLE STUDY. *Use* Religious Education

BIBLIOGRAPHIC SERVICES. *Use* Information Services

BIBLIOGRAPHICAL CENTERS. *Use* Libraries and Librarians

BIBLIOGRAPHY
See also subd. *Bibliography* under subjects, e.g., Accounting—Bibliography; Africa—Bibliography, etc.
LC ———; s.a. Libraries; Titles of books
SEARS ———; s.a. Indexing; Information storage and retrieval
RG ———; s.a. Books and reading—Best books; Reading lists
NYT BOOKS AND LITERATURE; s.a. Libraries and librarians; specific subjects of bibliographies, e.g., Religion and churches
PAIS ———; s.a. Documentation
BPI ———; s.a. Literature searching

BIBLIOTHERAPY. *Use* Therapeutics

BICULTURALISM. *Use* Civilization

BICYCLES AND BICYCLING
LC BICYCLES AND TRICYCLES; s.a. Cycling; Vehicles
SEARS ———; s.a. Bicycle racing; Motorcycles
RG BICYCLES; s.a. Bicycle racing; Cycling
NYT ———; s.a. Sports; Traffic (vehicular and pedestrian) and parking; Transportation
PAIS BICYCLE INDUSTRY; s.a. Cycling; Motorcycles
BPI BICYCLES; s.a. Leisure; Recreation

BIG BUSINESS
LC ———; s.a. Business; Competition; Industries, Size of
SEARS TRUSTS, INDUSTRIAL; s.a. Corporations; Industry
RG ———; s.a. Corporations—Size; Industries, Size of
NYT CORPORATIONS; s.a. Commerce; Economic conditions and trends (general); U.S.—Economic conditions and trends
PAIS CORPORATIONS—SIZE; s.a. Industries, Size of; Industry—Concentration ratios
BPI MONOPOLIES; s.a. Competition; Oligopolies

BIGAMY
LC ———; s.a. Marriage; Polygamy
SEARS MARRIAGE; s.a. Domestic relations; Sexual ethics
RG MARRIAGE; s.a. Divorce; Remarriage

BIGAMY, *cont.*
NYT ——; s.a. Divorce, separations and annulments; Marriages
PAIS ——; s.a. Polyandry; Polygamy
BPI MARRIAGE; s.a. Concubinage; Divorce

BIGOTRY. *See* Toleration

BILATERAL TRADE. *Use* Commercial Policy

BILINGUAL INSTRUCTION. *Use* Bilingualism; Education, Bilingual

BILINGUALISM
LC ——; s.a. Education, Bilingual; Language and languages
SEARS ——; s.a. Bilingual books
RG EDUCATION, BILINGUAL; s.a. Bilingual instruction; Language and languages—Study and teaching
NYT LANGUAGE AND LANGUAGES; s.a. Education and schools—Foreign study, teaching and travel
PAIS ——; s.a. Languages
BPI LANGUAGE AND LANGUAGES; s.a. Education; Teaching

BILLBOARDS
LC ——; s.a. Advertising, Outdoor; Signs and sign-boards
SEARS SIGNS AND SIGNBOARDS; s.a. Electric signs; Posters
RG ——; s.a. Advertising, Outdoor; Signs
NYT ADVERTISING—U.S.—OUTDOOR ADVERTISING; s.a. Signs and symbols
PAIS ADVERTISING, OUTDOOR; s.a. Signs and signboards
BPI ADVERTISING, OUTDOOR; s.a. Road signs; Signs

BILLING. *Use* Collecting of Accounts

BILLS, LEGISLATIVE. *Use* Legislation

BILLS AND NOTES. *See* Negotiable Instruments

BILLS OF CREDIT. *See* Credit

BILLS OF EXCHANGE. *Use* Acceptances; Banking; Checks (Banking); Foreign Exchange; Money; Negotiable Instruments

BILLS OF SALE. *Use* Sales

BIMETALLISM. *Use* Money

BIOCHEMISTRY
LC BIOLOGICAL CHEMISTRY; s.a. Biochemical engineering; Chemistry, Technical; Quantum biochemistry
SEARS ——; s.a. Chemical engineering; Chemistry
RG ——; s.a. Bioenergetics; Immunochemistry; Metabolism
NYT BIOLOGY AND BIOCHEMISTRY; s.a. Chemistry and chemicals
PAIS BIOLOGY
BPI ——; s.a. Enzymes; Molecular biology

BIOCLIMATOLOGY. *Use* Ecology; Man—Influence of Environment

BIOENERGETICS. *Use* Biochemistry

BIOENGINEERING. *Use* Biological Warfare

BIO-GEOGRAPHY. *See* Anthropo-Geography

BIOGRAPHY
Scope: Collections of biographies not limited to one country or to one class of people. See also subd. *Biography* under classes of persons, authors, musicians, etc., also special subjects with subd. *Biography*, e.g., Woman—Biography, and names of persons for biographies of individuals.
LC ——; s.a. Autobiographies; Christian biography; Military biography
SEARS ——; s.a. Anecdotes; Portraits
RG ——; s.a. Genealogy; Obituaries
NYT BIOGRAPHIES; s.a. Book reviews; Books and literature; names of biographees
PAIS ——; s.a. Directories—Biographical; Obituaries
BPI ——; s.a. Book industry—Biographies; Genealogy

BIOGRAPHY (As a literary form)
LC ——; s.a. Autobiography; Diaries; Literature
SEARS ——; s.a. Autobiographies; Literature
RG BIOGRAPHY; s.a. Autobiography; Diaries
NYT BIOGRAPHIES; s.a. Books and literature; Diaries; Writing and writers
PAIS BIOGRAPHY; s.a. Literature
BPI BIOGRAPHY; s.a. Books and reading; Geneology

BIOLOGICAL AND CHEMICAL WARFARE. *Use* Biological Warfare

BIOLOGICAL CHEMISTRY. *Use* Biochemistry; Chemistry

BIOLOGICAL CONTROL SYSTEMS. *Use* Biological Physics; Nervous System

BIOLOGICAL PHYSICS
LC ——; s.a. Cells; Electronics in biology
SEARS BIOPHYSICS; s.a. Bionics; Molecular biology
RG ——; s.a. Biological control systems; Molecular biology
NYT PHYSICS; s.a. Biology and biochemistry
PAIS BIOLOGY
BPI PHYSICS; s.a. Biology; Biomedical engineering

BIOLOGICAL WARFARE
LC ——; s.a. Bioengineering
SEARS ——; s.a. Communicable diseases; Tactics
RG ——; s.a. Chemical and biological weapons; Chemical warfare; War
NYT ——; s.a. Biology and biochemistry; Military art and science
PAIS ——; s.a. Military art and science
BPI BIOLOGICAL AND CHEMICAL WARFARE; s.a. Disarmament and arms control; Military art and science

BIOLOGY
LC ——; s.a. Anatomy, Human; Biometry; Evolution; Natural history
SEARS ——; s.a. Embryology; Microbiology
RG ——; s.a. Biological physics; Ecology; Life (biology)

NYT BIOLOGY AND BIOCHEMISTRY; s.a. Animals; Eugenics
PAIS ———; s.a. Genetics; Natural history
BPI ———; s.a. Genetics; Reproduction

BIOMECHANICS. *See* Human Engineering

BIOMEDICAL ENGINEERING. *Use* Biological Physics; Medicine

BIOMETRY
LC ———; s.a. Biomathematics; Entomology—Statistical methods; Mathematical statistics
SEARS SAMPLING (Statistics); s.a. Biology; Heredity; Statistics
RG STATISTICAL METHODS; s.a. subd. *Statistics* under usbjects, e.g., Heredity—Statistics; Vital statistics
NYT BIOLOGY AND BIOCHEMISTRY; s.a. Nature; Statistics
PAIS STATISTICS; s.a. Sampling; Vital statistics
BPI STATISTICS; s.a. Sampling (statistics); Variance analysis

BIONICS. *Use* Biological Physics; Cybernetics

BIOPHYSICS. *Use* Biological Physics

BIOSTATICS. *See* Biometry

BIOTECHNOLOGY. *See* Human Engineering

BIOTIC COMMUNITIES. *Use* Ecology

BIRDS. *Use* Flight; Wildlife Conservation

BIRDS—FLIGHT. *Use* Aerodynamics

BIRDS, INJURIOUS AND BENEFICIAL. *Use* Zoology, Economic

BIRDS OF PREY. *Use* Predatory Animals

BIRTH. *See* Labor (Obstetrics)

BIRTH (Philosophy). *Use* Life

BIRTH CONTROL
LC ———; s.a. Conception—Prevention; Condoms; Contraceptives; Veneral diseases—Prevention
SEARS ———; s.a. Birth rate; Children; Family; Illegitimacy; Sexual hygiene; Sterilization
RG ———; s.a. Abortion; Childbirth; Conception; Contraceptives; Malthusianism
NYT BIRTH CONTROL AND PLANNED PARENTHOOD; s.a. Abortion; Births; Population and vital statistics; Sex
PAIS ———; s.a. Contraceptives; Sterilization
BPI ———; s.a. Contraceptives; Family size; Sterilization (birth control)

BIRTH DEFECTS. *Use* Labor (Obstetrics)

BIRTH DEFECTS (Congenital defects). *Use* Genetics; Handicapped

BIRTH RATE. *Use* Birth Control; Demography; Population

BIRTHDAYS. *Use* Special Days, Weeks and Months

BIRTHS. *Use* Birth Control; Demography; Population; Vital Statistics

BISEXUALITY. *Use* Homosexuality

BLACK AMERICANS. *See* Negroes

BLACK ART. *Use* Art and Race

BLACK ART (Magic). *See* Occult Sciences

BLACK ARTISTS. *Use* Artists

BLACK ATHLETES. *Use* Athletes

BLACK AUTHORS. *Use* Black Literature; Negroes in Literature

BLACK BUSINESSMEN. *Use* Entrepreneur; Negroes and Business; Small Business

BLACK CAPITALISM. *Use* Black Nationalism; Black Power; Entrepreneur; Negroes and Business; New Business Enterprises; Small Business

BLACK CHILDREN. *See* Negro Children

BLACK COLLEGES
See also names of individual colleges or universities, e.g., Howard University.
LC NEGRO UNIVERSITIES AND COLLEGES; s.a. Art in Negro universities and colleges; Negro theological seminaries
SEARS COLLEGES AND UNIVERSITIES; s.a. Blacks—Education; Segregation in education
RG NEGRO COLLEGES AND UNIVERSITIES; s.a. Negroes—Education; Private schools, Negro
NYT COLLEGES AND UNIVERSITIES—U.S.—EQUAL EDUCATIONAL OPPORTUNITIES; s.a. Colleges and universities; Negroes (in U.S.)
PAIS NEGRO COLLEGES; s.a. Colleges and universities; Negro students
BPI NEGROES—EDUCATION; s.a. Colleges and universities; Discrimination in education

BLACK DIALECT. *See* Negro—English Dialects

BLACK FAMILIES. *See* Family

BLACK LITERATURE
LC NEGRO LITERATURE; s.a. American literature—Negro authors; Negro poetry; Negroes in literature
SEARS ———; s.a. American literature; Black authors; Black poetry
RG NEGRO LITERATURE; s.a. African literature; Publishers and publishing—Negro literature
NYT BOOKS AND LITERATURE; s.a. Negroes (general); Negroes (in U.S.)
PAIS NEGROES IN LITERATURE; s.a. African literature; Literature
BPI LITERATURE; s.a. Negro periodicals; Negroes in literature

BLACK MARKET
See also subd. *Black Market* under commodity, e.g., Black Market—Steel.
LC ———; s.a. Commerce; Price regulation; Supply and demand
SEARS COMMERCE; s.a. Markets; Prices
RG BLACK MARKETS; s.a. Profiteering; War profits

BLACK MARKET, *cont.*
NYT   Commodity and Industry Names, e.g., Tobacco, Food and Grocery Trade; s.a. Commerce; Currency
PAIS   BLACK MARKETS; s.a. Commerce, Foreign; Prices—Regulation; Priorities; Industrial
BPI   ———; s.a. Commerce; Food supply; Prices; Prices—Regulation

BLACK MUSIC. *Use* Music; Negro Music

BLACK MUSLIMS
LC   ———; s.a. Islam; Negroes—Religion; U.S.—Race question
SEARS   ———; s.a. Black nationalism; Blacks—Religion
RG   ———; s.a. Black Muslim Movement; Negroes—Religion
NYT   BLACK MUSLIMS (Organization); s.a. Negroes (in U.S.); Organizations, societies and clubs
PAIS   BLACK MUSLIM MOVEMENT; s.a. Negroes—Political activities; U.S.—Race relations
BPI   NEGROES

BLACK NATIONALISM
LC   ———; s.a. Black power; Negroes—Politics and suffrage
SEARS   ———; s.a. Blacks—Political activity; Blacks—Race identity
RG   NEGROES—NATIONALISM; s.a. Black power; Nationalism—Negro race
NYT   BLACK NATIONALISM (Political movement); s.a. Black power (slogan); Negroes (general)
PAIS   BLACK NATIONALIST MOVEMENT; s.a. Negroes—Political activities
BPI   NEGROES—POLITICS AND SUFFRAGE; s.a. Black capitalism; Negroes

BLACK POETRY. *Use* Black Literature

BLACK POWER
LC   ———; s.a. Negroes; Negroes—Civil rights; Negroes—Economic conditions
SEARS   ———; s.a. Black nationalism; Blacks—Civil rights; Blacks—Economic conditions
RG   ———; s.a. Black capitalism; Negroes—Nationalism
NYT   BLACK POWER (Slogan); s.a. Freedom and human rights; Minorities (ethnic, racial, religious); Negroes (general)
PAIS   NEGROES—POLITICAL ACTIVITIES; s.a. Civil rights
BPI   NEGROES—POLITICS AND SUFFRAGE; s.a. Black capitalism; Negroes

BLACK SONGS. *Use* Negro Music

BLACK STUDIES. *Use* Afro-American Studies; Area Studies

BLACK VETERANS. *See* Negroes as Soldiers

BLACKJACK (Game). *Use* Gambling

BLACKLISTING. *Use* Boycott; Discrimination in Employment; Employment

BLACKOUTS, ELECTRIC POWER. *See* Electric Power Plants

BLACKS. *Use* Black Power; Civil Rights; Negroes; Slavery in the United States; Woman; Youth

BLACKS (People and ethnic aspects). *Use* Negro Race

BLACKS—CIVIL RIGHTS. *Use* Equality

BLACKS—ECONOMIC CONDITIONS. *Use* Negroes and Business

BLACKS—EDUCATION. *Use* Afro-American Studies; Black Colleges; Busing; Discrimination in Education; Negro Studies; Segregation

BLACKS—HOUSING. *Use* Housing

BLACKS—POLITICAL ACTIVITY. *Use* Black Nationalism; Negroes

BLACKS—RACE IDENTITY. *Use* Black Nationalism; Ethnopsychology; Negro Race; Negroes; Race Awareness

BLACKS—RELIGION. *Use* Black Muslims

BLACKS—SEGREGATION. *Use* Discrimination; Segregation

BLACKS AND THE PRESS
LC   NEGRO NEWSPAPERS (American); s.a. Negro periodicals (American); Negro press
SEARS   AMERICAN NEWSPAPERS; s.a. Journalism; Reporters and reporting
RG   NEGRO PRESS; s.a. Journalism; Negro journalists
NYT   NEWS AND NEWS MEDIA—U.S.; s.a. names of newspapers, e.g., *N.Y. Amsterdam News*; Negroes (in U.S.)
PAIS   NEGRO PRESS; s.a. Negro journalists; Press
BPI   NEWSPAPERS, NEGRO; s.a. Black capitalism; Negro periodicals; Newspapers and negroes

BLACKS IN LITERATURE AND ART. *Use* Art and Race; Negroes in Literature

BLANK VERSE. *Use* Versification

BLANKET INDUSTRY. *Use* Beds and Bedding

BLASPHEMY. *Use* Ecclesiastical Law; Libel and Slander; Oaths; Religious Liberty

BLAST FURNACES. *Uses* Steel Industry and Trade

BLASTING
LC   ———; s.a. Explosives; Mines, Military
SEARS   EXPLOSIVES; s.a. Dynamite; Gunpowder
RG   ———; s.a. Atomic blasting; Nitroglycerin
NYT   EXPLOSIONS; s.a. Bombs and bomb plots; Explosives
PAIS   EXPLOSIVES; s.a. Bombs; Nuclear excavation
BPI   ———; s.a. Atomic blasting; Explosives

BLEACHING. *Use* Dyes and Dyeing; Laundries and Laundering; Textile Industry and Fabrics

BLIND
LC   ———; s.a. Physically handicapped
SEARS   ———; s.a. Blind—Institutional care; Vision
RG   ———; s.a. Libraries—Services to blind; Sports for the blind

NYT BLINDNESS AND THE BLIND; s.a. Color blindness; Disease names, e.g., Glaucoma; Handicapped
PAIS ——; s.a. Social service—Work with the blind; Talking books
BPI ——; s.a. Handicapped; Veterans, Disabled

BLIND—EDUCATION. *Use* Vocational Education; Vocational Guidance

BLIND—EMPLOYMENT. *Use* Vocational Rehabilitation

BLIND—DEAF. *Use* Deafness

BLINDNESS AND THE BLIND. *Use* Blind

BLOCK TRADING. *Use* Stock Exchange

BLOCKADE. *Use* Neutrality

BLOOD
LC ——; s.a. Anemia; Hematology
SEARS ——; s.a. Blood—Circulation; Physiology
RG ——; s.a. Arteries; Blood donors; Hemorrhage
NYT ——; s.a. Blood pressure; Blood vessels; Disease names, e.g., Leukemia
PAIS ——; s.a. Physiology
BPI ——; s.a. Anemia; Leukemia

BLOOD—TRANSFUSION. *Use* Surgery

BLOOD BROTHERHOOD. *Use* Society, Primitive

BLOOD DONORS. *Use* Blood

BLOOD PRESSURE
LC ——; s.a. Arteries; Blood—Circulation; Pressure
SEARS ——; s.a. Blood—Circulation
RG ——; s.a. Blood—Circulation, Disorders of; Hypertension
NYT ——; s.a. Gamma globulin; Heart (general material on cardiovascular disease)
PAIS BLOOD; s.a. Heart disease; Physiology
BPI ——; s.a. Cardiovascular system; Heart

BLOOD VESSELS. *Use* Arteries

BLUE LAWS. *See* Sabbath

BLUEPRINTS. *Use* Copying Processes; Drawings

BLUES (Songs, etc.). *Use* Jazz Music; Music; Negro Music

BOARDING HOMES. *See* Nursing Homes

BOARDING SCHOOLS. *Use* Private Schools

BOARDS OF EDUCATION. *See* Educational Administration

BOARDS OF TRADE. *Use* Trade and Professional Associations

BOATING. *Use* Boats and Boating

BOATS AND BOATING
LC ——; s.a. Aquatic sports; Ice-boats; Sailing; Ships
SEARS ——; s.a. Boat racing; Maritime law; Ocean travel; Steamboats; Water sports
RG ——; s.a. Navigation; Sailboat racing; Sailing
NYT BOATS AND YACHTS; s.a. Boating (yachting); Lifeboats and Liferafts; Ships and shipping
PAIS BOATING; s.a. Fishing boats; Marinas
BPI ——; s.a. Liferafts; Motorboats; Navigation; Yachts and yachting

BODY, HUMAN
See also parts of human body, e.g., Brain, Head, etc.
LC ——; s.a. Anatomy, Human; Human biology; Physiology; Posture
SEARS ANATOMY; s.a. Mind and body; Physiology
RG ——; s.a. Anatomy; Physiology
NYT ——; s.a. Biology and biochemistry; Exercise; Growth; Medicine and health
PAIS PHYSIOLOGY
BPI PHYSIOLOGY; s.a. Beauty, Personal; Growth; Reproduction

BODY AND MIND. *See* Mind and Body

BODY IMAGE. *Use* Perception

BODY MECHANICS. *See* Posture

BODY WEIGHT CONTROL. *See* Weight Control

BOHEMIANISM
LC ——; s.a. Hippies; Manners and customs; Subculture
SEARS ——; s.a. Collective settlements; Hippies
RG ——; s.a. Beatniks; Hippies
NYT MANNERS AND CUSTOMS; s.a. Beat generation; Beatniks
PAIS HIPPIES
BPI HIPPIES; s.a. Clothing and dress; Manners and customs

BOILERS. *Use* Heating

BOILING POINTS. *Use* Temperature

BOLSHEVISM. *See* Communism

BOMB SCARES. *Use* Terrorism

BOMBING, AERIAL. *Use* Air Warfare

BOMBS
LC ——; s.a. Ammunition; Ordnance
SEARS ——; s.a. Atomic bomb; Incendiary bombs
RG ——; s.a. Atomic bombs; Hydrogen bombs
NYT BOMBS AND BOMB PLOTS; s.a. Armament, defense and military forces; Atomic energy and weapons; War names, e.g., Korean war
PAIS ——; s.a. Armaments; Guided missiles
BPI ——; s.a. Atomic bombs; Blasting; Guided missiles

BOMBS AND BOMB PLOTS. *Use* Offenses Against Public Safety; Sabotage; Terrorism; Violence

BOND GRAPHS. *Use* System Analysis

BONDING (Bail). *See* Bail

BONDING (Technology). *See* Solder and Soldering

BONDING AND BONDSMEN. *Use* Bail; Suretyship and Guaranty

BONDS
LC ——; s.a. Finance; Stock exchange; Stocks
SEARS ——; s.a. Debts, Public; Investments

BONDS, *cont.*
RG ———; s.a. Finance, Public; Municipal bonds; Taxation of bonds, securities, etc.
NYT STOCKS AND BONDS; s.a. Company reports; Government bonds; Property and investments
PAIS ———; s.a. Investments; Securities
BPI ———; s.a. Investments; Municipal bonds; Negotiable instruments

BONDS, GOVERNMENT. *Use* Economic Assistance; Finance, Public; Investments; Municipal Government

BONDS, REVENUE. *Use* Municipal Government

BONDS, SCHOOL. *Use* Municipal Government

BONE GRAFTING. *Use* Surgery

BONES—DISEASES. *Use* Chiropractic

BONUS SYSTEM
Scope: Works on the distribution of money as employee bonus, as gift or reward for achievement.
LC ———; s.a. Incentives in industry; Profit sharing
SEARS PROFIT SHARING; s.a. Cooperation; Wages
RG ———; s.a. Incentives in industry; Wage payment plans
NYT BONUSES; s.a. names of businesses, industries and companies, e.g., New York Telephone Company; Labor—US—Overtime and premium pay
PAIS ———; s.a. Incentives in industry; Non-wage payments; Profit sharing
BPI ———; s.a. Incentives in industry; Profit sharing; Wages and salaries

BOOK CENSORSHIP. *See* Censorship

BOOK CLUBS. *Use* Reading

BOOK COLLECTING. *Use* Collectors and Collecting

BOOK DESIGN. *Use* Book Industries and Trade

BOOK FAIRS. *Use* Fairs

BOOK ILLUSTRATION. *See* Illustrated Books

BOOK INDUSTRIES AND TRADE
LC ———; s.a. Printing; Publishers and publishing
SEARS ———; s.a. Bookbinding; Paper making and trade
RG BOOK INDUSTRIES; s.a. Booksellers and bookselling; Copyright
NYT BOOKS AND LITERATURE—BOOK TRADE; s.a. Books and literature—Publishing, sales and distribution; Publications
PAIS BOOK INDUSTRY; s.a. Privately printed books; Publishing industry
BPI BOOK INDUSTRY; s.a. Best Sellers; Book design; Publishers and publishing

BOOK OF MORMON. *Use* Mormons and Mormonism

BOOK SELECTION. *Use* Books

BOOK TRADE. *See* Book Industries and Trade; Publishers and Publishing

BOOKBINDING. *Use* Book Industries and Trade; Leather Industry and Trade

BOOKKEEPERS. *See* Accountants

BOOKKEEPING. *Use* Accounting; Business Education

BOOKKEEPING MACHINES. *Use* Machine Accounting

BOOK-MAKING (Betting). *Use* Gambling; Horse Racing

BOOKS
LC ———; s.a. Bibliography—Best books; Book reviews under subject, e.g., Business—Book reviews; Books and reading for children; Illustrated books; Incunabula; Plots (drama, novel, etc.)
SEARS ———; s.a. Authorship; Book selection; Books and reading; Fiction; Paperback books
RG ———; s.a. Best sellers; Block books; Manuscripts; Textbooks
NYT BOOKS AND LITERATURE; s.a. Book reviews; Libraries and librarians; Publications; Writing and writers
PAIS ———; s.a. Reference books; Text books
BPI ———; s.a. Copyright; Paperback books; Printing—History; Publishers and Publishing; Textbooks

BOOKS—CENSORSHIP. *Use* Censorship; Liberty of Speech; Literature

BOOKS, PROHIBITED. *See* Censorship

BOOKS AND LITERATURE—CHILDREN AND YOUTH. *Use* Children's Literature

BOOKS AND LITERATURE—PUBLISHING, SALES AND DISTRIBUTION. *Use* Book Industries and Trade

BOOKS AND READING. *Use* Books; Education; Libraries and Librarians

BOOKS AND READING—BEST BOOKS. *Use* Bibliography

BOOKS AND READING FOR CHILDREN. *Use* Children's Literature

BOOKSELLERS AND BOOKSELLING. *Use* Book Industries and Trade; Mail-order Business; Publishers and Publishing

BOOKSELLING. *Use* Publishers and Publishing

BOOTS AND SHOES
LC ———; s.a. Leather industry and trade; Safety shoes
SEARS SHOES AND SHOE INDUSTRY; s.a. Clothing and dress; Leather industry and trade
RG SHOES; s.a. Slippers; Wooden shoes
NYT SHOES, BOOTS AND RUBBERS; s.a. Apparel; Leather and leather goods
PAIS SHOE INDUSTRY; s.a. Leather industry
BPI SHOES; s.a. Shoe factories; Shoe industry; Shoe stores

BORDER PATROLS. *Use* Police

BORING
Scope: Works on cutting earth or rock to determine the nature of strata penetrated, or to furnish an outlet for water, etc.
LC ———; s.a. Mining engineering; Wells

SEARS ——; s.a. Hydraulic engineering; Tunnels
RG DRILLING AND BORING (Earth and Rocks); s.a. Rock drills; Underwater drilling
NYT DRILLING AND BORING (Earth and Rock); s.a. Bridges and tunnels; Geology and Geophysics; Metals and minerals
PAIS DRILLING AND BORING; s.a. Mining methods; Petroleum industry—Underwater operations
BPI DRILLING AND BORING (Earth and Rocks); s.a. Gas, Natural—Well drilling; Petroleum—Well drilling

BOROUGHS. *Use* Local Government

BOSS RULE. *Use* Municipal Government

BOTANICAL CHEMISTRY. *Use* Chemistry

BOTANICAL GARDENS. *Use* Parks; Plants

BOTANY
LC ——; s.a. Biology; Plants
SEARS ——; s.a. Flower gardening; Trees
RG ——; s.a. Genetics (botany); Nature study
NYT PLANTS; s.a. Agriculture and agricultural products; Biology and biochemistry; Nature
PAIS PLANTS; s.a. Agriculture; Agricultural products
BPI PLANTS; s.a. Biology; Botanical gardens

BOTANY—ECOLOGY. *Use* Ecology

BOTANY, ECONOMIC. *Use* Weeds

BOTTLES. *Use* Beverages; Containers

BOTTLING. *Use* Beverages

BOUNDARIES
Scope: Subd. *Boundaries* under names of countries, e.g., U.S.—Boundaries.
LC ——; s.a. Geography; International law; State, The; Territory, National
SEARS ——; s.a. Geopolitics; International relations
RG ——; s.a. Atlases; Geography
NYT Names of countries; s.a. International relations; Waters, Territorial
PAIS ——; s.a. Jurisdiction (international law); Riparian rights
BPI ——; s.a. Geography; Territorial waters

BOUNTIES. *Use* Subsidies

BOUNTIES, MILITARY. *Use* Pensions, Military; Veterans

BOURGEOISIE. *See* Middle Classes

BOXES. *Use* Containers

BOXING. *Use* Self-Defense

BOYCOTT
LC ——; s.a. Labor disputes; Trade-unions
SEARS PASSIVE RESISTANCE; s.a. Nonviolence; Strikes and lockouts
RG ——; s.a. Labor disputes; School boycotts
NYT BOYCOTTS; s.a. Blacklisting; Commerce (trade boycotts); Labor
PAIS BOYCOTT (Commercial Policy); s.a. Labor disputes; Trade unions
BPI ——; s.a. Labor laws and legislation; Trade unions

BOYS
LC ——; s.a. Children; Youth
SEARS ——; s.a. Boy Scouts; Young men
RG ; s.a. Newsboys; Runaway boys and girls
NYT CHILDREN AND YOUTH; s.a. Hippies
PAIS CHILDREN; s.a. Negro children; Youth
BPI YOUTH; s.a. Children; Students

BRAHMANISM. *Use* Caste, Hinduism

BRAIN
LC ——; s.a. Head; Nervous system
SEARS ——; s.a. Apperception; Behavior; Dreams; Logic; Mind and body; Perception; Senses and Sensation
RG ——; s.a. Comprehension; Consciousness; Intellect; Memory
NYT ——; s.a. Intelligence; Mental health and disorders; Mind
PAIS INTELLIGENCE; s.a. Mental illness
BPI ——; s.a. Conditioned response; Electroencephalography

BRAIN—DISEASES. *Use* Amnesia; Cerebral Palsy; Paralysis

BRAIN DAMAGED CHILDREN. *Use* Handicapped; Mentally Handicapped Children

BRAIN DRAIN
LC ——; s.a. Professions; Scientists
SEARS IMMIGRATION AND EMIGRATION
RG ——; s.a. Immigration and emigration; Scientists—Supply and demand
NYT IMMIGRATION AND EMIGRATION—SCIENTIFIC AND TECHNICAL PERSONNEL; s.a. Labor; Science and technology
PAIS IMMIGRATION AND EMIGRATION—UNDERDEVELOPED STATES; s.a. Scientists
BPI ——; s.a. Immigration and emigration; Scientists

BRAINWASHING. *Use* Mental Suggestion; Progapanda; Will

BRAKES, AUTOMOBILE. *Use* Automobiles—Safety Measures

BRANCH FACTORIES. *Use* Factories

BRANCH STORES. *See* Chain Stores

BRAND MANAGEMENT. *See* Product Management

BRAND NAME GOODS. *Use* Trade-marks

BRANDED MERCHANDISE. *Use* Trade-marks

BRANDY INDUSTRY. *Use* Liquors

BRASS BANDS. *See* Bands (Music)

BRAZING. *Use* Solder and Soldering

BREACH OF CONTRACT. *Use* Contracts

BREACH OF PROMISE. *Use* Marriage Law

BREACH OF THE PEACE. *Use* Riots

BREAD. *Use* Baking

BREAD INDUSTRY. *Use* Baking

BREAKAGE, SHRINKAGE, ETC. (Commerce). *Use* Freight and Freightage

BREEDING
Scope: Propagation of plants or animals.
LC   ———; s.a. Genetics; Hybridization; Stock and stock breeding
SEARS   LIVESTOCK; s.a. Domestic animals; Plant breeding
RG   ———; s.a. Cattle breeding; Dog breeding, etc.; Eugenics
NYT   REPRODUCTION (Biological); s.a. Evolution; Genetics and heredity
PAIS   GENETICS; s.a. Heredity; Inbreeding
BPI   ———; s.a. Feeding and feeding stuffs; Livestock

BREWERIES. *Use* Beer and Brewing Industry

BREWING INDUSTRY. *Use* Beer and Brewing Industry; Beverages; Liquors

BRIBERY
LC   ———; s.a. Corruption (in politics); Criminal law
SEARS   CORRUPTION (in politics); s.a. Conflict of interests; Lobbying
RG   ———; s.a. Police corruption; Politics, Corruption in
NYT   ———; s.a. Crime and criminals; Frauds and swindling
PAIS   ———; s.a. Corruption (political); Criminal law
BPI   ———; s.a. Fraud; Political crimes and offenses; Politics, Corruption

BRIBERY, COMMERCIAL. *Use* Sales Management

BIRC-A-BRAC. *See* Art Objects

BRICKS
LC   ———; s.a. Brick trade; Tiles
SEARS   ———; s.a. Bricklaying; Clay industries
RG   ———; s.a. Brickmaking; Building materials
NYT   BRICK AND TILE; s.a. Ceramics and pottery; Floor coverings (for floor tiles)
PAIS   BRICK INDUSTRY; s.a. Building materials; Floor materials
BPI   ———; s.a. Brick industry; Building materials

BRIDAL CUSTOMS. *See* Marriage

BRIDES. *Use* Marriage; Woman

BRIDGES. *Use* Canals; Ports; Roads; Waterways

BRIGHT CHILDREN. *See* Child Study

BROADCASTING. *See* Radio Broadcasting and Programs; Television Broadcasting

BROADCASTING, EDUCATIONAL. *See* Television in Education

BROADCASTING INDUSTRY. *Use* Radio—Apparatus and Supplies

BROADCASTING STATIONS. *Use* Radio Stations

BROKEN HOMES. *Use* Divorce; Family; Parent and Child

BROKERS. *Use* Stock-Exchange; Wall Street

BROKERS—INSURANCE SELLING. *Use* Insurance

BROTHELS. *See* Prostitution

BROTHERHOOD OF MAN. *Use* Human Relations

BROTHERHOODS. *Use* Secret Societies

BROWNOUTS. *See* Electric Power Plants

BRUSH FIRES. *Use* Fires

BUDDHA AND BUDDHISM. *Use* Buddhism; Hinduism

BUDDHISM
LC   BUDDHA AND BUDDHISM; s.a. Dharma (Buddhism); Hinduism; Mahayana Buddhism; Religions; Zen (sect)
SEARS   BUDDHA AND BUDDHISM; s.a. Brahmanism; Theosophy
RG   BUDDHA AND BUDDHISM; s.a. Buddhists; Zen Buddhism
NYT   ———; s.a. Religion and churches
PAIS   ———; s.a. Communism and Buddhism; Sōka Gakkai (sect)
BPI   RELIGION

BUDDHISTS. *Use* Buddhism

BUDGET
Scope: Works on the budget or reports on the appropriations and expenditures of a government. For business budget see BUDGET IN BUSINESS.
LC   ———; s.a. County budgets; Expenditures, Public; Municipal budgets; Special funds
SEARS   ———(May subd. geographically); s.a. Finance; U.S.—Appropriations and expenditures
RG   ———; s.a. Government spending and policy; Program budgeting
NYT   U.S.—FINANCES—BUDGET; s.a. Budgets and budgeting; Finance; Politics and government (general)
PAIS   ———; s.a. Budget, Government; Capital budget; Performance budgeting; Program budgeting
BPI   ———; s.a. Program budgeting; subd. *Appropriations* and expenditures under names of government departments, agencies, etc.

BUDGET, BUSINESS. *Use* Budget in Business

BUDGET, FAMILY. *Use* Budgets, Household; Home Economics

BUDGET, GOVERNMENT. *Use* Finance, Public

BUDGET, HOUSEHOLD. *Use* Budgets, Household; Costs and Standard of Living

BUDGET, PERSONAL. *Use* Budgets, Household

BUDGET IN BUSINESS
LC   ———; s.a. Controllership; Finance; Program budgeting
SEARS   BUDGETS, BUSINESS; s.a. Business
RG   BUDGET, BUSINESS; s.a. Accounting; Corporations—Finance
NYT   BUDGETS AND BUDGETING; s.a. Corporations; Finance
PAIS   BUDGET, BUSINESS; s.a. Accounting—Budget, Business; Finance; Performance budgeting
BPI   BUDGET, BUSINESS; s.a. Advertising appropriations; Capital budget; Capital investments

BUDGETS, HOUSEHOLD
LC   HOME ECONOMICS—ACCOUNTING; s.a. Cost and standard of living; Finance, Personal
SEARS ——; s.a. Consumer credit; Cost and standard of living; Finance, Personal; Saving and Thrift
RG   BUDGET, HOUSEHOLD; s.a. Budget, Personal; Childrens' allowances; Domestic finance; Finance, Personal; Saving and savings
NYT   HOME ECONOMICS; s.a. Budgets and Budgeting; Savings
PAIS   BUDGET, FAMILY; s.a. Budget, Personal; Estate planning; Finance, Personal
BPI   BUDGET, HOUSEHOLD; s.a. Finance, Personal; Home economics; Saving

BUDGETS, MUNICIPAL. *Use* Municipal Government

BUDGETS AND BUDGETING. *Use* Accounting; Finance

BUGS (Listening devices). *See* Wire-tapping

BUILDING
LC   ——; s.a. Architecture; Construction industry; Janitors
SEARS ——; s.a. Engineering; Prefabricated houses; Public buildings; Sanitary engineering
RG   ——; s.a. Environmental engineering (buildings); House construction; Maintenance men
NYT   ——; s.a. Architecture and architects; Area planning and renewal; Housing; Office buildings
PAIS   ——; s.a. Architecture; Building service employees; Industrialized building
BPI   ——; s.a. Architecture; Buildings—Maintenance; Construction equipment; Industrial buildings

BUILDING—HEATING AND COOLING ASPECTS. *Use* Air Conditioning; Ventilation

BUILDING AND LOAN ASSOCIATIONS. *Use* Banks and Banking; Cooperative Societies; Loans, Personal

BUILDING DESIGN. *See* Architecture

BUILDING DESIGNERS. *Use* Architects

BUILDING INDUSTRY. *Use* Construction Indsutry

BUILDING MATERIALS. *Use* Strength of Materials

BUILDING SITES. *Use* Real Property

BUILDING SOCIETIES. *See* Building and Loan Associations

BUILDING TRADES. *Use* Construction Industry; Plaster and Plastering

BUILDINGS. *Use* Plant Layout

BUILDINGS OFFICE. *See* Office Buildings

BUILT-IN-FURNITURE. *Use* Furniture

BULBS. *Use* Floriculture; Gardening

BULK SALES. *Use* Sales; Transfer (Law)

BULLION. *See* Money

BULLS. *Use* Cattle

BURDEN OF PROOF. *Use* Trials

BUREAUCRACY. *Use* Civil Service; Public Administration

BURGLARY
LC   ——; s.a. Burglar—Alarms; Criminal law; Larceny; Electric alarms; Electronic alarm systems; Insurance, burglary; Offenses against property
SEARS ROBBERS AND OUTLAWS; s.a. Burglar alarms; Crime and criminals; Rogues and vagabonds
RG   BURGLARY AND BURGLARS; s.a. Automobiles—Protection against Theft; Brigands and robbers; Burglar alarms; Robberies and assaults
NYT   ROBBERIES AND THEFTS; s.a. Art—Thefts; Burglar alarms; Jewels and jewelry; Warning and detection devices and systems
PAIS   ——; s.a. Burglary prevention; Criminal law; Robbery; Theft
BPI   BURGLARY AND BURGLARS; s.a. Burglary protection; Crime and criminals; Theft

BURGLARY PROTECTION. *Use* Locks and Keys

BURIAL
LC   ——; s.a. Dead; Hygiene, Public
SEARS CATACOMBS; s.a. Cemeteries; Mounds and mound builders
RG   ——; s.a. Cemeteries; Funeral rites and ceremonies
NYT   CEMETERIES; s.a. Deaths; Funerals
PAIS   CEMETERIES; s.a. Funerals; National Cemeteries
BPI   ——; s.a. Cemeteries; Undertakers

BURIAL CUSTOMS. *See* Funeral Rites and Ceremonies

BURIAL STATISTICS. *See* Mortality; Vital Statistics

BURLESQUE (Theater). *Use* Vaudeville

BURNS. *Use* Fires

BURSARIES. *See* Scholarships

BURYING GROUNDS. *See* Cemeteries

BUSES. *Use* Automobiles; Local Transit; Motor Vehicles

BUSHINGS. *See* Bearings (Machinery)

BUSINESS
See also types of business activities, e.g., Retail trade, Mail-order business, etc.
LC   ——; s.a. Budget in business; Commerce; Economics; Management; New business enterprises
SEARS ——; s.a. Competition; Industry; Sales and salesmanship
RG   ——; s.a. Businessmen; Capitalism; Marketing; Small businesses
NYT   CORPORATIONS; s.a. Commerce (international trade only); Credit
PAIS   ——; s.a. Business tax; Interstate commerce; Manufacturing; Markets; Merchandising; Production
BPI   ——; s.a. Corporations; Occupations

BUSINESS, CHOICE OF. *See* Vocational Guidance

BUSINESS—POLITICAL ASPECTS. *Use* Business and Politics; Lobbying; Politics, Practical

BUSINESS, SMALL. *Use* Small Business

BUSINESS—SOCIAL ASPECTS. *Use* Industry and State; Wealth, Ethics of

BUSINESS ADMINISTRATION. *See* Business

BUSINESS AGENTS (Trade union). *Use* Trade—Unions

BUSINESS AND EDUCATION. *Use* Industry and Education

BUSINESS AND GOVERNMENT. *See* Business and Politics; Industry and State

BUSINESS AND POLITICS
LC ——; s.a. Politics, Practical
SEARS INDUSTRY AND STATE; s.a. Conflict of interest; Lobbying
RG INDUSTRY AND STATE; s.a. Government ownership; Military—Industrial complex
NYT ELECTIONS (U.S.)—BUSINESS ROLE IN POLITICS; s.a. Corporations; Elections (U.S.)—Finances; Politics and Government (general)
PAIS ——; s.a. Free enterprise; U.S.—President—Relations with business
BPI BUSINESS—POLITICAL ASPECTS; s.a. Banks and banking—Political activities; Business representatives in Washington; Lobbying

BUSINESS AND PROFESSIONAL WOMEN. *Use* Woman—Employment

BUSINESS ARITHMETIC. *Use* Accounting

BUSINESS BUDGETING. *See* Budget in Business

BUSINESS COLLEGES. *See* Business Education

BUSINESS COMBINATIONS. *See* Trusts, Industrial

BUSINESS CONDITIONS. *Use* Depressions; Economic History

BUSINESS CONSOLIDATION. *Use* Competition; Conglomerate Corporations; Trusts, Industrial

BUSINESS CORPORATIONS. *See* Corporations

BUSINESS CYCLES
LC ——; s.a. Depressions; Economic forecasting; Overproduction
SEARS ——; s.a. Economic conditions; Economic history
RG ——; s.a. Business depression; Economic stabilization
NYT ECONOMIC CONDITIONS AND TRENDS (General)
PAIS ——; s.a. Business depression; Business forecasting
BPI ——; s.a. Business depression; Economic stabilization

BUSINESS DEPRESSIONS. *Use* Business Cycles

BUSINESS DISTRICTS. *Use* City Planning; Urban Renewal

BUSINESS EDUCATION
LC ——; s.a. Bookkeeping; Industry and education; Secretaries; Vocational education
SEARS ——; s.a. Office management; Shorthand; Typewriting; English language—Business English
RG ——; s.a. Distributive education; Executives—Training
NYT COMMERCIAL EDUCATION; s.a. Education and schools
PAIS COMMERCIAL EDUCATION; s.a. names of business schools, e.g., Harvard University—Graduate School of Business Administration
BPI ——; s.a. Business schools and colleges; subd. *Study and teaching* under various subjects, e.g., Management—Study and teaching

BUSINESS ENTERPRISES
Scope: Work on business concerns as legal entities.
LC ——; s.a. Entrepreneur; International business enterprises
SEARS CORPORATIONS; s.a. Conglomerate corporations; Holding companies
RG ——; s.a. Limited partnerships; Trusts, Industrial
NYT CORPORATIONS; s.a. Banks and banking; Management, Industrial and institutional
PAIS CORPORATIONS; s.a. Interlocking directorates; Private companies
BPI CORPORATIONS; s.a. Corporation law; Holding companies

BUSINESS ENTERPRISES, NEW. *Use* New Business Enterprises

BUSINESS ENTERTAINING. *Use* Entertaining

BUSINESS ETHICS
LC ——; s.a. Business etiquette; Business intelligence; Wealth, Ethics of
SEARS ——; s.a. Competition; Professional ethics, Social ethics; Success
RG ——; s.a. Better business bureaus; Trade secrets
NYT ETHICS AND MORALS; s.a. Professions
PAIS ——; s.a. Trade practices; Unethical trade practices
BPI ——; s.a. Advertising ethics; Honesty; Speculation

BUSINESS ETIQUETTE. *Use* Business Ethics

BUSINESS EXECUTIVES. *See* Executives

BUSINESS FAILURES. *Use* Bankruptcy

BUSINESS FORECASTING
LC ——; s.a. Economic forecasting; Sales forecasting
SEARS ——; s.a. Business cycles
RG ——; s.a. Forecasts (economics); Stocks—Price forecasting
NYT U.S.—ECONOMIC CONDITIONS AND TRENDS; s.a. Marketing and merchandising; Sales and salesmen
PAIS ——; s.a. Economic forecasting; Sales estimates
BPI FORECASTS (Economic); s.a. Economic models; Sales estimates

BUSINESS GAMES. *See* Management Games

BUSINESS FORMS, BLANKS, ETC. *Use* Business Records

BUSINESS HISTORY. *Use* Economic History

BUSINESS HOURS. *Use* Sabbath

BUSINESS INTELLIGENCE. *Use* Business Ethics

BUSINESS LAW
LC ——; s.a. Commercial law; Forms (law)
SEARS COMMERCIAL LAW; s.a. Bankruptcy; Collecting of accounts; Debtor and creditor
RG COMMERCIAL LAW; s.a. Landlord and tenant; Trusts, Industrial—Law
NYT LAW AND LEGISLATION; s.a. Bankruptcies; Credit; Labor
PAIS COMMERCIAL LAW; s.a. Corporation—Legislation; Security (law)
BPI COMMERCIAL LAW; s.a. Contracts; Corporation law; Trade regulation

BUSINESS LETTERS. *Use* Commercial Correspondence; Letter Writing

BUSINESS MACHINES. *See* Office Equipment and Supplies

BUSINESS MANAGEMENT AND ORGANIZATION. *Use* Industrial Management; Management; Organization; Supervision of Employees

BUSINESS MATHEMATICS. *Use* Mathematics

BUSINESS MEN. *Use* Businessmen

BUSINESS MORTALITY. *Use* Bankruptcy

BUSINESS NAMES. *Use* Trade-marks

BUSINESS ORGANIZATION AND ADMINISTRATION. *Use* Management; Supervision of Employees

BUSINESS PLANNING. *Use* Industrial Management

BUSINESS RECORDS
LC ——; s.a. Business—Forms, blanks, etc.; Financial statements; Inventories; subd. *Records and correspondence* under specific business, e.g., Railroads—Records and correspondence
SEARS OFFICE MANAGEMENT; s.a. Industrial management
RG ——; s.a. Business—Forms, blanks, etc.; Microfilm records
NYT MANAGEMENT, INDUSTRIAL AND INSTITUTIONAL; s.a. Documents; Office equipment
PAIS ——; s.a. Office management; Records Management
BPI RECORDS; s.a. Files and filing; Sales records

BUSINESS REPORT WRITING. *Use* Report Writing

BUSINESS REPRESENTATIVES IN WASHINGTON. *Use* Business and Politics; Lobbying

BUSINESS SCHOOLS AND COLLEGES. *Use* Business Education; Colleges and Universities

BUSINESS STATISTICS. *Use* Statistics

BUSINESS TAX
LC ——; s.a. Licenses; Small business—Taxation
SEARS TAXATION; s.a. Business; Profit
RG TAXATION; s.a. Corporations—Taxation; Excess profits tax
NYT TAXATION; s.a. Commerce (international trade); Corporations
PAIS ——; s.a. Turnover tax; Value added tax
BPI CORPORATIONS—TAXATION; s.a. Corporate income tax; Excess profits tax; Taxation

BUSINESSMEN
LC ——; s.a. Capitalists and financiers; manufacturers; Merchants
SEARS CAPITALISTS AND FINANCIERS; s.a. Merchants; Millionaires
RG ——; s.a. Capitalists and financiers; Executives
NYT EXECUTIVES; s.a. Corporations; Management, Industrial and institutional
PAIS BUSINESS MEN; s.a. Executives; Negroes as business men
BPI ——; s.a. Capitalists and financiers; Entrepreneurs; Executives

BUSING
Scope: Works on transportation used to achieve school integration.
LC SCHOOL CHILDREN—TRANSPORTATION
SEARS BUSING (School integration); s.a. Blacks—Education; Segregation in education
RG SCHOOL CHILDREN—TRANSPORTATION FOR INTEGRATION; s.a. Public schools—Desegration; School boycotts
NYT EDUCATION AND SCHOOLS—U.S.—EQUAL EDUCATIONAL OPPORTUNITIES; s.a. Education and schools—U.S.—Transportation
PAIS SCHOOLS—TRANSPORTATION OF PUPILS; s.a. Education—Integration and segregation; Negroes—Integration and segregation
BPI PUBLIC SCHOOLS—DESEGRATION; s.a. Education; Negroes—Education

BUTCHERS. *Use* Meat Industry and Trade

BUYERS. *Use* Purchasing

BUYER'S GUIDES. *See* Consumer Education; Shopping and Shoppers

BUYING. *Use* Consumer Education; Industrial Management; Installment Plan; Materials Management; Purchasing; Shopping

BUYING HABITS. *Use* Consumers

BY-PRODUCTS. *See* Waste Products

C

C.I.F. CLAUSE. *Use* Risk; Shipment of Goods

C.O.D. SHIPMENTS. *Use* Shipment of Goods

CAB AND OMNIBUS SERVICE. *Use* Motor Vehicles

CABINET WORK. *Use* Furniture

CABLE CODES. *See* Ciphers

CABLES, SUBMARINE. *Use* Telecommunication

CAFETERIAS. *See* Restaurants, Lunchrooms, etc.

CAGE BIRDS. *Use* Birds

CAKE. *Use* Baking

CALAMITIES. *See* Disasters

CALCULATING MACHINES
Scope: All mechanical computers of pre-1945 vintage. See Computers for those developed after this date.
LC ———; s.a. Abacus; Computers; Digital counters; Mathematical instruments
SEARS ———; s.a. Cybernetics; Slide rule
RG CALCULATING DEVICES; s.a. Adding machines; Counting machines and devices
NYT DATA PROCESSING (Information processing) EQUIPMENT AND SYSTEMS; s.a. Adding machines; Electronics
PAIS ———; s.a. Computers; Electronic data processing equipment
BPI ———; s.a. Accounting machines; Desk calculators, Electronic

CALENDAR. *Use* Time

CALISTHENICS. *Use* Exercise; Gymnastics

CALLIGRAPHY
LC ———; s.a. Penmanship; Writing
SEARS WRITING; s.a. Alphabet
RG ———; s.a. Lettering; Penmanship; subd. *Writing* under names of languages, e.g., Arabic—Writing
NYT HANDWRITING; s.a. Art
PAIS GRAPHIC ARTS INDUSTRY
BPI PENMANSHIP; s.a. Lettering

CALLS (Commerce). *See* Stock-Exchange

CALUMNY. *See* Libel and Slander

CAMERAS
See also types and makes of cameras, e.g., Kodak cameras; Twin-lens cameras; Electric eye cameras; Miniature cameras; etc.
LC ———; s.a. Photography
SEARS ———; s.a. Photography—Equipment and supplies
RG ———; s.a. Photography—Apparatus and supplies; View finders
NYT PHOTOGRAPHY AND PHOTOGRAPHIC EQUIPMENT
PAIS CAMERA INDUSTRY; s.a. Photographic supplies industry; Photography
BPI ———; s.a. Moving picture cameras; Television cameras

CAMP COOKERY. *Use* Outdoor Life

CAMP SITES, FACILITIES, ETC. *Use* Tourist Trade

CAMPAIGN FUNDS
LC ———; s.a. Elections—(local subd.)—Campaign funds, e.g., Elections—Philadelphia—Campaign funds; Patronage, Political; U. S.—Officials and employees—Political activity

SEARS ———; s.a. Corruption (in politics); Politics, Practical
RG ———; s.a. Bribery; Politics, Corruption in
NYT ELECTIONS (U. S.)—FINANCES; s.a. Elections (U. S.)—Advertising; Elections (U. S.)—Business role in politics; Elections (U. S.)—Television and radio
PAIS ———; s.a. Corruption (political); Elections
BPI ———; s.a. Bribery; Politics, Corruption in

CAMPAIGN ISSUES. *Use* Electioneering; Political Parties; Politics, Practical

CAMPAIGN LITERATURE. *Use* Advertising, Political; Electioneering; Politics, Practical

CAMPING. *Use* Camps and Camping

CAMPS AND CAMPING
Scope: Camps used for works on camps with a definite program of activities. See Camping for works on technique of camping.
LC CAMPS; s.a. Backpacking; Camping; Outdoor life
SEARS CAMPS; s.a. Camping; Outdoor recreation; Tourist trade; Walking
RG CAMPS; s.a. Camp sites, facilities, etc.; Dance camps
NYT ———; s.a. Parks, playgrounds and other recreation areas; Trailers (auto) and trailer camps
PAIS ———; s.a. Parks; Recreation areas
BPI CAMPS; s.a. Camping; Campsites, facilities, etc.

CAMPS FOR THE HANDICAPPED. *Use* Handicapped

CAMPSITES, FACILITIES, ETC. *Use* Outdoor Life

CAMPUS DISORDERS. *See* Student Movements

CAMPUS POLICE. *Use* Police

CANALS. *Use* Waterways

CANCELLATIONS (Philately). *Use* Postage Stamps

CANCER
LC ———; s.a. Cancer research; Oneology; subd. *Cancer* under names of organs, e.g., Brain—Cancer
SEARS ———; s.a. Diseases; Tumors
RG ———; s.a. Sarcoma; Tumors
NYT ———; s.a. Atomic energy and weapons—Medical uses for; Tobacco, tobacco products and smoker's articles; types of cancer, e.g., Leukemia
PAIS ———; s.a. Krebiozen; Sickness
BPI ———; s.a. Cancer—Causes; Cancer—Therapy

CANDLES. *Use* Lighting

CANNED BEVERAGES. *Use* Berverages

CANNIBALISM. *Use* Society, Primitive

CANNING AND PRESERVING
LC ———; s.a. Agricultural processing; Food, canned; Food—Preservation; names of individual foods, e.g., Fishery products—Preservation
SEARS ———; s.a. Chemistry, Technical; Cookery
RG ———; s.a. Fruit—Preservation; Pickles and relishes
NYT CONTAINERS AND PACKAGING; s.a. Food and grocery trade; Fruit and vegetables

PAIS ——; s.a. Canned food industry
BPI ——; s.a. Blanching; Canned food industry; Canneries

CANNON. *See* Ordnance

CANON LAW. *Use* Catholic Church; Ecclesiastical Law

CANONIZATION
LC ——; s.a. Beatification; Catholic church
SEARS SAINTS; s.a. Fathers of the church; Martyrs
RG ——; s.a. Martyrs; Saints
NYT ROMAN CATHOLIC CHURCH—BEATIFICA-TION AND CANONIZATION; s.a. names of saints, inverted to given name, e.g., Gregory, Saint; Religion and churches
PAIS CLERGY; s.a. Religion; Roman Catholic church
BPI ——; s.a. Catholic church; Christianity

CANS. *Use* Containers

CANTEENS (Recreation centers). *See* Recreation

CANVASSING. *Use* Salesmen and Salesmanship

CANVASSING (Church Work). *Use* Social Surveys

CAPABILITY AND DISABILITY. *Use* Age (Law)

CAPITAL
LC ——; s.a. Banks and banking; Investments; Saving and investment
SEARS ——; s.a. Capitalism; Finance; Interest and usury; Trusts, Industrial; Wealth
RG ——; s.a. Liquidity (economics); Small business—Finance
NYT ECONOMICS; s.a. Banks and banking; Economic conditions and trends (general); Savings
PAIS ——; s.a. Money; Profits
BPI ; s.a. Corporations—Finance; Working capital

CAPITAL AND LABOR. *See* Industrial Relations

CAPITAL BUDGET. *Use* Budget; Budget in Business

CAPITAL EQUIPMENT. *See* Industrial Equipment

CAPITAL FORMATION. *See* Saving and Savings

CAPITAL GAINS TAX. *Use* Income Tax

CAPTIAL INVESTMENTS. *Use* Budget in Business; Investments; Machinery

CAPITAL LEVY. *Use* Taxation

CAPITAL PRODUCTIVITY. *Use* Machinery in Industry

CAPITAL PUNISHMENT
LC ——; s.a. Electrocution; Punishment
SEARS ——; s.a. Crime and criminals; Murder
RG ——; s.a. Crime prevention; Hanging
NYT ——; s.a. Crime and criminals; Prisons and prisoners; types of crimes, e.g., Murders and attempted murders
PAIS ——; s.a. Criminal law; Executions and executioners
BPI ——; s.a. Criminal law; Justice, Administration of

CAPITAL STOCK. *Use* Stock-Exchange

CAPITALISM
LC ——; s.a. Profit; Technocracy
SEARS ——; s.a. Capital; Industry and state; Labor and laboring classes; Monopolies; Trusts, Industrial
RG ——; s.a. Big business; Black capitalism
NYT ECONOMICS; s.a. Banks and banking; Corporations; Economic conditions and trends (general)
PAIS ——; s.a. Entrepreneurs; Free enterprise
BPI ——; s.a. Black capitalism; Entrepreneur

CAPITALISTS AND FINANCIERS
LC ——; s.a. Businessmen; Finance
SEARS ——; s.a. Millionaires; Stock-Exchange; Wealth
RG ——; s.a. Entrepreneurs; Rich, The
NYT FINANCE; s.a. Banks and banking; Executives; Property and investments
PAIS ——; s.a. Businessmen; Wealth
BPI ——; s.a. Businessmen; Millionaires

CAPITALIZATION (Finance). *See* Stock-Exchange; Valuation

CAPTURE AT SEA. *Use* Naval Art and Science

CARDIACS. *Use* Diseases

CARDINAL VIRTUES. *Use* Virtues

CARDIOVASCULAR SYSTEM. *Use* Arteries

CARDS AND CARD GAMES. *Use* Gambling; Recreation

CAREERS. *See* Occupations; Professions; Vocational Guidance

CARGO HANDLING
LC ——; s.a. Stowage; Unitized cargo system
SEARS MATERIALS HANDLING; s.a. Freight and freightage
RG FREIGHT HANDLING; s.a. Containerization (freight); Loading and unloading
NYT FREIGHT FORWARDING (Domestic and Foreign); s.a. Names of freight companies and specific commodities, e.g., Furniture; Railroads—U. S.—Freight; Ships and shipping
PAIS ——; s.a. Materials handling; Unitized cargo systems
BPI SHIPS—CARGO; s.a. Airplanes, Freight; Freight handling; Loading and unloading

CARICATURES AND CARTOONS
See also appropriate division under subjects, e.g. Marriage—Caricatures and cartoons; Divorce—Cartoons and caricatures; and subd. *Humor and caricature* under names of wars, e.g., European war, 1914-1918—Humor and caricature; and subd. *Portraits, caricatures,* or *cartoons* under names, e.g., Churchill, Winston—Cartoons, etc.
LC ——; s.a. Comic books, strips, etc.; Wit and humor, Pictorial
SEARS CARTOONS AND CARICATURES; s.a. Moving picture cartoons, Pictures
RG ——; s.a. Comics (book, strips, etc.); Satire
NYT CARTOONS AND CARTOONISTS; s.a. Art; names of cartoonists, e.g., Block, Herb; names of subjects of cartoons, e.g., Nixon, Richard M.
PAIS ——; s.a. Comics (books, strips, etc.)
BPI CARTOONS; s.a. Moving pictures—Animated cartoons; Television broadcasting—Cartoons

CARNIVALS. *Use* Festivals

CARNIVORA. *Use* Predatory Animals

CAROLS. *Use* Singing and Songs

CARPET INDUSTRY. *Use* Tapestry

CARRIERS
LC	——; s.a. Communications and traffic; Maritime law; Storage and moving trade
SEARS	FREIGHT AND FREIGHTAGE; s.a. Aeronautics, Commercial; Interstate commerce; Railroad—Rates
RG	——; s.a. Forwarding companies; Transportation
NYT	TRANSPORTATION; s.a. Freight forwarding (domestic and foreign); specific means of transportation, e.g., Ships and shipping
PAIS	——; s.a. Shipment of goods; Transportation—Regulation
BPI	——; s.a. Freight and freightage; Transportation

CARRIERS OF INFECTION. *Use* Communicable Diseases

CARS. *See* Automobiles; Motor Vehicles

CARS, TRANSIT AND COMMUTER. *Use* Railroads

CARTELS. *Use* Monopolies; Trusts, Industrial

CARTOGRAPHY
Scope:	Works on the general science of map making. For specific maps see subd. *Maps* under names of places e.g., U. S.—Maps.
LC	——; s.a. Geography, Mathematical; Maps
SEARS	MAP DRAWING; s.a. Charts; Topographical drawing
RG	——; s.a. Computers—Cartographic use; Mapping, Aerial
NYT	MAPS; s.a. Atlases; Geography
PAIS	MAPS; s.a. Atlases; Charts
BPI	——; s.a. Maps. Surveying, Aerial

CARTONS. *Use* Containers; Paper Making and Trade

CARTOONS AND CARICATURES. *Use* Caricatures and Cartoons

CARTRIDGES. *Use* Ammunition

CARVING (Art industries). *Use* Design

CARVING (Meat, etc.). *Use* Dinners and Dining; Table

CASH BUSINESS. *Use* Merchandising

CASINOS. *Use* Gambling

CASTE
LC	——; s.a. Manners and customs; Social classes
SEARS	——; s.a. Brahmanism; Hinduism
RG	——; s.a. Social classes; Untouchables
NYT	MANNERS AND CUSTOMS; s.a. India—Manners and customs; Sociology
PAIS	SOCIAL STATUS; s.a. Class struggle; Equality
BPI	——; s.a. Elite (social sciences); Social classes

CASUAL LABOR. *Use* Labor and Laboring Classes; Migrant Labor; Seasonal Industries

CASUALTY INSURANCE. *Use* Survivor's Benefits

CATACOMBS. *Use* Burial

CATALOGING. *Use* Indexing; Libraries and Librarians

CATALOGS. *Use* Indexing; Mail-order Business

CATARRH. *Use* Cold (Disease)

CATASTROPHES. *See* Disasters

CATECHISM. *Use* Theology

CATECHISMS. *Use* Religious Education

CATERERS AND CATERING
LC	——; s.a. Cookery; Food service
SEARS	——; s.a. Dinners and dining; Entertaining; Menus
RG	——; s.a. Cookery; Waiters and waitresses
NYT	CATERING; s.a. Food and grocery trade; Hotels, bars, motels, night clubs and restaurants
PAIS	CATERING INDUSTRY; s.a. subd. *Food service* under specific subjects, e.g., Schools—Food service
BPI	——; s.a. Concessions (food, etc.); Restaurants, lunchrooms, etc.

CATHARSIS. *Use* Psychoanalysis

CATHEDRALS. *Use* Abbeys

CATHOLIC CHURCH
LC	——; s.a. Anglo-Catholicism; Canonization; Church schools; Monasticism and religious orders; Ultramontanism; Virgin birth
SEARS	——; s.a. Baptism; Celibacy; Conversion, Religious; Jesus Christ; Liturgies; Saints; subd. *Catholic church* under subjects, e.g., Church and state—Catholic church
RG	——; s.a. Canon law; Mass
NYT	Specific types of Catholic churches, e.g., Greek Orthodox Church; s.a. Prayers and prayer books; Religion and churches
PAIS	ROMAN CATHOLIC CHURCH; s.a. Priests; Vatican
BPI	——; s.a. Mass; Papacy

CATHOLIC CHURCH IN THE U. S.
Scope:	Use similar headings for Catholic Church in other countries, e.g., Catholic Church in Spanish America, or Catholic Church in non-Catholic countries, etc.
LC	——; s.a. Americanism (Catholic controversy); Catholics, Negro
SEARS	——; s.a. Catholics in the U. S., and similar headings for Catholics in cities, e.g., Catholics in Boston.
RG	——; s.a. Catholics in the U. S.; Church union—U. S.
NYT	ROMAN CATHOLIC CHURCH—U. S.; s.a. Catholic charities; Orthodox churches; Religion and churches
PAIS	ROMAN CATHOLIC CHURCH; s.a. Priests; Roman Catholics
BPI	CATHOLIC CHURCH

CATHOLIC SCHOOLS. *Use* Church Schools

CATHOLICITY

Scope	Works emphasizing a unity and commonness of Christian ideas.
LC	——; s.a. Christian union; Ecumenical movement
SEARS	CHRISTIAN UNITY; s.a. Church; Community churches
RG	ECUMENICAL MOVEMENT; s.a. Church union; Religious cooperation
NYT	RELIGION AND CHURCHES; s.a. Names of specific denominations, e.g., Protestant Episcopal church
PAIS	ECUMENICAL MOVEMENT; s.a. Christianity and other religious; Roman Catholic church
BPI	ECUMENICAL MOVEMENT; s.a. Christianity

CATHOLICS, NEGRO. *Use* Catholic Church in the U. S.

CATHOLICS IN NON-CATHOLIC COUNTRIES. *Use* Minorities

CATTLE

LC	——; s.a. Dairy cattle; Stock and stock breeding
SEARS	——; s.a. Cattle—Breeds; Cattle breeding; Cows (limited to dairy cattle)
RG	——; s.a. Bulls; Dairying; Pastures
NYT	——; s.a. Livestock; Meat
PAIS	CATTLE INDUSTRY; s.a. Beef industry; Livestock industry
BPI	——; s.a. Livestock; Meat industry

CATTLE INDUSTRY. *Use* Cattle

CATTLE RUSTLING. *Use* Theft

CATTLE THIEVES. *Use* Theft

CATTLE TRADE. *Use* Meat Industry and Trade

CAUCUS. *Use* Legislative Bodies; Politics, Practical

CAUSATION. *Use* God

CAVERNS. *See* Caves

CAVES

LC	——; s.a. Speleology; Stalactites and stalagmites
SEARS	——; s.a. Cave drawing; Cave dwellers
RG	——; s.a. Cave fauna and flora; Ice caves
NYT	CAVES AND CAVERNS; Archeology and anthropology; Bats
PAIS	GEOLOGY
BPI	——

CELIBACY

LC	——; s.a. Chastity; Marriage; Single people; Virginity
SEARS	——; s.a. Monasticism and religious orders; Priests; Social life and customs
RG	——; s.a. Marriage of priests; Social ethics; Virginity
NYT	——; s.a. Ethics and morals; Marriages; Religion and churches; Sex
PAIS	SINGLE PEOPLE; s.a. Bachelors; Priests; Sexual ethics
BPI	——; s.a. Catholic church; Marriage; Sex (psychology)

CELLS

LC	——; s.a. Biological physics; Cytology; Reproduction
SEARS	——; s.a. Embryology; Genetics; Protoplasm
RG	——; s.a. Differentiation (biology); Membranes (biology)
NYT	BIOLOGY AND BIOCHEMISTRY (Life processes); s.a. Body, Human; Hormones; Reproduction (biological)
PAIS	BIOLOGY
BPI	——; s.a. Fertilization (biology); Tissue culture

CEMETERIES. *Use* Funeral Rites and Ceremonies

CENSORSHIP

See also subd.	*Censorship* under specific subjects, e.g., Books—Censorship; Libraries—Censorship; etc.
LC	——; s.a. Condemned books; Expurgated books; Liberty of the press; Literature and morals; Obscenity
SEARS	——; s.a. Free speech; Freedom of the press; Liberty of speech
RG	——; s.a. Government and the press; Information, Freedom of; Intellectual liberty; Prohibited books
NYT	——; s.a. Freedom of information, thought and expression; Pornography; Writing and writers
PAIS	——; s.a. Freedom of the press; Official secrets
BPI	——; s.a. Freedom of information; Freedom of the press

CENSORSHIP OF THE PRESS. *See* Press

CENSURES, ECCLESIASTICAL. *Use* Punishment

CENSUS. *Use* Demography; Population; Statistics; Vital Statistics

CENTENARIANS. *Use* Old Age

CENTRAL NERVOUS SYSTEM. *Use* Nervous System

CENTRALIZATION IN GOVERNMENT. *Use* Federal Government

CENTRALIZATION IN MANAGEMENT. *Use* Organization

CERAMICS

LC	——; s.a. Clay; Porcelain; Pottery; Urns
SEARS	——; s.a. Enamel and enameling; Glass; Tiles
RG	POTTERY; s.a. Ceramic sculpture; Glazes and glazing; Molds (for ceramic products)
NYT	CERAMICS AND POTTERY; s.a. Art objects; Tableware
PAIS	CERAMIC INDUSTRIES; s.a. Porcelain industry; Pottery industry
BPI	CERAMIC INDUSTRIES; s.a. Ceramic materials; Pottery industry; Tile industry

CEREBRAL PALSY

LC	——; s.a. Brain—Abnormalities and deformities; Paralysis
SEARS	——; s.a. Brain—Diseases
RG	CEREBROVASCULAR DISEASE; s.a. Cerebral palsied children; Paralysis
NYT	——; s.a. Brain; Handicapped; Mental health and disorders

CEREBRAL PALSY, *cont.*
PAIS ——; s.a. Disabled; Sickness
BPI   DISEASES; s.a. Brain; Handicapped

CEREMONIES. *See* Etiquette; Manners and Customs;
    Rites and Ceremonies

CERTAINTY. *Use* Logic

CERTIFICATES OF DEPOSIT. *Use* Banks and Banking;
    Negotiable Instruments

CERTIFIED PUBLIC ACCOUNTS. *See* Accountants

CHAIN STORES
LC   ——; s.a. Department stores; Franchises (retail
    trade); Stores, Retail
SEARS ——; s.a. Department stores; Retail trade
RG   ——; s.a. Grocery trade; Supermarkets
NYT   RETAIL STORES AND TRADE; s.a. Discount
    selling; Retail stores and trade—U. S.—Shopping
    centers
PAIS ——; s.a. subd. *Chain stores* under names of
    types of stores, e.g., Drug stores—Chain stores
BPI   ——; s.a. Supermarkets; Variety stores

CHAMBER MUSIC
Scope: Works on various combinations of two or more
    solo instruments.
LC   ——; s.a. Chamber orchestra; Monologues with
    music (chamber music)
SEARS ——; s.a. Instrumental music; Orchestral music
RG   ——; s.a. Ensemble playing; String quartets
NYT   MUSIC; s.a. Music—Concerts and recitals; Music—
    Orchestras and other music groups
PAIS MUSIC
BPI   MUSIC; s.a. Composers; Orchestras

CHANCE. *Use* Probabilities; Progress

CHANGE OF SEX. *Use* Sex

CHAPLAINS. *Use* Clergy

CHARACTER
LC   ——; s.a. Character tests; Conduct of life;
    Personality; Temperament; Virtue
SEARS ——; s.a. Behavior; Character education;
    Christian life; Self-control
RG   ——; s.a. Conscience; Duty; Individuality;
    Responsibility
NYT   PSYCHOLOGY AND PSYCHOLOGISTS; s.a.
    Ethics and morals; Intelligence; Mind
PAIS PSYCHOLOGY; s.a. Behavior (psychology);
    Ethics; Motivation (psychology)
BPI   PERSONALITY; s.a. Behavior (psychology);
    Conduct of life; Identity (psychology)

CHARACTER EDUCATION. *Use* Education; Ethics

CHARACTER TESTS. *Use* Character; Personality
    Tests; Will

CHARACTERISTICS. *See* National Characteristics

**CHARACTERS AND CHARACTERISTICS IN
    LITERATURE.** *Use* Fiction; Literature; Negroes
    in Literature; Plots (Drama, novel, etc.)

CHARGE ACCOUNT BANK PLANS. *Use* Consumer
    Credit

CHARGE ACCOUNTS (Retail trade). *Use* Acceptances;
    Credit

CHARITABLE BEQUESTS. *Use* Charitable Uses, Trusts
    and Foundations; Inheritance and Succession

CHARITABLE USES, TRUSTS AND FOUNDATIONS
Scope: Works dealing with legal aspects of the subject.
    General works are entered under *Endowments.*
    See also names of specific foundations, e.g., Ford
    Foundation
LC   ——; s.a. Charitable bequests; Legacies; Poor
    laws
SEARS CHARITIES—LAW AND REGULATIONS; s.a.
    Endowments—Law and regulations; Inheritance
    and succession
RG   FOUNDATIONS, CHARITABLE AND EDUCA-
    TIONAL; s.a. Corporations—Charitable contribu-
    tions; Money raising campaigns; Taxation,
    Exemption from
NYT   PHILANTHROPY; s.a. Foundations; Wills and
    estates
PAIS FOUNDATIONS; s.a. Corporations—Charities;
    Endowments
BPI   CHARITIES; s.a. Corporations—Charities;
    Foundations, Charitable and educational; Taxa-
    tion—Charitable deductions

CHARITIES
Scope: Privately supported welfare activities. See also
    tax supported activities under *Public Welfare*;
    methods employed in welfare work, public or
    private, under *Social Work.*
LC   ——; s.a. Friendly societies; International
    relief; Poor
SEARS ——; s.a. Begging; Charities, Medical; Charity
    organization; Gifts; Legal aid; Orphans, Poverty
RG   ——; s.a. Community chests; Fund raising;
    Giving
NYT   PHILANTHROPY; s.a. Catholic Charities;
    Foundations; Society
PAIS PHILANTHROPY; s.a. Church Charities; Corpora-
    tions—Charities; Endowments
BPI   ——; s.a. Corporations—Charities; Foundations,
    Charitable and educational; Gifts

CHARITY
LC   ——; s.a. Altruism; Humanity; Love (theology)
SEARS ——; s.a. Begging; Ethics
RG   KINDNESS, s.a. Giving; Hospitality; Humanity
NYT   PHILANTHROPY; s.a. Ethics and morals; Love
    (emotion)
PAIS PHILANTHROPY; s.a Church charities; Corpora-
    tions—Charities
BPI   PHILANTHROPY; s.a. Conduct of life

CHARITY ORGANIZATION. *Use* Charities

CHARTERS. *Use* Deeds; Municipal Government

CHARTOGRAPHY. *See* Cartography

CHARTS. *Use* Cartography; Graphic Methods; Maps

CHASSIDISM. *See* Jews

CHASTITY. *Use* Celibacy; Monastic and Religious Life
    of Women; Monasticism and Religious Orders

CHATTEL MORTGAGES. *Use* Mortgages

CHATTELS. *See* Property

CHAUVINISM AND JINGOISM. *Use* Imperialism;
Militarism; Nationalism; Patriotism

CHEATING (Education)
LC ——; s.a. Self-government (in education);
Students—Conduct of life
SEARS EDUCATION; s.a. School discipline; Students
RG CHEATING IN SCHOOL WORK; s.a. Self-
government in education; Students—Attitudes
NYT EDUCATION AND SCHOOLS—U.S.—STUDENT
ACTIVITIES AND CONDUCT; s.a. Children
and youth; Colleges and universities—Student
activities and conduct; Ethics and morals
PAIS CHEATING (Schoolwork); s.a. College students—
Discipline; School discipline
BPI EDUCATION; s.a. Schools

CHECK-CASHING SERVICES. *Use* Checks (Banking)

CHECK-OFF SYSTEM. *Use* Collective Bargaining

CHECKS (Banking)
LC CHECKS; s.a. Deposit banking; Negotiable
instruments; Travelers checks
SEARS BANKS AND BANKING; s.a. Bills of exchange;
Credit
RG CHECKS; s.a. Banks and banking; Clearing
houses
NYT BANKS AND BANKING; s.a. Check-cashing
services; Credit; Travelers checks
PAIS CHECKS; s.a. Banking—Checking accounts;
Banking—Credit transfers
BPI CHECKS; s.a. Negotiable instruments; Transfer
of funds

CHEMICAL AND BIOLOGICAL WEAPONS. *Use*
Biological Warfare; Chemical Warfare; Weapons

CHEMICAL ENGINEERING. *Use* Biochemistry

CHEMICAL INDUSTRIES
Scope: Industries based largely on chemical processes;
works dealing with the manufacture of chemicals
as such are entered under Chemicals. See also
names of specific industries, e.g., Petrochemicals
industry.
LC ——; s.a. Chemical engineering; Chemistry,
Technical
SEARS ——; s.a. Chemicals
RG ——; s.a. Chemical plants; Chemistry, Technical
NYT CHEMISTRY AND CHEMICALS; s.a. Fertilizer;
Waste materials and disposal
PAIS ——; s.a. Agricultural chemicals
BPI ——; Chemical engineers

CHEMICAL WARFARE
LC ——; s.a. Decontamination (gases, chemicals,
etc.); Smoke screens; War
SEARS ——; s.a. Gases, Asphyxiating and poisonous—
War use; Military art and science
RG ——; s.a. Chemical and biological weapons;
subd. *Chemical Warfare* under names of wars, e.g.,
European War, 1914–1918—Chemical warfare

NYT ——, s.a. Biological warfare; Military art and
science
PAIS ——; s.a. Gases, Asphyxiating and poisonous;
Napalm
BPI MILITARY ART AND SCIENCE; s.a. Chemicals;
Disarmament and arms control

CHEMICALS. *Use* Chemical Industries

CHEMICALS—SAFETY MEASURES. *Use* Hazardous
Substances

CHEMISTRY
Scope: Works on organic and inorganic chemistry. See
also headings beginning with Chemistry, e.g.,
Chemistry, Forensic; Chemistry, Organic;
Chemistry as a profession, etc.
LC ——; s.a. Acids; Biological chemistry; Combus-
tion; Physiological chemistry
SEARS ——; s.a. Biochemistry; Botanical chemistry;
Pharmacy
RG ——; s.a. Alchemy; Bases (chemistry); Surface
chemistry
NYT CHEMISTRY AND CHEMICALS; s.a. Biology
and biochemistry; Drugs and drug trade; Science
and technology
PAIS ——; s.a. Chemical industries; Science
BPI ——; s.a. Biochemistry; Electrochemistry;
Photochemistry

CHEMISTRY, MEDICAL AND PHARMACEUTICAL.
Use Antidepressants; Medicine; Therapeutics

CHEMISTRY, TECHNICAL. *Use* Biochemistry; Chemical
Industries

CHEMISTS. *Use* Drug Trade

CHEMOSURGERY. *Use* Surgery

CHEMOTHERAPY. *Use* Antibiotics

CHEMURGY. *Use* Substitute Products

CHICKENS. *See* Poultry Industry

CHIEF JUSTICES. *See* Judges *CHILD ABUSE LC uses CRUELTY TO CHILDREN*

CHILD AND MOTHER. *See* Mothers

CHILD AND PARENT. *See* Parent and Child

CHILD CUSTODY (Law). *Use* Marriage Law

CHILD DEVELOPMENT. *See* Child Study

CHILD DISCIPLINE. *See* Discipline of Children

CHILD GUIDANCE CLINICS. *Use* Child Psychiatry;
Mentally Handicapped Children; Problem
Children

CHILD LABOR
LC CHILDREN—EMPLOYMENT; s.a. Hours of
labor; Youth—Employment
SEARS ——; s.a. Age (law); Age and employment;
Apprentices; Industrial laws and legislation;
Night work; School attendance
RG CHILDREN—EMPLOYMENT; s.a. Child labor;
Youth—Employment
NYT LABOR—U.S.—CHILD LABOR; s.a. Labor—
U.S.—Youth, Employment of

CHILD LABOR, *cont.*
PAIS ———; s.a. Employment—Youth; Hours of labor
BPI ———; s.a. Age and employment; Child welfare

CHILD PLACING. *See* Adoption; Children

CHILD PSYCHIATRY
LC ———; s.a. Child guidance clinics; Child psychotherapy; Mentally ill children
SEARS ———; s.a. Adolescent psychiatry; Mentally handicapped children; Problem children
RG ———; s.a. Schizophrenia; School phobia
NYT MENTAL HEALTH AND DISORDERS; s.a. Children and youth—Behavior and training; Mental deficiency and defectives
PAIS MENTALLY ILL CHILDREN; s.a. Mentally handicapped children; Psychiatry
BPI PSYCHOTHERAPY; s.a. Children—Care and hygiene; Mental illness

CHILD PSYCHOLOGY. *Use* Child Study; Emotions

CHILD PSYCHOTHERAPY. *Use* Child Psychiatry

CHILD STUDY
Scope: Works on the psychology, personality, habits and mental development of the child.
LC ———; s.a. Education, Pre-school; Educational psychology; Exceptional children; Slow-learning children
SEARS ———; s.a. Adolescence; Discipline of children; Exceptional children; Home and school; Mentally handicapped children; Mentally handicapped children; Moving pictures and children; Problem children; Teaching
RG ———; s.a. Emotional problems of children; Parent-child relationship; Slow-learning children
NYT CHILDREN AND YOUTH—BEHAVIOR AND TRAINING; s.a. Mental Health and disorders; Psychology and psychologists
PAIS ———; s.a. Child psychology; Children, Gifted; Children, Research on; Socially handicapped children
BPI CHILDREN; s.a. Children—Care and hygiene; Infants

CHILD WELFARE
Scope: Works on the aid, support and protection of children by the state or by private welfare organizations.
LC ———; s.a. Abandoned children; Child labor; Cruelty to children; Maternal and infant welfare; Maternal deprivation; Parent and child
SEARS ———; s.a. Children—Institutional care; Foster home care
RG ———; s.a. Adoption; Detention homes; Foster grandparent program
NYT CHILDREN AND YOUTH; s.a. Baby sitters
PAIS ———; s.a. Day nurseries
BPI CHILDREN—CARE AND HYGIENE

CHILDBIRTH
LC ———; s.a. Childbirth—Psychology; Contraceptives; Obstetrics; Prenatal influences
SEARS ———; s.a. Medicine—Practice; Pregnancy
RG ———; s.a. Midwives; Pregnancy

NYT BIRTHS; s.a. Abortion; Birth control and planned parenthood
PAIS BIRTHS; s.a. Birth control; Fertility; Infant mortality
BPI LABOR (Obstetrics); s.a. Infants—Mortality; Pregnancy

CHILDISHNESS. *Use* Age (Psychology)

CHILDREN
See also headings beginning with Children, e.g., Children, Adopted; Children—Care and hygiene; Children—Diseases, etc.
LC ———; s.a. Abandoned children; Child study; Day nurseries; Discipline of children; Education of children; Foster home care; Prenatal influences; Runaway children
SEARS ———; s.a. Foster care; Heredity; Infants; Runaways
RG ———; s.a. Adoption; Baby sitters; Family; Infants; Negro children
NYT CHILDREN AND YOUTH; s.a. Birth control and planned parenthood; Children and youth—Lost, missing and runaway children; Families and family life
PAIS ———; s.a. Child welfare; Negro children; Runaway boys and girls; Youth
BPI ———; s.a. Child welfare; Day nurseries; Foster parents; Infants; Youth

CHILDREN, ABANDONED. *See* Abandoned Children

CHILDREN, ABNORMAL AND BACKWARD. *See* Handicapped

CHILDREN, ADOPTED. *Use* Adoption; Orphans

CHILDREN—CARE AND HYGIENE. *Use* Child Psychiatry

CHILDREN—DISCIPLINE. *See* Discipline of Children

CHILDREN—EMPLOYMENT. *Use* Child Labor; Education, Compulsory; Night Work

CHILDREN, EXCEPTIONAL. *Use* Exceptional Children

CHILDREN, GIFTED. *Use* Child Study; Exceptional Children

CHILDREN—GROWTH AND DEVELOPMENT. *Use* Growth

CHILDREN, HANDICAPPED. *Use* Exceptional Children; Handicapped; Mentally Handicapped Children

CHILDREN, ILLEGITIMATE. *See* Illegitimacy

CHILDREN—INSTITUTIONAL CARE. *Use* Abandoned Children; Child Welfare; Institutional Care; Orphans

CHILDREN—LANGUAGE. *Use* Verbal Behavior; Vocabulary

CHILDREN—LAW. *Use* Juvenile Delinquency; Parent and Child

CHILDREN—MANAGEMENT. *Use* Discipline of Children; Parent and Child; Home and School

CHILDREN, NEGRO. *See* Negro Children

CHILDREN, RESEARCH ON. *Use* Child Study

CHILDREN, VAGRANT. *Use* Juvenile Delinquency; Vagrancy

CHILDREN AND MOVING PICTURES. *See* Moving Pictures and Children

CHILDREN AND YOUTH. *Use* Adolescence; Boys; Child Welfare; Home and School; Parent and Child

CHILDREN AND YOUTH—BEHAVIOR AND TRAINING. *Use* Alienation (Social psychology); Conflict of Generations; Dropouts; Mental Illness; Moral Conditions; Problem Children; Violence; Youth Movement

CHILDREN AND YOUTH—LOST, MISSING AND RUNAWAY CHILDREN. *Use* Abduction; Children; Problem Children

CHILDREN AS MODELS. *Use* Models, Fashion

CHILDREN OF DIVORCED PARENTS. *Use* Divorce; Fathers; Mothers; Parent and child

CHILDREN OF MIGRANT LABORERS. *Use* Migrant Labor

CHILDREN'S BOOKS. *See* Children's Literature; Illustrated Books

CHILDREN'S COURTS. *See* Juvenile Delinquency

CHILDREN'S LITERATURE
See also subd. *Juvenile literature* under particular subjects, e.g., Astronomy—Juvenile literature.
LC ——; s.a. Books and reading for children; Literature
SEARS ——; s.a. Lullabies; Nursery rhymes
RG ——; s.a. Fairy tales; Story telling
NYT BOOKS AND LITERATURE—CHILDREN AND YOUTH; s.a. Children and youth; Libraries and librarians
PAIS ——; s.a. Children's periodicals; Literature
BPI ——; s.a. Book industry—Children's literature; Paperback books—Children's literature

CHILDREN'S PARTIES. *Use* Entertaining

CHIMNEYS. *Use* Ventilation

CHINAWARE. *See* Ceramics

CHINESE STUDIES (Sinology). *Use* Oriental Studies

CHIROPRACTIC
LC ——; s.a. Naturopathy; Osteopathy; Therapeutics, Physiological
SEARS OSTEOPATHY; s.a. Massage; Medicine—Practice
RG ——; s.a. Bones—Diseases; Orthopedia
NYT CHIROPRACTIC AND CHIROPRACTORS; s.a. Medicine and health; Osteopathy and Osteopaths
PAIS ——; s.a. Medicine; Osteopathy
BPI MEDICINE; s.a. Physicians; Physiology

CHIROTHERAPY. *See* Massage

CHIVALRY. *Use* Feudalism

CHOICE (Psychology). *Use* Decision Making; Fate and Fatalism

CHOICE OF PROFESSION. *See* Vocational Guidance

CHOIRS. *Use* Choral Music

CHORAL MUSIC
Scope: Collections of sacred and secular choral compositions are entered under heading Choruses.
LC ——; s.a. Choirs; Church music
SEARS ——; s.a. Conducting, Choral; Vocal music
RG ——; s.a. Choral groups and societies; Phonograph records—Choral music
NYT MUSIC; s.a. Opera; Recordings (disk and tape) and recording and playback equipment
PAIS MUSIC; s.a. Opera; Orchestras
BPI MUSIC; s.a. Composers; Opera

CHOREOGRAPHY. *Use* Ballet; Dancing

CHRIST. *See* Jesus Christ

CHRISTENING. *See* Baptism

CHRISTIAN ART AND SYMBOLISM. *Use* Art, Medieval; Art and Religion; Emblems; Liturgies; Signs and Symbols

CHRISTIAN BIOGRAPHY. *Use* Missionaries; Papcy; Saints

CHRISTIAN DEMOCRACY. *Use* Social Policy

CHRISTIAN EDUCATION. *See* Religious Education

CHRISTIAN ETHICS
LC ——; s.a. Commandments, Ten; Fear of God; Love (theology); Social ethics
SEARS ——; s.a. Christianity and economics; Sin
RG ——; s.a. Church and social problems; Humility
NYT ETHICS AND MORALS; s.a. Religion and churches
PAIS ——; s.a. Christianity and other religions; Moral education; Religion and ethics
BPI CHRISTIANITY; s.a. Ethics; Fairness

CHRISTIAN LIFE. *Use* Character; Religion

CHRISTIAN SCIENCE. *Use* Mental Healing

CHRISTIAN UNITY. *Use* Catholicity; Church

CHRISTIANITY
See also headings beginning with Christianity, e.g., Christianity and economics; Christianity and politics; etc.
LC ——; s.a. Baptism; Bible; Canonization; Catholicity; Christian ethics; Civilization, Christian; Ecumenical movement; Evangelicalism; Jesus Christ; Liturgies; Missionaries; Saints; Virgin birth
SEARS ——; s.a. Protestantism; Reformation
RG ——; s.a. Fundamentalism; Theology
NYT RELIGION AND CHURCHES; s.a. Names of specific denominations, e.g., Protestant Episcopal church
PAIS CHRISTIANITY AND OTHER RELIGIONS; s.a. Church; Religions
BPI ——; s.a. Catholic church; Protestantism

CHRISTIANITY AND OTHER RELIGIONS. *Use* Catholicity; Conversion, Religious; God; Religion; Theology

CHRISTMAS. *Use* Special Days, Weeks and Months

CHRISTMAS SHOPPING. *Use* Shopping

CHRISTMAS TREES. *Use* Trees

CHROMOSOMES. *Use* Genetics

CHRONICALLY ILL. *Use* Diseases; Sick

CHRONOLOGY. *Use* History; Time

CHURCH
See also headings beginning with Church, e.g., Church and education.

LC ——; s.a. Catholicity; Christianity; Dissenters, Religious; Evangelicalism; Nationalism and religion; Priesthood, Universal

SEARS ——; s.a. Christian unity; Religious Education; Theology

RG ——; s.a. Mission of the church; Women and the church

NYT RELIGION AND CHURCHES; s.a. Names of specific religious groups and denominations, e.g., Process Church——

PAIS CHURCHES; s.a. Clergy; Religion

BPI ——; s.a. Catholic church; Protestant church

CHURCH—AUTHORITY. *Use* Papacy; Ultramontanism

CHURCH AND EDUCATION. *Use* Church Schools; Religious Education

CHURCH AND LABOR. *Use* Labor and Laboring Classes

CHURCH AND POLITICS. *Use* Nationalism and Religion

CHURCH AND RACE PROBLEMS. *Use* Race Problems; School Ethics

CHURCH AND SCHOOLS. *Use* Religious Education

CHURCH AND SOCIAL PROBLEMS. *Use* Christian Ethics; Religion and Sociology; Social Problems; Sociology

CHURCH AND STATE. *Use* Dissenters, Religious; Ecclesiastical Law; Nationalism and Religion; Religious Education; Religious Liberty

CHURCH AND WAR. *See* War and Religion

CHURCH ATTENDANCE. *Use* Worship

CHURCH CALENDAR. *Use* Saints

CHURCH CHARITIES. *Use* Charity; Church Schools

CHURCH COLLEGES. *Use* Colleges and Universities

CHURCH DENOMINATIONS. *See* Sects

CHURCH HISTORY. *Use* Papacy; Protestantism; Sects

CHURCH LANDS. *Use* Land Tenure

CHURCH LAW. *See* Ecclesiastical Law

CHURCH MUSIC. *Use* Choral Music; Music

CHURCH OF JESUS CHRIST OF LATTER-DAY SAINTS. *Use* Mormons and Mormonism

CHURCH SCHOOLS
Scope: Works dealing with elementary and secondary schools whose pupils receive their entire education under church auspices, control or support.

LC ——; s.a. Church and education; Church colleges; Vacation schools, Religious

SEARS ——; s.a. Church and education; Private schools; Religious education

RG ——; s.a. Catholic schools; Education and state

NYT EDUCATION AND SCHOOLS—U.S.—SECTARIAN SCHOOLS; s.a. Education and schools—U.S.—Prep schools; Religious education

PAIS ——; s.a. Parochial schools; Roman Catholic church—Education

BPI ——; s.a. Catholic church; Schools

CHURCH UNION. *Use* Catholicity; Catholic Church in the U. S.

CHURCH WORK. *Use* Religious Education

CHURCH WORK WITH HOMOSEXUALS. *Use* Homosexuality

CHURCH WORK WITH MIGRANTS. *Use* Migrant Labor

CHURCH WORK WITH NARCOTIC ADDICTS. *Use* Nacrotic Addicts

CHURCH WORK WITH PROBLEM CHILDREN. *Use* Problem Children

CHURCH WORK WITH THE HANDICAPPED. *Use* Mentally Ill

CHURCHES. *Use* Church; Atheism; God; Preaching; Religion; Theology; Worship

CIGAR BANDS AND LABELS. *Use* Labels

CIGAR INDUSTRY. *Use* Smoking; Tobacco

CIGAR MANUFACTURE AND TRADE. *Use* Tobacco

CIGARETTES
LC ——; s.a. Cigars; Labels; Smoking

SEARS ——; s.a. Smoking; Tobacco habit

RG ——; s.a. Smoking; Tobacco

NYT TOBACCO, TOBACCO PRODUCTS AND SMOKERS ARTICLES; s.a. Cancer; Taxation—U. S.—Tax evasion

PAIS CIGARETTE INDUSTRY; s.a. Advertising—Cigarette industry; Smoking

BPI CIGARETS; s.a. Cigaret industry; Tobacco

CINEMA. *See* Moving Pictures

CINEMATOGRAPHY. *Use* Photography

CINEMATOGRAPHY (Photographic processes). *Use* Moving Pictures

CIPHERS
LC ——; s.a. Abbreviations; Morse Code

SEARS ——; s.a. Cryptography; Telegraph

RG CIPHER AND TELEGRAPH CODES; s.a. Abbreviations; Symbols

NYT CODES (Ciphers); s.a. Communications; Telegraphy

PAIS CIPHER AND TELEGRAPH CODES; s.a. Abbreviations; Signs and symbols

BPI NUMBERING SYSTEMS; s.a. Abbreviations

CIRCULAR LETTERS. *Use* Letter Writing

CIRCULATORY SYSTEM. *See* Cardiovascular system

CITIES AND TOWNS
Scope: Statistical and descriptive works on cities and towns. Theoretical and practical works are entered under Municipal government; legal treatises and collections of statutes are entered under Local government.
LC ———; s.a. Headings beginning with City, Municipal or Urban; Sociology, Urban; Urbanization; Villages
SEARS ———; s.a. Art, Municipal; City planning; Community life; Migration, Internal; Neighborhood; Tenement houses
RG ———; s.a. New cities and towns; Slums
NYT URBAN AREAS; s.a. Area planning and renewal
PAIS ———; s.a. Metropolitan areas; Suburbs
BPI ———; s.a. Urban renewal; Villages

CITIES AND TOWNS – CIVIC IMPROVEMENT. *Use* City Planning; Urban Renewal

CITIES AND TOWNS – LAWS AND LEGISLATION. *Use* Ordinances, Municipal

CITIZENS ASSOCIATIONS. *Use* Neighborhood

CITIZENS RADIO SERVICE. *Use* Radio, Short Wave; Radio Stations

CITIZENSHIP
LC ———; s.a. Aliens; Americanization; Civics; Emigration and immigration; Expatriation; Patriotism
SEARS ———; s.a. Constitutional law; Immigration and emigration; Nationality; Suffrage
RG ———; s.a. Citizenship, Education for; Education and democracy; Patriotism; Social ethics
NYT ———; s.a. Immigration and emigration; Refugees
PAIS ———; s.a. Expatriation; Nationality; Naturalization; Statelessness
BPI ———; s.a. Alien labor; Foreign visitors; Nationalization; Refugees

CITIZENSHIP, LOSS OF. *Use* Exiles

CITY AND COUNTRY. *Use* Country Life; Rural conditions; Villages

CITY GOVERNMENT. *See* Municipal Government; Mayors

CITY MANAGERS. *Use* Local Government; Mayors; Municipal Government; Municipal Officials and Employees

CITY ORDINANCES. *See* Ordinances, Municipal

CITY PLANNING
LC CITIES AND TOWNS–PLANNING; s.a. Architecture; Housing; Regional planning; Urban renewal
SEARS ———; s.a. Cities and towns–Civic improvement; Local transit; Social surveys; Tenement-houses; Urban renewal; Zoning
RG ———; s.a. Business districts; Traffic engineering; Urban renewal; subd. *City planning* under names of cities; Suburbs

NYT AREA PLANNING AND RENEWAL; s.a. Housing; Urban areas
PAIS ———; s.a. Neighborhood planning; Redevelopment, Urban; Regional planning
BPI ———; s.a. Business districts; Land subdivision; Social surveys; Urban renewal

CITY TRAFFIC. *Use* Streets; Traffic Safety

CITY TRANSIT. *See* Local Transit

CITY-COUNTY CONSOLIDATION. *Use* Local Government

CITY-STATE RELATIONS. *See* Municipal Government

CIVIC ART. *See* Art, Municipal

CIVIC IMPROVEMENT. *See* Urban Renewal

CIVIC RIGHTS. *See* Civil Rights

CIVICS. *Use* Citizenship; Patriotism; Social Ethics

CIVIL DEFENSE
LC ———; s.a. Air defenses; Civil; Disaster relief
SEARS ———; s.a. Air raid shelters; Rescue work
RG ———; s.a. Emergency communication systems; Radio in civil defense
NYT ———; s.a. U.S. armament and defense
PAIS ———; s.a. Atomic bomb shelters; Atomic warfare–Defense
BPI ———; s.a. Emergency broadcast system; Industrial defense

CIVIL DISOBEDIENCE. *Use* Government, Resistance to; Passive Resistance

CIVIL DISORDERS. *See* Riots

CIVIL ENGINEERING
LC ———; s.a. Harbors; Public works; Viaducts
SEARS ———; s.a. Bridges; Building, Iron and steel; Highway engineering; Mechanical engineering; Reclamation of land
RG ———; s.a. Dams; Piles and pile driving
NYT ENGINEERING AND ENGINEERS; s.a. Bridges and tunnels; Roads; Waterways
PAIS ———; s.a. Construction equipment; Engineering
BPI ———; s.a. Earthwork; Trestles; Tunnels and tunneling

CIVIL LAW. *Use* Liability (Law); Obligations

CIVIL LIBERTY. *See* Civil Rights; Liberty

CIVIL PROCEDURE. *Use* Judgments; Procedure (Law); Justice, Administration of; Trials

CIVIL RIGHTS
LC ———; s.a. Equality before law; Freedom of association; Liberty; Political rights; Suffrage
SEARS ———; s.a. Academic freedom; Constitutional law; Constitutions; Discrimination; Free speech; Justice, Administration of; Persecution
RG ———; s.a. Assembly, Right of; Information, Freedom of; Rule of law; subd. *Civil rights* under subjects, e.g., Employees–Civil rights
NYT FREEDOM AND HUMAN RIGHTS; s.a. Freedom of assembly; Freedom of information, thought and expression; Freedom of speech; Minorities (ethnic, racial, religious)

CIVIL RIGHTS, *cont.*
PAIS ——; s.a. Human rights; Legal rights; Petition, Right of; Religious liberty; Voting
BPI ——; s.a. Due process of law; Referendum; Women—Rights of women

CIVIL SERVICE
Scope: Works on career government service and laws governing it. Works on duties of civil service employees, salaries, etc., are entered under names of cities or agencies with subd. *Officials and employees,* e.g., Chicago—Officials and employees, or IRS—Officials and employees.
LC ——; s.a. Administrative law; Collective labor agreements—Municipal officials and employees; Misconduct in office; Trade unions—Government employees
SEARS ——; s.a. Civil service—Examinations; Political science; Public administration
RG ——; s.a. Conflict of interests (public office) Patronage, Political; Public officers
NYT GOVERNMENT EMPLOYEES AND OFFICIALS; s.a. Labor—U.S.—Union security; U.S.—Politics and government—Ethics in office; White collar workers
PAIS ——; s.a. Government employees; Municipal employees; Public officials
BPI ——; s.a. Bureaucracy; Government officials and employees; Local officials and employees

CIVIL SERVICE—EXAMINATIONS. *Use* Civil Service; Examinations; Municipal officials and Employees

CIVIL SERVICE ETHICS. *Use* Political Crimes and Offenses

CIVIL SERVICE PENSIONS. *Use* Pensions; Survivor's Benefits

CIVIL SERVICE REFORM. *Use* Patronage, Political

CIVIL SUPREMACY OVER MILITARY. *Use* Constitutions; Executive Power; Militarism

CIVIL WAR. *Use* Revolutions; War

CIVIL WAR (U.S.) (1861–65). *Use* Confederate States of America; Slavery

CIVILIZATION
Scope: Works on culture or civilization in general. Works on the civilization of a single country are entered under the name of country with subd. *Civilization,* e.g., U.S.—Civilization; or Civilization, Greek
LC ——; s.a. Ethnology; Manners and customs; Social history; Sociology; War and society
SEARS ——; s.a. Acculturation; Biculturalism; Inventions; Progress; Society, Primitive; War and civilization
RG ——; s.a. Humanism; Popular culture
NYT ——; s.a. Archeology and anthropology; Culture; Man
PAIS ——; s.a. Popular culture; Technology and civilization
BPI SOCIOLOGY; s.a. Culture; History; Social sciences

CIVILIZATION, CHRISTIAN. *Use* Christianity

CIVILIZATION, ISLAMIC. *Use* Islam

CIVILIZATION, MEDIEVAL. *Use* Feudalism

CIVILIZATION, MODERN—20TH CENTURY. *Use* Twentieth Century

CIVILIZATION, OCCIDENTAL. *Use* East and West

CIVILIZATION, ORIENTAL. *Use* East and West

CIVILIZATION, SECULAR. *Use* Secularism

CIVILIZATION AND TECHNOLOGY. *See* Technology

CIVILIZATION AND WAR. *See* War and Society

CIVIL-MILITARY RELATIONS. *Use* Militarism; Military Law

CLAIRVOYANCE
LC ——; s.a. Occult sciences; Psychical research; Psychometry (occult sciences)
SEARS ——; s.a. Fortune telling; Mind reading; Thought transference
RG ——; s.a. Extrasensory perception; Occult sciences
NYT PSYCHIC PHENOMENA; s.a. Occult sciences; Psychology and psychologists; Superstitions
PAIS EXTRASENSORY PERCEPTION; s.a. Occult sciences; Psychical research
BPI EXTRASENSORY PERCEPTION; s.a. Psychology

CLANS AND CLAN SYSTEM. *Use* Feudalism; Society, Primitive; Tribes and Tribal System

CLASS CONFLICT. *Use* Social Classes

CLASS DISTINCTION. *See* Elite (Social sciences); Social Classes

CLASS SIZE. *Use* Educational Administration

CLASS STRUGGLE. *Use* Aristocracy; Caste; Labor and Laboring classes; Revolutions; Upper Classes

CLASSICAL EDUCATION. *Use* Education; Humanism

CLASSIFICATION—BOOKS. *Use* Libraries and Librarians

CLASSIFIED INFORMATION. *See* Official Secrets

CLASSROOM MANAGEMENT. *Use* School Supervision; Teaching

CLASSROOM OBSERVATION. *See* Observation (Educational method)

CLASSROOMS. *Use* Schools

CLASSROOMS, PORTABLE. *Use* Schools

CLAY. *Use* Ceramics

CLAY INDUSTRIES. *Use* Bricks

CLEANING AND DYEING. *Use* Clothing and Dress; Dyes and Dyeing; Laundries and Laundering

CLEANING COMPOUNDS
LC ——; s.a. Scouring compounds; Soap
SEARS ——; s.a. Detergents, Synthetic; Soap
RG CLEANING COMPOSITIONS; s.a. Detergents; Polishing materials

NYT   CLEANSERS, DETERGENTS AND SOAPS; s.a. Cleaning and dyeing; Toiletries and Cosmetics

PAIS   CLEANING COMPOSITIONS; s.a. Cleaning equipment and supplies; Soap industry; Toilet goods industry

BPI   CLEANING COMPOSITIONS; s.a. Detergent pollution of water; Solvents

CLEANING INDUSTRY. *Use* Dyes and Dyeing; Laundries and Laundering

CLEANLINESS. *Use* Hygiene

CLEANSERS, DETERGENTS AND SOAPS. *Use* Cleaning Compounds; Disinfection and Disinfectants; Laundries and Laundering

CLEARING HOUSES. *Use* Banks and Banking; Checks (Banking); Trust Companies

CLEARING OF LAND. *Use* Land; Reclamation of Land

CLERGY
See also subd. *Clergy* Under church denominations, e.g., Catholic church—Clergy.

LC   ——; s.a. Confidential communications—Clergy; Priests; Theologians

SEARS   ——; s.a. Clergymen's wives; Monasticism and religious orders; Pastoral work; Preaching

RG   ——; s.a. Missionaries; Pastoral theology

NYT   RELIGION AND CHURCHES; s.a. Celibacy; names of specific religious groups, e.g., Mormons (Church of Jesus Christ of Latter-Day Saints)

PAIS   ——; s.a. Chaplains, Military; Women in the clergy

BPI   ——; s.a. Celibacy; Chaplains

CLERKS
LC   ——; s.a. Bank employees; Clerical occupations; Office practice

SEARS   ——; s.a. Salesmen and salesmanship

RG   OFFICE WORKERS; s.a. Employees; Secretaries

NYT   WHITE COLLAR WORKERS; s.a. Labor; Professions

PAIS   OFFICE EMPLOYEES; s.a. Secretaries; White collar employees

BPI   CLERKS (Retail trade); s.a. Occupations; Office workers; Salesmanship

CLIMATE
See also subd. *Climate* under names of places.

LC   CLIMATOLOGY; s.a. Acclimatization; Geography; Seasons; Soils and climate; Weather

SEARS   ——; s.a. Meteorology; Rain and rainfall

RG   ——; s.a. Paleoclimatology; Plants, Effects of climate on; Seasons

NYT   WEATHER; s.a. Atmosphere, Lower; Seasons and months; Space and upper atmosphere

PAIS   ——; s.a. Rainfall; Weather forecasting

BPI   ——; s.a. Meteorology; Weather control

CLIMBING PLANTS. *Use* Gardening

CLINICAL PSYCHOLOGY. *Use* Tests, Mental

CLINICS
Scope: Works dealing with institutions for treatment of non-resident patients.

LC   ——; s.a. Group medical practice; Naroctic clinics

SEARS   MEDICAL CARE; s.a. Children—Hospitals

RG   HEALTH FACILITIES; s.a. Mental health centers; Psychiatric clinics

NYT   MEDICINE AND HEALTH; s.a. Handicapped; Mental health and disorders

PAIS   ——; s.a. Child guidance clinics; Hospitals—Outpatient services

BPI   HOSPITALS; s.a. Medical centers

CLOCKS AND WATCHES. *Use* Time

CLOSED CIRCUIT TELEVISION. *Use* Television; Television in Education

CLOSED SHOP. *See* Open and Closed Shop

CLOTHES DRYERS. *Use* Laundries and Laundering

CLOTHING, PROTECTIVE. *Use* Safety Appliances

CLOTHING AND DRESS
Scope: Descriptive and historical works are entered under Costumes. See also names of items of clothing, e.g., Raincoats.

LC   ——; s.a. Men's clothing; Models, Fashion

SEARS   ——; s.a. Dressmaking; Tailoring

RG   ——; s.a. Fashion; Sewing

NYT   APPAREL; s.a. Cleaning and dyeing; Fur

PAIS   ——; s.a. Clothing industry; Emergency clothing supply

BPI   ——; s.a. Costumes; Fashion

CLOTHING TRADE. *Use* Tailoring

CLOWNS. *Use* Entertainers

CLUBS
LC   ——; s.a. Athletic clubs; Musical societies

SEARS   ——; s.a. Social group work; Women's clubs

RG   ——; s.a. Book clubs; Negroes—Clubs, societies, etc.

NYT   ORGANIZATIONS, SOCIETIES, AND CLUBS; s.a. Bridge (Card game); Colleges and universities—U. S.—Student activities and conduct

PAIS   ——; s.a. Country clubs; Travel clubs

BPI   ——; s.a. Businessmen's clubs; Health clubs

COACHING. *Use* Athletics; Sports

COAL. *Use* Mines and Mineral Resources

COAL GAS. *See* Gas

COAL INDUSTRY. *Use* Fuel

COAL MINERS (Gold miners, etc.). *Use* Mines and Mineral Resources

COAL MINES AND MINING. *Use* Mines and Mineral Resources

COAL-TAR INDUSTRY. *Use* Petroleum Industry and Trade

COAL-TAR PRODUCTS. *Use* Coke Industry; Gas; Oil and Fats

COALITION (Social sciences). *Use* Social Groups

COALITION GOVERNMENTS. *Use* Political Parties

COAST EROSION. *Use* Beaches; Erosion; Reclamation of Land; Seashore

COASTS
LC ————; s.a. Oceanography; Shore protection
SEARS SEASHORE; s.a. Ocean; Storms
RG ————; s.a. Estuaries; Seashore
NYT BEACHES; s.a. Coast erosion; Geology; Waters, Territorial
PAIS SHORE LINES; s.a. Oceanography; Shore protection
BPI TERRITORIAL WATERS; s.a. Maritime law; Shorelines

COASTWISE SHIPPING—LAW AND LEGISLATION. *Use* Maritime Law

COAT OF ARMS. *See* Genealogy

COCAINE HABIT. *Use* Nacrotic Habit

COCKTAILS. *Use* Liquors

CODES. *Use* Acronyms; Ciphers; Signs and Symbols

CODING THEORY. *Use* Programming (Electronic Computers)

COEDUCATION
LC ————; s.a. Education of women; Universities and colleges
SEARS ————; s.a. Colleges and universities; Education
RG ————; s.a. College students, Women; Education of women
NYT EDUCATION AND SCHOOLS; s.a. Colleges and universities; Women
PAIS ————; s.a. Colleges and universities; Women—Education
BPI EDUCATION OF WOMEN; s.a. Colleges and universities; Education

CO-EDS. *See* Education of Women

COFFEE HOUSES. *Use* Food Service; Hotels, Taverns, etc.; Restaurants, Lunchrooms, etc.

COGNITION. *Use* Apperception; Perception; Thought and Thinking

COINAGE. *Use* Coins; Money

COINAGE, INTERNATIONAL. *Use* Monetary Policy

COINS. *Use* Collectors and Collecting; Counterfeits and Counterfeiting; Money; Numismatics

COLD (Disease)
LC ————; s.a. Catarrh; Cough
SEARS ————; s.a. Influenza
RG ————; s.a. Communicable diseases; Virus diseases
NYT COLDS; s.a. Medicine and Health; names of cold infections, e.g., Influenza
PAIS SICKNESS; s.a. Communicable diseases
BPI ————; s.a. Drugs; Medicine

COLD WAR
LC INTERNATIONAL RELATIONS; s.a. World politics
SEARS PSYCHOLOGICAL WARFARE; s.a. World politics—1945-1965
RG WORLD POLITICS, 1945–; s.a. Communism and democracy; U.S.—Foreign relations—Russia
NYT INTERNATIONAL RELATIONS—COMMUNIST-WESTERN CONFRONTATION; s.a. Communism; Diplomacy; World government
PAIS INTERNATIONAL RELATIONS; s.a. East and west; World politics
BPI COMMUNISM AND DEMOCRACY; s.a. Isolationism; World politics

COLDS. *Use* Cold (Disease)

COLLABORATIONISTS. *See* Treason

COLLAGE. *Use* Art Objects

COLLATERAL LOANS. *See* Loans

COLLECTING. *See* Collectors and Collecting

COLLECTING OF ACCOUNTS
LC ————; s.a. Accounts current; Accounts receivable; Postal service—Collection of notes, etc.
SEARS ————; s.a. Business law; Commercial law; Credit management
RG ————; s.a. Billing; Debtor and creditor
NYT CREDIT—U.S.—CONSUMER CREDIT; s.a. Retail stores and trade
PAIS COLLECTION OF ACCOUNTS; s.a. Collection agencies; Debtor and creditor
BPI ————; s.a. Billing; Debtor and creditor

COLLECTIVE BARGAINING
See also appropriate subd., e.g., Collective bargaining—Railroads.
LC ————; s.a. Arbitration, Industrial; Collective labor agreements; Labor contract; Labor disputes; Labor laws and legislation; Management rights; Mediation and conciliation, Industrial; Negotiation; Trade-unions; Union security; Works councils
SEARS ————; s.a. Labor and laboring classes; Labor contracts; Labor unions; Strikes and lockouts; Trades and professional associations
RG ————; s.a. Arbitration, Industrial; Industrial relations; Trade unions
NYT ————; s.a. Labor—U.S.—Arbitration, conciliation and mediation; Labor—U.S.—Strikes; Labor—U.S.—Unionization
PAIS ————; s.a. Check-off system; Collective labor agreements; Employees' representation in management; Management—Rights and responsibilities; Right to work; subd. *Collective labor agreements* under subjects
BPI ————; s.a. Collective labor agreements; Open and closed shops; Strikes

COLLECTIVE EDUCATION. *Use* Collectivism

COLLECTIVE FARMING
LC COLLECTIVE FARMS; s.a. Agriculture, Co-operative; State farms
SEARS AGRICULTURE, COOPERATIVE; s.a. Agriculture—Societies; Collective settlements
RG COLLECTIVE FARMS; s.a. Agriculture, Co-operative; Cooperative associations

NYT AGRICULTURE AND AGRICULTURAL PRODUCTS; s.a. Communism; Economic conditions and trends (general); Kibbutzim

PAIS ——; s.a. Agricultural, Cooperative; State farming

BPI AGRICULTURE, COOPERATIVE; s.a. Farmers cooperative associations; Farm labor

COLLECTIVE LABOR AGREEMENTS. *Use* Collective Bargaining

COLLECTIVE PSYCHOTHERAPY. *See* Group Relations Training

COLLECTIVE SETTLEMENTS. *Use* Bohemianism; Collective Farming; Cooperation; Socialism; Subculture

COLLECTIVISM
LC ——; s.a. Collective education; Fascism; Government ownership; Individualism
SEARS COMMUNISM; s.a. Socialism
RG ——; s.a. Communism; Industrial democracy
NYT ECONOMIC CONDITIONS AND TRENDS (General); s.a. Agriculture and agricultural products; Communism
PAIS ——; s.a. Communism; Totalitarianism
BPI COMMUNISM; s.a. Socialism

COLLECTORS AND COLLECTING
See also subd. *Collectors and collecting* under names of objects, e.g., Postage stamps—Collectors and collecting; or for zoological specimens, the subd. *Collection and preservation* under names of specimens, e.g., Birds—Collection and preservation.
LC ——; s.a. Book collecting; Men as collectors
SEARS ——; Numismatics
RG ——; s.a. Display of antiques, art objects, etc.; Hobbies
NYT COLLECTORS AND COLLECTIONS; s.a. names of objects collected, e.g., Art
PAIS ——; s.a. Coins
BPI ——; s.a. Book collecting; Postage stamps

COLLEGE ATHLETICS. *Use* Athletics; Baseball; Basketball; Gymnastics; Sports; Track Athletics

COLLEGE CLUBS AND SOCIETIES. *Use* Students

COLLEGE COSTS
LC ——; s.a. Education—Finance; Student loan funds
SEARS ——; s.a. Colleges and universities—Finance; Scholarships, fellowships, etc.
RG COLLEGE EDUCATION—COST; s.a. Church colleges—Finance; Colleges and universities—Finance
NYT COLLEGES AND UNIVERSITIES—U.S.—FINANCES; s.a. Colleges and universities—U.S.—Enrollment; Scholarships and fellowships
PAIS COLLEGES AND UNIVERSITIES—FINANCE; s.a. Colleges and universities—Tuition; Education—Finance
BPI ——; s.a. Colleges and universities—Finance; Student aid

COLLEGE DEANS. *Use* Educational Administration

COLLEGE DEGREES. *See* Degrees, Academic

COLLEGE DISCIPLINE. *Use* Self-Government (In Education)

COLLEGE DROPOUTS. *Use* Dropouts.

COLLEGE EDUCATION. *Use* Education

COLLEGE EDUCATION, VALUE OF. *Use* College Graduates; Education

COLLEGE EDUCATION AND STATE. *Use* Education and State

COLLEGE EDUCATION COSTS. *See* College Costs

COLLEGE FRATERNITIES. *Use* Students

COLLEGE GRADUATES
Scope: Works relating to college graduates as a socioeconomic group only.
LC ——; s.a. Professions; Universities and colleges—Alumni
SEARS DEGREES, ACADEMIC; s.a. Education, Higher
RG ——; s.a. College education, Value of; Colleges and universities—Graduate work
NYT COLLEGES AND UNIVERSITIES—U.S.—GRADUATES AND GRADUATION; s.a. Labor—U.S.—Youth, Employment of; Professions; Sociology
PAIS ——; s.a. subd. *College Graduates* under specific subjects, e.g., Employment—College graduates
BPI ——; s.a. Business schools and colleges—Graduates; Engineering graduates

COLLEGE GRADUATES—EMPLOYMENT. *Use* Labor Supply

COLLEGE LIBRARIES. *Use* Libraries and Librarians

COLLEGE OFFICIALS. *Use* Educational Administration

COLLEGE PROFESSORS AND INSTRUCTORS. *Use* Educators; Learning and Scholarship; Personnel Service in Education; Teachers

COLLEGE RADIO STATIONS. *See* Radio Stations

COLLEGE SPORTS. *Use* Athletics; Baseball; Basketball; Sports; Track Athletics

COLLEGE STUDENTS. *Use* Negro Students; Students; Talented Students

COLLEGE STUDENTS—AID. *Use* Scholarships

COLLEGE STUDENTS—DISCIPLINE. *Use* Cheating (Education); Punishment; Student Movements

COLLEGE STUDENTS—ETHICS. *Use* Self-Government (In Education)

COLLEGE STUDENTS, MARRIED. *Use* Marriage

COLLEGE STUDENTS, MENTALLY SUPERIOR. *Use* Talented Students

COLLEGE STUDENTS—POLITICAL ACTIVITY. *Use* Student Movements; Students

COLLEGE STUDENTS, WOMEN. *Use* Coeducation; Education of Women

COLLEGE STUDENTS AND BUSINESS. *Use* Industry and Education

COLLEGE TEACHERS. *Use* Educators; Learning and Scholarship; Personnel Service in Education; Teachers

COLLEGE THEATER. *Use* Theater

COLLEGES AND UNIVERSITIES
See also names of types of schools, e.g., Business colleges; Community colleges; Evening and continuation schools; Junior colleges; Medical colleges; Municipal universities and colleges; and names of individual institutions.

LC	UNIVERSITIES AND COLLEGES; s.a. Adult education; Classical education; Education, Co-operative; Education, Higher; Educators; Learning and scholarship; Personnel service in education; Professional education; Self-government (in education); Students
SEARS	———; s.a. Coeducation; Education—Curricula; Scholarships, fellowships, etc.
RG	———; s.a. Free universities; Liberal education
NYT	———; s.a. Colleges and universities—Foreign study; Commercial education
PAIS	———; s.a. Degrees, Academic; University extension
BPI	———; s.a. Degrees, Academic

COLLEGES AND UNIVERSITIES—ACCREDITATION. *Use* Accreditation (Education)

COLLEGES AND UNIVERSITIES—ADMINISTRATION. *Use* Educational Administration; Educational Planning and Innovations; Educators

COLLEGES AND UNIVERSITIES—ADMINISTRATION—STUDENT PARTICIPATION. *Use* Self-Government (In Education)

COLLEGES AND UNIVERSITIES—BUSINESS AID. *Use* Industry and Education

COLLEGES AND UNIVERSITIES—COURSES OF STUDY. *Use* Education—Curricula

COLLEGES AND UNIVERSITIES—DESEGREGATION. *Use* Discrimination and Conduct; Negro Students

COLLEGES AND UNIVERSITIES—ENTRANCE REQUIREMENTS. *Use* Examinations

COLLEGES AND UNIVERSITIES—FEDERAL AID. *Use* Education and State

COLLEGES AND UNIVERSITIES—TUITION. *Use* College Costs

COLLISIONS, AUTOMOBILE. *See* Traffic Accidents

COLLISIONS AT SEA. *Use* Disasters; Maritime Law

COLONIAL COMPANIES. *Use* Colonization

COLONIALISM. *See* Colonies; Imperialism

COLONIES
See also subd. *Colonies* under names of countries, e.g., Great Britain—Colonies. Works on settling imigrants in colonial areas are entered under Colonization. For U.S. dependencies see heading U.S.-Territories and possessions

LC	———; s.a. Emigration and immigration; Land settlement; Protectorates
SEARS	———; s.a. Colonization; Penal colonies
RG	———; s.a. Imperialism; United Nations—Trusteeship Council
NYT	COLONIES AND TERRITORIES (General); s.a. Local government; names of colonies, e.g., Jamaica; Politics and government
PAIS	———; s.a. Imperialism; International trusteeships
BPI	———; s.a. Great Britain—Colonies; Immigration and emigration

COLONIZATION

Scope	Works on the policy of settling immigrants or nationals in colonial areas. See also subd. *Colonization* under countries or regions, e.g., Africa—Colonization.
LC	———; s.a. Agricultural colonies; Colonial companies; Land grants
SEARS	———; s.a. Immigration and emigration; Jews—Colonization
RG	———; s.a. Immigration and emigration; Imperialism
NYT	COLONIES AND TERRITORIES (General); s.a. Commonwealth of Nations; names of colonies, e.g., Tonga
PAIS	COLONIES; s.a. Imperialism; subd. *Territories and possessions* under names of individual countries
BPI	COLONIES; s.a. Great Britain—Colonies; Immigration and emigration

COLOR. *Use* Aesthetics; Optics

COLOR BLINDNESS. *Use* Blind

COLOR MOVING PICTURES. *Use* Moving Pictures

COLOR OF MAN

LC	———; s.a. Color variation—Biology; Ethnology; Melanism
SEARS	———; s.a. Man—Influence of environment; Somatology
RG	———; s.a. Albinos and albinism; Pigments (biology)
NYT	RACE; s.a. Biology and biochemistry; Evolution; Man
PAIS	RACES OF MAN; s.a. Nonwhite persons
BPI	RACE; s.a. Man; Race discrimination

COLOR PHOTOGRAPHY. *Use* Photography

COLOR PRINTING. *Use* Printing Industry

COLOR TELEVISION. *Use* Television

COMBAT. *Use* Battles

COMBATANTS AND NON-COMBATANTS (International law). *Use* Guerilla Warfare

COMBINATIONS, INDUSTRIAL. *See* Trusts, Industrial

COMBUSTION. *Use* Chemistry

COMEDIANS. *Use* Entertainers

COMEDY. *Use* Drama; Theater; Wit and Humor

COMIC OPERA. *See* Opera

COMICS (Books, strips, etc.). *Use* Caricatures and Cartoons

COMMANDMENTS, TEN. *Use* Bible; Christian Ethics

COMMEMORATIVE POSTAGE STAMPS. *Use* Postage Stamps

COMMENCEMENTS. *Use* Colleges and Universities; High Schools

COMMERCE
Scope: Domestic trade only.
LC ——; s.a. Black market; Business; Commercial crimes; Commercial law; Franchises (retail trade); Monopolies; Prices; Shipment of goods; Wholesale trade
SEARS ——; s.a. Interstate commerce; Retail trade
RG BUSINESS; s.a. Corporations; Free enterprise
NYT Names of commodities, companies or industries, e.g., Leather and leather goods; Genesco, Inc.; Steel and iron; etc.; s.a. Corporations; Credit; Retail stores and trade
PAIS BUSINESS; s.a. Barter; Interstate commerce
BPI ——; s.a. Interstate commerce; Markets; Retail trade

COMMERCE, FOREIGN. *Use* Barter; Commercial Policy; Foreign Trade

COMMERCIAL ART
Scope: Works on the application of art to business.
LC ——; s.a. Advertising; Art and industry; Photography, Advertising
SEARS ——; s.a. Art industries and trade; Posters; Textile design
RG ART, COMMERCIAL; s.a. Design, Industrial; Illustration of books and periodicals
NYT GRAPHIC ARTS; s.a. Advertising; Posters; Printing and allied trades
PAIS ——; s.a. Advertising art; Art and industry
BPI ADVERTISING; s.a. Creativity in advertising; Marketing

COMMERCIAL BUILDINGS. *See* Office Buildings

COMMERCIAL CORNERS. *See* Monopolies

COMMERCIAL CORRESPONDENCE
LC ——; s.a. Form letters; Sales letters
SEARS BUSINESS LETTERS; s.a. English language—Business English; Letter writing
RG LETTER WRITING; s.a. English language—Usage; Forms, blanks, etc.
NYT LETTERS; s.a. Secretaries
PAIS ——
BPI ——; s.a. Dictation; English language—Business english; Sales letters

COMMERCIAL CREDIT. *See* Credit

COMMERCIAL CRIMES
LC ——; s.a. Fraud; Price regulation; Restraint of trade
SEARS COMPETITION, UNFAIR; s.a. Interest and usury; Trusts, Industrial
RG COMPETITION, UNFAIR; s.a. Dumping (commercial policy); Restraint of trade

NYT COMMERCE—U.S.; s.a. Fair trade pricing; Frauds and swindling; Monopolies
PAIS ——; s.a. Competition, Unfair; Restraint of trade
BPI COMMERCIAL LAW; s.a. Fraud; Usury law

COMMERCIAL EDUCATION. *Use* Apprentices; Business Education; Occupational Training; Office Management; Secretaries; Technical Education; Vocational Education

COMMERCIAL JOURNALISM. *See* Journalism

COMMERCIAL LAW
See also subd. *Law* under commercial subjects, e.g., Accounting—Law, Banking—Law, etc.
LC ——; s.a. Arbitration and award; Commercial crimes; Debtor and creditor; Deeds; Liability (law); Licenses; Partnership; Sales; Suretyship and Guaranty; Vendors and purchasers
SEARS ——; s.a. Bankruptcy; Contracts
RG ——; s.a. Foreign trade regulation; Trusts, Industrial—Law; Warranty
NYT CORPORATIONS; s.a. Commerce; Fair trade pricing; Law and legislation
PAIS ——; s.a. Corporations—Legislation; Incorporation
BPI ——; s.a. Corporate law; subd. *Laws and regulations* under various subjects, e.g., Book industry—Laws and regulations

COMMERCIAL LEASES. *Use* Landlord and Tenant

COMMERCIAL PAPER. *See* Negotiable Instruments

COMMERCIAL PHOTOGRAPHY. *See* Photography, Commercial

COMMERCIAL POLICY
See also subd. *Commercial policy* under names of countries, e.g., U.S.—Commercial policy.
LC ——; s.a. Commercial treaties; Commodity control; Export controls; Favored nation clause
SEARS ——; s.a. Free trade and protection; International economic relations; Subsidies
RG ECONOMIC POLICY; s.a. Import quotas; Reciprocity; Tariff; subd. *Economic policy* under names of countries
NYT COMMERCE (subd. by geographic and market areas); s.a. International relations
PAIS ——; s.a. Bilateral trade; Commerce, Foreign; Government trading; Import quotas
BPI ——; s.a. Commodity control; Tariff; Underdeveloped areas—Commerce

COMMERCIAL PRODUCTS. *Use* Commodity Exchanges; Consumer Protection; New Products; Quality Control; Raw Materials; Substitute Products

COMMERCIAL RECORDS. *Use* Business Records

COMMERCIAL SCHOOLS. *See* Business Education; Commercial Education

COMMERCIAL TRAVELERS. *Use* Salesmen and Salesmanship

COMMERCIAL TREATIES AND AGREEMENTS. *Use* Commercial Policy; Tariff; Treaties

COMMERCIAL VEHICLES. *Use* Motor Vehicles

COMMERCIALS. *Use* Advertising; Television Broadcasting

COMMITTEES. *Use* Parliamentary Practice

COMMODITIES. *Use* Agricultural Processing; Farm Produce; New Products; Raw Materials

COMMODITY CONTROL. *Use* Commercial Policy; Raw Materials

COMMODITY EXCHANGES
LC ——; s.a. Commercial products; Markets
SEARS COMMERCIAL PRODUCTS; s.a. Marketing; Markets
RG ——; s.a. Grain trade; Speculation
NYT COMMODITIES AND COMMODITY EXCHANGES AND BROKERS; s.a. Commerce; Markets; Wall Street (NYC)
PAIS ——; s.a. Futures; Hedging
BPI ——; s.a. Markets; Speculation

COMMON CARRIERS. *See* Carriers

COMMON COLD. *See* Cold (Disease)

COMMON SENSE. *Use* Thought and Thinking; Wisdom

COMMONPLACES. *See* Terms and Phrases

COMMONS. *Use* Land Tenure; Pastures; Public Lands; Villages

COMMONS (Social order). *Use* Middle Classes

COMMUNAL SETTLEMENTS. *Use* Cooperative Societies; Subculture

COMMUNES. *See* Communal Settlements

COMMUNICABLE DISEASES
See also names of diseases, e.g., Cold (disease); Smallpox; etc.
LC ——; s.a. Biological warfare; Disease—Transmission; Disinfection and disenfectants; Epidemics; Hygiene, Public
SEARS ——; s.a. Communicable diseases—Prevention; Germ theory of disease; Public health; Vaccination
RG ——; s.a. Carriers of infection; Virus diseases
NYT MEDICINE AND HEALTH; s.a. Bacteria; Epidemics; Viruses
PAIS ——; s.a. Epidemiology; Public health; Sickness
BPI ——; s.a. Epidemics; Immunity; Quarantine

COMMUNICATION
Scope: Works on human communication in a broad sense. Works dealing with individual means of communication are entered under Language and Languages; Printing; Telecommunication, etc.
LC ——; s.a. Expression; Intercultural communication; Propaganda; Symbolism in communication; Visual aids
SEARS ——; s.a. Cybernetics; Mass media; Nonverbal communication
RG ——; s.a. Communication, Nonverbal; Popular culture; Speech; Verbal behavior
NYT COMMUNICATIONS; s.a. Culture; Mass communications
PAIS ——; s.a. Confidential communications; Cybernetics
BPI ——; s.a. Information theory; Mass media; Public speaking

COMMUNICATION (Theology). *Use* Preaching

COMMUNICATION AND TRAFFIC. *Use* Carriers; Telecommunication; Transportation

COMMUNICATION IN MANAGEMENT. *Use* Industrial Relations; Office Management; Organization; Personnel Management

COMMUNICATION SYSTEMS. *Use* Data Transmission Systems

COMMUNICATION THEORY. *See* Information Sciences

COMMUNICATIONS. *Use* Cybernetics; Information Sciences; Information Storage and Retrieval Systems; Telecommunication

COMMUNICATIONS, CONFIDENTIAL. *See* Ciphers; Confidential Communications

COMMUNICATIONS SATELLITES. *Use* Aerospace Industries; Artificial Satellites; Astronautics; Space Flight; Telecommunication; Television

COMMUNICATIVE DISORDERS. *Use* Speech

COMMUNISM
See also headings beginning with Communism and . . . , e.g., Communism and Islam.
LC ——; s.a. Collective farming; Collectivism; Communist party purges; Dictatorship of the proletariat; Proletariat; Social conflict; Tribes and tribal systems
SEARS ——; s.a. Anti-Communist movements; Individualism
RG ——; s.a. Communist countries; Socialism
NYT ——; s.a. International relations—Communist-Western confrontration; names of communist countries, e.g., Hungary
PAIS ——; s.a. Dialectical materialism; International, Third; Totalitarianism
BPI ——; s.a. Communist parties; Socialism

COMMUNISM AND DEMOCRACY. *Use* Cold War; Democracy; World Politics

COMMUNITY
Scope: A geographically defined social unit within a larger society.
LC ——; s.a. Cities and towns; Social groups; Sociology, Rural; Urban renewal
SEARS COMMUNITY LIFE; s.a. Community centers; Social settlements
RG ——; s.a. Neighborhoods; School and the community; Suburbs
NYT COMMUNITIES; s.a. Area planning and renewal; Community centers; Urban areas
PAIS COMMUNITY LIFE; s.a. Community development; Community organization
BPI ——; s.a. Cities and towns; Community development

COMMUNITY AND SCHOOL. *Use* Education and State; Home and School

COMMUNITY ANTENNA TELEVISION. *Use* Television

COMMUNITY CENTERS. *Use* Community; Neighborhood; Playgrounds; Recreation

COMMUNITY CHESTS. *Use* Charities

COMMUNITY CHURCHES. *Use* Catholicity

COMMUNITY COLLEGES. *See* Colleges and Universities

COMMUNITY FUNDS. *Use* Social Service

COMMUNITY LEADERSHIP. *Use* Leadership

COMMUNITY LIFE, RURAL. *Use* Country Life; Rural Conditions; Villages

COMMUNITY ORGANIZATIONS. *Use* Public Welfare; Social Service; Urban Renewal

COMMUNITY POWER. *Use* Local Government

COMMUNITY PROPERTY. *Use* Abandonment of Property; Marriage Law; Property

COMMUNITY PSYCHOLOGY. *Use* Social Psychology

COMMUNITY SCHOOLS. *See* Schools

COMMUNITY SURVEYS. *Use* Social Surveys

COMPANIES. *See* Partnership

COMPANION CROPS. *Use* Crops; Truck Farming

COMPANIONSHIP. *See* Human Relations

COMPANY REPORTS. *Use* Accounting; Bonds; Corporations; Report Writing; Stock Exchange

COMPANY UNIONS. *Use* Trade—Unions

COMPANY VACATIONS. *See* Vacations, Employee

COMPARATIVE RELIGION. *See* Religion

COMPASSES. *Use* Magnetism, Terrestrial

COMPENSATION. *See* Pensions; Personal Injuries; Wages and Salaries; Workmen's Compensation

COMPENSATORY EDUCATION. *Use* Education

COMPETITION
Scope: Works relating to business only.
LC   ——; s.a. Big business; Government competition; Laissez-faire; Supply and demand
SEARS ——; s.a. Business ethics; Trusts, Industrial
RG   ——; s.a. Business consolidation and mergers; Restraint of trade
NYT   CORPORATIONS; s.a. Consumer protection; Fair trade pricing; US—Economic conditions and trends—Business ethics
PAIS   ——; s.a. Monopoly; Oligopolies
BPI   ——; s.a. Monopolies; Oligopolies

COMPETITION, INTERNATIONAL. *Use* War—Economic Aspects

COMPETITION, UNFAIR. *Use* Commercial Crimes; Industrial Laws and Legislation; Monopolies; Patent Laws and Legislation; Trusts, Industrial

COMPETITIONS. *See* Rewards (Prizes, etc.)

COMPLAINTS (Retail trade). *Use* Consumers

COMPLEXES (Psychology). *Use* Psychoanalysis

COMPLEXION. *See* Beauty, Personal; Color of Man; Toilet

COMPOSERS. *Use* Music

COMPOSITE MATERIALS. *Use* Materials

COMPOSITION (Music). *Use* Music

COMPOSITION (Photography). *Use* Photography, Artistic

COMPOSITION (Rhetoric). *See* Letter-Writing

COMPOST. *Use* Fertilizers and Manures; Soils

COMPREHENSION
LC   ——; s.a. Apperception; Knowledge, Theory of; Memory
SEARS LEARNING, PSYCHOLOGY OF; s.a. Educational psychology; Thought and thinking
RG   ——; s.a. Learning, Psychology of; Reading comprehension
NYT   PSYCHOLOGY AND PSYCHOLOGISTS; s.a. Brain; Intelligence; Mind
PAIS   LEARNING ABILITY; s.a. Educational psychology
BPI   LEARNING, PSYCHOLOGY OF; s.a. Conditioned response; Though and thinking

COMPROMISE (Ethics). *Use* Ethics

COMPULSORY EDUCATION. *Use* Dropouts; Education, Compulsory; School Attendance

COMPULSORY MILITARY SERVICE. *See* Military Service, Compulsory

COMPULSORY SCHOOL ATTENDANCE. *See* Education, Compulsory

COMPUTER CONTROL. *See* Automation

COMPUTER GRAPHICS. *Use* Graphic Methods

COMPUTER INDUSTRY. *Use* Computers

COMPUTER LANGUAGES. *Use* Computers; Programming (Electronic computers)

COMPUTER LEASE AND RENTAL SERVICES. *Use* Electronic Data Processing

COMPUTER NETWORKS. *Use* Data Transmission Systems

COMPUTER PROGRAMMING. *Use* Computers; Electronic Data Processing; Information Storage and Retrieval Systems; Linear Programming; Programming (Electronic computers)

COMPUTER PROGRAMS. *Use* Programming

COMPUTER SOFTWARE. *See* Programming

COMPUTER STORAGE DEVICES. *Use* Data Tapes

COMPUTER SYSTEMS MANAGEMENT. *Use* System Analysis

COMPUTER-ASSISTED INSTRUCTION. *Use* Programmed Instruction

COMPUTER-BASED SERVICE COMPANIES. *Use* Information Services

COMPUTERS
Scope: Used for works about modern calculating machinery developed after 1945. For earlier models see Calculating machines.
LC ———; s.a. Computer industry; Computers and civilization; Cybernetics; Digital electronics; Electronic digital computers—Memory systems
SEARS ———; s.a. Electronic data processing; Information storage and retrieval systems; Programming languages (electronic computers)
RG ———; s.a. Computer languages; Data transmission; Memory devices (computers); Programming (computers)
NYT DATA PROCESSING (INFORMATION PROCESSING) EQUIPMENT AND SYSTEMS; s.a. Electronics; Science and technology
PAIS ———; s.a. Computer industry; Computer programming; Information processing systems
BPI ———; s.a. Computer industry; Computers—Memory systems; Data processing service centers; Electronic data processing; Information storage and retrieval systems

COMPUTERS—ACCOUNTING. *Use* Machine Accounting

COMPUTERS—EDUCATIONAL USE. *Use* Educational Technology; Programmed Instruction

COMPUTERS—INDUSTRIAL USE. *Use* Automation

COMRADESHIP. *Use* Human Relations

CONCENTRATION CAMPS
LC ———; s.a. Detention of persons; Political prisoners
SEARS ———; s.a. Camps, Military; Prisoners of war
RG ———; s.a. Political crimes and offenses; Prison camps
NYT MINORITIES—NAZI POLICIES; s.a. Jews; Torture
PAIS ———; s.a. Detention of persons; Prisoners of war
BPI ———; s.a. Military law; Prisoners of war

CONCEPT LEARNING. *Use* Learning, Psychology of

CONCEPTION. *Use* Reproduction

CONCEPTION—PREVENTION. *Use* Birth Control

CONCEPTS. *Use* Knowledge, Theory of

CONCERTS. *Use* Music

CONCESSIONS. *Use* Franchises (Retail trade); Licenses; Municipal Ownership

CONCESSIONS (Food, etc.). *Use* Caterers and Catering; Restaurants, Lunchrooms, etc.

CONCILIAR THEORY. *Use* Papacy

CONCORDATS. *Use* Ecclesiastical Law; Nationalism and Religion; Treaties

CONCRETE CONSTRUCTIONS. *Use* Construction Industry

CONCUBINAGE. *Use* Bigamy; Marriage Law

CONDEMNED BOOKS. *Use* Censorship

CONDITIONED RESPONSE
LC ———; s.a. Reflexes; Reinforcement (psychology)
SEARS BEHAVIORISM (Psychology); s.a. Behavior; Psychology
RG CONDITIONED RESPONSES; s.a. Operant conditioning; Reinforcement (psychology)
NYT PSYCHOLOGY AND PSYCHOLOGISTS; s.a. Brain; Intelligence; Mind
PAIS BEHAVIOR (Psychology); s.a. Psychology
BPI ———; s.a. Behavior (psychology); Learning, psychology of

CONDOMINIUM (Housing)
LC ———; s.a. Apartment houses, Cooperative; Joint tenancy
SEARS APARTMENT HOUSES; s.a. Housing; Landlord and tenant
RG APARTMENT HOUSES—CONDOMINIUM PLAN OWNERSHIP; s.a. Apartment houses—Cooperative ownership; Housing, Cooperative
NYT HOUSING; s.a. Building; Real Estate
PAIS CONDOMINIUM PLAN OWNERSHIP; s.a. subd. *Condominium plan* under specific subjects, e.g., Apartment houses—Condominium plan
BPI ———; s.a. Apartment houses, Cooperative; Housing, Cooperative

CONDUCT OF LIFE. *Use* Character; Ethics; Human Relations; Life; Vice; Virtues

CONDUCTING. *Use* Music

CONDUCTORS. *Use* Musicians; Orchestra

CONDUITS. *See* Aqueducts

CONFEDERATE STATES OF AMERICA
LC ———; s.a. U.S.—History—Civil war
SEARS ———; s.a. U.S.—History—Civil war
RG ———; s.a. South—History; U.S.—History—Civil war
NYT CIVIL WAR (U.S.) (1861-65); s.a. U.S.—History
PAIS SOUTHERN STATES; s.a. Insurgency; Civil war
BPI SOUTHERN STATES

CONFERENCES. *Use* Congresses and Conventions; Debates and Debating

CONFESSION. *Use* Sin

CONFIDENTIAL COMMUNICATIONS
LC ———; s.a. Clergy; Executive privilege (government information); Medical ethics; Professional secrets; Reporters and reporting; Self-incrimination
SEARS PRIVACY, RIGHT OF; s.a. Eavesdropping; Ethics; Professional
RG ———; s.a. Official secrets; Privacy, Right of
NYT POLITICS AND GOVERNMENT (General); s.a. Privacy, Invasion of; U.S.—Internal security
PAIS ———; s.a. Privacy; Secrecy (law)
BPI ———; s.a. Official secrets; Privacy, Right of

CONFLAGRATIONS. *See* Fires

CONFLICT, SOCIAL. *See* Social Conflict

CONFLICT OF GENERATIONS
LC ———; s.a. Age groups; Parent and child
SEARS ———; s.a. Human relations; Social conflict

RG GENERATION GAP; s.a. Social conflict; Youth-adult relationship

NYT CHILDREN AND YOUTH—BEHAVIOR AND TRAINING; s.a. Ethics and morals; Families and family life

PAIS ——; s.a. Age groups; Parent and child (law)

BPI PARENT-CHILD RELATIONSHIP; s.a. Conflict (psychology); Family

CONFLICT OF INTEREST. *Use* Business and Politics

CONFLICT OF INTERESTS. *Use* Bribery

CONFLICT OF INTERESTS (Public funds). *Use* Corruption (Politics)

CONFLICT OF JUDICIAL DEICISIONS. *Use* Judgments

CONFORMITY. *Use* Attitude (Psychology); Behavior (Psychology); Individualism; Individuality; Liberty; Propaganda

CONGLOMERATE CORPORATIONS

LC ——; s.a. Business enterprises; Competition; Consolidation and merger of corporations; Corporate reorganization

SEARS ——; s.a. Corporation law; Corporations; Trusts, industrial

RG ——; s.a. Bank consolidations and mergers; Diversification in industry; Government investigations—Conglomerate corporations

NYT CORPORATIONS; s.a. Company reports; Management, Industrial and institutional

PAIS CORPORATIONS, DIVERSIFIED; s.a. Bank mergers; Business consolidation; Corporate acquisitions; subd. *Consolidation* under specific industries, e.g., Coal industry—Consolidation, etc.

BPI ——; s.a. Corporate acquisitions and mergers; Monopolies

CONGREGATIONALISM. *Use* Dissenters, Religious

CONGRESSES AND CONVENTIONS

See also subd. *Conferences* or *Congresses* under subjects, e.g., City planning—Conferences.

LC ——; s.a. Meetings; Public meetings; Trade-union meetings

SEARS ——; s.a. International organizations; Parliamentary practice; Treaties

RG CONFERENCES; s.a. Conventions; International conferences

NYT CONVENTIONS AND CONFERENCES

PAIS CONFERENCES; s.a. Constitutional conventions; Conventions; Stockholders meetings

BPI ——; s.a. Sales meetings

CONJUGATION (Biology). *Use* Reproduction

CONQUEST, RIGHT OF. *Use* Territory, National

CONSANGUINITY. *Use* Tribes and Tribal System

CONSCIENCE. *Use* Character; Ethics

CONSCIENTIOUS OBJECTORS

LC ——; s.a. Nonviolence; Pacifism; War and religion

SEARS ——; s.a. Freedom of conscience; Military service, Compulsory

RG ——; s.a. Military service, Compulsory; Pacifism

NYT ——; s.a. U.S. Armament and defense—Draft and recruitment, Military

PAIS ——; s.a. Military service, Compulsory; Pacifism

BPI ——; s.a. Military service, Compulsory; Peace

CONSCIOUSNESS. *Use* Apperception; Brain Individuality; Mind and Body; Perception

CONSCRIPTION, MILITARY. *See* Military Service, Compulsory

CONSERVATION OF NATURAL RESOURCES

LC ——; s.a. Ecology; Natural resources

SEARS ——; s.a. Environmental policy; Nature conservation

RG CONSERVATION OF RESOURCES; s.a. Environmental policy; Reclamation of land

NYT NATURAL RESOURCES; s.a. Environment; Nature; U.S.—Environment

PAIS CONSERVATION OF RESOURCES; s.a. Flood control; Soil conservation

BPI CONSERVATION OF RESOURCES; s.a. Forest conservation; Petroleum—Conservation; Wilderness areas

CONSERVATION OF WILDLIFE. *See* Wildlife Conservation

CONSERVATISM. *Use* Right and Left (Political science)

CONSERVATIVE JUDAISM. *Use* Jews

CONSOLIDATION AND MERGER OF CORPORATIONS. *Use* Conglomerate Corporations; Trusts, Industrial

CONSPIRACIES. *Use* Subversive Activities

CONSPIRACY. *Use* Crime and Criminals; Racketeering; Treason

CONSTABLES. *Use* Police

CONSTELLATIONS. *Use* Astronomy

CONSTIPATION. *Use* Digestion

CONSTITUTIONAL CONVENTIONS. *Use* Congresses and Conventions; Constitutions

CONSTITUTIONAL LAW. *Use* Democracy; Rule of Law; Separation of Powers

CONSTITUTIONS

See also subd. *Constitution* under names of places, e.g., U.S.—Constitution.

LC ——; s.a. Civil supremacy over military; Constitutional history; Democracy; Monarchy; Separation of powers

SEARS ——; s.a. Civil rights; Constitutional law; Federal government; Political science

RG CONSTITUTIONAL HISTORY; s.a. Constitutional conventions; Constitutions, state; Privileges and immunities; U.S.—Supreme Court

NYT Subd. *Constitution* under names of countries; s.a. Law and legislation; Politics and government (general)

PAIS ——; s.a. subd. *Constitutions and constitutional history* under names of countries, states, etc.; Due process of law; Legal rights; State constitutions

CONSTITUTIONS, *cont.*
BPI ———; s.a. Representative government and representation; State government; War and emergency powers

CONSTRUCTION. *See* Building; Construction Industry; Engineering

CONSTRUCTION INDUSTRY
LC ———; s.a. Building; Contractors' operations; Seasonal industries
SEARS BUILDING; s.a. Concrete constructions; Engineering
RG CONSTRUCTION INDUSTRY; s.a. Building industry; Houses, Prefabricated
NYT BUILDING; s.a. Housing
PAIS BUILDING TRADES; s.a. Construction workers; subd. *Building trades* under specific subjects, e.g., Employment—Building trades
BPI BUILDING INDUSTRY; s.a. Construction workers; Contractors

CONSULAR SERVICE. *See* Diplomacy

CONSULATES. *See* Diplomacy

CONSUMER BEHAVIOR. *See* Consumers

CONSUMER CREDIT
Scope: Works on the economic aspects and methods of installment or deferrent payment financing in general.
LC ———; s.a. Charge account bank plans; Debtor and creditor; Finance charges; Layaway plan
SEARS ———; s.a. Credit; Installment plan
RG ———; s.a. Credit cards; Loans, Personal; Savings and loan associations
NYT CREDIT—U.S.—CONSUMER CREDIT; s.a. Consumer protection; Consumers and consumption; Credit cards
PAIS ———; s.a. Finance companies; Installment plan
BPI CREDIT; s.a. Finance charges; Installment plan; Loans, Bank—Installment payment

CONSUMER DEALS (Merchandising). *Use* Merchandising

CONSUMER EDUCATION
Scope: Works on the selection and most efficient use of consumer goods, and on means and methods of educating the consumer. See also specific problems, e.g., Food adulteration; Labels; etc.
LC ———; s.a. Consumers' leagues; Marketing; Purchasing; Shopping
SEARS ———; s.a. Buying; Home economics
RG ———; s.a. Consumer protection; Shopping and shoppers
NYT CONSUMER PROTECTION; s.a. Consumers and consumption; Food and grocery trade; Home economics
PAIS ———; s.a. Consumer protection; Shopping and shoppers
BPI ———; s.a. Consumer protection; Marketing (home economics)

CONSUMER GOODS. *Use* New Products

CONSUMER LOANS. *See* Loans, Personal

CONSUMER ORGANIZATIONS. *See* Cooperative Societies

CONSUMER PREFERENCES. *Use* Marketing

CONSUMER PROTECTION
Scope: Works on governmental and private activities which guard the consumer against dangers to his health, safety, or economic well being.
LC ———; s.a. Consumer education; Drugs—Adulteration and analysis; Food adulteration and inspection; Products liability; Quality of products
SEARS ———; s.a. Drugs—Adulteration and analysis; Food adulteration and inspection
RG ———; s.a. Better business bureaus; Commercial products—Safety devices and measures; Fraud; Labels—Laws and legislation
NYT ———; s.a. Consumers and consumption; Labeling and labels; Liability for products, Manufacturers'
PAIS ———; s.a. Better business bureaus; Product safety; Quality of products
BPI ———; s.a. Product safety; Safety packaging; Unit pricing

CONSUMER SURVEYS. *Use* Marketing

CONSUMERISM. *See* Consumer Education

CONSUMERS
Scope: Works on consumer behavior.
LC ———; s.a. Complaints (retail trade); Cooperation; Marketing; Purchasing
SEARS ———; s.a. Shopping; Youth as consumers
RG ———; s.a. Negro market; Youth market
NYT CONSUMERS AND CONSUMPTION; s.a. Marketing and merchandising; Market research; Retail stores and trade
PAIS ———; s.a. Consumption; Shopping and shoppers
BPI ———; s.a. Buying habits; Consumption (economics)

CONSUMERS' LEAGUES. *Use* Consumer Education; Cooperative Societies

CONSUMPTION (Economics)
Scope: Works on economic theories of consumption.
LC ———; s.a. Income; Luxury; National income; Overproduction; Prices; Substitution (economics); Supply and demand; Wealth
SEARS ———; s.a. Consumer education; Marketing
RG ———; s.a. Advertising; Consumers
NYT ECONOMICS; s.a. Consumers and consumption; Economic conditions and trends (general)
PAIS CONSUMPTION; s.a. Prices; Purchasing power
BPI ———; s.a. Market surveys; Supply and demand

CONTACT LENSES. *Use* Eye

CONTAGIOUS DISEASES. *See* Communicable Diseases

CONTAINER GARDENING. *See* Gardening

CONTAINER INDUSTRY. *Use* Containers; Packaging

CONTAINER SHIPS. *Use* Containers

CONTAINERIZATION (Freight). *Use* Cargo Handling; Containers

CONTAINERS
See also specific types of containers, e.g., Bottles; Boxes;
Cans; Cartons; Glass containers; Milk containers;
etc.
LC   ——; s.a. Containerization; Unitized cargo
system
SEARS   PACKAGING; s.a. Gift wrappings; Ships and
shipping
RG   ——; s.a. Containerization (freight); Packaging
NYT   CONTAINERS AND PACKAGING; s.a. Con-
tainerships; Freight forwarding (domestic and
foreign); Waste materials and disposal
PAIS   CONTAINER INDUSTRY; s.a. Box industry;
Glass container industry; Plastic containers
BPI   CONTAINERS (Shipping); s.a. Freight and
freightage

CONTAINERS AND PACKAGING. *Use* Canning and
Preserving

CONTAMINATION OF ENVIRONMENT. *See* Pollution

CONTEMPLATIVE ORDERS. *Use* Monastic and
Religious Life of Women; Monasticism and Religious Orders

CONTEMPORARY ART. *See* Modernism (Art)

CONTESTS AND PRIZES. *Use* Rewards (Prizes, etc.)

CONTINENTAL SHELF. *Use* Oceanography; Seashore;
Territorial Waters

CONTINUING EDUCATION CENTERS. *Use* Adult
Education; Evening and Continuation
Schools

CONTOUR FARMING. *Use* Farms and Farming

CONTRACEPTIVES. *Use* Birth Control

CONTRACT LABOR
LC   ——; s.a. Indentured servants; Native labor;
Peonage
SEARS ——; s.a. Convict labor; Slavery
RG   ——; s.a. Indentured servants; Labor, Compul-
sory
NYT   LABOR; s.a. Convict labor; Domestic service;
Service industries
PAIS   ——; s.a. Contracts for work and labor;
Slavery
BPI   LABOR AND LABORING CLASSES; s.a.
Alien labor; Peasantry

CONTRACT RESEARCH. *See* Industrial Research

CONTRACTIONS. *See* Abbreviations

CONTRACTORS. *Use* Construction Industry

CONTRACTS
LC   ——; s.a. Business law; Commercial law; Con-
venants; Deeds; Liberty of contract; Obligations
(law); Pledges (law); Public contracts; Renegotiation of government contracts
SEARS ——; s.a. Authors and publishers; Labor
contract; Mortgages
RG   ——; s.a. Contracts, Government; Installment
contracts; Municipal contracts
NYT   ——; s.a. U.S. armament and defense—Defense
contracts and production

PAIS   ——; s.a. Defense contracts; Service contracts
BPI   ——; s.a. Breach of contract; Contracts, Government—Renogotiation; Covenants, Restrictive;
Purchasing, Government; subd. *Procurement*
under subjects, e.g., U.S. Army—Procurement

CONTRACTS, GOVERNMENT. *Use* Contracts; Defense Contracts; Industry and State; Public
Works; Purchasing

CONTRACTUAL LIMITATIONS. *See* Contracts

CONTROL ENGINEERING. *See* Automatic Control

CONTROL EQUIPMENT. *See* Automatic Control

CONTROLLERSHIP. *Use* Accounting; Budget in
Business

CONVALESCENCE. *Use* Sick

CONVENTIONS. *Use* Congresses and Conventions;
Parliamentary Practice

CONVENTIONS (Treaties). *See* Treaties

CONVENTS AND NUNNERIES. *Use* Abbeys; Monastic
and Religious Life of Women

CONVERSION (Psychoanalysis). *Use* Mind and Body

CONVERSION, RELIGIOUS
LC   CONVERTS; s.a. Converts, Protestant; Peni-
tents; Proselytes and proselytizing, Jewish
SEARS CONVERTS; s.a. Conversion; Converts, Catholic
RG   CONVERSION; s.a. Evangelistic work; Revivals
NYT   RELIGION AND CHURCHES; s.a. Names of
religions and religious groups, e.g., Jews
PAIS   CHRISTIANITY AND OTHER RELIGIONS; s.a.
Jews—Converts to Christianity
BPI   RELIGION; s.a. Catholic church; Christianity

CONVEYANCING. *Use* Land Tenure; Mortgages; Real
Property; Transfer (Law)

CONVEYORS AND CONVEYOR BELTS. *Use*
Materials Handling

CONVICT LABOR. *Use* Contract Labor; Prisons and
Prisoners

CONVICTION. *See* Belief and Doubt

COOKBOOKS. *See* Cookery

COOKERY
See also types of cookery, e.g., Cookery (sea food);
Cookery (poultry); Cookery, Yugoslav; Outdoor
cookery, etc.
LC   ——; s.a. Dinners and dining; Food;
Gastronomy; Table
SEARS ——; s.a. Canning and preserving
RG   ——; s.a. Baking; Caterers and catering; Gastro-
nomy
NYT   COOKING; s.a. Food and grocery trade; names
of food, e.g., Meat
PAIS   FOOD; s.a. Cooks; Diet; Nutrition
BPI   ——; s.a. Flavoring materials; Menus

COOPERATION
Scope: Works on the theory and history of cooperation
and cooperative movements.

COOPERATION, *cont.*
LC ——; s.a. Chain stores, Voluntary; Mutualism; Profit-sharing
SEARS ——; s.a. Agriculture, Cooperative; International cooperation
RG ——; s.a. Collective settlements; Interracial cooperation
NYT COOPERATIVES; s.a. Cultural relations; International relations
PAIS COOPERATIVE MOVEMENT; s.a. International cooperation; Libraries, Cooperative movement
BPI ——; s.a. Agriculture, Cooperative; Cooperative stores

COOPERATION, INTERNATIONAL. *See* International Cooperation

COOPERATIVE EDUCATION. *Use* Education, Cooperative; Industry and Education

COOPERATIVE HOUSING. *See* Home Ownership

COOPERATIVE MOVEMENT. *Use* Cooperation

COOPERATIVE SOCIETIES
Scope: Works on the nature, organization and laws governing cooperative movements.
LC ——; s.a. Apartment houses, Cooperative; Consumers' leagues; Student cooperatives
SEARS ——; s.a. Banks and banking, Cooperative; Building and loan associations
RG COOPERATIVE ASSOCIATIONS; s.a. Credit unions; Marketing, Cooperative
NYT COOPERATIVES; s.a. Agriculture and agricultural products—U.S.—Cooperatives; Housing—U.S.—Cooperatives; Savings and loan associations
PAIS COOPERATIVE MOVEMENT; s.a. Agriculture, Cooperative; Communal settlements
BPI COOPERATIVE ASSOCIATIONS; s.a. Agriculture, Cooperative; Cooperative stores; Credit unions

COPY READING. *Use* Editing

COPY WRITING. *See* Advertising Copy

COPYING MACHINES. *Use* Copying Processes; Data Transmission Systems; Office Equipment and Supplies; Photography

COPYING PROCESSES
See also names of specific processes, e.g., Microphotography; Xerography; etc.
LC ——; s.a. Blue-prints; Documentation; Electrostatic printing; Office equipment and supplies; Photocopying processes; Photostat
SEARS COPYING PROCESSES AND MACHINES
RG ——; s.a. Electrostatics; Microfilm; Mimeograph; Transparencies—Copying
NYT COPYING MACHINES; s.a. Documents; Facsimile systems
PAIS ——; s.a. Documentation; Microforms; Office equipment; Printing, Electrostatic
BPI ——; s.a. Photomechanical processes

COPYRIGHT
LC ——; s.a. Authors and publishers; Trade regulation

SEARS ——; s.a. Books; Publishers and publishing
RG ——; s.a. Property, Intellectual; Royalties
NYT COPYRIGHTS; s.a. Books and literature—Book trade; Motion pictures—Screen rights; Writing and writers
PAIS ——; s.a. Property, Intellectual; Royalties
BPI ——; s.a. Intellectual property; Royalties

CORAL REEF ECOLOGY. *Use* Marine Ecology

CORDIALS (Liquor). *See* Liquors

CORE CURRICULUM. *See* Education—Curricula

CORNER STONES, LAYING OF. *Use* Rites and Ceremonies

CORNERS, COMMERCIAL. *See* Monopolies

CORONARY HEART DISEASE. *Use* Diseases

CORPORAL PUNISHMENT. *Use* Punishment

CORPORATE ACQUISITIONS AND MERGERS. *Use* Conglomerate Corporations

CORPORATE DEBT. *Use* Debtor and Creditor

CORPORATE IMAGE. *Use* Public Relations

CORPORATE INCOME TAX. *Use* Business Tax

CORPORATE LAW. *Use* Commercial Law

CORPORATE MERGERS. *See* Conglomerate Corporations

CORPORATE STATE. *Use* Industry and State; State, The; Trade Unions

CORPORATION LAW. *Use* Business Law; Commercial Law; Partnership

CORPORATION REPORTS. *Use* Report Writing; Stock Exchange

CORPORATIONS
Scope: Works on business associations organized as legal persons.
LC ——; s.a. Big business; Business; Business enterprises; Commercial law; Conglomerate corporations; Corporations, Foreign; Corporations, Nonprofit; Limited partnership; Monopolies; Partnership; Professional corporations; Stock-Exchange; Trust companies
SEARS ——; s.a. Guilds; Municipal corporations; Public utilities; Stock companies
RG ——; s.a. Corporations, Non-profit; Corporations—Reorganization; Executives; Limited partnership
NYT ——; s.a. Bankruptcies; Company reports; Law and legislation; Stocks and bonds
PAIS ——; s.a. Family corporations; Private companies; Stockholders; Trusts, Industrial
BPI ——; s.a. Holding companies; Incorporation; Liquidation; Stockholders

CORPORATIONS, DIVERSIFIED. *Use* Conglomerate Corporations

CORPORATIONS, GOVERNMENT
LC ——; s.a. Government competition; Juristic persons

SEARS GOVERNMENT OWNERSHIP; s.a. Industry and state; Municipal corporations; Public utilities
RG ——; s.a. Government corporations (heading used until 1971); Government ownership
NYT CORPORATIONS; s.a. Government employees and officials
PAIS GOVERNMENT CORPORATIONS; s.a. Government business enterprises; Government monopolies
BPI GOVERNMENT CORPORATIONS; s.a. Government business enterprises; Industry and state

CORPORATIONS, NONPROFIT. *Use* Corporations

CORPORATIONS, NONPROFIT—TAXATION. *Use* Taxation, Exemption from

CORPORATIONS, RELIGIOUS. *Use* Ecclesiastical Law

CORPORATIONS—REORGANIZATION. *Use* Bankruptcy

CORPULENCE. *Use* Weight Control

CORRECTION (Penology). *Use* Imprisonment; Prisons and Prisoners

CORRECTIONAL INSTITUTIONS. *Use* Imprisonment; Juvenile Delinquency; Prisons and Prisoners

CORRECTIVE TEACHING. *See* Teaching

CORRELATION (Statistics). *Use* Probabilities

CORRESPONDENCE. *See* Letter Writing

CORRESPONDENCE SCHOOLS AND COURSES
LC ——; s.a. Education subd. *Self-instruction* under names of languages, e.g., Spanish—Self-instruction or subd. *Methods—Self-instruction* under names of instruments, e.g., Flute—Methods—Self-instruction.
SEARS ——; s.a. Schools; Technical education
RG ——; s.a. Home study; University extension
NYT ——; s.a. Commercial education; Education and schools
PAIS CORRESPONDENCE EDUCATION; s.a. Education; Home study
BPI ——; s.a. Education; Schools

CORRUPTION (In politics)
LC ——; s.a. Conflict of interests (public office); Misconduct in office; Patronage, Political; Sale of public office
SEARS ——; s.a. Lobbying; Political ethics
RG POLITICS, CORRUPTION IN; s.a. Campaign funds; Conflict of interests (public funds)
NYT POLITICS AND GOVERNMENT (General); s.a. Crime and criminals (organized crime link to government corruption); Government employees and officials; U.S.—Politics and government—Ethics in office
PAIS CORRUPTION (Political); s.a. Elections—Corrupt practices; Political crimes and offenses
BPI POLITICS, CORRUPTION IN; s.a. Bribery; Campaign funds

CORSAIRS. *See* Maritime Law; Naval Art and Science

COSA NOSTRA. *Use* Crime and Criminals

COSMETICS
LC ——; s.a. Beauty, personal; Woman—Health and hygiene
SEARS ——; s.a. Beauty shops; Perfumes
RG ——; s.a. Make-up; Toilet preparations
NYT TOILETRIES AND COSMETICS; s.a. Beauty shops
PAIS COSMETIC INDUSTRY; s.a. Beauty culture; Toilet goods industry
BPI ——; s.a. Hair preparations; Toilet goods

COSMIC PHYSICS. *Use* Outer Space

COST. *Use* Valuation; Value

COST ACCOUNTING. *Use* Accounting

COST AND STANDARD OF LIVING
LC ——; s.a. Consumption (economic)—Surveys; Food prices; Luxury; Minimum wage; Poverty; Purchasing power
SEARS ——; s.a. Budgets, Household; Labor and laboring classes; Saving and thrift
RG COST OF LIVING; s.a. Domestic finance; Standard of living
NYT ECONOMIC CONDITIONS AND TRENDS (General); s.a. Income; Labor; Social conditions and welfare
PAIS ——; s.a. Economic conditions; Prices
BPI ——; s.a. Budget, Household; Wages and salaries

COST OF WAR. *See* War—Economic Aspects

COST WORK SYSTEM. *See* Prices

COSTUME
Scope: Works on modes or customs of dress among various nations at different periods; also works on fancy costumes and dress for special occasions. Works treating the subject from the viewpoint of utility are entered under Clothing and dress; prevailing style in dress is entered under Fashion.
LC ——; s.a. Arms and armor; Bohemianism; subd. *Costume* under classes of people, e.g., Physicians—Costume; and individual articles of apparel, e.g., Coats—Costume
SEARS ——; s.a. Dressmaking; Make-up, Theatrical; Men's clothing
RG ——; s.a. Fashion; Millinery
NYT COSTUMES, THEATRICAL; s.a. Apparel; Manners and customs
PAIS CLOTHING AND DRESS; s.a. Clothing industry; Fashion industry
BPI ——; s.a. Clothing and dress; Fashion

COTTAGE INDUSTRIES. *Use* Small Business

COTTAGES. *See* Home Ownership

COTTON MILLS—EMPLOYEES. *Use* Textile Workers

COTTON TEXTILE INDUSTRY. *Use* Textile Industry and Fabrics

COTTONSEED OIL INDUSTRY. *Use* Oils and Fats

COUGH. *Use* Cold (Disease)

COUNCIL AND SYNODS. *Use* Papacy

COUNSELING
LC ——; s.a. Family life education; Group counseling; Group relations training; Pastoral counseling
SEARS ——; s.a. Interviewing; Psychology, Pastoral; Social case work; Welfare work in industry
RG ——; s.a. Genetic counseling; Personnel service in education
NYT Specific subject area involved, e.g., Education and schools (for student counseling); Labor (for work counseling and training), Religion and churches (for pastoral counseling), etc.
PAIS ——; s.a. Marriage counseling; Vocational guidance
BPI ——; s.a. Employee counseling; Vocational guidance

COUNTER CULTURE. *Use* Culture; Social History; Subculture; Youth Movement

COUNTERFEITS AND COUNTERFEITING
LC ——; s.a. Money; Reproduction of money, documents, etc.–Law and legislation
SEARS ——; s.a. Forgery; Swindlers and swindling
RG ——; s.a. Forgery of works of art; Fraud
NYT COUNTERFEITING; s.a. Currency; Forgery
PAIS COUNTERFEITING; s.a. Money; Swindlers and swindling
BPI ——; s.a. Coins; Money

COUNTER-INSURGENCY. *See* Guerilla Warfare

COUNTER-IRRITANTS. *Use* Acupuncture

COUNTERPART FUNDS. *Use* Foreign Exchange

COUNTER-REVOLUTIONS. *Use* Revolutions

COUNTRY CLUBS. *Use* Clubs

COUNTRY HOMES. *Use* Home Ownership

COUNTRY LIFE
Scope: Works, popular and literary, on living in the country. Descriptive studies on living conditions in the country are entered under Rural conditions; studies on theory of social organization are entered under Sociology, Rural.
LC ——; s.a. Farmers; Farm life; Home economics, Rural; Rural conditions
SEARS ——; s.a. Outdoor life; Sociology, Rural
RG ——; s.a. City and country; Ranch life; Village life
NYT RURAL AREAS; s.a. Agriculture and agricultural products; Sociology
PAIS COMMUNITY LIFE, RURAL; s.a. Rural conditions; Villages
BPI FARMERS; s.a. Peasantry; Rural population

COUNTRY MUSIC. *Use* Music

COUNTY BUDGETS. *Use* Budget

COUNTY FINANCE. *Use* Finance, Public

COUNTY PLANNING. *See* Regional Planning

COUNTY TAXATION. *Use* Local Government

COUPS D'ÉTAT. *Use* Government, Resistance to; Revolutions

COURAGE. *Use* Morale

COURSES OF STUDY. *Use* Education–Curricula

COURSING. *Use* Hunting

COURT PROCEEDINGS. *See* Trials

COURT RULES. *Use* Procedure (Law)

COURTESY. *Use* Etiquette; Manners and Customs

COURTLY LOVE. *Use* Love

COURTS
See also types of courts, e.g., Appellate courts; Domestic relations courts; Juvenile courts; Traffic courts; Small claims courts; U.S. Supreme Court; etc.
LC ——; s.a. Bail; Judgements; Judicial power; Lawyers; Pleading; Pleas of guilty; Procedure (law); Witnesses
SEARS ——; s.a. Judges; Jury
RG ——; s.a. Appellate procedure; Criminal procedure; Pleas (criminal procedure)
NYT ——; s.a. Crime and criminals; Law and legislation; Legal profession
PAIS ——; s.a. Injunction; Trials
BPI ——; s.a. Judges; Justice, Administration of; Jury; Trials

COURTS, INTERNATIONAL. *Use* International Offenses

COURTS AND COURTIERS. *Use* Manners and Customs

COURTS MARTIAL AND COURTS OF INQUIRY. *Use* Military Law

COURTS OF PROBATE. *See* Probate Law and Practice

COURTSHIP. *Use* Dating (Social customs); Love

COVENANTS (Religion). *Use* Rites and Ceremonies

COVENANTS, RESTRICTIVE. *Use* Contracts

COVERS (Philately). *Use* Postage Stamps

COWBOYS. *Use* Horsemanship

CRAFTSMANSHIP. *Use* Handicraft

CRAFTS. *Use* Art and Industry

CRAFTS (Handicrafts). *See* Handicraft

CREATION. *Use* Earth; Evolution; God; Man

CREATION (Literary, Artistic, etc.). *Use* Intellect; Intellectual Property

CREATIVE ABILITY. *Use* Ability; Intellect

CREATIVE PHOTOGRAPHY. *Use* Photography, Artistic

CREATIVE WRITING. *Use* Advertising Copy; Authorship

CREATIVITY IN ADVERTISING. *Use* Commercial Art

CREDIBILITY. *See* Truth

CREDIT
LC ——; s.a. Acceptances; Checks; Debt, Public; Export credit; Finance; Finance charges; Interest and usury; Liquidity (economics); Monetary policy; Moratorium; Negotiable instruments; Promissory notes

SEARS ——; s.a. Agricultural credit; Installment plan
RG ——; s.a. Debtor and creditor; Discount; Loans, Personal
NYT ——; s.a. Bankruptcies; Banks and banking; Economic conditions and trends (general)
PAIS ——; s.a. Consumer credit; Loans, Bank; Small loans; Student loans
BPI ——; s.a. Charge accounts (retail trade); Credit counseling; Credit management; Finance companies

CREDIT CARDS. *Use* Banks and Banking; Consumer Credit

CREDIT COMPANIES. *See* Installment Plan

CREDIT COUNSELING. *Use* Credit

CREDIT MANAGEMENT. *Use* Collecting of Accounts; Credit

CREDIT UNIONS. *Use* Cooperative Societies; Loans, Personal

CREDITOR. *See* Debtor and Creditor

CREDULITY. *Use* Belief and Doubt; Errors

CREEDS. *Use* Theology

CREMATION. *Use* Funeral Rites and Ceremonies

CREOLE DIALECTS. *Use* Negro—English Dialects

CRIBS (Beds). *Use* Beds and Bedding

CRIME AND CRIMINALS
See also headings beginning with Crime or Criminals, e.g., Criminal psychology; and types of crime, e.g., Conspiracies; Homicide; Racketeering; Smuggling; Swindlers and swindling; etc.
LC ——; s.a. Amnesty; Arrest; Bail; Drug abuse and crime; Insanity, Moral; Juvenile delinquency; Law enforcement; Occasional criminals; Outlaws; Rehabilitation of criminals; Trials
SEARS ——; s.a. U.S. Federal Bureau of Investigation
RG ——; s.a. Mafia; Punishment; Victims of crime
NYT ——; s.a. Courts; False arrests, convictions and imprisonments; Loot and looting; Police (general); Prisons and prisoners
PAIS ——; s.a. Alcoholism and crime; Gangs; Mafia; Personnel management—Dishonesty problem; Recidivists; War criminals
BPI ——; s.a. Justice, Administration of; Prisoners; Prisons; Retail trade—Theft losses; Self-defense

CRIME PREVENTION. *Use* Law Enforcement

CRIME SYNDICATES. *See* Racketeering

CRIMES, POLITICAL. *See* Political Crimes and Offenses

CRIMES ABOARD AIRCRAFT. *Use* Offenses Against Public Safety

CRIMES AGAINST HUMANITY. *Use* International Offenses

CRIMES AGAINST PEACE. *Use* International Offenses; War (International law); War Crime Trials

CRIMES WITHOUT VICTIMS
LC ——; s.a. Criminal law; Moral conditions
SEARS CRIME AND CRIMINALS; s.a. Drugs and youth; Prostitution

RG CRIME AND CRIMINALS; s.a. Drug abuse; Prostitution
NYT CRIME AND CRIMINALS; s.a. Prostitution
PAIS CRIME AND CRIMINALS
BPI CRIME AND CRIMINALS; s.a. Justice, Administration of; Moral conditions

CRIMINAL CONSPIRACY. *Use* Conspiracy

CRIMINAL INVESTIGATION. *Use* Arrest; Crime and Criminals; Detectives; Justice, Administration of; Law Enforcement; Police; Privacy, Right of; Wire Tapping

CRIMINAL JUDGMENTS. *See* Judgments

CRIMINAL JUSTICE, ADMINISTRATION OF. *Use* Law Enforcement; Prisons and Prisoners

CRIMINAL LAW. *Use* Amnesty; Capital Punishment; Crime and Criminals; Crimes without Victims; Jury; Offenses against the Person and Property; Trials

CRIMINAL LIABILITY. *Use* Liability (Law)

CRIMINAL PROCEDURE. *Use* Judgments; Justice, Administration of; Procedure (Law)

CRIMINAL PSYCHOLOGY. *Use* Crime and Criminals

CRIMINAL REGISTERS. *Use* Arrest

CRIMINAL STATISTICS. *Use* Statistics

CRIMINALS. *See* Crime and Criminals

CRIMINOLOGY. *See* Crime and Criminals

CRIPPLES. *See* Handicapped

CRISIS, COMMERCIAL. *See* Depressions

CRITICAL PATH ANALYSIS. *Use* Graphic Methods; Operations Research; Production Control

CRITICISM. *Use* Literature

CRITICISM, TEXTUAL. *Use* Editing

CRO-MAGNON MAN. *Use* Man

CROPS
See also names of farm products, e.g., Corn; Hay; Maize; etc.
LC FIELD CROPS; s.a. Agricultural estimating and reporting; Crop yields; Crops and climate; Vegetation and climate
SEARS FARM PRODUCE; s.a. Agriculture—Economic aspects; Feeding and feeds; Forage plants; Marketing; Root crops
RG ——; s.a. Companion crops; Plants, Edible; Plants, Effect of climate on; Roots
NYT AGRICULTURE AND AGRICULTURAL PRODUCTS; s.a. Feed; Grain
PAIS AGRICULTURAL PRODUCTS; s.a. Food industry; Rotation of crops
BPI ——; s.a. Agriculture; Farm produce

CROSS AND CROSSES. *Use* Signs and Symbols

CROSS-COUNTRY RUNNING. *See* Track Athletics

CROSS-EXAMINATION. *Use* Trials; Witnesses

CROSSING OVER (Genetics). *Use* Genetics

CROWDS. *Use* Demonstrations; Mobs; Riots; Social Psychology

CROWN JEWELS. *Use* Jewelry

CROWN LANDS. *Use* Land

CRUELTY. *Use* Atrocities

CRUELTY TO CHILDREN. *Use* Abandoned Children; Child Welfare; Maternal Deprivation; Parent and Child

CRUISERS (Warships). *Use* Warships

CRUISING. *Use* Ocean Travel; Voyages and Travels

CRYING. *Use* Emotions

CRYOSURGERY. *Use* Operations, Surgical; Surgery

CRYPTOGRAPHY. *Use* Ciphers; Signs and Symbols

CRYSTALLOGRAPHY. *Use* Mineralogy

CUBISM. *Use* Art, Modern—20th Century; Modernism (Art)

CULTS. *Use* Rites and Ceremonies; Worship

CULTS AND SECTS. *See* Dissenters, Religious; Sects

CULTURAL ANTHROPOLOGY. *See* Ethnology

CULTURAL CENTERS. *Use* Recreation

CULTURAL EVOLUTION. *See* Social Change

CULTURAL LAG. *Use* Evolution; Progress; Social Change

CULTURAL RELATIONS. *Use* Acculturation; East and West; International Cooperation; Visitors, Foreign

CULTURE
Scope: Works of general nature only. Works limited to the culture of individual nations are entered under names of countries with appropriate subdivisions, Civilization or Social life and customs, e.g., Spain—Civilization, or India—Social life and customs.
LC   ——; s.a. Civilization; Counter cultures; Ethnology; Intellectual life; Subculture
SEARS   ——; s.a. Counter culture; Humanism; Manners and customs; Self-culture
RG   ——; s.a. History; Language and culture; subd. *Civilization, Intellectual life*, or *Popular culture* under names of countries
NYT   ——; s.a. Archeology and anthropology; names of groups, e.g., Indians, American; Sociology
PAIS   ——; s.a. Ethnic groups; Popular culture
BPI   ——; s.a. Culture diffusion; Intercultural education

CULTURE, POPULAR. *See* Popular Culture

CULTURE CONFLICT. *Use* Ethnopsychology

CULTURE CONTACT. *See* Acculturation

CULTURE DIFFUSION. *Use* Culture; Social Change

CUNNILINGUS. *Use* Sex

CURRENCY. *Use* Balance of Payments; Banks and Banking; Counterfeits and Counterfeiting; Foreign Exchange; Inflation (Finance); Money

CURRENCY CONVERTIBILITY. *Use* Currency Question; Foreign Exchange; Money

CURRENCY QUESTION
LC   ——; s.a. Currency convertibility; Finance; Foreign exchange problem
SEARS   ——; s.a. Inflation (finance); Money
RG   ——; s.a. Inflation (finance); Monetary policy; Money market
NYT   CURRENCY—INTERNATIONAL MONETARY SYSTEM; s.a. Commerce; Finance; U.S.—Finances
PAIS   MONEY; s.a. Exchange, Foreign; Inflation
BPI   MONEY; s.a. Barter; Inflation; Open market operations

CURRENT EVENTS
Scope: Works dealing with the study and teaching of current events; See History-Periodicals and History-Yearbooks for accounts and discussions of events themselves.
LC   ——; s.a. History, Modern—Study and teaching; History—Yearbooks; World politics
SEARS   ——; s.a. History, Modern—Study and teaching; History—Periodicals
RG   ——; s.a. History, Modern; World history
NYT   ——; s.a. History; News and news media
PAIS   ——; s.a. History
BPI   NEWS; s.a. History

CURRICULA (Courses of study). *See* Education—Curricula

CURRICULUM LABORATORIES. *Use* Education—Curricula

CURRICULUM MATERIALS CENTERS. *See* Instructional Materials Centers

CURRICULUM PLANNING. *Use* Education—Curricula; Educational Planning and Innovations

CUSTODIANSHIP ACCOUNTS. *Use* Trust Companies; Trusts and Trustees

CUSTOMER RELATIONS. *Use* Public Relations; Shopping

CUSTOMS. *See* Manners and Customs

CUSTOMS (Tariff). *See* Tariff

CUSTOMS ADMINISTRATION. *Use* Tariff

CUSTOMS APPRAISAL. *Use* Valuation

CUSTOMS UNIONS. *Use* Tariff

CUT FLOWERS. *Use* Floriculture

CUTTING. *See* Tailoring

CYBERNETICS
LC   ——; s.a. Automatic control; Communications; Computers; Electronic calculating machines

SEARS ——; s.a. Bionics; Calculating machines; Electronics; Systems engineering
RG ——; s.a. Man amplifiers; Perceptrons
NYT DATA PROCESSING (INFORMATION PROCESSING) EQUIPMENT AND SYSTEMS; s.a. Automation; Electronics
PAIS ——; s.a. Automation; System analysis

BPI ——; s.a. Information theory; Intelligence, Artificial

CYCLING. *Use* Bicycles and Bicycling

CYCLOTRON. *Use* Atoms; Nuclear Reactions

CYTOLOGY. *Use* Cells

D

DADAISM. *Use* Art, Modern—20th Century; Modernism (Art)

DAGUERROTYPES. *Use* Photography

DAIRY CATTLE. *Use* Cattle

DAIRYING. *Use* Agriculture; Cattle; Stock and Stock Breeding

DAMAGES. *Use* Liability (Law); Negligence; Obligations; Personal Injuries

DAMPNESS IN BUILDINGS. *Use* Ventilation

DAMS. *Use* Civil Engineering; Public Works; Water; Water Supply

DANCE ETIQUETTE. *Use* Dancing

DANCE MUSIC
LC ——; s.a. Bands (music); Dance-orchestra music; Folk dance music, Instrumental music; Instrumentation and orchestration (dance orchestra)
SEARS ——; s.a. Jazz music; Music, Popular (songs, etc.)
RG ——; s.a. Ballet music; Orchestral music; Phonograph records—Dance music; Rock groups
NYT MUSIC; s.a. Dancing
PAIS MUSIC; s.a. Dancing; Orchestras
BPI MUSIC; s.a. Bands; Orchestras

DANCE-ORCHESTRA MUSIC. *Use* Dance Music

DANCERS. *Use* Entertainers

DANCING
LC ——; s.a. Ballet; Ballroom dancing; Dance etiquette; Modern dance; Square dancing
SEARS ——; s.a. Folk dancing; Modern dance; Tap dancing
RG ——; s.a. Choreography; Dance music; Folk dancing; Modern dance
NYT ——; s.a. 'Happenings'; Opera
PAIS ——; s.a. Opera; Theater
BPI THEATER

DANGEROUS GOODS. *Use* Freight and Freightage; Hazardous Substances

DANGEROUS OCCUPATIONS. *See* Occupations, Dangerous

DARWINISM. *See* Evolution

DATA LIBRARIES. *Use* Information Services; Information Storage and Retrieval Systems

DATA PROCESSING. *Use* Automatic Control; Automation; Computers; Cybernetics; Data Tapes; Data Transmission Systems; Electronic Data Processing; Information Sciences; Information Storage and Retrieval Systems; Linear Programming; Machine Accounting; Mathematical Models; Programming (Electronic Computers); System Analysis

DATA TAPES
LC ——; s.a. Computer storage devices; Files and filing (documents); Programming
SEARS ELECTRONIC DATA PROCESSING; s.a. Information storage and retrieval systems
RG ——; s.a. Information storage and retrieval systems; Memory devices (computer)
NYT DATA PROCESSING (INFORMATION PROCESSING) EQUIPMENT AND SYSTEMS
PAIS ——; s.a. Computers; Information processing systems
BPI INFORMATION STORAGE AND RETRIEVAL SYSTEMS; s.a. Computers—Memory systems; Electronic data processing

DATA TRANSMISSION SYSTEMS
LC ——; s.a. Electronic data processing; Facsimile transmission; Information networks; Information sciences; Library information networks; Linear programming; Telecommunication
SEARS INFORMATION STORAGE AND RETRIEVAL SYSTEMS; s.a. Optical data processing; On line data processing
RG ——; s.a. Facsimile transmission; Telephone—Data transmission systems
NYT DATA PROCESSING (INFORMATION PROCESSING) EQUIPMENT AND SYSTEMS; s.a. Copying machines; Electronics
PAIS ——; s.a. Communication systems; Telephone—Data transmission systems
BPI ——; s.a. Computer networks; Facsimile transmission

DATING (Social customs)
LC ——; s.a. Courtship; Etiquette
SEARS ——; s.a. Love; Marriage

DATING (Social customs), *cont.*
RG   DATING; s.a. Courtship; Marriage
NYT DATING; s.a. Manners and customs; Marriages
PAIS SEXUAL ETHICS; s.a. Marriage; Single people
BPI MANNERS AND CUSTOMS; s.a. Marriage

DAUGHTERS
LC   ———; s.a. Adolescent girls; Education of women; Fathers and daughters; Mothers and daughters
SEARS PARENT AND CHILD, s.a. Girls; Young women
RG   ———; s.a. Coeducation; Girls; Parent-child relationship
NYT CHILDREN AND YOUTH; s.a. Families and family life; Women
PAIS PARENT AND CHILD (Law); s.a. Children; Youth
BPI PARENT-CHILD RELATIONSHIP; s.a. Children; Family; Girls

DAY CARE CENTERS. *Use* Nurseries; Woman—Employment

DAY NURSERIES. *Use* Child Welfare; Children; Education, Preschool; Nurseries; Public Welfare

DAYLIGHT SAVING. *Use* Time

DAYS. *Use* Special Days, Weeks and Months

DEAD. *Use* Burial; Deaths; Funeral Rites and Ceremonies; Obituaries

DEADLY SINS. *Use* Sin

DEAFNESS
LC   ———; s.a. Blind-deaf; Deaf—Institutional care; Deaf—Means of communications; Hearing disorders
SEARS ———; s.a. Deaf—Education; Hearing; Nonverbal communication
RG   ———; s.a. Hearing; Noise—Physiological effects; Television broadcasting and the deaf
NYT DEAFNESS AND DEAF-MUTES; s.a. Ears and hearing; Handicapped
PAIS DEAF; s.a. Employment—Deaf; Hearing aids
BPI DEAF; s.a. Hearing; Hearing aids; Sign language

DEALER AIDS. *Use* Salesmen and Salesmanship

DEANS (In schools). *Use* Educational Administration; Educators

DEATH
LC   ———; s.a. Autopsy; Dead; Death—Causes; Euthanasia; Future life; Future punishment; Inheritance and succession; Intermediate state; Obituaries; Violent death; Vital statistics; Wills
SEARS ———; s.a. Heaven; Hell; Mortality
RG   ———; s.a. Bereavement; Harakiri; Immortality
NYT ———; s.a. Biology and biochemistry; Mercy death (euthanasia)
PAIS ———; s.a. Suicide; Terminal care; Violent deaths
BPI ———; s.a. Life; Mortality

DEATH NOTICES. *See* Obituaries

DEATH OF GOD THEOLOGY. *Use* God

DEATH RATE. *See* Mortality; Vital Statistics

DEATH-BED MARRIAGE. *Use* Marriage Law

DEBATES AND DEBATING
LC   ———; s.a. Conversation; Oratory; Public speaking; Rhetoric
SEARS ———; s.a. Discussion groups; Parliamentary practice; Radio addresses, debates, etc.
RG   ———; s.a. Conferences; Forums (discussion and debate)
NYT DEBATING; s.a. Conversation; Speeches and statements (general)
PAIS DEBATING; s.a. Negotiation; Public speaking; Speeches, addresses, etc.
BPI PUBLIC SPEAKING; s.a. Discussion; Meetings

DEBENTURES. *See* Bonds

DEBT, IMPRISONMENT FOR. *Use* Prisons and Prisoners

DEBTOR AND CREDITOR
LC   ———; s.a. Acceptances; Business law; Commercial law; Debt; Deposits (law); Loans, Personal Moratorium; Mortgages; Obligations; Payment
SEARS ———; s.a. Bankruptcy; Collecting of accounts; Credit
RG   ———; s.a. Debt credit; Farm finance; Interest; Loan
NYT CREDIT; s.a. Bankruptcies; Finance
PAIS ———; s.a. Accounts receivable; Consumer credit; Liens; Security (law)
BPI ———; s.a. Bankruptcy; Collecting of accounts; Corporate debt; Payment

DEBTS, EXTERNAL. *Use* Debts, Public; Finance; International Finance

DEBTS, PUBLIC
LC   ———; s.a. Debts, External; Finance, Public; War, Cost of
SEARS ———; s.a. Bonds; Economics; Loans
RG   ———; s.a. Government spending policy; State finance
NYT U.S.—FINANCES; s.a. Credit; Finance
PAIS ———; s.a. Debts, External; Finance, Public
BPI ———; s.a. Fiscal policy; Monetary policy; War—Economic aspects

DECATHLON. *Use* Track Athletics

DECEDENTS' ESTATES. *Use* Inheritance and Succession; Probate Law and Practice; Wills

DECEIT. *See* Fraud

DECENDENTS' ESTATES. *Use* Inheritance and Succession; Probate Law and Practice

DECENTRALIZATION IN GOVERNMENT. *Use* Federal Government; Local Government; Metropolitan Government; Public Administration

DECIMAL SYSTEM. *Use* Weights and Measures

DECISION MAKING
LC   ———; s.a. Choice (psychology); Dilemma; Ethics; Experimental design; Games of strategy (mathematics); Methodology; Question-answering systems; Statistical decision

SEARS MANAGEMENT—METHODOLOGY; s.a. Executive ability; subd. *Methodology* under specific subjects

RG ——; s.a. Dilemma; Management games; Problem solving

NYT PSYCHOLOGY AND PSYCHOLOGISTS; s.a. Executives; Management, Industrial and institutional

PAIS ——; s.a. Game theory; Problem solving; subd. *Decision making* under specific subjects, e.g., Management—Decision making

BPI ——; s.a. Bayesian statistical decision theory; Games, Theory of; Make-or-buy decisions

DECKS. *Use* Roofs

DECLAMATION. *See* Voice

DECONTAMINATION (Gases, chemicals, etc.). *Use* Chemical Warfare

DECORATION, INTERIOR. *See* Interior Decoration

DECORATION AND ORNAMENT. *Use* Art Industries and Trade; Design; Interior Decoration; Jewelry

DECORATIONS OF HONOR. *Use* Emblems

DECORATIONS OF HONOR, ACADEMIC. *Use* Degrees, Academic

DECORATIVE ARTS. *See* Art Industries and Trade; Design

DECORATIVE LIGHTING. *Use* Lighting

DECOUPAGE. *Use* Handicrafts

DEDUCTION (Logic). *See* Logic

DEEDS
Scope: Works on property deeds.
LC ——; s.a. Abstracts of title; Charters; Vendors and purchasers
SEARS REAL ESTATE; s.a. Commercial law; Contracts; Land Tenure; Mortgages
RG LAND TITLES; s.a. Mortgages; Real property
NYT REAL ESTATE; s.a. Housing; Legal profession; Property and investments
PAIS ——; s.a. Land titles; Real property
BPI COMMERCIAL LAW; s.a. Contracts; Real property

DEEDS OF TRUST. *Use* Mortgages

DEEP SEA DIVING. *See* Underwater Exploration

DEFAMATION. *See* Libel and Slander

DEFECTIVE SPEECH. *See* Speech

DEFECTIVES. *See* Handicapped

DEFENSE (Criminal procedure). *Use* Legal Aid

DEFENSE, CIVIL. *See* Civil Defense

DEFENSE, RADAR. *See* Radar

DEFENSE CONTRACTS
LC ——; s.a. Research and development contracts; subd. *Procurement* under armies, navies, etc., e.g., U.S. Army—Procurement
SEARS INDUSTRIAL MOBILIZATION; s.a. Munitions

RG CONTRACTS, GOVERNMENT; s.a. Government spending policy; Military—Industrial complex
NYT U.S. ARMAMENT AND DEFENSE—DEFENSE CONTRACTS AND PRODUCTION; s.a. U.S.—Defense, Department of
PAIS ——; s.a. Accounting—Defense contracts; Military market; Purchasing, Military and naval
BPI CONTRACTS, GOVERNMENT; s.a. Purchasing, Military; Renegotiation of contracts; U.S.—Defense, Department of—Procurement

DEFENSE INFORMATION, CLASSIFIED. *Use* Official Secrets

DEFENSIVENESS (Psychology). *Use* Anxiety

DEFERRED COMPENSATION. *Use* Income Tax; Wages and Salaries

DEFICIENCY DISEASES. *Use* Diseases; Nutrition; Vitamins

DEFINITION (Logic). *Use* Logic; Semantics

DEFLATION (Finance). *Use* Depressions; Economic Policy; Inflation (Finance); Money

DEFOLIATION. *Use* Plants

DEFORMATION (Mechanics). *Use* Strength of Materials

DEGENERATION. *Use* Evolution; Vice

DEGREES, ACADEMIC
LC ——; s.a. Accreditation, Academic; College graduates; Decorations of honor, Academic; Education, Higher; Learning and scholarship; names of specific degrees, e.g., Bachelor of Arts; Students
SEARS ——
RG ——; s.a. Diplomas, Fraudulent
NYT COLLEGES AND UNIVERSITIES; s.a. names of institutions granting degrees, e.g., Yale University
PAIS ——; s.a. Education
BPI ——

DEISM. *Use* Atheism; God; Religion

DEITIES. *See* God

DELEGATED LEGISLATION. *Use* Legislation; Separation of Powers

DELEGATION OF AUTHORITY. *Use* Decision-making; Management

DELEGATION OF POWERS. *Use* Executive Power; Judicial Power; Separation of Powers

DELICATESSEN. *Use* Food Industry and Trade

DELINQUENTS. *Use* Crime and Criminals; Juvenile Delinquency; Vice

DELIVERY OF GOODS. *Use* Shipment of Goods

DELUSIONS. *See* Errors

DEMOCRACY
LC ——; s.a. Aristocracy; Constitutional law; Constitutions; Equality; Federal government; Republics

DEMOCRACY, *cont.*
SEARS ——; s.a. Liberty; Middle classes; Representative government and representation; Socialism
RG ——; s.a. Communism and democracy; Education and democracy; Liberty; Suffrage
NYT POLITICS AND GOVERNMENT (General); s.a. U.S.—Constitution; U.S.—Politics and government
PAIS ——; s.a. Communism and democracy; Equality
BPI ——; s.a. Equality; Representative government and representation

DEMOCRACY IN EDUCATION. *See* Self-Government (In education)

DEMOGRAPHY
LC ——; s.a. Geopolitics; Population forecasting; Vital statistics
SEARS POPULATION; s.a. Birth rate; Human ecology; Mortality
RG ——; s.a. Census; subd. *Population* under names of places, e.g., Europe—Population
NYT POPULATION AND VITAL STATISTICS; s.a. Immigration and emigration
PAIS POPULATION; s.a. Age groups; Census
BPI ——; s.a. Fertility; Population

DEMONSTRATION CENTERS IN EDUCATION. *Use* Educational Planning and Innovations

DEMONSTRATIONS
LC ——; s.a. Mobs; Public meetings; Riots
SEARS ——; s.a. Crowds; Youth movements
RG PROTESTS, DEMONSTRATIONS, ETC.; s.a. Student demonstrations; subd. *Protests, demonstrations,* etc. under names of cities and wars, e.g., Cambodian-Vietnamese conflict—American participation—Protests, demonstrations, etc. against
NYT POLITICS AND GOVERNMENT; s.a. Prisons and prisoners; Riots
PAIS DEMONSTRATIONS, POLITICAL; s.a. Riots; Student demonstrations
BPI PROTESTS, DEMONSTRATIONS, ETC.; s.a. Student demonstrations; Vietnam war—Protests, demonstrations, etc.

DEMYTHOLOGIZATION. *Use* Mythology

DENOMINATIONAL SCHOOLS. *See* Church Schools

DENOMINATIONS, RELIGIOUS. *See* Sects

DENTAL ECONOMICS. *Use* Dentistry

DENTAL EDUCATION. *Use* Dentistry

DENTAL HEALTH EDUCATION. *Use* Health Education

DENTAL HYGIENE. *Use* Dentistry

DENTISTRY
See also subd. *Dental care* under subject, e.g., Aged—Dental care.
LC ——; s.a. Dental economics; Enamel, Dental; Mouth; Teeth
SEARS ——; s.a. Teeth—Diseases; Water—Fluoridation
RG ——; s.a. Dental research; Orthodontics; Periodontia; Teeth—Care and hygiene; Toothpicks, Electric

NYT TEETH AND DENTISTRY; s.a. Gums; Mouth
PAIS DENTAL SERVICE; s.a. Dental education; Dentists; Medical service
BPI ——; s.a. Dental hygiene; Teeth

DENTISTS. *Use* Dentistry

DEODORANTS. *Use* Toilet

DEPARTMENT STORES
See also names of department stores, e.g., Neiman-Marcus Company.
LC ——; s.a. Chain stores; Stores, Retail; Variety stores
SEARS ——; s.a. Business; Retail trade; Salesmen and salesmanship
RG ——; s.a. Retail trade; Shopping centers; subd. *Stores* under names of cities, e.g., Houston—Stores
NYT RETAIL STORES AND TRADE; s.a. Discount selling; Marketing and merchandising
PAIS ——; s.a. Retail trade; subd. *Department stores* under specific subject, e.g., Advertising—Department stores
BPI ——; s.a. Appliance stores; Chain stores; Specialty stores; Stores, Retail; Variety stores

DEPENDENCIES. *See* Colonies

DEPENDENCY (Psychology). *Use* Human Relations

DEPORTATION. *Use* Aliens; Emigration and Immigration; Exiles

DEPOSIT BANKING. *Use* Banks and Banking; Checks (Banking)

DEPOSITIONS. *Use* Witnesses

DEPOSITS (Law). *Use* Debtor and Creditor; Suretyship and Guaranty

DEPRECIATION
Scope: Works on the depreciation of equipment and its business consequences.
LC ——; s.a. Accounting; Corporation reserves; Replacement of industrial equipment
SEARS ACCOUNTING; s.a. Bookkeeping
RG ——; s.a. Amortization deductions; Investment tax credit
NYT DEPRECIATION ALLOWANCES; s.a. Economics; Office equipment; Taxation
PAIS ——; s.a. Obsolescence; subd. *Depreciation* under specific subjects, e.g., Accounting—Depreciation
BPI ——; s.a. Economic life (of economic goods); Replacement of industrial equipment

DEPRESSION, BUSINESS. *See* Depressions

DEPRESSION, MENTAL
LC ——; s.a. Manic-depressive psychoses; Melancholia; Neuroses
SEARS INSANITY; s.a. Mental illness; Psychology, Pathological
RG ——; s.a. Antidepressants; Melancholy
NYT MENTAL HEALTH AND DISORDERS; s.a. Mind; Psychology and psychologists

PAIS   MENTAL ILLNESS; s.a. Mental hygiene; subd. *Mental illness* under specific subjects, e.g., Old age—Mental illness

BPI   ———; s.a. Manic-depressive psychoses; Mental illness

DEPRESSIONS
Scope: May be subdivided by date.
LC   ———; s.a. Business cycles; Deflation (finance); Overproduction
SEARS ———; s.a. Business cycles; Economics
RG   BUSINESS DEPRESSION; s.a. Business conditions; Panics
NYT   ECONOMIC CONDITIONS AND TRENDS; s.a. Economics; Labor
PAIS BUSINESS DEPRESSION; s.a. Business cycles; Economic conditions
BPI   BUSINESS DEPRESSION; s.a. Business cycles; Economic stabilization

DERELICTION (Civil law). *See* Abandonment of Property

DERVISHES. *Use* Islam

DESCENT. *See* Genealogy; Heredity

DESCRIPTION AND TRAVEL. *See* Travel

DESECRATION. *See* Religion

DESEGREGATION. *See* Segregation

DESEGRATION IN EDUCATION. *See* Discrimination in Education

DESERT ANIMALS. *Use* Animals

DESERT WARFARE. *Use* Military Art and Science

DESERTION, MILITARY. *Use* Military Law

DESERTION AND NON-SUPPORT. *Use* Abandoned Children; Alimony; Divorce; Marriage Law; Parent and Child

DESIGN
Scope: Works on the theory and purely ornamental features of design. See also specific types of design, e.g., Costume design; Textile design; etc.
LC   DESIGN, DECORATIVE; s.a. Art, Decorative; Art industries and trade; Carving (art industries); Design, Industrial; Glass, Ornamental; Human engineering; Illumination of books and manuscripts
SEARS DESIGN, DECORATIVE; s.a. Decoration and ornament
RG   DESIGN, DECORATIVE; s.a. Drawing
NYT   ———; s.a. Art; Interior decoration
PAIS DESIGN IN INDUSTRY; s.a. Art
BPI   ———

DESIGN, INDUSTRIAL
LC   ———; s.a. Design protection; Engineering models; Mechanical drawing; New products
SEARS ———; s.a. Art industries and trade; Commercial art
RG   ———; s.a. Human engineering; Systems engineering

NYT   DESIGN; s.a. Engineering and engineers; Graphic arts
PAIS DESIGN IN INDUSTRY; s.a. Human engineering; Systems engineering
BPI   DESIGN; s.a. Environmental engineering; Industrial design coordination

DESIGN IN INDUSTRY. *Use* Design, Industrial

DESIGN PROTECTION. *Use* Design, Industrial; Intellectual Property; Patent Laws and Legislation

DESIRE. *Use* Emotions; Will

DESPOTISM
LC   ———; s.a. Authoritarianism; Dictators
SEARS DICTATORS; s.a. Kings and rulers; Monarchy
RG   TYRANNY; s.a. Dictatorship; Fascism
NYT   POLITICS AND GOVERNMENT; s.a. Communism; Totalitarianism
PAIS DICTATORSHIP; s.a. Authority; Totalitarianism
PAIS DICTATORSHIP; s.a. Authority; Totalitarianism
BPI   POLITICAL SCIENCE; s.a. Authority; Dogmatism

DESSERTS. *Use* Dinners and Dining

DESTINY. *See* Fate and Fatalism

DESTITUTION. *See* Poverty

DETECTIVE AND MYSTERY STORIES. *Use* Fiction

DETECTIVES
LC   ———; s.a. Criminal investigation; Detective and mystery stories; House detectives; Watchmen
SEARS ———; s.a. Mystery and detective stories; Secret service
RG   ———; s.a. Electronics in criminal investigation, espionage, etc.; U.S. Federal Bureau of Investigation
NYT   DETECTIVES, PRIVATE; s.a. Crime and criminals; Police
PAIS ———; s.a. Criminal investigation; Police, Private
BPI   ———; s.a. Criminal investigation; Police

DETENTION, PREVENTIVE. *See* Imprisonment

DETENTION CAMPS. *See* Concentration Camps

DETENTION HOMES. *Use* Child Welfare; Juvenile Delinquency

DETENTION OF PERSONS. *Use* Arrest; Concentration Camps; Imprisonment

DETERGENT POLLUTION OF WATER. *Use* Water—Pollution

DETERGENTS. *Use* Cleaning Compounds

DETERMINISM AND INDETERMINISM. *See* Fate and Fatalism

DETRIBALIZATION. *Use* Tribes and Tribal System

DEVALUATION OF CURRENCY. *See* Currency Question

DEVELOPING COUNTRIES. *See* Underdeveloped Areas

DEVELOPMENT BANKS. *Use* Banks and Banking

DEVELOPMENT EDUCATION. *See* Acculturation

DEVELOPMENTAL READING. *Use* Reading

DEVIANT BEHAVIOR. *Use* Behavior (Psychology)

DEVOTIONAL EXERCISES. *Use* Liturgies; Worship

DIAGNOSIS. *Use* Medicine

DIALECTICS. *See* Logic

DIALECTS. *See* Language and Languages

DIAMONDS. *See* Jewelry; Precious Stones

DIARIES. *Use* Biography (As a literary form)

DICE. *Use* Gambling

DICTATION. *Use* Commercial Correspondence; Secretaries

DICTATORS. *Use* Despotism; Heads of State; Totalitarianism

DICTATORSHIP. *Use* Despotism; Totalitarianism

DICTATORSHIP OF THE PROLETARIAT. *Use* Communism; Proletariat; Totalitarianism

DICTION. *Use* Speech; Voice

DICTIONARIES. *Use* Handbooks; Vocabulary

DIESEL ENGINES. *Use* Motors

DIESEL MOTORS. *Use* Motors

DIET
LC	———; s.a. Beverages; Diet in disease; Food habits; Jews—Dietary laws; Nutrition; Zen (sect)
SEARS	———; s.a. Cookery; Digestion; Indigestion; names of diets, e.g., Salt free diet; Weight control
RG	———; s.a. Vegetarianism; Vitamins
NYT	FOOD AND GROCERY TRADE—DIET AND NUTRITION; s.a. Cooking; Weight
PAIS	———; s.a. Food; Nutrition
BPI	———; s.a. Food, Dietetic; Nutrition

DIET IN DISEASE. *Use* Diet; Sick; Therapeutics

DIFFERENTIATION (Biology). *Use* Cells; Embryology

DIFFUSION OF INNOVATIONS. *Use* Technological Innovations

DIGESTION
LC	———; s.a. Constipation; Digestive organs; Gastric juice
SEARS	———; s.a. Diet; Food; Indigestion; Physiological chemistry; Stomach
RG	———; s.a. Digestive system; Enzymes; Intestines; Stomach
NYT	STOMACH; s.a. Digestive tract
PAIS	PHYSIOLOGY
BPI	EATING; s.a. Physiology

DIGITAL COMPUTERS. *See* Computers

DIGITAL COUNTERS. *Use* Calculating Machines

DIGITAL ELECTRONICS. *Use* Computers

DIKES (Engineering). *Use* Reclamation of Land

DILEMMA. *Use* Decision Making

DIMOUTS. *See* Blackouts in War

DINNERS AND DINING
LC	———; s.a. Cookery; Desserts; Gastronomy; Table
SEARS	———; s.a. Carving (meat, etc.); Entertaining; Menus
RG	———; s.a. Caterers and catering; Outdoor meals
NYT	COOKING; s.a. Food and grocery trade; Hotels, bars, motels, night clubs and restaurants
PAIS	CATERING INDUSTRY; s.a. Food; Restaurants
BPI	———; s.a. Caterers and catering; Cookery; Menus

DIPLOMACY
See also subds. *Diplomatic and consular service* and *Foreign service* under names of countries.
LC	———; s.a. Ambassadors; Consuls; Diplomatic and consular service
SEARS	———; s.a. International law; Statesmen; Treaties
RG	———; s.a. International relations; Negro diplomats
NYT	———; s.a. Diplomatic immunity; International relations
PAIS	———; s.a. Attaches, Military; Attaches, Science
BPI	DIPLOMATS; s.a. Commercial treaties and agreements; International relations; World politics

DIPLOMAS, FRAUDULENT. *Use* Degrees, Academic

DIPLOMATIC AND CONSULAR SERVICE. *Use* Diplomacy

DIPLOMATIC ETIQUETTE. *Use* Etiquette

DIPLOMATIC IMMUNITY. *Use* Diplomacy

DIPLOMATICS. *Use* Historical Research

DIPSOMANIA. *See* Alcoholism

DIRECT ACTION. *Use* Demonstrations; Sabotage; Strikes and Lockouts

DIRECT TAXATION. *See* Income Tax; Taxation

DIRECTORIES. *Use* Handbooks

DIRECTORIES—BIOGRAPHICAL. *Use* Biography

DIRECTORS. *Use* Executives

DIRIGIBLE BALLOONS. *See* Airships

DISABILITY BENEFITS. *Use* Non-wage Payments; Workmen's Compensation

DISABLED. *Use* Amputees; Cerebral Palsy; Handicapped; Invalids; Paralysis

DISABLED—REHABILITATION. *Use* Occupational Therapy; Rehabilitation

DISALLOWANCE OF LEGISLATION. *Use* Veto

DISARMAMENT
LC	———; s.a. Armies, Cost of; Biological warfare; Chemical warfare; Disarmament—Inspection; Militarism; Pacifism; War, Cost of
SEARS	———; s.a. Arbitration, International; Sea—Power; Security, International
RG	———; s.a. Atomic weapons and disarmament; International security

NYT ARMS CONTROL AND LIMITATION AND DISARMAMENT; s.a. North Atlantic Treaty Organization (NATO); U.S. armament and defense

PAIS ARMAMENTS—LIMITATION; s.a. Peace; Strategic arms limitation talks

BPI DISARMAMENT AND ARMS CONTROL; s.a. International relations; Peace; World politics

DISASTER RELIEF

LC ———; s.a. Civil defense; Emergency housing; Food supply; International cooperation; Rescue work

SEARS ———; s.a. Civil defense

RG ———; s.a. Assistance in emergencies; Civil defense; Hospitals—Emergency services

NYT Specific kinds of disasters, e.g., Floods; s.a. Disaster insurance (flood, hurricane, etc.); Welfare work

PAIS ———; s.a. Emergency clothing supply; Red Cross; Relief work

BPI DISASTERS; s.a. Accidents; Relief work

DISASTERS

See also names of particular disasters, e.g., New England—Hurricane—1938; San Francisco—Earthquake and fire—1906; etc.

LC ———; s.a. Catastrophical, The; Collisions at sea; Disaster relief; Food supply; Mine accidents; Natural disasters

SEARS ———; s.a. Railroads—Accidents; Storms

RG ———; s.a. Fires; Hurricanes; Panic; Shipwrecks

NYT Specific kinds, e.g., Typhoons; s.a. Accidents and safety; Disaster insurance (flood, hurricane, etc.)

PAIS ———; s.a. Insurance, Disaster

BPI ———; s.a. Accidents; Relief work

DISCIPLINE, INDUSTRIAL. *See* Personnel Management

DISCIPLINE, MILITARY. *Use* Military Law; Morale

DISCIPLINE OF CHILDREN

LC ———; s.a. Children—Management; Discipline of infants; School discipline

SEARS CHILDREN—MANAGEMENT; s.a. Child study; Punishment; School discipline

RG CHILDREN—MANAGEMENT AND TRAINING; s.a. Moral education; Parent-child relationship

NYT CHILDREN AND YOUTH—BEHAVIOR AND TRAINING; s.a. Education and schools; Juvenile delinquency

PAIS SCHOOL DISCIPLINE; s.a. Infants; Moral education

BPI CHILDREN; s.a. Education; Schools

DISCOUNT. *Use* Acceptances; Credit; Interest and Usury; Prices

DISCOUNT SELLING. *Use* Chain Stores; Department Stores; Prices; Shopping

DISCOVERERS. *See* Discoveries (Geography); Explorers

DISCOVERIES (In geography)

See also subd. *Description and travel* under names of countries.

LC ———; s.a. Geography—History; Northwest Passage; Voyages and travels

SEARS ———; s.a. America—Discovery and exploration; Explorers; Scientific expeditions

RG ———; s.a. Antarctic exploration; Arctic exploration; Explorations

NYT GEOGRAPHY; s.a. Antarctic regions; Exploration and explorers; Maps

PAIS GEOGRAPHY

BPI VOYAGES AND TRAVELS; s.a. Geography

DISCOVERIES (In science). *See* Intellectual Property; Inventions

DISCRETE-TIME SYSTEMS. *Use* System Analysis

DISCRETIONARY INCOME. *Use* Income

DISCRIMINATION

Scope: General works on social discrimination based on race, religion, sex, social minority status, or other factors. See also headings beginning with Discrimination in . . . .

LC ———; s.a. Civil rights; Human relations; Prejudices and antipathies; Race awareness; Race problems; Segregation; Social problems

SEARS ———; s.a. Blacks—Segregation; Sex discrimination; Toleration

RG ———; s.a. Anti-Semitism; Minorities

NYT ———; s.a. Minorities (ethnic, racial, religious)

PAIS ———; s.a. Discrimination in education; Prejudice

BPI RACE DISCRIMINATION; s.a. Discrimination in employment; Discrimination in housing

DISCRIMINATION, RACIAL. *See* Race Discrimination

DISCRIMINATION IN EDUCATION

LC ———; s.a. Race discrimination; Race problems in school management; Segregation in education

SEARS ———; s.a. Blacks—Education; Busing (school integration); Segregation in education

RG ———; s.a. Equalization, Educational; Negroes—Education; School children—Transportation for integration

NYT EDUCATION AND SCHOOLS—U.S.—EQUAL EDUCATIONAL OPPORTUNITIES; s.a. Colleges and universities—U.S.—Racial integration and programs; Discrimination; Education and schools—U.S.—School buses; Minorities (ethnic, racial, religious)

PAIS ———; s.a. Education—Integration and segregation; Negroes—Education; Schools—Transportation of pupils

BPI ———; s.a. Negroes—Segregation; Public schools—Desegregation; Race discrimination

DISCRIMINATION IN EMPLOYMENT

See also subd. *Employment* under names of social and racial groups, e.g., Puerto Ricans—Employment; Woman—Employment.

LC ———; s.a. Equal pay for equal work; Labor and laboring classes; Open and closed shop; Recruiting of employees; Right to labor

SEARS ———

RG ———; s.a. Blacklisting; Minorities—Employment

NYT LABOR—U.S.—DISCRIMINATION; s.a. Minorities (ethnic, racial, religious); Negroes (in U.S.); Race

DISCRIMINATION IN EMPLOYMENT, *cont.*
PAIS ——; s.a. Age and employment; Blacklisting; Discrimination
BPI ——; s.a. Minorities—Employment; Race discrimination

DISCRIMINATION IN HOUSING
LC ——; s.a. Discrimination in public accomodations; Jews—Segregation; Real covenants
SEARS ——; s.a. Discrimination in public accomodations
RG ——; s.a. Housing—Desegregation; Negroes—Segregation
NYT HOUSING; s.a. Discrimination; Minorities (ethnic, racial, religious); Negroes (in U.S.)
PAIS ——; s.a. Negroes—Housing; Segregation, Social
BPI ——; s.a. Negroes—Segregation; Race discrimination

DISCRIMINATION IN PUBLIC ACCOMMODATIONS. *Use* Discrimination in Housing

DISCS. *See* Phonograph Records

DISCUSSION. *Use* Debates and Debating; Leadership

DISCUSSION GROUPS. *Use* Debates and Debating

DISEASES
See also names of specific diseases, e.g., Heart disease, and subd. *Diseases* under various subjects, e.g., Children—Diseases, Blood—Diseases, etc.
LC DISEASES—CAUSES AND THEORIES OF CAUSATION; s.a. Chronic diseases; Coronary heart disease; Deficiency diseases; Occupational diseases
SEARS ——; s.a. Communicable diseases; Epidemics; Medicine—Practice
RG DISEASES—CAUSES AND THEORIES OF CAUSATION; s.a. Animals as carriers of infection; Cardiacs; Traumatism
NYT MEDICINE AND HEALTH
PAIS SICKNESS; s.a. Chronically ill
BPI ——; s.a. Viruses

DISEASES, MENTAL. *See* Mental Illness

DISINFECTION AND DISINFECTANTS
LC ——; s.a. Air—Purification; Communicable diseases
SEARS ——; s.a. Antiseptics; Fumigation
RG ——; s.a. Germfree isolation; Hexachlorophene
NYT DISINFECTION AND ANTISEPTICS; s.a. Cleansers, detergents and soaps; Sanitation
PAIS COMMUNICABLE DISEASES
BPI ——; s.a. Antiseptics; Communicable diseases; Hospitals—Disinfection

DISINHERITANCE. *Use* Wills

DISK JOCKEYS. *Use* Radio Broadcasting and Programs

DISPENSARIES. *Use* Hospitals

DISPERSION STRENGTHENING. *Use* Strength of Materials

DISPLACEMENT (Psychology). *Use* Behavior (Psychology)

DISPLAY FIGURES. *See* Models, Fashion

DISPLAY OF MERCHANDISE. *Use* Merchandising; Packaging

DISPLAY SYSTEMS. *See* Information Services; Information Storage and Retrieval Systems

DISPUTATIONS, RELIGIOUS. *Use* Theology

DISSECTION. *Use* Anatomy, Human

DISSENTERS, RELIGIOUS
LC ——; s.a. Congregationalism; Established churches; Liberty; Liberty of conscience
SEARS RELIGION; s.a. Freedom of conscience; Protestantism; Sects
RG ——; s.a. Intellectual liberty; Religious liberty
NYT RELIGION AND CHURCHES; s.a. Freedom and human rights; Freedom of religion
PAIS DISSENTERS; s.a. Religion
BPI RELIGION; s.a. Church; Church and state

DISTANT EARLY WARNING SYSTEM. *Use* Radar

DISTILLATION. *Use* Alcohol; Liquors

DISTILLING INDUSTRY. *Use* Alcohol; Liquors

DISTRESS (Law). *Use* Landlord and Tenant

DISTRIBUTION. *Use* Marketing; Product Management

DISTRIBUTION (Probability theory). *Use* Probabilities; Statistics

DISTRIBUTION OF WEALTH. *See* Wealth

DISTRIBUTIVE EDUCATION. *Use* Business Education; Salesmen and Salesmanship

DIVERS AND DIVING. *Use* Underwater Exploration

DIVERSIFICATION IN INDUSTRY. *Use* Conglomerate Corporations

DIVIDENDS. *Use* Income; Investments; Stock Exchange

DIVINATION. *Use* Astrology; Occult Sciences; Prophecies

DIVINE HEALING. *See* Miracles

DIVINE RIGHT OF KINGS. *Use* Heads of State

DIVING, SUBMARINE. *Use* Oceanography

DIVISION OF LABOR. *Use* Labor and Laboring Classes; Machinery in Industry

DIVISION OF POWERS. *See* Federal Government; Separation of Powers

DIVORCE
LC ——; s.a. Adultery; Alienation of affections; Alimony; Bigamy; Broken homes; Divorce practice; Divorce suits; Legal cruelty; Marriage law; Single women
SEARS ——; s.a. Desertion and non-support; Domestic relations
RG ——; s.a. Children of divorced parents; Divorcees; Separation (law)
NYT DIVORCE, SEPARATIONS AND ANNULMENTS; s.a. Family and family life; Marriages
PAIS ——; s.a. Alimony; Marriage—Annulment; Remarriage; Separation (law)
BPI ——; s.a. Alimony; Desertion and non-support; Single people; Support (domestic relations)

DOCKS. *Use* Ports

DOCTORS OF THE CHURCH. *Use* Saints

DOCTRINES. *See* Theology

DOCUMENTATION
LC ——; s.a. Classification—Books; Information services; Précis writing; Public records
SEARS ——; s.a. Cataloging; Information science; Library science
RG ——; s.a. Archives; Information services
NYT DOCUMENTS; s.a. Books and literature; Indexes and indexing; Libraries and librarians
PAIS ——; s.a. Bibliography; Indexing
BPI ——; s.a. Archives; Information storage and retrieval systems

DOCUMENTS. *Use* Archives; Business Records; Copying Processes; Documentation; Files and Filing (Documents); Historical Research; Legal Aid; Public Records

DOG BREEDING. *Use* Breeding

DOGMATIC THEOLOGY. *See* Theology

DOGMATISM. *Use* Attitude (Psychology); Despotism

DO-IT-YOURSELF WORK. *Use* Industrial Arts; Recreation

DOLLS. *Use* Toys

DOMES. *Use* Roofs

DOMESTIC ANIMALS
Scope: General works on farm animals. Works limited to animals as pets are entered under Pets. Works on stock raising are entered under Livestock. See also names of individual animals, e.g., Cats; Goats; Reindeer; etc.
LC ——; s.a. Agriculture; Animal industry; Breeding; Domestication; Zoology, Economic
SEARS ——; s.a. Animals—Treatment; Veterinary medicine
RG ——; s.a. Livestock
NYT ANIMALS; s.a. Veterinary medicine
PAIS ——; s.a. Livestock industry
BPI ——; s.a. Livestock

DOMESTIC APPLIANCES. *See* Household Equipment and Furnishings

DOMESTIC ECONOMY. *See* Home Economics

DOMESTIC EDUCATION. *Use* Home Economics

DOMESTIC FINANCE. *Use* Budgets, Household; Cost and Standard of Living; Home Economics; Saving and Savings

DOMESTIC RELATIONS. *Use* Divorce; Family; Marriage; Marriage Law

DOMESTIC RELATIONS COURTS. *Use* Courts

DOMESTIC SECURITY. *See* Internal Security

DOMESTIC SERVICE. *Use* Contract Labor; Household Employees; Native Labor; Work

DOMESTICATION. *Use* Domestic Animals

DOMESTICS. *See* Household Employees

DOMINION OF THE SEA. *See* Sea Power

DONATIONS. *See* Charitable Uses, Trusts and Foundations

DOODLES (Sketches). *Use* Drawing

DOOR-TO-DOOR SELLING. *Use* Salesmen and Salesmanship

DOPING IN SPORTS. *Use* Sports

DORMANT PARTNERS. *Use* Partnership

DORMITORIES. *Use* Schools

DOUBLE JEOPARDY (Law). *Use* Justice, Administration of

DOUBLE SHIFTS (Public schools). *Use* Schools

DOUBT. *See* Belief and Doubt

DOUGH. *Use* Baking

DRAFT, MILITARY. *See* Military Service, Compulsory

DRAIN CLEANERS. *Use* Plumbing

DRAINAGE. *Use* Reclamation of Land; Refuse and Refuse Disposal

DRAINAGE, HOUSE. *Use* Plumbing

DRAMA
Scope: Works dealing with the subject of drama in general. Works on the history and criticism of the drama are entered under Drama—History and criticism. Works dealing with criticism of drama as presented on the stage are entered under Dramatic criticism. See also American drama and Negro drama.
LC ——; s.a. Acting; Classical drama; Comedy; Mystery and miracle plays—English; Plots (drama, novel, etc.)
SEARS ——; s.a. American drama, English drama, etc.; Moralities; Tragedy
RG ——; s.a. College and school drama; Dramas—Criticisms, plots, etc.; Pantomime; Religious drama
NYT THEATER; s.a. Books and literature; Opera
PAIS THEATER; s.a. Actors; Literature; Opera
BPI THEATER; s.a. Musical comedies, revues, etc.; Opera

DRAMA—CRITICISM, PLOTS, ETC. *Use* Plots (Drama, novel, etc.)

DRAMA, MODERN. *See* Drama

DRAMA—TECHNIQUE. *Use* Authorship

DRAMATIC CRITICISM. *Use* Drama; Moving Picture Plays

DRAMATIC PLOTS. *See* Plots (Drama, novel, etc.)

DRAPERY. *Use* Upholstery

DRAWING
LC ——; s.a. Architectural rendering; Blue-prints; Drawing, Psychology of; Figure drawing; Illustrators; Mechanical drawing; Projection
SEARS ——; s.a. Anatomy, Artistic; Commercial art; Landscape drawing; Pen drawing

DRAWING, *cont.*
RG ———; s.a. Architectural drawing; Black and white (art); Design; Doodles (sketches); Graffiti; Illustration of books and periodicals; Mechanical drawing; Perspective
NYT GRAPHIC ARTS
PAIS GRAPHIC METHODS; s.a. Art; Charts
BPI GRAPHIC METHODS; s.a. Art; Drawings; Engineering drawing

DREAMS
LC ———; s.a. Brain; Fantasy; Psychical research; Somnambulism; Superstition
SEARS ———; s.a. Mind and body; Psychoanalysis; Subconsciousness; Visions
RG ———; s.a. Sleep; Symbolism (psychology)
NYT ———; s.a. Psychology and psychologists; Sleep
PAIS PSYCHOLOGY
BPI SLEEP; s.a. Hypnotics; Insomnia

DREDGING. *Use* Engineering; Ports

DRESS. *See* Clothing and Dress; Costume

DRESS PATTERNS. *Use* Sewing

DRESSMAKING. *Use* Clothing and Dress; Fashion; Sewing

DRILLING AND BORING. *Use* Boring

DRINKING AND TRAFFIC ACCIDENTS. *Use* Liquor Problem; Traffic Accidents

DRINKING CUSTOMS. *Use* Manners and Customs

DRINKING WATER. *Use* Water

DRINKS. *See* Beverages; Liquors

DRIVEWAYS. *Use* Streets

DROP SHIPMENTS. *Use* Mail-order Business; Shipment of Goods

DROPOUTS
LC ———; s.a. College dropouts; High school dropouts; Personnel service in higher education; Youth
SEARS ———; s.a. Personnel service in education; School attendance; Youth
RG ———; s.a. Compulsory education; School attendance
NYT ———; s.a. Labor—U.S.—Youth; Children and youth—Behavior and training
PAIS STUDENT WITHDRAWALS; s.a. Colleges and universities; Employment—Student withdrawals
BPI ———; s.a. High school students; Students

DRUG ABUSE
Scope: Works on the misuse of drugs in a broad sense such as alcohol, marijuana, and narcotics. Works limited to hard drugs such as opium, heroin, etc. are entered under Narcotic habit.
LC ———; s.a. Alcoholism; Drug abuse and crime; Drug addicts; Drugs—Law and legislation
SEARS ———; s.a. Alcoholism; Drugs and youth; Narcotic habit
RG ———; s.a. Fetus, Effect of drugs on the; Narcotics and youth
NYT DRUG ADDICTION, ABUSE AND TRAFFIC; s.a. Alcoholism; Stimulants (drugs)

PAIS ———; s.a. Drugs and youth; subd. *Drug problem* under specific subjects, e.g., College students—Drug problem; Personnel management—Drug problem
BPI ———; s.a. Alcoholism; Narcotics and dangerous drugs, Control of

DRUG ABUSE AND CRIME. *Use* Crime and Criminals

DRUG ADDICTS. *Use* Narcotic Addicts; Narcotic Habit

DRUG ADDICTS—CARE AND TREATMENT. *Use* Narcotics, Control of

DRUG ALLERGY. *Use* Allergy

DRUG HABIT. *See* Drug Abuse; Narcotic Habit

DRUG INDUSTRY. *Use* Drug Trade

DRUG STORES. *Use* Drug Trade

DRUG TRADE
LC ———; s.a. Drugstores; Hospital pharmacies; Medical personnel; Narcotics, Control of; Pharmacy
SEARS PHARMACY; s.a. Chemists; Drugs; Pharmacology
RG DRUG INDUSRTY; s.a. Drug trade; Drugstores; Government investigations—Drug trade
NYT DRUGS AND DRUG TRADE; s.a. Food, drug and cosmetic regulation
PAIS ———; s.a. Drugstores; Medical profession; Pharmacists
BPI DRUG INDUSTRY; s.a. Drug stores; Drugs; Pharmaceutical research; Pharmacy technicians

DRUGS
Scope: The word Drugs is often used in a broad sense to include such items as sedatives, stimulants, and narcotics. The word Narcotics is mostly used for hard drugs, such as opium, heroin, etc. See also names of specific drugs, e.g., Alcohol; LSD; Marijuana; etc.
LC ———; s.a. Medicine—Formulae, receipts, prescriptions; Pharmacology; Poisons; Prescription pricing; Psychopharmacology
SEARS ———; s.a. Drugs—Physiological effect; Drugs—Psychological aspects; Medical care—Costs; Therapeutics
RG ———; s.a. Hallucinogenic drugs; Pharmacology; Prescriptions
NYT DRUGS AND DRUG TRADE
PAIS ———; s.a. Drugs—Legislation; Drugs—Prices; Prescriptions—Prices; Psychotropic drugs
BPI ———; s.a. Antibiotics; Drugs—Generic vs. brand names question; Drugs—Prices and sale; Medicine, Proprietary; Narcotics

DRUGS—ADULTERATION AND ANALYSIS. *Use* Consumer Protection

DRUGS—LAWS AND LEGISLATION. *Use* Narcotics, Control of

DRUGS AND DRUG TRADE. *Use* Drug Trade

DRUGS AND YOUTH. *Use* Crimes without Victims; Drug Abuse; Juvenile Delinquency

DRUGSTORES. *Use* Drug Trade

DRUM MAJORING. *Use* Bands (Music)

DRUNKENNESS. *See* Liquor Problem; Temperance

DRY FARMING. *Use* Farms and Farming

DRY GOODS. *Use* Textile Industry and Fabrics

DRYING OILS. *Use* Oils and Fats

DRYPOINT. *Use* Graphic Arts

DUAL ENROLLMENT. *Use* School Attendance

DUAL NATIONALITY. *Use* Nationality

DUAL PERSONALITY. *See* Mentally Ill

DUALISM. *Use* Idealism

DUE PROCESS OF LAW. *Use* Civil Rights; Constitutions; Equality; Justice, Administration of; Law; Persecution; Rule of Law

DUMB (Deaf mutes). *See* Deafness

DUMPING (Commercial policy). *Use* Commercial Crimes; Prices

DUNGEONS. *See* Prisons and Prisoners

DUPLICATING PROCESSES. *See* Copying Processes

DUST, RADIOACTIVE. *See* Radiation

DUST STORMS. *Use* Erosion

DUTIES. *See* Tariff; Taxation

DUTY. *Use* Character; Conduct of Life

DUTY FREE IMPORTATION. *Use* Tariff

DYES AND DYEING
See also names of specific dyes, e.g., Indigo, Henna, etc.
LC ——; s.a. Bleaching; Coloring matter
SEARS ——; s.a. Chemistry, Technical; Pigment; Textile chemistry
RG ——; s.a. Batik; Hair—Dyeing and bleaching
NYT DYES AND DYESTUFFS; s.a. Chemistry and chemicals; Cleaning and dyeing
PAIS DYE INDUSTRY; s.a. Chemical industries; Cleaning industry
BPI ——; s.a. Dye industry; Dyehouses

DYNAMICS. *Use* Aerodynamics; Force and Energy; Mechanical Engineering

DYNAMITE. *Use* Blasting

DYNAMOS. *Use* Motors

DYSPEPSIA. *See* Digestion

E

EAR—PROTECTION. *Use* Noise

EAR TRAINING. *Use* Music Education

EARLY CHILDHOOD EDUCATION. *See* Nurseries

EARS AND HEARING. *Use* Deafness; Hearing

EARTH
LC ——; s.a. Antarctic regions; Arctic regions; Geodesy; Geophysics; Magnetism, Terrestrial; Oceanography: Volcanoes
SEARS ——; s.a. Glacial epoch; Latitude; Longitude; Physical geography; Solar system; Universe
RG ——; s.a. Atmosphere; Creation; Earth movements
NYT ——; s.a. Geology; Gravitation and gravity; Seismology and seismographs
PAIS EARTH SCIENCES; s.a. Astronomy; Earthquakes; Geography; Geology
BPI ——; s.a. Geography; Geology; Meteorology; Seismological records

EARTH, EFFECT OF MAN ON. *See* Man—Influence on Nature

EARTH—INTERNAL STRUCTURE. *Use* Magnetism, Terrestrial

EARTH—MAGNETISM. *See* Magnetism, Terrestrial

EARTH—PHOTOGRAPHS FROM SPACE. *Use* Aerial Photography

EARTH CURRENTS. *Use* Magnetism, Terrestrial

EARTH SATELLITES. *See* Artificial Satellites

EARTH SCIENCES. *Use* Atmosphere; Atmosphere, Upper; Earth

EARTHENWARE. *See* Ceramics

EARTHQUAKES. *Use* Earth

EARTHWORK. *Use* Civil Engineering; Engineering

EAST (Near East). *See* Near East

EAST AND WEST
Scope: Works on acculturation and cultural conflict between Oriental and Occidental civilizations.
LC ——; s.a. Cold war; Eurasianism; Intercultural communication; Philosophy, Comparative
SEARS ——; s.a. Civilization, Occidental; Civilization, Oriental; Eastern question
RG ——; s.a. Acculturation; Cultural relations
NYT CULTURE; s.a. Far East
PAIS ——; s.a. Acculturation; International relations
BPI INTERCULTURAL EDUCATION; s.a. Far East; International relations

EASTERN QUESTION. *Use* Near East; World Politics

EAST-WEST TRADE (1945-). *Use* Foreign Trade

EATING. *Use* Cookery; Diet; Digestion; Food

EAVESDROPPING. *Use* Confidential Communications; Privacy, Right of; Wire tapping

ECCLESIASTICAL LAW
LC   ——; s.a. Asylum, Right of; Blasphemy; Concordats; Corporations, Religious; Privileges and immunities, Ecclesiastical; Sunday legislation; Theology, Practical
SEARS ——; s.a. Law; Sabbath; Tithes
RG   ——; s.a. Canon law; Marriage (canon law)
NYT RELIGION AND CHURCHES; s.a. subd. *Politics and government—Church—State Relations* under names of countries; Sunday observance
PAIS ——; s.a. Church and state; Churches
BPI   RELIGION; s.a. Church and state

ECCLESIASTICAL RITES AND CEREMONIES. *See* Liturgies; Rites and Ceremonies

ECCLESIASTICAL THEOLOGY. *See* Church

ECLIPSES, SOLAR. *Use* Sun

ECOLOGY
See also names of types of ecology, e.g., Botany—Ecology; Forest ecology; Fresh water ecology; Human ecology; Island ecology; Jungle ecology; Marine ecology; Mountain ecology; Social ecology; Zoology—Ecology, etc.
LC   ——; s.a. Acclimatization; Anthropo-geography; Bioclimatology; Biotic communities; Conservation of natural resources; Indicators (biology); Man—Influence of environment; Microclimatology; Predation (biology); Zoology, Economic
SEARS ——; s.a. Adaptation (biology); Geographical distribution of animals and plants
RG   ——; s.a. Food chains (ecology)
NYT ENVIRONMENT; s.a. Biology and biochemistry; Nature; Water pollution
PAIS ——; s.a. Environment
BPI   ——; s.a. Animal populations

ECONOMETRICS. *Use* Economics, Mathematical; Mathematics

ECONOMIC ASSISTANCE. *Use* Economic Assistance, Foreign; Industrialization; International Cooperation; International Finance; Underdeveloped Areas

ECONOMIC ASSISTANCE, DOMESTIC
Scope: Works on the relation between central and local governments.
LC   ——; s.a. Government lending; Grants-in-aid; Intergovernmental fiscal relations; subd. *Finance* under particular subjects, e.g., Roads—Finance; Work relief
SEARS ——; s.a. Federal aid to education; Poverty; Public works; Subsidies
RG   ——; s.a. Community development—U.S.; Federal aid; Negative income tax
NYT U.S.—ECONOMIC CONDITIONS AND TRENDS; s.a. U.S.—Finances; U.S.—Finances—Federal revenue sharing and grants-in-aid

PAIS GOVERNMENT LOANS AND GRANTS; s.a. Federal aid; Grants-in-aid; Research grants
BPI   FINANCE, PUBLIC; s.a. Bonds, Government; Fiscal policy; Grants-in-aid

ECONOMIC ASSISTANCE, FOREIGN
Scope: Works on international economic aid given in various forms.
LC   ECONOMIC ASSISTANCE; s.a. Exchange of patents and technical information; International cooperation; International relief; Investments, Foreign; Loans; U.N.—Economic assistance
SEARS ECONOMIC ASSISTANCE; s.a. Economic policy; International economic relations; Reconstruction—1939-1951; Underdeveloped areas
RG   ECONOMIC ASSISTANCE; s.a. Agricultural assistance; Economic relations; Industrialization; International cooperation
NYT FOREIGN AID; s.a. Commerce; Economic conditions and trends (general); specific subjects for which aid is given, e.g., Education and schools
PAIS ECONOMIC ASSISTANCE; s.a. Industrial development; subd. *Economic assistance program* under names of countries; Technical assistance; U.S.—Economic assistance programs; U.S.—International development agency
BPI   ECONOMIC ASSISTANCE; s.a. Economic assistance, American; Food relief; Technical assistance; Underdeveloped areas; U.S.—Agency for international development

ECONOMIC CHANGE. *Use* Progress

ECONOMIC CONCENTRATION. *See* Big Business

ECONOMIC CONDITIONS AND TRENDS. *Use* Business Cycles; Consumption (Economic); Cost and Standard of Living; Credit; Depressions; Economic Development; Economic History; Economics; Industrialization; Inflation (Finance); Overproduction; Welfare Economics

ECONOMIC CYCLES. *See* Business Cycles

ECONOMIC DEPRESSIONS. *See* Depressions

ECONOMIC DEVELOPMENT
Scope: Works on the theory and policy of economic development; for a particular area see the name of the area with the subds. *Economic conditions, Economic policy or Industries.*
LC   ——; s.a. Industrialization; Saving and investment; Statistics and dynamics (social sciences); Underdeveloped areas
SEARS ECONOMIC CONDITIONS; s.a. Business; Economic policy; Geography, Commercial; Natural resources
RG   ——; s.a. Development banks; Production
NYT ECONOMIC CONDITIONS AND TRENDS (General); s.a. Economics; Foreign aid
PAIS ——; s.a. Community development; Technical assistance; Underdeveloped states
BPI   ——; s.a. Industrialization; Underdeveloped areas

ECONOMIC DEVELOPMENT—SOCIAL ASPECTS. *Use* Social Change

ECONOMIC FORECASTING. *Use* Business Cycles;
Business Forecasting

ECONOMIC GEOGRAPHY. *Use* Geography

ECONOMIC HISTORY
LC ———; s.a. Automation—Economic aspects; subd.
Economic conditions under names of geographical
areas
SEARS ECONOMIC CONDITIONS; s.a. Business cycles;
Economic policy; Geography, Commercial; Labor
supply; Natural resources; Statistics
RG ———; s.a. Business conditions; Standard of
living
NYT ECONOMIC CONDITIONS AND TRENDS
(General); s.a. Economics; History; subd.
Economic Conditions and Trends under names
of countries
PAIS ———; s.a. Business history; Economic condi-
tions
BPI ———; s.a. Banks and banking—History; Industry—
History; subd. *Economic history* under names of
geographical areas

ECONOMIC HISTORY—MEDIEVAL. *Use* Feudalism

ECONOMIC IMPERIALISM. *See* Imperialism

ECONOMIC LIFE (Of economic goods). *Use* Depreciation; Machinery

ECONOMIC MODELS. *Use* Business Forecasting;
Economics, Mathematical; Operations
Research

ECONOMIC NATIONALISM. *Use* Nationalism

ECONOMIC PLANNING. *See* Economic Policy

ECONOMIC POLICY
Scope: Works on the policy of governments towards
economic problems. See also subds. *Commercial
policy* and *Economic policy* under names of
countries.
LC ———; s.a. Autarchy; Economic development;
Inflation (finance); Laissez-faire; Mercantile
system; Priorities, Industrial; Welfare economics
SEARS ———; s.a. Commercial policy; Free trade and
protection; Manpower policy; Subsidies; Tariff
RG ———; s.a. Deflation (finance); Industrialization
NYT ECONOMICS; s.a. Finance; U.S.—Finances—
Budget
PAIS ———; s.a. Full employment policies; Industrial
mobilization; Industry and state
BPI ———; s.a. Deflation; Economic stabilization;
Prices; Social policy

ECONOMIC RELATIONS. *Use* Economic Assistance,
Foreign; International Relations

ECONOMIC SECURITY. *Use* Guaranteed Annual Income; Insurance, Social; Minimum Wage; Social
Policy; Welfare Economics

ECONOMIC STABILIZATION. *Use* Business Cycles;
Depressions; Economic Policy; Overproduction

ECONOMIC STATISTICS. *Use* Economics, Mathematical; Statistics

ECONOMIC SURVEYS. *Use* Social Surveys

ECONOMICS
LC ———; s.a. Business; Commerce; Economic de-
velopment; Economic history; Economists;
Industry; Macroeconomics; Microeconomics;
Substitution (economics)
SEARS ———; s.a. Cost and standard of living; Depres-
sions; Economic conditions; Economic policy;
Government ownership; Industry; Labor and
laboring classes; Profit; Property
RG ———; s.a. Consumption (economics); Wealth,
Distribution of
NYT ———; s.a. Communism; Economic conditions
and trends (general); Finance
PAIS ———; s.a. Banking; Capitalism; Credit; Keynesian
economics
BPI ———; s.a. Economic policy; Finance; Keynesian
economics; Supply and demand

ECONOMICS, MATHEMATICAL
LC ———; s.a. Econometrics; Information theory in
economics; Interindustry economics
SEARS ECONOMICS; s.a. Statistics
RG ———; s.a. Economic models; Economic
statistics
NYT ECONOMICS; s.a. Mathematics; Statistics
PAIS ECONOMETRICS; s.a. Economic models; Input-
output data
BPI ———; s.a. Economic models; Statistics

ECONOMICS, PRIMITIVE. *Use* Society, Primitive

ECONOMICS OF WAR. *See* War—Economic Aspects

ECONOMISTS. *Use* Economics

ECONOMY. *See* Saving and Savings

ECUMENICAL MOVEMENT. *Use* Catholicity; Christianity

EDIBLE PLANTS. *See* Plants

EDITING
Scope: Works on the editing of books and texts.
LC ———; s.a. Authorship—Handbooks, manuals,
etc.; Copy-reading; Criticism, Textual; Printing,
Practical—Style manuals
SEARS JOURNALISM; s.a. Publishers and publishing
RG EDITORS AND EDITING; s.a. Publishers and
publishing; Style, Literary
NYT BOOKS AND LITERATURE; s.a. Books and
literature—Book trade—U.S.; Writing and
writers
PAIS EDITORS AND EDITING; s.a. Journalism; subd.
Editorial policy under specific media, e.g., News-
papers—Editorial policy
BPI ———; s.a. Authors and publishers; Publishers
and publishing

EDUCABILITY. *Use* Learning, Psychology of

EDUCATION
See also specific types of education, e.g., Adult education;
Audio-visual education; Business education;
Character education; Classical education; Com-
merical education; Compensatory education;
Domestic education; International education;
Legal education; Medical education; Military
education; Professional education; Religious
education; Technical education; Vocational
education

EDUCATION, *cont.*

LC ———; s.a. Academic achievement; Coeducation; Degrees, Academic; Education, Humanistic; Home and school; Illiteracy; Learning and scholarship; Manual training; Schools, Self-culture; Universities and colleges

SEARS ———; s.a. Books and reading; Correspondence schools and courses; Culture; Evening and continuation schools; Study, Method of

RG ———; s.a. Knowledge; Teaching

NYT EDUCATION AND SCHOOLS; s.a. Colleges and universities; Correspondence schools and courses

PAIS ———; s.a. Literacy; Research; Students; University extension

BPI ———; s.a. Business schools and colleges; Colleges and universities; High schools; Public schools

EDUCATION, ADULT. *Use* Adult Education; Evening and Continuation Schools

EDUCATION—AIDS AND DEVICES. *Use* Audio-Visual Education; Educational Technology; Instructional Materials Center; Moving Pictures in Education; Programmed Instruction; Radio in Education; Teaching; Television in Education

EDUCATION, BILINGUAL

LC ———; s.a. Bilingualism; Intercultural education

SEARS BILINGUALISM; s.a. Language and languages

RG ———; s.a. Bilingual instruction; Intercultural education

NYT EDUCATION AND SCHOOLS; s.a. Colleges and universities; Language and languages

PAIS ———; s.a. Bilingualism; Intercultural education

BPI EDUCATION; s.a. Language and languages; Schools

EDUCATION, BOARDS OF. *Use* Educational Administration

EDUCATION, COMPULSORY

LC ———; s.a. Children—Employment; Educational law and legislation; School census

SEARS ———; s.a. Evening and continuation schools; School attendance

RG COMPULSORY EDUCATION; s.a. School attendance; School phobia

NYT EDUCATION AND SCHOOLS

PAIS SCHOOL ATTENDANCE, COMPULSORY

BPI EDUCATION; s.a. Schools

EDUCATION, COOPERATIVE

Scope: Works dealing with the plan of instruction under which students spend alternating periods in school and in a practical occupation.

LC ———; s.a. Field work (educational method); Industry and education; Vocational education

SEARS APPRENTICES; s.a. Employees—Training; Vocational education

RG ———; s.a. Apprentices; Vocational education

NYT COLLEGES AND UNIVERSITIES; s.a. Commercial education; Education and schools; Labor

PAIS ———; s.a. Interns (business); Vocational education

BPI ———; s.a. Occupational training; Vocational education

EDUCATION—CURRICULA

See also subd. *Curricula* under specific types of education, e.g., Technical education—Curricula; University—Curricula. For course of study in particular subjects see subd. *Study and teaching* under subjects, e.g., Mathematics—Study and teaching.

LC ———; s.a. Curriculum laboratories; Curriculum planning

SEARS ———; s.a. Articulation (education)

RG COURSES OF STUDY; s.a. Curriculum planning; Schedules, School

NYT EDUCATION AND SCHOOLS; s.a. Colleges and universities; Commercial education

PAIS COLLEGES AND UNIVERSITIES—COURSES OF STUDY; s.a. Schools—Courses of study

BPI EDUCATION; s.a. Colleges and universities; Schools

EDUCATION, ELEMENTARY. *Use* Education, Preschool; Education, Primary; Exceptional Children

EDUCATION, EXPERIMENTAL. *Use* Education, Primary; Educational Planning and Innovations; Nongraded schools

EDUCATION—FEDERAL AID. *Use* Education and State

EDUCATION—FINANCE. *Use* College Costs; Education and State

EDUCATION, HIGHER

LC ———; s.a. Classical education; Education of adults; Higher education and state; Junior colleges; Universities and colleges; Women's colleges

SEARS ———; s.a. Adult education; College education, Value of; Colleges and universities; Technical education

RG COLLEGE EDUCATION; s.a. Liberal education; Professional education

NYT COLLEGES AND UNIVERSITIES; s.a. Commercial education

PAIS COLLEGES AND UNIVERSITIES; s.a. Degrees, Academic; University extension

BPI COLLEGES AND UNIVERSITIES; s.a. Education; Junior colleges

EDUCATION, HUMANISTIC. *Use* Education

EDUCATION, INDUSTRIAL. *See* Technical Education

EDUCATION — INTEGRATION AND SEGREGATION. *Use* Busing; Discrimination in Education

EDUCATION—METHODS. *See* Teaching

EDUCATION, MUSICAL. *See* Music Education

EDUCATION—PERSONNEL SERVICE. *See* Personnel Service in Education

EDUCATION, PHYSICAL. *See* Physical Fitness

EDUCATION, PRESCHOOL

LC ———; s.a. Agaszi method of education; Child study; Day nurseries; Nurseries; Nursery schools

SEARS NURSERY SCHOOLS; s.a. Day nurseries; Education, Elementary; Kindergartens

RG   PRESCHOOL CHILDREN—EDUCATION; s.a. Kindergarten; Montessori method of education; Nursery schools

NYT   NURSERY SCHOOLS; s.a. Children and youth—Behavior and training; Education and schools

PAIS   ——; s.a. Kindergartens; Nursery schools

BPI   PRESCHOOL EDUCATION; s.a. Child welfare; Day nurseries

EDUCATION, PRIMARY
LC   ——; s.a. Creative activities and seat work; Education, Elementary; Education of children; Kindergarten; Readiness for school

SEARS   EDUCATION, ELEMENTARY; s.a. Exceptional children; Montessori method of education; Nursery schools

RG   EDUCATION, ELEMENTARY; s.a. Education of children; Education, Experimental; Nursery schools; Open plan schools; Schools, Experimental; Special classes and special schools

NYT   EDUCATION AND SCHOOLS; s.a. Nursery schools

PAIS   ——; s.a. Children, Exceptional—Education; Children, Gifted—Education; Children, Handicapped—Education

BPI   EDUCATION; s.a. Children; Schools

EDUCATION, RELIGIOUS. *See* Religious Education

EDUCATION, RURAL. *Use* Rural Conditions

EDUCATION, SECONDARY
LC   ——; s.a. Education of adults; Eight year study; High schools; Junior high schools

SEARS   ——; s.a. Evening and continuation schools; Junior high schools; Private schools; Public schools

RG   ——; s.a. High schools; Private schools

NYT   EDUCATION AND SCHOOLS; s.a. Education and schools—U. S.—Prep schools

PAIS   ——; s.a. High schools; Schools, Private

BPI   HIGH SCHOOLS; s.a. Education; Public schools

EDUCATION—STUDY AND TEACHING. *Use* Educational Psychology; Observation (Educational method); Teachers, Training of

EDUCATION AND DEMOCRACY. *Use* Citizenship; Democracy

EDUCATION AND HEREDITY. *Use* Academic Achievement; Educational Psychology

EDUCATION AND INDUSTRY. *Use* Industry and Education

EDUCATION AND STATE
LC   ——; s.a. Academic freedom; Church schools; Community and school; Endowment of research; Federal aid to higher education; Nationalism and education; Private schools; Scholarships; State aid to education

SEARS   ——; s.a. Education—Finance; Federal aid to education; Scholarships, fellowships, etc.; State aid to education

RG   ——; s.a. Church schools; College education and state; Education—Federal aid; Negro colleges and universities—Federal aid; subd. *Federal aid* under types of school, e.g., High schools—Federal aid

NYT   EDUCATION AND SCHOOLS—U. S.—SCHOOL ADMINISTRATION AND COMMUNITY ROLE; s.a. Education and schools; Education and schools—U. S.—Sectarian schools; Politics and government

PAIS   ——; s.a. Colleges and universities—Federal aid; Negro colleges—Federal aid; Parochial schools—State aid

BPI   ——; s.a. Federal aid to education; Right to read program

EDUCATION MARKET. *Use* Textbooks

EDUCATION OF ADULTS. *Use* Adult Education

EDUCATION OF CHILDREN. *Use* Children; Education, Primary

EDUCATION OF GIRLS. *See* Education of Women

EDUCATION OF PRISONERS. *Use* Adult Education; Prisons and Prisoners

EDUCATION OF WOMEN
LC   ——; s.a. Coeducation; Women college graduates; Women college students

SEARS   ——; s.a. Coeducation; Girls; University students; Young women

RG   ——; s.a. Coeducation; College students, Women; Law students, Women; Negro students, Women

NYT   COLLEGES AND UNIVERSITIES—U. S.—WOMEN'S EDUCATION AND INSTITUTIONS; s.a. Colleges and universities—U. S.—Enrollment; Women

PAIS   WOMEN—EDUCATION; s.a. Coeducation; Women's colleges

BPI   ——; s.a. Colleges and universities; Graduate students; Students; Women—Employment

EDUCATION OF WORKERS. *Use* Adult Education; Evening and Continuation Schools

EDUCATIONAL ADMINISTRATION
LC   SCHOOL MANAGEMENT AND ORGANIZATION; s.a. Deans (in schools); Educational Planning; Personnel service in education; Principal-superintendent relationship; School boards; School supervisors, Training of; Self-government (in education); State boards of education; Teacher-principal relationship

SEARS   SCHOOL ADMINISTRATION AND ORGANIZATION; s.a. Articulation (education); Educators; School superintendents and principals; School supervision

RG   SCHOOL MANAGEMENT AND ORGANIZATION; s.a. College deans; Colleges and universities—Administration; Teacher-administrator relationships; Teachers and school boards

NYT   EDUCATION AND SCHOOLS—U. S.—ADMINISTRATION; s.a. Colleges and universities—Administration; Education and schools—(U. S.)—School administration and community role; Teachers and school employees

PAIS   SCHOOL ADMINISTRATION AND ORGANIZATION; s.a. College officials; Deans; Educators; Faculty participation in administration; School officials; School personnel management; School principals; School superintendents

EDUCATIONAL ADMINISTRATION, *cont.*
BPI   SCHOOL MANAGEMENT AND ORGANIZA-
TION; s.a. Class size

EDUCATIONAL ASSOCIATIONS. *Use* Teachers

EDUCATIONAL BROADCASTING. *Use* Radio in
Education; Television in Education

EDUCATIONAL DISCRIMINATION. *See* Discrimination in Education

EDUCATIONAL FILMS. *See* Moving Pictures in Education

EDUCATIONAL GAMES. *Use* Recreation

EDUCATIONAL GUIDANCE. *Use* Vocational Guidance

EDUCATIONAL INNOVATIONS. *Use* Educational
Planning and Innovations

EDUCATIONAL LAW AND LEGISLATION. *Use* Education, Compulsory; School Attendance

EDUCATIONAL MEDIA PERSONNEL. *Use* Audio-
Visual Education

EDUCATIONAL PLANNING AND INNOVATIONS
LC   EDUCATIONAL PLANNING; s.a. Demonstra-
tion centers in education; Education—Experi-
mental methods; Educational innovations;
Laboratory schools; Teaching demonstrations
SEARS EDUCATION—CURRICULA; s.a. Education—
Experimental methods; Free schools; Teaching—
Aids and devices
RG   EDUCATIONAL PLANNING; s.a. Curriculum
planning; Education, Experimental; Educational
innovations; Open plan schools; Schools, Experimental
NYT   EDUCATION AND SCHOOLS; s.a. Colleges
and universities—U.S.—Campus administration
PAIS   EDUCATIONAL PLANNING; s.a. Colleges and
universities—Administration; Innovation in
education
BPI   EDUCATIONAL PLANNING; s.a. Audio-visual
instruction; Programmed instruction; School
management and organization; Schools

EDUCATIONAL PSYCHOLOGY
LC   ——; s.a. Ability grouping in education;
Comprehension; Education and heredity;
Formal discipline; Listening; Rewards and
punishments in education; School psychologists;
Transfer of training
SEARS ——; s.a. Apperception; Attention; Heredity;
Imagination; Memory; Psychology, Applied
RG   PSYCHOLOGY, EDUCATIONAL; s.a. Intelli-
gence level; Learning, Psychology of; School
psychologists
NYT   PSYCHOLOGY AND PSYCHOLOGISTS; s.a.
Education and schools
PAIS   ——; s.a. Child study; Heredity; Learning
ability
BPI   PSYCHOLOGY; s.a. Child study; Education;
Learning, Psychology of; Teaching

EDUCATIONAL SURVEYS. *Use* Social Surveys

EDUCATIONAL TECHNOLOGY
LC   ——; s.a. Audio-visual education; Teaching—
Aids and devices

SEARS TEACHING—AIDS AND DEVICES; s.a. Audio-
visual materials; Moving pictures in education;
Teaching machines
RG   TEACHING—AIDS AND DEVICES; s.a.
Computers—Educational use; Instructional
materials centers
NYT   EDUCATION AND SCHOOLS; s.a. Education
and schools—U.S.—Teaching aids; Science and
technology
PAIS   EDUCATION—AIDS AND DEVICES; s.a.
Audio-visual equipment; Innovation in educa-
tion; Programmed instruction
BPI   TEACHING—AIDS AND DEVICES; s.a.
Electronics in education; Simulators; Teaching
machines; Television in education

EDUCATIONAL TESTS AND MEASUREMENTS. *Use*
Ability—Testing; Examinations; Grading and
Marking (Students); Occupational Aptitude
Tests; Personality Tests; Tests, Mental

EDUCATIONAL WORKSHOPS. *Use* Summer Schools

EDUCATORS
LC   ——; s.a. Deans (in schools); Education; Educa-
tional administration; Teachers
SEARS ——; s.a. Education; Teachers
RG   ——; s.a. College professors and instructors;
Negro educators
NYT   TEACHERS AND SCHOOL EMPLOYEES; s.a.
Colleges and universities; Education and schools;
names of specific educators, e.g., Montessori,
Maria; Piaget, Jean, etc.
PAIS   ——; s.a. School officials; Teachers
BPI   TEACHERS; s.a. College teachers; Education

EFFICIENCY, ADMINISTRATIVE. *Use* Decision
Making; Management

EFFICIENCY, INDUSTRIAL. *Use* Engineering; Factory
Management; Industrial Management; Manage-
ment; Organization; Performance Standards;
Production Control; Production Standards; Work
Measurement

EFFICIENCY, PERSONAL. *Use* Success

EGG INDUSTRY. *Use* Poultry Industry

EGO (Psychology). *Use* Psychoanalysis

EGYPTOLOGY. *Use* Oriental Studies

EIDETIC IMAGERY. *Use* Memory

EKISTICS. *Use* Human Ecology

ELASTICITY. *Use* Strength of Materials

ELECTION (Wills). *Use* Wills

ELECTION DISTRICTS. *Use* Apportionment (Election
law)

ELECTION FORECASTING. *Use* Elections; Public
Opinion

ELECTION LAW. *Use* Elections; Voters, Registration of

ELECTIONEERING
LC   ——; s.a. Advertising, Political; Radio in
politics; Television in politics

SEARS POLITICS, PRACTICAL; s.a. Campaign funds; Primaries; Television in politics
RG POLITICAL CAMPAIGNS; s.a. Campaign issues; Presidential campaigns
NYT ELECTIONS (U.S.); s.a. Presidential Election—Election of (year); U.S.—Politics and government
PAIS CAMPAIGNS, POLITICAL; s.a. Advertising, Political; Campaign literature
BPI POLITICS, PRACTICAL; s.a. Political advertising; Politics, Corruption in; Television and politics

ELECTIONS
LC ——; s.a. Advertising, Political; Apportionment (election law); Australian ballot; Ballot; Business and politics; Campaign management; Election forecasting; Election law; Elections, Nonpartisan; Local elections; Nominations for office; Plebiscite; Political parties; Politics, Practical; Voters, Registration of; Voting; subd. *Elections* under names of legislative bodies under names of countries, e.g., Great Britain—Parliament—Elections
SEARS ——; s.a. Presidents—U.S.—Election; Representative government and representation; Suffrage
RG ——; s.a. Campaign management; Suffrage
NYT ELECTIONS (U.S.); s.a. Presidential election of (year); U.S.—Politics and government
PAIS ——; s.a. Candidates; Local elections; Primaries
BPI ——; s.a. Campaign funds; Primaries; Referendum; Voting

ELECTIONS—CORRUPT PRACTICES. *Use* Corruption (In politics)

ELECTIONS, PRIMARY. *See* Political Parties

ELECTORAL COLLEGE. *Use* Presidents

ELECTRIC APPARATUS AND APPLIANCES. *Use* Electric Motors

ELECTRIC APPLIANCES AND EQUIPMENT (Fixtures). *Use* Lighting

ELECTRIC COMMUNICATION. *See* Telecommunication

ELECTRIC ENGINEERING. *Use* Electric Motors; Mechanical Engineering

ELECTRIC FISHING. *Use* Fisheries

ELECTRIC HEATING. *Use* Heating

ELECTRIC INDUSTRIES. *Use* Electric Power Plants

ELECTRIC LIGHT AND POWER. *Use* Electric Power Plants; Fuel; Lighting

ELECTRIC LIGHTING. *Use* Lighting

ELECTRIC LINES. *Use* Electric Power Plants

ELECTRIC MACHINERY. *Use* Electric Motors

ELECTRIC MACHINERY INDUSTRY. *Use* Machinery—Trade and Manufacture

ELECTRIC MEASUREMENTS. *Use* Weights and Measures

ELECTRIC MOTORS
LC ——; s.a. Armatures; Automobiles, Electric; Electric railway motors; Electric vehicles; Industrial electric trucks
SEARS ——; s.a. Electric apparatus and appliances; Electric machinery; Electric transformers; Electricity in mining
RG ——; s.a. Automobiles, Electric; Outboard motors
NYT ENGINEERING AND ENGINEERS; s.a. Electricity; Engines; Machinery, Industrial equipment and supplies
PAIS ELECTRIC MOTOR INDUSTRY; s.a. Electric engineering; Motor vehicles, Electric
BPI ——; s.a. Electric driving; Electronic apparatus and appliances

ELECTRIC NETWORKS. *Use* System Analysis

ELECTRIC POWER DISTRIBUTION. *Use* Electric Power Plants

ELECTRIC POWER FAILURES. *Use* Electric Power Plants

ELECTRIC POWER PLANTS
LC ——; s.a. Electric power systems; Interconnected electric utility systems; Water-power electric plants
SEARS ——; s.a. Electric power distribution; Electric power failures; Power transmission
RG ELECTRIC POWER DISTRIBUTION; s.a. Electric lines; Electric plants—Interconnection
NYT ELECTRIC LIGHT AND POWER; s.a. Atomic energy and weapons—Electric light and power; Electricity; Public utilities
PAIS ——; s.a. Atomic power plants; Electric generator sets
BPI ELECTRIC POWER DISTRIBUTION; s.a. Electric industries; Electric power plants—Interconnection

ELECTRIC POWER SYSTEMS. *Use* Electric Power Plants

ELECTRIC RAILROADS. *Use* Railroads

ELECTRIC SERVICE, RURAL. *Use* Rural Conditions

ELECTRIC SIGNS. *Use* Billboards; Signs and Symbols

ELECTRIC SUSPENSION. *Use* Bearings (Machinery)

ELECTRIC UTILITIES. *See* Electric Power Plants

ELECTRIC UTILITIES—GOVERNMENT OWNERSHIP. *Use* Municipal Ownership

ELECTRIC VEHICLES. *Use* Electric Motors

ELECTRICITY. *Use* Electric Motors; Electric Power Plants

ELECTRICITY IN AGRICULTURE. *Use* Rural Conditions

ELECTRIFICATION, RURAL. *See* Rural Conditions

ELECTROCHEMISTRY. *Use* Chemistry

ELECTROCUTION. *Use* Capital Punishment

ELECTROENCEPHALOGRAPHY. *Use* Brain

ELECTROMECHANICAL DEVICES. *Use* Mechanical Engineering

ELECTROMETALLURGY. *Use* Steel Industry and Trade

ELECTRONIC ANALOG COMPUTERS. *Use* Computers (Electronic computers)

ELECTRONIC APPARATUS AND APPLIANCES. *Use* Electric Motors

ELECTRONIC CALCULATING MACHINES. *Use* Cybernetics

ELECTRONIC DATA AND PROCESSING EQUIPMENT. *Use* Office Equipment and Supplies

ELECTRONIC DATA PROCESSING
LC ——; s.a. Automation; Data tapes; Electronic calculating machines; Electronic data processing departments; Information storage and retrieval systems; Linear programming; Programming (electronic computers); Programming languages (electronic computers)
SEARS ——; s.a. Computers; Information sciences; Programming languages (electronic computers)
RG ——; s.a. Artificial intelligence; Data processing service centers; Data transmission systems; Information systems, Management
NYT DATA PROCESSING (INFORMATION PROCESSING) EQUIPMENT AND SYSTEMS; s.a. Electronics; Research
PAIS INFORMATION PROCESSING SYSTEMS; s.a. Computer programming; Electronic data processing equipment; subd. *Information processing systems* under specific subjects, e.g., Banking—Information processing systems
BPI ——; s.a. Computer lease and rental services; Computer programming; Information storage and retrieval systems

ELECTRONIC DATA PROCESSING EQUIPMENT. *Use* Information Storage and Retrieval Systems

ELECTRONIC DIGITAL COMPUTERS. *Use* Computers

ELECTRONIC MUSIC. *Use* Music

ELECTRONIC OFFICE MACHINES. *Use* Office Equipment and Supplies

ELECTRONIC SURVEILLANCE. *See* Wiretapping

ELECTRONICS. *Use* Computers; Cybernetics; Data Transmission Systems; Electronic Data Processing; High-Fidelity Sound Systems; Information Storage and Retrieval Systems; Programming (Electronic computers); Radio—Apparatus and Supplies

ELECTRONICS IN CRIMINAL INVESTIGATION, ESPIONAGE, ETC. *Use* Detectives; Wiretapping

ELECTRONS. *Use* Atoms; Nuclear Physics

ELECTROSTATIC PRINTING. *Use* Copying Processes

ELECTROSURGERY. *Use* Surgery

ELECTROTHERAPEUTICS. *Use* Massage; Physical Therapy; Radiotherapy

ELECTROTYPING. *Use* Printing Industry

ELEMENTARY EDUCATION. *See* Education, Primary

ELEMENTARY EDUCATION OF ADULTS. *Use* Illiteracy

ELEMENTS. *Use* Nuclear Physics

ELITE (Social sciences)
LC ——; s.a. Caste; Leadership; Social classes; Social groups; Upperclasses
SEARS SOCIAL CLASSES; s.a. Aristocracy; Leadership; Nobility
RG ——; s.a. Leadership; Negro leadership
NYT SOCIAL SCIENCES; s.a. Nobility; Sociology
PAIS ——; s.a. Leadership; Social status
BPI ——; s.a. Executives; Leadership

ELOCUTION. *Use* Lectures and Lecturing; Speech; Voice

EMANCIPATION OF SLAVES. *See* Slavery

EMANCIPATION OF WOMEN. *See* Woman—Rights of Women

EMBARGO. *Use* International Offenses

EMBASSIES. *See* Diplomacy

EMBEZZLEMENT. *Use* Fraud; Theft

EMBLEMS
LC ——; s.a. Christian art and symbolism; Emblems, National; Genealogy, Regalia (insignia); Signs and symbols
SEARS INSIGNIA; s.a. Decorations of honor; Mottoes; Symbolism
RG ——; s.a. Corporations—Flags, insignia, etc.; Flags; Heraldry; Insignia
NYT FLAGS, EMBLEMS AND INSIGNIA
PAIS ——; s.a. Campaign insignia; Flags; Insignia; Signals and signaling
BPI ——; s.a. Industrial design coordination; Trademarks

EMBRIOLOGY. *Use* Embryology

EMBROIDERY. *Use* Beadwork; Sewing

EMBRYOLOGY
LC ——; s.a. Biology; Fetus; Genetics; Ontogeny; Ovulation; Spermatogenesis
SEARS ——; s.a. Cells; Protoplasm; Reproduction
RG ——; s.a. Differentiation (biology); Metamorphosis
NYT EMBRYOLOGY (Fetology); s.a. Biology and biochemistry; Pregnancy, Obstetrics and maternal welfare; Reproduction (biological)
PAIS BIOLOGY
BPI REPRODUCTION; s.a. Fertilization (biology)

EMBRYOLOGY, EXPERIMENTAL—MORAL AND RELIGIOUS ASPECTS. *Use* Medical Ethics

EMERGENCIES. *See* Accidents; First Aid in Illness and Injury

EMERGENCY COMMUNICATION SYSTEMS. *Use* Civil Defense; Telecommunication

EMERGENCY HOUSING. *Use* Disaster Relief

EMERGENCY MEDICAL SERVICES. *Use* First Aid in Illness and Injury; Rescue Work

EMERGENCY POWERS. *Use* Executive Power

EMERGENCY RELIEF. *See* Disaster Relief

EMIGRANTS. *See* Citizenship

EMIGRATION AND IMMIGRATION
Scope: Works on migration from one country to
another. For works on the movement of
population within a country see Migration—
Internal. See also names of nationalities, e.g.,
Italians in the U.S.
LC ——; s.a. Assimilation—Sociology; Asylum,
Right of; Colonies; Immigrants in literature;
Man—Migrations; Migration of nations; Popula-
tion transfers; Repatriation; subds. *Emigration
and immigration* and *Foreign population* under
names of countries
SEARS IMMIGRATION AND EMIGRATION; s.a.
Anthropogeography; Colonization; Naturaliza-
tion; Refugees; subds. *Immigration and emigra-
tion* and *Foreign population* under names of
countries
RG IMMIGRATION AND EMIGRATION; s.a.
Alien labor
NYT IMMIGRATION AND EMIGRATION; s.a.
Citizenship; Freedom and human rights; Popula-
tion and vital statistics
PAIS IMMIGRATION AND EMIGRATION; s.a.
Aliens; Deportation; Freedom of movement; Im-
migrants
BPI IMMIGRATION AND EMIGRATION; s.a. Civil
rights; Migration, Internal

EMIGRÉS. *Use* Asylum, Right of; Exiles

EMINENT DOMAIN. *Use* Abandonment of Property;
Land; Property; Public Lands; Real Property

EMINENT DOMAIN (International law). *Use* Nationalization

EMOTIONAL MATURITY. *Use* Emotions

EMOTIONAL PROBLEMS OF CHILDREN. *Use* Child
Study

EMOTIONALLY DISTURBED CHILDREN. *See*
Problem Children

EMOTIONS
See also names of specific emotions, e.g., Ambivalence;
Antipathy; Anxiety; Bashfulness; Crying; Desire;
Empathy; Envy; Fear; Frustration; Grief; Hate;
Jealousy; Laughter; Love; Melancholy; Pain;
Pleasure; Shame; Sympathy; Timidity; Worry.
LC ——; s.a. Avoidance (psychology); Belief and
doubt; Emotional maturity; Emotional problems
of children; Escape (psychology)
SEARS ——; s.a. Attitude (psychology); Joy and sorrow;
Prejudices and antipathies
RG ——; s.a. Moods; Motivation (psychology);
Psychology, Physiological; Temperament
NYT PSYCHOLOGY AND PSYCHOLOGISTS; s.a.
Children and youth—Behavior and training
PAIS BEHAVIOR (PSYCHOLOGY); s.a. Child
psychology; Motivation (psychology)
BPI ——; s.a. Personality; Psychology

EMPATHY. *Use* Emotions; Human Relations; Prejudices
and Antipathies

EMPERORS. *Use* Heads of State

EMPIRICISM. *Use* Knowledge, Theory of; Rationalism

EMPLOYEE ABSENTEEISM. *See* Absenteeism (Labor)

EMPLOYEE ATTITUDE. *Use* Attitude (Psychology)

EMPLOYEE BENEFITS. *See* Non-wage Payments

EMPLOYEE COMPETITIVE BEHAVIOR. *Use* Incentives
in Industry; Morale

EMPLOYEE COUNSELING. *Use* Counseling

EMPLOYEE INCENTIVES. *See* Incentives in Industry

EMPLOYEE MORALE. *Use* Incentives in Industry;
Industrial Sociology; Job Analysis; Morale

EMPLOYEE OWNERSHIP. *Use* Incentives in Industry

EMPLOYEE PENSION TRUSTS. *See* Pensions

EMPLOYEES. *Use* Clerks

EMPLOYEES, DISMISSAL OF. *Use* Labor Laws and
Legislation

EMPLOYEES—LEAVES OF ABSENCE. *Use* Vacations,
Employee

EMPLOYEES—MILITARY SERVICE. *Use* Military
Service, Compulsory

EMPLOYEES, RATING OF. *Use* Performance Standards

EMPLOYEES, RECRUITING OF. *See* Recruiting of
Employees

EMPLOYEES, RELOCATION OF. *Use* Labor Supply

EMPLOYEES, SUPERVISION OF. *See* Supervision of
Employees

EMPLOYEES, TEMPORARY. *Use* Employment

EMPLOYEES—TRAINING. *Use* Apprentices; Education,
Cooperative; Occupational Training; Technical
Education; Vocational Education

EMPLOYEES, TRANSFER OF. *Use* Labor Supply;
Migration, Internal

EMPLOYEES AS STOCKHOLDERS. *Use* Stock Exchange

EMPLOYEES' BENEFIT PLANS. *Use* Non-wage Payments

EMPLOYEES' INVENTIONS. *See* Inventions

EMPLOYEES' REPRESENTATION IN MANAGEMENT.
Use Collective Bargaining; Industrial Relations;
Personnel Management; Work Councils

EMPLOYEES' SAVINGS PLANS. *Use* Saving and Savings

EMPLOYEES' TRUSTS. *Use* Trusts and Trustees

EMPLOYER-EMPLOYEE RELATIONS. *See* Industrial
Relations

EMPLOYERS' LIABILITY. *Use* Liability (Law);
Negligence; Obligations; Occupations, Dangerous;
Personal Injuries; Workmen's Compensation

EMPLOYMENT
LC LABOR SUPPLY; s.a. Applications for employment; Economic policy; Employment (economic
theory); Employment forecasting; Free choice of
employment; Full employment policies; Recruiting of employees; Supplementary employment; Woman—Employment

EMPLOYMENT, *cont.*
SEARS   LABOR AND LABORING CLASSES; s.a.
         Economics; Labor supply; Manpower policy;
         subd. *Employment* under names of groups of
         people, e.g., Blacks–Employment; Unemployed
RG   ——; s.a. Discrimination in employment;
         Seasonal labor; Student employment; Working
         life, Length of
NYT   LABOR; s.a. Economics
PAIS   ——; s.a. Blacklisting; Employment–Socially
         handicapped; Full employment policies; Tem-
         porary employment; Unemployment
BPI   ——; s.a. Employees, Temporary; Labor
         supply; Part-time employment; Unemployment

EMPLOYMENT–DISABLED. *Use* Handicapped; Vocational Rehabilitation

EMPLOYMENT–MOTHERS. *Use* Mothers; Nurseries;
Woman-Employment

EMPLOYMENT–STUDENT WITHDRAWALS. *Use* Dropouts

EMPLOYMENT–WOMEN. *Use* Woman–Employment

EMPLOYMENT–YOUTH. *Use* Child Labor

EMPLOYMENT AGENCIES. *Use* Applications for
Positions; Labor Supply; Recruiting of Employees

EMPLOYMENT AND AGE. *See* Age and Employment

EMPLOYMENT DISCRIMINATION. *See* Discrimination in Employment

EMPLOYMENT FORECASTING. *Use* Employment;
Labor Supply

EMPLOYMENT IN FOREIGN COUNTRIES. *Use*
Americans in Foreign Countries

EMPLOYMENT INTERVIEWING. *Use* Applications for
Positions; Interviewing; Recruiting of Employees

EMPLOYMENT MANAGEMENT. *See* Personnel Management

EMPLOYMENT OF CHILDREN. *See* Child Labor

EMPLOYMENT OF WOMEN. *See* Woman–Employment

EMPLOYMENT REFERENCES. *Use* Applications for
Positions

EMPLOYMENT STABILIZATION. *Use* Guaranteed
Annual Income

EMPLOYMENT TAX. *See* Federal Tax

EMPLOYMENT TESTS. *Use* Occupational Aptitude
Tests

ENAMEL AND ENAMELING. *Use* Ceramics

ENCEPHALITIS. *Use* Brain

ENCOUNTER GROUPS. *See* Group Relations Training

ENCOUNTER THERAPY. *See* Behavior Therapy

ENCYCLOPEDIAS AND DICTIONARIES. *Use* Handbooks

ENDOWMENT OF RESEARCH. *Use* Education and
State; Science and State

ENDOWMENTS. *Use* Charitable Uses, Trusts and Foundations; Charities; Taxation, Exemption from

ENDURANCE, PHYSICAL. *See* Physical Fitness

ENERGY. *See* Force and Energy

ENERGY AND POWER. *Use* Fuel; Water Resources
Development

ENFORCEMENT OF LAW. *See* Law Enforcement

ENFRANCHISEMENT–WOMEN. *See* Voting; Woman–
Rights of Women; Women's Liberation Movement

ENGINEERING
See also names of specific engineering fields, e.g., Bio-
         chemical engineering; Civil engineering; Environ-
         mental engineering; Mechanical engineering;
         Military engineering; etc.
LC   ——; s.a. Architecture; Building; Construction
         industry; Earthwork; Engineering ethics; Ir-
         rigation; Technology; Tolerance (engineering)
SEARS   ——; s.a. Efficiency, Industrial; Mechanics;
         Reliability (engineering)
RG   ——; s.a. Computers–Engineering use; Tech-
         nology
NYT   ENGINEERING AND ENGINEERS; s.a. Science
         and technology
PAIS   ——; s.a. Dredging industry
BPI   ——; s.a. Reliability (engineering); Technology

ENGINEERING DESIGN
LC   ——; s.a. Design, Industrial; Engineering models;
         Structural design
SEARS   DESIGN, INDUSTRIAL; s.a. Human engineering;
         Systems engineering
RG   DESIGN, INDUSTRIAL; s.a. Human engineering;
         Structural engineering
NYT   DESIGN; s.a. Architecture and architects; En-
         gineering and engineers
PAIS   DESIGN IN INDUSTRY; s.a. Human engineering
BPI   ——; s.a. Design; Industrial design coordina-
         tion; Structural design

ENGINEERING INSPECTION. *Use* Quality Control

ENGINES. *Use* Electric Motors; Motors

ENGLISH AS A FOREIGN LANGUAGE. *See* Education, Bilingual

ENGLISH LANGUAGE. *Use* Americanisms; Negro-
English Dialects; Vocabulary

ENGLISH LANGUAGE–BUSINESS ENGLISH. *Use*
Commercial Correspondence

ENGLISH LANGUAGE–WORD FREQUENCY. *Use*
Vocabulary

ENGRAVING. *Use* Graphic Arts

ENLIGHTENMENT. *Use* Rationalism

ENSEMBLE PLAYING. *Use* Chamber Music; Orchestra

ENTAIL. *Use* Land Tenure

ENTERTAINERS
LC   ——; s.a. Actors; Clowns; Comedians; Dancers;
         Geishas; Musicians; Vaudeville

SEARS ——; s.a. Actors and actresses; Entertaining
RG ——; s.a. Magicians; Negro entertainers
NYT ENTERTAINMENT AND AMUSEMENTS; s.a. names of entertainers, e.g., Bassey, Shirley
PAIS ——; s.a. Amusement industry; Performing arts
BPI ——; s.a. Actors and actresses; Theater

ENTERTAINING
LC ——; s.a. Balls (parties); Campfire programs; Children's parties; Etiquette; Home economics; Leisure; Table
SEARS ——; s.a. Amusements; Dinners and dining; Games; Luncheons; Parties
RG ——; s.a. Caterers and catering; Hospitality
NYT PARTIES (Social); s.a. Games; Society
PAIS BUSINESS ENTERTAINING; s.a. Catering industry
BPI ——; s.a. Business entertaining

ENTERTAINING IN SALES PROMOTION. *Use* Sales Management

ENTERTAINMENTS. *Use* Amusements; Entertainers; Entertaining

ENTREPRENEUR
LC ——; s.a. Business enterprises; Capitalism; New business enterprises
SEARS CAPITALISM; s.a. Black businessmen; Capitalists and financiers; Small business
RG ——; s.a. Business enterprises; Capitalists and financiers; Corporations—Directors; Executives
NYT EXECUTIVES; s.a. fields of entrepreneurship, e.g., Food and grocery trade
PAIS ——; s.a. Capitalism; Executives
BPI ——; s.a. Black capitalism; Minority business enterprises

ENVIRONMENT. *Use* Acclimatization; Air—Pollution; Anthropo-geography; Conservation of Natural Resources; Ecology; Environmental Engineering; Environmental Policy; Human Ecology; Man—Influence of Environment; Man—Influence on Nature; Nature Conservation; Noise; Pollution; Public Health

ENVIRONMENT AND STATE. *See* Man—Influence on Nature

ENVIRONMENTAL EFFECTS. *See* Environmental Engineering

ENVIRONMENTAL ENGINEERING
LC ——; s.a. Design, Industrial; Human engineering
SEARS HUMAN ENGINEERING; s.a. Design, Industrial; Machinery—Design
RG ——; s.a. Life support systems (space environment); Life support systems (submarine environment)
NYT ENGINEERING AND ENGINEERS; s.a. Design; Environment
PAIS ——; s.a. Design in industry; Human engineering
BPI ——; s.a. Environmental engineering (buildings); Pollution

ENVIRONMENTAL HEALTH. *Use* Public Health

ENVIRONMENTAL POLICY
LC ——; s.a. Conservation of natural resources; Environmental health; Man—Influence on nature
SEARS ——; s.a. Man—Influence on nature; Natural resources; Pollution
RG ——; s.a. Environment—Laws and legislation; Human ecology; Pollution—Laws and legislation; Water pollution—Control
NYT ENVIRONMENT; s.a. Air pollution; Waste materials and disposal; Water pollution
PAIS ENVIRONMENT; s.a. Conservation of resources; Human ecology; Man—Influence on environment
BPI ——; s.a. Conservation of resources; Environmental health; Pollution

ENVIRONMENTAL POLLUTION. *See* Pollution

ENVY. *Use* Emotions

ENZYMES. *Use* Biochemistry; Digestion

EPIDEMICS. *Use* Communicable diseases; Public Health

EPIGRAMS. *Use* Proverbs; Quotations; Terms and Phrases; Wit and Humor

EPISTEMOLOGY. *See* Knowledge, Theory of

EPIZOA. *See* Parasites

EPOXY ADHESIVES. *Use* Adhesives

EPOXY RESINS. *Use* Plastics Industry and Trade

EQUAL PAY FOR EQUAL WORK
LC ——; s.a. Discrimination in employment; Wages; Woman—Employment
SEARS DISCRIMINATION IN EMPLOYMENT; s.a. Age and employment; Woman—Employment
RG ——; s.a. Discrimination in employment; Women—Equal rights
NYT LABOR; s.a. Labor—U. S.—Discrimination; Labor—U. S.—Women
PAIS ——; s.a. Discrimination in employment; Wages and salaries
BPI WAGES AND SALARIES—LAWS AND REGULATIONS; s.a. Discrimination in employment; Wages and salaries

EQUALITY
Scope: Works on political and social aspects of equality.
LC ——; s.a. Democracy; Individualism; Justice; Political science; Racial discrimination—Law and legislation; Socialism; Sociology; U. S. Constitution—14th amendment
SEARS ——; s.a. Blacks—Civil rights; Constitutional law; Democracy; Liberty; Social classes
RG ——; s.a. Civil rights; Due process of law; Individualism; Race relations
NYT FREEDOM AND HUMAN RIGHTS; s.a. Minorities (ethnic, racial, religious); Politics and government; U. S.—Constitution; Women
PAIS ——; s.a. Equality before the law; Legal rights; Women—Equal rights; Women's liberation movement
BPI ——; s.a. Civil rights; Democracy; Due process of law; Social classes

EQUALITY BEFORE THE LAW. *Use* Civil Rights; Equality; Justice, Administration of; Law; Rule of Law

EQUALITY OF STATES. *Use* Sovereignty

EQUALIZATION, EDUCATIONAL. *Use* Discrimination in Education

EQUATIONS. *Use* Mathematics

EQUESTRIANISM. *Use* Horsemanship

EQUIPMENT. *Use* Industrial Equipment

EQUIPMENT, REPLACEMENT OF. *Use* Depreciation; Machinery

EQUIPMENT AND SYSTEMS. *Use* Automatic Control

EREMITIC LIFE. *Use* Monasticism and Religious Orders

ERGOMANICS. *See* Human Engineering

EROSION
LC ——; s.a. Glaciers; Soil conservation; Weathering; Wind erosion
SEARS ——; s.a. Dust storms; Soil conservation
RG ——; s.a. Beach erosion; Coast changes
NYT ——; s.a. Coast erosion; Reclamation of land
PAIS SOIL EROSION; s.a. Agriculture; Soil conservation
BPI ——; s.a. Beach erosion; Geology

EROTIC LITERATURE. *Use* Erotica

EROTICA
LC ——; s.a. Erotic literature; Literature, Immoral; Love letters; Obscenity (law); Photography, Erotic; Sex in the performing arts
SEARS PORNOGRAPHY; s.a. Freedom of the press; Love poetry; Obscenity (law)
RG ——; s.a. Erotic literature; Immoral literature and pictures; Obscenity; Sex in moving pictures
NYT BOOKS AND LITERATURE; s.a. Art; Books and literature—Censorship—U. S.; Pornography and obscenity
PAIS SEX IN MOVING PICTURES; s.a. Censorship; Sex in advertising; Sex in literature
BPI PUBLISHERS AND PUBLISHING—EROTIC LITERATURE; s.a. Censorship; Freedom of the press; Literature; Sex in advertising

ERRORS
LC ——; s.a. Credulity; Errors, Scientific; Errors, Theory of; Errors and blunders, Literary; Fallibility; History—Errors, inventions, etc.; Medical delusions
SEARS ——; s.a. Superstitions
RG ERRORS, POPULAR; s.a. Fallacies (logic); Superstitions
NYT PSYCHOLOGY AND PSYCHOLOGISTS
PAIS PSYCHOLOGY
BPI ——

ERRORS, THEORY OF. *Use* Probabilities; Sampling (Statistics)

ERSATZ. *See* Substitute Products

ERUDITION. *See* Learning and Scholarship

ESCALATOR CLAUSE. *Use* Inflation (Finance)

ESCAPE (Psychology). *Use* Emotions

ESCHATOLOGY. *Use* Future Life; Heaven; Immortality; Theology

ESKIMOS. *Use* Native Races

ESSAYS. *Use* Literature

ESSENCES AND ESSENTIAL OILS. *Use* Oils and Fats

ESPIONAGE
LC ——; s.a. Intelligence service; Internal security; Official secrets; Sabotage; Spies; Trials (espionage); Wire-tapping
SEARS ——; s.a. Secret service; Spies; Subversive activities
RG ——; s.a. Intelligence service; Secret service; Trials (espionage)
NYT ——; s.a. U. S.—Intelligence agency
PAIS INTELLIGENCE SERVICE; s.a. Military intelligence; Spies
BPI ——; s.a. Industrial espionage; Secret service

ESTABLISHED CHURCHES. *Use* Dissenters, Religious

ESTATE PLANNING. *Use* Inheritance and Succession; Investments; Probate Law and Practice; Taxation, Exemption from; Trusts and Trustees; Wills

ESTATE TAX. *See* Inheritance and Succession

ESTATES (Law). *Use* Inheritance and Succession; Probate Law and Practice; Real Property; Wills

ESTHETICS. *Use* Aesthetics

ESTRANGEMENT (Social psychology). *See* Alienation (Social psychology)

ESTUARINE ECOLOGY. *Use* Marine Ecology

ETCHING. *Use* Graphic Arts

ETERNAL LIFE. *See* Future Life

ETERNITY. *Use* Future Life

ETHICAL PROBLEMS. *Use* Ethics

ETHICS
LC ——; s.a. Christian ethics; Communist ethics; Compromise (ethics); Conflict of generations; Decision-making (ethics); Ethical problems; Existentialism; Fairness; Human relations; Sexual ethics; Wealth, Ethics of
SEARS ——; s.a. Behavior; Character education; Honesty; Legal ethics; Medical ethics
RG ——; s.a. Conscience; Moral attitudes
NYT ETHICS AND MORALS; s.a. Philosophy; Pornography and obscenity; Religion and churches
PAIS ——; s.a. Political ethics; Social ethics
BPI ——; s.a. Business ethics; Conduct of life; Professional ethics

ETHICS, MEDICAL. *See* Medical Ethics

ETHICS, POLITICAL. *See* Political Crimes and Offenses

ETHICS, PRACTICAL. *See* Conduct of Life

ETHICS, PROFESSIONAL. *Use* Confidential Communications

ETHICS, SOCIAL. *See* Social Ethics

ETHNIC ATTITUDES. *Use* Ethnopsychology; Race Awareness

ETHNIC GROUPS. *Use* Culture; Ethnology; Minorities; Race Problems

ETHNIC PSYCHOLOGY. *See* Ethnopsychology

ETHNIC TYPES. *Use* Ethnology

ETHNOCENTRISM. *Use* Ethnopsychology; Prejudices and Antipathies

ETHNOGRAPHY. *See* Ethnology

ETHNOLOGY
LC ——; s.a. Ethnic types; Man, Prehistoric; Man, Primitive; Nativistic movements; Race; Totemism; Tribes and tribal system
SEARS ——; s.a. Acculturation; Color of man; Native races; Religion, Primitive; Society, Primitive; Totems and totemism
RG ——; s.a. Civilization; Culture; Ethnopsychology; Racial differences
NYT RACE; s.a. Archeology and anthropology; Minorities (ethnic, racial, religious); Population and vital statistics
PAIS RACES OF MAN; s.a. Anthropology; Civilization; Ethnic groups
BPI RACE; s.a. Man; Minorities

ETHNOPSYCHOLOGY
LC ——; s.a. Art and race; Culture conflict; Ethnic attitudes; Ethnocentrism; Race awareness; Social psychology
SEARS RACE PSYCHOLOGY; s.a. Blacks—Race identity; National characteristics; Nationalism
RG ——; s.a. Negroes—Psychology; Social psychology
NYT PSYCHOLOGY AND PSYCHOLOGISTS; s.a. Minorities (ethnic, racial, religious); Negroes (in U.S.); Race
PAIS ETHNIC GROUPS; s.a. Race problems; Race relations
BPI PSYCHOLOGY; s.a. Minorities; Race problems; Sociology

ETHOLOGY. *See* Character

ETIQUETTE
LC ——; s.a. Diplomatic etiquette; Forms of address; Military ceremonies, honors and salutes; Precedence; Table etiquette; Wedding etiquette
SEARS ——; s.a. Dating (social customs); Entertaining; Letter writing
RG ——; s.a. Courtesy; Salutations; Telephone etiquette
NYT MANNERS AND CUSTOMS; s.a. Society; Tips and tipping; Titles (personal)
PAIS DIPLOMATIC ETIQUETTE; s.a. Courtesy; Titles of honor and nobility
BPI MANNERS AND CUSTOMS; s.a. Courtesy

ETIQUETTES. *See* Labels

EUGENICS. *Use* Biology; Breeding; Genetics; Heredity

EURASIANISM. *Use* East and West

EURODOLLAR MARKET. *Use* Balance of Payments; Foreign Exchange; International Finance

EUROPEAN FREE TRADE ASSOCIATION. *Use* Free Trade and Protection

EUROPEAN WAR, 1914–1918
LC ——; s.a. History, Modern—20th century; World politics
SEARS ——; s.a. History, Modern—20th century; World politics
RG ——; s.a. International relations; World politics
NYT WORLD WAR I (1914–1918); s.a. Nineteen hundred fourteen (fifteen, etc.)
PAIS ——
BPI ——

EUTHANASIA. *Use* Aged, Killing of; Death; Medical Ethics; Murder

EVANGELICAL REVIVAL. *Use* Evangelicalism

EVANGELICALISM
LC ——; s.a. Apostles; Evangelical revival; Evangelists; Fundamentalism; Pietism
SEARS EVANGELISTIC WORK; s.a. Conversion; Missions; Revivals; Salvation Army
RG ——; s.a. Faith care; Fundamentalism; Paul, Saint—Teaching
NYT RELIGION AND CHURCHES
PAIS EVANGELISTIC WORK; s.a. Christianity and other religions; Churches; Fundamentalism
BPI CHRISTIANITY; s.a. Church

EVANGELISTIC WORK. *Use* Conversion, Religious; Missionaries

EVANGELISTS. *Use* Evangelicalism

EVENING AND CONTINUATION SCHOOLS
LC ——; s.a. Adult education; subd. *Evening and continuation schools* under names of cities
SEARS ——; s.a. Adult education; Education; Technical education
RG ——; s.a. Adult education; University extension
NYT EDUCATION AND SCHOOLS—U.S.—ADULT EDUCATION; s.a. Colleges and universities; Commercial education; Illiteracy
PAIS ——; s.a. Education, Adult; University extension
BPI ADULT EDUCATION; s.a. Education of workers; Occupational training

EVENING COLLEGES. *See* Evening and Continuation Schools

EVENING SCHOOLS. *See* Evening and Continuation Schools

EVICTION. *Use* Landlord and Tenant; Rent Laws

EVIDENCE. *Use* Logic; Truth; Wiretapping; Witnesses

EVOLUTION
LC ——; s.a. Anatomy, Comparative; Anthropology; Cultural lag; Degeneration; Man—Influence of environment; Man—Origin; Natural selection; Variation (biology)
SEARS ——; s.a. Biology; Genetics; Heredity; Man—Origin and antiquity; Natural selection
RG ——; s.a. Adaptation (biology); Creation; Species; Tennessee evolution controversy

EVOLUTION, *cont.*
NYT ——; s.a. Archeology and anthropology; Biology and biochemistry
PAIS ——
BPI ——; s.a. Man

EXAMINATIONS
LC ——; s.a. Educational tests and measurements; Multiple-choice examinations; True-false examinations
SEARS ——; s.a. Civil service—Examinations; Colleges and universities—Entrance requirements
RG ——; s.a. Physical examinations; Psychological examinations
NYT MENTAL TESTS; s.a. Colleges and universities—U.S.—Grading of students; Education and schools—U.S.—Evaluation of students; names of subjects or fields in which examinations are given, e.g., Engineering
PAIS ——; s.a. Bar examinations; Tests, Educational
BPI ——; s.a. Teaching

EXCEPTIONAL CHILDREN
LC ——; s.a. Child study; Gifted children; Handicapped children
SEARS ——; s.a. Education, Elementary; Problem children; Slow learning children
RG CHILDREN, EXCEPTIONAL; s.a. Minimal brain dysfunction; Problem children
NYT CHILDREN AND YOUTH—BEHAVIOR AND TRAINING; s.a. Education and schools—U.S.—Gifted children; Handicapped—Children and youth; Mental health and disorders
PAIS CHILDREN, EXCEPTIONAL; s.a. Children, Gifted; Children, Handicapped
BPI CHILDREN; s.a. Education

EXCESS PROFITS TAX. *Use* Business Tax

EXCHANGE. *Use* Barter; Foreign Trade; Supply and Demand

EXCHANGE, FOREIGN. *Use* Balance of Payments; Currency Question; Foreign Exchange

EXCHANGE OF PERSONS PROGRAMS. *Use* International Cooperation; Vistors, Foreign

EXCHANGES, COMMODITY. *See* Commodity Exchanges

EXCLUSION, RIGHT OF. *Use* Veto

EXCLUSIVE AND CONCURRENT LEGISLATIVE POWERS. *Use* Legislation; State Governments

EXCLUSIVE LICENSES. *Use* Licenses; Monopolies

EXECUTIONS AND EXECUTIONERS. *Use* Capital Punishment; Terrorism

EXECUTIVE ABILITY. *Use* Ability; Decision Making; Executives; Leadership; Management

EXECUTIVE ADIVSORY BODIES. *Use* Public Administration

EXECUTIVE AGREEMENTS. *Use* Executive Power; Treaties

EXECUTIVE IMPOUNDMENT OF APPROPRIATED FUNDS. *Use* Separation of Powers

EXECUTIVE PERFORMANCE. *See* Executives; Management

EXECUTIVE POWER
Scope: Works on the power of heads of government.
LC ——; s.a. Civil supremacy over military; Delegation of powers; Executive agreements; Heads of state; Implied powers (constitutional law); Prerogative, Royal; Presidents; Rule of law; Veto
SEARS ——; s.a. Monarchy; Political science; Presidents
RG ——; s.a. Executive privilege (government information); Presidents—U.S.—Powers and duties
NYT POLITICS AND GOVERNMENT (General); s.a. U.S.—Constitution; U.S.—President; U.S.—President, Executive office of the
PAIS ——; s.a. Emergency powers; Separation of powers
BPI ——; s.a. Presidents (U.S.); War and emergency powers

EXECUTIVE PRIVILEGE. *Use* Confidential Communications; Executive Power; Freedom of Information; Official Secrets

EXECUTIVES
LC ——; s.a. Businessmen; Elite (social sciences); Entrepreneur; Executive ability; Executives, Training of; Foreman; Government executives; Organization; Supervision of employees
SEARS EXECUTIVE ABILITY; s.a. Leadership; Personnel management
RG ——; s.a. Credit managers; Executive ability; Negro executives
NYT ——; s.a. Corporations; Management, Industrial and institutional
PAIS ——; s.a. Ability; Directors; Executives—Promotion; Women as executives
BPI ——; s.a. Executive ability; Leadership; Management

EXECUTORS AND ADMINISTRATORS. *Use* Inheritance and Succession; Probate Law and Practice; Trusts and Trustees; Wills

EXERCISE
See also particular types of exercise, e.g., Calisthenics; Isometric exercise; Reducing exercise; Running.
LC ——; s.a. Muscle strength; Physical education and training; Yoga, Hatha
SEARS ——; s.a. Gymnastics; Physical fitness; Weight control
RG ——; s.a. Gymnastics
NYT ——; s.a. Athletics; Physical education and training; Sports
PAIS PHYSICAL EDUCATION; s.a. Sports
BPI ——; s.a. Health clubs; Hygiene

EXERCISE FOR WOMEN. *Use* Woman—Health and Hygiene

EXHIBITIONS. *Use* Fairs

EXILES
LC ——; s.a. Citizenship, Loss of; Deportation; Expatriation; Governments in exile; Penal colonies; Refugees, Political; Statelessness; subd. *Exiles* under names of certain countries, e.g., Spain—Exiles

SEARS REFUGEES; s.a. Aliens; International law; Naturalization
RG ——; s.a. Emigrés; Refugees
NYT REFUGEES; s.a. Immigration and emigration
PAIS ——; s.a. Deportation; Refugees
BPI REFUGEES; s.a. Deportation

EXISTENTIAL PSYCHOLOGY. *Use* Psychiatry

EXISTENTIALISM
LC ——; s.a. Existential ethics; Existentialism in literature; Phenomenology; Relationism
SEARS ——; s.a. Metaphysics; Ontology; Philosophy, Modern
RG ——; s.a. Christianity and existentialism; Existentialist psychology; Situation ethics
NYT PHILOSOPHY; s.a. Ethics and morals
PAIS PHILOSOPHY; s.a. Ethics
BPI PHILOSOPHY; s.a. Ethics

EX-NUNS. *Use* Monastic and Religious Life of Women

EXPANSION (U.S. politics). *See* Imperialism

EXPATRIATION. *Use* Citizenship; Exiles; Nationality

EXPEDITIONS. *See* Discoveries (In geography); Explorers; Voyages and Travels

EXPENDITURES, PUBLIC. *Use* Budget; Public Administration

EXPERIENCE. *Use* Wisdom

EXPERIMENTAL DESIGN. *Use* Research

EXPERIMENTAL FILMS. *Use* Moving Pictures

EXPERIMENTAL THEATER. *Use* Theater

EXPLORATION, UNDERWATER. *See* Underwater Exploration

EXPLORATIONS. *Use* Discoveries (In geography); Explorers

EXPLORERS
LC ——; s.a. Adventure and adventures; Discoveries (in geography); Heroes
SEARS ——; s.a. America—Discovery and exploration; Travelers; Voyages and travels
RG EXPLORERS (American, Spanish, etc.); s.a. Explorations; subd. *Discovery and exploration* under names of places
NYT EXPLORATION AND EXPLORERS; s.a. Archeology and anthropology; names of explorers and places explored, e.g., Antarctic regions
PAIS GEOGRAPHY
BPI VOYAGES AND TRAVELS

EXPLOSIONS. *Use* Accidents; Atomic Energy; Blasting; Fires

EXPLOSIVES. *Use* Ammunition; Gunnery; Hazardous Substances; Ordnance

EXPORT CONTROL. *Use* Licenses

EXPORT CONTROLS. *Use* Commercial Policy; Free Trade and Protection

EXPORT CREDIT. *Use* Credit

EXPORT PREMIUMS. *Use* Subsidies

EXPORTS. *See* Tariff

EXPOSITIONS AND FAIRS. *Use* Fairs

EXPRESS HIGHWAYS. *Use* Roads; Traffic Safety

EXPRESSION. *Use* Communication

EXPRESSIONISM (Art). *Use* Art, Modern—20th Century; Modernism (Art)

EXPROPRIATION. *Use* Nationalization; Property

EXPURGATED BOOKS. *Use* Censorship

EX-SERVICEMEN. *See* Veterans

EXTEMPORANEOUS SPEAKING. *Use* Public Speaking; Speech

EXTENSION EDUCATION. *Use* Adult Education; Evening and Continuation Schools

EXTERMINATION OF PESTS. *See* Pests

EXTORTION. *Use* Abduction; Racketeering

EXTRADITION. *Use* Asylum, Right of

EXTRASENSORY PERCEPTION. *Use* Clairvoyance; Occult Sciences; Psychical Research; Thought Transference

EXTRATERRESTRIAL BASES. *Use* Space Flight

EXTRATERRESTIAL LIFE. *See* Life

EXTREMISM (Political science). *See* Right and Left (Political science)

EXTRUSION (Plastics). *Use* Plastics Industry and Trade

EYE
LC ——; s.a. Eye (in religion, folk-lore, etc.); Ophthalmology; Optics, Physiological
SEARS ——; s.a. Lenses; Optometry; Vision
RG ——; s.a. Eyeglasses; Retina; Sight
NYT EYES AND EYESIGHT; s.a. Blindness and the blind; Optical goods
PAIS EYES; s.a. Contact lenses; Eyeglasses; Sight
BPI ——; s.a. Eyeglasses; Lenses, Contact; Lenses, Plastic; Pupil (eye)

EYEGLASSES. *Use* Optical Trade

EYESIGHT. *See* Eye

F

FM BROADCASTING. *Use* Radio Broadcasting and Programs; Radio Stations

FM RADIO. *See* Radio—Apparatus and Supplies

F.O.B. CLAUSE. *Use* Risk; Shipment of Goods

FABLES. *Use* Folklore; Tales

FACSIMILE SYSTEMS. *Use* Copying Processes

FACSIMILE TRANSMISSION. *Use* Data Transmission Systems; Telecommunication

FACTOR ANALYSIS. *Use* Tests, Mental

FACTORIES
LC   ——; s.a. Chemical plants; Dairy plants; Factories—Location; Underground factories
SEARS   ——; s.a. Mills and millwork; Workshops
RG   ——; s.a. Automobile factories; Branch factories
NYT   U.S.—ECONOMIC CONDITIONS AND TRENDS—INDUSTRIAL RESEARCH; s.a. Industrial research; U.S.—Armament and defense; Zoning
PAIS   ——; s.a. Automobile assembly plants; Industrial buildings
BPI   ——; s.a. Foundries; Steel works; Textile mills

FACTORIES—DESIGN AND CONSTRUCTION. *Use* Plant Layout

FACTORIES—EQUIPMENT AND SUPPLIES. *Use* Industrial Equipment

FACTORY AND TRADE WASTE. *Use* Pollution; Refuse amd Refuse Disposal; Waste Products

FACTORY LAYOUT. *See* Plant Layout

FACTORY MANAGEMENT
Scope: Works limited to technical aspects of manufacturing processes.
LC   ——; s.a. Assembly line methods; Production engineering; Quality control
SEARS   ——; s.a. Motion study; Time study
RG   ——; s.a. Production control; Supervisors
NYT   MANAGEMENT, INDUSTRIAL AND INSTITUTIONAL; s.a. subd. *Economics* under names of areas; U.S.—Armament and defense—Material—Plants
PAIS   INDUSTRIAL MANAGEMENT; s.a. Efficiency, Industrial; Foremen and supervisors
BPI   ——; s.a. Industrial project management; Plant maintenance

FACTORY SYSTEM. *Use* Labor and Laboring Classes

FACULTY (Education). *See* Educators; Teachers

FACULTY ADVISORS. *Use* Personnel Service in Education

FACULTY PARTICIPATION IN ADMINISTRATION. *Use* Educational Administration

FADS. *Use* Fashion

FAILURE (Psychology). *Use* Success

FAIR EMPLOYMENT PRACTICE. *See* Discrimination in Employment

FAIR TRADE. *See* Prices

FAIR TRADE (Tariff). *See* Free Trade and Protection

FAIR TRADE PRICING. *Use* Commercial Crimes; Commercial Law; Competition

FAIRNESS. *Use* Ethics

FAIRS
See also subd. *Fairs* or *Exhibitions* under names of places or subjects, e.g., Lyons—Fairs; Book industry—Exhibitions; etc.
LC   ——; s.a. Agricultural exhibitions; Bazaars, Charitable; Bazaars, Oriental; Foreign trade promotion
SEARS   ——; s.a Exhibitions; Markets
RG   ——; s.a. Agricultural exhibitions; Book fairs; Exhibitions
NYT   EXPOSITIONS AND FAIRS; s.a. Conventions and conferences; Museums
PAIS   EXHIBITIONS; s.a. names of specific exhibitions, e.g., New York, New York—World's Fair, 1964–65.
BPI   EXHIBITIONS AND FAIRS; s.a. Exhibits

FAIRY TALES. *Use* Children's Literature; Fiction; Folklore; Tales

FAITH AND REASON. *Use* Knowledge, Theory of; Religion

FAITH CURE. *Use* Evangelicalism; Hypnotism; Mental Healing; Mental Suggestion; Miracles; Therapeutics, Suggestive

FAITHFULNESS. *See* Loyalty

FAKIRS. *Use* Yoga

FALL OF MAN. *Use* Sin

FALLACIES (Logic). *Use* Errors; Logic; Thought and Thinking

FALLIBILITY. *Use* Errors

FALLOUT, RADIOACTIVE. *See* Radiation

FALSE ADVERTISING. *See* Advertising, Fraudulent

FALSE ARRESTS, CONVICTIONS AND IMPRISONMENT. *Use* Crime and Criminals; Imprisonment

FALSE MESSIAH. *See* Messiah

FALSE SWEARING. *See* Witnesses

FALSE TESTIMONY. *Use* Witnesses

FALSEHOOD. *See* Truth

FAMILY
LC   ——; s.a. Children; Family social work; Foster day care; Joint family; Kinship; Marriage; Matriarchy; Negro families; Tribes and tribal system

SEARS ——; s.a. Domestic relations; Family life education; Home; Parent and child; Woman

RG ——; s.a. Birth control; Divorce; Family psychotherapy; Fathers; Marriage counseling

NYT FAMILIES AND FAMILY LIFE; s.a. Marriage; Population and vital statistics

PAIS ——; s.a. Family life; Farm families; Problem families; Single parent family

BPI ——; s.a. Broken homes; Family size; Mothers

FAMILY ALLOWANCES. *Use* Public Welfare; Welfare Economics

FAMILY CORPORATIONS. *Use* Corporations

FAMILY FARMS. *Use* Farms and Farming

FAMILY LIFE EDUCATION. *Use* Counseling; Family; Home Economics; Marriage

FAMILY PLANNING. *See* Population

FAMILY PSYCHOTHERAPY. *Use* Group Relations Training

FAMILY RECORDS. *Use* Genealogy

FAMILY SIZE. *Use* Abortion; Birth Control; Family; Population

FAMINES. *Use* Food Supply

FANCY DRESS. *See* Costume

FANTASTIC FICTION. *Use* Fiction; Literature

FANTASY. *Use* Dreams

FAR EAST. *Use* Oriental Studies

FARM ANIMALS. *See* Domestic Animals; Stock and Stock Breeding

FARM CROPS. *See* Crops; Farm Produce

FARM INCOME. *Use* Income

FARM LABOR. *Use* Collective Farming; Labor and Laboring Classes; Migrant Labor

FARM LIFE. *Use* Country Life; Peasantry; Rural Conditions

FARM MANAGEMENT. *Use* Farms and Farming

FARM MANURE. *Use* Fertilizers and Manures

FARM MECHANIZATION. *Use* Farms and Farming; Machinery in Industry

FARM OWNERSHIP. *Use* Absenteeism; Farms and Farming; Home Ownership; Land Tenure

FARM POPULATION. *Use* Rural Conditions

FARM PRODUCE
See also names of specific farm products, e.g., Butter; Eggs; Hay; etc.

LC ——; s.a. Field crops; Food industry and trade; Surplus agricultural commodities; Truck farming

SEARS ——; s.a. Agriculture; Food

RG ——; s.a. Fruit industry; Surplus products, Agricultural

NYT AGRICULTURE AND AGRICULTURAL PRODUCTS; s.a. Food and grocery trade; Markets

PAIS AGRICULTURAL PRODUCTS; s.a. Commodities; Produce trade; Tropical crops; Vegetable industry

BPI ——; s.a. Commodities; Crops

FARM PRODUCE—MARKETING. *Use* Prices

FARM TENANCY. *Use* Farms and Farming; Land; Land Tenure; Landlord and Tenant

FARMERS. *Use* Agriculture; Country Life; Peasantry

FARMERS COOPERATIVE ASSOCIATIONS. *Use* Collective Farming

FARMING. *See* Agriculture

FARMS—VALUATION. *Use* Real Property

FARMS, WORN-OUT. *Use* Abandonment of Property

FARMS AND FARMING

LC FARMS; s.a. Agriculture experiment stations; Family farms; Farm ownership; Land; Pastures; Plantations; Rural conditions; State farms

SEARS FARMS; s.a. Agriculture; Cooperatives; Dry farming; Farm management; Farm tenancy

RG FARMS; s.a. Contour farming; Terraces (agriculture); Tillage

NYT AGRICULTURE AND AGRICULTURAL PRODUCTS; s.a. Agricultural equipment; Fruit and vegetables; Rural areas

PAIS FARMS; s.a. Agriculture; Plantations

BPI FARMS; s.a. Farm management; Farm mechanization

FASCISM. *Use* Collectivism; Despotism; Totalitarianism

FASHION

Scope: Works on prevailing mode or style in dress. See Costume for historical works on styles of particular countries or periods.

LC ——; s.a. Dressmaking—Pattern books; Fashion as a profession; Men's clothing; Models, Fashion

SEARS ——; s.a. Dressmaking; Fashion shows; Tailoring

RG ——; s.a. Fads; Hairdressing

NYT APPAREL; s.a. Models (artists', fashion and photographers') and demonstrators; names of articles of apparel, e.g., Hats

PAIS FASHION INDUSTRY; s.a. Clothing and dress; Clothing industry

BPI ——; s.a. Clothing and dress; Tailors and tailoring

FASHION MODELS. *See* Models, Fashion

FASHIONABLE SOCIETY. *See* Upper Classes

FASTENINGS. *Use* Locks and Keys

FASTS AND FEASTS. *Use* Festivals; Rites and Ceremonies; Special Days, Weeks and Months

FATE AND FATALISM

LC ——; s.a. Fortune; Free will and determinism; God (Mohammedanism); Necessity (philosophy)

SEARS ——; s.a. Free will and determinism; Philosophy; Predestination; Theology

RG ——; s.a. Freedom (theology); Free will and determinism; Obedience

NYT PHILOSOPHY

PAIS PHILOSOPHY; s.a. Religion

BPI PHILOSOPHY; s.a. Choice (psychology); Religion

FATHERS
LC ———; s.a. Father and child; Fathers and daughters; Fathers and sons; Grandparents
SEARS ———; s.a. Family; Parent and child
RG ———; s.a. Broken homes; Children of divorced parents; Family life; Generation gap
NYT FAMILIES AND FAMILY LIFE; s.a. Children and youth
PAIS FAMILY; s.a. Conflict of generations; Family life; Father-separated children; Parent and child (law); Single parent family
BPI ———; s.a. Broken homes; Parent-child relationship

FATHERS, UNMARRIED. *Use* Illegitimacy; Parent and Child

FATHERS OF THE CHURCH. *Use* Canonization; Saints

FATIGUE, MENTAL. *Use* Job Analysis; Mental Hygiene; Work

FATS. *See* Oils and Fats

FAVORED NATION CLAUSE. *Use* Free Trade and Protection; Tariff

FEAR. *Use* Anxiety; Emotions; Neuroses

FEDERAL AID. *Use* Economic Assistance, Domestic

FEDERAL AID TO EDUCATION. *Use* Economic Assistance, Domestic; Education and State; Science and State

FEDERAL AID TO THE ARTS. *Use* Art and State

FEDERAL AND MUNICIPAL RELATIONS. *Use* Federal Government

FEDERAL AND STATE RELATIONS. *Use* Federal Government; State Governments; State Rights

FEDERAL BUDGET. *See* Budget

FEDERAL GOVERNMENT
LC ———; s.a. Federal-city relations; Federal-state controversies; Public administration; State governments; State rights; subd. *Constitution* under names of federal states, e.g., Australia—Constitution
SEARS ———; s.a. Democracy; Republics; State governments
RG ———; s.a. Federal and municipal relations; Intergovernmental tax relations
NYT U.S.—POLITICS AND GOVERNMENT; s.a. Politics and government (general); subd. *Politics and Government* under names of federal states, e.g., Canada—Politics and government
PAIS ———; s.a. Centralization in government; Intergovernmental relations; Intervention (federal government); Political science
BPI ———; s.a. Decentralization in government; Intergovernmental tax relations; subd. *Federal aid* under subjects, e.g., Housing—Federal aid

FEDERAL RESERVE SYSTEM. *Use* Banks and Banking; National Banks (U.S.)

FEDERALISM. *See* Federal Government

FEDERAL-STATE RELATIONS. *See* Federal Government

FEEBLE MINDED. *See* Mentally Ill

FEEDBACK CONTROL SYSTEMS. *Use* Automatic Control

FEEDING AND FEEDING STUFFS. *Use* Breeding; Crops

FEELING. *See* Perception

FEELINGS. *See* Emotions

FELLATIO. *Use* Sex

FELLOWSHIP. *Use* Social Ethics

FELLOWSHIPS. *See* Scholarships

FEMININE HEALTH. *See* Woman—Health and Hygiene

FEMININITY (Psychology). *Use* Woman; Women's Liberation Movement

FEMINISM. *See* Women's Liberation Movement

FENCES (Receivers of stolen goods). *See* Theft

FERROUS METAL INDUSTRIES. *See* Iron Industry and Trade

FERTILITY. *Use* Reproduction

FERTILITY, HUMAN. *Use* Childbirth; Demography; Reproduction; Vital Statistics

FERTILIZATION (Biology). *Use* Cells; Embryology; Reproduction

FERTILIZATION OF PLANTS. *Use* Plants

FERTILIZERS AND MANURES
LC ———; s.a. Compost; Farm manure; Green manuring; Sewage irrigation; Soil fertility; subd. *Fertilizers and manures* under names of crops, e.g., Potatoes—Fertilizers and manures
SEARS ———; s.a. Agricultural chemistry; Lime; Nitrates; Soils
RG ———; s.a. Potash industry and waste; Sewage disposal—Phosphate removal
NYT FERTILIZER; s.a. Cleansers; Phosphates; Potash
PAIS FERTILIZER INDUSTRY; s.a. Agricultural chemicals; Phosphate industry; Potash industry
BPI FERTILIZERS; s.a. Chemical industry; Phosphates; Potash industry

FESTIVALS
See also specific types of festivals, e.g., Music festivals, Drama festivals, etc.
LC ———; s.a. Holidays; Pageants; Popular culture; Procession
SEARS ———; s.a. Fasts and feasts; Holidays; Pageants
RG ———; s.a. Carnival; Parades
NYT ———; s.a. Carnivals; Entertainment and amusements
PAIS ———; s.a. Holidays; Parades
BPI ———; s.a. Anniversaries

FETAL DEATH. *See* Abortion

FETISHISM. *Use* Worship

FETUS. *Use* Embryology

FETUS, EFFECT OF DRUGS ON THE. *Use* Drug Abuse

FEUDALISM
LC ———; s.a. Chivalry; Civilization, Medieval; Land tenure; Middle ages; Tribes and tribal system
SEARS ———; s.a. Clans and clan system; Middle ages; Peasantry
RG ECONOMIC HISTORY—MEDIEVAL; s.a. Europe—History—476-1492; Middle ages—History
NYT HISTORY; s.a. Civilization; Culture
PAIS HISTORY
BPI POLITICAL SCIENCE; s.a. History

FIBER OPTICS. *Use* Optics

FICTION
See also American fiction; English fiction, etc. and subd. *Fiction* under historical events and characters, e.g., World War II—Fiction; Washington, George—Fiction; etc.
LC ———; s.a. Fantastic fiction; Literature; Negro fiction; Psychological fiction; Science fiction
SEARS ———; s.a. Fairy tales; Fantastic fiction; Historical fiction; Romances; Science fiction; Short stories
RG ———; s.a. Characters in literature; Gothic romances; Novelists; Science fiction
NYT BOOKS AND LITERATURE; s.a. Publications; Science fiction; Writing and writers
PAIS ———; s.a. Authorship; Books and reading; Literature
BPI ———; s.a. Books; Detective and mystery stories; Literature; Short story

FICTION—PLOTS. *See* Plots (Drama, novel, etc.)

FICTITIOUS NAMES. *See* Anonyms and pseudonyms

FIEFS. *See* Feudalism; Land Tenure

FIELD ATHLETICS. *See* Track Athletics

FIELD CROPS. *Use* Crops; Farm Produce

FIELD SPORTS. *See* Hunting; Sports; Track Athletics

FIELD WORK (Educational Method). *Use* Education, Cooperative

FIFTH COLUMN. *See* Subversive Activities

FIGHTING. *See* Battles; Boxing; Military Art and Science; Self-defense; War

FIGHTING (Psychology). *Use* Violence

FIGHTING, HAND TO HAND. *Use* Self-Defense

FIGURE DRAWING. *Use* Drawing

FIGURE PAINTING. *Use* Nude in Art

FIGURE SHAPING. *See* Weight Control

FILES AND FILING (Documents)
LC ———; s.a. Business records; Indexing; Management information systems; Office practice
SEARS ———; s.a. Indexing; Information storage and retrieval systems
RG ———; s.a. Computers—Indexing use; Indexing
NYT MANAGEMENT, INDUSTRIAL AND INSTITUTIONAL; s.a. Documents; Secretaries, stenographers and typists; White collar workers
PAIS ———; s.a. Office practice; Records
BPI ———; s.a. Indexing; Office methods; Records

FILIBUSTERS. *Use* Parliamentary Practice

FILICIDE. *Use* Murder

FILING SYSTEMS. *See* Files and Filing (Documents)

FILLING (Earthwork). *Use* Reclamation of Land

FILM ACTING. *See* Moving Pictures as a Profession

FILM ADAPTATIONS. *Use* Moving Picture Plays; Plots (Drama, novel, etc.)

FILM INDUSTRY. *See* Moving Picture Industry

FILMSTRIPS. *Use* Audio-Visual Materials; Moving Pictures in Education

FINANCE
LC ———; s.a. Commerce; Debtor and creditor; Economic policy; Interest and usury; Monetary policy; Money; subd. *Finance* under special subjects, e.g., Corporations—Finance
SEARS ———; s.a. Budget; Capital; Currency question; Inflation (finance); Prices; Stock exchange
RG ———; s.a. Credit; Eurodollar market; Foreign exchange; Investments
NYT ———; s.a. Banks and banking; Budgets and budgeting; Credit
PAIS ———; s.a. Banking, International; Debts, External; Finance, International; Special drawing rights
BPI ———; s.a. Banks and banking; Investments

FINANCE, PERSONAL. *Use* Budgets, Household; Insurance; Investments; Saving and Savings

FINANCE, PUBLIC
LC ———; s.a. Economic assistance, Domestic; Internal revenue; Local taxation; Taxation
SEARS FINANCE; s.a. Bonds; Debts, Public; Finance—(local subd.)—Laws and regulations; Internal revenue; Paper money; Taxation
RG FINANCE; s.a. Local finance; Municipal finance; State finance
NYT FINANCE; s.a. Government bonds; Taxation; U.S.—Internal revenue service (IRS)
PAIS ———; s.a. Budget, Government; County finance; Debts, Public; Local government—Finance
BPI ———; s.a. Bonds, Government; Local finance; Municipal finance

FINANCE CHARGES. *Use* Consumer Credit; Credit; Installment Plan; Interest and Usury; Loans, Personal

FINANCIAL JOURNALISM. *See* Journalism

FINANCIAL STATEMENTS. *Use* Accounting; Business Records

FINE ARTS. *See* Art; Arts, The

FINGER ALPHABET. *See* Deafness

FINISHES AND FINISHING
See also specific types of finishing, e.g., Metal finishing; Textile finishing; Wood finishing.
LC ———; s.a. Materials; Paint; Stains and staining
SEARS LACQUER AND LACQUERING; s.a. Painting, Industrial; Varnish and varnishing

FINISHES AND FINISHING, *cont.*
RG   FINISHING MATERIALS; s.a. Furniture—Finishing; Stains and staining
NYT   PAINTS, ENAMELS, VARNISHES, LACQUERS AND PROTECTIVE FINISHES; s.a. Interior decoration; Painting and decorating; Wood and wood products
PAIS   FINISHING MATERIALS; s.a. Materials; Painting industry; Polishing materials
BPI   ——; s.a. Finishing materials; Furniture polish; Varnish and varnishing

FIRE. *See* Fires

FIRE PROTECTION. *Use* Safety Appliances

FIREARMS
Scope: Works on weapons from which a missile (bullet, ball or shell) is propelled by the action of explosives. See also types of weapons, e.g., Flame throwers; Machine guns; Pistols; Rifles; Revolvers; Shotguns; etc.
LC   ——; s.a. Ammunition; Arms and Armor; Ballistics; Firearms industry and trade; Gunnery; Hunting; Munitions; Target practice
SEARS ——; s.a. Gunpowder; Shooting
RG   ——; s.a. Armaments
NYT   ——; s.a. Airlines—Hijacking; Armaments, defense and military forces; Weapons
PAIS   ——; s.a. Armaments
BPI   ——; s.a. Firearms industry; Gunnery

FIREPROOFING. *Use* Fires

FIRES
See also subd. *Fires and fire prevention* under names of cities.
LC   ——; s.a. Disasters; Fire (in religion, folklore, etc.); Incendiary bombs; Liability for fire damages; Life-saving at fires; Pyromania
SEARS ——; s.a. Fire prevention; Fireproofing; Forest fires; Insurance, Fire
RG   ——; s.a. Brush fires; Textile fabrics, Flammable
NYT   ——; s.a. Burns; Explosions; Fire insurance
PAIS   ——; s.a. Arson; Forest fires
BPI   ——; s.a. Arson; Fire extinction; Fire protection

FIRST AID IN ILLNESS AND INJURY
LC   ——; s.a. Accidents; Medical emergencies
SEARS FIRST AID; s.a. Accidents; Artificial respiration; Bandages and bandaging; Hospitals, Military; Rescue work; Sick
RG   ——; s.a. Ambulances; Respiration, Artificial
NYT   FIRST AID; s.a. Accidents and safety; Fires; Medicine and health
PAIS   ——; s.a. Accidents; Emergency medical services
BPI   ——; s.a. Accidents; subd. *Accidents* under various subjects, e.g., Sports—Accidents

FISCAL POLICY. *Use* Debts, Public; Economic Assistance, Domestic; Monetary Policy

FISH. *Use* Aquariums

FISH AS FOOD. *Use* Food

FISHERIES
See also types of fisheries, e.g., Crab fisheries; Lobster fisheries; Pearl fisheries; Shellfish fisheries.
LC   ——; s.a. Electric fishing; Fish trade; Fishways; Marine resources; Trawls and trawling
SEARS ——; s.a. Fish culture; Fishes; Marine resources; Natural resources; Whaling
RG   ——; s.a. Fishery research
NYT   FISHING AND FISH; s.a. Aquariums and oceanariums; Marine biology; Shellfish
PAIS   ——; s.a. Fish industry; Sea food industry
BPI   ——; s.a. European Economic Community; Fish industry; Fishery law and regulations

FISHING BOATS. *Use* Boats and Boating

FISHING DOCKS AND PIERS. *Use* Ports

FISHING LAWS AND LEGISLATION. *Use* Territorial Waters

FISHWAYS. *Use* Fisheries

FISSION, NUCLEAR. *See* Nuclear Reactions

FLAG DAY. *Use* Special Days, Weeks and Months

FLAGS. *Use* Emblems; Signs and Symbols

FLATS. *Use* Apartment Houses

FLAVORING MATERIALS. *Use* Cookery

FLEXOGRAPHY. *Use* Printing Industry

FLIGHT
LC   ——; s.a. Aeronautics; Flying machines; Space flight
SEARS ——; s.a. Aeronautics; Birds; Navigation
RG   ——; s.a. Gliding and soaring; subd. *Flight* under subjects, e.g., Birds—Flight
NYT   AERONAUTICS; s.a. Airplanes; Astronautics; Space and upper atmosphere
PAIS   AVIATION; s.a. Astronautics; Space flight
BPI   ——; s.a. Astronautics; Space flight

FLIGHT—PHYSIOLOGICAL ASPECTS. *Use* Aviation Medicine

FLOGGING. *See* Punishment

FLOOD CONTROL. *Use* Conservation of Natural Resources; Water Resources Development

FLOODS. *Use* Disaster Relief; Reclamation of Land

FLOORS
See also names of floor coverings, e.g., Carpets.
LC   ——; s.a. Carpentry; Parquet floors; Pavements, Mosaic
SEARS ——; s.a. Architecture—Details; Building
RG   ——; s.a. Flooring
NYT   FLOORS AND FLOORING; s.a. Floor coverings
PAIS   FLOOR MATERIALS; s.a. Building materials; Floor coverings
BPI   ——; s.a. Interior decoration

FLORA. *See* Plants

FLORICULTURE
LC ———; s.a. Annuals (plants); Flowers; Gardening; House plants; Plant breeding; Plant propagation; Plants, Cultivated; Window gardening
SEARS FLOWER GARDENING; s.a. Flowers; Greenhouses; Perennials; Plants, Ornamental
RG ———; s.a. Bulbs; Greenhouses; Nurseries (horticulture); Wild flowers
NYT PLANTS; s.a. Flowers and florists; Horticulture
PAIS ———; s.a. Cut flowers; Horticulture; Nurseries (horticultural)
BPI GARDENING; s.a. Florists; Flowers

FLORISTS. *Use* Floriculture

FLOW CHARTS. *Use* Graphic Methods; System Analysis

FLOW OF FUNDS. *Use* Gross National Product; National Income

FLOWER ARRANGEMENTS. *Use* Interior Decoration

FLOWER GARDENING. *Use* Annuals (Plants); Botany; Floriculture; Gardening; Horticulture

FLORESCENT LIGHTING. *Use* Lighting

FLUORIDATION. *See* Water

FLYING MACHINES. *Use* Airplanes; Flight

FOG DISPERSAL. *Use* Weather

FOLK ART. *Use* Art and Society; Art, Primitive; Folklore

FOLK DANCING. *Use* Dance Music; Dancing; Folklore

FOLK LITERATURE. *Use* Folklore

FOLK MEDICINE. *Use* Medicine

FOLK MUSIC. *Use* Folklore

FOLK PSYCHOLOGY. *See* Ethnopsychology

FOLK SONGS. *Use* Folklore; National Songs; Singing and Songs

FOLK SONGS, AFRICAN. *Use* Negro Music

FOLKLORE
See also divisions by race, nationality, or geography, e.g., Folklore, Gipsy; Folk songs, German; Folk music–Mexico.
LC ———; s.a. Animal lore; Geographical myths; Legends; Literature, Primitive; Marriage customs and rites; Mythology; Oral tradition
SEARS ———; s.a. Fairy tales; Folklore–U.S.; Folk songs; Legends; Plant lore; Sagas
RG ———; s.a. Fables; Folk art; Folk dancing; Folk literature; Folk music; Weather lore
NYT ART; s.a. Fairy tales; Music; Superstitions
PAIS ———; s.a. Arts; Literature; Music
BPI LITERATURE; s.a. Arts; Music

FOLKLORE OF STONES. *Use* Precious Stones

FOLKTALES. *See* Folklore; Tales

FOLKWAYS. *See* Manners and Customs

FOOD
See also names of foods, e.g., Bread; Fruit; Meat; Poultry; Seafood; Vegetables; etc.
LC ———; s.a. Food habits; Food substitutes; Gastronomy; Nutrition; Restaurants, lunchrooms, etc.; Survival and emergency rations
SEARS ———; s.a. Cookery; Digestion; Dinners and dining; Vitamins
RG ———; s.a. Diet; Food poisoning; Vegetarianism
NYT FOOD AND GROCERY TRADE; s.a. Agriculture and agricultural products; Cooking
PAIS ———; s.a. Fish as food; Food adulteration and inspection; Nutrition
BPI ———; s.a. Eating; Farm produce; Food contamination

FOOD, COST OF. *See* Cost and Standard of Living

FOOD–DIET AND NUTRITION. *Use* Weight Control

FOOD, DIETETIC. *Use* Diet

FOOD, DRIED. *Use* Food Industry and Trade

FOOD, ENRICHED. *Use* Vitamins

FOOD–LABELING. *Use* Food Industry and Trade

FOOD, RAW. *Use* Vegetables

FOOD ADDITIVES. *Use* Food Industry and Trade

FOOD ADULTERATION AND PROTECTION. *Use* Consumer Education

FOOD ADULTERATION AND INSPECTION. *Use* Consumer Protection; Food; Food Industry and Trade; Public Health

FOOD AID PROGRAMS. *See* Food Supply

FOOD ALLERGY. *Use* Allergy

FOOD CHAINS (Ecology). *Use* Ecology

FOOD CONTAMINATION. *Use* Bacteriology, Agricultural; Food

FOOD CONTROL. *See* Food Supply

FOOD HABITS. *Use* Diet; Food; Nutrition; Weight Control

FOOD INDUSTRY–PACKAGING. *Use* Packaging

FOOD INDUSTRY AND TRADE
Scope: Works on the processing of food in general and on the marketing of processed food products.
LC ———; s.a. Delicatessen; Food–Labeling; Food prices; Food supply; Produce trade
SEARS FARM PRODUCE; s.a. Canning and preserving; Food additives; Food, Dried
RG FOOD INDUSTRY; s.a. Canneries; Infants' food
NYT FOOD AND GROCERY TRADE; s.a. Agriculture and agricultural products; names of foods and other commodities, e.g., Butter
PAIS FOOD INDUSTRY; s.a. Food adulteration and inspection; Milk trade; Restaurants; Supermarkets
BPI FOOD INDUSTRY; s.a. Farm produce; Food service

FOOD PLANTS. *See* Plants

FOOD POISONING. *Use* Bacteriology, Agricultural; Food

FOOD PRICES. *Use* Cost and Standard of Living; Food Industry and Trade

FOOD RELIEF. *Use* Disasters; Economic Assistance, Foreign; Food Supply; International Co-operation; Public Welfare; Underdeveloped Areas

FOOD SERVICE

LC ——; s.a. Caterers and catering; Food industry and trade; Hotels, taverns, etc.; Industrial feeding; Restaurants, lunchrooms, etc.

SEARS RESTAURANTS, BARS, ETC.; s.a. Coffee houses

RG WAITERS AND WAITRESSES; s.a. Restaurants; subd. *Hotels, restaurants, etc.* under names of cities

NYT FOOD AND GROCERY TRADE; s.a. Hotels, bars, motels, night clubs and restaurants; names of places of service, e.g., Airlines

PAIS See subd. *Food service* under specific subjects, e.g., Schools—Food service

BPI ——; s.a. Restaurants; subd. *Food service* under various subjects, e.g., Airlines—Food service

FOOD SUBSTITUTES. *Use* Food; Substitute Products

FOOD SUPPLY

LC ——; s.a. Emergency food supplies; Food industry and trade; Produce trade; Rationing, Consumer; subd. *Famines* under certain countries, e.g., India—Famines

SEARS ——; s.a. Agriculture—Statistics; Famines; Food—Preservation; Meat industry and trade

RG ——; s.a. Assistance in emergencies; Black markets; Disaster relief; Nutrition problems; Production, Agricultural

NYT AGRICULTURE AND AGRICULTURAL PRO-DUCTS; s.a. Disasters; Food and grocery trade

PAIS ——; s.a. Food relief; Hunger; Rationing; Surplus agricultural products

BPI ——; s.a. Farm produce; Food relief

FOOD TRADE. *See* Crops; Farm Produce; Food In-dustry and Trade

FOOT WEAR. *See* Boots and Shoes

FOOTBALL COACHING, SOCCER COACHING, ETC. *Use* Athletics

FORAGE PLANTS. *Use* Crops; Pastures

FORCE AND ENERGY

LC ——; s.a. Man (physics); Mechanics; Pressure; Vital force

SEARS ——; s.a. Dynamics; Mechanics; Motion; Quan-tum theory

RG ——; s.a. Dynamics; Pressure

NYT PHYSICS; s.a. Atomic energy and weapons; Science and technology

PAIS POWER RESOURCES; s.a. Atomic power; Hydroelectric power

BPI PHYSICS; s.a. Mechanics

FORCED LABOR. *Use* Native Labor

FORCING (Plants). *Use* Gardening; Plants

FORECASTS. *Use* Prophecies

FORECASTS (Economic). *Use* Business Forecasting

FORECASTS (Social sciences). *Use* Social Sciences

FORECASTS (Technology). *Use* Technology

FORECLOSURE. *Use* Mortgages

FOREIGN AID. *Use* Agricultural Assistance; Economic Assistance, Foreign; Economic Development; Industrialization; War—Economic Aspects

FOREIGN AREA STUDIES. *See* Area Studies

FOREIGN COMMERCE. *See* Foreign Trade

FOREIGN CORRESPONDENTS. *Use* Journalism; Reporters and Reporting

FOREIGN ECONOMIC RELATIONS. *See* International Finance

FOREIGN EXCHANGE

LC ——; s.a. Balance of payments; Currency question; Forward exchange; International clearing; International finance; International liquidity

SEARS ——; s.a. Banks and banking; Bills of exchange; Finance; Money; Stock exchange

RG ——; s.a. Currency convertibility; Eurodollar market

NYT CURRENCY; s.a. Commerce; Credit; Currency—International monetary system

PAIS EXCHANGE, FOREIGN; s.a. Counterpart funds; Foreign funds control; Money of account

BPI ——; s.a. Arbitrage; Money—International aspects

FOREIGN POPULATION. *See* Emigration and Immi-gration; Migration of Nations

FOREIGN POPULATION AND RACE QUESTION. *Use* Minorities

FOREIGN RELATIONS. *Use* International Relations

FOREIGN STUDENTS IN [Name of country]. *Use* Visitors, Foreign

FOREIGN TRADE

Scope: Works on international trade only.

LC COMMERCE; s.a. Balance of trade; East-West trade (1945–); Government trading

SEARS COMMERCE; s.a. Exchange; Tariff

RG COMMERCE; s.a. Free trade and protection; Import quotas

NYT COMMERCE; s.a. International relations; Ships and shipping

PAIS COMMERCE, FOREIGN; s.a. Business; Shipping

BPI COMMERCE; s.a. Balance of payments; Foreign exchange

FOREIGN TRADE PROMOTION. *Use* Fairs; Industry and State; Subsidies

FOREIGN TRADE REGULATION. *Use* Commercial Law

FOREIGN VISITORS. *Use* Visitors, Foreign

FOREIGNERS. *Use* Aliens

FOREMEN AND SUPERVISORS. *Use* Executives; Factory Management; Industrial Management; Personnel Management; Supervision of Employees

FOREST CONSERVATION. *Use* Conservation of Natural Resources; Ecology; Nature Conservation; Trees

FOREST FIRES. *Use* Fires

FOREST PRODUCTS. *Use* Forests and Forestry; Raw Materials

FOREST RANGERS. *Use* National Parks and Reserves

FOREST RECREATION. *Use* Outdoor Life

FOREST RESERVES
LC   ——; s.a. Natural monuments; Outdoor recreation; Public lands; Wilderness areas
SEARS ——; s.a. Forests and forestry; National parks and reserves; Wilderness areas
RG   NATIONAL FORESTS; s.a. Forests, State; National parks and reserves; Wilderness areas
NYT   FORESTS AND FORESTRY; s.a. Parks, playgrounds and other recreation areas
PAIS   FORESTS, NATIONAL; s.a. Forests, Municipal; Forests, State
BPI   ——; s.a. Forests and forestry; U.S.—Forest service

FORESTATION. *See* Forests and Forestry

FORESTS, NATIONAL. *Use* Forest Reserves; National Parks and Reserves; Public Lands

FORESTS, STATE. *Use* Forest Reserves

FORESTS AND FORESTRY
See also names and types of woods, e.g., Plywood, Spruce.
LC   ——; s.a. Forest reserves; Lumber trade; Lumbering; Lumber resources; Paper making and trade; Public lands; Pulpwood industry; Reclamation of land; Timber; Trees
SEARS ——; s.a. Lumber and lumbering; Tree planting; Wood
RG   ——; s.a. Lumber industry; Rain forest; Reforestation; Trees
NYT   ——; s.a. Trees and shrubs; Woods and wood products
PAIS   FORESTRY; s.a. Afforestation; Lumber industry; Tree farming; Veneer industry; Wood pulp industry
BPI   ——; s.a. Forest products; Lumber industry; Lumbering; Pulpwood; Woodlots

FORGERY. *Use* Counterfeits and Counterfeiting; Fraud

FORGERY OF WORKS OF ART
LC   ——; s.a. Counterfeits and counterfeiting; Literary forgeries and mystifications; Reproduction of art objects
SEARS ——; s.a. Art
RG   ——; s.a. Art—Expertising; Reproductions of works of art
NYT   ART—FRAUDS; s.a. Forgery
PAIS   ——; s.a. Art; Crime and criminals; Forgery
BPI   ART; s.a. Forgery

FORGETFULNESS. *See* Memory

FORGING AND FORGINGS. *Use* Metal Industries

FORM (Art). *Use* Aesthetics

FORM LETTERS. *Use* Commercial Correspondence; Letter Writing

FORMS (Law). *Use* Business Law; Law

FORMS, BLANKS, ETC. *Use* Commercial Correspondence

FORMS OF ADDRESS. *Use* Etiquette; Letter Writing

FORTIFICATION. *Use* Military Art and Science

FORTITUDE. *Use* Morale

FORTUNE. *Use* Fate and Fatalism; Success

FORTUNE TELLING. *Use* Astrology; Clairvoyance; Occult Sciences; Prophecies

FORTUNES. *See* Income

FORUMS (Discussion and debate). *Use* Debates and Debating

FORWARD EXCHANGE. *Use* Foreign Exchange

FORWARDING COMPANIES. *Use* Carriers; Freight and Freightage; Shipment of Goods

FOSSIL MAN. *Use* Man

FOSTER CARE. *Use* Abandoned Children; Adoption; Child Welfare; Children

FOSTER DAY CARE. *Use* Family

FOSTER GRANDPARENT PROGRAM. *Use* Child Welfare

FOSTER PARENTS. *Use* Adoption; Children; Maternal Deprivation

FOUND OBJECTS (Art). *Use* Art Objects

FOUNDATIONS. *Use* Trusts and Trustees

FOUNDATIONS, CHARITABLE AND EDUCATIONAL. *Use* Charities; Charitable Uses, Trusts and Foundations; Trusts and Trustees

FOUNDATIONS, CHARITABLE AND EDUCATIONAL—TAXATION. *Use* Taxation, Exemption from

FOUNDATIONS (Structural). *Use* Plaster and Plastering; Walls

FOUNDLINGS. *Use* Orphans

FOWLS. *See* Poultry Industry

FRACTURE OF SOLIDS. *Use* Strength of Materials

FRACTURES. *Use* Surgery

FRANCHISE. *See* Elections; Voting

FRANCHISE SYSTEM. *Use* Franchises (Retail trade); Small Business

FRANCHISES, MUNICIPAL. *See* Municipal Ownership

FRANCHISES (Retail trade)
LC   ——; s.a. Retail trade; Small business
SEARS RETAIL TRADE; s.a. Chain stores; Commerce

FRANCHISES (Retail trade), *cont.*

RG   FRANCHISE SYSTEM; s.a. Small businesses; subd. *Franchise system* under subjects, e.g., Restaurants—Franchise system

NYT   Names of companies and industries granting and holding franchises, and products and services franchised; s.a. Retail stores and trade

PAIS   FRANCHISES; s.a. Concessions; Retail trade

BPI   FRANCHISE SYSTEM; s.a. Pyramid selling operations; Restaurants, lunchrooms, etc.—Chain and franchise operations

FRANKING PRIVILEGE. *Use* Postal Service

FRATERNITIES AND SORORITIES. *Use* Secret Societies; Students

FRAUD

LC   ——; s.a. Commercial crimes; Consumer protection; Imposters and imposture; Medicines, Patent, proprietary, etc.

SEARS ——; s.a. Forgery; Imposters and imposting; Patent medicines; Swindlers and swindling

RG   ——; s.a. Counterfeits and counterfeiting; Quacks and quackery

NYT   FRAUDS AND SWINDLING; s.a. Embezzlement and misappropriation; Extortion and blackmail; Hoaxes; Quackery

PAIS   ——; s.a. Counterfeiting; Embezzlement; Quacks and quackery

BPI   ——; s.a. Advertising, Fraudulent; Embezzlement; Tax fraud

FREE CHOICE OF EMPLOYMENT. *Use* Employment; Occupations; Professions

FREE CHURCHES. *See* Dissenters, Religious

FREE ENTERPRISE. *Use* Business; Business and Politics; Economics; Industry and State

FREE LOVE. *Use* Marriage; Sex

FREE PORTS AND TRADING ZONES. *Use* Merchant Marine; Ports; Tariff

FREE SCHOOLS. *Use* Educational Planning and Innovations

FREE SPEECH. *Use* Censorship; Civil Rights; Freedom of Information; Libel and Slander; Liberty of Speech

FREE THOUGHT. *Use* God; Rationalism; Religious Liberty

FREE TRADE AND PROTECTION

LC   ——; s.a. Export controls; Favored nation clause; Foreign trade; Reciprocity; Supply and demand

SEARS ——; s.a. Commerce; Commercial policy; Economic policy

RG   ——; s.a. Balance of trade; Import quotas

NYT   COMMERCE; s.a. International Relations; subd. *International trade and world market* under names of industries and products, e.g., Steel and iron—International trade and world market

PAIS   ——; s.a. European Free Trade Association; Tariff

BPI   ——; s.a. Tariff; U.S.—Commercial policy

FREE UNIVERSITIES. *Use* Colleges and Universities

FREE WILL AND DETERMINISM. *Use* Fate and Fatalism

FREEDMEN. *Use* Liberty; Slavery

FREEDOM (Theology). *Use* Fate and Fatalism; Religious Liberty

FREEDOM AND HUMAN RIGHTS. *Use* Black Power; Dissenters, Religious; Emigration and Immigration; Equality; Government, Resistance to; Liberty; Liberty of Speech; Minorities; Persecution; Prejudices and Antipathies; Privacy, Right of; Race Awareness; Race Discrimination; Race Problems; Religious Liberty; Segregation; Social Problems; Toleration; Woman—Rights of Women

FREEDOM OF ASSEMBLY. *Use* Civil Rights; Liberty of Speech; Riots

FREEDOM OF ASSOCIATION. *Use* Civil Rights; Liberty

FREEDOM OF CONSCIENCE. *Use* Conscientious Objectors; Dissenters, Religious; Liberty; Nationalism and Religion; Persecution; Public Opinion; Religious Liberty; Toleration

FREEDOM OF INFORMATION

LC   ——; s.a. Censorship; Civil rights; Executive privilege (government information); Liberty of speech; Liberty of the press; Public records; Reporters and reporting

SEARS ——; s.a. Censorship; Free speech; Freedom of the press; Moving pictures—Censorship; Radio—Censorship; Television—Censorship

RG   INFORMATION, FREEDOM OF; s.a. Intellectual liberty; Science, Freedom of

NYT   FREEDOM OF INFORMATION, THOUGHT AND EXPRESSION; s.a. Freedom of speech; Freedom of the press

PAIS   ——; s.a. Government and the press; Official secrets

BPI   ——; s.a. Freedom of the press; Government and the press

FREEDOM OF INQUIRY. *Use* Liberty; Persecution

FREEDOM OF MOVEMENT. *Use* Emigration and Immigration; Liberty

FREEDOM OF RELIGION. *Use* Dissenters, Religious; Liberty; Religious Liberty

FREEDOM OF SPEECH. *Use* Civil Rights; Libel and Slander; Liberty of Speech

FREEDOM OF TEACHING. *See* Academic Freedom

FREEDOM OF THE AIR. *See* Airspace (International law); Radio Broadcasting

FREEDOM OF THE PRESS. *Use* Censorship; Erotica; Freedom of Information; Government and the Press; Journalism; Libel and Slander; Liberty; Liberty of Speech; Newspapers; Obscenity; Political Crimes and Offenses; Press; Reporters and Reporting

FREEDOM OF THE SEAS
LC ———; s.a. Maritime law; Sea power; War, Maritime (international law)
SEARS MARITIME LAW; s.a. International law
RG ———; s.a. Maritime law; Territorial waters
NYT SHIPS AND SHIPPING—INTERNATIONAL INCIDENTS; s.a. International relations; Waters, Territorial
PAIS ———; s.a. Maritime law; Rule of the road at sea
BPI MARITIME LAW; s.a. Rule of the road at sea; Territorial waters

FREEDOM OF THE WILL. *See* Fate and Fatalism

FREEHOLD. *See* Land Tenure

FREEZING. *Use* Temperature

FREIGHT AND FREIGHTAGE
LC ———; s.a. Breakage, shrinkage, etc. (commerce); Carriers; Dangerous goods, Transportation of; Forwarding merchants
SEARS ———; s.a. Aeronautics, Commercial; Materials handling; Railroads—Rates
RG ———; s.a. Air freight service; Trucking
NYT FREIGHT FORWARDING (Domestic and foreign); s.a. names of commodities and companies, e.g., Wood and wood products; Transportation; Trucks and trucking industry
PAIS FREIGHT TRANSPORT; s.a. Forwarding companies; Motor transport; Unitized cargo systems
BPI ———; s.a. Shipment of goods; Shipping

FREIGHTERS. *Use* Merchant Marine

FREQUENCY THEORY. *Use* Probabilities

FRESH WATER ECOLOGY. *Use* Ecology; Water—Pollution

FRIENDLINESS. *See* Human Relations

FRIENDLY SOCIETIES. *Use* Charities; Insurance, Social

FRIENDSHIP. *Use* Human Relations

FRIGIDITY (Psychology). *Use* Sex

FRINGE BENEFITS. *See* Non-Wage Payments

FRONTIERS. *See* Boundaries

FROST PROTECTION. *Use* Horticulture

FROZEN GROUND. *Use* Soils

FRUIT CULTURE. *Use* Gardening

FRUIT INDUSTRY. *Use* Farm Produce

FRUIT PROCESSING. *Use* Agricultural Processing

FRUITS AND VEGETABLES. *Use* Bacteriology, Agricultural; Farms and Farming; Vegetables

FRUSTRATION. *Use* Emotions

FUEL
See also types of fuel, e.g., Charcoal; Coal; Coke; Gas; Wood; and subd. *Fuel* under subjects, e.g., Automobile engines—Fuel; Rockets—Fuel; etc.
LC ———; s.a. Fuel consumption; Gas as fuel; Liquid fuels; Nuclear fuel elements; Oil industries; Petroleum industry and trade; Smoke prevention; Wood as fuel
SEARS ———; s.a. Heating; Power resources
RG ———; s.a. Hydrogen, Liquid; Petroleum as fuel
NYT ———; s.a. Electric light and power; Energy and power; Heating
PAIS ———; s.a. Coal industry; Motor fuels; Nuclear fuels
BPI ———; s.a. Fuel cells; Heating

FUEL—SMOKELESS FUEL. *Use* Air—Pollution

FUEL OIL. *See* Petroleum Industry and Trade

FUGITIVES FROM JUSTICE. *Use* Arrest

FULL EMPLOYMENT POLICIES. *Use* Economic Policy; Employment; Manpower; Public Works; Work Relief

FUME CONTROL. *Use* Air—Pollution

FUMIGATION. *Use* Disinfection and Disinfectants

FUNCTIONAL REPRESENTATION. *Use* Lobbying; Representative Government and Representation

FUNCTIONS. *Use* Mathematics

FUND RAISING. *Use* Charities

FUNDAMENTALISM. *Use* Christianity; Evangelicalism; Protestantism

FUNDS. *See* Finance

FUNERAL RITES AND CEREMONIES
See also subd. *Funeral rites and ceremonies* under names of deceased persons, e.g., King, Martin Luther—Funeral rites and ceremonies
LC ———; s.a. Burial; Dead; Mourning customs; Obituaries
SEARS ———; s.a. Ancestor worship; Cremation; Manners and customs; Rites and ceremonies
RG ———; s.a. Burial at sea; Sepulchral monuments; Undertakers and undertaking
NYT FUNERALS; s.a. Cemeteries; Deaths
PAIS FUNERALS; s.a. Cremation; Dead bodies (law); Mortality
BPI DEATH; s.a. Religion; Undertakers

FUNGI—RESISTANCE AND SENSITIVITY. *Use* Antibiotics

FUR. *Use* Clothing and Dress

FUR TRADE. *Use* Hunting

FURNACES. *Use* Heating

FURNITURE
See also names of articles of furniture, e.g., Beds and bedding; etc.
LC ———; s.a. Art objects; Children's furniture; Furniture—Collectors and collecting; House furnishings; Interior decoration
SEARS ———; s.a. Antiques; Built-in-furniture; Garden ornaments and furniture; Upholstery
RG ———; s.a. Cabinet work; Joinery; Woodworking
NYT ———; s.a. Antiques; Household equipment and furnishings

FURNITURE, *cont.*
PAIS   FURNITURE INDUSTRY; s.a. Household
        furnishings; Interior decoration
BPI   ———; s.a. Cabinets (furniture); Furniture
        industry; Office furniture

FURNITURE—FINISHING. *Use* Finishes and Finishing

FUSION, NUCLEAR. *See* Nuclear Reactions

FUTURE INTERESTS. *Use* Property

FUTURE LIFE
LC   ———; s.a. Immortality; Pre-existence; Reincar-
        nation; Salvation; Soul

SEARS   ———; s.a. Eternity; Heaven; Immortality;
        Millenium; Spiritualism
RG   ———; s.a. Eschatology; Reincarnation;
        Resurrection
NYT   PHILOSOPHY; s.a. Deaths; Religion and
        churches
PAIS   DEATH; s.a. Mortality; Religion
BPI   MORTALITY; s.a. Death; Religion

FUTURE PUNISHMENT. *Use* Death

FUTURES. *Use* Commodity Exchanges

FUTURISM (Art). *Use* Modernism (Art)

G

G.I.'S. *See* Veterans

GALAXIES. *Use* Astronomy

GALLERIES AND MUSEUMS. *Use* Museums

GAMBLING
See also names of individual games, e.g., Blackjack (game);
    Dice; etc.
LC   ———; s.a. Book-making (betting); Pari-mutuel
        betting; Wagers
SEARS   ———; s.a. Cards; Horse racing; Probabilities
RG   ———; s.a. Casinos; Horse race betting; Proba-
        bilities
NYT   ———; s.a. Cards and card games; Horse racing—
        Betting; Lotteries
PAIS   ———; s.a. Betting; Lotteries
BPI   ———; s.a. Lotteries; Race tracks; Speculation

GAME AND GAME BIRDS. *Use* Birds; Hunting; Wildlife
    Conservation

GAME PRESERVES. *Use* Wildlife Conservation

GAME PROTECTION. *Use* Hunting; Wildlife Conserva-
    tion

GAME THEORY. *Use* Decision Making; Mathematical
    Models

GAMES. *Use* Amusements; Entertainment; Leisure;
    Physical Fitness; Probabilities; Recreation;
    Sports

GAMES (Management). *Use* Management Games

GAMES (Merchandising). *Use* Merchandising

GAMES OF CHANCE (Mathematics). *Use* Probabilities

GAMES OF STRATEGY (Mathematics). *Use* Decision
    Making

GAMING. *See* Gambling

GANGS. *Use* Crime and Criminals; Juvenile Delinquency;
    Subculture

GARBAGE AS FEED. *Use* Refuse and Refuse Disposal

GARDEN CITIES. *Use* Housing

GARDEN FARMING. *See* Truck Farming

GARDEN LIGHTING. *Use* Lighting

GARDEN ORNAMENTS AND FURNITURE. *Use*
    Furniture

GARDEN TOOLS, EQUIPMENT AND SUPPLIES. *Use*
    Tools

GARDENING
Scope: Practical works on the cultivation of flowers,
        fruits, lawns, vegetables, etc.
LC   ———; s.a. Annuals (plants); Forcing (plants);
        Plants, Cultivated; Plants, Potted; Topiary work;
        Truck farming; Weeds; Window gardening
SEARS   ———; s.a. Bulbs; Climbing plants; Flower gar-
        dening; Fruit culture; Grafting
RG   ———; s.a. Flower boxes, planters, etc.; House
        plants; Indoor gardening; Landscape gardening
NYT   HORTICULTURE; s.a. Flowers and florists;
        Fruits and vegetables; Plants; Trees and shrubs
PAIS   ———; s.a. Floriculture; Horticulture; Landscape
        gardening
BPI   ———; s.a. Flowers; Grounds maintenance; Horti-
        culture; Plants

GARMENT CUTTING. *Use* Tailoring

GAS
LC   ———; s.a. Automobile exhaust gas; Gas appli-
        ances; Gas companies
SEARS   ———; s.a. Coal-tar products; Fuel; Public utilities
RG   ———; s.a. Liquified natural gas; Motor fuels
NYT   GAS (Illuminating and fuel); s.a. Air pollution;
        Fuel; Public utilities
PAIS   GAS, NATURAL; s.a. Gases, Asphyxiating and
        poisonous; Liquified natural gas; Motor vehicles—
        Exhaust
BPI   ———; s.a. Coal tar products; Gas manufacture
        and works; Petroleum

GAS AND OIL ENGINES. *Use* Motors

GAS FITTING. *Use* Plumbing

GAS LIGHTING. *Use* Lighting

GASES, ASPHYXIATING AND POISONOUS. *Use* Gas; Hazardous Substances

GASES, ASPHYXIATING AND POISONOUS—WAR USE. *Use* Chemical Warfare

GASOLINE INDUSTRY. *Use* Oil Industries; Petroleum Industry and Trade

GASTRIC JUICE. *Use* Digestion

GASTRONOMY. *Use* Cookery; Dinners and Dining; Food

GAY LIBERATION MOVEMENT. *Use* Homosexuality

GEISHAS. *Use* Entertainers

GEMS. *Use* Jewelry; Mineralogy; Precious Stones

GENDARMES. *See* Police

GENEALOGY
LC ———; s.a. Peerage; Probate records; Titles of honor and nobility
SEARS ———; s.a. Biography; Register of births, etc.; Wills
RG ———; s.a. Family records; Heraldry
NYT ———; s.a. Nobility; Society
PAIS ———; s.a. Emblems; Family records; Heraldry
BPI ———; s.a. Biography

GENERAL STRIKE. *Use* Passive Resistance

GENERATION GAP. *Use* Conflict of Generations; Social Conflict

GENERATIVE ORGANS. *Use* Reproduction; Sex

GENES. *See* Genetics; Heredity

GENETIC CODE. *Use* Genetics; Heredity

GENETIC COUNSELING. *Use* Counseling; Genetics

GENETIC PSYCHOLOGY. *Use* Growth

GENETICS
LC ———; s.a. Breeding; Crossing over (genetics); Genetic code; Heredity, Human; Human chromosomes; Life; Man; Molecular genetics; Origin of Species; Variation (biology)
SEARS ———; s.a. Adaptation (biology); Chromosomes; Evolution; Natural selection; Reproduction
RG ———; s.a. Chromosomes; Genetic counseling; Genotype and phenotype; Human genetics; Linkage (genetics); Mutation (biology); Population genetics
NYT BIOLOGY AND BIOCHEMISTRY; s.a. Birth defects (congenital defects); Eugenics; Evolution
PAIS ———; s.a. Botany; Eugenics; Evolution; Heredity
BPI ———; s.a. Biology; Cells; Reproduction

GENIUS. *Use* Intellect; Wisdom

GENOCIDE. *Use* International Offenses; Murder; Race Problems; War Crime Trials

GEODESY. *Use* Earth

GEOGRAPHICAL ATLASES. *See* Atlases

GEOGRAPHICAL BOUNDARIES. *See* Boundaries

GEOGRAPHICAL DISTRIBUTION OF ANIMALS AND PLANTS. *Use* Ecology; Natural History

GEOGRAPHY
See also geographical terms; e.g., Lakes; Mountains; Plains; Rivers; Valleys; etc.
LC ———; s.a. Cartography; Climatology; Discoveries (in geography); Explorers; Physical geography; subd. *Description and travel* under names of countries and subd. *Description, Geography* under names of countries of antiquity, e.g., Sumeria—Description, Geography; Territory, National
SEARS ———; s.a. Atlases; Boundaries; Geophysics; Meterology; Voyages and travels
RG ———; s.a. Anthropogeography; Atlases; Earth
NYT ———; s.a. Atlases; Maps
PAIS ———; s.a. Area studies; Economic geography; Medical geography
BPI ———; s.a. Altitudes; Atlases; Maps

GEOGRAPHY, COMMERCIAL. *Use* Economic Development; Economic History

GEOGRAPHY—HISTORY. *Use* Discoveries (In geography)

GEOGRAPHY, MATHEMATICAL. *Use* Cartography

GEOGRAPHY, POLITICAL. *Use* Anthropo-geography; Boundaries; Demography; Territory, National; World Politics

GEOGRAPHY, SOCIAL. *See* Anthropogeography

GEOLOGY. *Use* Earth; Erosion; Mineralogy

GEOMAGNETISM. *See* Magnetism, Terrestrial

GEOMANCY. *Use* Occult Sciences

GEOMETRY. *Use* Mathematics

GEOPOLITICS. *Use* World Politics

GERIATRIC PSYCHIATRY. *Use* Psychiatry

GERIATRICS
LC ———; s.a. Geriatric nursing; Old age
SEARS AGED—DISEASES; s.a. Aged—Care and hygiene; Old age
RG AGED—CARE AND HYGIENE; s.a. Aged—Housing; Geriatrics as a profession; Physical education for the aged
NYT AGED AND AGE; s.a. Medicine and health; Nursing homes
PAIS OLD AGE—MEDICAL CARE; s.a. Old age; Social service—Work with the aged
BPI ———; s.a. Aged—Care and hygiene; Nurses and nursing

GERM THEORY OF DISEASE. *Use* Bacteria; Bacteriology; Communicable Diseases

GERM WARFARE. *See* Biological Warfare

GERMICIDES. *See* Disinfection and Disinfectants

GERMS. *See* Bacteriology

GERONTOLOGY. *Use* Old Age

GERRYMANDER. *Use* Apportionment (Election law); Representative Government and Representation

GESTALT PSYCHOLOGY. *Use* Perception; Senses and Sensation

GESTURE. *Use* Acting

GHOSTS. *Use* Occult Sciences

GIFT TAX. *Use* Inheritance and Succession

GIFT WRAPPING. *Use* Packaging

GIFTED CHILDREN. *Use* Exceptional Children; Talented Students

GIFTS. *Use* Charities

GIPSIES. *Use* Tribes and Tribal System

GIRLS. *Use* Coeducation; Daughters; Education of Women; Woman; Youth

GIVING. *Use* Charity

GLACIAL EPOCH. *Use* Earth

GLACIERS. *Use* Erosion

GLASS. *Use* Ceramics

GLASS BEADS. *Use* Beadwork

GLASS CONTAINERS. *Use* Containers

GLAZES AND GLAZING. *Use* Ceramics

GLIDERS. *Use* Airplanes

GLIDING AND SOARING. *Use* Flight

GLUES. *Use* Adhesives

GLUE-SNIFFING. *Use* Narcotic Habit

GOD
LC ———; s.a. Causation; Deism; Gods; Monotheism; Mythology; Secularization (theology); Theism
SEARS ———; s.a. Agnosticism; Creation; Free thought; Pantheism
RG ———; s.a. Atheism; Death of God theology; Gods and goddesses; Incarnation; Philosophy and religion; Theology
NYT RELIGION AND CHURCHES; s.a. Bible; Jesus Christ; Philosophy
PAIS RELIGION; s.a. Atheism; Christianity and other religions; Churches; Religious education
BPI RELIGION; s.a. Christianity; Church

GODS IN ART. *Use* Art and Religion

GOLD. *Use* Jewelry

GOLD AS MONEY. *Use* Money

GOLD MINES AND MINING. *Use* Mineralogy

GOLD STANDARD. *Use* Money

GOLDFISH. *Use* Aquariums

GOLDSMITHING. *Use* Jewelry

GONORRHEA. *Use* Sex

GOOD AND EVIL. *Use* Sin

GOTHIC ROMANCES. *Use* Fiction

GOVERNMENT, LOCAL. *See* Local Government

GOVERNMENT, MUNICIPAL. *See* Municipal Government

GOVERNMENT, PRIMITIVE. *Use* Society, Primitive

GOVERNMENT, RESISTANCE TO
LC ———; s.a. Guerilla warfare; Guerillas; Insurgency; Political crimes and offenses; Revolutions
SEARS ———; s.a. Political crimes and offenses; Political ethics
RG ———; s.a. Coups d'état; Protests, demonstrations, etc.
NYT POLITICS AND GOVERNMENT; s.a. Freedom—Human rights; U.S.—Politics and government—Civil disobedience and disorder; Right to dissent; War and revolution
PAIS ———; s.a. Civil disobedience; Passive resistance to government
BPI ———; s.a. Protests, demonstrations, etc.; Revolutions; Riots

GOVERNMENT AID TO BUSINESS. *Use* Business and Politics; Industry and State

GOVERNMENT AND THE PRESS
LC ———; s.a. Censorship; Freedom of information; Government information; Liberty of speech; Municipal documents; Press; Printing, Public; Propaganda
SEARS ———; s.a. Freedom of information; Government publications; Journalism; subd. *Government publications* under names of countries, cities, etc., e.g., U.S.—Government publications, etc.
RG ———; s.a. Local government and the press; Presidents—U.S.—Press conferences; Security classifications (government documents)
NYT FREEDOM OF THE PRESS; s.a. News and news media—U.S.—Government; News policies; Politics and government
PAIS ———; s.a. Freedom of information; Government periodicals; Reporters and reporting
BPI ———; s.a. Official secrets; Pentagon papers; State publications

GOVERNMENT ATTORNEYS. *Use* Justice, Administration of

GOVERNMENT BONDS. *Use* Bonds; Finance, Public; Investments; Municipal Government

GOVERNMENT BUSINESS ENTERPRISES. *Use* Corporations, Government; Municipal Ownership; Public Utilities; Public Works; Work Relief

GOVERNMENT COMPETITION. *Use* Competition; Corporations, Government; Nationalization

GOVERNMENT CORPORATIONS. *Use* Corporations, Government

GOVERNMENT EMPLOYEES AND OFFICIALS. *Use* Civil Service; Corruption (Politics); Municipal Officials and Employees; Patronage, Political; Public Administration

GOVERNMENT HOUSING. *See* Public Housing

GOVERNMENT INFORMATION. *Use* Government and the Press

GOVERNMENT LENDING. *Use* Loans

GOVERNMENT LIABILITY. *Use* Liability (Law);
State, The

GOVERNMENT LOANS AND GRANTS. *Use* Economic
Assistance, Domestic; Industry and State

GOVERNMENT MONOPOLIES. *Use* Corporations,
Government; Monopolies; Nationalization

GOVERNMENT OFFICIALS AND EMPLOYEES. *Use*
Civil Service

GOVERNMENT OWNERSHIP. *Use* Business and
Politics; Collectivism; Corporations, Government; Economics; Industry and State; Municipal Ownership; Nationalization; Public Lands;
Socialism

GOVERNMENT PRICE CONTROL. *See* Prices

GOVERNMENT PRICE REGULATION. *See* Prices

GOVERNMENT PROCUREMENT. *See* Purchasing

GOVERNMENT PUBLICATIONS
LC   ——; s.a. Government and the press; Govern-
ment publicity; Municipal documents; Printing,
Public; Propaganda
SEARS ——; s.a. subd. *Government publications* under
names of places, e.g., U.S.—Government publi-
cations; etc.
RG   ——; s.a. Security classification (government
documents); State publications
NYT U.S.—DEPARTMENTS AND AGENCIES—
PUBLICATIONS; s.a. Publications
PAIS ——; s.a. Government periodicals; Municipal
documents
BPI   ——; s.a. State publications

GOVERNMENT PUBLICITY. *Use* Government Publications; Propaganda

GOVERNMENT PURCHASING. *Use* Purchasing

GOVERNMENT RECORDS. *Use* Archives; Public Records

GOVERNMENT REGULATION OF COMMERCE. *See*
Commercial Policy; Industrial Laws and Legislation; Industry and State; Interstate Commerce

GOVERNMENT RESEARCH. *Use* Research

GOVERNMENT SECRECY. *See* Official Secrets

GOVERNMENT SPENDING POLICY. *Use* Budget;
Debts, Public; Defense Contracts

GOVERNMENT STATISTICS. *Use* Statistics

GOVERNMENT-SPONSORED RESEARCH. *Use*
Science and State

GOVERNMENT TRADING. *Use* Commercial Policy;
Foreign Trade

GOVERNMENTAL INVESTIGATIONS. *Use* Justice,
Administration of; Legislation; Loyalty

GOVERNMENTS IN EXILE. *Use* Exiles

GOVERNORS. *Use* State Governments

GRADING AND MARKING (Students)
LC   ——; s.a. Educational tests and measurements;
Promotion (school); School reports; Under-
achievers
SEARS ——; s.a. Educational tests and measurements;
Mental tests; School reports
RG   ——; s.a. Ability grouping in education; Per-
sonnel records in education; School reports and
records
NYT EDUCATION AND SCHOOLS—U.S.—GRADING
OF STUDENTS; s.a. Colleges and universities—
U.S.—Grading of students; Mental tests
PAIS ——; s.a. Ability grouping in education;
Students—Promotion; Tests, Educational
BPI   ——; s.a. Education; Teaching

GRADUATE STUDENTS. *Use* Scholarships; Students

GRAFFITI. *Use* Drawing

GRAFFITO DECORATION. *Use* Plaster and Plastering

GRAFT (In politics). *See* Corruption (In politics)

GRAFTING. *Use* Gardening

GRAIN HANDLING. *Use* Materials Handling

GRAIN TRADE. *Use* Commodity Exchanges

GRAMMAR. *Use* Language and Languages

GRAMOPHONE. *See* Phonograph Records

GRAND JURY. *Use* Jury; Trials

GRAND OPERA. *See* Opera

GRANTS-IN-AID. *Use* Economic Assistance, Domestic;
Subsidies

GRAPHY THEORY. *Use* Graphic Methods

GRAPHIC ARTS
LC   ——; s.a. Art—Technique; Art and industry;
Commercial art; Drawing; Painting; Printing
SEARS ——; s.a. Drawing; Engraving; Painting
RG   ——; s.a. Drawing; Drypoint; Etching; Prints
NYT ——; s.a. Art; Posters
PAIS GRAPHIC ARTS INDUSTRY; s.a. Lithography;
Photoengraving
BPI   ——; s.a. Etching (metals); Illustration of books,
periodicals, etc.; Printing; Prints

GRAPHIC METHODS
LC   ——; s.a. Critical path analysis; Graphic statics;
Organization charts; subd. *Graphic methods*
under specific subject, e.g., Algebra—Graphic
methods; etc.
SEARS ——; s.a. Drawing; Geometrical drawing;
Mechanical drawing; Statistics—Graphic methods
RG   ——; s.a. Flow charts; Nomography (mathemat-
ics); Organization charts
NYT GRAPHIC ARTS
PAIS ——; s.a. Charts; Computer graphics; System
analysis
BPI   ——; s.a. Flow charts; Graph theory

GRAPHOLOGY. *Use* Writing

GRAPHS. *See* Graphic Methods

GRASSES. *Use* Pastures; Weeds

GRASSLAND FARMING. *See* Pastures

GRAVES. *See* Burial; Cemeteries; Funeral Rites and Ceremonies

GRAVITATION AND GRAVITY. *Use* Earth; Magnetism, Terrestial

GRAZING LANDS. *Use* Pastures

GREASE. *See* Oils and Fats

GREAT POWERS. *Use* International Relations; World Politics

GREEK LETTER SOCIETIES. *Use* Secret Societies; Students

GREEN MANURING. *Use* Fertilizers and Manures

GREENBELTS. *Use* Regional Planning

GREENHOUSES. *Use* Floriculture; Horticulture

GREENS, EDIBLE. *Use* Vegetables

GREETINGS. *See* Etiquette

GRIEF. *Use* Emotions

GRIEVANCE PROCEDURES. *Use* Arbitration, Industrial; Industrial Relations; Labor Laws and Legislation

GROCERY TRADE. *Use* Chain Stores

GROOMING, PERSONAL. *Use* Beauty, Personal; Clothing and Dress

GROSS NATIONAL PRODUCT
LC   ——; s.a. Statistics; Wealth
SEARS   INCOME; s.a. Economics; Wealth
RG   ——; s.a. Income; Wealth, Distribution of
NYT   U.S.—ECONOMIC CONDITIONS AND TRENDS (General); s.a. Economics; Income; U.S.—Finances
PAIS   PRODUCTION; s.a. Income; Wealth
BPI   ——; s.a. Flow of funds; National income

GROTTOES. *See* Caves

GROUND SUPPORT SYSTEMS (Space flight). *Use* Astronautics; Space Flight

GROUNDS MAINTENANCE. *Use* Gardening

GROUP BEHAVIOR. *Use* Behavior Therapy; Group Relations Training; Riots; Social Groups

GROUP COUNSELING. *Use* Counseling; Group Relations Training

GROUP CREDITORS, INSURANCE. *Use* Installment Plan

GROUP DYNAMICS. *See* Social Groups

GROUP ENCOUNTERS. *See* Group Relations Training

GROUP GUIDANCE IN EDUCATION. *Use* Group Relations Training; Personnel Service in Education

GROUP MEDICAL PRACTICE. *Use* Medical Care

GROUP READING. *Use* Reading

GROUP RELATIONS TRAINING
LC   ——; s.a. Behavior; Group psychotherapy; Interpersonal relations; Social groups; Social interaction

SEARS   HUMAN RELATIONS
RG   ——; s.a. Group counseling; Group guidance in education; Social education
NYT   PSYCHOLOGY AND PSYCHOLOGISTS; s.a. Mental health and disorders
PAIS   ——; s.a. Counseling; Family psychotherapy; Group behavior; Human relations; Social psychology
BPI   ——; s.a. Groups (sociology); Psychotherapy

GROUP THERAPY. *See* Behavior Therapy; Group Relations Training

GROUPIES. *See* Music; Subculture; Youth

GROUPS, SOCIAL. *See* Social Groups

GROUPS (Sociology). *Use* Elite (Social sciences); Group Relations Training; Social Groups; Subculture

GROWTH
Scope: Works on development of the human organism.
LC   ——; s.a. Adulthood; Genetic psychology; Infants—Growth Maturation (psychology); Regeneration (biology)
SEARS   ——; s.a. Children—Growth; Physiology
RG   ——; s.a. Children—Growth and development; Maturity
NYT   ——; s.a. Body, Human; Stature
PAIS   STATURE; s.a. Body measurements; Physiology
BPI   ——; s.a. Physiology

GROWTH (Plants). *Use* Plants

GUARANTEED ANNUAL INCOME
LC   ——; s.a. Economic security; Employment stabilization; Income security; Negative income tax
SEARS   ——; s.a. Income; Wages—Annual wage
RG   ——; s.a. Negative income tax; Wages—Annual wage
NYT   LABOR—U.S.—MINIMUM WAGE; s.a. Income; Labor—U.S.—Wages and hours
PAIS   INCOME—GUARANTEED INCOME; s.a. Social and economic security; Unemployment, Seasonal; Wages and salaries
BPI   ——; s.a. Negative income tax; Wages and salaries

GUARANTEES AND WARRANTIES. *Use* Obligations

GUARANTY. *See* Suretyship and Guaranty

GUARDIAN AND WARD. *Use* Trusts and Trustees

GUERILLA WARFARE
LC   ——; s.a. Combatants and non-combatants (international law); Partisans
SEARS   ——; s.a. Tactics; War; World War, 1939–1945—Underground movements
RG   ——; s.a. Fedayeen; Guerillas
NYT   WAR AND REVOLUTION; s.a. Military art and science; names of guerilla forces, e.g., Tupamaros
PAIS   GUERILLAS; s.a. Insurgency; Military art and science; U.S.—Army—Special forces
BPI   ——; s.a. Government, Resistance to; subd. *Guerillas* under name of country

GUESTS. *See* Entertaining; Etiquette

GUIDANCE. *See* Personnel Service in Education; Vocational Guidance

GUIDANCE SYSTEMS (Flight). *Use* Ballistic Missiles

GUIDEBOOKS. *Use* Maps

GUIDED MISSILES. *Use* Aerospace Industries; Atomic Warfare; Ballistic Missiles; Ballistics; Bombs; Gunnery; Rockets (Aeronautics); Weapons

GUIDED MISSILES—DEFENSE. *Use* Radar

GUILD SOCIALISM. *Use* Socialism

GUILDS. *Use* Trade and Professional Associations; Trade Unions

GUMS. *Use* Dentistry

GUNNERY
LC ——; s.a. Artillery; Ballistics; Naval gunnery; Projectiles; Shooting, Military
SEARS ORDNANCE; s.a. Firearms; Rifles
RG FIREARMS; s.a. Bombing and gunnery ranges; Pistols; Revolvers; Shotguns
NYT ARMAMENT, DEFENSE AND MILITARY FORCES (General); s.a. Explosives; Firearms; Weapons
PAIS FIREARMS; s.a. Guided missiles; Rocket launchers (ordnance)
BPI ——; s.a. Explosives; Fire control (naval gunnery)

GUNNING. *See* Hunting

GUNS. *See* Firearms; Gunnery; Ordnance

GUTTERS. *Use* Streets

GYMNASTICS
LC ——; s.a. Callisthenics; Musico-callisthenics; Schools—Exercises and recreations; Swedish gymnastics
SEARS ——; s.a. Acrobats and acrobatics; Physical education and training; Physical fitness
RG ——; s.a. Exercise; Isometric exercise
NYT PHYSICAL EDUCATION AND TRAINING; s.a. Athletics; Exercise; Sports
PAIS PHYSICAL EDUCATION; s.a. College athletics; Sports
BPI EXERCISE; s.a. Athletics; Physical education and training

GYPSIES. *Use* Tribe and Tribal System

H

HABEAS CORPUS. *Use* Arrest; Bail

HABITATIONS, HUMAN. *See* Housing

HAGIOGRAPHY. *Use* Saints

HAIRDRESSING. *Use* Cosmetics; Dyes and Dyeing; Fashion; Toilet

HALACHA. *See* Talmud

HALLOWEEN. *Use* Special Days, Weeks and Months

HALLUCINATIONS AND ILLUSIONS. *Use* Insanity; Mental Illness; Mentally Ill; Occult Sciences; Psychical Research

HALLUCINOGENIC DRUGS. *Use* Antidepressants; Drugs

HAND TO HAND FIGHTING, ORIENTAL. *Use* Self-Defense

HANDBOOKS
Scope: Works of general miscellaneous information. See also subd. *Handbooks*, etc. under specific subjects, e.g., Needlework—Handbooks, etc.
LC HANDBOOKS, VADE-MECUMS, ETC.; s.a. Encyclopedias and dictionaries; Technical manuals
SEARS See subd. *Handbooks*, manuals, etc. under specific subject, e.g., Photography—Handbooks, manuals, etc.; s.a. Almanacs; Yearbooks
RG ——; s.a. Almanacs; Textbooks
NYT PUBLICATIONS; s.a. Almanacs; Books and literature; Textbooks
PAIS HANDBOOKS, VADE-MECUMS, ETC.; s.a. Dictionaries; subd. *Dictionaries* under subjects, e.g., Accounting—Dictionaries
BPI HANDBOOKS, MANUALS, ETC.; s.a. Directories; Reference books

HANDICAPPED
LC ——; s.a. Brain damaged children; Handicapped children; Invalids; Occupational therapy; Physical therapy; Veterans, Disabled
SEARS ——; s.a. Orthopedia; Physically handicapped; Sick; Socially handicapped
RG ——; s.a. Camps for the handicapped; Cerebral palsied children; Paralytics; Recreation for the handicapped
NYT ——; s.a. Birth defects (congenital defects); Mental deficiency and defectives; names of diseases, e.g., Epilepsy; types of handicaps, e.g., Blindness
PAIS DISABLED; s.a. Children, Handicapped; Employment—Disabled; Socially handicapped children
BPI ——; s.a. Blind; Deaf; Mentally handicapped; Veterans, Disabled

HANDICAPPED—EMPLOYMENT. *Use* Vocational Rehabilitation

HANDICAPPED—REHABILITATION. *See* Rehabilitation

HANDICRAFT.
See also kinds of handicraft, e.g., Basket making; Leather work; Origami; Weaving; etc.
LC ———; s.a. Art; Arts and crafts movement; Industrial arts; Manual training
SEARS ———; s.a. Occupational therapy; Paper crafts
RG ———; s.a. Artisans; Craftmanship
NYT HANDICRAFTS; s.a. Hobbies
PAIS HANDICRAFTS; s.a. Hobbies; Industrial arts
BPI ———; s.a. Arts and crafts; Hobbies

HANDWRITING. *Use* Alphabet; Calligraphy; Writing

HANGING. *Use* Capital Punishment

HAPPENINGS. *Use* Theater

HAPPENINGS (Art). *Use* Art, Modern—20th Century

HARAKIRI. *Use* Death

HARBORS. *Use* Civil Engineering; Merchant Marine; Ports

HARD-CORE UNEMPLOYED. *Use* Work Relief

HARD-CORE UNEMPLOYED, TRAINING. *Use* Occupational Training

HARDWARE. *Use* Locks and Keys; Metal Industries; Tools

HARNESS RACING. *Use* Horse Racing

HASSIDISM. *Use* Jews

HATE. *Use* Emotions

HATHA YOGA. *See* Yoga

HAUTE COUTURE. *See* Fashion

HAZARDOUS SUBSTANCES
LC ———; s.a. Chemicals—Safety measures; Industrial safety
SEARS LABELS; s.a. Explosives; Poisons
RG ———; s.a. Explosives; Gases, Asphyxiating and poisonous
NYT Names of substances, e.g., Explosives; Poisons; etc.
PAIS DANGEROUS GOODS; s.a. Poisons; Toxic and inflammable goods, Labeling of
BPI ———; s.a. Poisons, Industrial; Safety packaging

HAZING. *Use* Secret Societies

HEAD. *Use* Brain

HEADS OF STATE
LC ———; s.a. Dictators; Emperors; Executive power; Statesmen
SEARS KINGS AND RULERS; s.a. Presidents; Queens; subd. *Kings and rulers* under name of country, e.g., Great Britain—King and rulers
RG ———; s.a. Divine right of kings; Kings and rulers; Statesmen
NYT Names of individuals or countries s.a. Diplomacy; International relations; Nobility

PAIS ———; s.a. Kings and rulers; Monarchy; Visits of state
BPI POLITICAL SCIENCE; s.a. Presidents—U.S.

HEALING, MENTAL. *See* Mental Healing

HEALTH. *Use* Age; Hygiene; Physical Fitness; Woman—Health and Hygiene

HEALTH CARE. *See* Medical Care

HEALTH CENTERS. *Use* Medical Care

HEALTH CLUBS. *Use* Exercise

HEALTH EDUCATION
LC ———; s.a. Dental health education; Physical fitness; Schools of public health
SEARS ———; s.a. Physical health and education; School hygiene
RG ———; s.a. Health workers—Training; Television broadcasting—Health education programs
NYT MEDICINE AND HEALTH—U.S.—EDUCATION AND SCHOOLS; s.a. Medicine and health; Physical education and training; Sex education
PAIS PUBLIC HEALTH EDUCATION; s.a. Medical workers—Training; Physical education
BPI ———; s.a. Environmental health; Public health

HEALTH FACILITIES. *Use* Clinics; Hospitals; Medical Care

HEALTH INSURANCE. *See* Insurance, Health

HEALTH RESORTS, SPAS, ETC. *Use* Summer Resorts; Tourist Trade; Travel

HEALTH SERVICES. *Use* Clinics; Hospitals; Medical Care

HEALTH WORKERS — TRAINING. *Use* Health Education

HEARING
LC ———; s.a. Ear—Diseases; Hearing disorders; Music—Physiological aspects
SEARS ———; s.a. Deafness; Senses and sensations; Sound
RG ———; s.a. Deafness; Ear; Echolocation (physiology)
NYT EARS AND HEARING; s.a. Deafness and deaf-mutes; Sound
PAIS ———; s.a. Deaf; Hearing aids
BPI ———; s.a. Ear; Hearing aids

HEART. *Use* Arteries; Blood Pressure

HEART—TRANSPLANTS. *Use* Operations, Surgical

HEATING
LC ———; s.a. Electric heating; Radiant heating
SEARS ———; s.a. Hot water heating; Steam heating
RG ———; s.a. Insulation (heat); Solar heating
NYT ———; s.a. Fuel; Heat
PAIS HEATING AND VENTILATION; s.a. Furnaces; Heating from central stations; Oil burners
BPI ———; s.a. Boilers; Heaters; subd. *Heating, cooling*, etc. under subjects, e.g., Apartment houses—Heating; Factories—Heating; etc.

HEATING PIPES. *Use* Plumbing

HEAT-RESISTANT MATERIALS, ETC. *Use* Materials

HEAVEN
LC ———; s.a. Angels; Beatific vision; Hell; Immortality; Intermediate state
SEARS ———; s.a. Eschatology; Hell
RG ———; s.a. Future life; Hell
NYT RELIGION AND CHURCHES; s.a. Death; Philosophy
PAIS RELIGION; s.a. Death
BPI RELIGION; s.a. Death

HEAVY MINERAL. *Use* Mineralogy

HEBREW ART. *See* Art, Jewish

HEBREW LITERATURE. *Use* Jewish Literature; Talmud

HEBREWS. *See* Jews

HEDGING. *Use* Commodity Exchanges; Investments; Risk; Stock Exchange

HEIRLOOMS. *Use* Property

HEIRS. *See* Inheritance and Succession

HELICOPTERS. *Use* Aeronautics; Airplanes

HELIOGRAVURE. *See* Photography—Printing Processes

HELIPORTS. *Use* Airports

HELL. *Use* Death; Heaven; Immortality

HELLENISM. *Use* Humanism

HEMATOLOGY. *Use* Blood

HEMOGLOBINOPATHY. *Use* Anemia

HEMORRHAGE. *Use* Blood

HERALDRY. *Use* Emblems; Genealogy; Signs and Symbols

HERBICIDES. *Use* Pests; Weeds

HEREDITY
LC ———; s.a. Breeding; Heredity of disease; Human genetics; Inheritance of acquired characteristics
SEARS ———; s.a. Mendel's law; Natural selection; Variation (biology)
RG ———; s.a. Evolution; Population genetics
NYT BIOLOGY AND BIOCHEMISTRY; s.a. Eugenics; Evolution
PAIS ———; s.a. Eugenics; Genetics
BPI ———; s.a. Genetics

HERESY. *See* Sects; Theology

HERMETIC ART AND PHILOSOPHY. *See* Alchemy; Occult Sciences

HERMITS. *Use* Monasticism and Religious Orders

HEROISM. *Use* Explorers; Rescue Work; War

HIBERNATION. *Use* Sleep

HIDES AND SKINS. *Use* Leather Industry and Trade

HIEROGLYPHICS. *Use* Writing

HI-FI SYSTEMS. *See* High Fidelity Sound Systems

HIGH FASHION. *See* Fashion

HIGH FIDELITY AUDIO EQUIPMENT. *See* High Fidelity Sound Systems

HIGH FIDELITY SOUND SYSTEMS
LC ———; s.a. Sound—Recording and reproducing; Stereophonic sound systems
SEARS ———; s.a. Electronics; Sound—Recording and reproducing
RG ———; s.a. Loud speaking apparatus; Stereophonic sound systems
NYT RECORDING (DISK AND TAPE) AND RECORDING AND PLAYBACK EQUIPMENT; s.a. Electronics; Sound
PAIS ———; s.a. Electronics industry; Phonograph industry; Sound recording
BPI ———; s.a. Home electronics; Stereophonic sound systems

HIGH SCHOOL STUDENTS. *Use* Adolescence; Dropouts; High Schools; School Attendance; Schools; Students

HIGH SCHOOLS
Scope: Works on high schools of a particular city are entered under name of city, with subd. *Public schools*, e.g., Boston—Public schools.
LC ———; s.a. Accreditation (education); Education, Secondary; High school teachers; Public schools
SEARS ———; s.a. Commencements; Junior high schools
RG ———; s.a. Schools, Experimental; Trade Schools
NYT EDUCATION AND SCHOOLS (Name of place)—HIGH SCHOOLS; s.a. Commercial education; Education and schools—U.S.—Prep schools
PAIS ———; s.a. Education, Secondary; Folk high schools; High school students
BPI ———; s.a. High school students; Public schools

HIGH SOCIETY. *See* Upper Classes

HIGH TREASON. *See* Treason

HIGHER EDUCATION. *See* Education, Higher

HIGHER LAW. *See* Government, Resistance to

HIGH-FREQUENCY RADIO. *See* Radio, Short Wave

HIGHLAND CLANS. *See* Tribes and Tribal System

HIGHWAY BEAUTIFICATION. *See* Roads

HIGHWAY CONSTRUCTION. *See* Roads

HIGHWAY ENGINEERING. *Use* Civil Engineering; Roads

HIGHWAY SAFETY. *See* Traffic Safety

HIGHWAYS. *Use* Roads; Streets

HIJACKING OF AIRPLANES. *Use* Abduction; Kidnapping; Offenses Against Public Safety; Terrorism

HIKING. *Use* Backpacking; Outdoor Life; Walking

HINDUISM

LC   ——; s.a. Buddha and Buddhism; God (Hinduism); Sikhs—Religion; Women in Hinduism

SEARS   ——; s.a. Brahmanism; Caste; Veolas; Yoga

RG   ——; s.a. Hindus; Mysticism—Hinduism

NYT   ——; s.a. India

PAIS   ——; s.a. Hindus; India—Hindu-Muslim relations

BPI   ——; s.a. Krishna; Religion

HIPPIES. *Use* Bohemianism; Subculture; Vagrancy; Youth

HIRE-PURCHASE PLAN. *See* Installment Plan

HIRING HALLS. *Use* Trade Unions

HISTORICAL CRITICISM. *See* Historical Research

HISTORICAL FICTION. *Use* Fiction

HISTORICAL RESEARCH

See also subd. *History—Sources* under names of countries, e.g., U.S.—History—Civil war—Sources.

LC   ——; s.a. Diplomatics; Historiography; History—Methodology; Public records

SEARS HISTORY—RESEARCH; s.a. Archives; Charters

RG   HISTORY—SOURCES; s.a. Historians; Oral history; subd. *History—Historiography* under names of countries

NYT   RESEARCH; s.a. Books and literature; Documents; History; Oral history

PAIS   ——; s.a. History—Sources; History—Study and teaching; Libraries, Historical

BPI   ——; s.a. Historical literature; History

HISTORY

See also subd. *History* under names of places, e.g., U.S.—History; under specific subjects, e.g., Art—History; English language—History; and by period divisions, e.g., History, Ancient; History, Medieval; History, Modern

LC   ——; s.a. Chronology; Church history; Culture; Economic history; Historical fiction; Social history

SEARS ——; s.a. Constitutional history; Geography, Historical; Military history; World history

RG   ——; s.a. Civilization; Current events; Historical paintings; History in art

NYT   ——; s.a. Civilization; personal, place and event names

PAIS   ——; s.a. Local history; Oral history

BPI   ——; s.a. Historical research

HISTORY, ANCIENT. *Use* Bible

HISTORY—ERRORS, INVENTIONS, ETC. *Use* Errors

HISTORY — METHODOLOGY. *Use* Historical Research

HISTORY, MODERN. *Use* Current Events; Twentieth Century

HISTORY, NATURAL. *See* Natural History

HISTORY AND ART. *Use* Art and History

HISTRIONICS. *See* Acting

HIT AND RUN DRIVERS. *Use* Traffic Accidents

HITCHHIKING. *Use* Backpacking

HOAXES. *Use* Fraud

HOBBIES. *Use* Amusements; Handicraft; Leisure; Recreation; Retirement

HOCKEY. *Use* Winter Sports

HOLDING COMPANIES. *Use* Business Enterprises; Corporations; Trusts, Industrial

HOLIDAYS. *Use* Festivals; Manners and Customs; Special Days, Weeks and Months; Vacations, Employee

HOLINESS. *Use* Religion

HOLOCAUST. *See* Atrocities

HOLY SCRIPTURES. *See* Bible

HOLY SEE. *See* Catholic Church; Papacy

HOME. *Use* Family

HOME AND SCHOOL

LC   PARENT-TEACHER RELATIONSHIPS; s.a. Children—Management—Study and teaching; Community and school; Parent-teacher conferences

SEARS ——; s.a. Child study; Parents' and teachers' associations

RG   SCHOOL AND THE HOME; s.a. Home study; Parents and teachers associations

NYT   EDUCATION AND SCHOOLS—U.S.— SCHOOL ADMINISTRATION AND COMMUNITY ROLE; s.a. Children and youth; Teachers and school employees

PAIS   PARENT-TEACHER ASSOCIATIONS; s.a. Education; School and community

BPI   TEACHERS; s.a. Education; Schools

HOME DECORATION. *See* Interior Decoration

HOME ECONOMICS

LC   ——; s.a. Budgets, Household; Consumer education; Family life education; Household appliances; Household equipment and furnishings; Shopping

SEARS ——; s.a. Entertaining; Household employees; Mobile home living

RG   ——; s.a. Domestic finance; Storage in the home

NYT   ——; s.a. Budgets and budgeting; Families and family life

PAIS   ——; s.a. Budget, Family; Consumer education

BPI   ——; s.a. Consumer education; Marketing (home economics)

HOME FURNISHINGS. *See* Household Equipment and Furnishings

HOME NURSING. *Use* Invalids; Nurses and Nursing; Sick

HOME OWNERSHIP

LC   ——; s.a. Farm ownership; Homesites; Real property; Repairing—Amateurs' manuals

SEARS HOUSES; s.a. Farms; Mortgages
RG ———; s.a. Apartment houses—Cooperative ownership; House selling; Housing, Cooperative; Summer homes
NYT HOUSING; s.a. Mortgages; Real estate
PAIS ———; s.a. Condominium plan ownership; House buying; Real estate business
BPI ———; s.a. Condominium (housing); Country homes; Vacation houses

HOME RECEPTIONS. *See* Table

HOME RULE FOR CITIES. *See* Municipal Government

HOME STUDY. *Use* Correspondence Schools and Courses; Home and School

HOMELESS, THE. *Use* Begging; Poverty; Vagrancy

HOMES, INSTITUTIONAL. *Use* Institutional Care; Orphans

HOMES FOR THE AGED. *See* Nursing Homes; Old Age Homes

HOMESITES. *Use* Home Ownership

HOMESTEAD LAW. *Use* Land Tenure; Public Lands

HOMICIDE. *Use* Crime and Criminals; Murder

HOMILETICS. *See* Preaching

HOMONYMS. *Use* Vocabulary

HOMOSEXUALITY
LC ———; s.a. Bisexuality; Gay liberation movement; Lesbianism; Sodomy
SEARS ———; s.a. Lesbianism; Sexual ethics; subd. *Sexual behavior* under names of groups, e.g., Prisoners—Sexual behavior
RG ———; s.a. Church work with homosexuals; Lesbianism
NYT ———; s.a. Gay Activist Alliance (organization); Gay Liberation Movement (organization); Sex; Women
PAIS ———; s.a. Lesbianism
BPI ———; s.a. Sex (psychology)

HONESTY. *Use* Business Ethics; Ethics; Truth

HONEYBEES. *See* Bees

HONEYMOON. *Use* Marriage

HONOR SYSTEM. *See* Self-Government (Education)

HONORARY DEGREES. *See* Degrees, Academic

HORMONES. *Use* Cells

HORNBOOKS. *Use* Textbooks

HOROLOGY. *Use* Time

HOROSCOPE. *See* Astrology

HORSE BREEDING AND RACING. *Use* Horse-Racing; Horsemanship

HORSE RACE BETTING. *Use* Gambling; Horse-Racing

HORSEMANSHIP
LC ———; s.a. Coaching; Equestrianism; Horsemen; Jockeys; Jumping (horsemanship)
SEARS ———; s.a. Cowboys; Horse—Training; Rodeos
RG ———; s.a. Horse back trips; Polo; Rodeos
NYT HORSES; s.a. Horse Shows; Rodeos
PAIS HORSE BREEDING AND RACING; s.a. Horses
BPI ———; s.a. Horseback trips; Rodeos

HORSE-RACING
LC ———; s.a. Harness racing; Pari-mutuel betting; Race-horses
SEARS ———; s.a. Gambling
RG ———; s.a. Horse race betting; Jockeys; Race tracks
NYT ———; s.a. Gambling (illegal forms); Horse racing—Betting; Horses
PAIS HORSE BREEDING AND RACING; s.a. Book-making (betting); Racing
BPI ———; s.a. Race horses; Race tracks

HORSES. *Use* Domestic Animals; Stock and Stock Breeding

HORSEWOMEN. *See* Horsemanship

HORTICULTURE
Scope: Works on the scientific and economic aspects of the cultivation of fruits, vegetables, flowers, and ornamental plants.
LC ———; s.a. Arboculture; Frost protection; Greenhouse management; Plants, Potted; Truck farming
SEARS GARDENING; s.a. Flower gardening; Grounds maintenance; Organiculture; Plants, Cultivated; Window gardening
RG ———; s.a. Artificial light gardening; House plants; Nurseries (horticulture); Watering of plants
NYT ———; s.a. Plants; Trees and shrubs
PAIS ———; s.a. Floriculture; Nurseries (horticultural)
BPI ———; s.a. Gardening; Plants

HOSPITAL CARE. *Use* Hospitals; Medical Care

HOSPITALITY. *Use* Charity; Entertaining

HOSPITALIZATION. *Use* Insurance, Health

HOSPITALS
See also subd. *Hospitals* under names of cities, e.g., Philadelphia—Hospitals.
LC ———; s.a. Clinics; Dispensaries; Hospital care; Medical centers; Operating rooms; Public health; subd. *Hospitals* under types of illness, e.g., Incurables—Hospitals and asylums; Orthopedia—Hospitals and institutions
SEARS ———; s.a. Institutional care; Medical centers
RG ———; s.a. Children—Hospital care; Computers—Medical use; Missions, Medical; Nursing homes
NYT MEDICINE AND HEALTH; s.a. Mental Health and Disorders; names of hospitals, e.g., Mayo Clinic; Nursing homes
PAIS ———; s.a. Ambulance service; Health services; Hospitals—Home care program; Interns (medicine)
BPI ———; s.a. Hospital care; Medical care; Medical centers

HOSPITALS—EMERGENCY SERVICES. *Use* Ambulances

HOSPITALS, MILITARY. *Use* Veterans

HOSPITALS, PSYCHIATRIC. *Use* Mental Institutions

HOT WATER HEATING. *Use* Heating

HOT WATER SUPPLY. *Use* Plumbing

HOTELS, TAVERNS, ETC.
See also subd. *Hotels, Restaurants, etc.* under names of cities.
LC   ——; s.a. Caterers and catering; Coffee houses; Hotel management; Lodging houses; Motels; Restaurants, lunch rooms, etc.; Summer resorts
SEARS HOTELS, MOTELS, ETC.; s.a. Tourist trade
RG   ——; s.a. Airlines—Hotel operations; Hotel decoration; Restaurants
NYT   HOTELS, BARS, MOTELS, NIGHT CLUBS AND RESTAURANTS; s.a. Bars and barrooms; Travel and resorts; Vacations
PAIS   HOTELS; s.a. Motels; Tourist camps, hostels, etc.
BPI   HOTELS; s.a. Motels; Restaurants, lunchrooms, etc.

HOURS (Time). *See* Time

HOURS OF LABOR. *Use* Child Labor; Labor Laws and Legislation; Night Work; Vacations, Employee; Woman—Employment

HOURS OF WORK. *Use* Work

HOUSE BUYING. *Use* Home Ownership

HOUSE CONSTRUCTION. *Use* Building

HOUSE DECORATION. *Use* Household Equipment and Furnishings; Interior Decoration

HOUSE DETECTIVES. *Use* Detectives; Police

HOUSE DRAINAGE. *See* Plumbing

HOUSE FURNISHINGS. *Use* Furniture; Household Equipment and Furnishings; Interior Decoration; Upholstery

HOUSE FURNISHINGS INDUSTRY. *Use* Household Equipment and Furnishings

HOUSE PAINTING. *Use* Painting, Industrial

HOUSE PLANTS. *Use* Floriculture; Gardening; Horticulture

HOUSE SELLING. *Use* Home Ownership; Real Property

HOUSEHOLD APPLIANCES. *Use* Home Economics; Household Equipment and Furnishings; Laundries and Laundering

HOUSEHOLD EMPLOYEES
LC   SERVANTS; s.a. Master and servant; Wages
SEARS ——; s.a. Home economics; Labor and laboring classes
RG   ——; s.a. Housekeepers; Visiting housekeepers
NYT   DOMESTIC SERVICE; s.a. Housework
PAIS   DOMESTIC SERVICE; s.a. Housekeeping service (social work); Master and servant
BPI   SERVANTS; s.a. Home economics

HOUSEHOLD EQUIPMENT AND FURNISHINGS
See also names of specific items such as Carpets; Coverlets; Drapery; Furniture; Kitchen utensils; Vacuum cleaners, etc.

LC   HOUSE FURNISHINGS; s.a. Home economics; Household appliances
SEARS INTERIOR DECORATION; s.a. Household appliances; Household equipment and supplies
RG   HOUSEHOLD FURNISHINGS; s.a. Color in house decoration; House decoration
NYT   ——; s.a. Furniture; Interior decoration
PAIS   HOUSEHOLD FURNISHINGS; s.a. Home economics; Interior decoration
BPI   INTERIOR DECORATION; s.a. House furnishings industry

HOUSEHOLD EXPENSES. *See* Cost and Standard of Living

HOUSEHOLD FURNISHINGS. *Use* Furniture; Household Equipment and Furnishings; Interior Decoration; Upholstery

HOUSEHOLD MANAGEMENT. *See* Home Economics

HOUSEHOLD PESTS. *Use* Pests

HOUSEKEEPERS. *Use* Household Employees

HOUSEKEEPING. *See* Home Economics

HOUSES, APARTMENT. *See* Apartment Houses

HOUSES, PREFABRICATED. *Use* Construction Industry

HOUSEWIVES. *Use* Woman

HOUSEWORK. *Use* Home Economics; Household Employees; Woman

HOUSING
Scope: Works on the social and economic aspects of the housing problem.
LC   ——; s.a. Cities and towns—Planning; Discrimination in housing; Garden cities; Labor and laboring classes—Dwellings; Relocation (housing)
SEARS ——; s.a. Aged—Dwellings; Blacks—Housing; City planning; Home ownership; Landlord and tenants; Mortgages; Physically handicapped—Dwellings; Reclamation of land; Regional planning; Tenement houses
RG   ——; s.a. Housing projects—Relocation of tenants; Slums; subd. *Housing* under names of groups, e.g., Aged—Housing
NYT   ——; s.a. Area planning and renewal; Building; Urban areas
PAIS   ——; s.a. Apartment houses; Housing—Tenant relocation; Negroes—Housing; Residential location; Slums
BPI   ——; s.a. Apartment houses; Discrimination in housing; Relocation (housing); Residential mobility; Slums

HOUSING, COOPERATIVE. *Use* Condominium (Housing); Home Ownership

HOUSING, DISCRIMINATION IN. *See* Discrimination in Housing

HOUSING—FEDERAL AID. *Use* Mortgages; Public Housing; Subsidies

HOUSING—FINANCE. *Use* Mortgages; Subsidies

HOUSING AUTHORITIES. *Use* Public Housing

HOUSING FOR THE AGED. *See* Nursing Homes; Old Age Homes

HOUSING MANAGEMENT. *Use* Apartment Houses; Real Property

HOUSING PROJECTS. *Use* Public Housing

HUMAN ANATOMY. *See* Anatomy, Human

HUMAN BEHAVIOR. *Use* Behavior (Psychology); Leadership; Social Sciences; Virtues

HUMAN BIOLOGY. *Use* Man

HUMAN BODY. *See* Body, Human

HUMAN CAPITAL. *Use* Labor Supply; Man

HUMAN ECOLOGY
LC ———; s.a. Acclimatization; Anthropogeography; Conservation of natural resources; Demography; Ecology; Sociology
SEARS ———; s.a. Man—Influence of environment; Man—Influence on nature
RG ———; s.a. Ekistics; Environmental policy
NYT SOCIOLOGY; s.a. Environment; Man
PAIS ———; s.a. Environment; Man—Influence of environment
BPI ———; s.a. Environmental health; Population

HUMAN ENGINEERING
Scope: Works on engineering design as related to man's anatomical, physiological, and psychological capabilities and limitations. See Psychology, Applied for material on man's relation to his job.
LC ———; s.a. Design, Industrial; Environmental engineering; Psychology, Physiological
SEARS ———; s.a. Life support systems (space environment); Machinery—Design
RG ———; s.a. Environmental engineering (buildings); Human information processing
NYT ENGINEERING AND ENGINEERS; s.a. Design; Management, Industrial and institutional; Psychology and psychologists
PAIS ———; s.a. Design in industry; Environmental engineering
BPI ———; s.a. Human information processing; Man-machine systems

HUMAN FIGURE IN ART. *Use* Nude in Art

HUMAN FIGURE IN PHOTOGRAPHY. *Use* Nude in Art; Photography, Artistic

HUMAN GENETICS. *Use* Genetics; Heredity

HUMAN GEOGRAPHY. *See* Anthropo-Geography

HUMAN INFORMATION PROCESSING. *Use* Apperception; Human Engineering; Information Sciences; Perception

HUMAN RACE. *See* Anthropology; Man; Woman

HUMAN RELATIONS
LC INTERPERSONAL RELATIONS; s.a. Comradeship; Conduct of life; Dependency (psychology); Empathy; Family; Friendship; Psychology, Applied; Social distance; Supervision of employees; Teacher-student relationship; Toleration
SEARS ———; s.a. Behavior; Discrimination; Ethics; Prejudices and antipathies; Sympathy
RG ———; s.a. Alienation (social psychology); Brotherhood of man; Loneliness; Neighbors; Playmates; Race relations
NYT PSYCHOLOGY AND PSYCHOLOGISTS; s.a. Ethics and morals
PAIS ———; s.a. Group relations training; Race relations; Social psychology
BPI ———; s.a. Alienation (social psychology); Group relations training

HUMAN RESOURCE DEVELOPMENT. *See* Manpower

HUMAN RIGHTS. *Use* Civil Rights

HUMANISM
Scope: Works on culture founded on the study of classics and philosophical, intellectual, and religious movements centered on man rather than in nature or the supernatural.
LC ———; s.a. Classical education; Humanistic ethics; Learning and scholarship
SEARS ———; s.a. Culture; Humanism—20th century; Renaissance
RG ———; s.a. Classical education; Hellenism; Knowledge
NYT PHILOSOPHY; s.a. Books and literature; Culture; Religion and churches
PAIS ———; s.a. Culture
BPI PHILOSOPHY; s.a. Culture; Religion

HUMANITY. *Use* Charity

HUMILITY. *Use* Christian Ethics

HUMOR. *Use* Wit and Humor

HUMOROUS ILLUSTRATIONS. *See* Caricatures and Cartoons

HUNGER. *Use* Food Supply; Nutrition

HUNTING
LC ———; s.a. Game protection; Poaching; Trapping
SEARS ———; s.a. Fur trade; Game and game birds; Tracking and trailing
RG ———; s.a. Hunting with bow and arrow; Shooting; Whaling
NYT HUNTING AND TRAPPING; s.a. Firearms; Shooting (sport)
PAIS ———; s.a. Fur industry
BPI ———; s.a. Coursing; Game and game birds; Shooting

HURRICANE PROTECTION. *Use* Public Works; Regional Planning

HURRICANES. *Use* Disasters

HUSBAND AND WIFE. *Use* Family; Marriage; Marriage Law

HUSBANDRY. *See* Agriculture

HYBRIDIZATION. *Use* Breeding; Horticulture

HYDROELECTRIC POWER. *Use* Force and Energy; Water

HYDROGEN BOMB. *Use* Atomic Warfare; Bombs

HYDROLOGY. *Use* Water

HYDROTHERAPY. *Use* Baths; Physical Therapy; Therapeutics

HYGIENE

LC	——; s.a. Beauty, Personal; Children—Care and hygiene; Exercise; Hygiene, Public; Hygiene, Sexual; Medicine, Preventive; Sanitation; Toilet; Woman—Health and hygiene
SEARS	——; s.a. Hygiene, Rural; Infants—Care and hygiene; Military hygiene; Occupational diseases; School hygiene; Sexual hygiene
RG	——; s.a. Cleanliness; Health; Quarantine; Venereal diseases
NYT	MEDICINE AND HEALTH; s.a. Environment; Sanitation; Venereal diseases
PAIS	HEALTH; s.a. Environmental health; Industrial hygiene; Mental hygiene; Sanitation; Sex education
BPI	——; s.a. Hygiene, Industrial; Public health; Sex instruction

HYGIENE, MENTAL. *See* Mental Hygiene

HYGIENE, PUBLIC. *Use* Communicable Diseases; Medical Care; Public Health; Sanitation

HYGIENE, SEXUAL. *Use* Hygiene; Prostitution; Sex; Venereal Diseases

HYGIENE—STUDY AND TEACHING. *See* Health Education

HYMNS. *Use* Liturgies; Singing and Songs

HYPERSENSITIVITY (Immunology). *See* Allergy

HYPERTENSION. *Use* Blood Pressure

HYPNOTICS. *Use* Dreams; Hypnotism; Mental Suggestion; Narcotics

HYPNOTISM

LC	——; s.a. Magnetic healing; Mental suggestion; Sleep; Thought transference; Trance
SEARS	——; s.a. Mental healing; Mind and body; Subconscious; Therapeutics, Suggestive
RG	——; s.a. Faith cure; Medicine, magic, mystic, etc.
NYT	HYPNOSIS; s.a. Mental health and disorders; Psychic phenomena
PAIS	——
BPI	HYPNOTICS

HYPOTHESIS. *Use* Logic

HYPOTHESIS TESTING. *Use* Research

HYSTERIA. *Use* Insanity; Social Psychology

I

ICE CAVES. *Use* Caves

ICE SPORTS. *See* Winter Sports

ICEBOATS. *Use* Winter Sports

ICEBOXES. *Use* Cooling

ICONOGRAPHY. *See* Art

ICONS. *Use* Art and Religion

IDEALISM

LC	——; s.a. Dualism; Pragmatism; Transcendentalism
SEARS	——; s.a. Materialism; Positivism; Realism
RG	——; s.a. Humanism; Perfection (philosophy)
NYT	PHILOSOPHY; s.a. Ethics and morals
PAIS	PHILOSOPHY; s.a. Ethics
BPI	PHILOSOPHY; s.a. Ethics

IDEAS. *Use* Inventions; Intellectual Property

IDENTIFICATION (Psychology). *Use* Psychoanalysis

IDENTITY (Psychology). *Use* Character; Individuality

IDEOLOGY. *Use* Belief and Doubt; Knowledge, Theory of; Perception; Thought and Thinking

IDIOCY. *Use* Insanity

IDOLS AND IMAGES. *Use* Art, Primitive; Art and Religion; Worship

ILLEGALITY. *Use* Law

ILLEGITIMACY

LC	——; s.a. Legitimation of children; Paternity; Unmarried mothers
SEARS	——; s.a. Parent and child
RG	——; s.a. Fathers, Unmarried; Mothers, Unmarried
NYT	——; s.a. Abortion; Birth control and planned parenthood; Births
PAIS	——; s.a. Child welfare; Mothers, Unmarried
BPI	——; s.a. Child welfare; Mothers

ILLITERACY

LC	——; s.a. Elementary education of adults; Evening and continuation schools; New literates, Writing for
SEARS	——; s.a. Education
RG	——; s.a. Reading—Study and teaching; Underdeveloped areas—Education
NYT	——; s.a. Citizenship—U.S.; Elections (U.S.)—Voting
PAIS	——; s.a. Education; Literacy
BPI	READING—STUDY AND TEACHING; s.a. Adult education; Education

ILLUMINATING GAS. *See* Gas

ILLUMINATION OF BOOKS AND MANUSCRIPTS. *Use* Art, Medieval; Illustrated Books

ILLUSTRATED BOOKS
LC ———; s.a. Illustration of books; Picture books for children; Scientific illustration
SEARS ILLUSTRATION OF BOOKS; s.a. Decorative books; Illumination of books and manuscripts; Initials
RG ———; s.a. Newspapers—Illustrations; Picture books; Publishers and publishing—Illustrated books
NYT BOOKS AND LITERATURE; s.a. Graphic arts
PAIS BOOKS; s.a. Children's literature
BPI ILLUSTRATION OF BOOKS, PERIODICALS, ETC.; s.a. Children's literature; Illumination of books and manuscripts

ILLUSTRATION OF BOOKS AND PERIODICALS. *Use* Commercial Art; Graphic Arts

IMAGINATION. *Use* Intellect

IMMACULATE CONCEPTION. *Use* Virgin Birth

IMMIGRANTS. *Use* Aliens; Citizenship; Emigration and Immigration

IMMIGRATION AND EMIGRATION. *Use* Asylum, Right of; Brain Drain; Emigration and Immigration; Exiles; Nationality; Patriotism; Population; Race Problems

IMMIGRATION AND EMIGRATION—ISRAEL. *Use* Zionism

IMMORAL ART. *See* Art, Immoral

IMMORAL LITERATURE AND PICTURES. *Use* Art, Immoral; Censorship; Erotica

IMMORTALITY
Scope: Works dealing with the question of the endless existence of the soul. See Future life for works dealing with the character and forms of future existence.
LC ———; s.a. Future life; Heaven; Hell; Tree of life
SEARS ———; s.a. Eschatology; Future life; Soul; Theology
RG ———; s.a. Death; Eschatology; Future life; Reincarnation
NYT RELIGION AND CHURCHES; s.a. Philosophy
PAIS RELIGION; s.a. Death
BPI RELIGION; s.a. Death; Life

IMMUNITY. *Use* Allergy; Bacteriology; Communicable Diseases; Toxins and Antitoxins; Vaccination

IMMUNOCHEMISTRY. *Use* Biochemistry

IMPEACHMENT. *Use* Political Crimes and Offenses

IMPERIALISM
LC ———; s.a. Caesarism; Chauvinism and jingoism; Colonization; Militarism
SEARS ———; s.a. Colonies; subd. *Foreign relations* under names of countries, e.g., Russia—Foreign relations

RG ———; s.a. Colonies; subd. *Colonies* under names of countries, e.g., France—Colonies
NYT COLONIES AND TERRITORIES (General)
PAIS ———; s.a. Colonies; Political science
BPI ———; s.a. Colonies; Political science

IMPLEMENTS, UTENSILS, ETC. *Use* Tools

IMPLIED POWERS (Constitutional law). *Use* Executive Power; Judicial Power

IMPORT CONTROLS. *See* Tariff

IMPORT QUOTAS. *Use* Commercial Policy; Foreign Trade; Free Trade and Protection

IMPOSSIBILITY OF PERFORMANCE. *Use* Liability (Law)

IMPOSTERS AND IMPOSTING. *Use* Fraud

IMPOTENCE. *Use* Sex

IMPOUNDMENT OF APPROPRIATED FUNDS. *See* Separation of Powers

IMPRESSIONISM (Art). *Use* Art; Modernism (Art)

IMPRESSMENT. *Use* Seamen

IMPRISONMENT
LC ———; s.a. Arrest; Concentration camps; False imprisonment
SEARS PRISONS; s.a. Penal colonies; Reformatories
RG PRISONS; s.a. Indeterminate sentence; Parole; Punishment
NYT PRISONS AND PRISONERS; s.a. Crime and criminals; U.S.—Internal security—Preventive detention
PAIS ———; s.a. Correction (penology); Preventive detention
BPI PRISONS; s.a. Concentration camps; Prisoners; Prison riots

IMPULSE. *Use* Will

IN FORMA PAUPERIS. *Use* Legal Aid

INAUDIBLE SOUNDS. *See* Ultrasonics

INBREEDING. *Use* Breeding

INCARNATION. *Use* God; Immortality; Religion

INCENDIARY BOMBS. *Use* Bombs; Fires

INCENTIVES IN INDUSTRY
LC ———; s.a. Employee competitive behavior; Employee morale; Employee ownership; Performance awards; Personnel management
SEARS PROFIT SHARING; s.a. Cooperation; Wages
RG ———; s.a. Bonus system; Wage payment plans
NYT LABOR; s.a. Management, Industrial and institutional
PAIS ———; s.a. Bonus system; Cooperative movement; Performance awards
BPI ———; s.a. Bonus system; Piece work; Profit sharing

INCINERATION. *Use* Funeral Rites and Ceremonies; Refuse and Refuse Disposal

INCINERATORS. *Use* Air—Pollution

INCOME
LC —·——; s.a. Cost and standard of living; Farm income; Gross national product; Profit; Retirement income; Wealth; Welfare economics
SEARS ——; s.a. Capital; Profit; Property
RG ——; s.a. Guaranteed annual income; Purchasing power; Salaries
NYT ——; s.a. Economics; Finance
PAIS ——; s.a. Discretionary income; Dividends; Purchasing power
BPI ——; s.a. Consumption (economics); National income; Profit; Wages and salaries

INCOME TAX
Scope: Works on federal taxes.
LC ——; s.a. Internal revenue; Local government; Local taxation; Payroll tax
SEARS ——; s.a. Insurance, Unemployment; Internal revenue; Wealth
RG ——; s.a. Corporation—Taxation; Income tax, Municipal; Old age pensions—Taxation
NYT TAXATION; s.a. Income; Payroll taxes; Social insurance
PAIS ——; s.a. Payroll deductions; Tax returns; Taxation, Double; Taxation, Progressive
BPI ——; s.a. Capital gains tax; Deferred compensation—Taxation; Income tax—Collection; Negative income tax; Payroll deductions; Social security taxes

INCOMPATABILITY OF OFFICES. *Use* Separation of Powers

INCORPORATION. *Use* Commercial Law; Corporations

INCURABLES. *Use* Invalids

INDECENT ASSAULT. *Use* Assault and Battery

INDENTURED SERVANTS. *Use* Contract Labor; Slavery

INDENTURES. *See* Deeds

INDEPENDENT SCHOOLS. *See* Private Schools

INDETERMINATE SENTENCE. *Use* Imprisonment; Judgments; Prisons and Prisoners

INDEXES. *Use* Indexing

INDEXES, CARD. *See* Files and Filing (Documents)

INDEXING
See also subd. *Indexes* under specific subjects, e.g., Audiovisual aids—Indexes; Engineering—Indexes; etc.
LC ——; s.a. Abstracting; Documentation; Files and filing (documents); Punched card systems
SEARS ——; s.a. Bibliography; Catalogs; Periodicals—Indexes
RG ——; s.a. Computers—Indexing use; Indexes
NYT INDEXES AND INDEXING; s.a. Libraries and librarians; New York Times Index; subjects indexed, e.g., Books and literature
PAIS ——; s.a. Abstracting and indexing services; Cataloging
BPI ——; s.a. Indexes; Subject headings

INDIANS—SOCIAL LIFE AND CUSTOMS. *Use* Society, Primitive; Totemism

INDIANS, TREATMENT OF. *Use* Native Races

INDIFFERENTISM (Religion). *Use* Rationalism; Toleration

INDIGENOUS LABOR. *See* Native Labor

INDIGESTION. *Use* Diet; Digestion

INDIVIDUAL AND STATE. *Use* Individualism; State, The

INDIVIDUAL INSTRUCTION. *Use* Teaching

INDIVIDUALISM
LC ——; s.a. Collectivism; Equality; Persons; Self-interest; Solidarity
SEARS ——; s.a. Communism; Socialism
RG ——; s.a. Conformity; Individual and state
NYT PSYCHOLOGY AND PSYCHOLOGISTS; s.a. Sociology
PAIS ——; s.a. Conformity; Society and the individual
BPI ——; s.a. Self-reliance

INDIVIDUALITY
LC ——; s.a. Behavior (psychology); Character; Consciousness; Identity; Self
SEARS ——; s.a. Conformity; Personality; Self
RG ——; s.a. Personality; Self; Temperament
NYT PSYCHOLOGY AND PSYCHOLOGISTS; s.a. Sociology
PAIS INDIVIDUALISM; s.a. Conformity; Society and the individual
BPI SELF-ACTUALIZATION (Psychology); s.a. Identity (psychology)

INDOCTRINATION. *Use* Mental Suggestion; Propaganda

INDOOR GAMES. *Use* Amusements; Recreation

INDOOR GARDENING. *Use* Gardening

INDUCTION MOTORS. *See* Electric Motors

INDUSTRIAL ACCIDENTS. *Use* Occupations, Dangerous; Personal Injuries

INDUSTRIAL ARBITRATION. *See* Arbitration, Industrial

INDUSTRIAL ARTS
See also names of specific industries, arts, trades, e.g., Bookbinding; and subd. *Industries* under names of places, e.g., New Orleans—Industries.
LC ——; s.a. Artisans; Do-it-yourself work; Technical education
SEARS ——; s.a. Art industries and trade; Arts and crafts; Technology
RG ——; s.a. Arts and crafts; Technical education
NYT COMMERCIAL EDUCATION
PAIS ——; s.a. Handicrafts; Technical education
BPI TECHNICAL EDUCATION; s.a. Arts and crafts; Occupational training

INDUSTRIAL ARTS EDUCATION. *Use* Technical Education

INDUSTRIAL BUILDINGS. *Use* Building; Factories; Office Buildings; Plant Layout

INDUSTRIAL CONCILIATION. *See* Collective Bargaining

INDUSTRIAL COUNCILS. *Use* Works Councils

INDUSTRIAL DEFENSE. *Use* Civil Defense

INDUSTRIAL DEMOCRACY. *Use* Collectivism;
Socialism; Works Councils

INDUSTRIAL DESIGN. *See* Design, Industrial; Engineering Design

INDUSTRIAL DEVELOPMENT. *Use* Economic Assistance, Foreign; Industrialization; Regional
Planning; Underdeveloped Areas

INDUSTRIAL EDUCATION. *Use* Technical Education

INDUSTRIAL ENGINEERS. *Use* Plant Layout

INDUSTRIAL EQUIPMENT
See also subd. *Equipment and supplies* under appropriate
    subjects, e.g., Factories—Equipment and supplies.
LC   ——; s.a. Industrial equipment leases; In-
    stallation of industrial equipment; Replacement
    of industrial equipment
SEARS See subd. *Equipment and supplies* under appro-
    priate subjects
RG   ——; s.a. kinds of industrial equipment, e.g.,
    Construction machinery; Pumping machinery;
    etc.
NYT   MACHINERY, INDUSTRIAL EQUIPMENT
    AND SUPPLIES; s.a. Machine tools and dies;
    Tools and implements
PAIS   ——; s.a. Equipment; Office equipment
BPI   ——; s.a. Machinery in industry; Replacement
    of industrial equipment

INDUSTRIAL ESPIONAGE. *Use* Espionage; Spies

INDUSTRIAL FEEDING. *Use* Food Service

INDUSTRIAL GAMING. *See* Management Games

INDUSTRIAL HYGIENE. *Use* Hygiene

INDUSTRIAL LAWS AND LEGISLATION
Scope: Works on laws and legislation regulating indus-
    try. For works on theory of state regulation of
    industry see Industry and state and Laissez
    faire.
LC   ——; s.a. Law, Industrial; Right to labor; Trade
    regulations
SEARS INDUSTRY—LAW AND REGULATIONS; s.a.
    Competition, Unfair; Patents; Trademarks
RG   ——; s.a. Child labor laws and legislation; Labor
    courts; Labor laws and legislation
NYT   LAW AND LEGISLATION; s.a. Corporations;
    Labor; Trade practices and monopolies
PAIS   GOVERNMENT REGULATION OF BUSINESS;
    s.a. Competition, Unfair; Labor—Legislation
BPI   LABOR LAWS AND LEGISLATION; s.a.
    Child labor; Pensions—Regulation; Unfair
    labor practices; Wages and salaries—Laws and
    regulations

INDUSTRIAL MANAGEMENT
Scope: Works on the application of the principles of
    management to industrial enterprises, including
    problems of production, marketing, financial
    control, office management, etc. See Factory
    management for works limited to technical as-
    pects of manufacturing processes.

LC   ——; s.a. Big business; Industrial sociology;
    Management games; Management rights;
    Materials management; Network analysis
    (planning); New business enterprises; Office
    management; Operations research; Works
    council
SEARS ——; s.a. Buying; Marketing; Materials handling
RG   INDUSTRIAL MANAGEMENT AND ORGAN-
    IZATIONS; s.a. Business management and organ-
    ization; Business planning; Labor productivity
NYT   MANAGEMENT, INDUSTRIAL AND INSTITU-
    TIONAL; s.a. Labor
PAIS   ——; s.a. Foremen and supervisors; Industrial
    relations; Production
BPI   ——; s.a. Efficiency, Industrial; Personnel
    management; Production planning; Scheduling
    (management)

INDUSTRIAL MEDICINE. *Use* Occupations, Dangerous

INDUSTRIAL MOBILIZATION. *Use* Armaments; De-
fense Contracts; Economic Policy; Munitions;
Priorities, Industrial; U.S.—Defenses; War—
Economic Aspects

INDUSTRIAL ORGANIZATION. *Use* Industrial Management; Organization; Works Councils

INDUSTRIAL PLANTS. *See* Factories

INDUSTRIAL POLICE. *See* Police

INDUSTRIAL PRIORITIES. *See* Priorities, Industrial

INDUSTRIAL PROCUREMENT. *Use* Purchasing

INDUSTRIAL PRODUCTION. *See* Overproduction;
Supply and Demand

INDUSTRIAL PRODUCTIVITY CENTERS. *Use*
Industrial Research

INDUSTRIAL PROMOTION. *Use* Small Business

INDUSTRIAL PROPERTY. *Use* Patent Laws and Legislation; Property

INDUSTRIAL RELATIONS
LC   ——; s.a. Labor law; Management rights; Media-
    tion and conciliation, Industrial; Unfair labor
    practices
SEARS ——; s.a. Arbitration, Industrial; Employees'
    representation in management; Labor contracts;
    Labor unions; Strikes and lockouts
RG   ——; s.a. Arbitration, Industrial; Grievance
    procedures; Personnel management; Strikes
NYT   MANAGEMENT, INDUSTRIAL AND INSTI-
    TUTIONAL; s.a. Collective bargaining; Labor—
    U.S.—Arbitration, conciliation and mediation
PAIS   ——; s.a. Collective labor agreements; Com-
    munication in management; Grievance pro-
    cedures
BPI   ——; s.a. Collective bargaining; Trade unions

INDUSTRIAL RESEARCH
See also specific types of research, e.g., Fuel research;
    Market research, etc.
LC   RESEARCH, INDUSTRIAL; s.a. Industrial pro-
    ductivity centers; Inventions; New products
SEARS INDUSTRY—RESEARCH; s.a. Marketing;
    Patents; Technology

INDUSTRIAL RESEARCH, *cont.*
RG ——; s.a. Products, New; Technology transfer
NYT ——; s.a. Inventions and inventors; Research
PAIS ——; s.a. Products, New
BPI ——; s.a. Laboratories; Products, New

INDUSTRIAL SAFETY. *Use* Hazardous Substances; Occupations, Dangerous; Safety Appliances

INDUSTRIAL SOCIOLOGY
Scope: Works on social relations within industry, as distinguished from labor-management relations.
LC ——; s.a. Industry—Social aspects; Psychology, Industrial; Work
SEARS INDUSTRIAL MANAGEMENT; s.a. Personnel management; Psychology, Applied
RG PSYCHOLOGY, INDUSTRIAL; s.a. Employee morale; Job satisfaction
NYT SOCIOLOGY; s.a. Labor
PAIS SOCIOLOGY, INDUSTRIAL; s.a. Personnel management; Psychology, Industrial
BPI SOCIOLOGY, INDUSTRIAL

INDUSTRIAL UNIONS. *See* Trade Unions

INDUSTRIAL WASTE. *Use* Waste Products

INDUSTRIALIZATION
Scope: Works on the industrialization of individual countries are entered under the name of the area followed by the subd. *Industries*, e.g., Peru—Industries.
LC ——; s.a. Economic assistance, American; United Nations—Economic assistance; United Nations—Technical assistance
SEARS ——; s.a. Economic policy; Underdeveloped areas
RG ——; s.a. Economic development; Industrial development programs; Underdeveloped areas
NYT ECONOMIC CONDITIONS AND TRENDS (General); s.a. Foreign aid; United Nations (UN)
PAIS INDUSTRIAL DEVELOPMENT; s.a. Economic development; Technical assistance
BPI ——; s.a. Underdeveloped areas; United Nations—Industrial Development Organization

INDUSTRIALIZED BUILDING. *Use* Building

INDUSTRIAL-MILITARY COMPLEX. *See* Defense Contracts

INDUSTRIES. *See* Industry

INDUSTRIES, CHEMICAL. *See* Chemical Industries

INDUSTRIES, LOCATION OF. *Use* Industry

INDUSTRIES, PRIMITIVE. *Use* Society, Primitive

INDUSTRIES, SIZE OF. *Use* Big Business; Industry; Monopolies; Small Business; Trusts, Industrial

INDUSTRY
See also specific types of industries, e.g., Textile industry and subd. *Industries* under names of countries, e.g., U.S.—Industries.
LC ——; s.a. Big business; Entrepreneur; Industrial mobilization; Industries, Location of; Industry—Social aspects; Supply and demand

SEARS ——; s.a. Industrialization; Machinery in industry; Manufacturers
RG ——; s.a. Accidents, Industrial; Business enterprises, New; Economics; Location in business and industry
NYT U.S.—ECONOMIC CONDITIONS AND TRENDS; s.a. Corporations; Management, Industrial and institutional
PAIS ——; s.a. Factories; Industrial safety; Manufacturing; Raw materials
BPI ——; s.a. Industries, Size of; Production

INDUSTRY—HISTORY. *Use* Economic History

INDUSTRY—LAW AND REGULATIONS. *Use* Industrial Laws and Legislation

INDUSTRY—NATIONALIZATION. *Use* Industry and State

INDUSTRY (Psychology). *See* Work

INDUSTRY—SOCIAL ASPECTS. *Use* Industrial Sociology; Social Change

INDUSTRY AND EDUCATION
LC ——; s.a. Education, Cooperative
SEARS BUSINESS EDUCATION; s.a. Colleges and universities
RG BUSINESS AND EDUCATION; s.a. College students and business; Performance contracts (education)
NYT COMMERCIAL EDUCATION; s.a. Colleges and universities—U.S.—Professional schools; Education and schools
PAIS BUSINESS AND EDUCATION; s.a. Colleges and universities—Business aid; Education, Cooperative
BPI EDUCATION AND INDUSTRY; s.a. Business education; Cooperative education

INDUSTRY AND STATE
Scope: Works on theory of state regulation of industry, and general works on relations between government and business.
LC ——; s.a. Competition; Corporate state; Foreign trade promotion; Government ownership; Laissez-faire; Priorities, Industrial
SEARS ——; s.a. Agriculture and state; Economic policy; Government ownership; Railroads and state; Subsidies
RG ——; s.a. Business—Social aspects; Contracts, Government; Free enterprise; Military-industrial complex
NYT LABOR—U.S.; s.a. U.S.—Economic conditions and trends; U.S.—Politics and government
PAIS ——; s.a. Free enterprise; Government loans to industry; Government regulation of business; Industry—Nationalization; Public interest
BPI ——; s.a. Business—Social aspects; Capitalism; Government aid to business; Public utilities

INDUSTRY AND WAR. *See* War—Economic Aspects

INEFFICIENCY, INTELLECTUAL. *Use* Mentally Ill

INEQUALITY. *See* Equality

INERTIAL GUIDANCE SYSTEMS. *Use* Automatic Control; Ballistic Missiles

INFANT EDUCATION. *See* Education, Preschool

INFANT MORTALITY. *Use* Childbirth

INFANT WELFARE. *See* Maternal and Infant Welfare

INFANTICIDE. *Use* Murder

INFANTS. *Use* Child Study; Children; Discipline of Children; Maternal and Infant Welfare

INFANTS—CARE AND HYGIENE. *Use* Hygiene; Nurseries

INFANTS—GROWTH. *Use* Growth

INFANTS—MORTALITY. *Use* Childbirth; Mortality

INFANTS, PREMATURE. *Use* Childbirth; Labor (Obstetrics)

INFANTS' FOOD. *Use* Food Industry and Trade

INFECTIOUS DISEASES. *See* Communicable Diseases

INFERIORITY COMPLEX. *Use* Neuroses

INFLATION (Finance)
LC ———; s.a. Circular velocity of money; Economic policy; Escalator clause; Monetary policy; Price regulation
SEARS ———; s.a. Currency question; Finance; Paper money
RG ———; s.a. Deflation (finance); Wage-price policy
NYT ECONOMIC CONDITIONS AND TRENDS (General); s.a. Credit; Currency; U.S.—Economic conditions and trends
PAIS INFLATION; s.a. Accounting—Inflation problems; Wages, prices and productivity
BPI INFLATION; s.a. Prices—Economic aspects; Wage-price policy

INFLUENCE (Psychology). *Use* Behavior (Psychology); Propaganda

INFLUENZA. *Use* Cold (Disease)

INFORMATION, FREEDOM OF. *Use* Censorship; Civil Rights; Freedom of Information; Liberty of Speech

INFORMATION CENTERS. *See* Information Services

INFORMATION DISPLAY SYSTEMS. *Use* Information Storage and Retrieval Systems

INFORMATION MEASUREMENT. *Use* Information Sciences

INFORMATION NETWORKS. *Use* Data Transmission Systems

INFORMATION PROCESSING SYSTEMS. *Use* Automatic Control; Computers; Cybernetics; Electronic Data Processing; Information Services; Information Storage and Retrieval Systems; Libraries and Librarians

INFORMATION SCIENCES
LC INFORMATION SCIENCE; s.a. Documentation; Information measurement; Information theory; Library science
SEARS ———; s.a. Communication; Electronic data processing

RG DOCUMENTATION; s.a. Information storage and retrieval systems; Libraries—Automation
NYT DATA PROCESSING (Information processing) EQUIPMENT AND SYSTEMS; s.a. Communications; Electronics
PAIS INFORMATION SCIENCE; s.a. Cybernetics; Data transmission systems; Documentation; Information processing systems
BPI INFORMATION SCIENTISTS; s.a. Human information processing; Librarians; Uncertainty (information theory)

INFORMATION SERVICES
LC ———; s.a. Bibliographic services; Data libraries; Statistical services; subd. *Information services* under special subjects, e.g., Child welfare—Information services
SEARS INFORMATION STORAGE AND RETRIEVAL SYSTEMS; s.a. Documentation; subd. *Documentation* under subjects, e.g., Agriculture—Documentation
RG ———; s.a. Computer-based service companies; subd. *Information services* under subjects, e.g., Agriculture—Information services
NYT LIBRARIES AND LIBRARIANS—GOVERNMENT INFORMATION SERVICE LIBRARIES; s.a. names of information media, e.g., TV and radio; subjects of broadcasts or releases, e.g., Vietnam: U.S.—Information Agency
PAIS ———; s.a. Abstracting and indexing services; Information processing systems
BPI ———; s.a. Abstracting and indexing services; Information storage and retrieval systems

INFORMATION STORAGE AND RETRIEVAL SYSTEMS
LC ———; s.a. Abstracting; Data libraries; Data tapes; Data transmission systems; Documentation; Electronic data processing; Files and filing; Information services; Libraries and librarians; Optical data processing; Photoelectronic devices; Punched card systems
SEARS ———; s.a. Calculating machines; Electronic data processing; Library science
RG ———; s.a. Information display systems; Libraries—Automation; Microforms
NYT DATA PROCESSING (INFORMATION PROCESSING) EQUIPMENT AND SYSTEMS; s.a. Communications; Electronics; Libraries and librarians
PAIS INFORMATION PROCESSING SYSTEMS; s.a. Computer programming; Data processing centers; Electronic data processing equipment
BPI ———; s.a. Automatic data collection systems; Computers; Computers—Display systems; Electronic data processing

INFORMATION THEORY. *Use* Automatic Control; Communication; Cybernetics; Information Sciences

INFORMATION THEORY IN ECONOMICS. *Use* Economics, Mathematical

INFORMERS (Law). *Use* Witnesses

INHERITANCE (Biology). *See* Heredity

INHERITANCE AND SUCCESSION
LC ———; s.a. Charitable bequests; Charitable uses, trusts and foundations; Decedents' estates—Taxation; Legacies; Marriage law; Parent and child; Probate law and practice; Property; Trusts and foundations; Wealth
SEARS ———; s.a. Estate planning; Executors and administrators; Inheritance and transfer tax; Land tenure
RG INHERITANCE; s.a. Estate planning; Estates, Decedents; Reversion (law)
NYT WILLS AND ESTATES; s.a. Deaths; Taxation—Federal taxes (U.S.)—Inheritance and estate taxes
PAIS INHERITANCE; s.a. Estates (law)—Taxation; Gift tax; Probate law
BPI ———; s.a. Inheritance tax; Land tenure; Wills

INHERITANCE OF ACQUIRED CHARACTERISTICS. *Use* Heredity

INHERITANCE TAX. *Use* Inheritance and Succession

INHIBITION. *Use* Will

INITIALISMS. *See* Acronyms

INITIALS. *Use* Illustrated Books

INITIATIONS (Tribes, societies, etc.). *Use* Rites and Ceremonies; Secret Societies

INITIATIVE, RIGHT OF. *Use* Legislation

INJUNCTIONS. *Use* Courts; Strikes and Lockouts; Trade-Unions

INJURIES. *See* First Aid in Illness and Injury

INJURIES (Law). *See* Personal Injuries

INLAND NAVIGATION. *Use* Water Resources Development; Waterways

INNOVATION IN EDUCATION. *Use* Educational Planning and Innovations; Educational Technology

INNOVATIONS, TECHNOLOGICAL. *See* Technological Innovations

INNS. *Use* Hotels, Taverns, etc.; Restaurants, Lunchrooms, etc.

INOCULATION. *Use* Vaccination

INPUT-OUTPUT DATA. *Use* Economics, Mathematical; Linear Programming

INQUISITION. *Use* Persecution

INSANE ASYLUMS. *See* Mentally Ill

INSANITY
Scope: Works on the legal or sociological aspects of mental disorders. See Mental illness for works on medical aspects.
LC ———; s.a. Depression, Mental; Hysteria; Idiocy; Insane, Criminal and dangerous; Insane, Killing of; Mentally ill; Paranoia; Psychoses

SEARS ———; s.a. Hallucinations and illusions; Personality disorders; Psychology, Pathological; Suicide
RG ———; s.a. Psychiatry; Schizophrenia
NYT MENTAL HEALTH AND DISORDERS; s.a. Crime and criminals—U.S.—Insanity, Legal defense of; Mental deficiency and defectives
PAIS MENTAL ILLNESS; s.a. Mental institutions; Psychiatry
BPI ———; s.a. Mental illness; Schizophrenia

INSANITY, MORAL. *Use* Crime and Criminals

INSECT CONTROL. *Use* Pests

INSECTICIDES. *Use* Pests

INSECTS. *Use* Parasites

INSECTS, INJURIOUS AND BENEFICIAL. *Use* Zoology, Economic

INSIGNIA. *Use* Emblems

INSOLVENCY. *See* Bankruptcy

INSOMNIA. *Use* Sleep

INSPECTION. *Use* Quality Control

INSTALLMENT CONTRACTS. *Use* Contracts

INSTALLMENT PLAN
LC ———; s.a. Industrial loan associations; Insurance, Group creditors; Interest and usury; Sales, Conditional
SEARS ———; s.a. Buying; Consumer credit
RG ———; s.a. Credit
NYT CREDIT; s.a. Consumers and consumption; Retail stores and trade; Sales and salesmen
PAIS ———; s.a. Layaway plan; Retail trade
BPI ———; s.a. Finance companies; Loans, Bank—Installment payment

INSTITUTION MANAGEMENT. *Use* Office Management

INSTITUTIONAL ACCOUNTING. *Use* Accounting

INSTITUTIONAL CARE
LC ———; s.a. Hospitals; Mental institutions
SEARS ———; s.a. Mentally ill—Institutional care; Orphans and orphans' homes; Public welfare
RG HOMES, INSTITUTIONAL; s.a. Children—Institutional care; Old age homes
NYT MEDICINE AND HEALTH; s.a. Nursing and nurses; Nursing homes
PAIS HOMES, INSTITUTIONAL; s.a. Children—Institutional care; Nursing homes
BPI HOSPITALS; s.a. Medical centers; Nursing homes

INSTITUTIONAL INVESTMENTS. *Use* Investments

INSTITUTIONS, NONPROFIT. *Use* Public Institutions; Public Utilities

INSTITUTIONS, NONPROFIT—TAXATION. *Use* Taxation, Exemption from

INSTITUTIONS, PUBLIC. *Use* Public Institutions

INSTRUCTION. *See* Education; Teaching

INSTRUCTIONAL MATERIALS CENTERS
LC ——; s.a. Audio-visual education; Audio-visual materials centers; Librarians; Schools
SEARS ——; s.a. Libraries
RG ——; s.a. Audiovisual aids; Libraries and audiovisual materials
NYT EDUCATION AND SCHOOLS; s.a. Libraries and librarians
PAIS AUDIOVISUAL LIBRARY SERVICE; s.a. Audiovisual equipment; Librarians
BPI ——; s.a. Audiovisual materials; Librarians

INSTRUMENT INDUSTRY. *Use* Scientific Apparatus and Instruments

INSTRUMENTAL MUSIC. *Use* Bands (Music); Chamber Music; Dance Music; Music; Orchestra

INSTRUMENTATION AND ORCHESTRATION. *Use* Music; Orchestra

INSTRUMENTATION AND ORCHESTRATION (Dance orchestra). *Use* Dance Music; Jazz Music

INSULATION (Heat). *Use* Heating

INSURANCE
See also particular types of insurance, e.g., Insurance, Automobile; Insurance, Casualty; Insurance, Fire; Insurance, Moving; Insurance, War risk; etc.
LC ——; s.a. Insurance companies; Insurance policies; Liability (law); Reinsurance; Risk; Valuation
SEARS ——; s.a. Finance, Personal; Saving and thrift
RG ——; s.a. Investment trusts—Insurance; Risk (insurance)
NYT ——; s.a. names of particular insurance companies, e.g., Prudential Insurance
PAIS ——; s.a. Annuities; Insurance—Reinsurance
BPI ——; s.a. Brokers—Insurance selling; subd. *Insurance* under various subjects, e.g., Accountants—Insurance; Riots—Insurance; etc.

INSURANCE, ACCIDENT. *Use* Personal Injuries; Workmen's Compensation

INSURANCE, DENTAL. *Use* Insurance, Health

INSURANCE, EMPLOYERS' LIABILITY. *Use* Workmen's Compensation

INSURANCE, GROUP. *Use* Insurance, Life; Survivor's Benefits

INSURANCE, HEALTH
LC ——; s.a. Maternal and infant welfare; Medical care, Prepaid; Workmen's compensation
SEARS ——; s.a. Hospitalization; Workmen's compensation
RG ——; s.a. Insurance, Hospitalization; Maternity benefits; Medical service, State; Medicare program
NYT MEDICINE AND HEALTH—U.S.—HEALTH INSURANCE; s.a. Pregnancy, obstetrics and maternal welfare
PAIS ——; s.a. Insurance, Hospital; Insurance, Maternity; Maternal welfare
BPI ——; s.a. Insurance, Dental; Insurance, Medical expense; Medical care, Prepaid

INSURANCE, HOSPITAL. *Use* Insurance, Health

INSURANCE, INDUSTRIAL. *Use* Insurance, Life

INSURANCE, LIFE
LC ——; s.a. Insurance, Child; Insurance, Savings-bank life; Mortality; Survivors' benefits
SEARS ——; s.a. Insurance, Group; Insurance, Industrial
RG ——; s.a. Annuities; Risk (insurance)
NYT LIFE INSURANCE; s.a. Insurance
PAIS ——; s.a. Insurance, Credit life; Life insurance trusts
BPI ——; s.a. Insurance, Group life; Insurance trusts

INSURANCE, MATERNITY. *Use* Insurance, Health; Maternal and Infant Welfare

INSURANCE, OLD AGE. *See* Old Age Assistance

INSURANCE, SOCIAL
LC ——; s.a. Economic security; Friendly societies; Maternal and infant welfare; Non-wage payments; Public welfare; Social legislation; Welfare economics
SEARS ——; s.a. Insurance, Unemployment; Mothers' pensions; Workmen's compensation
RG ——; s.a. Old age pensions; Social security taxes
NYT SOCIAL INSURANCE; s.a. Aged and age; Pensions and retirement; Unemployment insurance
PAIS ——; s.a. Pensions, Old age; Transfer payments
BPI ——; s.a. Insurance, Unemployment; Old age pensions

INSURANCE, SURETY AND FIDELITY. *Use* Suretyship and Guaranty

INSURANCE, UNEMPLOYMENT. *Use* Insurance, Social

INSURANCE COMPANIES. *Use* Insurance

INSURANCE ENGINEERING. *Use* Safety Appliances

INSURANCE POLICIES. *Use* Insurance

INSURANCE TRUSTS. *Use* Insurance, Life; Survivor's Benefits

INSURGENCY. *Use* Government, Resistance to; Guerilla Warfare; Internal Security; Political Crimes and Offenses; Revolutions; Subversive Activities

INSURRECTIONS. *See* Revolutions

INTEGRAL ANALYSIS. *See* Mathematics

INTEGRATION, RACIAL. *See* Race Problems; Segregation

INTELLECT
LC ——; s.a. Creation (literary, artistic, etc.); Intellectual life; Reasoning (psychology); Senses and sensation; Wisdom
SEARS ——; s.a. Imagination; Memory; Perception; Reason
RG ——; s.a. Brain; Genius; Intelligence levels
NYT INTELLIGENCE; s.a. Intellectuals; Psychology and psychologists

INTELLECT, *cont.*
PAIS   INTELLIGENCE; s.a. Intellectuals; Thought and thinking
BPI   INTELLIGENCE; s.a. Creative ability; Thought and thinking

INTELLECT AND AGE. *See* Age (Psychology)

INTELLECTUAL COOPERATION. *Use* International Cooperation

INTELLECTUAL FREEDOM. *Use* Academic Freedom

INTELLECTUAL LIBERTY. *Use* Censorship; Dissenters, Religious; Freedom of Information; Liberty; Liberty of Speech

INTELLECTUAL LIFE. *Use* Culture; Popular Culture

INTELLECTUAL PROPERTY
LC   COPYRIGHT; s.a. Copyright—Infringements; Copyright—Performing rights; Creation (literary, artistic, etc.); Design protection; Inventions; Plagiarism
SEARS   COPYRIGHT; s.a. Inventions; Patents
RG   PROPERTY, INTELLECTUAL; s.a. Copyright
NYT   INVENTIONS AND INVENTORS; s.a. names of inventions and inventors
PAIS   PROPERTY, INTELLECTUAL; s.a. Copyright; Royalties
BPI   ——; s.a. Ideas in business; Patent law and legislation

INTELLECTUALS. *Use* Intellect; Learning and Scholarship; Professions

INTELLIGENCE. *Use* Brain; Comprehension; Conditioned Response; Intellect; Perception; Thought and Thinking; Wisdom

INTELLIGENCE, ARTIFICIAL. *Use* Cybernetics

INTELLIGENCE LEVEL. *Use* Ability-Testing; Educational Psychology

INTELLIGENCE LEVELS. *Use* Intellect

INTELLIGENCE SERVICE. *Use* Espionage; Secret Service; Spies

INTELLIGENCE TESTS. *Use* Ability—Testing; Character Tests; Occupational Aptitude Tests; Tests, Mental

INTEMPERANCE. *See* Liquor Problem; Temperance

INTERCHANGEABLE MECHANISMS. *Use* Machinery

INTERCONTINENTAL BALLISTIC MISSILES. *Use* Atomic Warfare; Ballistic Missiles

INTERCULTURAL COMMUNICATION. *Use* East and West

INTERCULTURAL EDUCATION. *Use* Acculturation; Afro-American Studies; East and West; Education, Bilingual; Minorities; Oriental Studies; Race Problems

INTERDENOMINATIONAL COOPERATION. *Use* Sects

INTEREST AND USURY
LC   ——; s.a. Commercial crimes; Debtor and creditor; Finance charges; Loans; Pawnbroking; Trials (usury)
SEARS   ——; s.a. Capital; Credit; Finance; Loans
RG   INTEREST; s.a. Installment plan; Loan sharks; Savings deposits—Interest; Usury
NYT   LOAN SHARKING; s.a. Banks and banking; Credit
PAIS   INTEREST; s.a. Discount; Interest—Rates— Legislation; Usury; Usury—Legislation
BPI   INTEREST; s.a. Bank deposits—Interest; Loans; Usury law

INTEREST GROUPS. *See* Lobbying

INTERFAITH MARRIAGE. *See* Marriage

INTERGOVERNMENTAL FISCAL RELATIONS. *Use* Economic Assistance, Domestic; Taxation

INTERGOVERNMENTAL RELATIONS. *Use* Federal Government

INTERINDUSTRY ECONOMICS. *Use* Economics, Mathematical; Linear Programming

INTERIOR DECORATION
LC   ——; s.a. Art, Decorative; House furnishings; Interior decoration—Amateurs' manuals; Interior decorators
SEARS   ——; s.a. Flower arrangements; Home economics; Mural painting and decoration
RG   ——; s.a. Decoration and ornament; Hotel decoration; House decoration
NYT   ——; s.a. Art designs; Furniture; Painting and decorating
PAIS   ——; s.a. Furniture industry; Household furnishings
BPI   ——; s.a. Office decoration; Restaurants, lunchrooms, etc.—Decoration

INTERLOCKING DIRECTORATES. *Use* Business Enterprises

INTERMARRIAGE OF RACES. *Use* Marriage; Race Problems

INTERMEDIATE STATE. *Use* Death; Heaven

INTERMENT. *See* Burial

INTERMURAL SPORTS. *Use* Athletics

INTERNAL REVENUE. *Use* Finance, Public; Income Tax; Taxation

INTERNAL SECURITY
LC   ——; s.a. Loyalty oaths; Offical secrets; Subversive activities; Treason
SEARS   ——; s.a. Subversive activities; U.S.—Defenses
RG   ——; s.a. Espionage; Insurgency; Subversive activities
NYT   Subd. *Internal Security* under names of countries, e.g., U.S.—Internal security; s.a. Oath of allegiance (U.S.)
PAIS   ——; s.a. Insurgency; Sabotage
BPI   U.S.—SUBVERSIVE ACTIVITIES CONTROL BOARD

INTERNATIONAL AGENCIES. *Use* International Cooperation

INTERNATIONAL AGREEMENTS. *See* Treaties

INTERNATIONAL AIRPORTS. *Use* Airports

INTERNATIONAL ARBITRATION. *See* Arbitration, International

INTERNATIONAL BALANCE OF PAYMENTS. *See* Balance of Payments

INTERNATIONAL BUSINESS ENTERPRISES. *Use* Business Enterprises; Corporations

INTERNATIONAL CLEARING. *Use* Balance of Payments; Foreign Exchange; International Finance

INTERNATIONAL CONFERENCES. *Use* Congresses and Conventions

INTERNATIONAL COOPERATION
See also names of international institutions, e.g., Food and Agricultural Organization; United Nations; World Federation of Trade Unions; World Health Organization; etc.

LC ———; s.a. Disaster relief; Intellectual cooperation; International agencies; International education

SEARS ———; s.a. Cultural relations; Exchange of persons programs; Reconstruction (1939–1951)

RG ———; s.a. Banks and banking international; Food relief; Medical relief work; subd. *International aspects* under subjects, e.g., Science—International aspects

NYT INTERNATIONAL RELATIONS; s.a. Cultural relations

PAIS ———; s.a. Economic assistance; International relief

BPI ———; s.a. Organization for Economic Cooperation and Development; Relief work

INTERNATIONAL COURTS. *Use* Arbitration, International; International Offenses

INTERNATIONAL DATE LINE. *Use* Time

INTERNATIONAL ECONOMIC RELATIONS. *Use* Balance of Payments; Commercial Policy; Economic Assistance, Foreign; International Finance; International Relations

INTERNATIONAL EDUCATION. *Use* International Cooperation

INTERNATIONAL EXCHANGE. *See* Foreign Exchange

INTERNATIONAL FINANCE
LC ———; s.a. Financial institutions, International; International clearing; Investments, Foreign; subd. *Foreign economic relations* under name of country, e.g., U.S.—Foreign economic relations—Libya

SEARS FOREIGN EXCHANGE; s.a. Balance of payments; Economic assistance; International economic relations

RG FINANCE, INTERNATIONAL; s.a. Banks and banking, International; Eurodollar market

NYT COMMERCE; s.a. Banks and banking; Currency—International monetary system

PAIS FINANCE, INTERNATIONAL; s.a. Balance of payments; Debts, External; Loans, Foreign

BPI FINANCE, INTERNATIONAL; s.a. Foreign exchange; Money—International aspects

INTERNATIONAL GRANTS-IN-AID. *See* Economic Assistance, Foreign

INTERNATIONAL LABOR ACTIVITIES. *Use* Trade Unions

INTERNATIONAL LABOR DAY. *See* Labor and Laboring Classes; Special Days, Weeks and Months

INTERNATIONAL LABOR LAWS AND LEGISLATION. *Use* Labor Laws and Legislation

INTERNATIONAL LANGUAGE. *See* Language and Languages

INTERNATIONAL LAW. *Use* Airspace (International law); Arbitration, International; Boundaries; Diplomacy; Exiles; Freedom of the Seas; International Offenses; Neutrality; Slavery; Sovereignty; State, The; Territorial Waters; Territory, National; Treaties; War (International law)

INTERNATIONAL LIQUIDITY. *Use* Balance of Payments; Foreign Exchange; International Finance

INTERNATIONAL OFFENSES
LC ———; s.a. Aggression (international law); Crimes against humanity; Crimes against peace; Genocide; International courts; Terrorism

SEARS INTERNATIONAL LAW; s.a. War crime trials

RG INTERNATIONAL LAW; s.a. International police; Intervention (international law); Sovereignty

NYT INTERNATIONAL CONTROL OF JUSTICE (UN) (WORLD COURT); s.a. International relations (The Hague); United Nations

PAIS COURTS, INTERNATIONAL; s.a. Jurisdiction (international law); Police, International

BPI INTERNATIONAL LAW; s.a. Arbitration, International; Embargo; Sanctions (international law)

INTERNATIONAL ORGANIZATION. *Use* International Relations; World Politics

INTERNATIONAL ORGANIZATIONS. *Use* Congresses and Conventions

INTERNATIONAL POLICE. *Use* International Offenses

INTERNATIONAL RELATIONS
Scope: Works on the theory of international relations. Historical accounts are entered under headings World Politics; Asia—Politics; Europe—Politics; etc. Works limited to relations between two countries are entered under names of countries with subd. *Foreign relations*, e.g., Kenya—Foreign relations.

INTERNATIONAL RELATIONS, *cont.*
LC   ——; s.a. Balance of payments; Cold war; Great powers; International cooperation; International economic relations; International offenses; Neutrality; Peaceful change (international relations); Security, International; War; World politics
SEARS   ——; s.a. Diplomacy; Peace; Treaties
RG   ——; s.a. Aggression (international law); Balance of power; Imperialism
NYT   ——; s.a. Arms control and limitation and disarmament; United Nations; U.S. Armament and defense
PAIS   ——; s.a. Arbitration, International; Foreign relations; International security
BPI   ——; s.a. Disarmament and arms control; International organization

INTERNATIONAL RELIEF. *Use* Charities; Economic Assistance, Foreign; International Cooperation

INTERNATIONAL SECURITY. *Use* Disarmament; International Relations

INTERNATIONAL TRAVEL REGULATIONS. *Use* Travel

INTERNATIONAL TRUSTEESHIPS. *Use* Colonies

INTERNATIONALISM. *Use* Communism; Nationalism

INTERNMENT CAMPS. *See* Concentration Camps

INTERNS (Business). *Use* Education, Cooperative

INTERNS (Medicine). *Use* Hospitals

INTERPELLATION. *Use* Parliamentary Practice

INTERPERSONAL RELATIONS. *Use* Group Relations Training; Human Relations; Toleration

INTERPLANETARY VOYAGES. *Use* Astronautics; Outer Space; Rockets (Aeronautics); Space Flight

INTERPOLATION. *Use* Mathematics

INTERPRETERS. *See* Translating and Interpreting

INTERRACIAL COOPERATION. *Use* Cooperation; Negro-Jewish Relations; Race Problems

INTERRACIAL MARRIAGE. *See* Marriage

INTERSTATE AGREEMENTS. *Use* State Governments

INTERSTATE COMMERCE
Scope: Works on interstate commerce in general and in the United States.
LC   ——; s.a. Restraint of trade; Transportation—Laws and regulations
SEARS   ——; s.a. Commerce; Railroads and state; Trusts, Industrial
RG   ——; s.a. Railroads and state—U.S.; Trade regulation
NYT   COMMERCE—U.S.; s.a. Transportation; U.S.—Interstate Commerce Commission
PAIS   ——; s.a. Business; Carriers
BPI   ——; s.a. Carriers; Trade regulation

INTERSTATE CONTROVERSIES. *Use* State Governments

INTERSTELLAR COMMUNICATION. *Use* Life; Outer Space

INTERVENTION (Federal government). *Use* Federal Government

INTERVENTION (International law). *Use* International Offenses; Neutrality; War (International law)

INTERVIEWING
LC   ——; s.a. Counseling; Employment interviewing (journalism); Interviewing in psychiatry; Questioning; Social casework
SEARS   ——; s.a. Applications for positions; Counseling; Journalism; Psychology, Applied; Reporters and reporting; Social psychology
RG   ——; s.a. Employment interviewing; Recruiting of employees; Reporters and reporting
NYT   LABOR; s.a. News and news media; Television and radio
PAIS   ——; s.a. Counseling; Interviewing (journalism)
BPI   ——; s.a. Interviewing (journalism); Personnel management—Interviewing; Recruiting of employees—Interviewing

INTERVIEWING (Journalism). *Use* Reporters and Reporting

INTERVIEWS. *Use* Social Psychology

INTESTINES. *Use* Digestion

INTOLERANCE. *See* Liberty; Religious Liberty; Toleration

INTOXICANTS. *See* Alcohol; Liquors

INTRACOASTAL WATERWAYS. *Use* Waterways

INTRODUCTION OF SPEAKERS. *Use* Lectures and Lecutring; Public Speaking; Speeches, Addresses, etc.

INTUITION (Psychology). *Use* Perception; Senses and Sensation

INVALIDS
LC   ——; s.a. Convalescence; Handicapped; Occupations; Veterans, Disabled
SEARS   PHYSICALLY HANDICAPPED; s.a. Occupational therapy; Sick
RG   SICK, THE; s.a. Incurables; Physicians and patients
NYT   HANDICAPPED; s.a. Aged and age; Medicine and health; Nursing homes
PAIS   DISABLED; s.a. Hospitals—Home care program; Nursing homes
BPI   HOME HEALTH CARE; s.a. Handicapped; Nursing homes; Veterans, Disabled

INVASION OF PRIVACY. *See* Privacy, Right of

INVENTIONS
LC   ——; s.a. Intellectual property; Inventions, Employees; Patent law and legislation; Research, Industrial; Technological innovations; Women as inventors
SEARS   ——; s.a. Civilization; Industry—Biography; Science; Science—Biography; Technology

RG — ; s.a. Industrial research; Patents; Patents and government developed inventions
NYT INVENTIONS AND INVENTORS; s.a. names of specific inventions and inventors, e.g., Duplicating machines; Research
PAIS — ; s.a. Ideas; Inventors; Patents
BPI — ; s.a. Patents; Technology transfer

INVENTORIES
LC — ; s.a. Business records; Inventories, Retail; Inventory control; Materials management; Stores or stock-room keeping
SEARS ACCOUNTING; s.a. Bookkeeping
RG — ; s.a. Booksellers and bookselling—Stock; Materials control
NYT ACCOUNTING AND ACCOUNTANTS; s.a. Retail stores and trade
PAIS INVENTORY; s.a. Accounting; Business; Stores systems
BPI INVENTORY CONTROL; s.a. Retail trade—Stock; Warehouses

INVENTORS. *Use* Inventions

INVESTMENT. *Use* Risk

INVESTMENT BANKING. *Use* Banks and Banking; Over-the-Counter Markets; Stock Exchange

INVESTMENT TAX CREDIT. *Use* Depreciation

INVESTMENT TRUSTS. *Use* Banks and Banking; Trust Companies; Trusts and Trustees

INVESTMENTS
LC — ; s.a. Bank investments; Capital investments; Estate planning; Investment of public funds; Legal investments; Over-the-counter markets; Real estate investments; Saving and investment; Saving and savings; Stock exchange; Wall Street
SEARS — ; s.a. Finance, Personal; Mortgages; Saving and thrift; Stocks; Trust companies
RG — ; s.a. Annuities; Bonds; Finance, Personal; Speculation; Trusts and trustees
NYT PROPERTY AND INVESTMENTS; s.a. Banks and banking; Government bonds; Stocks and bonds
PAIS — ; s.a. Bonds, Government; Dividends; Hedging; Speculation; subd. *Investment* under special subjects, e.g., Banking—Investment
BPI — ; s.a. Annuities; Bonds; Institutional investments; Saving; Securities; Speculation; Trusts and trustees—Investments

INVESTMENTS, FOREIGN. *Use* Economic Assistance, Foreign; International Finance; Underdeveloped Areas

INVOICES. *Use* Mail Order Business; Sales; Shipment of Goods

IRON AND STEEL INDUSTRY. *Use* Iron Industry and Trade; Metal Industries; Mines and Minerals; Steel Industry and Trade

IRON INDUSTRY AND TRADE
LC — ; s.a. Iron and steel workers; Metal trade; Steel industry and trade
SEARS — ; s.a. Iron ores; Ironwork; Steel industry and trade
RG — ; s.a. Iron industry and trade—Wages and hours; Iron mines and mining; Steel works
NYT STEEL AND IRON; s.a. Metals and minerals
PAIS IRON AND STEEL INDUSTRY; s.a. Scrap metal industry; Trade unions—Iron and steel industry
BPI IRON INDUSTRY; s.a. Iron workers; Steel industry; Steel workers

IRONING. *Use* Laundries and Laundering

IRONWORK. *Use* Building; Handicrafts; Metal Industries

IRONY. *Use* Wit and Humor

IRRADIATION. *Use* Radiation

IRRELIGION. *Use* Religion; Secularism

IRRIGATION. *Use* Engineering; Reclamation of Land; Soils; Water—Supply; Water Resources Development

ISLAM
See also headings beginning with Islam, e.g., Islam and race problem; and headings beginning with Muslim, e.g., Muslim authors; and subd. *Muslim* or *Islamic* under subjects, e.g., Architects, Muslim.
LC — ; s.a. Civilization, Arab; Civilization, Mohammedan; Hospitality (Islam); Islamic sects; Islamic literature; Jihad; Mohammedan law; Mohammedans; Mohammedanism; Shana (Mohammedan religious practices)
SEARS — ; s.a. Arab countries; Arabic literature; Bahaism; Black Muslims; Dervishes; Koran
RG — ; s.a. Civilization, Islamic; Islamic countries; Mosques; Mecca; Moors (people); Muslims; Ramadan
NYT MOHAMMEDANISM; s.a., Black Muslims; Middle East; Moslems; Pakistan
PAIS — ; s.a. Arab states; Black Muslim movement; Islam and politics; Islamic law; Muslims
BPI RELIGION; s.a. Arab countries

ISLAND ECOLOGY. *Use* Ecology

ISOLATIONISM. *Use* Cold War; World Politics

ISOMETRIC EXERCISES. *Use* Exercise

ISOTOPES. *Use* Radiation; Radiotherapy

ISRAEL, STATE OF. *Use* Jewish-Arab Relations; Jews—Political and Social Conditions; Zionism

ISRAELITES. *See* Jews

J

JAILS. *See* Prisons and Prisoners

JAZZ MUSIC
LC ——; s.a. Instrumentation and orchestration (dance orchestra); Jazz quintets; Jazz septets, etc; Piano music (jazz)
SEARS ——; s.a. Blues (songs, etc.); Dance music
RG ——; s.a. Phonograph records—Jazz music; Rock music (song, etc.)
NYT MUSIC
PAIS ——; s.a. Jazz musicians; Music
BPI MUSIC; s.a. Bands; Orchestras

JEALOUSY. *Use* Emotions; Love

JEST BOOKS. *See* Wit and Humor

JESUS CHRIST
LC ——; s.a. Christianity; God; Messiah; Millenium; Redemption; Virgin birth
SEARS ——; s.a. Atonement; Salvation; Trinity
RG ——; s.a. Messiah; Second advent
NYT ——; s.a. Assassination of Christ; Passion plays; Religion and churches
PAIS CHRISTIANITY AND OTHER RELIGIONS; s.a. Jesus movement; Roman Catholic Church
BPI CHRISTIANITY; s.a. Catholic Church; Protestantism

JET PLANES
LC ——; s.a. Jet plane sounds; Jet transports
SEARS ——; s.a. Short take off and landing aircraft
RG AIRPLANES, JET; s.a. Airplanes, Business; Sonic boom
NYT AIRPLANES—U. S.—COMMERCIAL AIR-CRAFTS; s.a. Airplanes—U. S.—SST (supersonic transport)
PAIS AIRPLANES, JET-PROPELLED; s.a. Airplanes, Supersonic; Shock waves
BPI AIRPLANES, JET PROPELLED; s.a. Airlines—Equipment and supplies—Jet equipment; Airplanes, Business—Jet planes; Jet airplane engines

JET PROPULSION. *Use* Ballistic Missiles; Rockets (Aeronautics)

JET TRANSPORTS. *Use* Jet Planes

JETTIES. *Use* Beaches; Reclamation of Land

JETTONS. *Use* Numismatics

JEWELRY
LC ——; s.a. Crown jewels; Jewelry making; Jewelry trade; Precious stones
SEARS ——; s.a. Decoration and ornament; Gems; Goldsmithing; Silversmithing
RG ——; s.a. Diamond cutting; names of pieces of jewelry, e.g., Necklaces
NYT JEWELS AND JEWELRY; s.a. Gold; Silver

PAIS JEWELRY BUSINESS; s.a. Gems; names of jewelry companies, e.g., Tiffany and Company
BPI ——; s.a. Gems; Jewelry industry; Jewelry stores

JEWISH QUESTION. *Use* Jews—Political and Social Conditions; Zionism

JEWISH RELIGION. *See* Jews

JEWISH THEOLOGY. *Use* Messiah; Talmud

JEWISH-ARAB RELATIONS
LC ——; s.a. Arabs in Palestine; Zionism
SEARS ——
RG ——; s.a. Jews in Arab states; Palestinian Arabs
NYT MIDDLE EAST—ISRAELI-ARAB CONFLICT; s.a. Arabs; Israel, State of
PAIS ISRAEL AND THE ARAB STATES; s.a. Jews—Arab states; Palestine—Jewish-Arab problem
BPI ISRAEL-ARAB COUNTRIES; s.a. Arab countries—Israel; Israeli-Arab war, 1967-

JEWISH LITERATURE
LC ——; s.a. Hebrew literature; Yiddish literature
SEARS ——; s.a. Bible; Talmud
RG ——; s.a. Booksellers and bookselling—Jewish literature; Yiddish literature
NYT BOOKS AND LITERATURE; s.a. Bible; Jews; Talmud
PAIS RELIGIOUS LITERATURE; s.a. Jewish press
BPI ——; s.a. Bible; Jews

JEWISH-NEGRO RELATIONS. *Use* Negro-Jewish Relations

JEWS
LC ——; s.a. Concentration camps; Conservative Judaism; Jewish Christians; Jewish sects; Reform Judaism; Religious Zionism; Sephardim
SEARS ——; s.a. Judaism; Talmud
RG ——; s.a. Church and state in Israel; Hasidism; Jewish theology; Maranos; Mysticism—Judaism; Recontructionist Judaism; Zionism
NYT ——; s.a. Religion and churches; Synagogues; Talmud
PAIS ——; s.a. Anti-Semitism; Communism and Judaism; Jews—Converts to Christianity; Judaism; Roman Catholic Church—Relations—Judaism
BPI ——; s.a. Discrimination; Jews in Russia; Prejudice

JEWS—CONVERTS TO CHRISTIANITY. *Use* Conversion, Religious

JEWS—DIETARY LAWS. *Use* Jews—Rites and Ceremonies

JEWS—HOLY DAYS. *Use* Jews—Rites and Ceremonies

JEWS—PERSECUTION. *Use* Atrocities; Jews—Political and Social Conditions

JEWS—POLITICAL AND SOCIAL CONDITIONS
LC ——; s.a. Jews—Diaspora; Jews—Economic conditions; Jews—Legal status, laws, etc.; Jews—Migration; Jews in Africa
SEARS JEWS—POLITICAL ACTIVITY; s.a. Jewish question; Jews—Economic conditions; Jews—Persecution; Jews—Social conditions; Jews in the U.S.
RG ——; s.a. Anti-Semitism; Jews—Nationalism; Zionism
NYT JEWS; s.a. Immigration and emigration; Israel, State of; Refugees
PAIS JEWS; s.a. Jewish-Negro relations; Jews—History
BPI JEWS; s.a. Discrimination; Jews in Russia

JEWS—RITES AND CEREMONIES
See also names of specific Jewish holidays, e.g., Passover; Hannukah; etc.
LC ——; s.a. Bar mitzvah; Jewish way of life; Menorah; Slaughtering and slaughterhouses—Jews; Worship (Judaism)
SEARS ——; s.a. Fasts and feasts—Judaism; Jews—Social life and customs
RG ——; s.a. Jews—Liturgy and ritual; Tradition (Judaism)
NYT JEWS—HOLY DAYS; s.a. Religion and churches
PAIS JEWS; s.a. Jews—Dietary laws
BPI JEWS; s.a. Jewish literature

JEWS — SEGREGATION. *Use* Discrimination in Housing

JEWS IN ARAB STATES. *Use* Jewish-Arab Relations

JEWS IN RUSSIA. *Use* Jews—Political and Social Conditions

JEWS IN THE U.S. *Use* Jews—Political and Social Conditions

JIHAD. *Use* Islam; War and Religion

JIU-JITSU. *Use* Self-Defense

JOB ANALYSIS
LC ——; s.a. Employee morale; Fatigue, Mental; Labor productivity; Performance standards
SEARS ——; s.a. Attitude (psychology); subd. *Attitudes* under names of group, e.g., Youth—Attitudes; etc.; Motion study; Time study
RG ——; s.a. Job satisfaction; Occupations
NYT LABOR; s.a. Labor—U.S.—Productivity; Management, Industrial and institutional
PAIS ——; s.a. Job satisfaction; Labor productivity; Personnel management
BPI ——; s.a. Job satisfaction; Performance; Production standards; Work design; Work measurement

JOB ASSIGNMENT. *Use* Personnel Management

JOB DESCRIPTIONS. *Use* Occupations

JOB DESIGN. *See* Job Analysis

JOB DISCRIMINATION. *See* Discrimination in Employment

JOB EVALUATION. *Use* Occupations; Personnel Management

JOB HUNTING. *Use* Applications for Positions

JOB PERFORMANCE STANDARDS. *See* Job Analysis; Performance Standards

JOB RÉSUMÉS. *See* Applications for Positions

JOB SATISFACTION. *Use* Attitude (Psychology); Industrial Sociology; Job Analysis; Work

JOB TRAINING. *See* Occupational Training

JOB VACANCIES. *Use* Applications for Positions; Labor Supply

JOBBERS (Securities). *Use* Stock Exchange

JOBS. *See* Employment; Occupations; Professions

JOCKEYS. *Use* Horse Racing; Horsemanship

JOGGING. *Use* Exercise; Walking

JOINERY. *Use* Furniture

JOINT ADVENTURES. *Use* Partnership

JOINT PRODUCTION COMMITTEES. *See* Works Councils

JOINT TENANCY. *Use* Condominium (Housing); Real Property

JOKES. *See* Wit and Humor

JOURNALISM
LC ——; s.a. Journalism, Journalistic ethics; Labor; Press; Radio journalism; Science news; Television broadcasting of news
SEARS ——; s.a. Blacks and the press; College and school journalism; Journalists, Radio broadcasting; Reporters and reporting
RG ——; s.a. Foreign correspondents; Interviewing; News; Radio broadcasting—News
NYT NEWS AND NEWS MEDIA; s.a. Freedom of the press; Photography and photographic equipment—News photography; Television and radio—Programs
PAIS ——; s.a. Negro journalists; News photographs; Newspapers; Radio; Trade journals
BPI ——; s.a. Negroes as journalists; News; Newsletters; Photography, Journalistic; Reporters; Reporting; Women as journalists

JOURNALISTIC PHOTOGRAPHY. *See* News Photographers

JOURNALISTS. *Use* Journalism; Press; Reporters and Reporting

JOY AND SORROW. *Use* Emotions

JUDAISM. *Use* Jews

JUDGE ADVOCATE. *Use* Military Law

JUDGE-MADE LAW. *Use* Judicial Power; Law; Legislation

JUDGES
LC ——; s.a. Bail; Courts; Judgments; Judicial behavior; Judicial corruption; Law; Law—Interpretation and construction; Lay judges

JUDGES, *cont.*
SEARS   ——; s.a. Courts; Lawyers
RG   ——; s.a. Judicial corruption; Negro judges
NYT   COURTS; s.a. Legal profession; Supreme
Court (U.S.)
PAIS   ——; s.a. Judges—Ethics; Judicial power;
Justices of the peace
BPI   ——; s.a. Courts; Justice, Administration of

JUDGMENT. *Use* Judges; Judgments; Logic; Thought
and Thinking; Wisdom

JUDGMENTS
Scope: Works on legal judgments.
LC   ——; s.a. Alternative convictions; Conflict of
judicial decisions; Judicial opinions; Sentences
(criminal procedure); Stare decisis
SEARS   COURTS; s.a. Judges; Punishment
RG   ——; s.a. Arrest of judgment; Indeterminate
sentence
NYT   COURTS; s.a. Law and legislation; Legal pro-
fession; Trials
PAIS   JUDGMENTS (Legal); s.a. Civil procedure;
Criminal procedure; Sentences (law)
BPI   JUSTICE, ADMINISTRATION OF; s.a.
Courts; Judges

JUDICIAL BEHAVIOR. *Use* Judges

JUDICIAL BONDS. *Use* Suretyship and Guaranty

JUDICIAL CORRUPTION. *Use* Judges

JUDICIAL OPINIONS. *Use* Judgments

JUDICIAL POWER
LC   ——; s.a. Delegation of powers; Implied
powers (constitutional law); Judge-made law;
Judicial review; Legislative bodies as courts;
Procedure (law)
SEARS   COURTS; s.a. Administrative law; Constitutional
law
RG   CONSTITUTIONAL LAW; s.a. Administrative
law; Judges; Separation of powers
NYT   COURTS; s.a. Law and legislation; Legal
profession; Politics and government
PAIS   ——; s.a. Judges; Separation of powers
BPI   CONSTITUTIONAL LAW; s.a. Judges; Justice,
Administration of

JUDICIAL REVIEW. *Use* Judicial Power; Legislation;
Rule of Law; Separation of Powers

JUDICIARY. *See* Courts; Judicial Power

JUDICIARY POWER. *Use* Courts; Judicial Power

JUDO. *Use* Self-Defense

JUKEBOXES. *Use* Music

JUMPING (Horsemanship). *Use* Horsemanship

JUNGLE ECOLOGY. *Use* Ecology

JUNIOR COLLEGES. *Use* Accreditation (Education);
Colleges and Universities; Education, Higher

JUNIOR HIGH SCHOOLS. *Use* Education, Secondary;
High Schools; Schools

JUNK YARDS. *Use* Refuse and Refuse Disposal

JURIES. *Use* Jury; Law

JURISDICTION. *Use* Law

JURISDICTION (International law). *Use* Boundaries;
International Offenses

JURISDICTION OVER SHIPS AT SEA. *Use* Maritime
Law

JURISPRUDENCE. *Use* Law

JURISTS. *See* Lawyers

JURY
LC   ——; s.a. Grand jury; Instructions to juries;
Lay judges; Trial practice
SEARS   ——; s.a. Criminal law; Law
RG   ——; s.a. Grand jury; Procedure (law)
NYT   JURIES AND JURY DUTY; s.a. Courts; Trials
PAIS   JURIES; s.a. Grand jury; Negro jurors
BPI   ——; s.a. Courts; Justice

JUSTICE. *Use* Equality; Judicial Power; Law; Rule
of Law

JUSTICE, ADMINISTRATION OF
LC   ——; s.a. Arbitration and award; Attorneys—
General; Equality before the law; Government
attorneys; Judges; Judicial process; Law enforce-
ment; Legal aid; Procedure (law); Trials; U.S.
marshals
SEARS   ——; s.a. Criminal investigations; Governmental
investigations
RG   ——; s.a. Arbitration and award; Civil pro-
cedure; Criminal procedure; Public prosecutors
NYT   LAW AND LEGISLATION; s.a. specific
phases, e.g., Search and seizure, etc.; Supreme
Court (U.S.)
PAIS   ——; s.a. Courts; Double jeopardy (law); Legal
procedure; Remedies (law)
BPI   ——; s.a. Civil rights; Due process of law

JUSTICES OF THE PEACE. *Use* Judges

JUVENILE COURTS. *Use* Courts

JUVENILE DELINQUENCY
LC   ——; s.a. Children, Vagrant; Delinquent girls;
Juvenile detention homes; Problem children;
Social work with delinquents and criminals
SEARS   ——; s.a. Drugs and youth; Juvenile delin-
quency—Case studies
RG   ——; s.a. Detention homes; Narcotics and
youth; Reformatories; Rehabilitation of
juvenile delinquents
NYT   ——; s.a. Children and youth—Crime and
criminals; Crime and criminals
PAIS   JUVENILE DELINQUENTS; s.a. Gangs;
Juvenile courts; Probation; Reformatories;
Youth and law
BPI   CHILDREN—LAW; s.a. Crime and criminals;
Prisoners; Youth

JUVENILE LITERATURE. *See* Children's Literature

K

KARATE. *Use* Self-Defense

KEYNESIAN ECONOMICS. *Use* Economics

KEYS. *See* Locks and Keys

KIBBUTZ. *See* Collective Farming

KIDNAPPING
LC   ——; s.a. Abduction; Ransom; Terrorism
SEARS OFFENSES AGAINST THE PERSON; s.a. Criminal law; Hijacking of airplanes
RG   ——; s.a. Guerrillas; Ransom
NYT   ——; s.a. Airlines—Hijacking; Ransom
PAIS   ——; s.a. Abduction; Air transport—Crimes
BPI   CRIME AND CRIMINALS; s.a. Criminal law; Kidnapping, Political

KINDERGARTEN. *Use* Education, Preschool; Education, Primary; Nurseries

KINDNESS. *Use* Charity

KINETIC ART. *Use* Art, Abstract; Modernism (Art); Optical Art

KINGS AND RULERS. *Use* Despotism; Heads of State; Presidents

KINSHIP. *Use* Family; Tribes and Tribal System

KNOWLEDGE, THEORY OF
LC   ——; s.a. Apperception; Comprehension; Education; Faith and reason; Logic; Senses and sensation; Thought and thinking
SEARS ——; s.a. Belief and doubt; Pragmatism; Truth
RG   ——; s.a. Concepts; Empiricism; Knowledge, Sociology of
NYT   PHILOSOPHY
PAIS   ——; s.a. Ideology
BPI   ——; s.a. Ideology; Subjectivity

KOLKHOZ. *See* Collective Farming

KORAN. *Use* Islam

KRISHNA. *Use* Hinduism

L

LABELS
See also subd. *Labeling* under names of products and industries, e.g., Cigarette industry—Labeling.
LC   ——; s.a. Cigar bands and labels; Cigarette package labels; Consumer education; Legal advertising; Marking devices; Packaging; Tobacco package labels; Trade-marks; Union labels
SEARS PACKAGING; s.a. Advertising
RG   ——; s.a. Labeling machines; Unit pricing
NYT   LABELING AND LABELS; s.a. Advertising—U.S.—Misleading and deceptive advertising
PAIS   ——; s.a. Marks of origin
BPI   LABELS AND LABELING; s.a. Labeling machines; Union labels

LABOR. *Use* Labor and Laboring Classes

LABOR (Obstetrics)
LC   ——; s.a. Childbirth; Infants, Premature; Labor, Complicated; Labor, Premature; Pregnancy, Protracted
SEARS CHILDBIRTH; s.a. Pregnancy
RG   CHILDBIRTH; s.a. Midwives; Obstetrics
NYT   PREGNANCY, OBSTETRICS AND MATERNAL WELFARE; s.a. Birth Defects; Births
PAIS   PREGNANCY; s.a. Births
BPI   ——; s.a. Pregnancy; Stillbirth

LABOR, COMPULSORY. *Use* Contract Labor; Native Labor; Slavery

LABOR, PREMATURE. *Use* Labor (Obstetrics)

LABOR, RIGHT TO. *See* Right to Labor

LABOR ABSENTEEISM. *See* Absenteeism (Labor)

LABOR AND LABORING CLASSES
See also names of types of laborers, e.g., Miners.
LC   ——; s.a. Alien labor; Automation; Casual labor; Church and labor; Contract labor; Equal pay for equal work; Incentives in industry; Industrial sociology; Manual labor; Night work; Occupational training; Proletariat; Right to labor; Seasonal labor; Socialism; Trade-unions; Work; Work relief
SEARS ——; s.a. Apprentices; Collective bargaining; Employment; Household employees; Industrial relations; Labor unions
RG   ——; s.a. Labor, Compulsory; Migrant labor; Skilled labor
NYT   LABOR; s.a. Labor—U.S.—Absenteeism; Management, Industrial and institutional; Service industries; White collar workers
PAIS   LABOR; s.a. Absenteeism (labor); Convict labor; Discrimination in employment; Labor productivity; Middle classes; Piece work; Technical workers; Unskilled labor

LABOR AND LABORING CLASSES, *cont.*
BPI ——; s.a. Division of labor; Factory system; Occupations; Unemployed

LABOR CONTRACT. *Use* Collective Bargaining; Contracts; Industrial Relations; Labor Laws and Legislation; Open and Closed Shop; Right to Labor

LABOR COST. *Use* Minimum Wage; Wages and Salaries

LABOR COURTS. *Use* Arbitration, Industrial; Collective Bargaining; Industrial Laws and Legislation

LABOR DISCIPLINE. *Use* Personnel Management

LABOR DISPUTES. *Use* Arbitration, Industrial; Boycott; Collective Bargaining; Collective Labor Agreements; Management Rights; Strikes and Lockouts

LABOR FORCE. *See* Employment; Labor Supply

LABOR GRIEVANCES. *See* Labor Laws and Legislation

LABOR INCENTIVES. *See* Incentives in Industry

LABOR JOURNALISM. *See* Journalism

LABOR LAWS AND LEGISLATION
LC ——; s.a. Boycott; Employees, Dismissal of; Grievance procedure; Industrial laws and legislation; International labor laws and legislation; Labor policy; Minimum wage; Open and closed shop; Picketing; subd. *Legal status, laws, etc.* under names of professions, e.g., Nurses and nursing—Legal status, laws, etc.; Unfair labor practices; Workmen's compensation; Works councils
SEARS LABOR LAW; s.a. Industrial law; Labor contract; Stikes and lockouts; subd. *Laws and regulations* under subject, e.g., Child labor—Laws and regulations
RG ——; s.a. Hours of labor; Work rules
NYT LABOR; s.a. Labor—U.S.—Minimum wage; Labor—U.S.—Strikes; Labor—U.S.—Wages and hours
PAIS LABOR—LEGISLATION; s.a. Collective bargaining; Industrial relations—Legislation; Unfair labor practices
BPI ——; s.a. Unfair labor practices; Wages and salaries—Laws and regulations

LABOR MARKET. *See* Employment; Labor Supply

LABOR MOBILITY. *Use* Labor Supply; Migrant Labor; Migration, Internal; Occupational Mobility; Rural Conditions

LABOR PRODUCTIVITY. *Use* Absenteeism (Labor); Automation; Industrial Management; Job Analysis; Labor and Laboring Classes; Machinery in Industry; Work Measurement

LABOR RELATIONS. *See* Industrial Relations

LABOR SAVING DEVICES, HOUSEHOLD. *See* Household Equipment and Furnishings

LABOR SUPPLY
LC ——; s.a. Absenteeism (labor); Economic history; Human capital; Job vacancies; Labor mobility; Manpower; Migration, Internal; Woman—Employment; Work relief

SEARS ——; s.a. Employment; Employment agencies; Manpower policy; Retraining, Occupational
RG ——; s.a. College graduates—Employment; Labor turnover; Occupational mobility; Unemployment
NYT LABOR—U.S.—UNEMPLOYMENT AND JOB MARKET; s.a. Labor—U.S.—Migratory labor; Labor—U.S.—Youth, Employment of; U.S.—Economic conditions and trends
PAIS ——; s.a. Employees, Transfer of; Labor mobility; Manpower utilization; Skilled labor
BPI ——; s.a. Employees, Relocation of; Employment; Labor mobility; Migrant labor

LABOR TURNOVER. *Use* Labor Supply; Occupational Mobility

LABOR UNIONS. *Use* Arbitration, Industrial; Collective Bargaining; Industrial Relations; Labor and Laboring Classes; Open and Closed Shop; Strikes and Lockouts; Trade Unions

LABORATORIES. *Use* Industrial Research; Scientific Apparatus and Instruments

LABORATORY SCHOOLS. *Use* Educational Planning and Innovations

LABORERS. *See* Labor and Laboring Classes; Labor Laws and Legislation; Labor Supply

LACQUER AND LACQUERING. *Use* Finishes and Finishing

LAICISM. *See* Secularism

LAISSEZ-FAIRE. *Use* Competition; Economic Policy; Industry and State

LAKES. *Use* Water; Waterways

LAMPS. *Use* Lighting

LAND
LC ——; s.a. Absenteeism; Farms; Land, Nationalization of; Land reform; Real property; Rent (economic theory)
SEARS ——; s.a. Agriculture—Economic aspect; Land tenure; Real estate; Reclamation of land
RG ——; s.a. Clearing of land; Farm tenancy; Landlord and tenant; Soils
NYT REAL ESTATE; s.a. Agriculture and agricultural products; Area planning and renewal; Reclamation of land
PAIS ——; s.a. Agriculture; Crown lands; Riparian rights
BPI ——; s.a. Eminent domain; Public lands; Real estate business; Zoning

LAND, NATIONALIZATION OF. *Use* Land; Land Tenure

LAND CONTRACTS. *Use* Mortgages

LAND GRANTS. *Use* Colonization; Public Lands

LAND RECLAMATION. *See* Reclamation of Land

LAND REFORM. *Use* Land; Social Policy

LAND SETTLEMENT. *Use* Colonies

LAND SPECULATION. *Use* Real Property

LAND SUBDIVISION. *Use* City Planning; Real Property; Suburbs

LAND TAX. *See* Real Property; Taxation

LAND TENURE
LC ———; s.a. Absenteeism; Administration of estates; Church lands; Commons; Deeds; Entail; Land, Nationalization of; Serfdom
SEARS ———; s.a. Farm tenancy; Feudalism; Landlord and tenant; Real estate
RG ———; s.a. Farm ownership; Homestead law
NYT REAL ESTATE; s.a. Mortgages
PAIS ———; s.a. Allotment of land; Farm ownership
BPI ———; s.a. Conveyancing; Land titles; Peasantry

LAND TITLES. *Use* Deeds; Land Tenure; Real Property; Transfer (Law)

LAND USE. *See* Land; Regional Planning

LAND VALUES. *Use* Real Property; Valuation

LANDLORD AND TENANT
LC ———; s.a. Abandonment of property; Absenteeism; Commercial leases; Condominium (housing); Distress (law); Land tenure; Leases; Real covenants; Real property; Rent control; Rent laws; Subtenants
SEARS ———; s.a. Apartment houses; Housing; Tenement houses
RG ———; s.a. Farm tenancy; Rent
NYT RENTS AND RENTING; s.a. Housing—U.S.—Rents and renting; Office building; Real estate
PAIS ———; s.a. Farm tenancy; Eviction
BPI ———; s.a. Rent; Rent strikes

LANDSCAPE. *Use* Landscape Protection

LANDSCAPE ARCHITECTURE. *Use* Architecture; Landscape Protection; Roads

LANDSCAPE GARDENING. *Use* Gardening; Landscape Protection; Trees

LANDSCAPE IMPROVEMENT. *Use* Regional Planning

LANDSCAPE PROTECTION
LC ———; s.a. Monuments—Preservation; Natural monuments; Regional planning
SEARS ———; s.a. Landscape architecture; Nature conservation; Views
RG ———; s.a. Conservation of resources; Nature (aesthetics); Roadside improvement
NYT U.S.—NATURAL RESOURCES; s.a. Landscaping; Nature; Roads
PAIS LANDSCAPE; s.a. Landscape gardening; Nature; Open space; Roadside improvement
BPI ———; s.a. Conservation of resources; Landscape architecture

LANGUAGE AND CULTURE. *Use* Culture

LANGUAGE AND LANGUAGES
See also names of lanugages, e.g., English language; Semitic language; and subd. *Languages* under names of countries, e.g., Canada—Languages; and subd. *Language* under names of groups, e.g., Children—Language.

LC ———; s.a. Accents and accentuation; Alphabet; Communication; Grammar, Comparative and general; Language—Philosophy; Language—Psychology; Language arts; Languages, Artificial; Linguistics; Negro-English dialects; Philology; Sign language; Slang; Sociolinguistics; Terms and phrases; Vocabulary; Words (new)
SEARS ———; s.a. Conversation; English language—Slang; Grammar; Language, Universal; Phonetics; Semantics; Translating and interpreting; Voice
RG ———; s.a. Americanisms (speech); Languages, Artificial; Languages, Modern; Rhetoric; Semantics
NYT ———; s.a. Slang; Speech
PAIS LANGUAGES; s.a. Bilingualism; Literature; Philology
BPI ———; s.a. Communication; English language—Slang; Literature

LANGUAGE ARTS. *Use* Communication; Language and Languages; Reading; Speech

LANGUAGE GAMES. *Use* Recreation

LANTERN SLIDES. *Use* Audio-visual Materials

LAPIDARY WORK. *Use* Precious Stones

LARCENY. *Use* Burglary; Theft

LARYNX. *Use* Voice

LASERS. *Use* Surgery; Technological Innovations; Telecommunication

LATIN ORIENT. *Use* Near East

LATITUDE. *Use* Earth

LATTER-DAY SAINTS. *See* Mormons and Mormonism

LAUGHTER. *Use* Emotions; Wit and Humor

LAUNCH VEHICLES (Astronautics). *Use* Rockets (Aeronautics)

LAUNDRIES AND LAUNDERING
LC LAUNDRIES; s.a. Hotel laundry service; Laundries, Hospital; Laundries, Military; Laundries, Public; Laundry machinery
SEARS LAUNDRY; s.a. Cleaning; Electric household equipment and supplies; Household appliances
RG LAUNDRY; s.a. Ironing; Laundry equipment
NYT ———; s.a. Cleaning and dyeing; Cleansers, detergents and soaps; Washing and ironing equipment
PAIS LAUNDRY INDUSTRY; s.a. Bleaching materials; Cleaning industry; Home economics; Washing machine industry
BPI LAUNDRIES, COMMERCIAL; s.a. Clothes dryers; Electric irons; Laundry equipment, Domestic; Washing machines

LAW
See also special branches of law, e.g., Administrative law, Civil law, Commercial law, Constitutional law, Corporation law, Criminal law, Ecclesiastical law, Internal revenue law, Maritime law, Military law, Public law, Space law; also subds. *Laws; Laws and legislation* or *Laws and regulations* under specific subjects, e.g., Telecommunication—Laws.

LAW, *cont.*
LC ——; s.a. Equality before law; Illegality; Judgments; Law—Psychology; Law—Vocational guidance; Law and politics; Law and socialism; Legal authorities; Legal correspondence; Legal instruments; Legal maxims; names of legal systems, e.g., Cannon law, Common law, Jewish law; Natural law; Roman law; Statutes; subds. *Cases* and *Cases—Digests* under legal subjects, e.g., Divorce—Cases; subd. *Terms and phrases* under branches of law, e.g., Civil law—Terms and phrases
SEARS ——; s.a. Jury; Justice; Law—Case studies; Law—Terminology; Law enforcement; Medical jurisprudence; Police
RG ——; s.a. Judges; Judicial corruption; Jurisprudence; Justice; Law—Philosophy; Law and ethics; Law schools; Legal literature; Procedure (law); Rule of law
NYT LAW AND LEGISLATION; s.a. Courts; Juries; Legal Profession; U.S.—Constitution; Supreme Court (U.S.)
PAIS ——; s.a. Bar examinations; Communism and law; Due process of law; Judge-made law; Judicial power; Jurisprudence; Law—Digests; Law—Interpretation and construction; Law—Language; Legal ethics; Legal literature; Sociological jurisprudence; U.S.—Supreme Court
BPI ——; s.a. Forms (law); Judges; Jurisdiction; Justice, Administration of; Lawyers; Legal education; Legal research

LAW AND LEGISLATION. *Use* Constitutions; Industrial Laws and Legislation; Legislation; Legislative Bodies; Lobbying; Narcotics, Control of; Rule of Law

LAW AND POLITICS. *Use* State, The

LAW AS A PROFESSION.
See also Lawyers

LAW ENFORCEMENT
LC ——; s.a. Criminal justice, Administration of; Federal aid to law enforcement agencies; Law; Peace officers; Sanctions, Administrative
SEARS ——; s.a. Police
RG ——; s.a. Crime prevention; Police
NYT POLICE; s.a. Crime and criminals; Law and legislation; UN—Military personnel
PAIS ——; s.a. Crime prevention; Sheriffs
BPI POLICE; s.a. Crime and criminals; Criminal investigation; Justice, Administration of

LAW EXAMINATONS. *Use* Lawyers

LAW OF SUCCESSION. *See* Inheritance and Succession

LAW OF SUPPLY AND DEMAND. *See* Supply and Demand

LAW OF THE SEA. *See* Maritime Law

LAW OFFICES. *Use* Lawyers

LAW PARTNERSHIP. *Use* Lawyers

LAW SCHOOLS. *Use* Law

LAWS. *See* Law

LAWYERS
LC ——; s.a. Attorney and client; Law examinations; Law—Vocational guidance; Law offices; Law partnership; Legal aid; Legal service corporations; Practice of law; Procedure (Law); Trials
SEARS ——; s.a. Judges; Law—Examinations, questions, etc.; Law as a profession; Legal ethics
RG ——; s.a. Law—Study and teaching; Malpractice; Negro lawyers
NYT LEGAL PROFESSION; s.a. Courts
PAIS LEGAL PROFESSION; s.a. Public defenders; Women as lawyers
BPI ——; s.a. Legal education; Tax consultants; Trust companies—Lawyers cooperation

LAY BROTHERS. *Use* Monasticism and Religious Orders

LAY JUDGES. *Use* Judges; Jury

LAYAWAY PLAN. *Use* Consumer Credit; Installment Plan

LEAD POISONING. *Use* Occupations, Dangerous

LEADERSHIP
LC ——; s.a. Community leadership; Discussion; Human behavior; Psychology, Military; Recreation leadership; Small groups; Social groups
SEARS ——; s.a. Ability; Executive ability; Management; Success
RG ——; s.a. Christian leadership; Negro leadership
NYT LEADERS AND LEADERSHIP; s.a. Executives
PAIS ——; s.a. Elite (social sciences); Negro leadership
BPI ——; s.a. Executives; Meetings; Sociology

LEAP YEAR. *Use* Special Days, Weeks and Months

LEARNED INSTITUTIONS AND SOCIETIES. *Use* Learning and Scholarship

LEARNERS, INDUSTRIAL. *Use* Apprentices

LEARNING. *Use* Academic Achievement; Learning and Scholarship

LEARNING, PSYCHOLOGY OF
LC ——; s.a. Ability; Comprehension; Concept learning; Educability; Learning by discovery; Paired-association learning; Sleep-learning; Thought and thinking; Transfer of training
SEARS ——; s.a. Animal intelligence
RG ——; s.a. Memory; Psychology, Educational
NYT PSYCHOLOGY AND PSYCHOLOGISTS; s.a. Education and schools
PAIS LEARNING AND SCHOLARSHIP; s.a. Education; Educational psychology; Learning ability
BPI ——; s.a. Conditioned response; Education; Memory

LEARNING ABILITY. *Use* Educational Psychology; Learning, Psychology of

LEARNING AND SCHOLARSHIP
See also Scholars, and names of specific institutions and societies, e.g., Society of Architectural Historians.
LC ——; s.a. Degrees, Academic; Scholarly publishing; Wisdom

SEARS ——; s.a. Culture; Degrees, Academic; Humanism; Professional education
RG ——; s.a. Intellectuals; Knowledge; Learned institutions and societies
NYT EDUCATION AND SCHOOLS; s.a. Colleges and universities; Culture; Organizations, societies and clubs; Research
PAIS ——; s.a. College teachers; Education; Research; Scientific societies
BPI EDUCATION; s.a. College professors and instructors; Research; Scientists; Societies

LEARNING BY DISCOVERY. *Use* Learning, Psychology of

LEARNING CENTERS. *See* Instructional Materials Centers

LEASED TERRITORIES. *Use* Territory, National

LEASES. *Use* Landlord and Tenant; Rent Laws

LEATHER INDUSTRY AND TRADE
LC ——; s.a. Boots and shoes—Trade and manufacture; Leather, Artificial; Leather embroidery; Leather garments; Leather work
SEARS ——; s.a. Bookbinding; Hides and skins; Shoes and shoe industry
RG LEATHER; s.a. Leather substitutes; Leather work; Shark leather; Tanning
NYT LEATHER AND LEATHER GOODS; s.a. Apparel; Hides and skins; Shoes
PAIS LEATHER INDUSTRY; s.a. Hides and skins; Shoe industry
BPI LEATHER INDUSTRY; s.a. Books, Leather bound; Leather substitutes

LEATHER SUBSTITUTES. *Use* Substitute Products

LEATHER WORK. *Use* Handicraft

LEAVE OF ABSENCE. *Use* Vacations, Employee

LECTURES AND LECTURING
LC ——; s.a. Elocution; Introduction of speakers; Lectures and lecturing—Audio-visual aids; Oratory; Radio addresses, debates, etc.
SEARS ——; s.a. Rhetoric; Speeches, addresses, etc.; Teaching
RG ——; s.a. Lecture method in teaching
NYT SPEECHES AND STATEMENTS; s.a. Colleges and universities—U.S.—Teachers and school employees; Debating
PAIS ——; s.a. Public speaking; Speeches, addresses, etc.
BPI PUBLIC SPEAKING; s.a. Television public speaking

LEFT (Political science). *See* Right and Left (Political science)

LEGACIES. *Use* Charitable Uses, Trusts and Foundations; Inheritance and Succession; Wills

LEGAL ADVERTISING. *Use* Labels

LEGAL AID
LC ——; s.a. Authentication; In forma pauperis; Legal assistance to the poor; Legalization; Public defenders; Social service

SEARS ——; s.a. Law—Documentation; Legal assistance to poor; Public welfare
RG ——; s.a. Defense (criminal procedure); Documentation; Justice, Administration of
NYT LEGAL AID FOR THE POOR; s.a. Crime—U.S.—Legal aid for the poor; Documents; Prisons and prisoners; Welfare work
PAIS ——; s.a. Legal documents; Poor—Legal status, laws, etc.; Public defenders
BPI ——; s.a. Justice; Administration of; Lawyers

LEGAL AUTHORITIES. *Use* Law

LEGAL CORRESPONDENCE. *Use* Law

LEGAL CRUELTY. *Use* Divorce

LEGAL EDUCATION. *Use* Lawyers

LEGAL ETHICS. *Use* Ethics; Law; Lawyers

LEGAL ETIQUETTE. *Use* Procedure (Law); Trials

LEGAL HOLIDAYS. *See* Special Days, Weeks and Months

LEGAL INSTRUMENTS. *Use* Law

LEGAL PROCEDURE. *Use* Justice, Administration of; Procedure (Law)

LEGAL PROFESSION. *Use* Courts; Judges; Lawyers; Probate Law and Practice

LEGAL RESEARCH. *Use* Law

LEGAL RESPONSIBILITY. *See* Liability (Law)

LEGAL RIGHTS. *Use* Civil Rights; Constitutions; Equality

LEGAL SECRETARIES. *Use* Secretaries

LEGAL SERVICE CORPORATIONS. *Use* Lawyers

LEGAL SERVICES FOR THE POOR. *See* Legal Aid

LEGAL TENDER. *Use* Money

LEGATES, PAPAL. *Use* Papacy

LEGENDS. *Use* Folklore; Mythology; Tales

LEGISLATION
LC ——; s.a. Bills, Legislative; Delegated legislation; Exclusive and concurrent legislative powers; Initiative, Right of; Judicial review; Legislation on particular subjects, e.g., Sunday laws; Repeal of legislation; Separation of powers
SEARS ——; s.a. Governmental investigations; Law; Legislative bodies
RG ——; s.a. Constitutional law; Lobbying; Parliamentary practice; Referendum
NYT LAW AND LEGISLATION; s.a. U.S.—Congress (Senate); U.S.—Constitution—Amendments, Constitutional; U.S.—Law and legislation
PAIS ——; s.a. Judge-made law; Legislative power; Legislators; subd. *Legislation* under specific subjects, e.g., Civil rights—Legislation; U.S. Congress—Power and duties
BPI ——; s.a. Government investigations; Referendum; Representative government and representation; U.S.—Congress

LEGISLATIVE BODIES
LC   ——; s.a. Legislative bodies as courts; Legislative councils; Parliamentary practice; Right and left (political science)
SEARS ——; s.a. Parliamentary practice; Representative government and representation
RG   ——; s.a. Caucus; Parliamentary practice
NYT LAW AND LEGISLATION; s.a. Local government; Politics and government; U.S.—Congress (House of Representatives); U.S.—Congress (Senate)
PAIS LEGISLATIVE COUNCILS; s.a. Caucus; Parliamentary procedure; Representative government
BPI   LEGISLATION; s.a. Parliamentary practice; Political science; State legislatures

LEGISLATIVE COUNCILS. *Use* Legislative Bodies

LEGISLATIVE HEARINGS. *Use* Legislation; Loyalty

LEGISLATIVE INVESTIGATIONS. *See* Legislation; Loyalty

LEGISLATIVE POWER. *Use* Legislation

LEGISLATIVE PROCEDURE. *See* Parliamentary Practice

LEGISLATORS. *Use* Legislation

LEGISLATURES—APPORTIONMENT. *Use* Apportionment (Election law)

LEGITIMACY (Law). *See* Illegitimacy

LEGITIMACY OF GOVERNMENTS. *Use* Revolutions; Sovereignty; State, The

LEGITIMATION OF CHILDREN. *Use* Illegitimacy

LEISURE
LC   ——; s.a. Church and leisure; Leisure class; Leisure in literature; Luxury; Time allocation
SEARS ——; s.a. Hobbies; Recreation; Retirement
RG   ——; s.a. Recreation; Time, Use of
NYT ——; s.a. Entertainment and amusements; Parks, playgrounds and other recreation areas; Recreation
PAIS ——; s.a. Games; Recreation
BPI   ——; s.a. Hobbies; Recreation; Retirement

LENDING. *See* Loans

LENSES. *Use* Optical Trade

LENSES, CONTACT. *Use* Eye

LESBIANISM. *Use* Homosexuality; Sex

LESSON PLANNING. *Use* Teaching

LETTER WRITING
See also Letters for collections of literary letters.
LC   ——; s.a. Circular letters; Commercial correspondence; Form letters; Government correspondence; Love-letters
SEARS ——; s.a. Business letters; Rhetoric; Style, Literary
RG   ——; s.a. Etiquette; Forms of address; Lobbying; Newspapers—Letter to the editor
NYT LETTERS; s.a. Advertising—U.S.—Direct mail advertising; Writing and writers

PAIS COMMERCIAL CORRESPONDENCE; s.a. Letter services; Letters
BPI   COMMERCIAL CORRESPONDENCE; s.a. Sales letters

LETTERING. *Use* Alphabet; Design

LETTERS. *Use* Air Mail Service; Commercial Correspondence; Letter Writing; Postal Service

LETTERS (Belles-lettres). *Use* Literature

LETTERS OF CREDIT. *See* Credit; Negotiable Instruments

LEUKEMIA. *Use* Anemia; Blood

LEVANT. *Use* Near East

LIABILITY (Law)
LC   ——; s.a. Criminal liability; Employers' liability; Impossibility of performance; Liability for sport accidents [and similar headings]; Limited liability; Negligence; Personal injuries; Suretyship and guaranty; Warranty
SEARS CIVIL LAW; s.a. Commercial law; subd. *Laws and regulations* under subjects, e.g., Animals—Laws and regulations
RG   ——; s.a. Insurance, Liability; Limited partnership; Torts
NYT LAW AND LEGISLATION; s.a. Liability insurance; Manufacturers' liability for products
PAIS LIABILITY; s.a. Government liability; Municipal liability; Negligence; Partnership; Private companies; subd. *Liability* under subjects, e.g., Executives—Liability
BPI   LIABILITY; s.a. Damages; Employers liability; Products liability

LIAR PARADOX. *Use* Logic

LIBEL AND SLANDER
LC   ——; s.a. Blasphemy; Liability for credit information; Liberty of speech; Liberty of the press; Personality (law); Publicity (law); Seditious libel; Trials (slander)
SEARS ——; s.a. Free speech; Journalism; Privacy, Right of
RG   ——; s.a. Press law; Trials (libel)
NYT ——; s.a. Freedom of speech; Freedom of the press
PAIS ——; s.a. Freedom of speech; Press law
BPI   ——; s.a. Free speech; Freedom of the press

LIBERAL EDUCATION. *Use* Colleges and Universities; Education, Higher

LIBERALISM. *Use* Liberty; Right and Left (Political science)

LIBERTY
LC   ——; s.a. Assembly, Right of; Conformity; Dissenters, Religious; Freedom of association; Freedom of movement; Liberalism; Liberty of conduct; Liberty of conscience; Life and death, Power over; Natural law; Political rights; Social control; Teaching, Freedom of

SEARS ——; s.a. Anarchism and anarchists; Civil rights; Democracy; Equality; Freedom of conscience; Intellectual freedom; Political science; Religious liberty; Slavery

RG ——; s.a. Civil rights; Democracy; Free speech; Freedom of the press; Liberalism; Liberty of conscience; Religious liberty

NYT FREEDOM AND HUMAN RIGHTS; Freedom of information, thought and expression; Freedom of religion

PAIS ——; s.a. Academic freedom; Conscientious objectors; Freedom of information

BPI ——; s.a. Civil rights; Equality; Freedom of association; Intellectual liberty

LIBERTY (Theology). *See* Religious Liberty

LIBERTY OF CONSCIENCE. *Use* Dissenters, Religious; Persecution; Religious Liberty; Toleration

LIBERTY OF CONTRACT. *Use* Contracts

LIBERTY OF INFORMATION. *See* Freedom of Information

LIBERTY OF SPEECH

LC ——; s.a. Freedom of information; Legislative bodies—Freedom of debate; Liberty of speech in the church; Liberty of the press; Press laws; Sedition

SEARS FREE SPEECH; s.a. Books—Censorship; Civil rights; Freedom of assembly; Freedom of information; Freedom of the press; Intellectual freedom; Libel and slander

RG FREE SPEECH; s.a. Academic freedom; Government and the press; Information, Freedom of

NYT FREEDOM OF SPEECH; s.a. Books and literature—Censorship; Censorship; Freedom and human rights; Freedom of information, Thought and expression; Freedom of inquiry; Freedom of the press; News and news media

PAIS FREEDOM OF SPEECH; s.a. Assembly, Right of; Freedom of the press; Liberty

BPI FREE SPEECH; s.a. Censorship; Freedom of information; Freedom of the press; Intellectual liberty

LIBERTY OF THE PRESS. *Use* Censorship; Freedom of Information; Libel and Slander; Liberty of Speech; Press

LIBRARIANS. *Use* Libraries and Librarians

LIBRARIANSHIP. *Use* Libraries and Librarians

LIBRARIES—AUTOMATION. *See* Information Sciences; Information Storage and Retrieval Systems

LIBRARIES AND AUDIO-VISUAL MATERIALS. *Use* Audio-visual Education

LIBRARIES AND LIBRARIANS
See also types of libraries, e.g., Art; Business; Medical; Public; Rental; Research; School, etc.

LC LIBRARIES; s.a. Archives; Audio-visual library service; Audio-visual materials; Bibliographical centers; Bibliography; Librarians; Libraries, Universities and colleges; Libraries and readers; Libraries and state; Library legislation; Library schools; Library science; Library technicians

SEARS LIBRARIES; s.a. Classification—Books; Documentation; Information sciences; Instructional materials centers; Libraries, College and university; Library administration; Library education; Library service; Library surveys; State aid to libraries

RG LIBRARIES; s.a. Books and reading; Cataloging; College libraries; Librarianship; Libraries—Federal aid; Libraries and schools; Library education; Library schools and education

NYT ——; s.a. Books and literature; Indexes and indexing; subd. *Libraries and Librarians* under subject, e.g., Medicine and health—Libraries and librarians

PAIS LIBRARIES; s.a. Cataloging; Information processing systems; Libraries, Colleges; Libraries—State aid; Libraries and education; Library research; Subject headings

BPI LIBRARIES; s.a. College libraries; Federal aid to libraries; Indexing; Information services; Information storage and retrieval systems; Library use studies; Library science as a profession; Processing (libraries)

LIBRARIES AND MOVING PICTURES. *Use* Moving Pictures in Education

LIBRARY INFORMATION NETWORKS. *Use* Data Transmission Systems

LIBRARY SCIENCE. *Use* Documentation; Information Sciences; Information Storage and Retrieval Systems; Libraries and Librarians

LIBRARY SERVICE. *Use* Libraries and Librarians

LIBRARY TECHNICIANS. *Use* Libraries and Librarians

LIBRETTISTS. *Use* Opera

LICENCE SYSTEM. *Use* Liquor Problem

LICENSES
Scope: Works on licenses as means of controlling trades and industries, or of producing revenue. See also subd. *Licenses* under names of industries and occupations, e.g., Automobile drivers—Licenses.

LC ——; s.a. Business tax; Concessions; Copyright licenses; Exclusive licenses; Export control; Patent licenses

SEARS COMMERCIAL LAW; s.a. subd. *Laws and regulations* under specific subjects, e.g., Liquor traffic—Laws and regulations

RG ——; s.a. Municipal finance

NYT ——

BPI ——; s.a. Taxation

LIENS. *Use* Debtor and Creditor; Mortgages; Property

LIFE

LC ——; s.a. Birth (philosophy); Death (biology); Evolution; Life (biology); Life and death, Power over; Life on other planets; Plurality of worlds; Spontaneous generation

SEARS ——; s.a. Death; Future life; Immortality; Life (biology); Life—Philosophy; Life on other planets; Middle age; Old age; Ontology; Space biology

LIFE, *cont.*

RG ———; s.a. Conduct of life; Death; Genetics; Interstellar communication; Life on Mars; Reproduction

NYT BIOLOGY AND BIOCHEMISTRY; s.a. Ethics and morals; Reproduction (biological)

PAIS ———; s.a. Ethics; Genetics; Longevity; Philosophical anthropology; Space, Outer

BPI ———; s.a. Conduct of life; Death; Life (biology); Old age

LIFE (Biology). *Use* Biology; Life; Middle Age; Old Age

LIFE AFTER DEATH. *See* Future Life; Immortality

LIFE AND DEATH, POWER OVER. *Use* Liberty

LIFE EXPECTANCY. *Use* Old Age

LIFE IMPRISONMENT. *Use* Prisons and Prisoners

LIFE INSURANCE. *Use* Annuities; Insurance, Life; Survivor's Benefits

LIFE ON OTHER PLANETS. *Use* Astronomy; Life; Outer Space

LIFE SPAN, PRODUCTIVE. *Use* Age and Employment

LIFE SUPPORT SYSTEMS (Space environment). *Use* Environmental Engineering; Human Engineering; Space flight

LIFE-SAVING. *Use* Rescue Work

LIGHT. *Use* Optics

LIGHTING

See also subd. *Lighting* under names of cities and subjects, e.g., Chicago—Lighting, Theaters—Lighting, Restaurants, lunchrooms, etc.—Lighting.

LC ———; s.a. Decorative lighting; Electric lighting; Garden lighting; Gas lighting; Lighting industry; Optics

SEARS ———; s.a. Candles; Fluorescent lighting; Lamps

RG ———; s.a. Lighting, Architectural and decorative; Skylights

NYT ———; s.a. Electric appliances and equipment (fixtures); Electric light and power; Streets

PAIS ———; s.a. Electric lamps; Street lighting

BPI ———; s.a. Office lighting

LIME. *Use* Fertilizers and Manures

LIMITATION OF ARMAMENT. *See* Disarmament

LIMITED COMPANIES. *See* Corporations

LIMITED LIABILITY. *Use* Liability (Law)

LIMITED PARTNERSHIPS. *Use* Business Enterprises; Corporations; Liability (Law); Partnership

LIMOUSINES. *See* Motor Vehicles

LINE OF BALANCE (Management). *Use* Production Control

LINEAR PROGRAMMING

LC ———; s.a. Interindustry economics; Recursive programming; Scheduling (management); Stochastic programming

SEARS PROGRAMMING (Electronic computers); s.a. Economics; Electronic data processing; Management; Mathematics

RG INPUT-OUTPUT ANALYSIS. s.a. Computer programming; Data transmission systems

NYT MATHEMATICS; s.a. Data processing (information processing) equipment and systems; Economics

PAIS ———; s.a. Input-output data; Programming (mathematics)

BPI ———; s.a. Simplex method; Transportation problem (programming)

LINGUISTIC TABOO. *See* Taboo

LINGUISTICS. *Use* Language and Languages

LINKAGE (Genetics). *Use* Genetics

LINOLEUM. *Use* Floors

LIP READING. *See* Deafness

LIQUID FUELS. *Use* Fuel

LIQUID METALS. *Use* Metal Industries

LIQUIDATION. *Use* Bankruptcy; Corporations; Partnership

LIQUIDITY (Economics). *Use* Banks and Banking; Credit; Money

LIQUOR. *Use* Alcohol; Alcoholism; Bars and Barrooms; Beverages; Liquor Problem; Liquors; Temperance

LIQUOR INDUSTRY. *Use* Alcohol; Beer and Brewing Industry; Liquors

LIQUOR LAWS. *Use* Liquors; Liquor Problem

LIQUOR PROBLEM

LC ———; s.a. Alcohol and children; Alcohol and Jews; Alcohol and Negroes; Alcohol and women; Alcoholics; Licence system; Local option; Social problems

SEARS ———; s.a. Alcoholism; Temperance

RG ———; s.a. Alcohol—Physiological effects; Alcohol and youth; Liquor laws and regulations

NYT ALCOHOLISM; s.a. Liquor; Liquor—Children and youth; Traffic (vehicular and pedestrian) and parking—U.S.—Drunken and reckless driving

PAIS ———; s.a. Alcohol and youth; Drinking and traffic accidents; Prohibition

BPI ———; s.a. Alcoholism; Insurance, Liquor law liability; Personnel management—Alcohol problem

LIQUORS

LC ———; s.a. Adulterations; Brewing industry; Liquor laws; Liquor traffic; Wine and wine making

SEARS ———; s.a. Alcohol; Distillation; Liquor traffic—Laws and regulations; Stimulants

RG ———; s.a. Cocktails; Cookery—Liquors; Liquers; Liquor laws and regulations

NYT LIQUOR; s.a. Alcohol; Beverages; Wines

PAIS LIQUOR INDUSTRY; s.a. Brandy industry; Distilling industry; Wine industry

BPI ———; s.a. Liquor industry; Wine and wine making

LISTENING. *Use* Educational Psychology

LISTENING DEVICES—LAW AND LEGISLATION. *See* Wiretapping

LITERACY. *Use* Education; Illiteracy

LITERACY TESTS (Election law). *Use* Voting

LITERARY AGENTS. *Use* Publishers and Publishing

LITERARY CRITICISM. *Use* Literature

LITERARY FORGERIES AND MYSTIFICATIONS. *Use* Forgery of Works of Art

LITERARY LANDMARKS. *Use* Literature

LITERARY PRIZES. *Use* Literature; Rewards (Prizes, etc.)

LITERARY PROPERTY. *See* Copyright; Intellectual Property

LITERARY RESEARCH. *Use* Literature

LITERATURE
See also types of literature, e.g., Classical literature; Christian literature; Pastoral literature; etc.; and national literatures, e.g., English literature; German literature; etc.

LC ——; s.a. America—Literatures; Authorship (language arts); Characters and characteristics in literature; Letters; Literature, Comparative; Literature, Immoral; Literary landmarks; Literary prizes; Literature, Modern; Literature—Terminology; Literature and science; Literature and technology; Negro literature; Negroes in literature; Plots (drama, novel, etc.); Sex in literature

SEARS ——; s.a. Black literature; Books—Censorship; Drama; Fantastic fiction; Poetry; Pornography; Religion in literature; Science fiction; Women in literature and arts

RG ——; s.a. Censorship; Characters in literature; Essays; Fiction; Literary criticism; Literary research; Literature—Appreciation and interpretation; Literature—Psychology; Literature—Themes; Literature and morals; Literature and science

NYT BOOKS AND LITERATURE; s.a. Book reviews; Pornography; Science fiction; Writing and writers

PAIS ——; s.a. African literature; Authors; Censorship; Criticism; Literature and society; Obscenity; Pornography

BPI ——; s.a. Censorship; Fiction; Language and languages; Obscenity; Science fiction

LITERATURE, IMMORAL. *Use* Censorship; Erotica

LITERATURE, PRIMITIVE. *Use* Folklore

LITERATURE—STORIES, PLOTS, ETC. *Use* Plots (Drama, novel, etc.)

LITERATURE AND MORALS. *Use* Censorship

LITERATURE AND RADIO. *See* Radio Broadcasting and Programs

LITERATURE AS A PROFESSION. *Use* Authorship

LITERATURE SEARCHING. *Use* Bibliography

LITHOGRAPHY. *Use* Graphic Arts; Printing Industry

LITTLE LEAGUES. *Use* Baseball

LITTORAL DRIFT. *Use* Beaches

LITURGIES
LC ——; s.a. Hymns; Liturgical movement; Liturgy and literature; Responsive worship; subd. *Liturgy and rituals* under names of churches; Worship programs

SEARS ——; s.a. Christian art and symbolism; Devotional exercises; Mass; Rites and ceremonies; Worship

RG ——; s.a. Catholic church—Liturgy and ritual; Liturgical language; Liturgical movement

NYT RELIGION AND CHURCHES; s.a. Prayer and prayer books; Protestant Episcopal Church; Roman Catholic Church

PAIS RELIGION; s.a. Christianity and other religions; Roman Catholic Church

BPI RELIGION; s.a. Catholic church; Christianity; Protestantism

LIVESTOCK. *Use* Cattle; Domestic Animals; Meat Industry and Trade; Pastures

LIVESTOCK BREEDING. *Use* Stock and Stock Breeding

LIVESTOCK JUDGING. *Use* Stock and Stock Breeding

LOADING AND UNLOADING. *Use* Cargo Handling; Materials Handling

LOAN. *Use* Debtor and Creditor

LOAN SHARKING. *Use* Interest and Usury; Loan, Personal; Loans

LOANS
Scope: Mostly works on small loans. For works on government loans see Debts, Public.
LC ——; s.a. Amortization; Bank loans; Government lending; Loans, Personal; Lombard loans; Mortgage loans

SEARS ——; s.a. Building and loan associations; Consumer credit; Interest and usury

RG ——; s.a. Interest; Mortgages; Pawnbroking

NYT CREDIT; s.a. Banks and banking; Loan sharking; Savings and loan associations

PAIS ——; s.a. Debtor and creditor; Interest; Usury

BPI ——; s.a. Government loans and grants; Savings and loan association; Usury laws

LOANS, FOREIGN. *Use* Economic Assistance, Foreign; International Finance

LOANS, PERSONAL
Scope: Works on loans to individuals for personal rather than business uses, for consumption rather than production purposes.
LC ——; s.a. Banks and banking, Cooperative; Building and loan associations; Consumer credit; Industrial loan associations; Instalment plan; Loan sharking; Pawnbroking

SEARS LOANS; s.a. Credit; Interest and usury

RG ——; s.a. Credit unions; Savings and loan associations

LOANS, PERSONAL, *cont.*
NYT   CREDIT; s.a. Banks and banking; Credit unions; Savings and loan associations
PAIS   LOANS; Debtor and creditor; Interest
BPI   ——; s.a. Finance charges; Student loans

LOBBYING
LC   ——; s.a. Bribery; Business and politics; Functional representation; Legislation; Lobbyists; Political letter writing; Political science; Propaganda; Public relations and law; Pressure groups; Social control; Social pressure
SEARS   ——; s.a. Corruption (politics); Politics, Practical
RG   ——; s.a. Lobbyists; Pressure groups; Protests, demonstrations, etc.
NYT   LOBBYING AND LOBBYISTS; s.a. Law and legislation; Local government; Politics and government; Taxation
PAIS   ——; s.a. Letter writing, Political; Pressure groups
BPI   ——; s.a. Business—Political aspects; Business representatives in Washington; Politics, Corruption in

LOCAL ADMINISTRATION. *See* Local Government

LOCAL ELECTIONS. *Use* Elections; Voters, Registration of

LOCAL FINANCE. *Use* Finance, Public; Metropolitan Government; Municipal Government

LOCAL GOVERNMENT
Scope: General works on local government; others are entered under County government, Metropolitan government, Municipal government, and Villages.
LC   ——; s.a. Administrative and political divisions; Boroughs; Cities and towns; Community power; Local officials and employees; Local laws; Mayors; Municipal officials and employees; Municipal ownership; Ordinances, Municipal; Parishes (local government); Politics, Practical; Representative government and representation
SEARS   ——; s.a. Administrative law; Civil service; Political science; Public administration
RG   ——; s.a. Assessment; City manager plan; Decentralization in government; Government employees; Income tax, Municipal; Municipal employees; Parishes
NYT   ——; s.a. Rural areas; U.S.—Politics and government—Local government; Urban areas; Taxation
PAIS   ——; s.a. County taxation; City-county consolidation; Government employees; Local taxation; Municipal officials; Special districts; Water districts
BPI   ——; s.a. Income tax—[local subd.]; Local officials and employees; Metropolitan areas; School districts

LOCAL HISTORY. *Use* History

LOCAL LAWS. *Use* Local Government

LOCAL OFFICIALS AND EMPLOYEES. *Use* Civil Service; Local Government

LOCAL OPTION. *Use* Liquor Problem

LOCAL TAXATION. *Use* Finance, Public; Income Tax; Taxation

LOCAL TRANSIT
See also subd. *Transit systems* under names of areas.
LC   ——; s.a. Taxicabs; Railroads, Elevated; Underpasses; Urban transportation
SEARS   ——; s.a. Buses; Public utilities; Street railroads, etc.; Subways; Tunnels
RG   ——; s.a. Motor bus lines; Moving platforms
NYT   TRANSIT SYSTEMS—[local subd.]; s.a. Buses; Taxicabs and taxicab drivers; Transit authority, N.Y.C. (NYCTA); Transportation
PAIS   ——; s.a. City planning—Transportational aspects; Street cars; Underground construction
BPI   ——; s.a. Motor bus lines; Subways

LOCATION OF BUSINESS. *See* Industry

LOCKOUTS. *Use* Strikes and Lockouts

LOCKS AND KEYS
LC   ——; s.a. Fastenings; Watch keys
SEARS   ——; s.a. Burglary protection
RG   ——; s.a. Automobile locks and keys; Boat locks and keys
NYT   ——; s.a. Robberies and thefts
PAIS   ——; s.a. Burglary protection; Hardware industry
BPI   ——; s.a. Burglary protection; subd. *Security measures* under various subjects, e.g., Retail stores—Security measures

LODGING HOUSES. *Use* Hotels, Taverns, etc.

LOGARITHMS. *Use* Mathematics

LOGIC
LC   ——; s.a. Certainty; Definition (logic); Hypothesis; Liar paradox; Logic, symbolic and mathematical; Sufficient reason; Syllogism; Truth
SEARS   ——; s.a. Probabilities; Thought and thinking
RG   ——; s.a. Evidence; Fallacies (logic)
NYT   ——; s.a. Brain; Mind; Philosophy
PAIS   KNOWLEDGE, THEORY OF; s.a. Philosophy; Problem solving; Thought and thinking
BPI   ——; s.a. Judgement (logic); Problem solving; Thought and thinking

LOGIC, SYMBOLIC AND MATHEMATICAL
LC   ——; s.a. Algebra, Abstract; Logic machines; Metamathematics; Pragmatics; Probabilities
SEARS   ——; s.a. Algebra, Boolean; Mathematics; Set theory
RG   ——; s.a. Algebra, Boolean; Mathematics
NYT   MATHEMATICS; s.a. Logic
PAIS   MATHEMATICS
BPI   ——; s.a. Switching theory

LOGISTICS. *Use* Military Art and Science; Naval Art and Science

LOGOGRAPHY. *Use* Signs and Symbols

LOMBARD LOANS. *Use* Loans

LONELINESS. *Use* Human Relations

LONGEVITY. *Use* Age; Life; Old Age

LOOT AND LOOTING. *Use* Crime and Criminals; Theft

LORD'S DAY. *See* Sabbath

LOST TRIBES OF ISRAEL. *Use* Mormons and Mormonism

LOTTERIES. *Use* Gambling

LOUD SPEAKING APPARATUS. *Use* High-Fidelity Sound Systems

LOVE
LC ——; s.a. Courtly love; Courtship; Love (Judaism); Love, Maternal; Love, Platonic; Love feasts; Love in art; Love letters; Yoga, Bhakti
SEARS ——; s.a. Behavior; Dating (social customs) Friendship; Marriage; Love (theology); Love poetry
RG ——; s.a. Courtly love; Jealousy; Love, Maternal; Love, Platonic; Love in literature
NYT LOVE (Emotion); s.a. Families and family life; Marriages; Philosophy
PAIS MARRIAGE; s.a. Remarriage
BPI EMOTIONS; s.a. Marriage

LOVE (Theology). *Use* Charity; Christian Ethics

LOVE, MATERNAL. *Use* Love; Maternal Deprivation; Mothers

LOVE, PLATONIC. *Use* Love

LOVE-LETTERS. *Use* Erotica; Letter-Writing

LOVE POETRY. *Use* Erotica

LOW TEMPERATURE. *Use* Temperature

LOYALTY
Scope: Works on loyalty as a virtue and loyalty to the state.
LC ——; s.a. Allegiance; Conduct of life; Legislative hearings; Loyalty-Security program, 1947– ; Turncoats
SEARS ——; s.a. Behavior; Governmental investigations; Internal security; Patriotism; Treason
RG ——; s.a. Americanism; Loyalty, Oaths of; Patriotism
NYT ETHICS AND MORALS; s.a. Loyalty oaths and tests; Oath of allegiance; U.S.—Politics and government—Ethics in office
PAIS ——; s.a. Americanism; Loyalty investigations; Loyalty oaths; Patriotism
BPI ——; s.a. Government investigations; Loyalty, Organizational

LOYALTY OATHS. *Use* Academic Freedom; Internal Security; Oaths; Patriotism

LOYALTY TESTS. *See* Loyalty

LUBRICATION AND LUBRICANTS
See also subd. *Lubrication* under subjects, e.g., Compressors—Lubrication.
LC ——; s.a. Lubricating oils; Oil reclamation; Metal working lubricants; Petroleum products
SEARS ——; s.a. Bearings (machinery); Machinery; Oils and fats
RG ——; s.a. Petroleum industry
NYT LUBRICANTS; s.a. Names of lubricants, e.g., Oil (petroleum) and gasoline; etc.
PAIS LUBRICATING OILS; s.a. Oils and fats; Petroleum industry
BPI ——; s.a. Bearings (machinery)

LUGGAGE. *Use* Travel

LULLABIES. *Use* Singing and Songs

LUMBER AND LUMBERING. *Use* Forests and Forestry; Trees

LUNACY. *See* Insanity

LUNAR BASES. *Use* Space Flight

LUNAR EXPEDITIONS. *See* Space Flight

LUNAR EXPLORATIONS. *Use* Space Flight

LUNAR PROBES. *Use* Outer Space; Space Flight

LUNATIC ASYLUMS. *See* Mentally Ill

LUNCHEONS. *Use* Caterers and Catering; Entertaining; Table

LUNCHROOMS AND CAFETERIAS. *Use* Restaurants, Lunchrooms, etc.

LUXURY
LC ——; s.a. Consumption (economics); Leisure class; Luxury in literature
SEARS CONSUMPTION (Economics); s.a. Millionaires; Wealth
RG ——; s.a. Leisure class; Wealth
NYT U.S.—ECONOMIC CONDITIONS AND TRENDS; s.a. Consumers and consumption; Finance; Leisure
PAIS LUXURIES; s.a. Cost and standard of living; Wealth
BPI WEALTH; s.a. Consumption (economics); Profit

LYING. *Use* Truth

LYRIC DRAMA. *See* Opera

M

MACHINE ACCOUNTING
LC ——; s.a. Accounting machines; Bookkeeping machines; Tabulating machines
SEARS CALCULATING MACHINES; s.a. Computers; Slide machines
RG ACCOUNTING—MECHANICAL AIDS; s.a. Adding machines; Computers—Business use
NYT ADDING MACHINES; s.a. Accounting and accountants; Data processing (information processing) equipment and systems; Office equipment
PAIS CALCULATING MACHINES; s.a. Computers—Accounting; Office equipment
BPI ACCOUNTING MACHINES; s.a. Calculating machines; Office equipment and supplies

MACHINE AGE. *See* Machinery in Industry

MACHINE DATA STORAGE AND RETRIEVAL. *See* Information Storage and Retrieval Systems

MACHINE INDUSTRY. *See* Machinery—Trade and Manufacture

MACHINE PARTS. *Use* Machinery

MACHINE THEORY. *Use* Mathematical Models

MACHINE TOOL INDUSTRY. *Use* Machinery—Trade and Manufacture

MACHINE TOOLS. *Use* Machinery; Mechanical Engineering; Tools

MACHINE TOOLS AND DIES. *Use* Industrial Equipment

MACHINE TRANSLATING. *Use* Translating and Interpreting

MACHINERY
See also types of machinery used in particular industries or for special purposes, e.g., Agricultural machinery; Bearings (machinery); Cutting machines; Electrical machinery; Folding machines; Tractors; etc.
LC ——; s.a. Interchangeable mechanisms; Jigs and fixtures; Machinery, Automatic; Machinery—Quality control; Replacement of industrial equipment; Technological innovations
SEARS ——; s.a. Lubrication and lubricants; Machine tools; Machinery—Design; Machinery—Models; Power transmission; Tools
RG ——; s.a. Industrial equipment; Obsolescence; Repair parts
NYT MACHINERY, INDUSTRIAL EQUIPMENT AND SUPPLIES; s.a. Machine tools and dies; Tools and implements
PAIS ——; s.a. Equipment, Replacement of; Obsolescence; Repair parts
BPI ——; s.a. Capital investments; Depreciation; Economic life (of economic goods); Machine parts; Replacement of industrial equipment

MACHINERY, AUTOMATIC. *Use* Machinery in Industry

MACHINERY—TRADE AND MANUFACTURE
LC ——; s.a. Electric machinery industry; Tool and die industry
SEARS MACHINERY; s.a. Automation; Manufacturers
RG MACHINERY INDUSTRY; s.a. Agricultural machinery industry and trade; Machine tool industry
NYT MACHINERY, INDUSTRIAL EQUIPMENT AND SUPPLIES; s.a. Machine tools and dies
PAIS MACHINERY INDUSTRY; s.a. Bearings; Equipment industry; Machine parts industry; Machine tool industry; Mechanical engineering; Tool industry
BPI MACHINERY INDUSTRY; s.a. Machine tool industry; Wages and salaries—Machinery industry

MACHINERY IN INDUSTRY
Scope: Works on social and economic aspects of mechanization in the industrial world, in the machine age, etc.
LC ——; s.a. Capital productivity; Industrial equipment; Labor productivity; Mechanization, Military; Plant layout; Technocracy; Technological innovations; Technology—Philosophy
SEARS ——; s.a. Industry; Labor and laboring classes; Mechanical engineering; Technology and civilization
RG ——; s.a. Automation; Unemployment, Technological
NYT AUTOMATION
PAIS ——; s.a. Division of labor; Mechanization
BPI ——; s.a. Farm mechanization; Machinery, Automatic

MACROBIOTICS. *See* Zen (Sect)

MACROECONOMICS. *Use* Economics

MADNESS. *See* Insanity

MADONNA. *See* Virgin Birth

MAFIA. *Use* Crime and Criminals; Racketeering

MAGIC. *Use* Occult Sciences

MAGIC, MYSTIC AND SPAGIRIC. *Use* Medicine

MAGICIANS. *Use* Entertainers

MAGISTRATES. *See* Judges

MAGNETIC ANOMALIES. *Use* Magnetism, Terrestrial

MAGNETIC HEALING. *Use* Hypnotism

MAGNETIC RECORDERS AND RECORDING. *Use* Phonograph Records

MAGNETIC RECORDINGS (Data Storage). *See* Data Tapes

MAGNETIC STORMS. *Use* Magnetism, Terrestrial

MAGNETIC SUSPENSION. *Use* Bearings (Machinery)

MAGNETISM, TERRESTRIAL
LC ——; s.a. Compass; Earth currents; Magnetic anomalies; Magnetic storms; Sun-spots
SEARS COMPASS; s.a. Magnetism; Navigation
RG ——; s.a. Auroras; Geomagnetic observatories
NYT MAGNETISM AND MAGNETS; s.a. Compasses; Earth; Gravitation and gravity
PAIS EARTH—INTERNAL STRUCTURE; s.a. Navigation
BPI MAGNETISM

MAIL ORDER BUSINESS
LC ——; s.a. Advertising, Direct-mail; Drop shipments; Postal service—U.S.—Unordered merchandise; Sales letters
SEARS ——; s.a. Advertising; Business; Salesmen and salesmanship
RG ——; s.a. Booksellers and bookselling; Postal service—Unordered merchandise
NYT ADVERTISING—U.S.—DIRECT MAIL ADVERTISING; s.a. Credit—U.S.—Consumer Credit; Retail stores and trade—U.S.
PAIS ——; s.a. Insurance—Mail order selling; names of mail order firms, e.g., Sears, Roebuck and Company
BPI ——; s.a. Advertising, Mail; Catalogs; Unordered merchandise

MAIL SERVICE. *See* Postal Service

MAINTENANCE OF PRICES. *See* Prices

MAJORITIES. *Use* Minorities; Representative Government and Representation; Voting

MAKE-OR-BUY DECISIONS. *Use* Decision Making; Purchasing

MAKE UP. *Use* Beauty, Personal; Cosmetics; Toilet

MAKE UP, THEATRICAL. *Use* Costume; Theater

MALADJUSTED CHILDREN. *See* Problem Children

MALNUTRITION. *Use* Nutrition

MALPRACTICE. *Use* Lawyers; Medical Ethics

MALTHUSIANISM. *Use* Birth Control; Population

MAN
LC ——; s.a. Anthropo-geography; Cro-Magnon man; Fossil man; Heredity, Human; Human biology; Human capital; Man—Origin; Man (theology); Men; Men in literature; Persons
SEARS ——; s.a. Anatomy—Comparative; Anthropology; Anthropometry; Cave dwellers; Color of man; Creation; Ethnology; Heredity; Human ecology; Man—Origin and antiquity; Progress; Soul
RG ——; s.a. Civilization; Evolution; Man—Constitution; Man—Migrations; Man, Prehistoric; Man, Primitive; Neanderthal race

NYT ——; s.a. Archeology and anthropology; Body, Human; Civilization; Evolution
PAIS MEN; s.a. Archeology; Anthropology; Civilization; Evolution; Genetics; Society, Primitive
BPI ——; s.a. Ecology; Evolution; Men

MAN—CONSTITUTION. *Use* Temperament

MAN, ERECT POSITION OF. *See* Posture

MAN—INFLUENCE OF ENVIRONMENT
LC ——; s.a. Acclimatization; Anthropo-geography; Bioclimatology; Dwellings—Psychological aspects; Man—Influence of climate
SEARS ——; s.a. Adaptation (biology); Anthropogeography; Color of man; Weightlessness
RG ——; s.a. Altitude, Influence of; Environmental health; Weather—Mental and physiological effects
NYT ENVIRONMENT; s.a. Archeology and anthropology; Evolution; Weather
PAIS ——; s.a. Environmental health; Human ecology
BPI ENVIRONMENTAL HEALTH; s.a. Climate; Ecology; Industry and weather

MAN—INFLUENCE ON NATURE
LC ——; s.a. Environmental policy; Human ecology; Pollution
SEARS ——; s.a. Environmental policy; Nature conservation; Pollution
RG ——; s.a. Environmental policy; Pollution
NYT NATURE; s.a. Air pollution; Environment; Water pollution
PAIS ——; s.a. Environment; Nature
BPI ENVIRONMENTAL POLICY; s.a. Conservation of resources; Pollution

MAN—MIGRATIONS. *Use* Anthropo-geography; Emigration and Immigration; Migration of Nations

MAN—ORIGIN. *Use* Evolution

MAN, PREHISTORIC. *Use* Archaeology; Ethnology; Man

MAN, PRIMITIVE. *Use* Anthropology; Ethnology; Man; Society, Primitive

MAN—SEXUAL BEHAVIOR. *Use* Sex

MAN (Theology). *Use* Soul

MAN AMPLIFIERS. *Use* Cybernetics

MAN IN SPACE. *See* Space Flight

MANAGEMENT
Scope: For works on the application of management principles to particular fields see specific subjects, e.g., Industrial management; Office management; Personnel management.
LC ——; s.a. Decision-making; Delegation of authority; Executive ability; Linear programming; Planning; subd. *Management* under specific subjects, e.g., Engineering—Management; System analysis

MANAGEMENT, *cont.*
SEARS ——; s.a. Business; Efficiency, Industrial; Operations research; Supervision of employees
RG ——; s.a. Executive ability; Leadership; Management games
NYT MANAGEMENT, INDUSTRIAL AND INSTITUTIONAL; s.a. Corporations; Executives
PAIS ——; s.a. Authority; Efficiency, Administrative; Executives; Leadership; Management—Decentralization
BPI ——; s.a. Organization

MANAGEMENT, EMPLOYEES REPRESENTATION IN. *See* Works Councils

MANAGEMENT, INDUSTRIAL. *See* Industrial Management

MANAGEMENT, PRODUCT. *See* Product Management

MANAGEMENT, SCIENTIFIC. *See* Management

MANAGEMENT GAMES
LC ——; s.a. Decision-making; Industrial management; Management—Simulation methods
SEARS MANAGEMENT—RESEARCH; s.a. Management—Study and teaching
RG ——; s.a. Decision making; Simulation methods
NYT MANAGEMENT, INDUSTRIAL AND INSTITUTIONAL; s.a. Psychology and psychologists
PAIS GAMES (Management); s.a. Role playing; System simulation
BPI OPERATIONAL GAMING; s.a. Decision making; Problem solving

MANAGEMENT INFORMATION SYSTEMS. *Use* Files and Filing (Documents)

MANAGEMENT OF FACTORIES. *See* Factory Management

MANAGEMENT RIGHTS
Scope: Works dealing with hiring and production methods, which management may claim to be outside the scope of collective bargaining.
LC ——; s.a. Industrial management; Industrial relations
SEARS INDUSTRIAL RELATIONS; s.a. Collective bargaining; Personnel management
RG INDUSTRIAL MANAGEMENT AND ORGANIZATION; s.a. Industrial relations; Labor disputes
NYT LABOR; s.a. Management, industrial and institutional; U.S.—Economic conditions and trends
PAIS MANAGEMENT—RIGHTS AND RESPONSIBILITIES; s.a. Industrial relations; Unfair labor practices
BPI ——; s.a. Industrial relations; Trade unions

MANIA. *See* Insanity

MANIC-DEPRESSIVE PSYCHOSES. *Use* Depression, Mental; Mental Illness; Mentally Ill

MANICURING. *Use* Toilet

MANIKINS. *Use* Models, Fashion

MAN-MACHINE SYSTEMS. *Use* Human Engineering

MANNED SPACE FLIGHTS. *Use* Astronautics; Space Flight

MANNEQUINS. *See* Models, Fashion

MANNERS. *See* Etiquette

MANNERS AND CUSTOMS
See also subd. *Social life and customs* under names of places and ethnic groups, e.g., Berbers—Social life and customs; Morocco—Social life and customs.
LC ——; s.a. Bohemianism; Courts and courtiers; Culture; Holidays; see also specific customs, e.g., Marriage customs; Kissing; Mourning customs
SEARS ——; s.a. Etiquette; Moral conditions; Social classes; Travel
RG ——; s.a. Clothing and dress; Dating; Drinking customs; Taboo
NYT ——; s.a. Social conditions and welfare; Society
PAIS SOCIAL LIFE AND CUSTOMS; s.a. Rites and ceremonies
BPI ——; s.a. Clothing and dress; Courtesy

MANPOWER
Scope: Works on the strength of a country in terms of available personnel and manpower in particular fields, e.g., Chemists.
LC ——; s.a. Full employment policies; Labor supply; Manpower development and training; Military service, Compulsory
SEARS LABOR SUPPLY; s.a. Child labor; Manpower policy; Retraining, Occupational; Unemployed; Women—Employment
RG ——; s.a. Labor supply; Vocational education; subd. *Population* under names of countries
NYT LABOR—U.S.—UNEMPLOYMENT AND JOB MARKET; s.a. Professions; White collar workers
PAIS LABOR SUPPLY; s.a. Employment; Manpower utilization
BPI ——; s.a. Employment; Labor supply

MANPOWER POLICY. *Use* Economic Policy; Employment; Labor Supply; Manpower; Occupational Training

MANSLAUGHTER. *See* Assassination; Murder

MANUAL LABOR
See also particular types of manual laborers, e.g., Carpenters.
LC ——; s.a. Labor and laboring classes; Manual training; Work
SEARS LABOR AND LABORING CLASSES; s.a. Apprentices; Industrial arts education
RG WORK; s.a. Skilled labor; Vocational education
NYT LABOR
PAIS ——; s.a. Labor; Technical workers
BPI LABOR AND LABORING CLASSES; s.a. Occupations; Skilled labor; Work

MANUAL TRAINING. *Use* Handicraft; Technical Education; Vocational Education

MANUFACTURERS. *Use* Industry; Trademarks

MANUFACTURERS' LIABILITY FOR PRODUCTS. *Use* Liability (Law)

MANUFACTURING. *Use* Industry

MANURES. *See* Fertilizers and Manures

MANUSCRIPTS. *Use* Archives; Books; Writing

MAP DRAWING. *Use* Cartography

MAP READING. *See* Maps

MAPPING, AERIAL. *Use* Aerial Photography

MAPS
Scope: Works about maps and their history; for collections of maps see Atlases; for maps of regions, countries, cities, etc. see subd. *Maps* under names of places.
LC ——; s.a. Discoveries (geography); Maps, Pictorial; Maps, Statistical; Surveys—Plotting; World maps; Zoning maps
SEARS ——; s.a. Atlases, Historical; Automobiles—Road guides; Map drawing; Military geography
RG ——; s.a. Maps, Decorative; Maps, Military; Military topography
NYT ——; s.a. Atlases; Geography; Guidebooks
PAIS ——; s.a. Charts; Geography; Surveying
BPI ——; s.a. Cartography; Mapping, Aerial; Surveying, Aerial; Topography

MARANOS. *Use* Jews

MARCHES (Demonstration). *See* Demonstrations

MARGARINE INDUSTRY. *Use* Oils and Fats

MARGINAL UTILITY. *Use* Value

MARGINS (Security trading). *Use* Stock Exchange

MARINAS. *Use* Boats and Boating; Ports

MARINE BIOLOGY. *Use* Aquariums; Fisheries; Marine Biology; Natural History; Oceanography; Underwater Exploration

MARINE ECOLOGY
LC ——; s.a. Coral reef ecology; Estuarine ecology; Marine pollution; Marine radioecology; Natural resources
SEARS ——; s.a. Ecology; Marine biology; Marine mineral resources
RG ——; s.a. Fisheries; Marine resources
NYT MARINE BIOLOGY; s.a. Oceans and oceanography; Seaweed; Water pollution
PAIS MARINE RESOURCES; s.a. Marine biology; Ocean bottom
BPI MARINE RESOURCES; s.a. Ecology; Ocean mining

MARINE ENGINEERING. *Use* Mechanical Engineering

MARINE LAW. *See* Maritime Law

MARINE PARKS AND RESERVES. *Use* National Parks and Reserves

MARINE POLLUTION. *Use* Marine Ecology; Oil—Pollution; Water—Pollution

MARINE RESEARCH. *Use* Oceanography; Underwater Exploration

MARINE RESOURCES. *Use* Marine Ecology

MARINE SERVICE. *Use* Naval Art and Science

MARINERS. *See* Seamen

MARIONETTES. *Use* Theater

MARITIME DISCOVERIES. *See* Discoveries (Geography)

MARITIME LAW
LC ——; s.a. Access to the sea (International law); Carriers; Coastwise shipping—Law and legislation; Collisions at sea; Freedom of the seas; Jurisdiction over ships at sea; Neutrality; Wreck
SEARS ——; s.a. Freight and freightage; Merchant marine; Salvage
RG ——; s.a. Boats and boating—Laws and regulations; Pirates; Privateering; Territorial waters
NYT ——; s.a. Boating (yachting); Ships and shipping; Waters, Territorial
PAIS ——; s.a. Pirates; Shipmasters
BPI ——; s.a. Rule of the road at sea; Salvage; Territorial waters

MARITIME WORKERS. *Use* Seamen

MARKET GARDENING. *See* Truck Farming

MARKET RESEARCH. *Use* Marketing Research

MARKET STATISTICS. *Use* Statistics

MARKET SURVEYS. *Use* Consumption (Economics); Marketing Research; Public Opinion

MARKETING
LC ——, s.a. Consumer preferences; Inventory control; Market surveys; Merchandising; New products; Physical distribution of goods; Product management; Sales forecasting; Shipment of goods; subd. *Marketing* under names of commodities, e.g., Farm produce—Marketing
SEARS ——; s.a. Market surveys; Sales management; Salesman and salesmanship; subd. *Marketing* under names of commodities
RG ——; s.a. Advertising; Consumer surveys; Distribution of goods; Wholesale trade
NYT MARKETING AND MERCHANDISING; s.a. Retail stores and trade; Sales and salesmen
PAIS ——; s.a. Consumers; Consumption; Distribution; Products, New; Shipment of goods
BPI ——; s.a. Distribution of goods; Marketing managers; Merchandising; Order processing; Price policy; Product planning; Salesmanship

MARKETING, COOPERATIVE. *Use* Cooperative Societies

MARKETING (Home economics). *Use* Consumer Education; Home Economics; Purchasing; Shopping; Shopping and Shoppers

MARKETING OF FARM PRODUCE. *See* Crops

MARKETING OF LIVESTOCK. *Use* Stock and Stock Breeding

MARKETING RESEARCH
LC ———; s.a. Advertising—Psychological aspects; Marketing research—Simulation methods; Marketing research—Statistical methods; Merchandising; Motivation research (marketing); Sampling (statistics)
SEARS MARKETING; s.a. Advertising—Research; Consumers; Industrial research; Marketing—Psychological aspects; Motivation (psychology)
RG MARKET RESEARCH; s.a. Market surveys
NYT MARKET RESEARCH; s.a. Marketing and merchandising; Psychology and psychologists
PAIS MOTIVATION RESEARCH; s.a. Advertising research; Market research
BPI MARKET RESEARCH; s.a. Advertising research; Electronic data processing—Market research; Motivation (psychology)

MARKETS. *Use* Barter; Black Market; Business; Commerce; Commodity Exchanges; Fairs

MARKS OF ORIGIN. *Use* Labels; Trademarks

MARRIAGE
LC ———; s.a. Age (law); Adultery; Alimony; Bigamy; Dating (social customs); Divorce; Domestic relations; Free love; Honeymoon; Husband and wife; Love; Marriage in literature; Married people; Married students; Matrimonial advertisements; Miscegenation; Questions and answers—Wedding; Sex in marriage; Teen-age marriage
SEARS ———; s.a. Celibacy; Family life and education; Marriage, Mixed
RG ———; s.a. College student, Married; Intermarriage of races; Marriage customs and rites; Marriages, Mixed; Sex relations; Weddings
NYT MARRIAGES; s.a. Families and family life; Manners and customs; Society
PAIS ———; s.a. College students, Married; Family; Marriage counselling; Polyandry; Polygamy; Sexual ethics; Weddings
BPI ———; s.a. Brides; Family; Sex (psychology); Weddings

MARRIAGE—ANNULMENT. *Use* Divorce; Marriage Law

MARRIAGE, MIXED. *Use* Marriage

MARRIAGE COUNSELING. *Use* Counseling; Family; Marriage

MARRIAGE CUSTOMS AND RITES. *Use* Etiquette; Marriage; Rites and Ceremonies

MARRIAGE LAW
LC ———; s.a. Adultery; Death-bed marriage; Divorce; Husband and wife; Parent and child (law); Posthumous marriage; Settlements (law)
SEARS MARRIAGE—LAWS AND REGULATIONS; s.a. Dating (social customs); Desertion and nonsupport; Domestic relations; Inheritance and succession; Parent and child
RG ———; s.a. Husbands; Marriage (canon law); Married women; Separation (law); Wives
NYT MARRIAGES; s.a. Divorce, separations and annulments

PAIS ———; s.a. Breach of promise; Child custody (law); Domestic relations; Married women
BPI ———; s.a. Community property; Concubinage; Divorce; Husband and wife

MARRIAGE OF PRIESTS. *Use* Celibacy

MARRIAGE SETTLEMENTS. *See* Marriage Law

MARRIAGE STATISTICS. *See* Vital Statistics

MARRIED WOMEN. *Use* Woman—Rights of Women

MARRIED WOMEN—EMPLOYMENT. *Use* Woman—Employment

MARSHES. *Use* Reclamation of Land

MARTIAL LAW. *Use* Military Law

MARTYRS. *Use* Canonization; Persecution; Saints

MARXISM. *See* Communism; Economics; Socialism

MARY, VIRGIN. *Use* Virgin Birth

MASONRY. *Use* Plaster and Plastering; Walls

MASONS (Secret order). *See* Secret Societies

MASS. *Use* Catholic Church; Liturgies

MASS COMMUNICATION. *See* Communication

MASS CULTURE. *See* Popular Culture

MASS MEDIA. *Use* Communication; Press; Radio Broadcasting and Programs; Television Broadcasting

MASS PSYCHOLOGY. *See* Social Psychology

MASS SOCIETY. *Use* Sociology

MASS TRANSIT. *See* Local Transit

MASSACRES. *Use* Persecution; Violence

MASSAGE
LC ———; s.a. Chiropractic; Mechanotherapy; Medicine—Practice; Vibration (therapeutics)
SEARS ———; s.a. Electrotherapeutics; Physical therapy
RG ———; s.a. Chiropractors; Therapeutics
NYT ———; s.a. Medicine and health
PAIS ———; s.a. Chiropractic; Osteopathy
BPI ———

MASTICATION. *See* Digestion

MASTURBATION. *Use* Sex

MATERIA MEDICA. *Use* Medicine; Therapeutics

MATERIAL HANDLING. *Use* Materials Handling; Plant Layout

MATERIALS
Scope: Works on materials utilized in engineering and in industry.
LC ———; s.a. Materials management; Materials—Testing; Mechanical wear; Structural dynamics; Weathering
SEARS ———; s.a. Building materials; Raw materials; Strength of materials
RG ———; s.a. Composite materials; Heat-resistant materials; etc.
NYT ENGINEERING AND ENGINEERS; s.a. Building; Materials testing and research

PAIS ——; s.a. Raw materials; Strategic materials
BPI ——; s.a. Building materials; Raw materials; subd. *Materials* under specific subjects, e.g., Automobiles–Materials

MATERIALS CONTROL. *Use* Inventories; Materials Management

MATERIALS HANDLING
LC ——; s.a. Cargo handling; Materials management; Motor trucks; Shipment of goods
SEARS ——; s.a. Freight and freightage; Industrial management; Trucks
RG ——; s.a. Freight handling; Grain handling
NYT MATERIALS HANDLING EQUIPMENT; s.a. Agricultural equipment; Conveyors and conveyor belts; Freight forwarding (domestic and foreign)
PAIS ——; s.a. Cargo handling
BPI ——; s.a. Conveyancing machinery; Loading and unloading

MATERIALS MANAGEMENT
LC ——; s.a. Materials; Purchasing
SEARS INDUSTRIAL MANAGEMENT; s.a. Buying
RG MATERIALS CONTROL; s.a. Inventories; Materials handling
NYT MANAGEMENT, INDUSTRIAL AND INSTITUTIONAL; s.a. Retail stores and trade
PAIS ——; s.a. Computers–Materials management; Industrial management
BPI MATERIAL CONTROL; s.a. Inventory control; Stores systems

MATERIALISM. *Use* Idealism

MATERNAL AND INFANT WELFARE
LC ——; s.a. Insurance, Maternity; Maternity leave; Mothers' pensions; Unmarried mothers
SEARS MOTHERS; s.a. Child welfare; Infants; Insurance, Social
RG MATERNITY BENEFITS; s.a. Child welfare; Orphans and orphan asylums
NYT PREGNANCY, OBSTETRICS AND MATERNAL WELFARE
PAIS MATERNAL WELFARE; s.a. Child welfare; Mothers, Unmarried
BPI MATERNITY BENEFITS; s.a. Child welfare

MATERNAL DEPRIVATION
LC ——; s.a. Love, Maternal; Maternal rejection; Mother and child
SEARS MOTHERS; s.a. Cruelty to children; Parent and child
RG ——; s.a. Foster parents; Love, Maternal; Mothers; Step parents
NYT CHILDREN AND YOUTH–CHILD ABUSE; s.a. Families and family life; Illegitimacy; Orphans and orphanages
PAIS MOTHERS; s.a. Child welfare; Cruelty to children
BPI MOTHERS; s.a. Child welfare; Orphans and orphan asylums

MATERNAL LOVE. *See* Love

MATERNAL REJECTION. *Use* Maternal Deprivation

MATERNAL WELFARE. *Use* Insurance, Health; Maternal and Infant Welfare

MATERNITY. *See* Labor (Obstetrics); Mothers

MATERNITY BENEFITS. *Use* Maternal and Infant Welfare; Woman–Employment

MATERNITY INSURANCE. *See* Insurance, Health

MATERNITY LEAVE. *Use* Vacations, Employee

MATERNITY WELFARE. *See* Maternal and Infant Welfare

MATHEMATICAL ANALYSIS. *Use* Mathematics

MATHEMATICAL ECONOMICS. *See* Economics, Mathematical

MATHEMATICAL INSTRUMENTS. *Use* Calculating Machines

MATHEMATICAL LOGIC. *See* Logic, Symbolic and Mathematical

MATHEMATICAL MODELS
LC ——; s.a. Game theory; subd. *Mathematical models* under subjects, e.g., Human behavior–Mathmatical models
SEARS MATHEMATICS–STUDY AND TEACHING; s.a. Operations research; Programming (electronic computers)
RG ——; s.a. Machine theory; Systems analysis
NYT MATHEMATICS; s.a. Data processing (information processing) electronic equipment and systems
PAIS MATHEMATICS; s.a. Game theory; System analysis
BPI ——; s.a. Games, Theory of; Systems analysis

MATHEMATICAL STATISTICS. *Use* Biometry; Sampling (Statistics)

MATHEMATICS
See also headings beginning with Mathematical; and the subd. *Mathematics* under specific subjects, e.g., Physics–Mathematics.
LC ——; s.a. Business mathematics; Engineering mathematics; Linear programming; Logic, symbolic and mathematical; Mathematical instruments; Numerical calculations; Probabilities; Ready reckoners; Scientific recreations
SEARS ——; s.a. Arithmetic; Geometry; Logarithms; Mathematics–Tables, etc.; Number games
RG ——; s.a. Combinations; Economics, Mathematical; Equations; Harmonic functions; Mathematical recreations; Numerical analysis; Permutations; Tables, calculations, etc.
NYT ——
PAIS ——; s.a. Business mathematics; Econometrics
BPI ——; s.a. Engineering mathematics; Functions; Interpolation; Mathematical analysis

MATRIARCHY. *Use* Family

MATRIMONIAL ADVERTISEMENTS. *Use* Marriage

MATRIMONIAL CRUELTY. *See* Divorce

MATRIMONY. *See* Marriage

MATTRESSES. *Use* Beds and Bedding

MATURATION (Psychology). *Use* Age (Psychology); Growth

MATURITY. *Use* Growth

MAXIMS. *Use* Proverbs; Quotations

MAYORS
See also subd. *Mayors* under names of cities, e.g., London—Mayors.
LC ——; s.a. Municipal corporation; Municipal government
SEARS MUNICIPAL GOVERNMENT; s.a. Cities and towns; Local government
RG ——; s.a. Local government; Negro mayors
NYT ——; s.a. Local government; U.S.—Politics and government—Local government
PAIS ——; s.a. City managers; Municipal officials
BPI ——; s.a. Local officials and employees; Municipal government

MEADOWS. *Use* Pastures

MEANING (Psychology). *Use* Semantics

MEASUREMENT. *Use* Weights and Measures

MEASUREMENT, MENTAL. *See* Tests, Mental

MEAT INDUSTRY AND TRADE
See also kinds of meat, e.g., Beef; Lamb (meat); Veal, etc.
LC ——; s.a. Butchers; Cattle trade; Packing houses; Slaughtering and slaughter houses; Stock and stock breeding; Stockyards
SEARS ——; s.a. Cold storage; Food supply; Meat inspection; Packaging
RG ——; s.a. Cattle industry; Slaughtering and slaughterhouses
NYT MEAT; s.a. Cattle; Food and grocery trade; Livestock
PAIS MEAT INDUSTRY; s.a. Beef industry; Packing industry; Pork industry; Slaughtering
BPI MEAT INDUSTRY; s.a. Meat packing house workers; Pork industry; Stockyards

MECCA. *Use* Islam

MECHANICAL BRAINS. *See* Computers; Cybernetics

MECHANICAL DRAWING. *Use* Design, Industrial; Drawing; Graphic Methods

MECHANICAL ENGINEERING
LC ——; s.a. Automobile mechanics; Aviation mechanics (persons); Civil engineering; Electromechanical devices; Mechanical engineers; Mechanics, Applied
SEARS ——; s.a. Electric engineering; Marine engineering; Mechanical movements; Power (mechanics)
RG ——; s.a. Automobile mechanics (persons); Computers—Engineering use; Dynamics; Machine tools
NYT ENGINEERING AND ENGINEERS
PAIS ——; s.a. Engineering; Machinery industry; Mechanics (persons)
BPI ——; s.a. Mechanics; Power transmission; Vibrations

MECHANICAL HANDLING. *See* Materials Handling

MECHANICAL MOVEMENTS. *Use* Mechanical Engineering

MECHANICAL WEAR. *Use* Materials

MECHANICS. *Use* Engineering; Force and Energy

MECHANICS, APPLIED. *Use* Mechanical Engineering

MECHANICS, CELESTRIAL. *Use* Astronomy

MECHANICS (Persons). *Use* Mechanical Engineering

MECHANIZATION. *Use* Machinery in Industry

MECHANOTHERAPY. *Use* Massage; Osteopathy

MEDALS. *Use* Collectors and Collecting; Numismatics; Rewards (Prizes, etc.)

MEDIA CENTERS (Education). *See* Instructional Materials Centers

MEDIATION, INDUSTRIAL. *See* Arbitration, Industrial; Collective Bargaining; Industrial Relations

MEDIATION, INTERNATIONAL. *Use* Arbitration, International

MEDICAID. *Use* Medical Care; Old Age Assistance

MEDICAL CARE
See also subd. *Medical care* under specific subjects, e.g., Poor—Medical care.
LC ——; s.a. Group medical practice; Hospital care; Hygiene, Public; Medical cooperation; Medical social work; Social medicine
SEARS ——; s.a. Charities, Medical; Hospitals; Institutional care; Medical centers; Medicine, State; Nurses and nursing; Public health; Woman—Health and hygiene
RG MEDICAL SERVICE; s.a. Health agencies, Voluntary; Health facilities; Medical social work; Medicine, Group practice; Physicians
NYT MEDICINE AND HEALTH; s.a. Medicaid; Medicine and health—U.S.—Health insurance; Welfare work
PAIS MEDICAL SERVICE; s.a. Health services; Medicaid program; Medical profession—Group practice; Old age—Medical care; Social service, Medical
BPI ——; s.a. Aged—Medical care; Insurance, Health; Medicaid; Medical care, Prepaid; Medical service, State; Medicare; Public health

MEDICAL CARE, PREPAID. *Use* Insurance, Health

MEDICAL CENTERS. *Use* Hospitals; Institutional Care

MEDICAL EDUCATION. *Use* Education

MEDICAL ELECTRONICS. *Use* Radiotherapy

MEDICAL EMERGENCIES. *Use* Accidents; First Aid in Illness and Injury; Rescue Work

MEDICAL ETHICS
LC ——; s.a. Confidential communications—Physicians; Medical laws and legislation; Nursing ethics; Pastoral medicine
SEARS ——; s.a. Medicine—Laws and regulations; Professional ethics

RG ———; s.a. Embryology, Experimental—Moral and religious aspects; Euthanasia; Transplantation of organs, tissues, etc.—Moral and religious aspects

NYT MEDICINE AND HEALTH—U.S. LAW AND LEGISLATION; s.a. Ethics and morals

PAIS ———; s.a. Medical profession—Legislation; Professional ethics

BPI ———; s.a. Pharmaceutical ethics

MEDICAL FOLKLORE. *See* Medicine

MEDICAL GROUP PRACTICE. *See* Medical Care

MEDICAL JURISPRUDENCE. *Use* Autopsy; Law

MEDICAL LAWS AND LEGISLATION. *Use* Medical Ethics

MEDICAL PROFESSION. *Use* Drug Trade; Medicine; Nurses and Nursing; Osteopathy

MEDICAL RELIEF WORK. *Use* Internationa Cooperation

MEDICAL SERVICE. *Use* Dentistry; Health; Insurance; Medical Care; Nurses and Nursing

MEDICAL SOCIAL WORK. *Use* Medical Care; Social Service

MEDICAL TECHNOLOGY. *Use* Medicine

MEDICAL WORKERS—TRAINING. *Use* Health Education

MEDICARE PROGRAM. *Use* Insurance, Health

MEDICINE
See also types of diseases, e.g., Venereal disease.

LC ———; s.a. Acupuncture; Anatomy; Bacteriology; Chemistry, Medical and pharmaceutical; Chiropractic, Medical personnel; Medicine in literature; Medicine, Magic, mystic and spagiric; Medicine, Psychosomatic; Pastoral medicine; Surgeons

SEARS ———; s.a. Aviation medicine; Hospitals; Hygiene; Materia medica; Medical technology; Medicine as a profession; Mind and body; Osteopathy; Physical therapy; Quacks and quackery; Radiotherapy; Surgery; Therapeutics

RG ———; s.a. Biomedical engineering; Diagnosis; Folk medicine; Medicine, Popular; Medicine and religion

NYT MEDICINE AND HEALTH; s.a. Body, Human; Drugs and drug trade; Surgery and surgeons

PAIS ———; s.a. Interns (medicine); Medical profession; Medicine and religion; Medicine, Preventive; Nurses and nursing

BPI ———; s.a. Drugs; Medicine, Primitive; Physicians

MEDICINE, DENTAL. *See* Dentistry

MEDICINE, FORENSIC. *Use* Autopsy

MEDICINE—FORMULAE, RECEIPTS, PRE-SCRIPTIONS. *Use* Drugs

MEDICINE, INDUSTRIAL. *Use* Occupations, Dangerous

MEDICINE, MAGIC, MYSTIC AND SPAGIRIC. *Use* Medicine; Mental Healing; Therapeutics, Suggestive

MEDICINE, OCCULT. *See* Mental Healing

MEDICINE, PREVENTIVE. *Use* Hygiene; Toxins and Antitoxins

MEDICINE, PSYCHOSOMATIC. *Use* Mind and Body; Neuroses; Psychoanalysis

MEDICINE AND HEALTH. *Use* Geriatrics

MEDICINE AND RELIGION. *Use* Mental Healing

MEDICINES, PATENT, PROPRIETARY, ETC. *Use* Analgesics; Antibiotics; Drugs; Fraud

MEDIEVAL ART. *See* Art, Medieval

MEDITATION. *Use* Mind and Body; Thought and Thinking; Yoga; Zen (sect)

MEDIUMS. *Use* Occult Sciences; Psychical Research

MEETINGS. *Use* Congresses and Conventions; Debates and Debating; Parliamentary Practice

MEGAVITAMIN THERAPY. *See* Vitamins

MELANCHOLY. *Use* Depression, Mental; Emotions

MELANISM. *Use* Color of Man

MELODY. *Use* Music

MELTING POINTS. *Use* Temperature

MEMBRANES (Biology). *Use* Cells

MEMOIRS. *See* Biography

MEMORIAL DAY. *Use* Special Days, Weeks, and Months

MEMORY

LC ———; s.a. Association of ideas; Comprehension; Intellect; Mnemonics; Music-Memorizing, Recollection (psychology); Reproduction (psychology)

SEARS ———; s.a. Attention; Brain; Educational psychology; Mental discipline

RG ———; s.a. Amnesia; Eidetic imagery; Recall (psychology); Recognition (psychology)

NYT ———; s.a. Mind; Psychology and psychologists

PAIS PSYCHOLOGY; s.a. Thought and thinking

BPI ———

MEMORY DEVICES (Computers). *Use* Computers; Cybernetics; Data Tapes

MEN. *Use* Man

MENDEL'S LAW. *Use* Heredity

MENDICANCY. *See* Begging

MENOPAUSE. *Use* Woman—Health and Hygiene

MENORAH. *Use* Jews—Rites and Ceremonies

MEN'S CLOTHING
See also names of individual articles of apparel, e.g., Hats.

LC ———; s.a. Grooming for men; Men's furnishing goods

SEARS ———; s.a. Clothing and dress; Tailoring

RG CLOTHING AND DRESS—MEN; s.a. Grooming, Personal

MEN'S CLOTHING, *cont.*
NYT   APPAREL—U.S.—MEN'S AND BOY'S WEAR
PAIS   CLOTHING INDUSTRY; s.a. Fashion industry
BPI   CLOTHING AND DRESS—MEN; s.a. Fashion

MEN'S WEAR. *See* Men's Clothing

MENSTRUATION. *Use* Reproduction; Woman—Health and Hygiene

MENTAL DEFICIENCIES AND DEFECTIVES. *Use* Handicapped; Mentally Handicapped Children; Mentally Ill

MENTAL DISCIPLINE. *Use* Memory

MENTAL DEPRESSION. *See* Depression, Mental

MENTAL DISORDERS. *See* Mental Illness

MENTAL HEALING
LC   ——; s.a. Medicine, magic, mystic and spagiric; Mesmerism; Pastoral medicine; Psychotherapy; Subconsciousness
SEARS   ——; s.a. Christian Science; Faith cure; Hypnotism; Mental suggestion; Therapeutics, Suggestive
RG   FAITH CURE; s.a. Medicine and religion; Medicine, Magic, mystic, etc.
NYT   MENTAL HEALTH AND DISORDERS; s.a. Occult sciences; Superstitions
PAIS   PSYCHOTHERAPY; s.a. Mental hygiene
BPI   PSYCHOTHERAPY; s.a. Mental hygiene

MENTAL HEALTH AND DISORDERS. *Use* Amnesia; Anxiety; Attitude (Psychology); Behavior Therapy; Brain; Depression, Mental; Insanity; Mental Hygiene; Mental Illness; Mental Institutions; Mentally Handicapped; Mentally Ill; Neuroses

MENTAL HEALTH LAWS. *Use* Mental Illness

MENTAL HOSPITALS. *See* Mentally Ill

MENTAL HYGIENE
LC   ——; s.a. Fatigue, Mental; Nervous system—Hygiene; Relaxation; Social psychiatry; Worry
SEARS   MENTAL HEALTH; s.a. Mental illness; Mind and body; Psychology, Pathological; Psychology, Physiological
RG   ——; s.a. Adjustment, Social; Child psychiatry
NYT   MENTAL HEALTH AND DISORDERS; s.a. Mental deficiency and defectives; Mind; Psychology and psychologists
PAIS   ——; s.a. Community mental health services; Volunteer workers in mental health
BPI   ——; s.a. Psychiatry; Psychology; Psychotherapy

MENTAL ILLNESS
Scope: Works mainly on types of mental disorder; see Mentally ill for works on persons so afflicted.
LC   ——; s.a. Mental deficiency; Mental hygiene; Mental illness—Genetic aspects; Mental illness—Public opinion; Mental illness and law; Paranoia; Social psychiatry
SEARS   ——; s.a. Hallucinations and illusions; Insanity; Mental health; Mentally handicapped; Psychology, Pathological
RG   ——; s.a. Mental health law; Neuroses; Psychoses

NYT   MENTAL HEALTH AND DISORDERS; s.a. Children and youth—Behavior and training; Mental deficiency and defectives
PAIS   ——; s.a. Mental hygiene—Legislation; subd. *Mental illness* under specific subjects, e.g, Youth—Mental illness; Rural population—Mental illness
BPI   ——; s.a. Manic-depressive psychoses; Schizophrenia

MENTAL INSTITUTIONS
LC   PSYCHIATRIC HOSPITALS; s.a. Asylums; Mentally ill—Home care; Public institutions; subd. *Hospitals* under names of cities.
SEARS   MENTALLY ILL—INSTITUTIONAL CARE; s.a. Hospitals; Institutional care
RG   HOSPITALS, PSYCHIATRIC; s.a. Children—Hospitals, Psychiatric; Hospitals, Psychiatric; Hospitals, Psychiatric—Outpatient service; Hospitals—Psychiatric service; Mentally handicapped—Institutional care
NYT   MENTAL HEALTH AND DISORDERS; s.a. Medicine and health; names of hospitals
PAIS   ——; s.a. Mentally ill—Commitment and detention; Mentally ill—Rehabilitation; Psychiatric clinics
BPI   HOSPITALS, PSYCHIATRIC; s.a. Mental illness—Therapy; Mentally handicapped—Institutional care

MENTAL SUGGESTION
LC   ——; s.a. Autogenic training; Hypnotism; Subliminal perception; Subliminal projection; Thought transference
SEARS   ——; s.a. Brainwashing; Mental healing; Mind and body; Therapeutics, Suggestive; Will
RG   SUGGESTION; s.a. Faith cure; Hypnotism
NYT   PSYCHIC PHENOMENA; s.a. Hypnosis; Occult sciences
PAIS   HYPNOTISM; s.a. Indoctrination
BPI   HYPNOTICS; s.a. Advertising, Subliminal

MENTAL TELEPATHY. *See* Thought Transference

MENTAL TESTS. *Use* Ability—Testing; Personality Tests; Tests, Mental

MENTALLY HANDICAPPED. *Use* Mental Illness; Mentally Ill

MENTALLY HANDICAPPED CHILDREN
LC   ——; s.a. Child psychiatry; Mentally ill children; Mentally retarded children
SEARS   ——; s.a. Child psychiatry; Child study; Handicapped children; Slow learning children
RG   ——; s.a. Brain damaged children; Child guidance clinics; Children—Hospitals, Psychiatric; Mongolism
NYT   MENTAL DEFICIENCY AND DEFECTIVES; s.a. Education and schools—U.S.—Mentally retarded; Handicapped—Children; Mental health and disorders
PAIS   ——; s.a. Children, Handicapped; Mentally ill children
BPI   MENTALLY HANDICAPPED; s.a. Handicapped

MENTALLY ILL

Scope: Works mainly on persons suffering from mental disorders, their care and treatment. See Mental illness for works on types of mental disorders.

LC ———; s.a. Inefficiency, Intellectual; Insanity, Mentally handicapped; Mentally ill—Care and treatment; Mentally ill—Home care; Psychoses

SEARS MENTALLY HANDICAPPED; s.a. Hallucinations and illusions; Mentally handicapped children; Mentally ill—Institutional care; Personality disorders

RG ———; s.a. Church work with the handicapped; Hospitals—Psychiatric service; Mentally handicapped; Mentally handicapped—Institutional care; Mentally ill—Care and treatment; Personality, Disorders of

NYT MENTAL HEALTH AND DISORDERS; s.a. Handicapped; Mental deficiency and defectives

PAIS ———; s.a. Employment—Mentally handicapped; Mentally handicapped; Mentally ill—Care and treatment; Mentally ill—Rehabilitation

BPI ———; s.a. Antidepressants; Manic-depressive psychoses; Mentally handicapped; Schizophrenia

MENTALLY ILL CHILDREN. *Use* Child Psychiatry; Mentally Handicapped Children; Problem Children

MENTALLY RETARDED CHILDREN. *Use* Exceptional Children; Mentally Handicapped Children

MENUS. *Use* Caterers and Catering; Cookery; Dinners and Dining; Table

MERCANTILE MARINE. *See* Merchant Marine

MERCANTILE SYSTEM. *Use* Economic Policy

MERCENARY TROOPS. *Use* Soldiers

MERCHANDISE, NEW. *See* New Products

MERCHANDISING

LC ———; s.a. Display of merchandise; Merchandising—Mathematical models

SEARS MARKETING; s.a. Retail trade; Sales management; Show windows

RG ———; s.a. Cash business; Samples (merchandising); Show windows

NYT MARKETING AND MERCHANDISING; s.a. Market research; Retail stores and trade; Sales and salesmen

PAIS ———; s.a. Game (merchandising); Premiums; Show windows

BPI ———; s.a. Business; Consumer deals (merchandising); Markets; Retail trade; Show windows; Showrooms

MERCHANT MARINE

LC ———; s.a. Freighters; Merchant seamen; Merchant ships, American (British, etc.); Ocean liners; Shipping; Steamboats

SEARS ———; s.a. Harbors; Insurance, Marine; Maritime law; Ocean travel; Ports; Seamen; Shipping; Transportation

RG ———; s.a. Shipping—International aspects; Training ships

NYT SHIPS AND SHIPPING; s.a. Free ports and trading zones; Freight forwarding (domestic and foreign)

PAIS SHIPPING; s.a. Freight vessels; Tank ships

BPI ———; s.a. Shipping; Ship subsidies

MERCHANT SEAMEN. *Use* Seamen

MERCHANTS. *Use* Businessmen

MERCY DEATH (Euthanasia). *Use* Aged, Killing of; Death; Medical Ethics; Murder

MERCY MISSIONS. *Use* Rescue Work

MERGERS. *See* Conglomerate Corporations

MERGERS, INDUSTRIAL. *See* Trusts, Industrial

MERRY-GO-ROUND. *Use* Amusement Parks

MESMERISM. *Use* Mental Healing

MESSIAH

LC ———s.a. Jesus Christ—Messiahship; Messianic era (Judaism); Pseudo-Messiahs; Superman

SEARS BIBLE—PROPHECIES—MESSIAH; s.a. Jesus Christ—Messiahship; Judaism

RG ———; s.a. Christianity; Jewish theology

NYT RELIGION AND CHURCHES; s.a. Bible; Jesus Christ

PAIS RELIGION; s.a. Christianity and other religions; Jews; Messianism

BPI RELIGION; s.a. Christianity; Jews

METABOLISM. *Use* Biochemistry; Nutrition

METAL FINISHING. *Use* Finishes and Finishing

METAL INDUSTRIES

See also specific industries, e.g., Copper industry, Mercury industry, etc.

LC METAL TRADE; s.a. Hardware; Iron industry and trade; Liquid metals; Metals; Metallurgy; Mineral industries

SEARS IRON INDUSTRY AND TRADE; s.a. Ironwork; Mineralogy; Precious metals; Steel industry and trade; Transmutation (chemistry)

NYT METALS AND MINERALS; s.a. Dowsing; Iron and steel; Water pollution—Metals and minerals; Welding and welders

PAIS METAL TRADES; s.a. Iron founding; Iron ores; Metal-working machinery; Smelting

BPI METAL INDUSTRY; s.a. Forging and forgings; Solder and soldering; Steel metallurgy

METAL WORK. *Use* Handicraft; Solder and Soldering

METALLURGY. *Use* Metal Industries; Steel Industry and Trade

METAMATHEMATICS. *Use* Logic, Symbolic and Mathematical

METAMORPHOSIS. *Use* Embryology

METAPHYSICS. *Use* Existentialism

METAPSYCHOLOGY. *See* Psychical Research

METEORITES. *Use* Mineralogy

METEOROLOGICAL SATELLITES. *Use* Artificial
Satellites

METEOROLOGY. *Use* Atmosphere; Weather

METER. *See* Versification

METHADONE. *Use* Narcotic Addicts

METHODOLOGY. *Use* Decision Making; Logic

METRIC SYSTEM. *Use* Weights and Measures

METROPOLITAN AREAS. *Use* Cities and Towns; Local
Government; Metropolitan Government;
Regional Planning; Suburbs; Urban Renewal;
Urbanization

METROPOLITAN GOVERNMENT
See also names of central cities; and subd. *Politics and
government* under names of metropolitan areas.

LC ———; s.a. Metropolitan areas; Metropolitan
finance; Municipal powers and services beyond
corporate limits; Public administration; Special
districts

SEARS ———; s.a. Metropolitan areas; Metropolitan
finance; Urban renewal

RG ———; s.a. Decentralization in government; Local
government; Local taxation; Regional planning;
subd. *Metropolitan district* under names of cities

NYT LOCAL GOVERNMENT; s.a. Area planning
and renewal; subd. *Finance* under names of
metropolitan areas; Urban Areas

PAIS ———; s.a. Cities and towns—Growth; Local
government—Finance; Metropolitan government
—Finance

BPI MUNICIPAL GOVERNMENT; s.a. Cities and
towns; Local finance; Metropolitan areas;
Suburbs

MICROBES. *See* Bacteria; Bacteriology

MICROBIOLOGY. *Use* Bacteriology; Biology

MICROCLIMATOLOGY. *Use* Ecology

MICROECONOMICS. *Use* Economics

MICROFILM. *Use* Copying Processes

MICROFORMS. *Use* Information Storage and Retrieval
Systems

MICROORGANISMS. *Use* Bacteria; Bacteriology

MICROPHONES. *Use* Radio—Apparatus and Supplies;
Sound and Sound Recording

MICROSCOPES AND MICROSCOPY. *Use* Optical Trade

MICROWAVE COMMUNICATION SYSTEMS. *Use*
Radio, Short Wave; Telecommunication;
Television

MIDDLE AGE
LC ———; s.a. Aging; Longevity; Middle age—Sexual
behavior; Old age

SEARS ———; s.a. Age and employment; Life (biology);
Old age

RG ———; s.a. Aging; Working life, Length of

NYT AGE AND AGED; s.a. Biology and biochemistry

PAIS AGE GROUPS; s.a. Age; Middle age market

BPI ———; s.a. Aging; Old age

MIDDLE AGES. *Use* Feudalism

MIDDLE CLASSES
LC ———; s.a. Commons (social order); Democracy;
Proletariat; Social classes

SEARS ———; s.a. Democracy; Labor and laboring classes

RG ———; s.a. Labor and laboring classes; Social
classes

NYT SOCIAL CONDITIONS AND WELFARE; s.a.
Labor; Sociology

PAIS ———; s.a. Class struggle; Social status

BPI ———; s.a. Groups (sociology)

MIDDLE EAST. *Use* Arab Countries; Islam; Jewish-Arab
Relations; Near East

MIDDLE-INCOME CLASS. *See* Middle Classes

MIDWIVES. *Use* Childbirth; Labor (Obstetrics)

MIGRANT LABOR
Scope: Works on casual or seasonal workers who move
from place to place in search of employment.
For works on population movements within a
country for permanent settlement see Migration,
Internal.

LC ———; s.a. Casual labor; Children of migrant
laborers; Migration, Internal; Rural conditions;
Seasonal industries; Transients, Relief of; Unemployment, Seasonal

SEARS ———; s.a. Agricultural laborers; Labor and
laboring classes; Labor supply; Social problems;
Unemployed

RG ———; s.a. Children of migrant laborers; Church
work with migrants

NYT LABOR—U.S.—MIGRATORY LABOR; s.a.
Labor—U.S.—Unemployment and job market

PAIS ———; s.a. Agricultural labor; Labor mobility

BPI ———; s.a. Alien labor; Farm labor; Migration,
Internal

MIGRATION. *Use* Emigration and Immigration; Migration of Nations; Population

MIGRATION, INTERNAL
See note under Migrant labor.

LC ———; s.a. Cities and towns—Growth; Labor
mobility; Rural-urban migration; Student
mobility

SEARS ———; s.a. Cities and towns; Colonization; Labor
supply; Population; Sociology, Rural; Sociology,
Urban

RG ———; s.a. Cities and towns—Growth; Negroes—
Migration; Occupational mobility

NYT LABOR; s.a. Rural areas; Urban areas

PAIS LABOR MOBILITY; s.a. Employees, Transfer
of; Occupational mobility; Residential mobility

BPI ———; s.a. Labor mobility; Residential mobility;
Rural-urban migration

MIGRATION OF NATIONS
Scope: Works on mass migrations of peoples.

LC ———; s.a. Civilization; Emigration and immigration (modern); Man—Migrations (prehistoric);
Population transfers

SEARS IMMIGRATION AND EMIGRATION; s.a. Anthropogeography; Colonization; Race problems
RG MAN—MIGRATIONS; s.a. Colonies; Imperialism
NYT IMMIGRATION AND EMIGRATION; s.a. Refugees; War and revolution
PAIS MIGRATION; s.a. Aliens; Immigrants; Immigration and emigration
BPI IMMIGRATION AND EMIGRATION; s.a. Alien labor; History

MIGRATORY WORKERS. *See* Migrant Labor

MILITARISM
LC ——; s.a. Chauvinism and jingoism; Civil supremacy over military; Military-civil relations; Military ethics; Sociology, Military; War, Cost of
SEARS ARMIES; s.a. Conscientious objectors; Military policy; Military service, Compulsory
RG ——; s.a. Disarmament; Imperialism; War
NYT MILITARY ART AND SCIENCE; s.a. Armament, defense and military forces (general); U.S.—Armament and defense; War and revolution
PAIS ——; s.a. Military occupation; Military service, Compulsory; War
BPI MILITARY ART AND SCIENCE; s.a. Disarmament and arms control; War

MILITARY ART AND SCIENCE
See also types of warfare: Air warfare; Biological warfare; Chemical warfare; Desert warfare; Guerilla warfare; Night fighting (military science); Psychological warfare; Street fighting (military science), etc.
LC ——; s.a. Ambushes and surprises; Armed forces; Battles; Military history; Morale; Ordnance; Revolutions; Soldiers; Spies; Unified operations (military science); War games
SEARS MILITARY ART AND SCIENCES; s.a. Armies; Arms and armor; Civil defense; Fortification; Military training camps; Naval art and science; Tactics
RG ——; s.a. Industrial mobilization; Strategy
NYT ——; s.a. Armament, defense and military forces (general); U.S.—Armament and defense
PAIS ——; s.a. Logistics; Militarism; Military history; Military tactics; Military training; War—Strategy
BPI ——; s.a. Aeronautics, Military; Gunnery; Logistics; Strategy; Tactics

MILITARY BIOGRAPHY. *Use* Soldiers

MILITARY CAREER. *See* Military Service as a Profession

MILITARY CEREMONIES, HONORS AND SALUTES. *Use* Etiquette

MILITARY CONTRACTS. *See* Defense Contracts

MILITARY COURTS. *Use* Military Law

MILITARY DISCIPLINE. *Use* Morale

MILITARY DRAFT. *See* Military Service, Compulsory

MILITARY EDUCATION. *Use* Military Service as a Profession

MILITARY ETHICS. *Use* Militarism; Morale

MILITARY GOVERNMENT. *Use* Public Administration

MILITARY HISTORY. *Use* Battles; Military Art and Science

MILITARY INTELLIGENCE. *Use* Espionage

MILITARY LAW
LC ——; s.a. Judge advocate; Military courts; Military privileges and immunities
SEARS ——; s.a. Courts martial and courts of inquiry; Desertion, Military; Military offenses
RG ——; s.a. Capitulations, Military; Discipline, Military; Military service, Compulsory; subd. *Desertion* under names of army, e.g., U.S. Army—Desertion
NYT U.S.—ARMAMENT AND DEFENSE—COURTS-MARTIAL
PAIS ——; s.a. Civil-military relations; Courts martial; Martial law; Trials (military offenses)
BPI ——; s.a. Courts martial; Martial law

MILITARY LIFE. *Use* Armed Forces; Soldiers

MILITARY MARKET. *Use* Defense Contracts

MILITARY OCCUPATION. *Use* Militarism

MILITARY OFFENSES. *Use* Military Law

MILITARY PENSIONS. *See* Pensions, Military

MILITARY PERSONNEL. *See* Military Service as a Profession; Soldiers

MILITARY POWER. *See* Disarmament; Militarism; Military Art and Science

MILITARY RESERVES. *Use* Military Service as a Profession

MILITARY SCHOOLS. *Use* Military Service as a Profession; Private Schools

MILITARY SECRETS. *See* Official Secrets

MILITARY SERVICE, COMPULSORY
LC ——; s.a. Recruiting and enlistment; subd. *Army—Recruiting, enlistment, etc.* under names of countries
SEARS ——; s.a. Conscientious objectors; Military law
RG ——; s.a. Conscientious objectors; subd. *Recruiting and enlistment* under names of armies
NYT U.S.—ARMAMENT AND DEFENSE—DRAFT AND RECRUITMENT, MILITARY
PAIS ——; s.a. Conscientious objectors; Militarism; U.S.—Selective service system
BPI ——; s.a. Employees—Military service; Military training

MILITARY SERVICE, VOLUNTARY. *Use* Military Service as a Profession

MILITARY SERVICE AS A PROFESSION
See also names of military schools, e.g., U.S. Military Academy, West Point.
LC ——; s.a. Aeronautics; Military—Study and teaching; Military posts; Military reserves; U.S. Navy—Vocational guidance
SEARS ——; s.a. Military education; Military training camps; Soldiers

MILITARY SERVICE AS A PROFESSION, *cont.*

RG   MILITARY SERVICE; s.a. Military service, Voluntary; Military schools; Soldiers

NYT   U.S. ARMAMENT AND DEFENSE—DRAFT AND RECRUITMENT, MILITARY; s.a. U.S. armament and defense—Education and schools; U.S. armament and defense—Reserves—ROTC; Veterans

PAIS   ——; s.a. Military service, Voluntary; Military training; Servicemen

BPI   MILITARY SERVICE; s.a. Military education; Servicemen; Soldiers

MILITARY SYMBOLS. *Use* Signs and Symbols

MILITARY TRAINING. *Use* Military Art and Science; Military Service as a Profession; Military Service, Compulsory

MILITARY TRIBUNALS. *See* Military Law

MILITARY-CIVIL RELATIONS. *Use* Militarism

MILITARY-INDUSTRIAL COMPLEX. *Use* Business and Politics; Defense Contracts; Industry and State; Militarism; War—Economic Aspects

MILK TRADE. *Use* Food Industry and Trade

MILLENIUM. *Use* Future Life; Jesus Christ; Messiah

MILLINERY. *Use* Clothing and Dress; Costume

MILLIONARIES. *Use* Businessmen; Luxury; Wealth

MILLS AND MILLWORK. *Use* Factories

MIME. *Use* Theater

MIMEOGRAPH. *Use* Copying Processes

MIND. *Use* Brain; Comprehension; Intellect; Memory; Perception; Thought and Thinking

MIND AND BODY

LC   ——; s.a. Ability, Influence of age on; Body and soul in literature; Conversion (psychoanalysis); Mental hygiene; Nervous system; No-mind (Buddhism); Other minds (theory of knowledge); Self

SEARS ——; s.a. Consciousness; Phrenology; Psychoanalysis; Sleep; Temperament

RG   ——; s.a. Medicine, Psychosomatic; Meditation

NYT   MIND; s.a. Body, Human; Brain; Psychology and psychologists

PAIS   PSYCHOLOGY; s.a. Physiology

BPI   ——; s.a. Psychology, Physiological

MIND READING. *Use* Clairvoyance; Psychical Research; Thought Transference

MINE ACCIDENTS. *Use* Disasters

MINE SAFETY. *Use* Mines and Mineral Resources

MINERAL INDUSTRIES. *Use* Metal Industries; Mineralogy

MINERAL OILS. *Use* Oil Industries; Oils and Fats

MINERALOGY

See also names of minerals, e.g., Feldspar; Quartz.

LC   ——; s.a. Artificial minerals; Heavy mineral; Marine mineral resources; Nonmetallic minerals; Soil mineralogy

SEARS ——; s.a. Crystallography; Gems; Metals; Precious stones

RG   ——; s.a. Meteorites; Soils—Mineral content

NYT   METALS AND MINERALS; s.a. Precious metals

PAIS   MINERAL INDUSTRIES; s.a. Mineralogists; Mines and mineral industries

BPI   MINES AND MINERAL RESOURCES; s.a. Geology; Gold mines and mining; Marine resources

MINERALS IN THE BODY. *Use* Nutrition

MINES AND MINERAL RESOURCES

See also specific types of mines and mining, e.g., Coal mines and mining.

LC   ——; s.a. Coal miners (gold miners, etc.); Mine safety; Mining industry and finance; Mining law; Ores; Raw materials; Spoil banks

SEARS ——; s.a. Boring; Mine surveying; Miners; Mining engineering; Ore deposits

RG   ——; s.a. Mine accidents and explosion; Mining claims; Ore deposits; Prospecting; Strip mining

NYT   METALS AND MINERALS; s.a. Accidents and safety; Coal; Engineering and engineers, Finance—Law and legislation; Iron and steel; Precious stones; Strip mining

PAIS   ——; s.a. Mineral rights; Mining industry—Finance; Mining industry—Safety measures; Oil and gas leases; Trade unions—Miners

BPI   ——; s.a. Coal mines and mining; Iron mines and mining; Mine safety; Miners; Mining leases

MINIATURE OBJECTS. *Use* Art Objects; Models and Model making; Toys

MINIATURE PLANTS. *Use* Plants

MINIMUM WAGE

LC   WAGES—MINIMUM WAGE; s.a. Economic security

SEARS ——; s.a. Wages—Laws and regulations

RG   ——; s.a. Labor cost; Labor laws and legislation

NYT   LABOR—U.S.—MINIMUM WAGE; s.a. Labor—U.S.—Wages and hours

PAIS   ——; s.a. Social and economic security

BPI   ——; s.a. Cost and standard of living; Social and economic security

MINING CLAIMS. *Use* Mines and Mineral Resources

MINISTERIAL RESPONSIBILITY. *Use* Representative Government and Representation

MINISTERS (Diplomatic agents). *See* Diplomacy

MINISTRY. *See* Clergy

MINORITIES

Scope: Works dealing with the condition, protection, rights, etc., of racial, religious and other minorities; see also names of minority groups living in a country or city dominated by another nationality, e.g., Mexicans in the U.S.; Puerto Ricans in New York City; etc.

LC ——; s.a. Assimilation (sociology); Catholics in non-Catholic countries; Ethnic attitudes; Jews—Diaspora; Majorities; Minorities—Employment; Muslims in non-Moslem countries; Native races; Persecution; Prejudices and antipathies; Race awareness; Religious liberty; Segregation; subd. *Education* under names of minority groups; subd. *Foreign population and race question* under names of places; Toleration

SEARS ——; s.a. Discrimination; Ethnopsychology; Nationalism; Race problems; Segregation

RG ——; s.a. Intercultural education; Race discrimination

NYT MINORITIES (Ethnic, racial, religious); s.a. Discrimination; Freedom and human rights; Negroes (U.S.)

PAIS ——; s.a. Ethnic groups; Race relations

BPI ——; s.a. names of specific minorities, e.g., Jews; Race discrimination

MINORITIES—EMPLOYMENT. *Use* Discrimination in Employment

MINORITY BUSINESS ENTERPRISES. *Use* Entrepreneur; Negroes and Business; New Business Enterprises; Small Business

MINORITY STOCKHOLDERS. *Use* Stock Exchange

MIRACLES

LC ——; s.a. Modernist-fundamentalist controversy; Psychology, Religious; Saints—Legends; Shrines

SEARS ——; s.a. Apparitions; Bible—Evidences, authority, etc.; Supernatural

RG ——; s.a. Faith cure; Stigmatization

NYT RELIGION AND CHURCHES; s.a. Occult sciences; Psychic phenomenon; Superstitions

PAIS RELIGION

BPI RELIGION

MIRV. *Use* Ballistic Missiles

MISAPPROPRIATIONS. *Use* Theft

MISCARRIAGE. *See* Abortion

MISCEGENATION. *Use* Marriage

MISCONDUCT IN OFFICE. *Use* Civil Service; Corruption (In politics)

MISREPRESENTATION (Law). *See* Fraud

MISSILES. *Use* Ballistic Missiles; Ordnance

MISSIONARIES
See also subd. *Missions* under names of churches, denominations and religious orders.

LC ——; s.a. Church growth; Missionaries, Lay; Missionaries' wives; Missions (to the Blind, to Jews, to Hindus, etc.); Native clergy

SEARS ——; s.a. Christian biography; Clergy; Evangelistic work; Missions

RG ——; s.a. Children of missionaries; Missions

NYT RELIGION AND CHURCHES

PAIS CHRISTIANITY AND OTHER RELIGIONS

BPI CHRISTIANITY

MISSIONS, MEDICAL. *Use* Hospitals

MISTAKES. *See* Errors

MNEMONICS. *Use* Memory

MOB VIOLENCE. *Use* Mobs; Riots

MOBILITY. *See* Migration, Internal; Occupational Mobility; Social Classes

MOBS

LC ——; s.a. Crowds; Panic; Riot control

SEARS CROWDS; s.a. Demonstrations; Riots

RG ——; s.a. Mob violence; Panic

NYT RIOTS

PAID CROWDS; s.a. Demonstrations, Political; Mob violence

BPI ——; s.a. Protests, demonstrations, etc.; Riots

MODEL KITS. *Use* Toys

MODEL MAKING. *See* Models and Model Making

MODELS (Artists', fashion and photographers') AND DEMONSTRATORS. *Use* Fashion; Models, Fashion

MODELS, FASHION

LC ——; s.a. Artists and models in art; Manikins; Models, Artists'; Pattern making; Style manikins

SEARS ——; s.a. Clothing and dress; Fashion

RG MODELS (Persons); s.a. Children as models; Fashion shows

NYT MODELS (Artists', fashion and photographers') AND DEMONSTRATORS; s.a. Apparel; Photography and photographic equipment

PAIS MODELS (Persons); s.a. Clothing industry; Fashion industry

BPI MODELS (Persons); s.a. Clothing and dress; Fashion

MODELS (Patents). *Use* Patent Laws and Legislation

MODELS (Persons). *Use* Models, Fashion

MODELS AND MODEL MAKING
See also subd. *Models* under subjects, e.g., Machinery—Models.

LC ——; s.a. Architectural models; Model theory; Model makers, Operations research; Pattern-making

SEARS ——

RG MODEL MAKING; s.a. Economic models; Mathematical models

NYT MODELS AND REPLICAS

PAIS MODELS; s.a. Economic models

BPI ——; s.a. Linear models; Simulation methods

MODERN ART. *See* Art, Modern—20th Century; Modernism (Art)

MODERN DANCE. *Use* Dancing

MODERN LANGUAGES. *See* Language and Languages

MODERNISM (Art)

LC ——; s.a. The arts, Modern; Cubism; Dadaism; Expressionism (art); Futurism (art); Post-Impressionism (art)

MODERNISM (ART), *cont.*
SEARS ART, MODERN; s.a. Art, Abstract; Art, Modern
       —19th century; Art, Modern—20th century;
       Kinetic art
RG   ———; s.a. Impressionism (art); Surrealism
NYT   ART; s.a. Art objects; Decoupage
PAIS   ART
BPI   ART; s.a. Drawings; Painting

MOHAMMEDAN COUNTRIES. *Use* Arab Countries

MOHAMMEDANISM. *Use* Islam

MOLECULAR BIOLOGY. *Use* Biochemistry; Biological
       Physics; Genetics

MONACHISM. *See* Monasticism and Religious Orders

MONARCHS. *See* Heads of State

MONARCHY. *Use* Constitutions; Despotism

MONASTERIES. *Use* Abbeys

MONASTIC AND RELIGIOUS LIFE OF WOMEN
LC   ———; s.a. Chastity, Vow of; Ex-nuns; Nuns in
       campus ministry; Obedience, Vow of; Vows;
       Women—Religious life; Zen (sect)
SEARS MONASTICISM AND RELIGIOUS ORDERS
       FOR WOMEN; s.a. Convents; Ex-nuns
RG   NUNS; s.a. Contemplative orders; Sisterhoods
NYT   RELIGION AND CHURCHES—U.S.—WOMEN;
       s.a. Roman Catholic religious orders
PAIS   CONVENTS AND NUNNERIES; s.a. Religious
       orders
BPI   RELIGION

MONASTICISM AND RELIGIOUS ORDERS
See also names of religious orders, e.g., Dominicans,
       Jesuits, etc.
LC   ———; s.a. Ascetism; Celibacy; Chastity; Eremitic
       life; Lay brothers; Monasteries and state;
       Monastic and religious life; Obedience, Vow of;
       Poverty, Vow of; Zen (sect)
SEARS ———; s.a. Monasteries; Religious life
RG   MONASTICISM; s.a. Contemplative orders;
       Hermits
NYT   RELIGION AND CHURCHES; s.a. Protestant
       Episcopal Church; Religious education; Roman
       Catholic religious orders
PAIS   RELIGIOUS ORDERS; s.a. Monasteries; subd.
       Religious life and customs under names of
       countries
BPI   RELIGION

MONETARY POLICY
LC   ———; s.a. Coinage, International; Credit; Fiscal
       policy; Monetary unions; names of specific
       monetary unions, e.g., European Payments
       Union
SEARS CURRENCY QUESTION; s.a. Finance; Inflation
       (finance); Money
RG   ———; s.a. Currency question; Fiscal policy
NYT   CURRENCY—U.S.; s.a. Credit; Economics;
       U.S.—Economic conditions and trends
PAIS   ———; s.a. Fiscal policy; Monetary unions;
       Money—International aspects
BPI   ———; s.a. Debts, Public; European Economic
       Community—Money; Fiscal policy; Under-
       developed areas—Money

MONEY
LC   ———; s.a. Bimetallism; Currency convertibility;
       Deflation (finance); Foreign exchange; Gold
       standard; Inflation (finance); Legal tender;
       Money, Primitive; Wealth
SEARS ———; s.a. Bills of exchange; Coinage; Credit
       question; Currency question; Paper money
RG   ———; s.a. Coins; Liquidity (economics); Paper
       money
NYT   CURRENCY; s.a. Banks and banking; Credit;
       Finance
PAIS   ———; s.a. Bank-notes; Capital; Gold as money;
       Purchasing power
BPI   ———; s.a. Barter; Finance; Open market
       operations

MONEY—INTERNATIONAL ASPECTS. *Use* Balance
       of Payments; Foreign Exchange; International
       Finance; Monetary Policy

MONEY, OLD AND RARE. *Use* Numismatics

MONEY MARKET. *Use* Currency Question; Monetary
       Policy

MONEY RAISING CAMPAIGNS. *Use* Charitable Uses,
       Trusts and Foundations

MONGOLISM. *Use* Mentally Handicapped Children

MONKEYS. *Use* Apes

MONKS. *See* Monasticism and Religious Orders

MONOPOLIES
LC   ———; s.a. Big business; Commercial crimes;
       Exclusive licenses; Government monopolies;
       Press monopolies; Price policy; Restraint of
       trade; Shipping conferences; Trade regulation
SEARS ———; s.a. Capitalism; Commerce; Competition,
       Unfair; Corporation law; Railroads—Consolida-
       tion; Trusts, Industrial
RG   ———; s.a. Competition; Patents—Licensing;
       Price maintenance by industry
NYT   TRADE PRACTICES AND MONOPOLIES; s.a.
       Cartels; U.S.—Economic conditions and trends
PAIS   MONOPOLY; s.a. Cartels; Industry—Concen-
       tration ratios
BPI   ———; s.a. Oligopolies; Price fixing; Restraint of
       trade; Trusts, Industrial

MONOTHEISM. *Use* God; Religion

MONTESSORI METHOD OF EDUCATION. *Use*
       Education, Preschool; Education, Primary

MONUMENTS. *Use* Architecture

MOODS. *Use* Emotions

MOON. *Use* Artificial Satellites; Astrology; Space Flight

MOORS (People). *Use* Islam

MORAL ATTITUDES. *Use* Ethics; Virtues

MORAL CONDITIONS
See also subd. *Moral conditions* under names of
       places, e.g., U.S.—Moral conditions.
LC   ———; s.a. Arts and morals, The; Sex customs;
       Social history
SEARS ———; s.a. Social conditions; Vice

RG   ——; s.a. Subd. *Moral aspects* under subjects, e.g., Moving pictures—Moral aspects; subd. *Moral conditions* under names of places

NYT   ETHICS AND MORALS; s.a. Children and youth—Behavior and training; Manners and customs; Social conditions and welfare

PAIS   ——; s.a. Social conditions

BPI   ——

MORAL PHILOSOPHY. *See* Ethics

MORALE

LC   ——; s.a. Fortitude; Military discipline; Military ethics; Psychology, Military; Teacher morale

SEARS   ——; s.a. Courage; Psychological warfare

RG   ——; s.a. Discipline, Military; subd. *Morale* under names of armed forces, e.g., U.S.—armed forces—Morale

NYT   PSYCHOLOGY AND PSYCHOLOGISTS; s.a. Mind

PAIS   ——; s.a. Employee morale; Social psychology

BPI   ——; s.a. Alienation (social psychology); Employee competitive behavior

MORALE, NATIONAL. *Use* Alienation (Social psychology)

MORALITIES. *Use* Drama

MORALITY. *See* Ethics

MORALS. *See* Conduct of Life; Ethics; Moral Conditions

MORATORIUM. *Use* Credit; Debtor and Creditor

MORMONS AND MORMONISM

LC   ——; s.a. Book of Mormon; Church of Jesus Christ of Latter Day Saints; Converts, Mormon; Kingdom of God (Mormonism); Lost tribes of Israel

SEARS   ——

RG   ——; s.a. Polygamy; Religion

NYT   MORMONS (Church of Jesus Christ of Latter-Day Saints); s.a. Religion and churches

PAIS   ——; s.a. Religion

BPI   ——; s.a. Christianity; Religion

MORPHINE HABIT. *Use* Narcotic Habit

MORSE CODE. *Use* Ciphers

MORTALITY

LC   ——; s.a. Children—Mortality; Death (biology); Insurance, Life—Mathematics; Men—Mortality; Mortality, Law of; Negroes—Mortality; Occupational mortality; Violent deaths; War—Casualties (statistics, etc.)

SEARS   ——; s.a. Death; Old age; Population; Vital statistics

RG   ——; s.a. Infant mortality; subd. *Mortality* under names of diseases, e.g., Multiple sclerosis—Mortality

NYT   DEATH; s.a. Population and vital statistics

PAIS   ——; s.a. Fetus, Death of; Population; Suicide

BPI   ——; s.a. Demography; Infants—Mortality; Life span, Productive

MORTGAGE BANKS. *Use* Banks and Banking

MORTGAGES

LC   ——; s.a. Chattel mortgages; Deeds of trust; Foreclosure; Housing—Finance; Mortgage loans; Priorities of claims and liens; Settlement costs; Veterans—Loans

SEARS   ——; s.a. Agricultural credit; Contracts; Investments; Loans; Property; Real estate

RG   ——; s.a. Debtor and creditor; Insurance, Mortgage guaranty; Land contracts

NYT   ——; s.a. Housing; Real estate

PAIS   ——; s.a. Liens; Ship mortgages; Veterans—Housing—Finance

BPI   ——; s.a. Bankruptcy; Conveyancing; Home ownership—Finance

MORTUARY CUSTOMS. *See* Funeral Rites and Ceremonies

MORTUARY STATISTICS. *See* Mortality

MOSLEMS. *Use* Islam

MOSQUES. *Use* Islam

MOTELS. *Use* Hotels, Taverns, etc.; Tourist Trade

MOTHERS

LC   ——; s.a. Maternal and infant welfare; Maternal deprivation; Mother and child; Mothers and daughters; Mothers and sons; Mothers—Employment; Mothers in art; Mothers-in-law; Pregnancy—Nutrition aspects; Prenatal care; Stepmothers

SEARS   ——; s.a. Family; Parent and child; Woman

RG   ——; s.a. Childbirth; Foster parents; Love, Maternal

NYT   FAMILIES AND FAMILY LIFE; s.a. Children and youth; Mother's Day; Women

PAIS   ——; s.a. Employment—Mothers; Parent and child (law); Women

BPI   ——; s.a. Children; Family; Women

MOTHERS—EMPLOYMENT. *Use* Woman—Employment

MOTHERS, UNMARRIED. *Use* Illegitimacy; Maternal and Infant Welfare; Parent and Child

MOTHERS' PENSIONS. *Use* Insurance, Social; Maternal and Infant Welfare

MOTION. *Use* Force and Energy

MOTION PICTURES. *Use* Audio-visual Materials; Moving Picture Industry; Moving Picture Plays; Moving Pictures; Moving Pictures as a Profession; Plots (Drama, novel, etc.)

MOTION STUDY. *Use* Job Analysis; Work Measurement

MOTIVATION (Psychology). *Use* Behavior (Psychology); Character; Emotions; Marketing Research; Propaganda; Teaching

MOTOR CARS. *See* Automobiles; Motor Vehicles

MOTOR ENGINES. *See* Motors

MOTOR FUELS. *Use* Fuel; Gas

MOTOR TRANSPORT. *Use* Freight and Freightage; Materials, Handling

MOTOR VEHICLES
LC ———; s.a. Automobiles; Cab and omnibus service; Commercial vehicles; Taxicabs; Transportation, Automotive
SEARS AUTOMOBILES; s.a. Buses; Motorcycles; Trucks
RG ———; s.a. Lunar vehicles; Snowmobiles and snowmobiling; Taxicabs
NYT AUTOMOBILES; s.a. Military vehicles; Transportation; Trucks
PAIS ———; s.a. Motor transport; Snowmobiles; Taxicabs
BPI ———; s.a. Automobiles; Motor trucks

MOTOR VEHICLES, ELECTRIC. *Use* Electric Motors

MOTOR VEHICLES—EXHAUST. *Use* Air—Pollution; Gas

MOTOR VEHICLES—SAFETY MEASURES. *Use* Automobiles—Safety Measures; Traffic Safety

MOTORBOATS. *Use* Boats and Boating

MOTORCYCLES. *Use* Bicycles and Bicycling; Motor Vehicles

MOTORS
LC ———; s.a. Alcohol motors; Diesel motors; Dynamos; Hydraulic motors; Outboard motors; subd. *Motors* under subjects, e.g., Aeroplanes—Motors
SEARS ENGINES; s.a. Electric motors; Gas and oil engines
RG Names of types of motors, e.g., Automobile engines; Electric motors; etc.; s.a. Machinery
NYT ENGINES; s.a. Automobiles—U.S.—Engines; Boats and yachts; Shipbuilding, conversion and repair
PAIS ENGINES; s.a. Diesel engines; Motors, Outboard
BPI ———; s.a. Automobile engines; Gas and oil engines

MOTTOES. *Use* Emblems; Proverbs

MOUND AND MOUND BUILDERS. *Use* Anthropology; Archaeology; Burial

MOUNTAINEERING. *Use* Outdoor Life

MOURNING CUSTOMS. *Use* Funeral Rites and Ceremonies

MOVIE THEATRES. *See* Moving Picture Industry

MOVIES. *See* Moving Pictures

MOVING INDUSTRY. *Use* Storage and Moving Trade

MOVING PICTURE ACTING. *Use* Moving Pictures as a Profession

MOVING PICTURE AUDIENCES. *Use* Moving Picture Industry

MOVING PICTURE CAMERAS. *Use* Cameras

MOVING PICTURE CRITICISM. *Use* Moving Picture Plays

MOVING PICTURE DIRECTORS. *Use* Moving Picture Industry; Moving Pictures as a Profession

MOVING PICTURE INDUSTRY
LC MOVING-PICTURE INDUSTRY; s.a. Moving-picture audiences; Moving-pictures, American (French, etc.); Moving-pictures—Production and direction
SEARS ———; s.a. Moving picture theaters; Theater—Production and direction
RG ———; s.a. Moving picture production and direction; Moving pictures—Setting and scenery
NYT MOTION PICTURES; s.a. Motion pictures—Personnel; Motion pictures—U.S.
PAIS MOVING PICTURES; s.a. Moving picture audiences; Moving picture directors
BPI ———; s.a. Collective labor agreements—Actors and actresses; Moving picture producers and directors; Television film companies

MOVING PICTURE JOURNALISM. *Use* News Photographers

MOVING PICTURE PHOTOGRAPHY. *Use* Moving Pictures; Photography

MOVING PICTURE PLAYS
LC MOVING-PICTURE PLAYS; s.a. Film adaptations; Moving-pictures—Evaluation; Moving-pictures in industry; Moving-pictures—Plots, themes, etc.; Newspapers—Sections, columns, etc.—Reviews
SEARS ———; s.a. Dramatic criticism; Moving pictures—History and criticism; Moving pictures—Moral and religious aspects; Moving pictures—Psychological aspects; Moving pictures—Stories, plots, etc.
RG ———; s.a. Moving picture criticism; Moving picture plays—Criticism, plots, etc.; Moving pictures in psychotherapy; Television broadcasting—Moving pictures
NYT MOTION PICTURES; s.a. Motion pictures—Reviews and other data on specific productions; Moving pictures—Censorship; Television and radio—Programs—Motion pictures
PAIS MOVING PICTURES; s.a. Moving picture criticism; Moving pictures—Social aspects
BPI MOVING PICTURES; s.a. Newspapers—Moving picture news; Television broadcasting—Moving pictures

MOVING PICTURE PRODUCERS. *Use* Moving Picture Industry; Moving Pictures as a Profession

MOVING PICTURE THEATRES. *Use* Moving Picture Industry; Theaters

MOVING PICTURES
LC MOVING-PICTURES; s.a. Cinematography (photographic processes); Color moving-pictures; Historical films; Moving-picture cartoons; Moving-picture journalism; Moving-pictures and television; Moving-pictures, Three dimensional; Photography—Moving-pictures; Women in moving-pictures; Youth in moving-pictures
SEARS ———; s.a. Audio-visual materials; Experimental films; Moving picture photography; Moving pictures, Documentary; Sound—Recording and reproducing

RG ——; s.a. Moving picture industry; Moving pictures, Experimental; Moving pictures—Silent films; Moving pictures—Sound recording; Negroes in moving pictures; Realism in moving pictures

NYT MOTION PICTURES; s.a. Entertainment and amusements; Multimedia

PAIS ——; s.a. Sex in moving pictures; Television—Moving pictures

BPI ——; s.a. Newspapers—Moving picture news; Television broadcasting—Moving pictures

MOVING PICTURES—AWARDS. *Use* Rewards (Prizes, etc.)

MOVING PICTURES—PLOTS, THEMES, ETC. *Use* Moving Picture Plays; Plots (Drama, novel, etc.)

MOVING PICTURES AND CHILDREN
Scope: Works dealing with the effect of moving pictures on children and youth.
LC MOVING-PICTURES AND CHILDREN; s.a. Child study; Mass media and children; Moving-pictures for children; Violence in moving pictures
SEARS ——; s.a. Children; Television and children
RG ——; s.a. Moving pictures for children; Moving pictures—Moral aspects
NYT MOTION PICTURES—U.S.; s.a. Children and youth—Behavior and training
PAIS ——; s.a. Children, Research on; Television and children
BPI MOVING PICTURES; s.a. Television and children

MOVING PICTURES AS A PROFESSION
LC MOVING-PICTURES AS A PROFESSION; s.a. Acting as a profession; Moving-picture acting; Moving-picture actors and actresses
SEARS ——; s.a. Acting as a profession
RG MOVING PICTURE ACTORS AND ACTRESSES; s.a. Moving picture authorship; Moving picture directors
NYT MOTION PICTURES—PERSONNEL; s.a. Motion pictures—U.S.
PAIS ACTORS; s.a. Moving picture directors
BPI MOVING PICTURE INDUSTRY; s.a. Actors and actresses; Moving picture producers and directors

MOVING PICTURES IN EDUCATION
LC MOVING-PICTURES IN EDUCATION; s.a. Moving-pictures in higher education; Moving-pictures in teacher training; Museums and moving-pictures; Teachers in moving-pictures; Visual education
SEARS ——; s.a. Audio-visual education; Libraries and moving pictures; Teaching—Aids and devices
RG ——; s.a. Moving pictures in health education; Moving pictures—Study and teaching
NYT EDUCATION AND SCHOOLS—U.S.—TEACHING AIDS; s.a. Motion pictures
PAIS ——; s.a. Audio-visual instruction; Education—Aids and devices
BPI ——; s.a. Audio-visual instruction; Filmstrips

MOVING TRADE. *See* Storage and Moving Trade

MUGGING. *See* Crime and Criminals; Offenses Against the Person

MULTI-MEDIA CENTERS. *Use* Audio-visual Education; Instructional Materials Centers

MULTI-NATIONAL CORPORATIONS. *Use* Business Enterprises

MULTIPLE ARTS. *Use* Arts, The

MULTIPLE CONSCIOUSNESS. *See* Mentally Ill

MUNICIPAL ADMINISTRATION. *See* Mayors; Municipal Government

MUNICIPAL BONDS. *Use* Bonds

MUNICIPAL BUDGETS. *Use* Budget; Municipal Government

MUNICIPAL BUILDINGS. *Use* Public Works

MUNICIPAL CHARTERS. *Use* Municipal Government

MUNICIPAL CORPORATIONS. *Use* Corporations; Corporations, Government; Mayors; Municipal Government

MUNICIPAL DUMPS. *Use* Refuse and Refuse Disposal

MUNICIPAL EMPLOYEES. *Use* Civil Service; Local Government; Municipal Officials and Employees

MUNICIPAL ENGINEERING. *Use* Public Works

MUNICIPAL FINANCE. *Use* Finance, Public; Licenses; Municipal Government

MUNICIPAL FRANCHISES. *Use* Municipal Ownership

MUNICIPAL GOVERNMENT
See also subd. *Politics and government* under names of cities.
LC ——; s.a. Cities and towns; Local finance; Mayors; Metropolitan government; Municipal budgets; Municipal charters; Municipal corporations; Municipal home rule; Municipal ownership; Municipal services; Ordinances, Municipal; School bonds
SEARS ——; s.a. Bonds; Charters; Intergovernmental tax relations; Municipal corporations; Municipal finance; Public administration
RG ——; s.a. Bonds, Revenue; Boss rule; City manager plan; Intergovernmental fiscal relations; Municipal corporations; Municipal finance; Municipal incorporation; State and municipal relations; subd. *Finance* under names of cities
NYT LOCAL GOVERNMENT; s.a. Government bonds; Politics and government; Urban areas
PAIS ——; s.a. Bonds, Government; Budgets, Municipal; Local government—Finance; Municipal charters; Municipal incorporation; State and municipal relations
BPI ——; s.a. Bonds, Industrial development; Bonds, School; Local finance; Municipal bonds; Municipal finance; subd. *Finance* under names of cities

MUNICIPAL IMPROVEMENT. *See* City Planning; Urban Renewal

MUNICIPAL INCOME TAX. *See* Income Tax

MUNICIPAL LAW. *Use* Ordinances, Municipal

MUNICIPAL OFFICIALS AND EMPLOYEES

LC ———; s.a. Public officers; subd. *Officials and employees* under names of cities

SEARS CIVIL SERVICE; s.a. Civil service—Examinations; Civil service—U.S.; Local government

RG MUNICIPAL OFFICERS; s.a. City managers; Mayors

NYT LOCAL GOVERNMENT; s.a. Government employees and officials; names of cities; U.S.—Politics and government—Local government

PAIS MUNICIPAL OFFICIALS; s.a. City managers; Municipal employees

BPI ———; s.a. Mayors; Strikes—Municipal employees

MUNICIPAL ORDINANCES. *Use* Ordinances, Municipal

MUNICIPAL OWNERSHIP

LC ———; s.a. Government business enterprises; Municipal franchises; Service at cost (public utilities)

SEARS ———; s.a. Corporations; Government ownership; Public utilities

RG GOVERNMENT OWNERSHIP; s.a. Municipal contracts

NYT LOCAL GOVERNMENT; s.a. Government employees and officials; Public utilities; Public works

PAIS Subd. *Municipal ownership* under specific subjects, e.g., Electric utilities—Municipal ownership; s.a. Concessions

BPI GOVERNMENT OWNERSHIP; s.a. Electric utilities—Government ownership; Government corporations; Municipal government; Public works

MUNICIPAL POWERS AND SERVICES BEYOND CORPORATE LIMITS. *Use* Metropolitan Government; Suburbs

MUNICIPAL RECORDS. *Use* Public Records

MUNICIPAL SERVICES. *Use* Municipal Government; Public Utilities

MUNICIPAL TAXATION. *Use* Taxation

MUNICIPAL UTILITIES. *See* Public Utilities

MUNICIPALITIES. *See* Cities and Towns; Municipal Government

MUNITIONS

LC ———; s.a. Defense contracts; Firearms industry and trade; Tear gas munitions; Weapons systems

SEARS ———; s.a. Industrial mobilization; War—Economic aspects; Weapons

RG ———; s.a. Atomic weapons; subd. *Equipment and supplies* under names of wars, e.g., Vietnamese war, 1959- —Equipment and supplies

NYT ARMAMENT, DEFENSE AND MILITARY FORCES; s.a. Firearms; U.S. armament and defense

PAIS ———; s.a. Ammunition; Armaments

BPI ———; s.a. Firearms industry; Weapons systems

MURDER

LC ———; s.a. Aged, Killing of; Filicide; Infanticide; Patricide; Poisoning; Strangling; Trials (murder)

SEARS ———; s.a. Capital punishment; Medical jurisprudence; Offenses against the person

RG ———; s.a. Commandments, Ten—Murder; Euthanasia

NYT MURDERS AND ATTEMPTED MURDERS; s.a. Capital punishment; Mercy death (euthanasia)

PAIS ———; s.a. Assassination; Genocide

BPI ———; s.a. Assassination; Homicide

MUSCLE STRENGTH. *Use* Exercise; Physical Fitness

MUSEUMS

See also types of museums, e.g., Science museum; names of museums, e.g., Smithsonian Institution; and subd. *Galleries and museums* under names of cities.

LC ———; s.a. Museum conservation methods; subd. *Museum* under appropriate subject, e.g., Indians of North America—Museums

SEARS ———; s.a. Art—Galleries and museums

RG ———; s.a. Museum techniques

NYT ———; s.a. Subjects of exhibits, e.g., Art

PAIS ———; Arts market

BPI ———; s.a. Art—Galleries and museums

MUSIC

See also types of music, e.g., Chamber music; Church music; Dance music; Instrumental music; Jazz music; Military music; and national subds., e.g., Music, American (French, etc.); Folk music, American (Spanish, etc.).

LC ———; s.a. Concert music; Country music; Electronic music; Improvisation (music); Instrumentation and orchestration; Music (popular songs, etc.); Music—Negroes; Music—Performance; Music and race; Music in theatre; Music therapy; Musical criticism; Musical instruments; Negroes—Songs and music; Orchestra

SEARS ———; s.a. Black music; Concerts; Music—History and criticism; Music—Psychology; Music and literature; Musical instruments, Mechanical; Musical revues, comedies, etc.; Spirituals

RG ———; s.a. Blues (songs, etc.); Composition (music); Ensemble playing; Mass (music); Melody; Music, Electronic; Music, Incidental; Music, Influence of; Music and color; Orchestral music; Phonograph records—(type of music, e.g., Electronic music); Religion and music; Rock music

NYT ———; s.a. Culture; Dancing; Entertainment and amusements; Opera; Recordings (disk and tape) and recording and playback equipment; Theater

PAIS ———; s.a. Communism and music; Jukeboxes; Music festivals; Opera; Orchestras

BPI ———; s.a. Composers; Copyright—Music; Music, Popular (songs, etc.); Orchestras; Rock groups

MUSIC—ANALYSIS, APPRECIATION. *Use* Music Education

MUSIC—CONCERTS AND RECITALS. *Use* Chamber Music

MUSIC—ECONOMIC ASPECTS
LC   ——; s.a. Music as a profession; Music trade
SEARS   ——; s.a. Music as a profession; Musicians
RG   ——; s.a. Composers; Music publishing; Musicians
NYT   MUSIC; s.a. Music—Festivals; Music—Orchestras and other music groups
PAIS   MUSIC TRADES; s.a. Music market; Musical instruments industry
BPI   MUSIC; s.a. Composers; Copyright—Music; Musicians

MUSIC, ELECTRONIC. *Use* Music

MUSIC—INSTRUCTION AND STUDY. *Use* Music Education

MUSIC—NEGROES. *Use* Negro Music

MUSIC—ORCHESTRA AND OTHER MUSIC GROUPS. *Use* Chamber Music; Orchestra

MUSIC, POPULAR (Songs, etc.). *Use* Dance Music; Music; Singing and Songs

MUSIC, VOCAL. *See* Singing and Songs

MUSIC AS A PROFESSION. *Use* Music—Economic Aspects; Music Education; Musicians

MUSIC EDUCATION
LC   MUSIC—INSTRUCTION AND STUDY; s.a. Ear training; Instrumental music—Instruction and study; Music—Analytical guides; Music—Instruction and study—Programmed instruction; Music—Manuals, textbooks; Music—Memorizing; subd. *Instruction and study* under names of musical instruments
SEARS   MUSIC—STUDY AND TEACHING; s.a. Music—Analysis, appreciation; Music as a profession; Music—Examinations, questions, etc.; Musical form; Musical notation
RG   MUSIC—INSTRUCTION AND STUDY; s.a. Music students; School music
NYT   MUSIC; s.a. Education and schools—U.S.—Music
PAIS   ——; s.a. Names of music schools, e.g., Julliard School of Music, New York
BPI   MUSIC—INSTRUCTION AND STUDY

MUSIC FESTIVALS. *Use* Music; Music—Economic Aspects; Singing and Songs

MUSIC HALLS (Variety theaters, cabarets, etc.). *Use* Theaters; Vaudeville

MUSIC MARKET. *Use* Music—Economic Aspects

MUSIC PUBLISHING. *Use* Music—Economic Aspects; Publishers and Publishing

MUSIC THERAPY. *Use* Occupational Therapy

MUSICAL COMEDIES, REVUES, ETC. *Use* Drama; Music; Opera; Vaudeville

MUSICAL INSTRUMENTS. *Use* Music

MUSICAL INSTRUMENTS INDUSTRY. *Use* Music—Economic Aspects

MUSICAL PERFORMANCE. *See* Music

MUSICAL REVUES, COMEDIES, ETC. *Use* Drama; Music; Opera; Vaudeville

MUSICIANS
Scope: For works on the attainments of women see Women as musicians; for biographical works, see Musicians, Women.
LC   ——; s.a. Artists; Flute-players, pianists, singers and similar headings; Music as a profession; Music critics; Musicians—Biography
SEARS   ——; s.a. Composers; Conductors; Entertainers
RG   ——; s.a. Singers; Street musicians
NYT   MUSIC; s.a. Musicians, American Federation of (AFM); names of individual musicians, e.g., Bernstein, Leonard
PAIS   ——; s.a. Composers; Trade unions—Musicians
BPI   ——; s.a. Composers; Rock groups

MUSLIMS. *Use* Islam

MUSLIMS IN NON-MOSLEM COUNTRIES. *Use* Minorities

MUTATION (Biology). *Use* Evolution; Genetics

MUTUALISM. *Use* Cooperation; Socialism

MYSTERIES, RELIGIOUS. *Use* Secret Societies

MYSTERY AND DETECTIVE STORIES. *Use* Detectives

MYSTERY AND MIRACLE PLAYS—ENGLISH. *Use* Drama

MYSTICISM. *Use* Religion; Theology; Yoga

MYTHOLOGY
See also various divisions, e.g., Mythology, Germanic; Mythology, Japanese; Mythology, Classical.
LC   ——; s.a. Animals, Mythical; Demythologization; Folk-lore; Geographical myths; Myth; Religion, Primitive; Totemism
SEARS   ——; s.a. Ancestor worship; Art and mythology; Classical antiquities; Indians of North America—Religion and mythology; Symbolism
RG   ——; s.a. Gods and goddesses; Legends; Mythology, Greek
NYT   MYTHS; s.a. Archeology and anthropology; Books and literature; Religion and churches; Superstitions
PAIS   FOLKLORE; s.a. Religion
BPI   RELIGION; s.a. Anthropology; Archeology

N

NAMES, PERSONAL. *Use* Anonyms and Pseudonyms

NAPALM. *Use* Chemical Warfare

NARCOANALYSIS
LC ———; s.a. Narcotics; Psychoanalysis
SEARS PSYCHOANALYSIS; s.a. Psychology, Physiological
RG ———; s.a. Narcotics; Psychology, Physiological
NYT DRUGS AND DRUG TRADE; s.a. Drug addiction, abuse and traffic
PAIS ———; s.a. Crime and criminals
BPI NARCOTICS; s.a. Psychology

NARCOLEPSY. *Use* Sleep

NARCOTIC ADDICTS
See note under Narcotics.
LC ———; s.a. Church work with narcotic addicts; Narcotics, Control of
SEARS NARCOTIC HABIT; s.a. Narcotics and youth
RG ———; s.a. Methadone; Narcotics and crime
NYT DRUG ADDICTION, ABUSE AND TRAFFIC; s.a. Drugs and drug trade; Prisons and prisoners; Robberies and thefts
PAIS DRUG ADDICTS; s.a. Drug abuse; Drugs and youth; Narcotics and crime
BPI ———; s.a. Drug abuse

NARCOTIC HABIT
See also under Narcotics.
LC ———; s.a. Cocaine habit; Glue-sniffing; Morphine habit; Opium habit
SEARS ———; s.a. Drug abuse
RG ———; s.a. Drug abuse; Narcotics and youth; Narcotics laws
NYT DRUG ADDICTION, ABUSE AND TRAFFIC; s.a. Drugs and drug trade; Prisons and prisoners; Robberies and thefts
PAIS DRUG ADDICTS; s.a. Drugs; Narcotics and crime
BPI ———; s.a. Drug abuse; Narcotic addicts

NARCOTIC LEGISLATION. *Use* Narcotics, Control of

NARCOTICS
Scope: The word Drugs is often used in a broad sense to include such items as alcohol, sedatives, LSD, and marihuana; the word Narcotics is mostly used for hard drugs such as opium, heroin, etc. See also names of specific narcotics, e.g., Hashish.
LC ———; s.a. Hypnotics; Insomnia; Sedatives; Therapeutics
SEARS ———; s.a. Drugs; Materia medica; Stimulants
RG ———; s.a. Drugs; Hypnotics; Opium trade
NYT DRUG ADDICTION, ABUSE AND TRAFFIC; s.a. Drugs and drug trade
PAIS ———; s.a. Drug abuse; Drugs
BPI ———; s.a. Narcotic addicts; Narcotics and dangerous drugs, Control of

NARCOTICS, CONTROL OF
LC ———; s.a. Drugs—Laws and legislation; Narcoanalysis; Narcotic addicts; Narcotic clinics
SEARS NARCOTICS—INSTITUTIONAL CARE; s.a. Narcotics—Laws and legislation
RG ———; s.a. Narcotic addicts—Rehabilitation; Narcotic laws
NYT DRUG ADDICTION, ABUSE AND TRAFFIC; s.a. Drugs and drug trade; Law and legislation
PAIS DRUG ADDICTS—CARE AND TREATMENT; s.a. Drug trade; Drugs—Legislation; Narcotic legislation
BPI NARCOTICS AND DANGEROUS DRUGS, CONTROL OF; s.a. Narcotic addicts; Narcotics—Law

NARCOTICS AND CRIME. *Use* Narcotic Addicts; Narcotic Habit

NARCOTICS AND YOUTH. *Use* Drug Abuse; Juvenile Delinquency; Narcotic Addicts; Narcotic Habit

NATION—STATE. *See* Nationalism

NATIONAL ACCOUNTING. *Use* National Income

NATIONAL ANTHEMS. *See* National Songs

NATIONAL BANKS (U.S.)
See also names of national banks, e.g., Bank of England.
LC ———; s.a. Banks and banking, Central; Banks of issue—U.S.
SEARS BANKS AND BANKING—U.S.; s.a. Federal reserve banks
RG BANKS AND BANKING—U.S.; s.a. Banking law; U.S.—Federal reserve board
NYT BANKS AND BANKING—U.S.; s.a. U.S.—Federal reserve system
PAIS BANKING, NATIONAL; s.a. Banking; Federal reserve system
BPI BANKS AND BANKING; s.a. Banking laws and regulations; Federal reserve act

NATIONAL CEMETERIES. *Use* Burial

NATIONAL CHARACTERISTICS
LC ———; s.a. Anthropology; Ethnopsychology; Race awareness; Social psychology; Uncle Sam (nickname)
SEARS ———; s.a. Nationalism; Race psychology
RG ———; s.a. Acculturation; Ethnopsychology
NYT RACE; s.a. Archeology and anthropology; names of races; e.g., Arabs
PAIS ———; s.a. Nationalism; Races of man
BPI ———; s.a. Nationalism; Race

NATIONAL CONSCIOUSNESS. *See* Nationalism

NATIONAL CONVENTIONS. *Use* Congresses and Conventions; Political Parties

NATIONAL DEBTS. *See* Debts, Public

NATIONAL DEFENSE. *Use* U.S.—Defenses

NATIONAL FORESTS. *Use* Forest Reserves

NATIONAL HOLIDAYS. *See* Special Days, Weeks and Months

NATIONAL HYMNS. *See* National Songs

NATIONAL INCOME
LC   ——; s.a. Gross national product; Multiplier (economics); Purchasing power
SEARS INCOME; s.a. Consumption (economic)
RG   INCOME; s.a. Gross national product; Wealth, Distribution of
NYT   Subd. *Government revenue and national income* under names of countries; s.a. Economics; Income
PAIS   INCOME; s.a. Finance; National accounting; Production—Statistics
BPI   ——; s.a. Flow of funds; Gross national product

NATIONAL MILITARY PARKS. *See* National Parks and Reserves

NATIONAL MUSIC. *Use* Singing and Songs

NATIONAL PARKS AND RESERVES
See also names of national parks, e.g., Yellowstone National Park.
LC   ——; s.a. Forest rangers; Forest reserves; Military reservations
SEARS ——; s.a. Forest reserves; Natural monuments
RG   ——; s.a. Marine parks and reserves; Wilderness areas; Wildlife conservation
NYT   PARKS, PLAYGROUNDS AND OTHER RECREATION AREAS; s.a. Forests (state and national); Wildlife sanctuaries
PAIS   PARKS, NATIONAL; s.a. Forests, National; Public lands
BPI   PARKS; s.a. Recreation areas; Wilderness areas

NATIONAL PLANNING. *See* Social Policy

NATIONAL PRODUCT, GROSS. *See* Gross National Product

NATIONAL RESOURCES. *See* Natural Resources

NATIONAL SECURITY. *See* Internal Security

NATIONAL SOCIALISM. *Use* Socialism; Totalitarianism

NATIONAL SONGS
LC   ——; s.a. Political ballads and songs; State songs (American); War—Songs
SEARS ——; s.a. Folk songs; Patriotic poetry
RG   ——; s.a. Anthems; names of songs, e.g., Star Spangled Banner (song); Political poetry; State songs
NYT   MUSIC
PAIS   MUSIC AND STATE; s.a. Music
BPI   MUSIC

NATIONAL STATE. *Use* Nationalism; Nationality; State, The

NATIONAL TERRITORY. *See* Territory, National

NATIONALISM
See also subd. *Nationalism* under names of countries, continents and groups, e.g., Europe—Nationalism; Spain—Nationalism; Basques—Nationalism.
LC   ——; s.a. Autonomy; Chauvinism and jingoism; National state; Patriotism; Regionalism
SEARS ——; s.a. Citizenship; Minorities; National characteristics; Sectionalism (U.S.); State, The
RG   ——; s.a. Americanism; Internationalism; Zionism
NYT   Names of specific countries; s.a. Minorities; Politics and government; Race
PAIS   ——; s.a. Economic nationalism; Nationality; Patriotism; Self-determination, National
BPI   ——; s.a. Minorities; Race

NATIONALISM, BLACK. *See* Black Nationalism

NATIONALISM—JEWS. *Use* Zionism

NATIONALISM—NEGROES. *See* Black Nationalism; Negro Race

NATIONALISM AND EDUCATION. *Use* Education and State

NATIONALISM AND RELIGION
LC   ——; s.a. Church and state; Religion and state; Theocracy
SEARS CHURCH AND STATE; s.a. Christianity and politics; Freedom of conscience; Religion in the public schools
RG   CHURCH AND STATE; s.a. Church property; Concordats
NYT   RELIGION AND CHURCHES; s.a. subd. *Politics and government—Church-state relations* under name of country, e.g., Spain Politics and government—Church-state relations
PAIS   CHURCH AND STATE; s.a. Church and politics; Religious liberty
BPI   RELIGION AND STATE; s.a. Church and state; Church

NATIONALITY
LC   NATIONALITIES, PRINCIPLE OF; s.a. National state; Option of nationality; Self-determination, National
SEARS CITIZENSHIP; s.a. Aliens; Naturalization
RG   CITIZENSHIP; s.a. Aliens; Naturalization
NYT   CITIZENSHIP; s.a. Immigration and emigration; Minorities; Race
PAIS   ——; s.a. Dual nationality; Expatriation
BPI   NATIONALISM; s.a. Immigration and emigration; Minorities

NATIONALIZATION
See also subd. *Government ownership* under names of industries, e.g., Electric utilities—Government ownership.
LC   GOVERNMENT OWNERSHIP; s.a. Government competition; Government monopolies
SEARS GOVERNMENT OWNERSHIP; s.a. Industry and state; Municipal ownership; Railroads and state
RG   GOVERNMENT OWNERSHIP; s.a. Railroads and state; Socialism

NATIONALIZATION, *cont.*
NYT POLITICS AND GOVERNMENT; s.a. Nationalization of industry; Socialism
PAIS ———; s.a. Government ownership; Political science
BPI GOVERNMENT OWNERSHIP; s.a. Government corporations; Eminent domain (international law)

NATIONS, NEW. *Use* State, The

NATIVE CLERGY. *Use* Missionaries

NATIVE LABOR
Scope: For works dealing with native labor in particular colonial areas, see *Labor and laboring classes* with appropriate regional subdivision, e.g., Labor and laboring classes—Morocco.
LC ———; s.a. Contract labor; Forced labor
SEARS CONTRACT LABOR; s.a. Household employees; Peonage
RG LABOR, COMPULSORY; s.a. Native races; also subd. *Native races* under names of places e.g. Philippines—Native races
NYT Subd. *Labor* under name of country, e.g., Italy—Labor; s.a. Domestic service; Labor
PAIS CONTRACT LABOR; s.a. Contracts for work and labor; Migrant labor
BPI LABOR AND LABORING CLASSES; s.a. Alien labor; Labor supply; Migrant labor

NATIVE RACES
Scope: Works on the relations between the governing authorities and the aboriginal inhabitants of colonial or other areas.
LC ———; s.a. Ethnology; Native labor; also subd. *Government relations* under Indians of North America, and under names of tribes, e.g., Sioux—Government relations
SEARS ———; s.a. Ethnology; Race problems
RG ———; s.a. Indians, Treatment of; United Nations—Trusteeship council
NYT RACE; s.a. Minorities; Population and vital statistics
PAIS ———; s.a. Eskimos; Indians; Maoris; also subds. *Native races*, and *Race question* under names of countries and subjects, e.g., Alaska—Native races; South Africa—Race question
BPI RACE PROBLEMS; s.a. Cultural relations

NATIVISTIC MOVEMENTS. *Use* Ethnology

NATURAL CHILDBIRTH. *See* Childbirth; Labor (Obstetrics)

NATURAL DISASTERS. *Use* Disasters

NATURAL HISTORY
Scope: Popular works describing animals, plants, minerals, and nature in general. For detailed studies of birds, flowers, etc. see *Nature study*.
LC ———; s.a. Animal lore; Biology; Plant lore; Zoology
SEARS ———; s.a. Geographical distribution of animals and plants; Marine biology
RG ———; s.a. Botany; Wildlife conservation
NYT NATURE—HISTORY; s.a. Horticulture; Natural resources

PAIS ———; s.a. Animals; Nature
BPI NATURE; s.a. Animals; Plants

NATURAL LAW. *Use* Law; Liberty

NATURAL MONUMENTS. *Use* Forest Reserves; Landscape Protection; National Parks and Reserves; Nature Conservation

NATURAL RESOURCES
Scope: May subdivide geographically, e.g., Natural resources—France.
LC ———; s.a. Afforestation; Conservation of natural resources; Economic development; Environmental policy; Fisheries; Marine ecology; Nature conservation; Raw materials; Reclamation of land; Wind power
SEARS ———; s.a. Forests and forestry; Mines and mineral resources
RG ———; s.a. Power resources; Wildlife conservation
NYT Subd. *Natural resources* under names of geographical areas, e.g., Rhine Valley—Natural resources; s.a. Economic conditions and trends; Forests and forestry
PAIS ———; s.a. Conservation of resources; Wilderness areas
BPI ———; s.a. Conservation of resources; Marine resources; Power resources

NATURAL SCENERY. *See* Landscape Protection

NATURAL SCIENCE. *See* Natural History; Science

NATURAL SELECTION. *Use* Evolution; Genetics; Heredity

NATURALIZATION. *Use* Aliens; Citizenship; Emigration and Immigration; Nationality

NATURE. *Use* Conservation of Natural Resources; Ecology; Landscape Protection; Man—Influence on Nature; Natural History; Nature Conservation; Outdoor Life

NATURE, EFFECT OF MAN ON. *See* Man—Influence on Nature

NATURE CONSERVATION
LC ———; s.a. Landscape protection; Man—Influence on nature; Wildlife conservation
SEARS ———; s.a. Conservation of natural resources; Natural monuments
RG ———; s.a. Conservation of resources; Forest conservation; Reclamation of land
NYT NATURE; s.a. Environment; names of specific subjects, e.g., Animals
PAIS CONSERVATION OF RESOURCES; s.a. Nature; Wildlife conservation
BPI CONSERVATION OF RESOURCES; s.a. Natural resources; Power resources; Wildlife, Conservation of

NATURE PHOTOGRAPHY. *Use* Photography

NATURE STUDY. *Use* Botany; Natural History

NATUROPATHY. *Use* Chiropractic; Therapeutics

NAVAL ART AND SCIENCE
See also subd. *Navies* under names of countries, e.g., Norway—Navies.

LC   ——; s.a. Marine service; Naval battles; Naval history; Seamen
SEARS   ——; s.a. Navies; Pirates; Sea power
RG   ——; s.a. Seamanship; Signals and signaling; Submarine warfare
NYT   U.S.—ARMAMENT AND DEFENSE—NAVY; s.a. Military art and science; Ships and shipping; Submarines and submersibles
PAIS   ——; s.a. Capture at sea; Military art and science; Naval warfare; Submarines, Atomic-powered; War
BPI   ——; s.a. Aircraft carriers; Anti-submarine warfare; Logistics; Military art and science; Warships

NAVAL HISTORY. *Use* Sea-Power

NAVAL LAW. *See* Maritime Law

NAVAL WARFARE. *See* Naval Art and Science

NAVIES. *Use* Armed Forces; Naval Art and Science; Sea-Power

NAVIGATION. *Use* Boats and Boating; Flight; Magnetism, Terrestrial; Radar

NAVIGATION (Astronautics). *Use* Space Flight

NAVIGATORS. *See* Discoveries (Geography); Explorers; Seamen

NEANDERTHAL RACE. *Use* Anthropology; Evolution; Man

NEAR EAST
Scope: Works dealing with the Mediterranean countries east of the Adriatic. See also appropriate subd. Near East or Middle East under subjects, e.g., Socialism—Near East.
LC   ——; s.a. Arab countries; Latin Orient; Levant
SEARS   ——; s.a. Eastern question
RG   MIDDLE EAST
NYT   MIDDLE EAST; s.a. Mediterranean area
PAIS   ——; s.a. Arab states
BPI   MIDDLE EAST

NECESSITY (Philosophy). *Use* Fate and Fatalism

NECROLOGIES. *See* Obituaries

NECROSCOPY. *See* Autopsy

NEEDLEWORK. *Use* Sewing; Tapestry

NEGATIVE INCOME TAX
LC   ——; s.a. Economic assistance, Domestic; Wages—Annual wage
SEARS   GUARANTEED ANNUAL INCOME; s.a. Income; Taxation
RG   ——; s.a. Guaranteed annual income; Wages—Annual wage
NYT   TAXATION; s.a. Income
PAIS   INCOME—GUARANTEED INCOME; s.a. Income tax; Wages and salaries—Guaranteed wage
BPI   ——; s.a. Guaranteed annual income; Taxation

NEGLIGENCE
LC   ——; s.a. Accident law; Employers' liability; Occupations, Dangerous
SEARS   LAW; s.a. Workmen's compensation
RG   ——; s.a. Liability (law); Torts

NYT   ACCIDENTS AND SAFETY; s.a. Law and legislation
PAIS   ——; s.a. Law; Liability
BPI   ——; s.a. Damages; Personal injuries; Products liability

NEGOTIABLE INSTRUMENTS
LC   ——; s.a. Acceptances; Banking law; Certificates of deposit; Letters of credit; Promissory notes
SEARS   ——; s.a. Bonds; Commercial law
RG   ——; s.a. Checks; Credit
NYT   BANKS AND BANKING; s.a. Credit; Stocks and bonds
PAIS   ——; s.a. Bills of exchange; Warehouse receipts
BPI   ——; s.a. Checks; Transfer of funds

NEGOTIATION. *Use* Collective Bargaining

NEGRO AUTHORS. *Use* Negroes in Literature

NEGRO BUSINESSMEN. *Use* Negroes and Business

NEGRO CATHOLICS. *See* Catholic Church in the U.S.

NEGRO CHILDREN
LC   ——
SEARS   CHILDREN; s.a. Segregation in education; Youth
RG   ——; s.a. Discrimination in education; Negro youth; Socially handicapped children
NYT   CHILDREN AND YOUTH; s.a. Negroes (general); Negroes (in U.S.)
PAIS   ——; s.a. Children; Negro youth
BPI   NEGROES; s.a. Discrimination in education; Public schools—Desegregation

NEGRO COLLEGES. *Use* Black Colleges; Education and State; Negro Students

NEGRO CONSUMERS. *See* Negroes and Business

NEGRO FAMILIES. *Use* Family

NEGRO JOURNALISTS. *Use* Blacks and the Press

NEGRO LEADERSHIP. *Use* Elite (Social sciences)

NEGRO LITERATURE. *Use* Black Literature; Literature

NEGRO MARKET. *Use* Consumers; Negroes and Business

NEGRO MINSTRELS. *Use* Negro Music

NEGRO MUSIC
Scope: Songs of African Negroes are entered under heading *Folk songs, African.*
LC   ——; s.a. Negro minstrels; Negro musicians; Negro songs; Negro spirituals
SEARS   BLACK MUSIC; s.a. Black musicians; Black songs; Spirituals
RG   ——; s.a. Blues (songs, etc.); Jazz music
NYT   MUSIC; s.a. Negroes (general); Negroes (in U.S.)
PAIS   MUSIC; s.a. Jazz music
BPI   MUSIC; s.a. Negroes

NEGRO NATIONALISM. *See* Black Muslims; Black Nationalism

NEGRO POETRY. *Use* Black Literature

NEGRO PRESS. *Use* Blacks and the Press

NEGRO RACE
LC ———; s.a. Color of man
SEARS NEGRO RACE (anthropological and biological aspects); s.a. Blacks (people and ethnic aspects); Blacks—Race identity; Race awareness
RG ———; s.a. Nationalism—Negro race; Negroes—Nationalism
NYT NEGROES (General); s.a. Negroes (in U.S.); Race
PAIS NEGROES; s.a. Minorities; Race relations
BPI NEGROES; s.a. Minorities; Race discrimination

NEGRO SPIRITUALS. *Use* Negro Music

NEGRO STUDENTS
LC ———; s.a. Negroes—Education; Students
SEARS BLACKS—EDUCATION; s.a. Black colleges; College students; Segregation in education
RG ———; s.a. Colleges and universities—Desegregation; Negro student militants
NYT COLLEGES AND UNIVERSITIES—U.S.—EQUAL EDUCATION; s.a. Education—U.S.—Equal education; Negroes (in U.S.)
PAIS ———; s.a. Negro colleges; Students
BPI NEGROES—EDUCATION; s.a. Discrimination in education; Public schools—Desegregation

NEGRO UNIVERSITIES AND COLLEGES. *Use* Black Colleges

NEGRO VETERANS. *Use* Negroes as Soldiers; Veterans

NEGRO YOUTH. *Use* Negro Children; Youth

NEGRO-ENGLISH DIALECTS
LC ———; s.a. Creole dialects
SEARS ENGLISH LANGUAGE—DIALECTS; s.a. Americanisms
RG ———; s.a. Americanisms (speech); English language—Dialects
NYT LANGUAGE AND LANGUAGES—ENGLISH
PAIS ENGLISH LANGUAGE; s.a. Languages
BPI ENGLISH LANGUAGE; s.a. Language and languages; Negroes

NEGRO-JEWISH RELATIONS
LC ———; s.a. subd. *Race question* under names of places, e.g., California—Race question
SEARS JEWISH QUESTION; s.a. Race problems
RG JEWS AND NEGROES; s.a. Interracial cooperation; Race relations
NYT NEGROES (In U.S.); s.a. Jews; Minorities
PAIS JEWISH-NEGRO RELATIONS; s.a. Negroes; Race relations
BPI NEGROES; s.a. Jews; Minorities

NEGROES
Scope: Works on Negroes in the U.S. For works on Negroes in particular states or localities see Negroes—(local subdivision). For works on Negroes of other continents or countries see Negroes in (name of country).
LC ———; s.a. Negro race; Segregation; U.S.—Race question; also headings beginning with the word Negro, e.g., Negroes—Economic conditions; Negroes as farmers, (as soldiers, etc.); Negroes in literature

SEARS BLACKS; s.a. Black Muslims; Black nationalism; Blacks—Political activity; Blacks—Race identity
RG ———; s.a. Black power; Interracial cooperation; Race relations
NYT NEGROES (In U.S.); s.a. Negroes (general); Race
PAIS ———; s.a. Afro-American studies; Black Muslim movement; Minorities
BPI ———; s.a. Black capitalism; Race discrimination

NEGROES—ECONOMIC CONDITIONS. *Use* Black Power; Discrimination in Employment; Negroes and Business; Poverty

NEGROES—EDUCATION. *Use* Black Colleges; Busing; Discrimination in Education; Negro Students

NEGROES—HOUSING. *Use* Discrimination in Housing; Housing; Tenements

NEGROES—INTEGRATION AND SEGREGATION. *Use* Busing; Civil Rights

NEGROES—MIGRATION. *Use* Migration, Internal

NEGROES—RACE IDENTITY. *Use* Black Power; Race Awareness

NEGROES—SEGREGATION. *Use* Discrimination in Education; Discrimination in Housing; Race Discrimination; Segregation

NEGROES AND BUSINESS
LC NEGROES AS BUSINESSMEN; s.a. Negroes as consumers; Negroes—Economic conditions
SEARS BLACK BUSINESSMEN; s.a. Blacks—Economic conditions; Consumers
RG NEGRO BUSINESSMEN; s.a. Black capitalism; Negro executives
NYT LABOR—U.S.—MINORITIES; s.a. Management, Industrial and institutional; Negroes (in U.S.); U.S.—Economic conditions and trends—Negroes (in U.S.)
PAIS NEGROES AS BUSINESSMEN; s.a. Advertising—Negroes, Appeal to; Businessmen; Negro market
BPI NEGROES AS BUSINESSMEN; s.a. Black capitalism; Minority business enterprises; Negro market; Negroes as executives; Television advertising—Negroes, Appeal to

NEGROES AS SOLDIERS
LC ———; s.a. European war, 1914–1918—Negroes; U.S.—History—Revolutionary [Civil war, etc.]—Negro troops; Negroes as seamen; World war, 1939-1945—Negroes
SEARS SOLDIERS; s.a. U.S. Army—Military life; Veterans
RG U.S.—ARMY—NEGROES; s.a. Negro veterans; Vietnamese War, 1957—Negroes
NYT U.S. ARMAMENTS AND DEFENSE—MINORITIES; s.a. Negroes (in U.S.); Race; Veterans
PAIS ———; s.a. U.S.—Armed forces—Negroes; Veterans
BPI SOLDIERS; s.a. Negroes; Veterans

NEGROES IN ART. *Use* Art and Race

NEGROES IN FICTION. *See* Negroes in Literature

NEGROES IN LITERATURE
LC ——; s.a. Characters and characteristics in literature; Negro authors
SEARS BLACKS IN LITERATURE AND ART; s.a. Black authors; Black literature
RG ——; s.a. Characters in literature; Negroes in children's literature
NYT BOOKS AND LITERATURE; s.a. Negroes (general); Negroes (in U.S.)
PAIS ——; s.a. African literature; Literature
BPI ——; s.a. Children's literature; Council on interracial books for children

NEGROES IN MOVING PICTURES. *Use* Moving Pictures

NEIGHBORHOOD
LC ——; s.a. Adjoining landowners; Community; Neighborliness; Social groups
SEARS COMMUNITY LIFE; s.a. Cities and towns; City planning; Community centers; Neighborhood schools
RG NEIGHBORHOODS; s.a. Citizens associations; Community life
NYT URBAN AREAS; s.a. Area planning and renewal; Community centers
PAIS NEIGHBORHOODS; s.a. Cities and towns; Neighborhood planning
BPI ——; s.a. Community development; Community life

NEIGHBORS. *Use* Human Relations

NEOFASCISM. *See* Totalitarianism

NEPOTISM. *Use* Patronage, Political

NERVOUS SYSTEM
LC ——; s.a. Mind and body; Nerves; Neurology; Relfexes
SEARS ——; s.a. Brain; Psychology, Pathological
RG ——; s.a. Biological control systems; Receptors, Neural; Synapses
NYT NERVES AND NERVOUS SYSTEM; s.a. Brain; Mental health and disorders
PAIS PHYSIOLOGY
BPI PSYCHOLOGY, PHYSIOLOGICAL; s.a. Brain; Physiology

NET NATIONAL PRODUCT. *See* National Income

NETBALL. *Use* Basketball

NETWORK ANALYSIS (Planning). *Use* Industrial Management; Operations Research

NEUROLOGY. *Use* Nervous System

NEUROSES
LC ——; s.a. Depression, Mental; Inferiority complex; names of particular neuroses, e.g., Anxiety, etc.; Traumatic neuroses
SEARS ——; s.a. Anxiety; Fear; Medicine, Psychosomatic
RG ——; s.a. Mentally ill; Psychoses; Traumatism; Shock

NYT MENTAL HEALTH AND DISORDERS; s.a. Medicine and health; Psychiatry and psychiatrists
PAIS MENTAL ILLNESS; s.a. Behavior (psychology); Mental hygiene; Mentally ill
BPI MENTAL ILLNESS; s.a. Depression, Mental; Psychology

NEUROTHERAPY. *Use* Osteopathy; Therapeutics

NEUTRALISM. *See* Neutrality

NEUTRALITY
See also subd. *Neutrality* under names of countries and of neutralized areas, e.g., Switzerland—Neutrality.
LC ——; s.a. Asylum, Right of; Blockade; Intervention (international law); Security, International; War (international law)
SEARS ——; s.a. International law; International relations
RG ——; s.a. Intervention (international law); Territorial waters
NYT ——; s.a. International relations; names of wars, e.g., World War II
PAIS ——; s.a. Commerce, Foreign; International law
BPI ——; s.a. Commerce; Maritime Law

NEUTRONS. *Use* Atoms; Nuclear Physics

NEW BUSINESS ENTERPRISES
LC ——; s.a. Industrial management; New products
SEARS BUSINESS; s.a. Commercial products; Corporations; Industrial management
RG BUSINESS ENTERPRISES, NEW. s.a. Products, New; Small business
NYT U. S.—ECONOMIC CONDITIONS AND TRENDS—SMALL BUSINESS; s.a. Executives; Labor—U. S.—Minorities
PAIS ——; s.a. Business; Industry
BPI ENTREPRENEUR; s.a. Black capitalism; Minority business enterprises; Products, New

NEW CITIES AND TOWNS. *Use* Cities and Towns

NEW LEFT. *See* Right and Left (Political science)

NEW LIFE STYLE. *See* Subculture

NEW PRODUCTS
LC ——; s.a. Design, Industrial; Research, Industrial
SEARS COMMERCIAL PRODUCTS
RG PRODUCTS, NEW; s.a. Design, Industrial; Quality of products
NYT MARKETING; s.a. Market research; Retail stores and trade
PAIS PRODUCTS, NEW; s.a. Commodities; Consumer goods; Design in industry; Product management
BPI PRODUCTS, NEW; s.a. Marketing; Product planning

NEW STATES. *See* State, The

NEW THOUGHT. *Use* Therapeutics, Suggestive

NEW TOWNS. *See* City Planning

NEWS. *Use* Current Events; Journalism

NEWS AGENCIES. *Use* Newspapers; Press

NEWS AND NEWS MEDIA. *Use* Blacks and the Press; Government and the Press; Journalism; Liberty of Speech; Newspapers; Press; Radio Stations; Reporters and Reporting; Television Broadcasting

NEWS BROADCASTS. *Use* Radio Broadcasting and Programs

NEWS PHOTOGRAPHERS
LC ———; s.a. Moving picture journalism; Photography, Commercial; Photography, Journalistic
SEARS PHOTOGRAPHY, JOURNALISTIC; s.a. Reporters and reporting
RG ———; s.a. Vietnamese war, 1957- —War correspondents and photographers
NYT PHOTOGRAPHY AND PHOTOGRAPHIC EQUIPMENT—NEWS PHOTOGRAPHY; s.a. News and news media
PAIS ———; s.a. Journalism; Photographers
BPI ———; s.a. Photographers; Photography, Journalistic

NEWSLETTERS. *Use* Journalism

NEWSPAPER—LETTERS TO THE EDITOR. *Use* Letter Writing

NEWSPAPERS
See also subd. by country, e.g., American (English, French, etc.) newspapers.
LC ———; s.a. Advertising, Newspaper; Foreign news; Journalistic ethics; News agencies
SEARS ———; s.a. Freedom of the press; Journalism; Periodicals
RG ———; s.a. Freedom of the press; Journalism; Newspaper publishers and publishing
NYT NEWS AND NEWS MEDIA; s.a. Freedom of the press; names of newspapers, e.g., Washington Post
PAIS ———; s.a. Press; Reporters and reporting
BPI ———; s.a. Audit bureau of circulation; Advertising, Newspaper; Freedom of the press

NEWSPAPERS, NEGRO. *Use* Blacks and the Press

NEWSPAPERS—OPINION POLLS. *Use* Public Opinion

NEWSPRINT. *Use* Paper Making and Trade

NICOTINE. *Use* Tobacco

NIGHT SCHOOLS. *See* Evening and Continuation Schools

NIGHT WORK
LC ———; s.a. Children—Employment; Shift systems
SEARS HOURS OF LABOR; s.a. Child labor; Woman—Employment
RG HOURS OF LABOR—SHIFT SCHEDULES; s.a. Overtime; Staggered hours
NYT LABOR; s.a. Labor—U. S.—Overtime and premium pay; Labor—U. S.—Wages and hours

PAIS ———; s.a. Hours of labor; Overtime
BPI HOURS OF LABOR; s.a. Hours of labor—Shift schedules; Overtime

NIHILISM. *Use* Terrorism

NITRATES. *Use* Fertilizers and Manures

NITRIFICATION. *Use* Bacteriology, Agricultural

NOBILITY. *Use* Aristocracy; Elite (Social sciences); Genealogy; Heads of State; Social Classes; Upper Classes

NOISE
See also subd. *Noise* under various subjects, e.g., Airplanes—Noise; Electronic noise; Radio noise; Traffic noise, etc.
LC ———; s.a. City noise; Jet plane sounds; Sound control; Traffic noise
SEARS ———; s.a. Noise pollution
RG ———; s.a. Noise control; Sound
NYT ———; s.a. Environment
PAIS ———; s.a. Municipal transport; Shock waves
BPI ———; s.a. Ear—Protection; Sound proofing

NOMADS. *Use* Society, Primitive; Tribes and Tribal System

NOMINATIONS FOR OFFICE. *Use* Politics, Practical

NONCONFORMITY. *See* Behavior (Psychology)

NONGRADED SCHOOLS
LC ———; s.a. Ability grouping in education; Grading and marking (students)
SEARS ———; s.a. Ability grouping in education; Education—Experimental methods
RG UNGRADED CLASSES; s.a. Ability grouping in education; Education—Organization by years; Grading and marking (students)
NYT EDUCATION AND SCHOOLS; s.a. Education and school—U.S.—Grading of students
PAIS SCHOOLS; s.a. Ability grouping in education; Grading and marking (students)
BPI EDUCATION; s.a. Schools

NONLINEAR THEORIES. *Use* System Analysis

NONMETALLIC MINERALS. *Use* Mineralogy

NONOBJECTIVE ART. *See* Art, Abstract; Modernism (Art)

NONPUBLIC SCHOOLS. *See* Church Schools

NONRESISTANCE. *Use* Nonviolence; Pacifism

NONSENSE VERSE. *Use* Wit and Humor

NONSUPPORT. *Use* Alimony

NONVERBAL COMMUNICATION. *Use* Communication; Deafness

NONVIOLENCE
LC ———; s.a. Boycott; Conscientious objectors; Evil, Nonresistance to; Pacifism
SEARS ———; s.a. Passive resistance; War and religion
RG ———; s.a. Pacifism; Passive resistance to government

NYT NONVIOLENCE (in connection with political issues, social change, etc.); s.a. Arms control and limitation and disarmament; War and revolution

PAIS PACIFISM; s.a. Passive resistance to government; Peace

BPI CONSCIENTIOUS OBJECTORS; s.a. Peace

NON-WAGE PAYMENTS

LC ———; s.a. Insurance, Social; Restricted stock options; Vacations, Employee; Welfare funds (trade-unions)

SEARS PROFIT SHARING; s.a. Cooperation; Wages

RG ———; s.a. Bonus system; Profit sharing

NYT LABOR; s.a. Labor—U. S.—Profitsharing; Pensions and retirement

PAIS ———; s.a. Employees' benefit plans; subd. *Benefits* under specific occupations, e.g., Executives—Benefits; Tipping

BPI ———; s.a. Disability benefits; Welfare funds (trade-unions)

NONWHITE PERSONS. *Use* Color of Man

NONWOVEN FABRICS. *Use* Substitute Products

NOVELS. *See* Fiction; Plots (Drama, novel, etc.)

NUCLEAR ENERGY. *See* Atomic Energy; Nuclear Reactions

NUCLEAR FISSION. *Use* Atomic Energy; Nuclear Reactions

NUCLEAR FUELS. *Use* Fuel; Nuclear Rockets

NUCLEAR FUSION. *Use* Atomic Energy; Nuclear Reactions

NUCLEAR PHYSICS

LC ———; s.a. Atomic energy; Atomic mass; Nuclear reactions; Radiation; Radioactivity

SEARS ———; s.a. Atoms; Electrons; Neutrons; Protons; Transmutation (chemistry)

RG ———; s.a. Particles (nuclear physics); Scattering (physics)

NYT NUCLEAR RESEARCH; s.a. Atomic energy and weapons; Elements; Physics

PAIS ———; s.a. Atomic research; Particle accelerators; Physics

BPI PHYSICS; s.a. Accelerators (electrons, etc.); Atomic power plants; Nuclear reactions

NUCLEAR PROPULSION. *Use* Nuclear Reactions; Nuclear Rockets

NUCLEAR REACTIONS

LC ———; s.a. Nuclear fission; Nuclear fusion; Radioactivity

SEARS ATOMIC ENERGY; s.a. Nuclear propulsion; Nuclear reactors; Radioisotopes

RG ———; s.a. Radioactive dating

NYT ATOMIC ENERGY AND WEAPONS; s.a. Cyclotrons; Nuclear research; Radiation

PAIS ATOMIC POWER; s.a. Nuclear engineering; Nuclear physics

BPI ———; s.a. Atomic blasting; Atomic power plants

NUCLEAR REACTORS. *Use* Atomic Energy

NUCLEAR RESEARCH. *Use* Atomic Energy; Atoms; Nuclear Physics; Nuclear Reactions; Radiation

NUCLEAR ROCKETS

LC ———; s.a. Nuclear fuels; Photon rockets; Space vehicles—Propulsion systems

SEARS ROCKETS (Aeronautics); s.a. Artificial satellites—Launching; Ballistic missiles

RG ROCKETS, ATOMIC POWERED; s.a. Space vehicles—Atomic power plants; Space vehicles—Propulsion systems

NYT ATOMIC ENERGY AND WEAPONS—U. S.—ROCKET PROPULSION; s.a. Nuclear research; Rockets and rocket propulsion

PAIS ROCKETS, ATOMIC POWERED; s.a. Atomic warfare

BPI ROCKETS, ATOMIC POWERED; s.a. Atomic weapons; Rockets

NUCLEAR TEST BAN. *See* Disarmament

NUCLEAR WARFARE. *See* Atomic Warfare

NUCLEAR WEAPONS. *See* Atomic Weapons

NUDE IN ART

LC ———; s.a. Figure painting; Human figure in art; Photography of the nude

SEARS NUDITY IN PERFORMING ARTS; s.a. Performing arts

RG ———; s.a. Human figure in art; Human figure in photography; Sex in art; Women in art

NYT NUDISM AND NUDITY, s.a. Art; Pornography; Theater—Censorship

PAIS NUDITY; s.a. Art

BPI NUDISM; s.a. Art

NULLIFICATION. *Use* State Rights

NUMBERS, RANDOM. *Use* Sampling (Statistics)

NUMERICAL CONTROL. *Use* Automatic Control

NUMISMATICS

Scope: Works dealing with coins, medals, tokens, etc., collectively; also works dealing with coins alone. See *Coins* for lists of coins, specimens, etc.

LC ———; s.a. Coin hoards; Collectors and collecting Jettons; Medals

SEARS ———; s.a. Coins; Seals (numismatics)

RG ———; s.a. Coins; Medals

NYT MONEY, OLD AND RARE; s.a. Medals

PAIS ———; s.a. Coins; Medals

BPI COINS; s.a. Medals; Mints

NUNCIOS, PAPAL. *Use* Papacy

NUNS. *Use* Monastic and Religious Life of Women

NURSERIES

LC ———; s.a. Children—Care and hygiene; Day nurseries; Infants—Care and hygiene; Play schools

NURSERIES, *cont.*
SEARS DAY NURSERIES; s.a. Children—Institutional care; Kindergarten; Nursery schools
RG   NURSERY SCHOOLS; s.a. Day nurseries; Play schools
NYT   DAY CARE CENTERS FOR CHILDREN; s.a. Children—Behavior and Training
PAIS NURSERY SCHOOLS; s.a. Child welfare; Day Nurseries; Education, Preschool
BPI   DAY NURSERIES; s.a. Child welfare; Children—Care and hygiene

NURSERIES (Horticulture). *Use* Floriculture; Horticulture

NURSERIES, DAY. *See* Nurseries

NURSERY RHYMES. *Use* Children's Literature

NURSERY SCHOOLS. *Use* Education, Preschool; Education, Primary; Nurseries

NURSES AND NURSING
LC   ——; s.a. Care of the sick; Children—Care and hygiene; Geriatric nursing; Home nursing; Sick; Surgical nursing; subd. *Hospitals, charities, etc.* and *Medical and sanitary affairs* under names of wars, e.g., Crimean war—Medical and sanitary affairs; Therapeutics.
SEARS ——; s.a. Cookery for the sick; First aid; Institutional care; Practical nurses and nursing; School nurses
RG   ——; s.a. Medical service; Nurse and patient; School nursing

NYT   NURSING AND NURSES; s.a. Medicine and health—U. S.—Professional personnel; Nursing homes
PAIS NURSING; s.a. Hospitals—Home care program; Practical nursing; Public health nursing
BPI   ——; s.a. Home health care; Medical care

NURSING ETHICS. *Use* Medical Ethics

NURSING HOMES
LC   ——; s.a. Geriatric nursing; Invalids; Rest homes; Sick
SEARS AGED—DWELLINGS; s.a. Institutional care; Nurses and nursing; Retirement
RG   ——; s.a. Aged—Housing; Old age homes
NYT   ——; s.a. Aged and age; Medicine and health
PAIS ——; s.a. Old age homes; Old age—Housing
BPI   ——; s.a. Nurses and nursing; Old age homes

NUTRITION
LC   ——; s.a. Artificial feeding; Cookery; Deficiency diseases; Food habits; Food supply; Minerals in the body; Survival and emergency rations; Therapeutics
SEARS ——; s.a. Digestion; Metabolism; Physiological chemistry; Weight control
RG   ——; s.a. Starvation; subd. *Nutrition* under names of groups, e.g., Aged—Nutrition, etc.; Vitamins
NYT   FOOD AND GROCERY TRADE—DIET AND NUTRITION; s.a. Weight
PAIS ——; s.a. Diet; Hunger
BPI   ——; s.a. Diet; Food; Malnutrition

NYLON. *Use* Substitute Products

O

OTC. *See* Over-the-counter Markets

OATH OF ALLEGIANCE. *Use* Internal Security; Loyalty; Oaths

OATHS
Scope: Works on judicial or official oaths; for works on profane language see Swearing; for works in the legal and theological sense see Blasphemy.
LC   ——; s.a. Affidavits; Perjury; Vows
SEARS LAW; s.a. Internal security; Witnesses
RG   ——; s.a. Loyalty, Oaths of; Promises
NYT   ——; s.a. Loyalty oaths and tests; Oath of allegiance; Perjury
PAIS ——; s.a. Law; Loyalty oaths
BPI   LOYALTY; s.a. Loyalty, Organizational

OBEDIENCE, VOW OF. *Use* Monastic and Religious Life of Women; Monasticism and Religious Orders

OBESITY. *See* Weight Control

OBITUARIES
LC   ——; s.a. Biography; Dead; Funeral sermons
SEARS ——; s.a. Biography
RG   ——; s.a. Bereavement; Biography; Funeral rites and ceremonies
NYT   DEATHS; s.a. Funerals
PAIS ——; s.a. Biography; Death
BPI   BIOGRAPHY; s.a. Death

OBJECTIVE TESTS. *See* Personality Tests; Tests, Mental

OBLIGATIONS
LC   OBLIGATIONS (Law); s.a. Debtor and creditor; Natural obligations
SEARS CIVIL LAW; s.a. Contracts
RG   LIABILITY (Law); s.a. Damages; Torts
NYT   CONTRACTS; s.a. Guarantees and warranties; Legal profession; Liability for products, Manufacturers'

PAIS   LAW; s.a. Damages; Liability; Products liability

BPI   LIABILITY; s.a. Damages; Employers liability; Products liability

OBSCENITY
LC   OBSCENITY (Law); s.a. Art, Immoral; Erotic literature; Postal service—Laws and regulations; Trials (obscenity)

SEARS   OBSCENITY (Law); s.a. Pornography

RG   OBSCENITY (Law); s.a. Censorship; Postal censorship

NYT   PORNOGRAPHY AND OBSCENITY; s.a. Books and literature—Censorship and bans; Magazines—Censorship and bans

PAIS   ——; s.a. Censorship; Pornography

BPI   ——; s.a. Censorship; Freedom of the press

OBSERVATION (Educational method)
LC   ——; s.a. Interaction analysis in education; Teachers, Training of

SEARS   EDUCATION—STUDY AND TEACHING; s.a. Student teaching

RG   EDUCATION—STUDY AND TEACHING; s.a. Student teaching; Teachers—Education

NYT   EDUCATION AND SCHOOLS; s.a. Teachers and school employees

PAIS   TEACHERS—RATING; s.a. Teachers—Training

BPI   TEACHERS, TRAINING OF; s.a. Education; Teaching

OBSOLESCENCE. *Use* Depreciation; Machinery; Technological Innovations

OBSTETRICS. *Use* Childbirth; Labor (Obstetrics)

OCCULT SCIENCES
LC   ——; s.a. Astrology; Clairvoyance; Divination; Geomancy; Ghosts; Supernatural

SEARS   ——; s.a. Apparitions; Fortune telling; Palmistry; Spiritualism; Witchcraft

RG   ——; s.a. Hallucinations and illusions; Magic; Mediums; Parapsychology; Satanism

NYT   ——; s.a. Astrology; Psychic phenomena; Superstitions

PAIS   ——; s.a. Extrasensory perception

BPI   OCCULT LITERATURE; s.a. Extrasensory perception

OCCUPATION, CHOICE OF. *See* Vocational Guidance

OCCUPATIONAL APTITUDE TESTS
LC   ——; s.a. Employment tests; Vocational qualifications

SEARS   ABILITY TESTING; s.a. Educational tests and measurements; Mental tests

RG   APTITUDE TESTS; s.a. Educational tests and measurements; Intelligence tests

NYT   MENTAL TESTS; s.a. Labor—U. S.—Discrimination

PAIS   EMPLOYMENT TESTS; s.a. Tests, Ability; Tests, Mental

BPI   ABILITY TESTS; s.a. Occupations; Personality tests

OCCUPATIONAL DISEASES. *Use* Occupations, Dangerous; Workmen's Compensation

OCCUPATIONAL MOBILITY
Scope: Includes works on freedom from social pressure in the choice of particular occupations or professions, e.g., the ambition of the child of a carpenter to become a doctor.

LC   ——; s.a. Labor supply; Migration, Internal; Social mobility; Vocational interests

SEARS   OCCUPATIONS; s.a. Labor turnover

RG   ——; s.a. Labor mobility; Labor turnover

NYT   LABOR

PAIS   ——; s.a. Labor mobility; Labor turnover

BPI   ——; s.a. Labor mobility; Migrant labor

OCCUPATIONAL MORTALITY. *Use* Mortality; Occupations, Dangerous

OCCUPATIONAL RETRAINING. *See* Occupational Training

OCCUPATIONAL THERAPY
LC   ——; s.a. Art therapy; Industrial arts; Invalids; Invalids—Occupations; Music therapy; Recreational therapy

SEARS   ——; s.a. Handicraft; Physical therapy; Rehabilitation; Therapeutics

RG   ——; s.a. Recreational therapy; Rehabilitation

NYT   HANDICAPPED

PAIS   ——; s.a. Disabled—Rehabilitation; Retraining, Occupational

BPI   VOCATIONAL REHABILITATION; s.a. Occupational training

OCCUPATIONAL TRAINING
Scope: Works on teaching people a skill after formal education; for teaching a skill during the educational process see Vocational education; for on the job training use Employees—Training; for retraining use Retraining, Occupational.

LC   ——; s.a. Manpower policy; Occupational therapy; Retraining, Occupational; Technical education

SEARS   ——; s.a. Employees—Training; Technical education

RG   VOCATIONAL EDUCATION; s.a. Education, Cooperative; Retraining, Occupational; Trade schools

NYT   LABOR; s.a. Commercial education

PAIS   EMPLOYEES—TRAINING; s.a. Apprenticeship; Retraining, Occupational; Vocational education

BPI   ——; s.a. Employees, Training of; Hard-core unemployed, Training

OCCUPATIONS
See also types of occupations, e.g., Clerks.

LC   ——; s.a. Civil service positions; Free choice of employment; Occupations and race; Job descriptions; (name of field) as a profession, e.g., Music as a profession; Occupational mobility

SEARS   ——; s.a. Handicrafts; Job analysis; Professions

RG   ——; s.a. Professions; subd. *Occupations* under names of groups, e.g., Women—Occupations

OCCUPATIONS, *cont.*

NYT   LABOR; s.a. Names of trades, e.g., Carpentry and carpenters; Professions

PAIS   ——; s.a. Job analysis; Professionalism

BPI   ——; s.a. Job evaluation; Professions; Vocational guidance

OCCUPATIONS, DANGEROUS

See also subd. *Diseases and hygiene* under types of workers, e.g., Printers—Diseases and hygiene; etc.

LC   ——; s.a. Accident law; Employers liability; Industrial accidents; Medicine, Industrial

SEARS   ——; s.a. Accidents; Occupational diseases

RG   OCCUPATIONS, HAZARDOUS; s.a. Accidents, Industrial; Industrial safety; Lungs—Dust diseases

NYT   LABOR; s.a. Medicine and health; Workmen's compensation insurance

PAIS   ——; s.a. Accidents, Industrial; Industrial medicine; Workmen's compensation

BPI   ——; s.a. Employers liability; Lead poisoning; Personal injuries

OCCUPATIONS AND RACE. *Use* Discrimination in Employment; Occupational Mobility

OCEAN. *Use* Marine Ecology; Oceanography; Seashore; Underwater Exploration

OCEAN LINERS. *Use* Merchant Marine; Ocean Travel

OCEAN TRAVEL

LC   ——; s.a. Merchant ships. Steamboat lines; Travel; Voyages and travel; Yachts and yachting

SEARS   ——; s.a. Sailing; Ships; Yachts and yachting

RG   ——; s.a. Cruising; Shipwrecks; Voyages

NYT   OCEAN VOYAGES; s.a. Boats and yachts; Ships and shipping; Travel and resorts

PAIS   OCEAN LINERS; s.a. Cruising; Shipping—Passenger service; Yachting

BPI   ——; s.a. Steamship lines; Steamships; Yachts and yachting

OCEANOGRAPHY

Scope: Works on the scientific study of the ocean and its phenomena. See Ocean for geographical descriptions of the world's oceans.

LC   ——; s.a. Coasts; Diving, Submarine; Marine biology; names of oceans, e.g., Arctic ocean; Submarine geology

SEARS   ——; s.a. Marine mineral resources; Ocean waves; Seashore; Underwater explorations

RG   ——; s.a. Marine pollution; Marine sediments; Meteorology, Maritime; Sounding and Soundings; Waves

NYT   OCEANS AND OCEANOGRAPHY; s.a. Marine biology; Tides; Water pollution

PAIS   ——; s.a. Continental shelf; Marine research; Ocean bottom; Sea water

BPI   ——; s.a. Diving, Submarine; Marine resources; Ocean bottom

OCEANOLOGY. *See* Oceanography

OFFENSES AGAINST PROPERTY. *Use* Offenses Against the Person and Property

OFFENSES AGAINST PUBLIC SAFETY

LC   ——; s.a. Crimes aboard aircraft; Sabotage

SEARS   ——; s.a. Hijacking of airplanes

RG   CRIME AND CRIMINALS; s.a. Airplane hijacking; Riots

NYT   CRIME AND CRIMINALS; s.a. Bombs and bomb plots; Riots

PAIS   See names of offenses against public safety, e.g., Sabotage; s.a. Air transport—Crimes

BPI   CRIME AND CRIMINALS; s.a. Aeronautics—Crimes; Arson

OFFENSES AGAINST THE PERSON AND PROPERTY

See also specific offenses against persons, e.g., Abduction; Assassination; False imprisonment; Homicide; Kidnapping; etc. and specific offenses against property, e.g., Arson; Burglary; Poaching; Robbery; etc.

LC   OFFENSES AGAINST THE PERSON; s.a. Offenses against property

SEARS   OFFENSES AGAINST THE PERSON; s.a. Crime and criminals

RG   OFFENSES AGAINST THE PERSON; s.a. Criminal law; Justice, Administration of

NYT   CRIME AND CRIMINALS

PAIS   CRIME AND CRIMINALS; s.a. Criminal law

BPI   CRIME AND CRIMINALS; s.a. Offenses against property

OFFICE ADMINISTRATION. *See* Office Management

OFFICE BUILDINGS

See also subd. *Office buildings* under names of cities.

LC   ——; s.a. Employees' buildings and facilities; Landlord and tenant; Offices; Real estate management

SEARS   ——; s.a. Industrial buildings; Skyscrapers

RG   ——; s.a. Bank buildings; County buildings; Office layout; Skyscrapers

NYT   OFFICE BUILDINGS AND OTHER COMMERCIAL PROPERTIES; s.a. Area planning and renewal; Buildings; Urban areas

PAIS   ——; s.a. Buildings; Real estate business

BPI   ——; s.a. Condominium (office buildings); Real estate management

OFFICE DECORATION. *Use* Interior Decoration

OFFICE EMPLOYEES

LC   CLERKS; s.a. Bank employees; Clerical occupations; Receptionists

SEARS   CLERKS; s.a. Salesmen and salesmanship

RG   OFFICE WORKERS; s.a. Corporation secretaries; Secretaries

NYT   WHITE COLLAR WORKERS; s.a. Professions; Secretaries

PAIS   ——; s.a. Secretaries; White collar employees

BPI   OFFICE WORKERS; s.a. Secretaries, Private; Typists; Wages and salaries—Office workers

OFFICE EQUIPMENT AND SUPPLIES

LC   ——; s.a. Electronic office machines; Office practice—Automation; Writing—Materials and instruments

SEARS ——; s.a. Calculating machines; Typewriters
RG ——; s.a. Calculating machines, Electronic; Computers—Business use
NYT OFFICE EQUIPMENT; s.a. Adding machines
PAIS OFFICE EQUIPMENT; s.a. Computers; Copying processes; Electronic data and processing equipment
BPI ——; s.a. Accounting machines; Addressing machines and devices; Copying machines

OFFICE LANDSCAPING. *See* Interior Decoration; Office Buildings

OFFICE LAYOUT. *Use* Interior Decoration; Office Buildings; Office Management

OFFICE MACHINES. *See* Office Equipment and Supplies

OFFICE MANAGEMENT
LC ——; s.a. Business records; Institution management; Office layout; Office procedures; Organization; Public records; Supervision of employees
SEARS ——; s.a. Business education; Personnel management; Secretaries
RG ——; s.a. Communication in management; Job satisfaction
NYT MANAGEMENT, INDUSTRIAL AND INSTITUTIONAL; s.a. Commercial education; White collar workers
PAIS ——; s.a. Files and filing (documents); Industrial management; Management; Office practice; Shorthand reporting
BPI ——; s.a. Files and filing; Office methods; Personnel management; Transcription departments

OFFICE PRACTICE. *Use* Clerks; Files and Filing (Documents); Office Management; Secretaries

OFFICE PRACTICE—AUTOMATION. *Use* Office Equipment and Supplies

OFFICE PRACTICE IN GOVERNMENT. *Use* Public Administration

OFFICE RECORDS. *See* Business Records

OFFICE WORK—TRAINING. *See* Business Education

OFFICE WORKERS. *Use* Clerks; Office Employees; Secretaries

OFFICIAL PUBLICATIONS. *See* Government and the Press; Government Publications

OFFICIAL SECRETS
LC ——; s.a. Censorship; Confidential communications; Defense information, Classified; Executive privilege (government information); Freedom of information
SEARS INTERNAL SECURITY; s.a. Government and the press; Government publications
RG ——; s.a. Defense information, Classified; Government and the press
NYT POLITICS AND GOVERNMENT; s.a. Espionage; News and news media; U. S.—Internal security
PAIS ——; s.a. Secrecy (law); Security classification (government documents)

BPI ——; s.a. Pentagon papers; Security classification (government documents)

OFFICIALS AND EMPLOYEES. *Use* Municipal Officials and Employees

OFFSET PRINTING. *Use* Printing Industry

OIL—POLLUTION
LC OIL POLLUTION OF RIVERS, HARBORS, ETC.; s.a. Oil tagging; Water—Pollution
SEARS ——; s.a. Marine pollution; Pollution
RG OIL POLLUTION OF RIVERS, HARBORS, ETC.; s.a. Marine pollution; Water pollution
NYT WATER POLLUTION—OIL; s.a. Air pollution; Oil (petroleum) and gasoline
PAIS OIL POLLUTION OF RIVERS, HARBORS, ETC.; s.a. Petroleum industry; Water pollution
BPI OIL POLLUTION OF RIVERS, HARBORS, ETC; s.a. Petroleum waste; Pollution control in industry

OIL AND GAS LEASES. *Use* Mines and Mineral Resources; Petroleum Industry and Trade

OIL BURNERS. *Use* Heating

OIL COMPANIES. *Use* Petroleum Industry and Trade

OIL FIELDS
LC ——; s.a. Oil sands; Oil wells; Petroleum; Secondary recovery of oil
SEARS PETROLEUM; s.a. Petroleum industry and trade
RG OIL LANDS; s.a. Petroleum; Petroleum in submerged lands
NYT OIL (Petroleum) AND GASOLINE; s.a. Fuel; names of companies, e g , Gulf Oil Corporation
PAIS ——; s.a. Petroleum industry
BPI OIL LANDS; s.a. Oil fuel industry; Petroleum industry

OIL INDUSTRIES
LC ——; s.a. Names of individual oils, e.g. Cottonseed oil; etc.
SEARS PETROLEUM INDUSTRY AND TRADE
RG ——; s.a. Fuel industry; Petroleum industry and trade
NYT OIL (Petroleum) AND GASOLINE; s.a. Fields of use, e.g., Heating; Fuel; Taxation
PAIS PETROLEUM INDUSTRY; s.a. Gasoline industry; Oil fuel industry
BPI ——; s.a. Mineral oils; Oils and fats

OIL LANDS. *Use* Oil Fields; Petroleum Industry and Trade

OIL POLLUTION OF RIVERS, HARBORS, ETC. *Use* Oil—Pollution; Water—Pollution

OIL RECLAMATION. *Use* Lubrication and Lubricants; Petroleum Industry and Trade

OIL REFINERIES. *See* Petroleum Industry and Trade

OIL SANDS. *Use* Oil Fields

OIL WELLS. *See* Oil Fields; Petroleum Industry and Trade

OILS AND FATS
Scope: Works on the technological aspects of oils and fats. See Oil industries for works on the economic aspects. See also names of particular oils and fats, e.g. Butter.
LC   ——; s.a. Coal-tar products; Drying oils; Lubrication and lubricants; Oil industries
SEARS   ——; s.a. Essences and essential oils; Petroleum
RG   OILS AND FATS, EDIBLE; s.a. Essences and essential oils; Foods—Fat content
NYT   ——; s.a. Food and grocery trade
PAIS   ——; s.a. Cottonseed oil industry; Margarine industry
BPI   ——; s.a. Essences and essential oils; Mineral oils

OILSEED INDUSTRY. *See* Oil Industries

OLD AGE
LC   ——; s.a. Age (psychology); Aged; Aging; Geriatrics; Old age assistance
SEARS   ——; s.a. Life (biology); Physiology; Retirement
RG   ——; s.a. Centenarians; Gerontology; Mortality; Retirement
NYT   AGED AND AGE; s.a. Longevity; Medicine and health
PAIS   ——; s.a. Age and employment; Longevity; Working life, Length of
BPI   ——; s.a. Aged; Aging; Life expectancy; Retirement

OLD AGE—DISEASES. *See* Geriatrics

OLD AGE—HOUSING. *Use* Nursing Homes; Old Age Homes

OLD AGE—MEDICAL CARE. *Use* Medical Care

OLD AGE ASSISTANCE
LC   ——; s.a. Aged—Medical care; Retirement pensions; subd. *Salaries, pensions, etc.* under names of industries, professions, trades, etc., e.g., Teachers—Salaries, pensions, etc.; Welfare funds (trade-union)
SEARS   OLD AGE PENSIONS; s.a. Annuities; Pensions; Saving and thrift
RG   ——; s.a. Insurance, Social; Old age pensions; Retirement income; Social security taxes
NYT   MEDICINE AND HEALTH—U. S.—HEALTH AND HOSPITAL INSURANCE AND RELATED GOVERNMENT AID; s.a. Aged and age; Labor—U. S.—Pensions and retirement; Medicaid; Pensions and retirement; Social insurance
PAIS   ——; s.a. Insurance, Social; Pensions, Old age; Public welfare
BPI   OLD AGE; s.a. Aged—Care and hygiene; Old age pensions; Retirement; Self-employed, Pensions

OLD AGE HOMES
LC   ——; s.a. Public institutions; Rest homes; subd. *Charities* under religious denominations, fraternal orders, etc., e.g., Daughters of Israel—Charities

SEARS   AGED—DWELLINGS; s.a. Aged—Institutional care; Public welfare
RG   ——; s.a. Aged—Housing; Nursing homes
NYT   NURSING HOMES; s.a. Aged and age; Medicine and health
PAIS   ——; s.a. Nursing homes; Old age—Housing
BPI   ——; s.a. Aged; Nursing homes

OLD AGE PENSIONS. *Use* Insurance, Social; Old Age Assistance; Pensions; Retirement; Saving and Savings; Survivor's Benefits; Welfare Economics

OLDER WORKERS. *See* Age and Employment; Discrimination in Employment

OLIGOPOLIES. *Use* Big Business; Competition; Monopolies; Prices

OMENS. *Use* Signs and Symbols

ON LINE DATA PROCESSING. *Use* Data Transmission Systems

ONANISM. *See* Sex

ONTOGENY. *Use* Embryology

ONTOLOGY. *Use* Existentialism; Life

OP ART. *See* Optical Art

OPEN AND CLOSED SHOP
LC   ——; s.a. Collective bargaining; Union label; Union shop; Yellow dog contract
SEARS   ——; s.a. Labor contract; Labor unions
RG   ——; s.a. Discrimination in employment; Labor laws and legislation—U.S.; Right to labor
NYT   LABOR; s.a. Labor—U.S.—Union security
PAIS   ——; s.a. Collective labor agreements; Trade unions
BPI   ——; s.a. Collective labor agreements; Trade unions

OPEN CORRIDOR SCHOOLS. *See* Nongraded Schools

OPEN MARRIAGE. *See* Adultery; Family; Subculture

OPEN PLAN SCHOOLS. *Use* Education, Primary; Educational Planning and Innovations

OPEN PULPITS. *Use* Preaching

OPEN SEA. *See* Freedom of the Seas

OPEN-PIT MINING. *See* Mines and Mineral Resources

OPERA
Scope: For collections of miscellaneous librettos see Librettos; for works on history and criticism and on libretto writing see Libretto.
LC   ——; s.a. Ballet; Musical reviews, comedies, etc.; Opera, English; Opera, Italian; etc.; Radio operas
SEARS   ——; s.a. Music—History and criticism; Operas—Librettos; Operas—Stories, plots, etc.; Operetta; Vocal music
RG   ——; s.a. Librettists
NYT   ——; s.a. Music
PAIS   ——; s.a. Music
BPI   ——; s.a. Music

OPERA HOUSES. *Use* Theaters

OPERANT CONDITIONING. *Use* Conditioned Response

OPERATING ROOMS. *Use* Hospitals; Operations, Surgical; Surgery

OPERATIONAL ANALYSIS. *See* Operations Research

OPERATIONAL GAMING. *Use* Management Games

OPERATIONS, SURGICAL
Scope: Works on the risks and accidents of surgical operations, treatment of patients after operations, mortality, and other generalities.
LC ———; s.a. Postoperative care; Surgery, Aseptic and antiseptic; Surgery, Operative; Surgical nursing
SEARS SURGERY; s.a. Orthopedia; Transplantation of organs, tissues, etc.
RG SURGERY; s.a. Anesthesia; subd. *Surgery* under names of organs and parts of body, e.g., Throat—Surgery
NYT SURGERY AND SURGEONS; s.a. Anesthesia; Heart—Transplants
PAIS SURGERY; s.a. Surgeons; Transplantation of organs, tissues, etc.
BPI SURGERY; s.a. Anesthetics; Cryosurgery

OPERATIONS RESEARCH
LC ———; s.a. Network analysis (planning); Research, Industrial; Simulation methods; Systems engineering
SEARS ———; s.a. Models and model making; Queing theory; Systems engineering
RG ———; s.a. Critical path analysis; Network analysis (planning); Systems management
NYT SYSTEMS ANALYSIS; s.a. Engineering and engineers; Industrial research
PAIS ———; s.a. Economic models; Industrial management; PERT (network analysis); Research; Systems in management
BPI ———; s.a. Critical path analysis; Industrial research; Mathematical models; Simulation methods; Systems in management

OPERETTA. *Use* Opera

OPHTHALMOLOGY. *Use* Eye

OPIATES. *See* Narcotics

OPINION, PUBLIC. *See* Public Opinion

OPIUM HABIT. *Use* Narcotic Habit

OPIUM TRADE. *Use* Narcotics, Control of

OPTICAL ART
LC ———; s.a. Kinetic art; Visual perception
SEARS ART, MODERN—20TH CENTURY; s.a. Art, Abstract
RG ART, MODERN; s.a. Art, Abstract; Paintings
NYT ART; s.a. Art objects
PAIS ART
BPI ART; s.a. Artists; Paintings

OPTICAL DATA PROCESSING. *Use* Data Transmission Systems; Information Storage and Retrieval Systems

OPTICAL INDUSTRY. *Use* Optical Trade; Optics

OPTICAL INSTRUMENTS. *Use* Optical Trade; Scientific Apparatus and Instruments

OPTICAL TRADE
LC ———; s.a. names of individual instruments, e.g., Eriometer, Spectroscope; Optical instruments
SEARS SCIENTIFIC APPARATUS AND INSTRUMENTS; s.a. Optical data processing; Photography—Equipment and supplies
RG ———; s.a. Lenses; Measuring instruments, Optical; Photographic apparatus industry and trade
NYT OPTICAL GOODS; s.a. Eyeglasses; Microscopes and microscopy; Telescopes
PAIS ———; s.a. Optical instruments industry; Scientific apparatus and instruments
BPI OPTICAL INDUSTRY; s.a. Optical instruments; Remote sensing systems

OPTICS
LC ———; s.a. Color; Spectrum analysis
SEARS ———; s.a. Light; Photometry
RG ———; s.a. Perspective; Reflection (optics)
NYT ———; s.a. Eyes and eyesight; Light; Optical goods
PAIS LIGHTING; s.a. Light amplifiers
BPI ———; s.a. Electron optics; Fiber optics; Spectrum analysis

OPTICS, PHYSIOLOGICAL. *Use* Eye

OPTOMETRY. *Use* Eye

ORACLES. *Use* Prophecies

ORAL COMMUNICATION. *Use* Speech

ORAL HISTORY. *Use* Historical Research

ORAL TRADITION. *Use* Folklore

ORATIONS. *Use* Oratory; Public Speaking; Speeches, Addresses, etc.

ORATORY
Scope: Works dealing with the rhetorical aspects of speeches. See Public speaking for works dealing with the problems of speaking effectively in public. For collections of speeches see After dinner speeches; Orations; Speeches, addresses, etc.
LC ———; s.a. Classical orations; Debates and debating; Persuasion (rhetoric); subd. *Oratory* under names of persons, e.g., King, Martin Luther—Oratory; Voice; Voice culture
SEARS PUBLIC SPEAKING; s.a. Lectures and lecturing; Orations; Preaching; Rhetoric
RG ———; s.a. Baccalaureate addresses; Public speaking; Rhetoric; Speeches, addresses, etc.
NYT SPEECHES AND STATEMENTS (general); s.a. Debating; Speech
PAIS PUBLIC SPEAKING; s.a. Debating; Speeches, addresses, etc.
BPI PUBLIC SPEAKING; s.a. Television public speaking

ORBITING VEHICLES. *See* Artificial Satellites (American; Russian; etc.); Astronautics; Space Flight

ORCHESTRA
LC ——; s.a. Bands (music); Dance music; Orchestral music; subd. *Orchestras and bands* under names of universities and colleges, e.g., Baruch College—Orchestras and bands
SEARS ORCHESTRAS; s.a. Conductors (music); Instrumentation and orchestration
RG ORCHESTRAS; s.a. Bands (music); Ensemble playing; Instrumental music
NYT MUSIC—ORCHESTRAS AND OTHER MUSIC GROUPS; s.a. Music
PAIS ORCHESTRAS; s.a. Music; Opera
BPI ORCHESTRAS; s.a. Bands; Composers

ORCHESTRATION. *See* Music

ORDER PROCESSING. *Use* Marketing

ORDINANCES, MUNICIPAL
LC ——; s.a. Model ordinances; Municipal corporations; Statutes
SEARS CITIES AND TOWNS—LAWS AND LEGISLATION; s.a. Administrative law; Municipal government
RG MUNICIPAL ORDINANCES; s.a. Administrative law; Local government
NYT LOCAL GOVERNMENT
PAIS MUNICIPAL ORDINANCES; s.a. Municipal law; subd. *Ordinances* under specific subjects, e.g., Zoning—Ordinances
BPI MUNICIPAL GOVERNMENT; s.a. Local government; Zoning

ORDNANCE
LC ——; s.a. Atomic weapons; subd. *Ordnance and ordnance stores* under names of armies and navies, e.g., U.S. Army—Ordnance and ordnance stores; Weapons
SEARS ——; s.a. Bombs; Projectiles
RG ——; s.a. Armaments; Weapons systems
NYT ARMAMENT, DEFENSE AND MILITARY FORCES; s.a. Arms control; Missiles; U.S. armament and defense
PAIS ——; s.a. Armaments; Rocket launchers (ordnance)
BPI ——; s.a. Gunnery; Weapons systems

ORE DRESSING. *Use* Steel Industry and Trade

ORES. *Use* Mines and Mineral Resources

ORGANICULTURE. *Use* Horticulture

ORGANIZATION
LC ——; s.a. Industrial organization; Planning
SEARS MANAGEMENT; s.a. Efficiency, Industrial; Office management
RG INDUSTRIAL MANAGEMENT AND ORGANIZATION; s.a. Business management and organization; Communication in management; Organizational change
NYT MANAGEMENT, INDUSTRIAL AND INSTITUTIONAL; s.a. Executives
PAIS ORGANIZATION, THEORY OF; s.a. Industrial management; Management
BPI ——; s.a. Centralization in management; Industrial management; Management

ORGANIZATIONS, SOCIETIES, AND CLUBS. *Use* Clubs; Secret Societies; Trade and Professional Associations

ORGANIZED CRIME. *See* Crime and Criminals; Racketeering

ORGANIZED LABOR. *See* Trade-Unions

ORGANOTHERAPY. *Use* Therapeutics

ORGANS, ARTIFICIAL. *See* Artificial Organs

ORGASM. *Use* Sex

ORIENT. *See* Near East

ORIENT AND OCCIDENT. *See* East and West

ORIENTAL STUDIES
LC ——; s.a. Assyriology; Byzantine studies; Egyptology; Oriental philology
SEARS CIVILIZATION, ORIENTAL; s.a. Art, Oriental; East and west
RG ——; s.a. Area studies; Chinese studies (Sinology)
NYT AREA STUDIES; s.a. Language and languages—(name of language), e.g., Language and Languages—Japanese; names of areas, e.g., Far East
PAIS ——; s.a. Area studies; Asia; subd. *Languages* under name of specific countries, e.g., China (People's Republic)—Languages
BPI INTERCULTURAL EDUCATION; s.a. Asia; China; Far East

ORIGAMI. *Use* Handicraft

ORIGIN OF LIFE. *See* Life

ORIGIN OF MAN. *See* Man

ORIGIN OF SPECIES. *Use* Evolution; Genetics

ORNAMENTAL PLANTS. *See* Plants

ORNITHOLOGY. *Use* Birds

ORPHANS
LC ORPHANS AND ORPHAN-ASYLUMS; s.a. Abandoned children; Foundlings; Maternal and infant welfare; Maternal deprivation; subd. *Orphans and orphan-asylums* under names of cities, e.g., Boston—Orphans and orphan-asylums; Survivors benefits
SEARS ORPHANS AND ORPHANS' HOMES; s.a. Charities; Institutional care; Public welfare
RG ORPHANS AND ORPHAN ASYLUMS; s.a. Children, Adopted; Homes, Institutional
NYT ORPHANS AND ORPHANAGES; s.a. Adoptions; Children and youth
PAIS ——; s.a. Child welfare; Children—Institutional care
BPI ORPHANS AND ORPHAN ASYLUMS; s.a. Adoption; Child welfare

ORTHODONTIA. *See* Dentistry

ORTHODONTICS. *Use* Dentistry

ORTHODOX CHURCHES. *Use* Catholic Church in the U.S.

ORTHOPEDIA. *Use* Chiropractic; Operations, Surgical; Osteopathy; Surgery

OSTEOPATHY
LC ——; s.a. Chiropractic; Mechanotherapy; Neurotherapy
SEARS ——; s.a. Massage; Medicine—Practice
RG ORTHOPEDIA; s.a. Chiropractic; Medical service
NYT OSTEOPATHY AND OSTEOPATHS; s.a. Medicine and health
PAIS ——; s.a. Chiropractic; Medical profession
BPI MEDICINE; s.a. Medical care; Physicians

OUTBOARD MOTORS. *Use* Boats and Boating; Electric Motors; Motors

OUTDOOR COOKERY. *Use* Cookery; Outdoor Life

OUTDOOR LIFE
LC ——; s.a. Camping; Country life; Outdoor cookery; Outdoor recreation; Picnicing; Vagrancy
SEARS ——; s.a. Camping; Hiking; Nature study; Outdoor cookery
RG ——; s.a. Camp cookery; Cookery, Outdoor; Forest recreation; Mountaineering, Wilderness survival
NYT CAMPS AND CAMPING; s.a. Nature; Parks, playgrounds and other recreation areas; Recreation
PAIS CAMPS AND CAMPING; s.a. Playgrounds; Recreation areas
BPI CAMPING; s.a. Barbecue cookery; Campsites, facilities, etc.; Outdoor education; Parks

OUTER SPACE
See also names of specific projects, e.g., Apollo project.
LC ——; s.a. Interplanetary voyages; Interstellar communication; Lunar probes; Manned space flight; Space flight
SEARS ——; s.a. Astronomy; Space environment; Space sciences
RG SPACE, OUTER; s.a. Interstellar communication; Rockets, Interplanetary

NYT SPACE AND UPPER ATMOSPHERE; s.a. Aerospace industries and sciences; Astronautics
PAIS SPACE, OUTER; s.a. Airspace (international law); Astronautics
BPI SPACE FLIGHT; s.a. Astronautics; Atmosphere, Upper

OUTLAWS. *Use* Crime and Criminals

OUTPUT STANDARDS. *See* Production Standards

OVERPRODUCTION
LC ——; s.a. Industry; Supply and demand; Technocracy
SEARS BUSINESS CYCLES; s.a. Depressions; Prices
RG SUPPLY AND DEMAND; s.a. Business depression; Consumption (economics)
NYT CONSUMERS AND CONSUMPTION; s.a. Economic conditions and trends (general)
PAIS BUSINESS DEPRESSION; s.a. Business cycles; Economic conditions
BPI BUSINESS DEPRESSION; s.a. Business cycles; Economic stabilization

OVER-THE-COUNTER MARKETS
LC ——; s.a. Investment banking; Stock-exchange
SEARS STOCK EXCHANGE; s.a. Securities; Speculation
RG STOCKS—MARKETING; s.a. Investments; Speculation
NYT STOCKS AND BONDS—U.S.—OVER-THE-COUNTER TRADING; s.a. Commodities and commodity exchanges and brokers
PAIS SECURITIES-OVER-THE-COUNTER MARKETING; s.a. Stock exchanges
BPI SECURITIES-OVER-THE-COUNTER MARKETING; s.a. Securities; Stock market

OVERTIME. *Use* Night Work; Wages and Salaries

OVERWEIGHT. *See* Weight Control

OVULATION. *Use* Embryology

OWNERSHIP. *See* Property

P

PACIFISM
Scope: Works on the renunciation on moral grounds of offensive or defensive military action.
LC ——; s.a. Evil, Non-resistance to; Passive resistance to government; War and religion
SEARS ——; s.a. Conscientious objectors; Nonviolence
RG ——; s.a. Conscientious objectors; Peace; Vietnamese War, 1957- —Protests, demonstrations, etc., against

NYT NONVIOLENCE; s.a. Armament, defense and military forces; Arms control and limitation and disarmament; War and revolution
PAIS ——; s.a. Conscientious objectors; Peace movements; War and religion
BPI CONSCIENTIOUS OBJECTORS; s.a. Disarmament and arms control; Peace

PACKAGE DESIGN. *Use* Design

PACKAGING

LC   ——; s.a. Aerosols; Containers; Display of merchandise; Packing for shipment; Shipment of goods; subd. *Packaging* under subjects, e.g., Confectionery—Packaging; Wrapping machines; Wrapping materials

SEARS ——; s.a. Gift wrapping; Retail trade

RG   ——; s.a. Labels; Meat—Pre-packaging; Pressure packaging

NYT   CONTAINERS AND PACKAGING; s.a. Food and grocery trade; Labeling and labels

PAIS   ——; s.a. Container industry; Food industry—Packaging; Labels

BPI   ——; s.a. Food packages; Packing for shipment; Sealing (packaging); Valves, Aerosol

PACKING HOUSES. *Use* Meat Industry and Trade

PACKING INDUSTRY. *See* Meat Industry and Trade

PAGEANTS. *Use* Festivals

PAID VACATIONS. *See* Vacations, Employee

PAIN. *Use* Emotions

PAIN-RELIEVING DRUGS. *Use* Analgesics

PAINT. *Use* Finishes and Finishing; Painting, Industrial

PAINTING. *Use* Art; Artists

PAINTING, INDUSTRIAL

LC   ——; s.a. House painting; Sign painting

SEARS ——; s.a. Finishes and finishing; Varnish and varnishing; Wood finishing

RG   PAINTING, INDUSTRIAL AND PRACTICAL; s.a. Boats—Painting; Paint spraying

NYT   PAINTING AND DECORATING; s.a. Building; Interior decoration; Paints, enamels, varnishes, lacquers, and protective finishes

PAIS   PAINTING INDUSTRY; s.a. Finishing materials; Varnish and varnishing

BPI   ——; s.a. Automobiles—Painting and finishing; Paint

PAINTING AND DECORATING. *Use* Interior Decoration

PAINTING AND LITERATURE. *See* Art and Literature

PAINTING INDUSTRY. *Use* Finishes and Finishing; Painting, Industrial

PAINTINGS, ABSTRACT. *See* Art, Abstract

PAIRED-ASSOCIATION LEARNING. *Use* Learning, Psychology of

PALEOGRAPHY. *Use* Writing

PALEONTOLOGY. *Use* Archaeology

PALESTINIAN ARABS. *Use* Jewish-Arab Relations

PALMISTRY. *Use* Occult Sciences

PALSY. *See* Paralysis

PANARABISM. *Use* Arab Countries

PANELING. *Use* Walls

PANIC. *Use* Disasters; Mobs

PANTHEISM. *Use* God; Religion

PANTOMIME. *Use* Acting; Ballet; Drama

PAPACY

LC   ——; s.a. Apostolic succession; Authority (religion); Catholic church; Church—Foundation; Council and synods; Conciliar theory; Legates, Papal; Ultramontanism

SEARS ——; s.a. Christian biography; Church history; Popes

RG   CHURCH—AUTHORITY; s.a. Nuncios, Papal; Popes—Primacy

NYT   ROMAN CATHOLIC CHURCH; s.a. names of Popes; Religion and churches

PAIS   ——; s.a. Roman Catholic church; Vatican

BPI   ——; s.a. Catholic church

PAPAL LEGATES. *See* Papacy

PAPER CRAFTS. *Use* Handicraft

PAPER INDUSTRY. *Use* Paper Making and Trade

PAPER MAKING AND TRADE

LC   ——; s.a. Cartons; Crepe paper; Newsprint; Waste paper; Wood—Pulp industry

SEARS ——; s.a. Book industries and trade; Paper crafts; Wood pulp

RG   PAPER INDUSTRY; s.a. Containers; Paper making

NYT   PAPER, PAPERBOARD AND PULP; s.a. Forests and forestry; Stationery; Wood

PAIS   PAPER INDUSTRY; s.a. Newsprint paper; Paper bag industry; Paper recycling; Waste paper industry

BPI   PAPER INDUSTRY; s.a. Paper making; Paper products industry; Wood pulp

PAPER MONEY. *Use* Finance, Public; Inflation (Finance); Money

PAPER RECYCLING. *Use* Paper Making and Trade

PAPER TEXTILES. *Use* Substitute Products

PAPERBACK BOOKS. *Use* Books

PARABLES. *Use* Tales

PARACHUTING

LC   ——; s.a. Airborne troops; Parachute troops; Parachutes—Testing equipment; Skydiving

SEARS PARACHUTE TROOPS; s.a. Aeronautics, Military; Parachutes

RG   ——; s.a. Airdrop; Forest fire patrol, Aerial

NYT   PARACHUTES AND PARACHUTE JUMPING; s.a. Airplanes

PAIS   ——; s.a. Aviation, Military; Parachute troops

BPI   PARACHUTES

PARADES. *Use* Festivals

PARALYSIS

LC   ——; s.a. Apoplexy; Cerebral palsy; Obstetrical paralysis; Paralysis, Facial; Paraplegia; Tetraplegia

SEARS CEREBRAL PALSY; s.a. Brain—Diseases; Poliomyelitis

RG   ——; s.a. Paralytics; Parkinson's disease; Poliomyelitis

NYT ———; s.a. Handicapped
PAIS CEREBRAL PALSY; s.a. Disabled
BPI ———; s.a. Apoplexy; Paraplegics

PARALYSIS, CEREBRAL. *See* Cerebral Palsy

PARALYTICS. *Use* Handicapped; Paralysis

PARANOIA. *Use* Insanity; Mental Illness

PARAPLEGICS. *Use* Paralysis

PARAPSYCHOLOGY. *Use* Psychical Research

PARASITES
See also names of parasitic orders, classes and individual
    parasites, e.g., Bats, Cestoda, Ticks, etc.
LC ———; s.a. Parasitic birds; Parasitic plants;
Parasitism; Worms, Intestinal and parasitic
SEARS ———; s.a. Bacteriology; Insects, Injurious and
beneficial
RG ———; s.a. Symbiosis
NYT ———; s.a. Insects; names of diseases caused by
parasites, e.g., Scabies; Pests and pesticides
PAIS PESTS
BPI ———; s.a. Insects, Injurious and beneficial

PARASITISM (Social sciences). *Use* Social Problems

PARATROOPS. *See* Parachuting

PARCEL POST. *Use* Postal Service

PARDON. *Use* Amnesty; Prisons and Prisoners

PARENT AND CHILD
LC ———; s.a. Acknowledgment of children; Adop-
tion; Child study; Children of divorced parents;
Desertion and non-support; Discipline of children;
Father separated children; Illegitimacy; Marriage
law; Maternal deprivation; Mothers; Step children
SEARS ———; s.a. Children—Management; Cruelty to
children; Inheritance and succession
RG PARENT AND CHILD (law); s.a. Family;
Fathers, Unmarried; Support (domestic rela-
tions)
NYT FAMILIES AND FAMILY LIFE; s.a. Adoptions;
Children and youth
PAIS PARENT AND CHILD (Law); s.a. Child wel-
fare; Illegitimacy; Mothers, Unmarried; Parents;
Paternity; Single parent family
BPI PARENT-CHILD RELATIONSHIP; s.a. Adop-
tion; Broken homes; Child welfare; Children—
Law

PARENT-TEACHER RELATIONSHIPS. *Use* Home and
School

PARENTS WITHOUT PARTNERS. *See* Parent and Child

PARESIS. *See* Paralysis

PARI-MUTUEL BETTING. *Use* Gambling; Horse-racing

PARISH SCHOOLS. *See* Church Schools

PARISHES (Local government). *Use* Local Government

PARKINSON'S DISEASE. *Use* Paralysis

PARKS
LC ———; s.a. Picnic grounds; Public lands; subd.
Parks under names of cities

SEARS ———; s.a. Botanical gardens; National parks and
reserves
RG ———; s.a. Amusement parks; Playgrounds
NYT PARKS, PLAYGROUNDS AND OTHER RE-
CREATION AREAS; s.a. Beaches; Forests;
Recreation
PAIS ———; s.a. Recreation areas; Wilderness areas
BPI ———; s.a. Amusement parks; Botanical gardens;
Zoological gardens

PARKS, NATIONAL. *Use* National Parks and Reserves;
Public Lands

PARLIAMENTARY GOVERNMENT. *See* Representative Government and Representation

PARLIAMENTARY PRACTICE
See also subd. *Rules and practice* under individual legis-
    lative bodies, e.g., U.S. Congress—Rules and
    practice.
LC ———; s.a. Committees; Congresses and conven-
tions; Interpellation; Legislation; Rules of order;
Veto
SEARS ———; s.a. Debates and debating; Legislative
bodies; Public meetings
RG ———; s.a. Conventions; U.S.—Congress—Senate—
Rules and practice
NYT Subd. *Politics and government* under names of
countries, e.g., Algeria—Politics and government;
s.a. Filibusters and debate curbs; Speeches and
statements (general)
PAIS PARLIAMENTARY PROCEDURE; s.a. Amend-
ments (parliamentary practice); Filibusters
BPI ———; s.a. Filibusters (political science); Meetings

PARLIAMENTS. *See* Legislative Bodies

PAROCHIAL SCHOOLS. *Use* Church Schools; Private
Schools; Religious Education

PAROCHIAL SCHOOLS—STATE AID. *Use* Education
and State

PARODY. *Use* Wit and Humor

PAROLE. *Use* Imprisonment; Prisons and Prisoners

PARQUET FLOORS. *Use* Floors

PARTIES. *Use* Entertaining

PARTIES, POLITICAL. *See* Political Parties

PARTISANS. *Use* Guerilla Warfare

PARTITIONS. *Use* Walls

PART-TIME EMPLOYMENT. *Use* Employment

PARTNERSHIP
LC ———; s.a. Agency (law); Articles of partnership;
Corporation law; Dormant partners; Liability
(law); Liquidation
SEARS COMMERCIAL LAW; s.a. Corporations; Stock
companies
RG ———; s.a. Joint adventures; Limited partnership
NYT CORPORATIONS; s.a. Banks and banking—U.S.
—Holding companies; Labor; Law and legislation
PAIS ———; s.a. Business; Private companies; Stock
companies
BPI ———; s.a. Corporations; Holding companies;
Joint adventure; Trusts, Industrial

PARTURITION. *Use* Reproduction

PARTY AFFILIATION. *Use* Political Parties

PASSION PLAYS. *Use* Jesus Christ

PASSIONS. *See* Emotions

PASSIVE RESISTANCE
LC ———; s.a. Boycott; General strike; Pacifism
SEARS ———; s.a. Nonviolence
RG PASSIVE RESISTANCE TO GOVERNMENT; s.a. Protests, demonstrations, etc.; Tax evasion
NYT NONVIOLENCE; s.a. International relations
PAIS PASSIVE RESISTANCE TO GOVERNMENT; s.a. Government, Resistance to; Political science
BPI BOYCOTT; s.a. Strikes

PASTIMES. *See* Amusements; Recreation

PASTORAL COUNSELING. *Use* Counseling; Therapeutics, Suggestive

PASTORAL WORK. *Use* Clergy; Preaching

PASTRY. *Use* Baking

PASTURES
LC ———; s.a. Commons; Meadows; Pasture, Right of; Public lands; Stock and stock breeding
SEARS ———; s.a. Agriculture; Forage plants; Grasses
RG ———; s.a. Grazing; Stock ranges
NYT AGRICULTURE AND AGRICULTURAL PRODUCTS; s.a. Livestock; Rural areas
PAIS GRAZING LANDS; s.a. Farms; Livestock industry
BPI FARMS; s.a. Cattle; Cattle industry; Livestock

PATENT LAWS AND LEGISLATION
See also subd. *Patents* under names of industries, trades or articles protected, e.g., Atomic power—Patents; Automobiles—Patents, etc.
LC ———; s.a. Competition, Unfair; Copyright; Design protection; Industrial laws and legislation; Industrial property; Models (patents); Patents—Government owned; Technological innovations
SEARS PATENTS; s.a. Copyright; Publishers and publishing; Trademarks
RG ———; s.a. Inventions; Patents and government-developed inventions; Patents—Licensing
NYT PATENT LAW; s.a. Inventions and inventors; Trademarks and trade names
PAIS PATENT LAW; s.a. Copyright; Inventions; Patents; Trademarks and names
BPI PATENT LAWS AND REGULATIONS; s.a. Intellectual property; Inventions, Employees; Patents—Licensing; Royalties

PATENT LICENSES. *Use* Licenses; Monopolies

PATENT MEDICINES. *Use* Analgesics; Fraud

PATERNITY. *Use* Illegitimacy; Parent and Child

PATERNITY SUITS. *See* Acknowledgement of Children

PATIENTS. *See* Sick

PATRIARCHY. *See* Family

PATRICIDE. *Use* Murder

PATRIOTISM
LC ———; s.a. Chauvinism and jingoism; Civics; Conduct of life; Ethics; Patriotic societies
SEARS ———; s.a. Loyalty; Nationalism
RG ———; s.a. Allegiance; Citizenship
NYT CITIZENSHIP; s.a. Immigration and emigration; Loyalty oaths and tests
PAIS ———; s.a. Loyalty oaths; Nationalism
BPI ———; s.a. Loyalty; Nationalism

PATRON SAINTS. *Use* Saints

PATRONAGE, POLITICAL
LC ———; s.a. Civil service reform; Corruption (in politics)
SEARS CIVIL SERVICE; s.a. Corruption (in politics); Political ethics
RG ———; s.a. Campaign funds; Nepotism; Political ethics
NYT GOVERNMENT EMPLOYEES AND OFFICIALS—PATRONAGE; s.a. Politics and government
PAIS PATRONAGE; s.a. Corruption (political); Political science
BPI POLITICS, PRACTICAL; s.a. Campaign funds; Lobbying; Politics, Corruption in

PATTERN MAKING. *Use* Models and Model Making

PATTERNS (Dress). *Use* Sewing

PAUPERISM. *See* Poverty

PAVEMENTS. *Use* Roads; Streets

PAWNBROKING. *Use* Interest and Usury; Loans; Loans, Personal

PAYMENT. *Use* Debtor and Creditor

PAYROLL DEDUCTIONS. *Use* Income Tax

PAYROLL TAX. *Use* Income Tax

PAYROLLS. *Use* Wages and Salaries

PEACE. *Use* Arbitration, International; Conscientious Objectors; Disarmament; International Relations; Nonviolence

PEACE MOVEMENTS. *Use* Pacifism

PEACE OFFICERS. *Use* Law Enforcement; Police

PEACE TREATIES. *Use* Treaties

PEACE OF MIND. *Use* Anxiety

PEASANT UPRISINGS. *Use* Revolutions

PEASANTRY
LC ———; s.a. Agricultural laborers; Contract labor; Country life; Feudalism; Peasant uprisings; Plantations; Rural conditions; Village communities
SEARS ———; s.a. Farm life—U.S.; Plantation life; Sociology, Rural
RG ———; s.a. Land tenure; Plantations; Rural population
NYT AGRICULTURE AND AGRICULTURAL PRODUCTS; s.a. Rural areas; Sociology

PAIS ——; s.a. Agricultrual labor; Farmers
BPI ——; s.a. Land tenure, Rural population

PEDAGOGY. *See* Education; Teaching

PEDDLERS AND PEDDLING. *Use* Sales; Salesmen and Salesmanship

PEDESTRIANS. *Use* Traffic Safety

PEDIATRIC PSYCHIATRY. *See* Child Psychiatry

PEDIGREES. *See* Genealogy

PEDOLOGY (Child study). *See* Children

PEERAGE. *Use* Genealogy

PEN DRAWING. *Use* Drawing

PENAL COLONIES. *Use* Colonies; Exiles; Imprisonment; Prisons and Prisoners

PENAL DISCIPLINE. *See* Prisons and Prisoners

PENAL INSTITUTIONS. *See* Prisons and Prisoners

PENALTIES (Criminal law). *See* Punishment

PENOLOGY. *See* Judgments; Punishment

PENSIONS
LC ——; s.a. Civil list; Civil service pensions; Industrial laws and legislation; Non-wage payment; Old age assistance; Old age pensions; Pension trusts; Retirement; subds. *Pensions* and *Salaries, pensions, etc.* under appropriate subjects, e.g., Lawyers—Pensions; Welfare economics
SEARS ——; s.a. Annuities; Insurance, Social; Mother's pensions
RG ——; s.a. Old age pensions; Survivors' benefits; subd. *Pensions* under names of groups of employees
NYT PENSIONS AND RETIREMENT; s.a. Social insurance; Veterans
PAIS ——; s.a. Pensions, Old age; Retirement income; Trusts and trustees
BPI ——; s.a. Insurance, Social; Old age pensions; Pension funds and funding; Pension trusts

PENSIONS, MILITARY
LC ——; s.a. Bounties, Military; Insurance, War risk; subd. *Pay, allowances* under armies, navies, etc., e.g., U.S. Air Force—Pay, allowances, etc.; Survivors benefits; War victims—Law and legislation
SEARS ——; s.a. Veterans
RG VETERANS—BENEFITS; s.a. Survivors' benefits
NYT PENSIONS AND RETIREMENT; s.a. U.S. armament; Veterans
PAIS ——; s.a. Veterans—Benefits
BPI ——; s.a. Pensions; Veterans

PENSIONS, NAVAL. *See* Pensions, Military

PEONAGE. *Use* Contract Labor; Native labor; Slavery

PEOPLE'S DEMOCRACY. *Use* Communism; Socialism; Totalitarianism

PERCEPTION
LC ——; s.a. Awareness; Cognition; Intuition (psychology); Senses and sensation; Social perception; Subliminal perception; Thought and thinking; Whole and parts (psychology)
SEARS ——; s.a. Apperception; Consciousness; Gestalt psychology; Intellect; Intuition
RG ——; s.a. Body image; Consciousness; Human information processing; Orientation
NYT INTELLIGENCE; s.a. Brain; Mind; Psychology and psychologists
PAIS INTELLIGENCE; s.a. Extrasensory perception
BPI ——; s.a. Human information processing; Ideology

PERCEPTRONS. *Use* Cybernetics

PERENNIALS. *Use* Floriculture

PERFECTION (Philosophy). *Use* Idealism

PERFORATED CARD SYSTEMS. *See* Information Storage and Retrieval Systems

PERFORMANCE. *Use* Job Analysis; Performance Standards; Production Standards; Work Measurement

PERFORMANCE AWARDS. *Use* Incentives in Industry

PERFORMANCE CONTRACTS (Education). *Use* Academic Achievement; Industry and Education

PERFORMANCE STANDARDS
LC ——; s.a. Employees, Rating of; Job analysis
SEARS EFFICIENCY, INDUSTRIAL; s.a. Job analysis
RG ——
NYT LABOR—U.S.—PRODUCTIVITY; s.a. Labor; Quality control (industrial and laboratory processes)
PAIS JOB ANALYSIS; s.a. Employees—Rating; Performance
BPI ——; s.a. Performance; Performance contracts (education)

PERFORMING ARTS. *Use* Amusements; Arts, The; Ballet; Entertainers; Music; Theater

PERFUMES. *Use* Cosmetics; Toilet

PERIODICALS. *Use* Newspapers; Press; Publishers and Publishing

PERIODICITY. *Use* Time

PERIODONTIA. *Use* Dentistry

PERJURY. *Use* Oaths; Witnesses

PERMUTATIONS. *Use* Mathematics

PERSECUTION
See also subd. *Persecution* under names of groups, e.g., Jews—Persecution.
LC ——; s.a. Inquisition; Liberty of conscience; Massacres; Martyrdom; Political crimes and offenses
SEARS ——; s.a. Atrocities; Freedom of conscience; Religious liberty
RG ——; s.a. Martyrs

PERSECUTION, *cont.*
NYT   FREEDOM AND HUMAN RIGHTS; s.a. Freedom of inquiry; Minorities
PAIS   RELIGIOUS LIBERTY
BPI   CIVIL RIGHTS; s.a. Due process of law; Religion

PERSIAN GULF REGION. *Use* Arab Countries; Petroleum Industry and Trade

PERSON. *See* Individualism; Man

PERSONAL APPEARANCE. *See* Clothing and Dress; Toilet

PERSONAL BUDGETS. *See* Budgets, Personal

PERSONAL DEVELOPMENT. *Use* Success

PERSONAL HYGIENE. *See* Hygiene

PERSONAL INJURIES
LC   ——; s.a. Accident law; Employers' liability; Industrial accidents; Negligence; Occupations, Dangerous; Sports—Accidents and injuries
SEARS WORKMEN'S COMPENSATION; s.a. Insurance, Accident; Insurance, Health
RG   ——; s.a. Damages; Liability (law)
NYT   ACCIDENTS AND SAFETY; s.a. names of sports, e.g., Boating; types of disasters, e.g., Floods; Workmen's compensation insurance
PAIS   ——; s.a. Damages; Workmen's compensation
BPI   ——; s.a. Claims; Damages; Insurance, Workmen's compensation

PERSONAL LIBERTY. *See* Liberty

PERSONAL LOANS. *See* Loans, Personal

PERSONAL OBLIGATIONS. *See* Obligations

PERSONAL PROPERTY. *Use* Property

PERSONALITY. *Use* Character; Emotions; Individuality; Temperament

PERSONALITY (Law). *Use* Libel and Slander

PERSONALITY DISORDERS. *Use* Insanity; Mentally Ill; Mentally Handicapped Children

PERSONALITY TESTS
LC   ——; s.a. Character tests; Projection (psychology); Self-evaluation; types of tests, e.g., Maze tests
SEARS MENTAL TESTS; s.a. Ability testing; Educational tests and measurements
RG   ——; s.a. Character tests
NYT   MENTAL TESTS; s.a. Education and schools; U.S. armament and defense—Draft, recruitment and mobilization
PAIS   TESTS, MENTAL; s.a. Tests, Ability
BPI   ——; s.a. Self-evaluation

PERSONNEL ADMINISTRATION. *See* Personnel Management

PERSONNEL CLASSIFICATION. *See* Job Analysis

PERSONNEL MANAGEMENT
LC   ——; s.a. Industrial relations; Industrial sociology; Interviewing; Job analysis; Labor passports; Management rights; Personnel directors; Personnel records; Research, Industrial; subds. *Personnel management* and *Personnel records* under subjects, e.g., Hospitals—Personnel management; Supervision of employees; U.S. Army Reserve—Personnel records
SEARS ——; s.a. Absenteeism (labor); Employees' representation in management; Factory management; Foremen; Recruiting of employees
RG   ——; s.a. Communication in management; Incentives in industry; Industrial research; Labor discipline
NYT   LABOR
PAIS   ——; s.a. Foremen and supervisors; Industrial relations; Labor discipline; Personnel research
BPI   ——; s.a. Job assignment; Job evaluation; Personnel departments; Personnel managers; Psychology, Industrial; Supervision of employees

PERSONNEL RECORDS IN EDUCATION. *Use* Grading and Marking (Students)

PERSONNEL SERVICE IN EDUCATION
LC   ——; s.a. Faculty advisors; Group guidance in education; School social work; Student counselors
SEARS ——; s.a. Dropouts; School psychologists
RG   ——; s.a. Group guidance in education; Student counselors
NYT   EDUCATION AND SCHOOLS; s.a. Colleges and universities; Labor—U.S.—Youth
PAIS   ——; s.a. College teachers; Counseling; School counselors
BPI   COUNSELING; s.a. College teachers; Education; Vocational guidance

PERSPECTIVE. *Use* Drawing; Optics

PERSUASION (Rhetoric). *Use* Oratory; Public Speaking

PEST CONTROL. *Use* Pests; Zoology, Economic

PESTICIDES. *Use* Pests; Zoology, Economic

PESTS
See also names of pests, e.g., Boll-weevil; Moles (animals).
LC   ——; s.a. Bacteriology, Agricultural; Insect control; Parasites; Pest control; Rodenticides; Zoology, Economic
SEARS AGRICULTURAL PESTS; s.a. Fungi; Fungicides; Household pests; Pest control—Biological control; Pesticides and environment
RG   ——; s.a. Agricultural pests; Household pest control; Insect control; Insects, Injurious and beneficial—Resistance to control; Parasites—Insects; Spraying and dusting
NYT   PESTS AND PESTICIDES
PAIS   ——; s.a. Insecticides; Pesticides
BPI   PEST CONTROL; s.a. Herbicides; Insects, Injurious and beneficial; Pesticides

PETROCHEMICALS. *Use* Petroleum Industry and Trade

PETROGLYPHS. *Use* Art, Primitive; Writing

PETROLEUM. *Use* Gas; Oil Fields

PETROLEUM—CONSERVATION. *Use* Conservation of
Natural Resources; Petroleum Industry and Trade

PETROLEUM, SYNTHETIC. *Use* Petroleum Industry
and Trade

PETROLEUM AS A FUEL. *Use* Fuel; Petroleum
Industry and Trade

PETROLEUM INDUSTRY AND TRADE
LC ——; s.a. Coal-tar industry; Fuel, Colloidal; Oil
  fields—Production methods; Oil industries; Oil-
  shale industry; Petroleum; Petroleum in submerged lands; Petroleum mining; Petroleum,
  Synthetic; Petroleum workers; Secondary recovery of oil
SEARS ——; s.a. Gasoline; Petroleum as a fuel; Petroleum pollution of water; Wells
RG PETROLEUM INDUSTRY; s.a. Oil lands;
  Petroleum laws and legislation; Petroleum
  products; Petroleum—Proration; Petroleum
  refineries
NYT OIL (Petroleum) AND GASOLINE; s.a. Names
  of oil companies; Environment
PAIS PETROLEUM INDUSTRY; s.a. Bituminous
  sand; Fuel; Gasoline industry; Oil and gas leases;
  Oil fields; Petroleum engineering
BPI PETROLEUM INDUSTRY; s.a. Lubricating oil
  industry; Oil companies; Oil pollution of rivers,
  harbors, etc.; Oil reclamation; Petrochemicals;
  Petroleum—Conservation; Petroleum supply

PETROLEUM PRODUCTS. *Use* Lubrication and Lubricants; Oils and Fats

PETROLEUM WASTE. *Use* Oil—Pollution

PETS. *Use* Animals; Aquariums; Domestic Animals

PHARMACEUTICAL ETHICS. *Use* Medical Ethics

PHARMACEUTICAL INDUSTRY. *See* Drug Trade

PHARMACOLOGY. *Use* Chemistry; Drug Trade; Drugs

PHARMACY. *Use* Drug Trade

PHENOMENOLOGY. *Use* Existentialism

PHILANTHROPY. *Use* Begging; Charitable Uses, Trusts
and Foundations; Charities; Charity

PHILOLOGY. *Use* Language and Languages

PHILOSOPHICAL ANTHROPOLOGY. *Use* Life

PHILOSOPHY. *Use* Aesthetics; Apperception; Belief and
Doubt; Ethics; Fate and Fatalism; Humanism;
Idealism; Knowledge, Theory of; Logic; Rational-
ism; Truth; Will

PHILOSOPHY, MORAL. *See* Ethics

PHILOSOPHY AND RELIGION. *Use* Future Life; God;
Heaven

PHONETICS. *Use* Language and Languages; Sound and
Sound Recording; Speech; Voice

PHONOGRAPH RECORDS
LC PHONORECORDS; s.a. High-fidelity sound
  systems; Phonotapes; Sound—Recording and
  reproducing; Talking books
SEARS ——; s.a. Audio-visual materials; Sound—Record-
  ing and reproducing; Talking books
RG ——; s.a. Copyright—Phonograph records; Tape
  recordings
NYT RECORDINGS (Disk and tape) AND RECORD-
  ING AND PLAYBACK EQUIPMENT; s.a.
  Entertainment and amusements
PAIS ——; s.a. Sound recording; Talking books
BPI ——; s.a. Libraries—Phonograph record collec-
  tions; Magnetic recorders and recording; Radio
  broadcasting—Music

PHOSPHATES INDUSTRY. *Use* Fertilizers and Manures

PHOTO JOURNALISM. *See* Journalism

PHOTOCHEMISTRY. *Use* Chemistry

PHOTOCOPYING PROCESSES. *Use* Copying Processes;
Photography—Printing Processes

PHOTOENGRAVING. *Use* Graphic Arts; Photography—
Printing Processes

PHOTOGRAMMETRY. *Use* Aerial Photography

PHOTOGRAPHERS. *Use* News Photographers

PHOTOGRAPHIC APPARATUS INDUSTRY AND
TRADE. *Use* Cameras; Optical Trade

PHOTOGRAPHIC INDUSTRY. *Use* Photography

PHOTOGRAPHIC SURVEYING. *Use* Aerial Photography

PHOTOGRAPHY
See also other headings beginning with the word Photog-
  raphy, e.g., Photography—Lighting; Photography,
  Close-up; Photography, Trick; Photography of
  animals, birds, flowers, etc.
LC ——; s.a. Cameras; Cinematography; Nature
  photography; Stereoscope
SEARS ——; s.a. Slides (Photography); Telephotography
RG ——; s.a. Color photography; Daguerrotypes;
  Moving picture photography; Telephotography
NYT PHOTOGRAPHY AND PHOTOGRAPHIC
  EQUIPMENT; s.a. Copying machines;
  Microforms
PAIS ——; s.a. Camera industry; Microfilms; Micro-
  forms
BPI ——; s.a. Cameras; Photographic industry;
  Photomechanical processes; Transparencies

PHOTOGRAPHY, ADVERTISING. *Use* Commercial Art;
Photography, Commercial

PHOTOGRAPHY, AERIAL. *Use* Aerial Photography

PHOTOGRAPHY—ANIMATED PICTURES. *See* Moving
Pictures

PHOTOGRAPHY, ARTISTIC
LC ——; s.a. Photography—Landscapes;
  Photography of the nude; Photography of
  women

PHOTOGRAPHY, ARTISTIC, *cont.*
SEARS ——; s.a. Art
RG ——; s.a. Composition (photography); Creative photography; Human figure in photography
NYT PHOTOGRAPHY AND PHOTOGRAPHIC EQUIPMENT; s.a. Art
PAIS PHOTOGRAPHY; s.a. Art
BPI PHOTOGRAPHY; s.a. Art

PHOTOGRAPHY, COMMERCIAL
LC ——; s.a. Photography, Advertising; Photography, Industrial
SEARS ——; s.a. Photography, Journalistic; Photography—Scientific applications
RG ——; s.a. Photography as a profession; Photography, Fashion; Photography in advertising
NYT PHOTOGRAPHY AND PHOTOGRAPHIC EQUIPMENT; s.a. Advertising
PAIS ——; s.a. News photographs; Photography in industry
BPI PHOTOGRAPHY, INDUSTRIAL; s.a. Advertising; Photography, Journalistic

PHOTOGRAPHY, FASHION. *Use* Photography, Commercial

PHOTOGRAPHY, INDUSTRIAL. *Use* Photography, Commercial

PHOTOGRAPHY, JOURNALISTIC. *Use* Journalism; News Photographers; Photography, Commercial

PHOTOGRAPHY—PRINTING PROCESSES
LC PHOTOMECHANICAL PROCESSES; s.a. Chemigraph; Photocopying processes; Photogravure; Photolithography
SEARS PHOTOMECHANICAL PROCESSES; s.a. Photoengraving
RG PHOTOMECHANICAL PROCESSES; s.a. Copying processes; Phototypesetting
NYT PRINTING AND ALLIED TRADES; s.a. Copying machines; Photography and photographic equipment
PAIS ——; s.a. Copying processes; Photoengraving
BPI PHOTOMECHANICAL PROCESSES; s.a. Copying processes; Photoengraving; Xerography

PHOTOGRAPHY, SUBMARINE. *Use* Underwater Exploration

PHOTOGRAPHY AS A PROFESSION. *Use* News Photographers; Photography, Commercial

PHOTOGRAPHY OF THE NUDE. *Use* Nude in Art; Photography, Artistic

PHOTOMECHANICAL PROCESSES. *Use* Copying Processes; Photography; Photography—Printing Processes

PHOTOMETRY. *Use* Optics

PHOTOPLAYS. *See* Moving Picture Plays

PHOTOSTAT. *Use* Copying Processes

PHOTOTELEGRAPHY. *Use* Telecommunication

PHOTOTHERAPY. *Use* Radiotherapy

PHOTOTYPESETTING. *Use* Photography—Printing Processes

PHRASEOLOGY. *Use* Semantics

PHYSICAL DISTRIBUTION OF GOODS. *Use* Marketing; Shipment of Goods

PHYSICAL EDUCATION. *Use* Athletics; Exercise; Gymnastics; Health Education; Posture; Self-defense; Sports; Winter Sports

PHYSICAL FITNESS
LC ——; s.a. Athletics; Gymnastics for women; Muscle strength; Physical education and training; Reading—Physiological aspects
SEARS ——; s.a. Exercise; Games; Health education; Physical education and training
RG ——; s.a. Exercise; Gymnastics; Health; Physical education and training
NYT EXERCISE; s.a. Athletics; Physical education and training
PAIS PHYSICAL EDUCATION; s.a. Health; Sports; subd. *Health* under specific subjects, e.g., Executives—Health
BPI ——; s.a. Exercise; Outdoor education; Physical education and training

PHYSICAL GEOGRAPHY. *Use* Earth; Geography

PHYSICAL HEALTH AND EDUCATION. *Use* Health Education

PHYSICAL THERAPY
LC ——; s.a. Baths; Electrotherapeutics; Occupational therapy; Therapeutics, Physiological; Thermotherapy; Vibration (therapeutics)
SEARS ——; s.a. Hydrotherapy; Radiotherapy
RG ——; s.a. Recreational therapy; Therapeutics
NYT MEDICINE AND HEALTH; s.a. Handicapped; Massage; names of diseases, e.g., Infantile paralysis (poliomyelitis)
PAIS ——; s.a. Massage; Medicine
BPI PHYSIOLOGY; s.a. Medicine

PHYSICALLY HANDICAPPED. *Use* Amputees; Blind; Deaf; Handicapped; Invalids; Vocational Rehabilitation

PHYSICIANS. *Use* Chiropractic; Medical Care; Medicine; Osteopathy

PHYSICS. *Use* Astrophysics; Biological Physics; Force and Energy; Nuclear Physics; Ultrasonics

PHYSIOLOGICAL CHEMISTRY. *Use* Chemistry; Digestion; Nutrition; Toxins and Antitoxins; Vitamins

PHYSIOLOGY. *Use* Anatomy, Human; Body, Human; Growth; Mind and Body; Nervous System

PHYSIOTHERAPY. *See* Physical Therapy

PICKETING. *Use* Labor Laws and Legislation; Strikes and Lockout; Trade-Unions

PICKPOCKETS. *Use* Theft

PICNIC GROUNDS. *Use* Amusement Parks; Parks; Playgrounds

PICTURE BOOKS. *See* Children's Literature

PIECE WORK. *Use* Incentives in Industry; Wages and Salaries

PIERS. *Use* Ports

PIETISM. *Use* Evangelicalism

PIGEON POST. *Use* Air Mail Service

PIGMENT. *Use* Dyes and Dyeing

PIGMENTS (Biology). *Use* Color of Man

PILGRIMAGES TO MECCA. *Use* Islam

PILLAGE. *Use* Theft

PILLOWS. *Use* Beds and Bedding

PILOTS AND PILOTAGE. *Use* Ports; Seamen

PIMPS. *Use* Prostitution

PIPES. *Use* Plumbing

PIPES, STEEL. *Use* Steel Industry and Trade

PIPES, TOBACCO. *Use* Tobacco

PIRATES. *Use* Maritime Law; Naval Art and Science

PISTOLS. *Use* Arms and Armor; Firearms

PITCHING (Baseball). *Use* Baseball

PLAGIARISM. *Use* Intellectual Property

PLANETARIUMS. *Use* Astronomy

PLANETS. *Use* Astronomy

PLANNED PARENTHOOD. *Use* Abortion; Birth Control; Family

PLANNING. *Use* Management; Organization

PLANNING, ECONOMIC. *See* Economic Policy

PLANNING, REGIONAL. *See* Regional Planning

PLANT BREEDING. *Use* Floriculture; Plants

PLANT ENGINEERING. *Use* Plant Layout

PLANT LAYOUT
LC ———; s.a. Assembly line methods; Factories—Design and construction; Machinery in industry; Plant engineering
SEARS INDUSTRIAL BUILDINGS; s.a. Design, Industrial; Systems engineering; Workshops
RG FACTORIES—DESIGN; s.a. Design, Industrial; Human engineering
NYT ENGINEERING AND ENGINEERS; s.a. Buildings
PAIS DESIGN IN INDUSTRY; s.a. Industrial buildings; Machinery in industry
BPI ———; s.a. Assembly line methods; Industrial engineers; Material handling

PLANT LORE. *Use* Folklore; Plants

PLANT MAINTENANCE. *Use* Factory Management

PLANTATION LIFE. *Use* Peasantry; Slavery

PLANTATIONS. *Use* Farms and Farming

PLANTING. *See* Gardening

PLANTS
LC ———; s.a. Annuals (plants); Botany; Fertilization of plants; Floriculture; Flowers in literature; Forcing (plants); Growth (plants); Miniature plants; Plant-soil relationship; Plants, Edible; Shrubs; Transmutation of plants; Weeds

SEARS ———; s.a. Plant breeding; Plant—Diseases; Plants, Cultivated; Tree planting; names of particular types of plants, e.g., Climbing plants; Desert plants; Forage plants; Freshwater plants; House plants; Marine plants; Poisonous plants; Tropical plants
RG ———; s.a. Berry bearing plants; Botany—Ecology; Plant lore; Plants, Effect of air pollution on; Plants, Effect of smog on; Plants, Ornamental
NYT ———; s.a. Horticulture; Trees and shrubs
PAIS ———; s.a. Botanical gardens; Defoliation; Horticulture; Plants—Diseases and pests
BPI ———; s.a. Crops; Flowers; Fruit; Gardening; Horticulture; Trees; Vegetables

PLANTS, EDIBLE. *Use* Crops

PLANTS, INDUSTRIAL. *See* Factories

PLANTS, ORNAMENTAL. *Use* Floriculture; Gardening; Horticulture; Plants

PLASTER AND PLASTERING
LC PLASTERING; s.a. Calcimining; Graffito decoration; Rabitz construction
SEARS ———; s.a. Mortar; Stucco
RG MASONRY; s.a. Foundations; Plaster work
NYT PAINTING AND DECORATING; s.a. Building
PAIS ———; s.a. Building trades
BPI PLASTER; s.a. Masonry, Cement

PLASTIC PRODUCTS. *See* Plastics Industry and Trade

PLASTIC SURGERY. *Use* Surgery

PLASTICS. *Use* Substitute Products

PLASTICS INDUSTRY AND TRADE
See also names of plastics, e.g., Bakelite; Celluloid.
LC ———; s.a. Plastics; Plastics machinery; Plastics plants; Plastics workers
SEARS PLASTICS; s.a. Chemistry, Organic—Synthesis; Polymers and polymerization; Rubbers, Artificial; Synthetic products
RG PLASTICS INDUSTRY; s.a. Epoxy resins; Plastics; Polymers
NYT PLASTICS
PAIS PLASTICS INDUSTRY; s.a. Chemical industries; Wages and salaries—Plastics industry
BPI PLASTICS INDUSTRY; s.a. Extrusion (plastics); Plastics; Polyethylene; Polypropylene

PLATFORMS, POLITICAL. *Use* Political Parties

PLATONIC LOVE. *See* Love

PLAY. *Use* Recreation

PLAY CENTERS. *See* Playgrounds

PLAY SCHOOLS. *Use* Nurseries

PLAY WRITING. *See* Moving Picture Plays

PLAYBILLS. *Use* Posters

PLAYGROUNDS
LC ———; s.a. Athletic fields; Physical education facilities; Picnic grounds; School hygiene; subd. *Playgrounds* under names of cities
SEARS ———; s.a. Community centers; Social settlements; Vacation schools

PLAYGROUNDS, *cont.*
RG ——; s.a. Athletic fields; Parks; Swings
NYT PARKS, PLAYGROUNDS AND OTHER RE-
  CREATION AREAS; s.a. Beaches; Forests
  (for State and national forests); Recreation
PAIS ——; s.a. Parks; Recreation areas
BPI ——; s.a. Athletic fields; Parks

PLAYHOUSES. *See* Theaters

PLAYS. *See* Drama

PLEAS (Criminal procedure). *Use* Courts

PLEASURE. *Use* Emotions

PLEBISCITE. *Use* Elections

PLEDGES (Law). *Use* Contracts

PLOTS (Drama, novel, etc.)
Scope: Works dealing with the construction and analysis
  of plots as a literary vehicle. Collections of plots
  are entered under Drama, Literature, etc., with
  subd. *Stories, plots,* etc., e.g., Drama—Stories,
  plots, etc.; Literature—Stories, plots, etc.
LC ——; s.a. Amateur theatricals—Plots, themes,
  etc.; Film adaptations; Literature, Comparative—
  Themes, motives, etc; Moving pictures—Plots,
  themes, etc.; Musical revues, comedies, etc.—
  Stories, plots, etc.
SEARS PLOTS (Drama, fiction, etc.); s.a. Characters
  and characteristics in literature; Literature—
  Stories, plots, etc.
RG ——; s.a. Drama—Criticism, plots, etc.; Moving
  pictures—Themes
NYT BOOKS AND LITERATURE; s.a. Motion pic-
  tures; Theater; Writing and writers
PAIS LITERATURE; s.a. Books; Motion pictures
BPI LITERATURE; s.a. Books and reading; Theater

PLUMBING
LC ——; s.a. Heating pipes; Hotwater supply;
  Sanitation, Household; Solder and soldering;
  Steam-pipes; Water-pipes
SEARS ——; s.a. Drainage, House; Gas fitting; Sanitary
  engineering; Sewerage
RG ——; s.a. Boats—Sanitation; Pipe joints; Water
  distribution
NYT PLUMBING AND PLUMBERS; s.a. Drain clean-
  ers; Housing; Pipe; Sanitation
PAIS ——; s.a. Pipe fitting; Sanitary engineering
BPI ——; s.a. Pipes; Plumbers; Plumbing industry

PLURALITY OF WORLDS. *Use* Astronomy

POACHING. *Use* Hunting

POETICS. *Use* Versification

POETRY. *Use* Literature

POISON GASES. *See* Gas

POISONING AND POISONS. *Use* Drugs; Hazardous
  Substances; Toxins and Antitoxins

POLEMICS. *Use* Public Opinion

POLICE
See also subd. *Police* under names of cities; e.g., Chicago—
Police.

LC ——; s.a. Constables; Detectives; House
  detectives; Mobile communication system; Peace
  officers; Police-fire integration; Police patrol;
  Store detectives; Television in police work
SEARS ——; s.a. Crime and criminals; Criminal investi-
  gation; Detectives; Law enforcement; Police,
  State; Secret service
RG ——; s.a. Agents provocateurs; Negro police;
  Police communication systems; Police depart-
  ments; Police, Private; Public safety officers
NYT POLICE (General Material in U.S.); s.a. U.N.—
  Military personnel
PAIS ——; s.a. Border patrols; Campus police; Com-
  puters—Police communication systems; Police
  departments—Administration; Police questioning;
  Watchmen
BPI ——; s.a. Factory guards; Police, Private;
  Secret service; Store detectives

POLICE, INTERNATIONAL. *Use* International Offenses

POLICE, PRIVATE. *Use* Detectives; Police

POLICE CORRUPTION. *Use* Bribery

POLICE POWER. *Use* Rule of Law

POLICE STATE. *See* Totalitarianism

POLIOMYELITIS. *Use* Paralysis

POLISHING MATERIALS. *Use* Cleaning Compounds;
  Finishes and Finishing

POLITICAL ADVERTISING. *Use* Advertising, Political;
  Electioneering

POLITICAL CAMPAIGNS. *Use* Advertising, Political;
  Electioneering; Politics, Practical

POLITICAL CLUBS AND ASSOCIATIONS. *Use* Political
  Parties

POLITICAL CONVENTIONS. *Use* Political Parties

POLITICAL CRIMES AND OFFENSES
LC ——; s.a. Atrocities; Civil service ethics; Communist party purges; Concentration camps;
  Offenses against heads of state; Political atrocities; Political ethics; Regicides; Sedition;
  Treason
SEARS ——; s.a. Anarchism and anarchists; Corruption
  (in politics); Government, Resistance to; Persecu-
  tion; Political prisoners; Revolution
RG ——; s.a. Asylum, Right of; Conscientious ob-
  jectors; Freedom of the press; Insurgency; Polit-
  ical ethics; Politics, Corruption in; Subversive
  activities; Terrorism
NYT CRIME AND CRIMINALS; s.a. Ethics and
  morals; Politics and government
PAIS ——; s.a. Corruption (political); Impeachment;
  Political purges; Prisoners, Political; Refugees,
  Political
BPI POLITICS, CORRUPTION IN; s.a. Assassination;
  Bribery; Campaign funds; Kidnapping, Political;
  Political defectors; Political prisoners

POLITICAL DEFECTORS. *Use* Asylum, Right of; Political Crimes and Offenses

POLITICAL ECONOMY. *See* Economics

POLITICAL ETHICS. *Use* Corruption (in politics); Ethics; Government, Resistance to; Patronage, Political; Political Crimes and Offenses; Social Ethics

POLITICAL FORECASTS. *Use* Public Opinion

POLITICAL LETTER WRITING. *Use* Lobbying

POLITICAL MURDER. *See* Assassination

POLITICAL OFFENSES. *See* Political Crimes and Offenses

POLITICAL PARTICIPATION. *Use* Political Parties; Politics, Practical

POLITICAL PARTIES
See also names of parties; and subd. *Politics and government* under names of countries, cities, etc.
LC   ——; s.a. Coalition governments; Party affiliation; Party discipline; Political clubs; Political conventions; Right and left (political science)
SEARS ——; s.a. Political conventions; Politics, Practical; Primaries; Right and left (political science)
RG   ——; s.a. Communist parties; National conventions (political); Party affiliation; Platforms, Political; Political clubs and associations; Representative government and representation
NYT POLITICS AND GOVERNMENT; s.a. Elections
PAIS ——; s.a. Campaigns, Political; Party discipline; Political clubs and associations; Political parties—Conventions; Popular fronts
BPI   ——; s.a. Platforms, Political; Political clubs and associations; Political participation; Primaries

POLITICAL PARTIES—FINANCES. *Use* Advertising, Political

POLITICAL PATRONAGE. *See* Patronage, Political

POLITICAL PRISONERS. *Use* Political Crimes and Offenses

POLITICAL PSYCHOLOGY. *Use* Propaganda; Public Opinion; Social Psychology

POLITICAL QUESTIONS AND JUDICIAL POWER. *Use* Politics, Practical; Rule of Law; Separation of Powers

POLITICAL RIGHTS. *Use* Civil Rights; Liberty

POLITICAL SATIRE. *Use* Wit and Humor

POLITICAL SCIENCE. *Use* Communism; Constitutions; Democracy; Despotism; Equality; Executive Power; Federal Government; Imperialism; Legislative Bodies; Liberty; Lobbying; Local Government; Nationalism; Public Administration; Representative Government and Representation; Revolutions; Right and Left (Political science); Separation of Powers; State, The; World Politics

POLITICS, CORRUPTION IN. *Use* Bribery; Corruption (in politics); Electioneering; Lobbying; Patronage, Political; Political Crimes and Offenses; Wiretapping

POLITICS, PRACTICAL
Scope: Works dealing with practical political methods in general, electioneering, political machines, etc.

LC   ——; s.a. Advertising, Political; Business and politics; Caucus voting; Electioneering; Nominations for office; Patronage, Political; Political parties; Political questions and judicial power; Political rights, Loss of; subd. *Politics and government* under names of places
SEARS ——; s.a. Campaign funds; Campaign literature; subd. *Political activity* under groups of people, e.g., College students—Political activity
RG   CAMPAIGN MANAGEMENT; s.a. Political campaigns; Pressure groups; Suffrage
NYT POLITICS AND GOVERNMENT; s.a. Elections (U.S.); Local government; U.S.—Politics and government—Local government
PAIS POLITICAL PARTICIPATION; s.a. Campaigns, Political; Lobbying; Primaries
BPI   ——; s.a. Business—Political aspects; Lobbying; Voting

POLITICS AND BUSINESS. *See* Business and Politics

POLITICS AND GOVERNMENT. *Use* Colonies; Demonstrations; Government, Resistance to; Government and the Press; Metropolitan Government; Municipal Government; Nationalization; Official Secrets; Patronage, Political; Political Crimes and Offenses; Political Parties; Politics, Practical; Public Administration; State Rights; Voting

POLITENESS. *See* Etiquette

POLLS. *See* Elections; Public Opinion; Voting

POLLUTION
See also types of pollution, e.g., Air pollution; Marine pollution; Noise pollution; Soil pollution; Space pollution; Water pollution.
LC   ——; s.a. Environmental engineering; Environmental policy; Factory and trade waste; Man—Influence on nature; Refuse and refuse disposal
SEARS ——; s.a. Automobiles—Pollution control devices; Radioactive fallout
RG   ——; s.a. Pesticides and the environment
NYT ENVIRONMENT; s.a. Waste materials and disposal
PAIS ——; s.a. Sanitation
BPI   ——; s.a. Petroleum waste

POLLUTION—LAWS AND LEGISLATION. *Use* Environmental Policy

POLYANDRY. *Use* Bigamy; Marriage

POLYGAMY. *Use* Bigamy; Marriage; Mormons and Mormonism

POLYMERS AND POLYMERIZATION. *Use* Plastics Industry and Trade

PONY EXPRESS. *Use* Postal Service

POOR. *Use* Begging; Charities; Poverty; Public Welfare; Social History; Social Problems

POOR—LEGAL STATUS, LAWS, ETC. *Use* Legal Aid

POOR RELIEF. *See* Charities; Public Welfare

POPES. *Use* Papacy; Ultramontanism

POPULAR CULTURE
Scope: Works on literature, art, and music produced for the general public, i.e. for mass consumption.
LC ——; s.a. Civilization; Communication; Intellectual life
SEARS CULTURE; s.a. Manners and customs
RG ——; s.a. Subd. *Popular culture* under names of countries
NYT CULTURE; s.a. Festivals; names of cultural centers and organizations
PAIS ——; s.a. Subd. *Popular culture* under names of countries
BPI CULTURE

POPULAR FRONTS. *Use* Political Parties

POPULARIZATION OF SCIENCE. *See* Science

POPULATION
See also subd. *Population* under names of places.
LC ——; s.a. Conception—Prevention; Demography; Emigration and immigration; Ethnology; Human ecology; Migrations—Internal; Population forecasting; Population research; Population transfers; Rural population; Vital statistics
SEARS ——; s.a. Birth rate; Eugenics; Migration; Sterilization; Vital statistics
RG ——; s.a. Birth control; Census; Malthusianism; Population, Increase of
NYT POPULATION AND VITAL STATISTICS; s.a. Birth control; Families and family life; Immigration; Zero population growth
PAIS ——; s.a. Age groups; Census; Mortality; Population research
BPI ——; s.a. Birth rate; Demography; Family size

PORCELAIN. *Use* Ceramics

PORNOGRAPHY AND OBSCENITY. *Use* Art, Immoral; Censorship; Erotica; Ethics; Obscenity

PORTABLE RADIOS. *Use* Radio—Apparatus and Supplies

PORTS
LC HARBORS; s.a. Breakwaters; Dredging; Merchant marine; Piers; Port districts; Shore protection; Wharves
SEARS HARBORS; s.a. Docks; Navigation; Pilots and pilotage; Transportation
RG ——; s.a. Fishing docks and piers; Harbors; Piers; subd. *Harbor* under names of port cities; Terminals
NYT ——; s.a. Ships and shipping; Stevedoring
PAIS ——; s.a. Port authorities; Shipping
BPI ——; s.a. Bridges—Foundations and piers; Docks; Free ports and zones; Marinas

POSITIVISM. *Use* Rationalism

POSSESSION (Law). *Use* Property

POST OFFICE. *See* Postal Service

POSTAGE RATES. *Use* Postal Service

POSTAGE STAMPS
LC ——; s.a. Cancellations (philately); Commemorative postage stamps; Postage stamp design; Postage stamp printing; Postage stamps—Forgeries; Precancels
SEARS ——; s.a. Collectors and collecting; Postage stamps—Collectors and collecting
RG ——; s.a. Covers (philately); Postmarks
NYT STAMPS, COVERS AND CACHETS (Postal); s.a. Collectors and collections; Postal service
PAIS ——; s.a. Postage stamps—Collectors and collecting
BPI ——; s.a. Advertising media—Postage stamps; Postal rates

POSTAL CENSORSHIP. *Use* Obscenity

POSTAL SERVICE
LC ——; s.a. Carriers; Franking privilege; Letter mail handling; Mail sorting; Pigeon post; Postage stamps; Postal conventions; Postal service buildings; Postal service—Rates
SEARS ——; s.a. Air mail service; Pony express; Postal savings banks; Postal service—laws and regulations; Railway mail service
RG ——; s.a. Franking privilege; Mail boats; Parcel post; Postal rates; Post office buildings
NYT ——; s.a. Postal service—U.S.—Unordered merchandise
PAIS ——; s.a. Air mail service; Franking privilege; Postage rates
BPI ——; s.a. Advertising media—Postage stamps; Postal laws and regulations; Postal rates

POSTERS
LC ——; s.a. Bill-posting; Commercial art; Playbills; Posters, American (Belgian, French, etc.); subd. *Posters* under historical events and periods
SEARS ——; s.a. Advertising; Commercial art; Signs and signboards
RG ——; s.a. Billboards; Signs and signboards
NYT ——; s.a. Art; Graphic arts
PAIS ——; s.a. Advertising, Outdoor; Signs and Signboards
BPI ——; s.a. Advertising, Outdoor; Signs

POSTHUMOUS MARRIAGE. *Use* Marriage Law

POSTIMPRESSIONISM (Art). *Use* Art, Modern—20th Century; Modernism (Art)

POSTMARKS. *Use* Postage Stamps

POSTMORTEM EXAMINATIONS. *See* Autopsy

POSTOPERATIVE CARE. *Use* Operations, Surgical

POSTURE
LC ——; s.a. Man—Attitude and movement; School hygiene
SEARS ——; s.a. Physical education and training
RG ——; s.a. Body, Human; Stature
NYT STATURE; s.a. Body, Human; Medicine and health
PAIS STATURE; s.a. Body measurements; Physical education

BPI   PHYSICAL FITNESS; s.a. Physical education and training; Physiology

POTASH INDUSTRY. *Use* Fertilizers and Manures

POTTERY. *Use* Ceramics

POULTRY INDUSTRY
See also names of domesticated birds, e.g., Capons and caponizing; Ducks; Geese.
LC   ——; s.a. Egg trade; Incubators; Poultry houses and equipment; Poultry industry; Poultry plants
SEARS POULTRY; s.a. Domestic animals—Food; Poultry—Equipment and supplies
RG   ——; s.a. Cookery—Poultry; Poultry feeders
NYT   POULTRY; s.a. Agriculture and agricultural products; Eggs; Food and grocery trade
PAIS ——; s.a. Egg industry; Farm buildings; Turkey industry
BPI   ——; s.a. Poultry as food; Poultry, Frozen

POVERTY
LC   ——; s.a. Begging; Charities and poor; Cost and standard of living; Poor; Poor laws; Poverty, Vow of; Social conflict; Social problems; subds. *Economic conditions*; *Social conditions* under names of countries; Unemployed; Vagrancy
SEARS ——; s.a. Charities; Economic assistance, Domestic; Labor and laboring classes; Wealth
RG   ——; s.a. Homeless, The; Poor; Public welfare; Slums
NYT   U.S.—ECONOMIC CONDITIONS
PAIS ——; s.a. Beggars and begging; Employment—Poor; Poor
BPI   ——; s.a. Child welfare; Public welfare

POVERTY, VOW OF. *Use* Monasticism and Religious Orders

POWER, EXECUTIVE. *See* Executive Power

POWER, LEGISLATIVE. *See* Legislation

POWER (Mechanics). *Use* Mechanical Engineering

POWER (Political science). *Use* Separation of Powers

POWER (Social sciences). *Use* Sociology

POWER PLANTS, ELECTRIC. *See* Electric Power Plants

POWER RESOURCES. *Use* Force and Energy; Fuel; Natural Resources; Nature Conservation; Raw Materials

POWER TOOLS. *Use* Tools

POWER TRANSMISSION. *Use* Electric Power Plants; Mechanical Engineering

PRACTICAL JOKES. *Use* Wit and Humor

PRACTICAL NURSING. *Use* Nurses and Nursing

PRACTICAL POLITICS. *See* Politics, Practical

PRAGMATISM. *Use* Idealism; Rationalism

PRAYER. *Use* Worship

PRAYERS IN THE PUBLIC SCHOOLS. *See* Education and the State; Religious Education

PREACHING
LC   ——; s.a. Communication (theology); Homiletical illustrations; Open pulpits; Oratory; Preaching, Extemporaneous; Preaching, Jewish; Preaching, Lay; Theology, Practical
SEARS ——; s.a. Pastoral work; Rhetoric; Sermons
RG   ——; s.a. Bible—Homiletical use; Communication (theology)
NYT   RELIGION AND CHURCHES; s.a. Sermons; Speeches and statements (general)
PAIS RELIGION; s.a. Churches; Public speaking
BPI   CLERGY; s.a. Public speaking; Religion

PRECEDENCE. *Use* Etiquette

PRECIOUS METALS. *Use* Metal Industries; Mineralogy

PRECIOUS STONES
Scope: Works of mineralogical or technological interest; see Gems for works on engraved stones and jewels from the point of view of antiquities or art; see also names of stones, e.g., Opals.
LC   ——; s.a. Folk-lore of stones; Jewelry; Precious stones, Artificial
SEARS ——; s.a. Gems; Jewelry; Mineralogy
RG   ——; s.a. Lapidary work
NYT   JEWELS AND JEWELRY; s.a. Metals and minerals; Robberies and thefts; Treasure, Sunken
PAIS ——; s.a. Diamond industry; Gems
BPI   ——; s.a. Gems; Mines and mineral resources

PRÉCIS WRITING. *Use* Documentation; Report Writing

PREDATION (Biology). *Use* Ecology

PREDATION (Zoology). *Use* Predatory Animals; Zoology, Economic

PREDATORY ANIMALS
Scope: Works on carnivorous animals which prey on domestic animals or game. See also names of carnivorous animals, e.g., Coyotes.
LC   ——; s.a. Birds of prey; Carnivora
SEARS ANIMALS; s.a. Zoology, Economic
RG   ANIMALS, PREDATORY; s.a. Birds of prey; Predation (zoology)
NYT   ANIMALS; s.a. Nature; Wildlife sanctuaries
PAIS ——; s.a. Animals; Wild life
BPI   ANIMALS; s.a. Wildlife, Conservation of

PREDESTINATION. *Use* Fate and Fatalism

PREDICTIONS. *Use* Prophecies

PREEXISTENCE. *Use* Future Life; Soul

PREFERRED STOCKS. *Use* Stock Exchange

PREGNANCY. *Use* Childbirth; Embryology; Labor (Obstetrics); Maternal and Infant Welfare; Reproduction

PREHISTORIC ART. *See* Art, Primitive

PREHISTORY. *See* Society, Primitive

PREJUDICE. *Use* Discrimination; Prejudices and
Antipathies; Race Awareness; Toleration

PREJUDICES AND ANTIPATHIES
LC ——; s.a. Antisemitism; Empathy; Ethnocentrism
SEARS ——; s.a. Emotions; Human relations; Race awareness
RG PREJUDICE; s.a. Race prejudice; Racism
NYT DISCRIMINATION; s.a. Freedom and human rights; Minorities (ethnic, racial, religious)
PAIS PREJUDICE; s.a. Anti-Americanism; Discrimination
BPI PREJUDICES; s.a. Favoritism (personnel management); Race discrimination

PREMARITAL EXAMINATIONS. *Use* Venereal Diseases

PREMIUMS. *Use* Merchandising; Sales Management

PRENATAL CARE. *Use* Maternal and Infant Welfare; Mothers

PREROGATIVE, ROYAL. *Use* Executive Power

PRESCHOOL EDUCATION. *See* Education, Preschool

PRESCRIPTIONS. *Use* Drugs

PRESERVATION OF FORESTS. *See* Forests and Forestry; Natural Resources; Nature Conservation

PRESIDENTIAL CAMPAIGNS. *Use* Advertising, Political; Electioneering; Presidents

PRESIDENTIAL ELECTION OF (Year). *Use* Elections

PRESIDENTIAL LIBRARIES. *Use* Archives

PRESIDENTIAL PRIMARIES. *See* Political Parties

PRESIDENTS
See also names of individual presidents, e.g., Kennedy, John Fitzgerald.
LC ——; s.a. Executive power; Heads of state; Presidents—U.S.; subd. *Presidents* under countries, e.g., Mexico—Presidents
SEARS ——; s.a. Executive power; Kings and rulers; President—U.S.
RG ——; s.a. Executive power; Heads of state; Presidential campaigns
NYT U.S.—PRESIDENTS
PAIS U.S.—PRESIDENT; s.a. Electoral college
BPI PRESIDENTS (U.S.); s.a. Corporations—Presidents; Executives; Veto

PRESS
LC ——; s.a. Amateur journalism; Journalists—Legal status, laws, etc.; Liberty of the press; Newspapers; Periodicals; Press and politics; Press law; Public opinion; Publicity
SEARS NEWSPAPERS; s.a. Blacks and the press; Freedom of information; Freedom of the press; Government and the press; Journalism; News agencies; Reporters and reporting

RG ——; s.a. Confidential communications—Press; Freedom of the press; Local government and the press; Newspapers and politics; Presidents—U.S.—Press conferences; Underground press
NYT NEWS AND NEWS MEDIA; s.a. Freedom of the press; Politics and government; Press conferences; Publications; U.S.—Presidents—Press conference
PAIS ——; s.a. Advertising, Political; Government and the press; Journalism; Reporters and reporting; U.S.—President—Relations with the press
BPI NEWSPAPERS; s.a. Government and the press; Journalism; Libel and slander; Mass media; Presidents (U.S.)—Press relations; Press conferences

PRESS, NEGRO. *See* Blacks and the Press

PRESS AND GOVERNMENT. *See* Government and the Press

PRESS CENSORSHIP. *See* Liberty of Speech

PRESS CONFERENCES. *Use* Public Relations; Reporters and Reporting

PRESS LAW. *Use* Libel and Slander; Liberty of Speech

PRESS MONOPOLIES. *Use* Monopolies

PRESS PHOTOGRAPHERS. *See* News Photographers

PRESS RELEASES. *Use* Public Relations

PRESSURE GROUPS. *Use* Lobbying; Politics, Practical; Representative Government and Representation; Social Groups

PRESTIGE. *Use* Elite (Social sciences); Social Classes

PRE-TRIAL DETENTION. *See* Arrest

PRE-TRIAL PROCEDURE. *Use* Procedure (Law); Trials

PREVENTION OF CRIME. *See* Crime and Criminals

PREVENTIVE DETENTION. *Use* Arrest; Bail; Imprisonment

PRICE FIXING. *Use* Commercial Crimes; Monopolies; Prices

PRICE LABELS. *See* Labels

PRICE MAINTENANCE. *Use* Prices

PRICE POLICY. *Use* Marketing; Monopolies; Prices

PRICE REGULATION. *Use* Black Market; Commercial Crimes; Inflation (Finance); Prices; Rent Laws

PRICE TAGS. *See* Prices

PRICES
See also subd. *Prices* under names of products and other subjects, e.g., Eggs—Prices.
LC ——; s.a. Agricultural price supports; Black market; Consumption (economics); Cost and standard of living; Overproduction; Price discrimination; Price indexes; Price maintenance; Price regulation; Rebates; Supply and demand
SEARS ——; s.a. Competition, Unfair; Farm produce—Marketing; Retail trade; Wage-price policy

RG ——; s.a. Dumping (commercial policy); Inflation (finance); Price maintenance by industry; Price marks; Value (economic theory)
NYT ECONOMIC CONDITIONS AND TRENDS; s.a. Commerce; Discount selling, Labor—U.S.—Wages and hours; Retail stores and trade
PAIS ——; s.a. Competition, Unfair; Discount houses (retail trade); Discount, Trade; Oligopolies; Purchasing power; Unit pricing; Wages and salaries—Regulation
BPI ——; s.a. Cost and standard of living; Discount houses (retail trade); Discount, Trade; Price cutting; Price fixing; Price policies; Value; Wages and salaries

PRIESTS. *Use* Catholic Church; Catholic Church in the U.S.; Celibacy; Church; Clergy

PRIMARIES. *Use* Electioneering; Elections; Political Parties; Politics, Practical; Voters, Registration of; Voting

PRIMARY EDUCATION. *See* Education, Primary

PRIMATES. *Use* Apes

PRIMITIVE ART. *See* Art, Primitive

PRINTERS MARKS. *Use* Trade-marks

PRINTING. *Use* Book Industries and Trade; Commercial Art; Graphic Arts; Printing Industry; Publishers and Publishing

PRINTING, ELECTROSTATIC. *Use* Copying Processes

PRINTING, PUBLIC. *Use* Government and the Press; Government Publications

PRINTING INDUSTRY
LC ——; s.a. Advertising layout and typography; Book industry and trade; Photography—Printing processes; Printers; Printing machinery and supplies; Printing, Practical; Serigraphy; Trade-unions—Printing industry
SEARS PRINTING; s.a. Color printing; Electrotyping; Offset printing; Printing as a trade; Typesetting; U.S.—Government publications
RG ——; s.a. Lithography; Printing—Legibility; Proofreading; Strikes—U.S.—Printers; Type and type founding
NYT PRINTING AND ALLIED TRADES; s.a. Graphic arts; Paper—Newsprint; Publications
PAIS ——; s.a. Government publications; Printing industry, Public; Typesetting; U.S.—Government Printing Office; subd. *Printing industry* under specific subjects, e.g., Computers—Printing industry
BPI ——; s.a. Advertising—Printing; Book industry; Flexography; Silk screen printing; Wages and salaries—Printing industry

PRINTS. *Use* Graphic Arts

PRIORITIES, INDUSTRIAL
LC ——; s.a. Economic policy; Industrial procurement; Rationing, Consumer; Trade regulation; World War, 1939-1945—Rationing

SEARS INDUSTRY AND STATE; s.a. Industrial mobilization; War—Economic aspects
RG PRIORITIES AND ALLOCATIONS, INDUSTRIAL; s.a. Black markets; War profits
NYT LABOR; s.a. Armament and defense; Economic conditions and trends (general); War and revolution
PAIS ——; s.a. Black markets; War and emergency powers
BPI INDUSTRY AND STATE; s.a. Subsidies; Trade regulation

PRISON CAMPS. *Use* Concentration Camps

PRISON LABOR. *See* Convict Labor

PRISON RIOTS. *Use* Imprisonment

PRISONERS. *Use* Prisons and Prisoners

PRISONERS OF WAR. *Use* Concentration Camps

PRISONS AND PRISONERS
See also subd. *Prisons* under names of cities.
LC PRISONS; s.a. Amnesty; Arrest; Bail; Capital punishment; Correctional institutions; Criminal justice, Administration of; Indeterminate sentence; Juvenile delinquency; Legal aid; Life imprisonment; Narcotic addicts; Prison discipline; Prison sentences; Prisoners; Reformatories; Rehabilitation of criminals; Riots; Suretyship and guaranty; Vice
SEARS PRISONS; s.a. Convict labor; Crime and criminals; Education of prisoners; Parole; Penal colonies; Reformatories; Social case work
RG PRISONS; s.a. Indeterminate sentence; Justice, Administration of; Parole; Penal colonies; Prison riots; Prisoners—Treatment; Probation; Punishment
NYT ——; s.a. Amnesties; Crime and criminals; Police; Probation and parole
PAIS PRISONS; s.a. Correction (penology); Crime and criminals—Punishment; Debt, Imprisonment for; Imprisonment; Jails; Pardon; Prisoners; Prisoners, Discharged
BPI PRISONS, s.a. Parole; Prison riots; Prisoners

PRIVACY, RIGHT OF
LC ——; s.a. Eavesdropping; Privileged communications (libel and slander); Secrecy (law)
SEARS ——; s.a. Criminal investigation; Eavesdropping; Libel and slander; Wiretapping
RG ——; s.a. Confidential communications; Wiretapping
NYT PRIVACY, INVASION OF; s.a. Freedom and human rights; Law and legislation; Libel and slander
PAIS PRIVACY; s.a. Confidential communications; Privileges and immunities; Secrecy (law)
BPI ——; s.a. Libel and slander; Official secrets; U.S.—Congress—Privileges and immunities

PRIVATE BRANDS. *Use* Trade-marks

PRIVATE COMPANIES. *Use* Business Enterprises; Corporations; Liability (Law); Partnership

PRIVATE POLICE. *See* Police

PRIVATE PRESSES. *Use* Publishers and Publishing

PRIVATE SCHOOLS
LC ——; s.a. Boarding schools; Church schools; Education, Secondary; Schools
SEARS ——; s.a. Black colleges; Church schools; Education, Secondary
RG ——; s.a. Education and state; Military schools
NYT EDUCATION AND SCHOOLS—U.S.—PREP SCHOOLS; s.a. Colleges and universities; Education and schools—U.S.—Sectarian schools
PAIS SCHOOLS, PRIVATE; s.a. Boarding schools; Education; Parochial schools
BPI ——; s.a. Church schools; Schools

PRIVATE SECRETARIES. *Use* Secretaries

PRIVATEERING. *Use* Maritime Law; Naval Art and Science

PRIVILEGED COMMUNICATIONS. *See* Confidential Communications; Privacy, Right of

PRIVILEGES AND IMMUNITIES. *Use* Constitutions; International Law

PRIZES (Rewards). *See* Rewards (Prizes, etc.)

PROBABILITIES
LC ——; s.a. Average; Chance; Errors, Theory of; Frequency theory; Games of chance (mathematics); Logic; Uncertainty (information theory)
SEARS ——; s.a. Gambling; Insurance, Life; Sampling (statistics)
RG ——; s.a. Distribution (probability theory); Risk
NYT STATISTICS; s.a. Gambling; Games
PAIS MATHEMATICS; s.a. Statistics
BPI ——; s.a. Correlation (statistics); Reliability engineering; Sampling (statistics)

PROBATE LAW AND PRACTICE
LC ——; s.a. Decedents' estates; Estates (law); Probate courts
SEARS PROBATE LAW; s.a. Estate planning; Inheritance and succession; Wills
RG ——; s.a. Executors and administrators
NYT LAW AND LEGISLATION; s.a. Legal profession; Wills and estates
PAIS PROBATE LAW; s.a. Estates (law); Inheritance; Probate courts
BPI PROBATE LAW; s.a. Estate planning; Estates (law); Wills

PROBATION. *Use* Juvenile Delinquency; Prisons and Prisoners; Punishment; Social Service

PROBLEM CHILDREN
Scope: Works on children with behavior difficulties due to emotional instability or social environment.
LC ——; s.a. Child guidance clinics; Church work with problem children; Juvenile delinquency
SEARS ——; s.a. Child study; Juvenile delinquency
RG ——; s.a. Child psychiatry; Mentally ill children; Runaway boys and girls
NYT CHILDREN AND YOUTH—BEHAVIOR AND TRAINING; s.a. Children and youth—Crime and criminals; Children and youth—Lost, missing and runaway children; Juvenile delinquency
PAIS ——; s.a. Juvenile delinquents; Social service—Work with youth
BPI CHILD WELFARE; s.a. Child study; Orphans and orphan asylums

PROBLEM SOLVING. *Use* Decision Making; Logic; Thought and Thinking

PROCEDURE (Law)
LC ——; s.a. Civil procedure; Court rules; Judicial powers; Jury; Legal etiquette; Trials
SEARS JUSTICE, ADMINISTRATION OF; s.a. Courts; Courts martial and courts of inquiry
RG ——; s.a. Appellate procedure; Conduct of court proceedings; Criminal procedure
NYT LAW AND LEGISLATION; s.a. Courts; Crime and criminals; Legal profession
PAIS LEGAL PROCEDURE; s.a. Administrative procedure; Pre-trial procedure
BPI LAW; s.a. Courts; Lawyers

PROCURERS. *See* Prostitution

PRODUCE TRADE. *Use* Farm Produce; Food Industry and Trade; Food Supply

PRODUCT MANAGEMENT
LC ——; s.a. Inventories, Retail; Marketing management; New products
SEARS MARKETING; s.a. Sales management
RG MARKETING; s.a. Inventories; Products, New
NYT MARKETING AND MERCHANDISING; s.a. Market research; Sales
PAIS ——; s.a. Distribution; Products, New
BPI MARKETING; s.a. Marketing managers; Product planning; Products, New

PRODUCT QUALITY. *See* Quality Control

PRODUCT SAFETY. *Use* Consumer Protection

PRODUCTION. *Use* Economic Development; Gross National Product; Industrial Management; Industry; Overproduction; Production Standards; Supply and Demand

PRODUCTION CONTROL
LC ——; s.a. Critical path analysis; Line of balance (management); subd. *Production control* under subjects, e.g., Weapons systems—Production control
SEARS QUALITY CONTROL; s.a. subd. *Quality control* under specific industries, e.g., Factory management; Industrial management
RG ——; s.a. Critical path analysis; Quality control
NYT QUALITY CONTROL (Industrial and laboratory processes); s.a. Economic conditions and trends (general); Labor—U.S.—Productivity
PAIS ——; s.a. Efficiency, Industrial; Quality control
BPI ——; s.a. Inventory control; Quality control; Scheduling (management)

PRODUCTION ENGINEERING. *Use* Factory Management

PRODUCTION PLANNING. *Use* Industrial Management

PRODUCTION STANDARDS
LC ——; s.a. Motion study; Performance; subd. *Production standards* under subjects, e.g, Turning—Production standards; Work
SEARS JOB ANALYSIS; s.a. Efficiency, Industrial; Time study
RG ——; s.a. Work measurement
NYT STANDARDS AND STANDARDIZATION; s.a. Labor; Management, Industrial and institutional
PAIS PRODUCTION; s.a. Efficiency, Industrial; Time and motion study
BPI ——; s.a. Motion study; Time study

PRODUCTS, CERTIFICATION OF. *Use* Quality Control

PRODUCTS, NEW. *Use* Industrial Research; Marketing; New Business Enterprises; New Products; Product Management

PRODUCTS LIABILITY. *Use* Liability (Law); Negligence; Obligations

PRODUCTS OF LIABILITY. *Use* Consumer Protection

PROFESSIONAL ASSOCIATIONS. *Use* Professions; Trade and Professional Associations

PROFESSIONAL CORPORATIONS. *Use* Corporations; Professions

PROFESSIONAL EDUCATION. *Use* Colleges and Universities; Education, Higher; Learning and Scholarship; Professions

PROFESSIONAL ETHICS. *Use* Business Ethics; Ethics; Medical Ethics, Professions

PROFESSIONAL SECRETS. *Use* Confidential Communications

PROFESSIONALISM. *Use* Occupations

PROFESSIONS
See also names of professions, e.g., Librarianship; Agriculture as a profession; Music as a profession; etc.
LC ——; s.a. Brain drain; College graduates; Free choice of employment; Intellectuals; Manpower; Professional corporations; Professional education; Professional ethics; Professionalism in sports
SEARS ——; s.a. Labor and laboring classes; Occupations; Vocational guidance
RG ——; s.a. Negro women—Occupations; Woman—Occupations
NYT ——; s.a. Labor; White collar workers
PAIS ——; s.a. Occupations; Self-employed
BPI ——; s.a. Occupations; Professional associations

PROFIT. *Use* Business Tax; Economics; Income; Risk

PROFIT SHARING. *Use* Bonus System; Cooperation; Incentives in Industry; Non-wage Payments; Wages and Salaries

PROFITEERING. *Use* Black Market; Racketeering; War—Economic Aspects

PROGRAM BUDGETING. *Use* Budget

PROGRAMMED INSTRUCTION
See also subd. *Programmed instruction* under subjects, e.g., Trigonometry—Programmed instruction.
LC ——; s.a. Computer-assisted instruction; Educational planning; Learning, Psychology of; Teaching machines
SEARS ——; s.a. Teaching—Aids and devices; Teaching machines
RG ——; s.a. Computers—Educational use; Teaching machines
NYT EDUCATION AND SCHOOLS; s.a. Education and schools—U.S.—Teaching aids; Teaching machines
PAIS ——; s.a. Education—Aids and devices
BPI ——; s.a. Teaching—Aids and devices; Teaching machines

PROGRAMMED LEARNING. *See* Programmed Instruction

PROGRAMMING (Electronic computers)
LC ——; s.a. Coding theory; Computer programming management; Data tapes; Electronic analog computers—Programming; Linear programming; Mathematical models
SEARS ——; s.a. Computer programs; Electronic data processing; Programming languages (electronic computers)
RG COMPUTER PROGRAMMING; s.a. Computer languages; Punched card systems
NYT DATA PROCESSING (INFORMATION PROCESSING) EQUIPMENT AND SYSTEMS; s.a. Electronics
PAIS COMPUTER PROGRAMMING
BPI COMPUTER PROGRAMMING; s.a. Computer languages; Punched card systems

PROGRAMS, RADIO. *See* Radio Broadcasting and Programs

PROGRESS
LC ——; s.a. Cultural lag; Social problems; Social stability; War and stability
SEARS ——; s.a. Civilization; War and civilization
RG ——; s.a. Change; Science and civilization
NYT CIVILIZATION; s.a. Man; Science and technology
PAIS SOCIAL PROGRESS; s.a. Social change; Technology and civilization
BPI ——; s.a. Economic change; Technological change

PROGRESSIVE EDUCATION. *See* Educational Planning and Innovations

PROHIBITED BOOKS. *Use* Censorship

PROHIBITION. *Use* Alcoholism; Liquor Problem; Temperance

PROJECTILES. *Use* Ballistics; Gunnery; Ordnance

PROJECTION (Psychology). *Use* Personality Tests

PROLETARIAT
LC   ——; s.a. Dictatorship of the proletariat; Middle classes; Plebs (Rome)
SEARS ——; s.a. Labor and laboring classes; Socialism
RG   LABOR AND LABORING CLASSES; s.a. Socialism; Work
NYT   LABOR; s.a. Politics and government; Sociology; subd. *Labor* under names of countries or areas, e.g., Italy—Labor
PAIS   LABOR; s.a. Poor; Socialism
BPI   LABOR AND LABORING CLASSES; s.a. Communism; Political science; Socialism

PROMISCUITY. *Use* Sex

PROMISES. *Use* Oaths

PROMISSORY NOTES. *Use* Credit; Negotiable Instruments

PROMOTION OF SPECIAL EVENTS. *Use* Special Days, Weeks and Months

PROMOTIONAL ALLOWANCES. *Use* Sales Management

PROOFREADING. *Use* Editing; Printing Industry

PROPAGANDA
See also types of propaganda, e.g., Propaganda, American; Propaganda, Anti-American.
LC   ——; s.a. Advertising; Anti-Communist movements; Conformity; Government publicity; Lobbying; Persuasion (psychology); Public opinion; Publicity; Rumor; subd. *Psychological aspects* under names of wars, e.g., World War, 1939–1945—Psychological aspects
SEARS ——; s.a. Advertising; Political psychology; Psychology, Applied; Social psychology
RG   ——; s.a. Moving pictures—Propaganda films; Political attitudes; Public opinion; subd. *Propaganda* under names of wars
NYT   GOVERNMENT AND POLITICS; s.a. News and news media; Psychology and psychologists
PAIS   ——; s.a. Brainwashing; Communication; Political parties—Propaganda; Psychological warfare; Public opinion
BPI   ——; s.a. Influence (psychology); Motivation (psychology); Persuasion; Radio broadcasting—Propaganda

PROPERTY
See also types of property, e.g., Church property; Community property; Industrial property; Intellectual property; Personal property; Primitive property; Real property; Socialist property.
LC   ——; s.a. Abandonment of property; Absenteeism; Acquisition of property; Bailments; Economics; Future interests; Income; Offenses against property; Possession (law); Property and socialism; Real property; Things (law); Transfer (law); Wealth
SEARS ——; s.a. Assessment; Eminent domain; Inheritance and succession
RG   ——; s.a. Heirlooms; Joint tenancy; Mortgages; Vested rights; Wills

NYT   PROPERTY AND INVESTMENTS; s.a. Wills and estates
PAIS   ——; s.a. Expropriation; Liens; Property tax; Trademarks and names
BPI   ——; s.a. Eminent domain; Patent laws and regulations; Right of property; Trademarks

PROPERTY, INTELLECTUAL. *Use* Copyright; Intellectual Property

PROPERTY, LITERARY. *See* Intellectual Property

PROPERTY, REAL. *See* Real Property

PROPERTY—VALUATION. *See* Valuation

PROPERTY INSURANCE. *Use* Valuation

PROPHECIES
LC   ——; s.a. Apocalyptic literature; Second sight; subd. *Prophecies* under specific subjects, e.g., Bible—Prophecies; History—Prophecies; Supernatural
SEARS ——; s.a. Astrology; Divination; Fortune telling; Oracles
RG   ——; s.a. Forecasting; Prophets
NYT   PREDICTIONS; s.a. Astrology; Fortune telling
PAIS   FORECASTING; s.a. Political forecasting; Population forecasting
BPI   FORECASTS

PROPHETS. *Use* Bible; Prophecies

PROPORTIONAL REPRESENTATION. *Use* Apportionment (Election law); Minorities; Representative Government and Representation

PROPRIETARY RIGHTS. *See* Property

PROSELYTES AND PROSELYTIZING. *See* Conversion, Religious

PROSODY. *See* Versification

PROSPECTING. *See* Mines and Mineral Resources

PROSPERITY. *Use* Luxury; Success; Wealth

PROSTHESIS. *Use* Amputees; Artificial Organs

PROSTHODENTICS. *See* Dentistry

PROSTITUTION
LC   ——; s.a. Hygiene, Sexual; Prostitutes in literature; Sex and law; Trials (pimps)
SEARS ——; s.a. Sexual ethics; Woman—Social conditions
RG   ——; s.a. Illegitimacy; Sex crimes
NYT   ——; s.a. Sex crimes; Vice
PAIS   ——; s.a. Sexual ethics; Venereal diseases
BPI   ——; s.a. Moral conditions; Sex

PROTECTION. *See* Free Trade and Protection

PROTECTION OF WILDLIFE. *See* Wildlife Conservation

PROTECTORATES. *Use* Colonies

PROTEST MARCHES. *See* Demonstrations

PROTESTANTISM
See also names of Protestant denominations, e.g., Lutheran church; Methodist Episcopal Church; Protestant Episcopal Church in the U.S.A.

LC ——; s.a. Anglo-Catholicism; Dissenters, Religious; Jesus Christ; Liturgies; Protestant churches; Reformation
SEARS ——; s.a. Christianity; Church history
RG ——; s.a. Evangelicalism
NYT RELIGION AND CHURCHES
PAIS PROTESTANTS; s.a. Fundamentalism; Protestant church
BPI ——; s.a. Religion

PROTESTANTISM, EVANGELICAL. *See* Evangelicalism

PROTESTS, DEMONSTRATIONS, ETC. *Use* Demonstrations; Government, Resistance to; Lobbying; Mobs; Passive Resistance; Riots

PROTONS. *Use* Atoms; Nuclear Physics

PROTOPLASM. *Use* Embryology

PROVERBS
LC ——; s.a. Maxims; Mottoes; Sea proverbs; subd. *Quotations, maxims, etc.* under subjects, e.g., Musk—Quotations, maxims, etc.
SEARS ——; s.a. Epigrams; Folklore; Quotations
RG ——; s.a. Aphorisms and apothegms; Maxims
NYT QUOTATIONS AND PROVERBS; s.a. Slogans, mottoes and catch-phrases
PAIS SLOGANS
BPI SLOGANS

PROXIES. *Use* Stock Exchange

PRUNING. *Use* Trees

PSEUDONYMS. *Use* Anonyms and Pseudonyms

PSYCHIATRIC HOSPITALS. *Use* Mental Institutions; Mentally Ill

PSYCHIATRY
Scope: Works on clinical aspects of mental disorders, including therapy. See Mental illness for popular works on the subject and Psychology, Pathological for systematic descriptions of mental disorders.
LC ——; s.a. Existential psychology; Geriatric psychiatry; Neuroses; Psychiatry in literature; Psychoses; Shock therapy
SEARS ——; s.a. Adolescent psychiatry; Child psychiatry; Insanity; Psychotherapy
RG ——; s.a. Group psychotherapy; Mental hygiene; Social psychiatry
NYT MENTAL HEALTH AND DISORDERS; s.a. Mental deficiency and defectives; Psychology and psychologists
PAIS ——; s.a. Hospitals—Psychiatric services; Mental hygiene
BPI MENTAL ILLNESS—THERAPY; s.a. Hospitals, Psychiatric; Psychotherapy

PSYCHIATRY, CHILD. *See* Child Psychiatry

PSYCHIC ENERGIZERS. *See* Antidepressants

PSYCHICAL RESEARCH
Scope: Investigations of phenomena that appear to be beyond the normal sense of perception.

LC ——; s.a. Mental suggestion; Mind and body; Second sight; Spiritualism; Subconsciousness; Thought transference
SEARS ——; s.a. Apparitions; Dreams; Hallucinations and illusions; Mind reading
RG ——; s.a. Clairvoyance; Mediums, Parapsychology
NYT PSYCHIC PHENOMENA; s.a. Mind; Occult science; Psychology and psychologists
PAIS OCCULT SCIENCES; s.a. Extrasensory perception; Hypnotism
BPI EXTRASENSORY PERCEPTION

PSYCHOANALYSIS
LC ——; s.a. Catharsis; Ego (psychology); Group psychoanalysis; Identification (psychology); Mind and body; Narcoanalysis; Neuroses; Repression (psychology); subd. *Psychology* under classes of persons, e.g., Authors—Psychology
SEARS ——; s.a. Hypnotism; Medicine, Psychosomatic; Subconsciousness
RG ——; s.a. Complexes (psychology); Dreams; Symbolism (psychology)
NYT MENTAL HEALTH AND DISORDERS; s.a. Medicine and health; Psychology and psychologists
PAIS ——; s.a. Hypnotism
BPI PSYCHOTHERAPY; s.a. Mental illness—Therapy; Psychology

PSYCHODRAMA. *Use* Group Relations Training

PSYCHOLOGICAL TESTS. *See* Personality Tests; Tests, Mental

PSYCHOLOGICAL WARFARE. *Use* Cold War; Military Art and Science; Morale; Propaganda; War

PSYCHOLOGY. *Use* Age (Psychology); Alienation (Social psychology); Behavior (Psychology); Behavior Therapy; Character; Conditioned Response; Dreams; Emotions; Ethnopsychology; Mind and Body; Psychoanalysis; Senses and Sensation; Temperament

PSYCHOLOGY, APPLIED. *Use* Educational Psychology; Group Relations Training; Human Relations; Industrial Sociology; Interviewing; Propaganda; Public Relations; Social Psychology

PSYCHOLOGY, CHILD. *See* Child Study

PSYCHOLOGY, EDUCATIONAL. *Use* Educational Psychology; Learning, Psychology of; Teaching; Thought and Thinking

PSYCHOLOGY, ETHNIC. *See* Ethnopsychology

PSYCHOLOGY, INDUSTRIAL. *Use* Industrial Sociology; Personnel Management

PSYCHOLOGY, MILITARY. *Use* Leadership; Morale

PSYCHOLOGY, NATIONAL. *See* Ethnopsychology; National Characteristics

PSYCHOLOGY, PASTORAL. *Use* Clergy; Counseling; Therapeutics, Suggestive

PSYCHOLOGY, PATHOLOGICAL. *Use* Depression, Mental; Insanity; Mental Hygiene; Mental Illness; Psychiatry

PSYCHOLOGY, PHYSIOLOGICAL. *Use* Human Engineering; Mind and Body; Narcoanalysis; Nervous System; Senses and Sensation

PSYCHOMETRICS. *Use* Tests, Mental

PSYCHONEUROSES. *See* Neuroses

PSYCHOPHARMACOLOGY. *Use* Antidepressants; Drugs

PSYCHOSES. *Use* Insanity; Mental Illness; Mentally Ill; Neuroscs; Psychiatry

PSYCHOTHERAPY. *Use* Behavior Therapy; Child Psychiatry; Group Relations Training; Mental Healing; Mental Hygiene; Psychiatry; Psychoanalysis; Therapeutics, Suggestive

PSYCHOTROPIC DRUGS. *Use* Analgesics; Drugs

PTOMAINES. *Use* Toxins and Antitoxins

PUBERTY. *Use* Adolescence; Sex

PUBLIC ADMINISTRATION
Scope: Works on the principles and techniques involved in the conduct of public business. See also subd. *Politics and government* under names of places.
LC ———; s.a. Administrative agencies; Decentralization in government; Federal government; Metropolitan government; Military government; Office practice in government; Public officers
SEARS ———; s.a. Administrative law; Civil service; Local government; Political science
RG ———; s.a. Executive advisory bodies; Municipal government
NYT POLITICS AND GOVERNMENT; s.a. Local government; U.S.—Departments and agencies; U.S.—Finances
PAIS ———; s.a. Administrative remedies; Independent regulatory commissions
BPI ADMINISTRATION, PUBLIC; s.a. Bureaucracy; Expenditures, Public; Government officials and employees

PUBLIC ASSISTANCE. *See* Public Welfare

PUBLIC AUTHORITIES. *See* Corporations, Government

PUBLIC BATHS. *Use* Baths

PUBLIC BUILDINGS. *Use* Architecture; Art and State; Public Works

PUBLIC CONTRACTS. *Use* Contracts; Purchasing

PUBLIC DEBTS. *See* Debts, Public

PUBLIC DEFENDERS. *Use* Lawyers; Legal Aid

PUBLIC DOCUMENTS. *See* Government and the Press; Government Publications

PUBLIC FINANCE. *See* Finance, Public

PUBLIC HEALTH
LC HYGIENE, PUBLIC; s.a. Cities and towns—Planning—Hygienic aspects; Communicable diseases; Health education; Hygiene; Public health laws; Public health nursing; Quarantine; Sewage disposal; subd. *Sewerage* under names of cities; Venereal diseases
SEARS ———; s.a. Food adulteration and inspection; Medical care; Occupational diseases
RG ———; s.a. Cleaning of cities, towns, etc.; Epidemics; Hospitals
NYT MEDICINE AND HEALTH; s.a. Environment; Sanitation
PAIS ———; s.a. Environmental health; Sanitation
BPI ———; s.a. Environmental health; Pollution; Vaccination

PUBLIC HOUSING
LC ———; s.a. Housing authorities; Public housing—Rent; Public housing—Social aspects
SEARS HOUSING; s.a. Apartment houses; City planning; Social problems; Tenement houses
RG HOUSING PROJECTS, GOVERNMENT; s.a. Housing—Federal aid; Mortgages
NYT HOUSING; s.a. Area planning and renewal; Urban areas
PAIS HOUSING PROJECTS, GOVERNMENT; s.a. Housing; Housing authorities
BPI HOUSING PROJECTS, GOVERNMENT; s.a. Housing—Federal aid; Housing projects; Housing projects, Municipal

PUBLIC INSTITUTIONS
See also types of public institutions, e.g., Hospitals; Old age homes; Prisons; Schools
LC ———; s.a. Institutional care
SEARS INSTITUTIONAL CARE; s.a. Charities; Public welfare
RG ———; s.a. State institutions
NYT Types and names of institutions, e.g., Libraries
PAIS INSTITUTIONS, PUBLIC
BPI INSTITUTIONS, NONPROFIT

PUBLIC INTEREST. *Use* Industry and State; State, The

PUBLIC LANDS
See also subd. *Public lands* under names of places.
LC ———; s.a. Commons; Forest reserves; Homestead law—U.S.; Land grants; Pasture, Right of; Pastures; Reclamation of land; Squatters
SEARS GOVERNMENT OWNERSHIP; s.a. Forest reserves; National parks and reserves
RG ———; s.a. Submerged lands; Wilderness areas
NYT NATURE; s.a. Forests and forestry; Parks, playgrounds and other recreation areas; Wildlife sanctuaries
PAIS ———; s.a. Forests, National; Parks, National; Territorial waters
BPI ———; s.a. Eminent domain; Parks; Wilderness areas

PUBLIC MEETINGS. *Use* Congresses and Conventions; Demonstrations; Parliamentary Practice

PUBLIC OFFICIALS. *Use* Civil Service; Municipal Officials and Employees; Public Administration

PUBLIC OPINION
See also subds. *Public opinion* and *Foreign opinion* under names of countries, e.g., U.S.—Foreign opinion or subjects, e.g., Vietnamese conflict—Public opinion.
LC ———; s.a. Polemics; Press; Public opinion polls; Public relations; Rumor; Scale analysis (psychology); Social pressure

SEARS ———; s.a. Attitude (psychology); Freedom of conscience; Political psychology; Public opinion—Research; Publicity

RG ———; s.a. Attitudes; Political forecasting; Student opinion

NYT ———; s.a. names of polling organizations, e.g., Gallup Poll; subjects of polls, e.g., Elections

PAIS ———; s.a. Election forecasting; Market surveys; Propaganda

BPI ———; s.a. Employees—Opinion polls; Newspapers—Opinion polls; Public opinion polls

PUBLIC OWNERSHIP. *See* Municipal Ownership

PUBLIC PLAYGROUNDS. *See* Playgrounds

PUBLIC PROSECUTORS. *Use* Justice, Administration of

PUBLIC RECORDS

LC ———; s.a. Archives; subd. *Public records* under names of government agencies

SEARS ARCHIVES; s.a. Documentation; History—Sources

RG ———; s.a. Archives, subd. *Public records* under names of government agencies

NYT DOCUMENTS; s.a. subd. *Archives and records* under names of places

PAIS GOVERNMENT RECORDS; s.a. Archives; Municipal records

BPI GOVERNMENT RECORDS; s.a. Business—Reports to government; Freedom of information

PUBLIC RELATIONS

Scope: Works on the policies and methods which promote the standing in the community of an individual or organization.

LC ———; s.a. Advertising, Public service; Industrial publicity; Lobbying; Press conferences; Press releases; subd. *Public relations* under names of organizations

SEARS ———; s.a. Propaganda; Psychology, Applied; Publicity

RG ———; s.a. Corporate image; Customer relations; Television in politics

NYT PUBLIC RELATIONS AND PUBLICITY; s.a. News and news media

PAIS ———; s.a. Advertising; Press; Public opinion

BPI ———; s.a. Advertising, Corporate image; Press conferences; Publicity

PUBLIC SAFETY, CRIMES AGAINST. *See* Offenses Against Public Safety

PUBLIC SAFETY OFFICERS. *Use* Police

PUBLIC SCHOOLS. *Use* Education; Education, Secondary; High Schools; Schools

PUBLIC SCHOOLS—DESEGRATION. *Use* Busing; Discrimination in Education; Negro Children; Negro Students

PUBLIC SCHOOLS AND RELIGION. *Use* Religious Education

PUBLIC SERVICE CORPORATIONS. *See* Public Utilities

PUBLIC SPEAKING

Scope: Works dealing with the problems of speaking effectively in public.

LC ———; s.a. Debates and debating; Extemporaneous speaking; Introduction of speakers; Oratory; Persuasion (rhetoric); Stage fright

SEARS ———; s.a. Acting; Lectures and lecturing; Orations; Preaching

RG ———; s.a. Argument; Lectures and lecturing; Rhetoric

NYT SPEECHES AND STATEMENTS (General); s.a. Debating; Speech

PAIS ———; s.a. Debating

BPI ———; s.a. Speech; Television public speaking; Voice

PUBLIC TRUSTEES. *Use* Trusts and Trustees

PUBLIC UTILITIES

See also types of public utilities, e.g., Electric utilities; Gas; Water supply.

LC ———; s.a. Industry and state; Local transit; Municipal ownership; Public service; Service at cost (public utilities); Strikes and lockouts—Public utilities

SEARS ———; s.a. Corporation law; Corporations

RG ———; s.a. Government investigations—Public utilities

NYT ———; s.a. Taxation

PAIS ———; s.a. Government business enterprises; Municipal services

BPI ———; s.a. Government business enterprises; Institutions, Nonprofit

PUBLIC WELFARE

Scope: Works on tax-supported welfare activities. See Charities for privately supported activities and Social service for works on methods employed in welfare work, private or public.

LC ———; s.a. Community organizations; Disaster relief; Food relief; Legal aid; Old age homes; Poor; Psychiatric social work; Public institutions; Social service; subd. *Poor* under names of cities; Welfare economics; Work relief

SEARS ———; s.a. Day nurseries; Institutional care; Legal assitance to the poor; Orphans and orphans' homes; Poverty; Unemployed

RG ———; s.a. Insurance, Social; Old age assistance

NYT WELFARE WORK (U.S. Only); s.a. Social conditions and welfare

PAIS ———; s.a. Family allowances; Transients, Relief of

BPI ———; s.a. Child welfare; Family allowances

PUBLIC WORKS

See also subd. *Public works* under names of places, e.g., Chicago—Public works.

LC ———; s.a. Contracts, Letting of; Full employment policies; Hurricane protection; Municipal buildings; Municipal ownership; Work relief

SEARS ———; s.a. Economic assistance, Domestic; Municipal engineering; Public buildings

RG ———; s.a. Dams

NYT ———; s.a. Building; Labor—U.S.—Unemployment and job market; Roads

PUBLIC WORKS, *cont.*
PAIS ——; s.a. Civil engineering; Government business enterprises
BPI ——; s.a. Government business enterprises; Public works—Federal aid

PUBLIC WORSHIP. *Use* Worship

PUBLICATIONS. *Use* Book Industries and Trade; Books; Government Publications; Press; Publishers and Publishing

PUBLICITY. *Use* Advertising; Propaganda; Public Relations

PUBLICITY (Law). *Use* Libel and Slander

PUBLISHERS AND PUBLISHING
LC ——; s.a. Book industries and trade; Editing; Music printing; Newspaper publishing; Periodicals, Publishing of; Private presses
SEARS ——; s.a. Booksellers and bookselling; Copyright; Printing
RG ——; s.a. Best sellers; Literary agents
NYT BOOKS AND LITERATURE—BOOK TRADE; s.a. Copyrights; Publications; Writing and writers
PAIS PUBLISHING INDUSTRY; s.a. Bookselling; Pamphlets
BPI ——; s.a. Authors and publishers; Books

PULPWOOD INDUSTRY. *Use* Forests and Forestry

PUNCHED CARD SYSTEMS. *Use* Indexing; Information Storage and Retrieval Systems; Programming (Electronic computers)

PUNISHMENT
See also particular forms of punishment, e.g., Hanging.
LC ——; s.a. Amnesty; Censures, Ecclesiastical; Discipline of children; Judgments; Punishment in literature; Rewards and punishment in education
SEARS ——; s.a. Crime and criminals; Probation
RG ——; s.a. School discipline
NYT CRIME AND CRIMINALS; s.a. Prisons and prisoners

PAIS See particular forms of punishment, e.g., Capital punishment
BPI ——; s.a. Justice, Administration of; Prisoners

PUNISHMENT OF CHILDREN. *See* Discipline of Children

PUNS AND PUNNING. *Use* Wit and Humor

PUPPETS AND PUPPET PLAYS. *Use* Theater

PURCHASING
See also subd. *Procurement* under government agencies, e.g., U.S. Navy—Procurement.
LC ——; s.a. Consumer education; Consumers; Government purchasing; Industrial procurement; Materials management; Public contracts; Purchasing departments
SEARS BUYING; s.a. Consumers; Contracts; Shopping
RG ——; s.a. Buyers; Contracts, Government; Purchasing, Industrial, Quality of products
NYT Commodities purchased; s.a. Economic conditions and trends; Income
PAIS ——; s.a. Consumers; Purchasing agents; Purchasing, Industrial; Purchasing, Military and naval; Shopping and shoppers
BPI ——; s.a. Make-or-buy decisions, Marketing (home economics); Men as purchasers; Purchasing departments; Purchasing, Government; Purchasing, Industrial; Women as purchasers

PURCHASING, GOVERNMENT. *Use* Contracts; Purchasing

PURCHASING, MILITARY. *Use* Defense Contracts

PURCHASING POWER. *Use* Consumption (Economics); Cost and Standard of Living; Income; Money; National Income; Prices

PUTS AND CALLS. *Use* Stock Exchange

PYRAMID SELLING OPERATIONS. *Use* Franchises (Retail trade)

PYROMANIA. *Use* Fires

Q

QUACKERY. *Use* Fraud

QUALITY CONTROL
See also subd. *Quality control* under specific activities and specific industries, e.g., Foundries—Quality control.
LC ——; s.a. Engineering inspection; Factory management; Quality of products
SEARS ——; s.a. Reliability (engineering); Sampling (statistics)

RG ——; s.a. Commercial products, Certification of; Products, New
NYT QUALITY CONTROL (Industrial and laboratory processes); s.a. Consumer protection; Liability for products, Manufacturers'
PAIS ——; s.a. Production control; Standardization
BPI ——; s.a. Inspection; Products, Certification of; Quality of products

QUALITY OF PRODUCTS. *Use* Consumer Protection; New Products; Quality Control

QUANTUM THEORY. *Use* Force and Energy

QUARANTINE. *Use* Communicable Diseases; Hygiene; Public Health

QUEING THEORY. *Use* Operations Research

QUESTION-ANSWERING SYSTEMS. *Use* Decision Making

QUESTIONING. *Use* Interviewing; Teaching

QUILTING. *Use* Handicraft; Sewing

QUILTS. *Use* Beds and Bedding

QUIZ SHOWS. *Use* Rewards (Prizes, etc.); Television Programs

QUOTATIONS
See also subd. *Quotations, maxims, etc.* under subjects, e.g., Music—Quotations, maxims, etc.; Law—Quotations.
LC ——; s.a. Aphorisms and apothegms; Maxims; Terms and phrases
SEARS ——; s.a. Epigrams; Folklore; Proverbs
RG ——; s.a. Aphorisms and apothegms; Children—Sayings; Proverbs
NYT QUOTATIONS AND PROVERBS; s.a. Language and languages; Slogans, mottoes and catch-phrases
PAIS SLOGANS
BPI SLOGANS; s.a. Words

R

RACE. *Use* Anthropology; Color of Man; Ethnology; National Characteristics; Native Races; Negro Race; Race Discrimination; Race Problems

RACE AND ART. *See* Art and Race

RACE AWARENESS
LC ——; s.a. Art and race; Awareness; Ethnic attitudes; Music and Race; Negro race—Race identity; Negroes—Race identity; Race awareness in literature; Race discrimination—Psychological aspects
SEARS ——; s.a. Blacks—Race identity; Ethnology; Prejudices and antipathies; Race problems; Race psychology
RG ETHNOPSYCHOLOGY; s.a. Negroes—Nationalism; Negroes—Psychology; Race attitudes
NYT RACE; s.a. Discrimination; Freedom and human rights; Minorities (ethnic, racial, religious); Prejudices and antipathies
PAIS INTERCULTURAL EDUCATION; s.a. National characteristics; Prejudice, Racial; Race problems
BPI RACE DISCRIMINATION; s.a. Intercultural education; Minorities; Prejudices; Race problems

RACE DISCRIMINATION
LC ——; s.a. Discrimination in employment; Discrimination in housing; Segregation
SEARS RACE PROBLEMS; s.a. Discrimination; Minorities; Social problems; subd. *Race relations* under names of places, e.g., Chicago—Race relations
RG ——; s.a. Discrimination in housing; Negroes—Segregation; Race prejudice
NYT DISCRIMINATION; s.a. Freedom and human rights; Minorities (ethnic, racial, religious); Prejudices and antipathies; Race
PAIS ——; s.a. Discrimination in housing; subd. *Integration and segregation* under specific subjects, e.g., Education—Integration and segregation
BPI ——; s.a. Discrimination in education; Discrimination in employment; Discrimination in housing

RACE HORSES. *Use* Horse-Racing

RACE PROBLEMS
LC ——; s.a. Antisemitism; Church and race problems (yellow-peril); Intercultural education; Racial attitude of American presidents; Social service and race problems; subd. *Native races* under names of continents and countries; and subd. *Race question* under names of places, e.g., Los Angeles—Race question
SEARS ——; s.a. Acculturation; Ethnology; Immigration and emigration; Native races; Race psychology; subd. *Race relations* under names of places, e.g., U.S.—Race relations
RG ——; s.a. Intermarriage of races; subd. *Race question* under names of places
NYT DISCRIMINATION; s.a. Freedom and human rights; Minorities (ethnic, racial, religious); Race
PAIS ——; s.a. Minorities; Race relations
BPI ——; s.a. Genocide; Intercultural education; Minorities

RACE PREJUDICE. *Use* Prejudices and Antipathies; Race Discrimination

RACE PROBLEMS IN SCHOOL MANAGEMENT. *Use* Discrimination in Education

RACE PSYCHOLOGY. *Use* Ethnopsychology; Race Awareness; Social Psychology

RACE RELATIONS. *Use* Equality; Human Relations; Minorities; Race Problems

RACE TRACKS. *Use* Gambling; Horse-Racing

RACIAL DIFFERENCES. *Use* Ethnology

RACIAL DISCRIMINATION. *Use* Equality; Race Discrimination

RACIAL PSYCHOLOGY. *See* Ethnopsychology

RACING. *Use* Horse-Racing

RACISM. *Use* Prejudices and Antipathies

RACKETEERING
LC ——; s.a. Conspiracy; Extortion
SEARS ——; s.a. Crime and criminals; Criminal law
RG ——; s.a. Mafia; Profiteering
NYT RACKETEERING AND RACKETEERS; s.a. Crime and criminals; Extortion
PAIS ——; s.a. Criminal syndicalism; Mafia
BPI CRIME AND CRIMINALS; s.a. Conspiracy; Criminal law

RADAR
LC ——; s.a. Distant early warning system; Surveillance radar; Tracking radar
SEARS ——; s.a. Air defenses; Ballistic missile early warning system; Navigation; Radio
RG ——; s.a. Radar defense networks; Radar in aviation; subd. *Radar equipment* under subjects, e.g., Motor vehicles—Radar equipment
NYT ——; s.a. Airlines—Accidents and safety; Missiles; Ships and shipping—Accidents and safety; U.S. armament and defense
PAIS ——; s.a. Guided missiles—Defense; Navigation; Radar aids to navigation
BPI ——; s.a. Airplanes, Military—Radar equipment; Navigation; Pulse techniques (electronics)

RADIANT HEATING. *Use* Heating

RADIATION
See also types of rays, e.g., Alpha rays; Beta rays; Cathode rays; Cosmic rays; Delta rays; Electromagnetic rays; Gamma rays; Infrared rays; Ultraviolet rays; X-rays; and names of radioactive elements, e.g., Plutonium.
LC ——; s.a. Bacteria, Effect of radiation on; Fetus, Effect of radiation on; Food, Effect of radiation on; Nervous system, Effect of radiation on; Nuclear reactions; Radiation—Dosage; Radiogenetics; Radiology; Radiotherapy; Radium; Shielding (radiation); Soils, Radioactive substances in; Van Allen radiation belt
SEARS ——; s.a. Atomic medicine; Nuclear physics; Radiation—Psychological effect; Radiation—Safety measures; Radioactivity; Sound; Spectrum
RG ——; s.a. Atomic bomb shelters; Irradiation; Plants, Effect of radiation on; Radioactive fallout; Radioactive pollution; Scattering (physics); Transmutation (chemistry)
NYT ——; s.a. Astronautics; Atomic energy and weapons; Electrons; Isotopes; Nuclear research; Radiation effects and hazards; Space—Radiation
PAIS ——; s.a. Atomic weapons—Tests; Radiation—Physiological effect; Radioactive substances
BPI ——; s.a. Atomic power plants—Safety measures; Electronic ovens, Baking—Radiation hazards; Radioactivity; Solar radiation

RADIATION THERAPY. *See* Radiotherapy

RADICALISM. *Use* Right and Left (Political science)

RADICALS AND RADICALISM. *See* Revolutions; Right and Left (Political science)

RADIO. *Use* Radio, Short Wave; Radio Broadcasting and Programs

RADIO—APPARATUS AND SUPPLIES
LC ——; s.a. Amplifiers, Vacuum-tube; Loud speakers, radio-antennas, etc.; Portable radios; Radio industry and trade; Transistor radios
SEARS ——; s.a. Electric industries; Radio industry and trade; Transistors
RG RADIO APPARATUS; s.a. Microphones; Radio industry; Radio receivers—Frequency modulation receivers; Radio receivers, Portable; Radio telephone on ships, boats, etc.
NYT TV AND RADIO—EQUIPMENT AND PROCESSES; s.a. Amplification systems; Electronics; Microphones
PAIS RADIO APPARATUS INDUSTRY
BPI RADIO APPARATUS; s.a. Broadcasting industry; Radio antennas; Radio apparatus industry; Radio receivers

RADIO—CENSORSHIP. *Use* Freedom of Information; Radio Broadcasting and Programs

RADIO, SHORT WAVE
LC ——; s.a. Citizens radio service; Microwaves; Radio pulse line modulation
SEARS ——; s.a. Amateur radio stations; Microwave communication systems
RG RADIO COMMUNICATION, SHORT WAVE; s.a. Citizens radio service; Radio apparatus, Short wave
NYT TELEVISION AND RADIO; s.a. Communications; News and news media
PAIS RADIO; s.a. Microwaves; Radio operators, Amateur
BPI ——; s.a. Microwave communication systems; Radio communication

RADIO ADVERTISING. *Use* Advertising; Radio Broadcasting and Programs

RADIO AND CHILDREN. *Use* Radio in Education

RADIO BROADCASTING AND PROGRAMS
LC RADIO BROADCASTING; s.a. News broadcasts; Public interest radio programs; Public service radio programs; Radio adaptations; Radio and literature; Radio—Censorship; Radio in politics; Radio journalism; Radio Programs; Radio programs—Rating; Subscription radio broadcasting
SEARS RADIO BROADCASTING; s.a. Radio advertising; Radio and music; Radio authorship; Radio plays; Radio scripts; Television broadcasting
RG RADIO BROADCASTING—PROGRAMS; s.a. Audiences; Disc jockeys; Radio broadcasting—Censorship; Radio broadcasting—Music; Radio broadcasting—Public service programs; Radio broadcasting—Sports; Radio laws and regulations; Radio plays
NYT TELEVISION AND RADIO—PROGRAMS; s.a. Freedom of information, thought and expression
PAIS RADIO; s.a. F.M. broadcasting; Radio audiences; Radio—Political uses; Radio—Program rating; Radio—Programs; Radio—Public service programs; Radio—Regulation; Science news

BPI RADIO BROADCASTING—PROGRAMMING; s.a. Radio advertising; Radio and politics; Radio broadcasting—Disk jockeys; Radio broadcasting—F.M. programs; Radio broadcasting—Programs; Radio broadcasting—Public service programs

RADIO IN EDUCATION
LC ——; s.a. Audio-visual education; Radio and children; Radio broadcasting; Radio programs for children; Teaching—Aids and devices; Television and children; Television in education
SEARS ——; s.a. Audio-visual education; Teaching—Aids and devices
RG ——; s.a. Audio-visual instruction; Radio broadcasting—Social aspects; Teaching—Aids and devices
NYT TELEVISION AND RADIO—NONCOMMERCIAL TELEVISION AND RADIO; s.a. Audio-visual devices; Children and youth; Education and schools—U.S.—Teaching aids
PAIS ——; s.a. Education; Education—Aids and devices; Radio programs
BPI ——; s.a. Educational broadcasting; Educational broadcasting stations

RADIO FACSIMILE. *Use* Telecommunication

RADIO IN POLITICS. *Use* Advertising, Political; Electioneering; Radio Broadcasting and Programs

RADIO INDUSTRY AND TRADE. *Use* Radio—Apparatus and Supplies

RADIO PROGRAMS. *Use* Radio Broadcasting and Programs; Radio in Education

RADIO RECEIVERS. *Use* Radio—Apparatus and Supplies

RADIO SCRIPTS. *Use* Radio Broadcasting and Programs

RADIO STATIONS
See also names of radio stations, e.g., British Broadcasting Corporation (BBC).
LC ——; s.a. Aeronautical radio stations; F.M. broadcasting; Marine radio stations; Radio relay stations; Radio stations, Short wave; Radio—Transmitters and transmission
SEARS ——; s.a. Amateur radio stations
RG ——; s.a. Citizens radio service; Radio transmitters
NYT TELEVISION AND RADIO—STATIONS AND NETWORKS; s.a. Communications; News and news media
PAIS ——; s.a. Radio stations, Illegal; Radio stations, Military
BPI BROADCASTING STATIONS; s.a. Broadcasting stations—F.M. stations; Educational broadcasting stations; Mobile radio stations

RADIO TELEGRAPH. *Use* Telecommunication

RADIO TRANSMITTERS. *Use* Radio Stations

RADIOACTIVE DATING. *Use* Nuclear Reactions

RADIOACTIVE FALLOUT. *Use* Atomic Warfare; Pollution; Radiation

RADIOACTIVE SUBSTANCES. *Use* Radiation; Radiotherapy

RADIOACTIVITY. *Use* Nuclear Physics; Nuclear Reactions; Radiation; Radiotherapy

RADIOBIOLOGY. *Use* Radiotherapy

RADIOGENETICS. *Use* Radiation

RADIOLOGY, MEDICAL. *Use* Radiotherapy

RADIOTELEPHONE. *Use* Artificial Satellites

RADIOTHERAPY
LC ——; s.a. Electrotherapeutics; Radiation—Dosage; Radiology, Medical; Short wave therapy; Tracers (biology); X-rays—Therapeutic use
SEARS ——; s.a. Medical electronics; Phototherapy; Radiobiology; Radiologists; Radium
RG ——; s.a. Cancer—Therapy; Diagnosis, Radioscopic; Radioactive tracers; X-rays—Therapeutic applications
NYT MEDICINE AND HEALTH; s.a. Biology and biochemistry; Radiation; Radium; X-Rays
PAIS ——; s.a. Atomic medicine; Medicine; Radioactivity; X-rays
BPI RADIOISOTOPES—MEDICAL USE; s.a. Atomic medicine; Chest radiology; Isotopes; Radioactive substances; Radiography

RADIUM. *Use* Radiation; Radiotherapy

RAFFIA WORK. *Use* Basket Making; Handicrafts

RAGTIME MUSIC. *See* Jazz Music

RAILROADS
LC ——; s.a. Car trusts; Electric locomotives; Electric railroads; Locomotive engineers; Porters; Railroad companies; Railroad construction workers; Railroad land grants; Railroad motorcars; Railroad—Rates; Railroads—Accounts, bookkeeping, etc.; also names of individual railroads
SEARS ——; s.a. Electric railroads; Interstate commerce; Railroad engineering; Railroads—Electrification; Railroads—Employees; Railroads—Statistics; Railway mail service
RG ——; s.a. Railroad travel; Railroads—Private cars; Railroads—Trains; Railroads—Wages and hours; Strikes—U.S.—Railroads; Train ferries
NYT ——; s.a. Freight forwarding; Transit systems; Transportation
PAIS ——; s.a. Accounting—Railroads; Railroads, Electric, Railroads—Finance; Railroads—Freight cars; Railroads—Passenger cars; Strikes—Railroads; Trade unions—Railroad employees; Railroads—Passenger service—Financial aspects; Unit trains
BPI ——; s.a. Cars, Transit and commuter; Collective bargaining—Railroads; Freight and freightage; Railroad construction; Railroads and state; Railroads—Securities; Subways; Tank cars

RAILROADS—ACCIDENTS. *Use* Disasters

RAILROADS—CONSOLIDATION. *Use* Monopolies; Trusts, Industrial

RAILROADS, ELECTRIC. *Use* Railroads

RAILROADS, ELEVATED. *Use* Local Transit

RAILROADS—FREIGHT. *See* Cargo Handling; Freight and Freightage

RAILROADS, MINIATURE. *Use* Amusement Parks

RAILROADS—MODELS. *Use* Toys

RAILROADS—RATES. *Use* Freight and Freightage

RAILROADS AND STATE. *Use* Industry and State; Interstate Commerce

RAILWAY MAIL SERVICE. *Use* Postal Service

RAIN AND RAINFALL. *Use* Water

RAIN FOREST. *Use* Forests and Forestry

RAIN MAKING. *Use* Weather

RAMADAN. *Use* Islam; Special Days, Weeks and Months

RANCH LIFE. *Use* Country Life

RANK. *See* Elite (Social sciences); Social Classes

RANSOM. *Use* Abduction; Kidnapping

RAPE. *Use* Assault and Battery; Sex

RAPID READING. *Use* Reading

RAPID TRANSIT. *Use* Local Transit; Transportation

RARE ANIMALS. *Use* Wildlife Conservation

RARE EARTHS. *Use* Mines and Mineral Resources

RATIONALISM
LC   ———; s.a. Agnosticism; Atheism; Free thought; Indifferentism (religion); Positivism; Rationalists
SEARS ———; s.a. Belief and doubt; Realism; Reason; Secularism; Skepticism
RG   ———; s.a. Empiricism; Enlightenment
NYT   PHILOSOPHY
PAIS PHILOSOPHY
BPI   PHILOSOPHY; s.a. Knowledge, Theory of

RATIONING, CONSUMER. *Use* Food Supply; Priorities, Industrial; War—Economic Aspects

RAW MATERIALS
LC   ———; s.a. Animal products; Farm produce; Strategic materials
SEARS ———; s.a. Commercial products; Forest products; Materials; Mines and mineral resources
RG   ———; s.a. Natural resources; Power resources
NYT   COMMERCE; s.a. Economic conditions and trends (general); names of specific materials, e.g., metals and minerals; U.S. economic conditions and trends
PAIS ———; s.a. Commodities; Strategic materials
BPI   ———; s.a. Commodity control; Natural resources

RAYONS. *Use* Substitute Products

READERS (Books). *Use* Textbooks

READINESS FOR SCHOOL. *Use* Education, Primary

READING
LC   ———; s.a. American school reading readiness tests; Developmental reading; Group reading; Illiteracy; Oral reading; Rapid reading; Readers and speakers; Reading comprehension; Reading disability; Reading machines; Reading, Psychology of; Reading, Teachers of
SEARS ———; s.a. Rapid reading; Readability (literary style); Reading—Remedial teaching
RG   ———; s.a. Reading disability; Speed reading; Supplementary reading
NYT   ———; s.a. Books and literature; Education and schools; Language and languages
PAIS ———; s.a. Books and reading; Reading clinics; Reading—Study and teaching
BPI   ———; s.a. Book clubs; Books and reading; Reading—Study and teaching

READING LISTS. *Use* Bibliography

READY RECKONERS. *Use* Mathematics

REAL COVENANTS. *Use* Discrimination in Housing; Landlord and Tenant

REAL ESTATE. *Use* Real Property

REAL PROPERTY
LC   ———; s.a. Abandonment of property; Absenteeism; Apartment houses; Condominiums (housing); Deeds; Estates (law); Farms—Valuation; Land subdivision; Land titles; Landlord and tenant; Office buildings; Real property tax; Real property valuation; Vendors and purchasers
SEARS REAL ESTATE; s.a. Assessments; Commercial law; Eminent domain; Farms
RG   ———; s.a. Building sites; Joint tenancy; Real estate business; Real estate investment; subd. *Real estate operations* under subjects, e.g., Corporations—Real estate operations
NYT   REAL ESTATE; s.a. Housing; Property and investments; Taxation—Real estate; Trespass; Zoning
PAIS ———; s.a. Government purchasing of real property; House selling; Housing management; Land; Mortgages; Real estate sales tax; Real property, Exchange of
BPI   ———; s.a. Conveyancing; Eminent domain; Home ownership; Land tenure; Land value taxation; Real estate management; Real property—Taxation

REALISM. *Use* Idealism; Rationalism

REALITY. *Use* Truth

REALTY. *See* Real Property

REAPPORTIONMENT (Election law). *See* Apportionment (Election law)

REASON. *Use* Intellect; Rationalism; Thought and Thinking; Wisdom

REASON OF STATE. *Use* State, The

REBATES. *Use* Prices

REBELLIONS. *See* Revolutions

REBELS (Social psychology). *See* Alienation (Social psychology)

REBIRTH. *See* Future Life

RECALL. *Use* Representative Government and Representation

RECALL (Psychology). *Use* Amnesia; Memory

RECEIVING STOLEN GOODS. *Use* Theft

RECEPTIONISTS. *Use* Office Employees; Secretaries

RECIDIVISTS. *Use* Crime and Criminals

RECIPES. *See* Cookery

RECIPROCITY. *Use* Commercial Policy; Free Trade and Protection; Tariff

RECLAMATION OF LAND
LC ——; s.a. Beaches; Clearing of land; Conservation of natural resources; Dikes (engineering); Hydraulic engineering; Jetties; Land; Natural resources; Nature conservation; Seashore; Shore protection; Soils; Waste lands
SEARS ——; s.a. Civil engineering; Drainage; Floods; Sand dunes; Soils
RG ——; s.a. Land utilization; Marshes
NYT ——; s.a. Area planning and renewal; Coast erosion; Forests and forestry; Housing
PAIS ——; s.a. Conservation of resources; Filling (earthwork); Irrigation
BPI ——; s.a. Conservation of resources; Irrigation; Public lands

RECOGNITION (Psychology). *Use* Memory

RECOLLECTION (Psychology). *Use* Memory

RECONSTRUCTION. *Use* Slavery

RECONSTRUCTION (1939-1951). *Use* Economic Assistance, Foreign; International Cooperation

RECORD PLAYERS. *See* Phonograph Records

RECORDINGS (Disk and tape) AND RECORDING AND PLAYBACK EQUIPMENT. *Use* High-fidelity Sound Systems; Phonograph Records

RECORDS. *Use* Archives; Business Records; Files and Filing (Documents)

RECORDS, PHONOGRAPH. *See* Phonograph Records

RECORDS MANAGEMENT. *Use* Business Records

RECORDS OF BIRTHS, ETC. *See* Vital Statistics

RECREATION
See also subd. *Recreation* under groups of persons, e.g., Soldiers—Recreation.
LC ——; s.a. Aged—Recreation; Amusements; Collectors and collecting; Educational games; Family recreation; Industrial recreation; Language games; Popular culture; Recreation and state; Recreational therapy
SEARS ——; s.a. Community centers; Indoor games; Outdoor recreation; Playgrounds; Vacations

RG ——; s.a. Art, Amateur; Cultural centers; Games; Play; School buildings as social centers; subd. *Collectors and collecting* under names of things collected, e.g., Rocks—Collectors and collecting
NYT ——; s.a. Cards and card games; Children and youth—Behavior and training; Community centers; Entertainment and amusements; Parks, playgrounds and other recreation areas
PAIS ——; s.a. Camps and camping; Leisure; Recreation areas; Recreation centers; Sports
BPI ——; s.a. Amusement parks; Do-it-yourself work; Hobbies; Leisure; Parks; Resorts; Vacations

RECREATION AREAS. *Use* Amusement Parks; National Parks and Reserves; Parks; Playgrounds

RECREATIONAL THERAPY. *Use* Occupational Therapy; Physical Therapy; Therapeutics

RECREATIONS. *See* Amusements; Sports

RECRUITING AND ENLISTMENT. *Use* Military Service, Compulsory

RECRUITING OF EMPLOYEES
LC ——; s.a. Civil service recruiting; Employment interviewing; Interviewing; subd. *Recruiting* under names of professions, e.g., Lawyers—Recruiting
SEARS ——; s.a. Employment agencies; Personnel management
RG ——; s.a. Applications for positions; Discrimination in employment
NYT LABOR—U.S.—UNEMPLOYMENT AND JOB MARKET, ETC; s.a. White collar workers
PAIS RECRUITING OF LABOR; s.a. Employment; Personnel management
BPI ——; s.a. Employment agencies; Executives—Recruiting; Youth and business

RECURSIVE PROGRAMMING. *Use* Linear Programming

RED TIDE. *Use* Algae; Toxins and Antitoxins

REDEMPTION. *Use* Jesus Christ

REDEVELOPMENT, URBAN. *Use* City Planning; Regional Planning; Tenement-Houses; Urban Renewal

REDUCING DRUGS. *Use* Weight Control

REDUCING EXERCISES. *Use* Exercise; Weight Control

REFEREES (Law). *Use* Bankruptcy

REFERENCE BOOKS. *Use* Handbooks

REFERENCE GROUPS. *Use* Social Groups

REFERENDUM. *Use* Elections; Legislation; Representative Government and Representation; Voting

REFLEXES. *Use* Conditioned Response; Nervous System

REFLEXOTHERAPY. *Use* Acupuncture

REFORESTATION. *Use* Forests and Forestry; Trees

REFORM, SOCIAL. *See* Social Problems

REFORMATION. *Use* Protestantism

REFORMATORIES. *Use* Imprisonment; Juvenile Delinquency

REFORMERS. *Use* Right and Left (Political science)

REFRIGERATION INDUSTRY. *Use* Air Conditioning

REFUGEES. *Use* Aliens; Asylum, Right of; Citizenship; Emigration and Immigration; Exiles

REFUGEES, POLITICAL. *Use* Asylum, Right of; Political Crimes and Offenses

REFUSE AND REFUSE DISPOSAL

LC ———; s.a. Garbage as feed; Incineration; Sewage as fertilizer; Waste products

SEARS ———; s.a. Drainage; Factory and trade waste; Pollution; Sanitation; Sewerage; Water pollution

RG ———; s.a. Municipal dumps; Refuse, Utilization of; Sewage; Street cleaning; Trade waste disposal; Waste disposal in the ocean; Water reuse

NYT WASTE MATERIALS AND DISPOSAL; s.a. Environment; Sewage and industrial wastes; Water pollution—Sewage

PAIS REFUSE DISPOSAL; s.a. Junk yards; Salvage (waste, etc.); Sewage disposal

BPI REFUSE DISPOSAL; s.a. Refuse collection; Salvage (waste, etc.); Sewage disposal; Sludge; Waste products

REGALIA (Insignia). *Use* Emblems

REGENERATION (Biology). *Use* Growth

REGICIDE. *Use* Assassination; Political Crimes and Offenses

REGIONAL PLANNING

LC ———; s.a. Cities and towns—Planning; City planning and redevelopment law; Greenbelts; Hurricane protection; Metropolitan government; Redevelopment, Urban; Suburbs

SEARS ———; s.a. City planning; Landscape protection; Social surveys

RG ———; s.a. Landscape improvement; Metropolitan areas; Urban renewal

NYT AREA PLANNING AND RENEWAL; s.a. Housing; Rural areas; Urban areas

PAIS ———; s.a. City planning; Rural planning

BPI ———; s.a. City planning; Industrial development programs; Zoning

REGIONALISM. *Use* Nationalism

REGISTERS OF BIRTHS, ETC. *Use* Genealogy; Vital Statistics

REHABILITATION

Scope: Works on the physical, medical, psychiatric, educational and vocational methods of restoring persons to normal activity.

LC ———; s.a. Occupational therapy; Rehabilitation centers; Rehabilitation counselling; Sheltered workshops; subd. *Rehabilitation* under specific groups, e.g., Amputees—Rehabilitation

SEARS See subd. *Rehabilitation* under specific groups, e.g., Physically handicapped—Rehabilitation

RG ———; s.a. Vocational rehabilitation

NYT See specific subjects of rehabilitation, e.g., Handicapped, Prisons and prisoners, etc.; s.a. Medicine and health; Psychology and psychologists

PAIS ———; s.a. Disabled—Rehabilitation; Vocational rehabilitation

BPI ———; s.a. Prisoners—Rehabilitation; Vocational rehabilitation

REHABILITATION OF CRIMINALS. *Use* Crime and Criminals; Prisons and Prisoners

REHABILITATION OF JUVENILE DELINQUENTS. *Use* Juvenile Delinquency

REINCARNATION. *Use* Future Life; Immortality; Soul

REINFORCEMENT (Psychology). *Use* Conditioned Response

REINSURANCE. *Use* Insurance

REJECTION, MATERNAL. *See* Maternal Deprivation

RELATIONISM. *Use* Existentialism

RELAXATION. *Use* Mental Hygiene; Recreation

RELAY RACING. *Use* Track Athletics

RELIABILITY (Engineering). *Use* Engineering; Quality Control

RELICS AND RELIQUARIES. *Use* Art Objects; Saints

RELIEF (Aid). *See* Public Welfare

RELIEF WORK. *Use* Disaster Relief; International Cooperation

RELIGION

See also particular religions, e.g., Bahaism, Brahminism; Buddha and Buddhism; Catholic Church; Christianity; Confucius and Confucianism; Druids and Druidism; Hinduism; Judaism; Islam or Mohammedanism; Mormons and Mormonism; Paganism; Protestantism; Shinto; Zoroastrianism; see also specific denominations, e.g., Anglican Church

LC ———; s.a. Baptism; Belief and doubt; Canonization; Catholicity; Church; Dissenters, Religious; Ecclesiastical law; Future life; God; Idols and images; Irreligion; Jesus Christ; Liturgies; Messiah; Miracles; Monastic and religious life; Monastic and religious life of women; Monasticism and religious orders; Mysticism; Preaching; Religion and sociology; Religious education; Religious liberty; Rites and ceremonies; Sacrilege; Saints; Sanctification; Sects; Secularism; Sin; Soul; Supernatural; Worship

SEARS ———; s.a. Agnosticism; Christian life; Deism; Monotheism; Pantheism; Revelation; Theism; Theology; Worship

RG ———; s.a. Faith; Holiness; Religion, Primitive; Sacraments; Salvation; Secularism; Spiritual life

NYT RELIGION AND CHURCHES; s.a. Freedom of religion

PAIS ———; s.a. Atheism; Christianity and other religions; Churches; Religious orders

BPI ———

RELIGION, PRIMITIVE. *Use* Ethnology; Mythology; Society, Primitve; Taboo; Totemism

RELIGION—STUDY AND TEACHING. *See* Theology

RELIGION AND ART. *See* Art and Religion

RELIGION AND ECONOMICS. *Use* Wealth, Ethics of

RELIGION AND ETHICS. *Use* Christian Ethics

RELIGION AND LAW. *Use* Religious Liberty

RELIGION AND NATIONALISM. *See* Nationalism and Religion

RELIGION AND SCIENCE. *Use* Theology

RELIGION AND SOCIOLOGY
LC ——; s.a. Non church-affiliated people; Religion and social status; Sociology, Biblical; subd. *Religious life and customs* under names of places
SEARS SOCIOLOGY, CHRISTIAN; s.a. Church and social problems
RG ——; s.a. Church and social problems; Social action; Sociology, Christian
NYT RELIGION AND CHURCHES; s.a. Sociology; subd. *Politics and government—Church-state relations* under names of places, e.g., Sweden—Politics and government—Church-state relations
PAIS ——; s.a. Church and social problems
BPI RELIGION; s.a. Sociology

RELIGION AND STATE. *Use* Nationalism and Religion; Religious Education; Religious Liberty

RELIGION AND WAR. *See* War and Religion

RELIGIOUS EDUCATION
Scope: Works dealing with instruction in religion in schools and private life.
LC ——; s.a. Catechists; Church and schools; Monasticism; Schools—Prayers; Sunday schools; Worship (Religious education)
SEARS ——; s.a. Bible—Study; Catechisms; Church and education; Church work; Theology—Study and teaching
RG ——; s.a. Bible study; Church and education; Church schools; Public schools and religion; Sunday school lessons; Theological education
NYT ——; s.a. Education and schools—U.S.—Issue of religious practices in public schools; Religion and churches
PAIS ——; s.a. Church and education; Discussion in religious education; Parochial schools; Religion and the public schools; Religious education—Audio-visual aids; Roman Catholic Church—Education
BPI RELIGION; s.a. Church; Church and state; Religious literature

RELIGIOUS FREEDOM. *See* Religious Liberty

RELIGIOUS LIBERTY
LC ——; s.a. Blasphemy; Nationalism and religion; Persecution; Religion and law; Religion and state; Religious liberty (international law); Sabbath legislation; Sunday legislation
SEARS ——; s.a. Civil rights; Free thought; Freedom of conscience; Minorities; Toleration

RG ——; s.a. Church and state; Dissenters, Religious; Freedom (theology); Liberty of conscience; Toleration
NYT FREEDOM OF RELIGION; s.a. Freedom and human rights; Freedom of information, thought and expression; Religion and churches
PAIS ——; s.a. Civil rights; Liberty
BPI RELIGION AND STATE: s.a. Church and state; Religion

RELIGIOUS LIFE. *See* Monastic and Religious Life of Women

RELIGIOUS LIFE AND CUSTOMS. *Use* Rites and Ceremonies

RELIGIOUS ORDERS. *Use* Monastic and Religious Life of Women; Monasticism and Religious Orders; Sects

RELIGIOUS RITES. *See* Rites and Ceremonies

RELOCATION (Housing). *Use* Housing

REMAND HOMES. *See* Juvenile Delinquency

REMARRIAGE. *Use* Bigamy; Divorce

REMEDIAL TEACHING. *Use* Teaching

REMEDIES (Law). *Use* Justice, Administration of

REMODELING (Architecture). *Use* Architecture

RENAISSANCE. *Use* Humanism

RENT. *Use* Landlord and Tenant; Rent Laws

RENT (Economic theory). *Use* Land

RENT LAWS
LC RENT CONTROL; s.a. Eviction; Price regulation; Public housing—Rent; Rent charges; Rent strikes; Rent subsidies
SEARS APARTMENT HOUSES—LAWS AND REGULATIONS; s.a. Landlord and tenant; Public welfare; Tenement houses
RG ——; s.a. Apartment houses; Landlord and tenant
NYT RENTS AND RENTING; s.a. Evictions; Housing—N.Y.C.—Rents and renting; Housing—U.S.—Rents and renting
PAIS RENT—REGULATION; s.a. Eviction; Landlord and tenant
BPI RENT—LAWS AND REGULATIONS; s.a. Landlord and tenant; Leases; Rent

RENT STRIKES. *Use* Landlord and Tenant; Rent Laws; Strikes and Lockouts

RENT SUBSIDIES. *Use* Rent Laws; Subsidies

REPATRIATION. *Use* Emigration and Immigration

REPEAL OF LEGISLATION. *Use* Legislation

REPENTANCE. *Use* Sin

REPLACEMENT OF INDUSTRIAL EQUIPMENT. *Use* Depreciation; Industrial Equipment; Machinery

REPORT WRITING
LC ——; s.a. Business report writing; Précis writing; School reports; Social casework reporting

REPORT WRITING, *cont.*
SEARS ——; s.a. Authorship
RG REPORTS; s.a. Corporation reports; Note taking
NYT WRITING AND WRITERS; s.a. Company reports; Education and schools
PAIS ——; s.a. Authorship; Business reports
BPI ——; s.a. Corporations—Reports and yearbooks; Reports

REPORTERS AND REPORTING
LC ——; s.a. Journalism; News photographers; Newspaper court reporting; Newspapers; Note-taking; Press; Shorthand reporting; subd. *Reporters and reporting* under names of legislative bodies, e.g., Congress—Reporters and reporting
SEARS ——; s.a. Blacks and the press; Government and the press; Journalism
RG ——; s.a. Foreign correspondents; Press conferences
NYT NEWS AND NEWS MEDIA; s.a. Freedom of information, thought and expression; Freedom of the press; Publications
PAIS ——; s.a. Freedom of information; Journalists
BPI REPORTERS; s.a. Confidential communications; Interviewing (journalism); Reporting

REPORTS, SCIENTIFIC AND TECHNICAL. *See* Technical Writing

REPRESENTATION, PROPORTIONAL. *See* Representative Government and Representation

REPRESENTATIVE GOVERNMENT AND REPRESENTATION
LC ——; s.a. Democracy; Functional representation; Majorities; Ministerial responsibility; Minorities; Pressure groups
SEARS ——; s.a. Constitutions; Elections; Legislative bodies; Political parties; Recall; Republics; Suffrage; Voting
RG ——; s.a. Apportionment (election law); Referendum
NYT Subd. *Politics and government* under names of places, e.g., Great Britain—Politics and government; s.a. Elections (U.S.); Local government; World government
PAIS REPRESENTATIVE GOVERNMENT; s.a. Majorities; Political science; Proportional representation
BPI ——; s.a. Gerrymander; Majorities; Proportional representation; Referendum

REPRESSION (Psychology). *Use* Psychoanalysis

REPRODUCTION
Scope: General works on sexual and asexual reproduction in animals and plants.
LC ——; s.a. Breeding; Conjugation (biology); Fertility, Human; Generative organs; Genetics; Life; Menstruation; Parthenogenesis; Parturition; Reproduction, Asexual; Sex; Sexual cycle
SEARS ——; s.a. Cells; Embryology; Pregnancy; Reproductive systems; Sex
RG ——; s.a. Conception; Fertility; Spawning; Spermatozoa; Spontaneous generation

NYT REPRODUCTION (Biological); s.a. Animals; Biology and biochemistry
PAIS BIOLOGY; s.a. Artificial insemination; Births; Fertility
BPI ——; s.a. Fertility; Fertilization (biology); Sterility

REPRODUCTION PROCESSES. *See* Copying Processes

REPROGRAPHY. *See* Copying Processes

REPUBLICS. *Use* Democracy; Representative Government and Representation

RESCUE WORK
LC ——; s.a. Ambulances; Disaster nursing; Lifesaving; Medical emergencies; Survival and emergency rations
SEARS ——; s.a. Civil defense; First aid; Space rescue operation
RG ——; s.a. First aid in illness and injury; Survival after airplane accidents, shipwrecks, etc.
NYT RESCUES; s.a. Accidents and safety; Heroism; Mercy missions
PAIS ——; s.a. Ambulance service; Emergency medical services
BPI ——; s.a. Accidents; Lifesaving equipment

RESEARCH
LC Inventions; subd. *Research* under subjects, e.g., Insurance, Social—Research; types of research, e.g., Advertising research, Medical research, etc.
SEARS ——; s.a. Learning and scholarship; Operations research; subd. *Research* under subjects, e.g., Medicine—Research
RG ——; s.a. Experimental design; Research—Federal aid; Scholarships and fellowships; Science—Methodology
NYT ——; s.a. subd. *Scholarships and fellowships* under specific fields, e.g., Medicine and health—Scholarships and fellowships
PAIS ——; s.a. Research grants; Sampling; Science; Surveys
BPI ——; s.a. Government research; Hypothesis testing (statistics); Technology and state

RESEARCH—FEDERAL AID. *Use* Science and State

RESEARCH, INDUSTRIAL. *Use* Industrial Research; Inventions; New Products

RESEARCH GRANTS. *Use* Scholarships; Science and State

RESERVOIRS. *Use* Water—Supply; Water Resources Development

RESIDENTIAL LOCATION. *Use* Housing

RESIDENTIAL MOBILITY. *Use* Migration, Internal

RESISTANCE TO GOVERNMENT. *See* Government, Resistance to

RESORTS. *Use* Recreation; Summer Resorts; Tourist Trade; Travel

RESPIRATION, ARTIFICIAL. *Use* First Aid in Illness and Injury

RESPONSIBILITY. *Use* Character

RESPONSIBILITY (Law). *See* Liability (Law)

RESPONSIBILITY, LEGAL. *See* Liability (Law)

RESPONSIVE WORSHIP. *Use* Liturgies

REST. *Use* Sleep

REST HOMES. *Use* Nursing Homes; Old Age Homes

RESTAURANTS, LUNCHROOMS, ETC.
LC ——; s.a. Caterers and catering; Dinner and dining; Hotels, taverns, etc.; Restaurant management; School lunchrooms, cafeterias, etc; subd. *Restaurants, lunchrooms, etc.* under names of cities; Table
SEARS RESTAURANTS, BARS, ETC.; s.a. Bars and barrooms; Coffee houses; Inns
RG RESTAURANTS; subd. *Hotels, restaurants, etc.* under names of cities; Waiters and waitresses
NYT HOTELS, BARS, MOTELS, NIGHT CLUBS AND RESTAURANTS; s.a. Beverages; Food
PAIS RESTAURANTS; s.a. Food industry; Restaurants—Drive-in restaurants
BPI ——; s.a. Concessions (food, etc.); Franchises (retail trade); Lunchrooms and cafeterias

RESTRAINT OF TRADE. *Use* Commercial Crimes; Competition; Interstate Commerce; Monopolies; Trusts, Industrial

RESTRICTED STOCK OPTIONS. *Use* Non-wage Payments; Stock Exchange

RÉSUMÉS (Employment). *Use* Applications for Positions

RESURRECTION. *Use* Future Life

RETAIL FRANCHISES. *See* Franchises (Retail trade)

RETAIL STORES. *See* Retail Trade

RETAIL TRADE. *Use* Chain Stores; Commerce; Consumers; Department Stores; Franchises (Retail Trade); Installment Plan; Inventories; Mail-order Business; Marketing; Merchandising; Packaging; Prices; Shopping and Shoppers; Small Business

RETAIL TRADE—BUSINESS HOURS. *Use* Sabbath

RETAIL TRADE—THEFT LOSSES. *Use* Theft

RETAINING WALLS. *Use* Walls

RETARDED CHILDREN. *See* Child Study; Exceptional Children; Handicapped; Mentally Handicapped Children

RETENTION (Psychology). *See* Memory

RETINA. *Use* Eye

RETIRED MILITARY PERSONNEL. *Use* Veterans

RETIREMENT
LC ——; s.a. Age and employment; Civil service retirement; Leisure; Old age; Retired military personnel; Retirement income; subd. *Retirement* under classes of persons, e.g., Clergy—Retirement
SEARS ——; s.a. Annuities; Leisure; Old age; Old age pensions

RG ——; s.a. Hobbies; Pensions, Industrial; Retirement income, Teachers, Retired; subd. *Pensions* under groups, e.g., Congressmen—Pensions
NYT PENSIONS AND RETIREMENT; s.a. Age and aged; Income; Social insurance
PAIS ——; s.a. Old age; Pensions; subd. *Retirement* under specific subjects, e.g., City managers—Retirement
BPI ——; s.a. Aged; Executives—Retirement; Pension funds and funding; Pensions; Self-employed—Pensions

RETIREMENT INCOME. *Use* Income; Old Age Assistance; Pensions

RETIREMENT PENSIONS. *See* Pensions

RETRAINING, OCCUPATIONAL. *Use* Labor Supply; Manpower; Occupational Training; Vocational Rehabilitation; Work Relief

REVELATION. *Use* Miracles; Religion; Theology

REVENUE. *Use* Taxation

REVENUE, INTERNAL. *See* Taxation

REVENUE SHARING. *See* Federal Government

REVERSION (Law). *Use* Inheritance and Succession

REVIVALISTS. *See* Evangelicalism

REVIVALS. *Use* Evangelicalism

REVOLUTION (Theology). *Use* Social Change

REVOLUTIONS
See also France—History—Revolution, 1789–1799; Russia—History—Revolution, 1919–1921; U.S.—History—Revolution; and similar historical headings.
LC ——; s.a. Counterrevolutions; Legitimacy of governments; Literature and revolutions; Peasant uprisings; Revolutionists; Right and left (political science); Social conflict; State of siege; Terrorism
SEARS ——; s.a. Class struggle; Political science
RG ——; s.a. Coups d'etat; Government, Resistance to
NYT WAR AND REVOLUTION; s.a. Armament, defense and military forces; International relations; Military art and science
PAIS REVOLUTION; s.a. Civil war; Insurgency
BPI ——; s.a. Political science; War

REVOLVERS. *Use* Firearms; Gunnery

REWARDS (Prizes, etc.)
See also names of awards, e.g., National Book Award, Nobel Prizes, Pulitzer Prizes, etc.
LC ——; s.a. Aeronautics—Awards; Literary Prizes; Moving pictures—Awards; Prize contests in advertising; Quiz shows; School contests; subd. *Competitions* under subjects, e.g., Art—Competitions; Suggestion systems
SEARS ——; s.a. Literary prizes

REWARDS (Prizes, etc), *cont.*
RG   REWARDS, PRIZES, ETC.; s.a. Advertising awards; Television awards; subd. *Awards, prizes, etc.* under names of subjects, e.g., Agriculture—Awards, prizes, etc.
NYT   Subd. *Awards and honors* under subjects, e.g., Books and literature—Awards and honors; s.a. Contests and prizes
PAIS REWARDS, PRIZES, ETC.; s.a. Medals
BPI   REWARDS, PRIZES, ETC.; s.a. Advertising awards; Public relations awards

REWARDS AND PUNISHMENT IN EDUCATION. *Use* Discipline of Children; Educational Psychology; School Supervision

RHETORIC. *Use* Debates and Debating; Language and Languages; Lectures and Lecturing; Oratory; Preaching; Public Speaking; Speech

RHYME. *Use* Versification

RICH, THE. *Use* Wealth

RIDING. *See* Horsemanship; Horse-Racing

RIFLES. *Use* Arms and Armor; Fire Arms; Gunnery

RIGHT AND LEFT (Political science)
LC   ——; s.a. Legislative bodies; Political parties
SEARS ——; s.a. Conservatism; Political parties; Reformers; Revolutions
RG   ——; s.a. Conservatism; Liberalism
NYT   POLITICS AND GOVERNMENT (General); s.a. U.S.—Politics and government—Fringe political movements; War and revolution; World government
PAIS ——; s.a. Political science; Radicalism
BPI   POLITICAL SCIENCE; s.a. Political parties

RIGHT OF ASYLUM. *See* Asylum, Right of

RIGHT OF PRIVACY. *See* Privacy, Right of

RIGHT OF PROPERTY. *Use* Property

RIGHT TO DISSENT. *Use* Government, Resistance to

RIGHT TO LABOR
LC   ——; s.a. Discrimination in employment; Industrial laws and legislation; Industry and state; Socialism; Unemployed; Work
SEARS DISCRIMINATION IN EMPLOYMENT; s.a. Labor contract; Open and closed shops
RG   ——; s.a. Discrimination in employment; Labor and laboring classes
NYT   LABOR—U.S.—UNION SECURITY (FOR 'RIGHT TO WORK' LAWS); s.a. Labor—U.S.—Discrimination; Management, Industrial and institutional
PAIS RIGHT TO WORK; s.a. Industrial relations; Open and closed shop
BPI   ——; s.a. Discrimination in employment; Open and closed shop

RIGHT TO WORK. *Use* Open and Closed Shop; Right to Labor

RIGHTS OF WOMEN. *See* Woman—Rights of Women

RIME. *Use* Versification

RIOT CONTROL. *Use* Demonstrations; Mobs; Riots

RIOTS
LC   ——; s.a. Assembly, Right of; Breach of the peace; Government, Resistance to; Mobs; Spectator control; Street fighting (military science); subd. *Riots* under names of cities and names of special riots, e.g., Draft riot, 1863; Tear gas munitions
SEARS ——; s.a. Crowds; Demonstrations; Freedom of assembly
RG   ——; s.a. Mob violence; Prison riots; Riot control
NYT   ——; s.a. Crime and criminals; Prisons and prisoners; U.S.—Politics and government
PAIS ——; s.a. Demonstrations, Political; Group behavior; Riots—Prevention
BPI   ——; s.a. Protests, demonstrations, etc.; Riot control

RIOTS, PRISON. *See* Prisons and Prisoners; Riots

RIPARIAN RIGHTS. *Use* Boundaries

RISK
LC   ——; s.a. C.I.F. clause; F.O.B. clause; Profit; Risk (insurance); Speculation
SEARS INVESTMENT; s.a. Insurance; Probabilities; Speculation
RG   ——; s.a. Hedging; Risk (insurance)
NYT   PROPERTY AND INVESTMENTS; s.a. Insurance; Stocks and bonds
PAIS ——; s.a. Economics; Speculation
BPI   ——; s.a. Hedging; Insurance—Risks; Insurance—Substandard risks; Insurance—War risk; Speculation; subd. *Risk* under type of insurance, e.g., Life insurance—Risk

RITES AND CEREMONIES
LC   ——; s.a. Corner stones, Laying of; Covenants (religion); Cults; Fasts and feasts; Initiations (into tribes, societies, etc.); Municipal ceremonies; Ritual; subd. *Ceremonies and practices* under subjects, e.g., Catholic Church—Ceremonies and practices; Taboo
SEARS ——; s.a. Baptism; Funeral rites and ceremonies; Manners and customs; Marriage customs and rites; Sacraments; Secret societies; subd. *Rites and ceremonies* under groups of people, e.g., Jews—Rites and ceremonies
RG   ——; s.a. Catholic Church—Liturgy and ritual; Funeral rites and ceremonies; Liturgies; Marriage customs and rites
NYT   MANNERS AND CUSTOMS; s.a. Marriages; Religion and churches
PAIS ——; s.a. Cults
BPI   MANNERS AND CUSTOMS; s.a. Religion

RITUAL. *Use* Rites and Ceremonies

RIVERS. *Use* Water; Water Resources Development; Waterways

ROAD ACCIDENTS. *See* Traffic Accidents

ROAD MAPS. *See* Maps

ROAD SIGNS. *Use* Billboards; Signs and Symbols; Traffic Safety

ROADS
LC ———; s.a. Civil engineering; Cycling paths; Highway communications; Highway research; Indian trails; Landscape architecture; Landscape protection; Private roads; Public works; Roadside rest areas; Toll roads
SEARS ———; s.a. Pavements; Roadside improvements; Soils (engineering); Streets
RG ———; s.a. Highway engineering; Pavements; Trails
NYT ———; s.a. Autos—Travel; Bridges and tunnels (for access roads); Traffic (vehicular and pedestrian) and parking
PAIS HIGHWAYS; s.a. Bridges; Express highways; Highway engineers
BPI ———; s.a. Pavements; Road construction; Streets

ROADS—SAFETY DEVICES AND MEASURES. *Use* Traffic Safety

ROBBERIES AND ASSAULTS. *Use* Burglary; Theft

ROBOTS. *See* Automation

ROCK GROUPS. *Use* Bands (Music); Dance Music; Music; Musicians; Singing and Songs

ROCK 'N ROLL. *See* Dance Music; Music; Singing and Songs

ROCKET FLIGHT. *See* Space Flight

ROCKET LAUNCHERS. *Use* Gunnery; Rockets (Aeronautics)

ROCKETRY. *Use* Nuclear Rockets; Rockets (Aeronautics)

ROCKETS (Aeronautics)
LC ———; s.a. Ballistic missiles; Jet propulsion; Nuclear rockets; Rocketry; Rockets (ordnance); Space ships
SEARS ———; s.a. Artificial satellites—Launching; Guided missiles; Space vehicles
RG ROCKETS; s.a. Rocket propulsion; Rockets, Atomic powered
NYT ROCKETS AND ROCKET PROPULSION; s.a. Aeronautics; Airplanes; Astronautics
PAIS ROCKETS; s.a. Airplanes, Rocket-propelled; Interplanetary flight; Rockets, Interplanetary
BPI ROCKETS; s.a. Launch vehicles (astronautics); Propellants; Rocket engines; Space vehicles—Propulsion systems

ROCKETS, INTERPLANETARY. *Use* Outer Space

RODENTICIDES. *Use* Pests

RODEOS. *Use* Horsemanship

ROGUES AND VAGABONDS. *Use* Burglary; Fraud; Outdoor Life; Vagrancy

ROLE PLAYING. *Use* Management Games

ROLLING MILLS. *Use* Steel Industry and Trade

ROMAN CATHOLIC CHURCH. *Use* Baptism; Canonization; Catholic Church; Catholic Church in the U. S.; Catholicity; Jesus Christ; Liturgies; Papacy; Saints; Ultramontanism; Virgin Birth

ROMAN CATHOLIC CHURCH—EDUCATION. *Use* Church Schools; Religious Education

ROMAN CATHOLIC RELIGIOUS ORDERS. *Use* Abbeys; Monastic and Religious Life of Women; Monasticism and Religious Orders

ROMAN CATHOLICS. *Use* Catholic Church; Catholic Church in the U. S.

ROMANCES. *Use* Fiction

ROOFS
LC ———; s.a. Arches; Architecture, Domestic; Decks; Framing, Building; Graphic statics; Tiles, Roofing; Vaults
SEARS ———; s.a. Architecture—Details; Building; Building, Iron and steel; Carpentry
RG ———; s.a. Domes; Roofing
NYT ROOFING AND SIDING; s.a. Building; Housing
PAIS ROOFING MATERIALS; s.a. Building materials
BPI ———; s.a. Roofing; Shingles

ROOMING HOUSES. *See* Hotels, Taverns, etc.

ROOT CROPS. *Use* Crops; Vegetables

ROTATION OF CROPS. *Use* Crops

ROW HOUSES. *Use* Apartment Houses

ROYALTIES. *Use* Copyright; Intellectual Property; Patent Laws and Legislation

ROYALTY. *See* Heads of State

RUBBER, SYNTHETIC. *Use* Substitute Products

RUGS. *Use* Floors; Tapestry

RULE OF LAW
LC ———; s.a. Act of state; Administrative discretion; Civil rights; Judicial review; Political questions and judicial power
SEARS LAW; s.a. Administrative law; Constitutional law; Justice, Administration of
RG ———; s.a. Administrative law; Executive power; Police power
NYT LAW AND LEGISLATION; s.a. Legal profession; Politics and government (general)
PAIS ———; s.a. Administrative law; Due process of law
BPI DUE PROCESS OF LAW; s.a. Courts; Justice, Administration of

RULE OF THE ROAD AT SEA. *Use* Freedom of the Seas; Maritime Law

RULERS. *See* Heads of State

RULES OF ORDER. *Use* Parliamentary Practice

RUMOR. *Use* Propaganda; Public Opinion

RUNAWAYS. *Use* Children; Problem Children; Youth

RUNNING. *Use* Exercise; Track Athletics

RURAL AREAS. *Use* Country Life; Farms and Farming; Migration, Internal; Peasantry; Rural Conditions; Villages

RURAL CONDITIONS
See also subd. *Rural conditions* under names of places.
LC   ——; s.a. Country life; Education, Rural; Electricity in agriculture; Rural youth; School supervision, Rural; Social history; Sociology, Rural; Urbanization; Villages
SEARS   FARM LIFE; s.a. Migrant labor; Outdoor life; Peasantry; Rural schools
RG   COUNTRY LIFE; s.a. City and country; Education, Rural; Farm life; Rural population; Rural schools
NYT   RURAL AREAS; s.a. Education and schools—U. S.; Housing; Population and vital statistics; Real estate; U. S.—Economic conditions
PAIS   ——; s.a. Community life, Rural; Farm population; Rural education; Rural electrification; Rural-urban migration
BPI   ——; s.a. Education, Rural; Electric service, Rural; Electricity on the farm; Farms; Labor mobility; Migration, Internal; Peasantry; U. S.—Rural conditions; U. S.—Rural electrification administration; Villages

RURAL LIFE. *See* Country Life; Rural Conditions
RURAL POPULATION. *Use* Peasantry; Population
RURAL SCHOOLS. *Use* Rural Conditions
RURAL-URBAN MIGRATION. *Use* Migration, Internal; Urbanization

S

SABBATH
Scope: Works on laws regarding the observance of the Sabbath.
LC   SABBATH LEGISLATION; s.a. Ecclesiastical law; Sabbath (Jewish law); Sabbath—Biblical teaching; Sunday; Sunday legislation; Sunday schools
SEARS   ——; s.a. Judaism; Retail trade
RG   ——; s.a. Business hours; Store hours; Sunday
NYT   SUNDAY OBSERVANCE; s.a. Labor—U.S.—Discrimination
PAIS   SUNDAY LEGISLATION; s.a. Jews; Retail trade—Business hours; Weekly rest-day
BPI   SUNDAY LEGISLATION; s.a. Jews; Retail trade—Hours of business

SABOTAGE
LC   ——; s.a. Criminal syndicalism; Direct action; Trials (sabotage)
SEARS   ——; s.a. Offenses against public safety; Strikes and lockouts; Subversive activities
RG   ——; s.a. Internal security; Subversive activities; Terrorism; Treason
NYT   ——; s.a. Airlines—Hijacking; Bombs and bomb plots; Espionage
PAIS   ——; s.a. Subversive activities; Syndicalism
BPI   ——; s.a. Terrorism; Violence

SACCHARIN. *Use* Substitute Products

SACRAMENTS. *Use* Baptism; Religion; Rites and Ceremonies

SACRIFICE. *Use* Worship

SACRILEGE. *Use* Religion; Taboo

SAFE-DEPOSIT COMPANIES. *Use* Trust Companies

SAFETY. *Use* Accidents

SAFETY, INDUSTRIAL. *See* Industry

SAFETY APPLIANCES
See also subds. *Safety appliances, Safety measures* or *Safety devices and measures* under subject, e.g., Railroads—Safety appliances, etc.; and names of specific appliances, e.g., Clothing, Protective; Automobile seat belts, etc.
LC   ——; s.a. Accidents—Prevention; Employers' liability; Safety education, Industrial; Safety regulations
SEARS   ——; s.a. Accidents—Prevention; Safety education
RG   SAFETY DEVICES AND MEASURES; s.a. Accidents—Prevention; Fire protection; Industrial safety—Laws and regulations; Safety laws and legislation
NYT   ACCIDENTS AND SAFETY; s.a. Accidents and safety—Industrial and occupational hazards; Traffic (vehicular and pedestrian) and parking—U. S.—Automobile safety features and defects
PAIS   SAFETY EQUIPMENT; s.a. Industrial safety; Safety measures
BPI   SAFETY EQUIPMENT; s.a. Industrial safety; Safety laws and regulations

SAFETY MEASURES. *Use* Safety Appliances

SAFETY PACKAGING. *Use* Consumer Protection; Hazardous Substances

SAFETY SHOES. *Use* Boots and Shoes

SAGAS. *Use* Folklore; Tales

SAILING. *Use* Boats and Boating; Ocean Travel

SAILORS. *See* Seamen

SAINTS

LC ———; s.a. Church calendar; Hagiography; Martyrs; Miracles; Patron saints

SEARS ———; s.a. Apostles; Christian biography; Fathers of the church

RG ———; s.a. Canonization; Doctors of the church; Relics and reliquaries

NYT ROMAN CATHOLIC CHURCH—BEATIFICATIONS AND CANONIZATIONS; s.a. names of specific saints, e.g., Paul, Saint; Religion and churches

PAIS RELIGION

BPI CATHOLIC CHURCH; s.a. Christianity

SALARIES. *Use* Income; Wages and Salaries

SALES

LC ———; s.a. Bulk sales; Special sales; Vendors and purchasers

SEARS SALES AND SALESMANSHIP; s.a. Commercial law; Peddlers and peddling

RG ———; s.a. Bills of sale

NYT SALES AND SALESMEN; s.a. Property and investments

PAIS ———; s.a. Auctions; Invoices

BPI ———; s.a. Auctions; Special sales

SALES, CONDITIONAL. *Use* Instalment Plan

SALES FORECASTING. *Use* Business Forecasting; Marketing; Sales Management

SALES LETTERS. *Use* Commercial Correspondence; Letter-writing; Mail-order Business

SALES MANAGEMENT

LC ———; s.a. Expense accounts; Merchandising; Sales forecasting; Sales meetings; Sales reporting; Salesmen and salesmanship

SEARS ———; s.a. Industrial management; Marketing; Show windows

RG ———; s.a. Entertaining in sales promotion; Premiums

NYT SALES AND SALESMEN; s.a. Advertising; Marketing and merchandising

PAIS ———; s.a. Bribery, Commercial; Merchandising; Promotional allowances

BPI ———; s.a. Retail trade—Manufacturers demonstrations; Sales promotion

SALES MEETINGS. *Use* Congresses and Conventions; Sales Management

SALES PROMOTION. *Use* Advertising; Marketing; Sales Management

SALESMEN AND SALESMANSHIP

Scope: Works on technique of salesmanship and occupation of salesman in general. Works on sales personnel in retail stores are entered under Clerks (Retail trades).

LC ———; s.a. Commercial travelers; Dealer aids; Distributive education; Merchandising; Sales management; Telephone selling

SEARS ———; s.a. Mail-order business; Peddlers and peddling

RG ———; s.a. Automobile salesmen; Canvassing

NYT SALES AND SALESMEN; s.a. Marketing and merchandising

PAIS ———; s.a. Canvassing; Sales management

BPI SALESMEN; s.a. Door-to-door selling; Salesmanship

SALINE WATER. *Use* Water

SALOONS. *See* Bars and Barrooms; Restaurants, Lunchrooms, etc.

SALT WATER. *Use* Water

SALUTATIONS. *Use* Etiquette; Letter-writing

SALVAGE. *Use* Maritime Law

SALVAGE (Waste, etc.). *Use* Refuse and Refuse Disposal; Waste Products

SALVATION. *Use* Future Life; Jesus Christ; Religion; Sin

SAMPLES (Merchandising). *Use* Merchandising

SAMPLING (Statistics)

LC ———; s.a. Analysis of variance; Biometry; Errors, Theory of; Mathematical statistics; Numbers, Random; Probabilities

SEARS ———; s.a. Probabilities; Quality control; Statistics

RG SAMPLING (Statistical Methods)

NYT STATISTICS; s.a. Data processing (information processing) equipment and supplies

PAIS SAMPLING; s.a. Market research; Statistics

BPI ———; s.a. Variance analysis; Work sampling

SANCTIFICATION. *Use* Religion

SANCTIONS (International law). *Use* International Law; International Offenses

SANCTIONS, ADMINISTRATIVE. *Use* Law Enforcement

SANCTUARY (Law). *See* Asylum, Right of

SAND DUNES. *Use* Beaches; Reclamation of Land; Seashore

SANITATION

LC ———; s.a. Air—Purification; Hygiene, Public; Sanitary chemistry; subd. *Sanitation* under specific subjects, e.g., Theaters—Sanitation

SEARS ———; s.a. Disinfection and disinfectants; Public health; School hygiene; Ventilation

RG ———; s.a. Refuse and refuse disposal; Sewer cleaning

NYT ———; s.a. Air pollution; Waste materials and disposal

PAIS ———; s.a. Pollution; Refuse disposal; Sewage disposal

BPI ———; s.a. Pollution; Sanitary engineering; Sewerage

SANITATION, HOUSEHOLD. *Use* Ventilation

SATANISM. *Use* Occult Sciences

SATELLITES, ARTIFICIAL. *Use* Artificial Satellites; Astronautics; Space Flight; Telecommunication

SATIRE. *Use* Caricatures and Cartoons; Wit and Humor

SAVING AND INVESTMENT. *Use* Economic Development; Wealth

SAVING AND SAVINGS

LC	SAVING AND INVESTMENT; s.a. Capital; Cost and standard of living; Investments
SEARS	SAVING AND THRIFT; s.a. Finance, Personal; Insurance, Industrial; Old age pensions
RG	———; s.a. Domestic finance; Investments; Thrift
NYT	SAVINGS; s.a. Banks and banking; Property and investments
PAIS	SAVING; s.a. Employees' savings plans; Savings plans
BPI	SAVING; s.a. Savings banks; Savings deposits

SAVINGS AND LOAN ASSOCIATIONS. *Use* Consumer Credit; Cooperative Societies; Loans; Loans, Personal

SAVINGS BANKS. *Use* Banking; Saving and Savings

SAYINGS. *See* Proverbs; Quotations

SCALE ANALYSIS (Psychology). *Use* Psychology; Public Opinion

SCALES (Weighing instruments). *Use* Weights and Measures

SCATTERING (Physics). *Use* Nuclear Physics; Radiation

SCENARIOS. *See* Moving Picture Plays; Plots (Drama, novel, etc.)

SCENERY. *See* Landscape Protection

SCENERY (Stage). *See* Theater

SCHEDULING (Management). *Use* Industrial Management; Linear Programming; Operations Research; Production Control

SCHISM. *Use* Dissenters, Religious; Sects

SCHIZOPHRENIA. *Use* Insanity; Mental Illness; Mentally Ill

SCHOLARSHIP. *Use* Academic Achievement; Learning and Scholarship

SCHOLARSHIPS

LC	———; s.a. College costs; Education and state; Research grants; Student aid; subd. *Scholarships, fellowships, etc.* under subjects, e.g., Medicine—Scholarships, fellowships, etc.; Talented students
SEARS	SCHOLARSHIPS, FELLOWSHIPS, ETC.; s.a. Education and state; Student loan funds
RG	SCHOLARSHIPS AND FELLOWSHIPS; s.a. Student aid; names of specific scholarships, e.g. Nieman fellowship
NYT	SCHOLARSHIPS AND FELLOWSHIPS; s.a. Colleges and universities—U. S.—Finances; fields or subjects in which scholarships and fellowships are awarded, e.g., Medicine and health
PAIS	SCHOLARSHIPS AND FELLOWSHIPS; s.a. College students—Aid; Graduate students—Aid
BPI	SCHOLARSHIPS AND FELLOWSHIPS; s.a. Student loans

SCHOLASTIC SUCCESS. *See* Academic Achievement

SCHOOL ADMINISTRATION AND ORGANIZATION. *Use* Educational Administration; Self-Government (In education); School Supervision

SCHOOL AND COMMUNITY. *Use* Community; Home and School

SCHOOL AND THE HOME. *Use* Home and School

SCHOOL ATHLETICS. *Use* Athletics; Sports

SCHOOL ATTENDANCE

LC	———; s.a. Dropouts; Dual enrollment; Educational law and legislation; Elementary school dropouts; High school dropouts; School day; School year
SEARS	———; s.a. Child labor; Education, Compulsory
RG	———; s.a. Compulsory education; School phobia
NYT	EDUCATION AND SCHOOLS—U. S.—ENROLLMENT; s.a. Education and schools—U. S.—Student activities and conduct; Labor—U. S.—Youth
PAIS	———; s.a. Colleges and universities—Attendance; Student withdrawals
BPI	SCHOOLS; s.a. Dropouts

SCHOOL BOARDS. *Use* Educational Administration; Schools

SCHOOL BONDS. *Use* Local Government

SCHOOL BOOKS. *See* Handbooks; Textbooks

SCHOOL BOYCOTTS. *Use* Boycott; Busing

SCHOOL CENSUS. *Use* Education, Compulsory

SCHOOL CHILDREN. *Use* Schools

SCHOOL CHILDREN—TRANSPORTATION FOR INTEGRATION. *Use* Busing; Discrimination in Education

SCHOOL CONTESTS. *Use* Rewards (Prizes, etc.)

SCHOOL COUNSELORS. *Use* Personnel Service in Education

SCHOOL DISCIPLINE. *Use* Cheating (Education); Discipline of Children; Punishment; School Supervision; Self-Government (In education)

SCHOOL DISTRICTS. *Use* Local Government

SCHOOL DROPOUTS. *See* Dropouts

SCHOOL HYGIENE. *Use* Health Education; Hygiene

SCHOOL MANAGEMENT AND ORGANIZATION. *Use* Educational Administration; Educational planning and Innovations; School Supervision; Self-government (In education)

SCHOOL MUSIC. *Use* Music Education

SCHOOL NURSES. *Use* Nurses and Nursing

SCHOOL OFFICIALS. *Use* Educational Administration; Educators

SCHOOL PHOBIA. *Use* Child Psychiatry; Dropouts; Education, Compulsory; School Attendance

SCHOOL PLAYGROUNDS. *See* Playgrounds

SCHOOL PRINCIPALS. *Use* Educational Administration; School Supervision

SCHOOL PSYCHOLOGISTS. *Use* Educational Psychology; Personnel Service in Education

SCHOOL REPORTS. *Use* Grading and Marking (Students); Report Writing

SCHOOL SAFETY PATROLS. *Use* School Supervision; Traffic Accidents

SCHOOL SOCIAL WORK. *Use* Personnel Service in Education; Social Service

SCHOOL SPORTS. *Use* Athletics

SCHOOL SUPERINTENDENTS AND PRINCIPALS. *Use* Educational Administration; School Supervision; Teachers

SCHOOL SUPERVISION
Scope: Works on the supervision of instruction.
LC ———; s.a. Classroom management; Educational administration; New schools; Rewards and punishment in education; School safety patrols; School size; School supervisors, Training of; Teacher-principal relationships; Teaching
SEARS ———; s.a. School administration and organization; School superintendents and principals; Self-government in education
RG SCHOOL SUPERVISION AND SUPERVISORS; s.a. School discipline; Supervisors of student teaching
NYT EDUCATION AND SCHOOLS—U.S.—ADMINISTRATION; s.a. Education and schools—U.S.—School administration and community role
PAIS ———; s.a. School administration and organization; School discipline; School principals
BPI SCHOOLS; s.a. School management and organization

SCHOOL TEACHING. *See* Teaching

SCHOOL YEAR. *Use* School Attendance; Summer Schools

SCHOOLS
See also types of schools, e.g., Church schools, Correspondence schools and courses, Junior high schools, High schools, Private schools, Public schools, Trade schools, etc. For schools of a particular city, see subd. *Schools* under the name of the city.
LC ———; s.a. Double shifts (public schools); Education, Primary; Education, Secondary; New schools; School boards; School buildings; School children; School hygiene; School sites; School size
SEARS ———; s.a. School buildings; School children—Food; School children—Transportation; School hygiene; Schools—Assignment of pupils
RG ———; s.a. Classrooms; Play schools; Public schools—Health service; Schedules, School; School children; School nurses; Summer schools
NYT EDUCATION AND SCHOOLS; s.a. Children and youth; Commercial education
PAIS ———; s.a. Classrooms, Portable; Dormitories; High school students; School health; School nursing; Vacation schools

BPI ———; s.a. Public schools; School buildings; Students

SCHOOLS—COURSES OF STUDY. *Use* Education—Curricula

SCHOOLS, NONGRADED. *See* Nongraded schools

SCHOOLS—PRAYERS. *Use* Religious Education

SCHOOLS, PRIVATE. *Use* Private Schools

SCHOOLS—TRANSPORTATION OF PUPILS. *Use* Busing; Discrimination in Education

SCHOOLS OF EDUCATION. *Use* Teachers, Training of

SCHOOLS OF PUBLIC HEALTH. *Use* Health Education

SCIENCE
See also branches of science, e.g., Astronomy, Crystallography, Space sciences; and classes of scientists, e.g., Chemists; Physicists.
LC ———; s.a. Science and civilization; Science news; Scientists; Technology
SEARS ———; s.a. Science—Methodology; Science and the humanities; Scientific apparatus and instruments
RG ———; s.a. Communication in science; Religion and science; Specialization
NYT SCIENCE AND TECHNOLOGY; s.a. Inventions
PAIS ———; s.a. Communication in science; Communism and science; Research; Women as scientists
BPI ———; s.a. Brain drain; Newspapers—Science news; Technology

SCIENCE, FREEDOM OF. *Use* Freedom of Information

SCIENCE—METHODOLOGY. *Use* Research

SCIENCE AND ART. *See* Art and Science

SCIENCE AND CIVILIZATION. *Use* Progress

SCIENCE AND STATE
LC ———; s.a. Endowment of research; Research and development contracts; State encouragement of science, literature and art
SEARS ———; s.a. Federal aid to education; Industry and state
RG ———; s.a. Research—Federal aid; Technology and state
NYT SCIENCE AND TECHNOLOGY; s.a. Government employees and officials; Politics and government
PAIS ———; s.a. Government-sponsored research; Technocracy
BPI ———; s.a. National Science Foundation; Research

SCIENCE AND TECHNOLOGY. *Use* Brain Drain; Progress; Science and State; Technological Innovations; Technology

SCIENCE AND THE HUMANITIES. *Use* Art and Science

SCIENCE FICTION. *Use* Fiction; Literature

SCIENCE NEWS. *Use* Journalism; Technical Writing

SCIENCES, OCCULT. *See* Occult Sciences

SCIENTIFIC APPARATUS AND INSTRUMENTS
See also names of particular classes of instruments, e.g.,
Astronomical instruments; Optical instruments;
etc; and names of particular instruments, e.g.,
Sextant.
LC   ——; s.a. Instrument industry; Research—Equipment and supplies; Scientific satellites
SEARS   ——
RG   ——; s.a. Instruments
NYT   LABORATORIES AND SCIENTIFIC EQUIPMENT; s.a. Instruments
PAIS   ——
BPI   ——; s.a. Testing apparatus

SCIENTIFIC EXPEDITIONS. *Use* Discoveries
(In geography); Voyages and Travels

SCIENTIFIC INSTRUMENTS. *See* Scientific Apparatus
and Instruments

SCIENTIFIC LITERATURE. *Use* Technical Writing

SCIENTIFIC MANAGEMENT. *See* Industrial Management; Management; Operations Research

SCIENTIFIC PROPERTY. *See* Patent Laws and Legislation

SCIENTIFIC RESEARCH. *See* Research

SCIENTIFIC SATELLITES. *Use* Artificial Satellites;
Scientific Apparatus and Instruments

SCIENTIFIC SOCIETIES. *Use* Learning and Scholarship

SCIENTIFIC WRITING. *See* Technical Writing

SCIENTISTS. *Use* Brain Drain; Learning and Scholarship; Science

SCOTTISH CLANS. *See* Tribes and Tribal System

SCOURING COMPUNDS. *Use* Cleaning Compounds

SCOUTS AND SCOUTING. *Use* Military Art and
Science; Soldiers

SCRAP METAL INDUSTRY. *Use* Iron Industry and
Trade

SCRAP METALS. *Use* Waste Products

SCREENPLAYS. *See* Moving Picture Plays

SCRIPTURES, HOLY. *See* Bible

SEA. *See* Oceanography

SEA LAW. *See* Maritime Law

SEA TRAVEL. *See* Ocean Travel

SEA WARFARE. *See* Naval Art and Science

SEA WATER. *Use* Water

SEA WATER—POLLUTION. *Use* Water—Pollution

SEAFARING LIFE. *Use* Seamen; Voyages and Travels

SEA-FISHERIES. *See* Fisheries

SEAFOOD INDUSTRY. *Use* Fisheries

SEALING (Packages). *Use* Adhesives; Packaging

SEALING (Technology). *Use* Solder and Soldering

SEALS (Numismatics). *Use* Numismatics

SEAMANSHIP. *Use* Naval Art and Science; Seamen

SEAMEN
LC   ——; s.a. Impressment; Merchant seamen;
Negroes as seamen; Seamanship; Soldiers;
Veterans; Voyages and travels
SEARS   ——; s.a. Naval biography; Pilots and
pilotage
RG   ——; s.a. Maritime workers; Seafaring life
NYT   SHIPS AND SHIPPING; s.a. Boating (yachting);
U.S. armament and defense—Navy
PAIS   ——; s.a. Maritime workers; Merchant marine
officers
BPI   ——; s.a. Maritime workers; Merchant seamen

SEAPLANE BASES. *Use* Airports

SEAPLANES. *Use* Airplanes

SEA-POWER
LC   ——; s.a. Disarmament; Freedom of seas;
Naval battles; Naval history; subd. *History, Naval*
under names of countries
SEARS   ——; s.a. Naval art and science
RG   ——; s.a. Carriers; Navies; Warships
NYT   U.S. ARMAMENT AND DEFENSE—NAVY;
s.a. Arms control and limitation and disarmament; Ships and shipping
PAIS   ——; s.a. Navies; Warships
BPI   NAVIES; s.a. Aircraft carriers; Warships; subd.
Navy under names of countries, e.g., U.S.—Navy

SEARCH AND RESCUE WORK. *See* Rescue Work

SEAS, FREEDOM OF THE. *See* Freedom of the Seas

SEASHORE
LC   ——; s.a. Coast changes; Coasts; Seashore
ecology; Submerged lands
SEARS   ——; s.a. Ocean; Sand dunes
RG   ——; s.a. Beaches; Shore protection
NYT   BEACHES; s.a. Coast erosion; Parks, playgrounds
and other recreation areas; Reclamation of
land
PAIS   SHORE LINES; s.a. Beaches; Continental shelf;
Reclamation of land
BPI   SHORELINES; s.a. Beach erosion; Continental
shelf

SEASIDE RESORTS. *Use* Beaches; Summer Resorts

SEASONAL INDUSTRIES
LC   ——; s.a. Casual labor; Migrant labor; Unemployment, Seasonal
SEARS   MIGRANT LABOR; s.a. Labor and laboring
classes; Unemployed
RG   ——; s.a. Construction industry; Seasonal labor
NYT   LABOR—U.S.—MIGRATORY LABOR; s.a.
Agriculture and agricultural products; Seasons
and months
PAIS   SEASONAL LABOR; s.a. Migrant labor; Unemployment, Seasonal
BPI   SEASONAL LABOR; s.a. Summer employment;
Unemployment, Seasonal

SEASONS. *Use* Climate; Weather

SEAWEED. *Use* Marine Ecology; Weeds

SECESSION. *Use* State Rights

SECOND ADVENT. *Use* Jesus Christ

SECOND SIGHT. *Use* Clairvoyance; Prophecies; Psychical Research; Thought Transference

SECONDARY EDUCATION. *See* Education, Secondary

SECONDARY SCHOOLS. *See* Education, Secondary; High Schools; Private Schools

SECRECY (Law). *Use* Official Secrets; Privacy, Right of

SECRET SERVICE
LC ——; s.a. Espionage; Intelligence service; Police
SEARS ——; s.a. Detectives; Espionage; Spies
RG ——; s.a. Intelligence service; World War, 1939–1945—Secret service
NYT U.S.—SECRET SERVICE; s.a. Government employees and officials; U.S.—Internal security
PAIS ——; s.a. Intelligence service; U.S.—Secret service
BPI ——; s.a. Espionage; Industrial espionage; U.S.—Central Intelligence Agency

SECRET SOCIETIES
See also names of societies, e.g., Ku Klux Klan.
LC ——; s.a. Brotherhoods; Greek letter societies; Hazing; Indians of North America—Secret societies; Initiations (into trades, societies, etc.); Mysteries, Religious
SEARS ——; s.a. Fraternities and sororities; Rites and ceremonies; Societies
RG ——
NYT ORGANIZATIONS, SOCIETIES AND CLUBS; s.a. Colleges and universities—U.S.—Fraternities and sororities
PAIS SOCIETIES, SECRET
BPI Names of societies, e.g., Freemasons

SECRETARIAL PRACTICE. *See* Office Management

SECRETARIES
LC ——; s.a. Clerks; Commercial correspondence; Corporation secretaries; Dictation (office practice); Files and filing (documents); Legal secretaries; Medical secretaries; Private secretaries; Receptionists; Social secretaries
SEARS ——; s.a. Business education; Office management
RG ——; s.a. Office workers; names of types of secretaries, e.g., School secretaries
NYT SECRETARIES, STENOGRAPHERS AND TYPISTS; s.a. Commercial education; White collar workers
PAIS ——; s.a. Office employees; Office practice
BPI SECRETARIES, PRIVATE; s.a. Corporations—Secretaries; Dictation; Office methods; Secretarial services

SECRETS (Law). *Use* Confidential Communications; Official Secrets

SECRETS, MILITARY. *See* Official Secrets

SECRETS, OFFICIAL. *See* Official Secrets

SECTIONALISM (U.S.). *Use* Nationalism

SECTS
Scope: Works on religious sects. See also names and types of specific sects, e.g., Black Muslims; Mennonites, Methodist Church; etc.
LC ——; s.a. Apostasy; Cults and sects; Heresies and heretics—Modern period; Interdenominational cooperation; Schism
SEARS ——; s.a. Church history; Religions
RG ——; s.a. Dissenters, Religious
NYT RELIGION AND CHURCHES
PAIS ——; s.a. Religion; Religious orders
BPI RELIGION

SECULARISM
LC ——; s.a. Anti-clericalism; Civilization, Secular; Rationalism; Secularization (theology)
SEARS AGNOSTICISM; s.a. Belief and doubt; Ethics
RG ——; s.a. Agnosticism; Irreligion
NYT ETHICS AND MORALS; s.a. Religion and churches; Sociology
PAIS RELIGION; s.a. Ethics
BPI RELIGION; s.a. Theology

SECURITIES. *Use* Bonds; Investments; Over-the-Counter Markets; Stock-exchange

SECURITIES, TAX EXEMPT. *Use* Taxation, Exemption from

SECURITIES EXCHANGE. *See* Stock-exchange

SECURITY, INTERNAL. *See* Internal Security

SECURITY, INTERNATIONAL. *Use* Disarmament; International Relations; Neutrality

SECURITY (Law). *Use* Business Law; Debtor and Creditor

SECURITY, SOCIAL. *See* Insurance, Social

SECURITY CLASSIFICATION (Government documents). *Use* Government and the Press; Government Publications; Official Secrets

SEDATIVES. *Use* Anesthesia and Anesthetics; Antidepressants; Barbiturates; Narcotics

SEDITION. *Use* Liberty of Speech; Political Crimes and Offenses; Revolutions; Treason

SEGREGATION
LC ——; s.a. Minorities; Race discrimination; Segregation in education; Segregation in transportation; subd. *Segregation* under names of ethnic groups, e.g., Negroes—Segregation
SEARS ——; s.a. Blacks—Education; Blacks—Segregation; Discrimination
RG SEGREGATION, SOCIAL; s.a. Busing (school integration); Discrimination in housing; Negroes—Segregation
NYT MINORITIES (Ethnic, racial, religious); s.a. Discrimination; Freedom and human rights; Negroes (in U.S.)
PAIS SEGREGATION, SOCIAL; s.a. Discrimination in housing; Integration and segregation of Negroes
BPI ——; s.a. Discrimination in education; Negroes—Segregation

SEGREGATION, SOCIAL. *Use* Segregation

SEGREGATION IN EDUCATION. *Use* Black Colleges; Busing; Discrimination in Education; Negro Children; Negro Students; Segregation

SEGREGATION IN HOUSING. *See* Discrimination in Housing

SEGREGATION IN TRANSPORTATION. *Use* Segregation

SEISMOLOGY AND SEISMOGRAPHS. *Use* Earth

SELECTIVE SERVICE. *See* Military Service, Compulsory

SELF. *Use* Individuality; Mind and Body; Thought and Thinking; Will

SELF EDUCATION. *Use* Education

SELF MANAGEMENT IN INDUSTRY. *See* Industrial Relations; Works Councils

SELF-ACTUALIZATION (Psychology). *Use* Individuality

SELF-CONTROL. *Use* Character; Will

SELF-CULTURE. *Use* Adult Education; Education

SELF-DEFENSE
See also names of specific forms of self defense, e.g., Boxing; Jiu-Jitsu; Judo; Karate; Wrestling; etc.
LC ———; s.a. Hand to hand fighting, Oriental
SEARS ———
RG ———; s.a. Fighting, Hand to hand
NYT PHYSICAL EDUCATION AND TRAINING; s.a. Athletics; Sports
PAIS ———; s.a. Physical education
BPI ———

SELF-DETERMINATION, NATIONAL. *Use* Nationalism; Nationality; Sovereignty

SELF-EMPLOYED. *Use* Professions; Small Business

SELF-EMPLOYED PENSIONS. *Use* Pensions

SELF-EVALUATION. *Use* Ability—Testing; Personality Tests; Tests, Mental

SELF-GOVERNMENT. *See* Democracy; Representative Government and Representation

SELF-GOVERNMENT (In Education)
LC ———; s.a. Cheating (education); College discipline; Student-administrator relationships; Student ethics; Student participation in administration
SEARS ———; s.a. School administration and organization; School discipline
RG ———; s.a. College discipline; Colleges and universities—Administration—Student participation; School management and organization
NYT COLLEGES AND UNIVERSITIES—U.S.—CAMPUS ADMINISTRATION; s.a. Colleges and universities—U.S.—Student activities and conduct; Education and schools—U.S.—Student activities and conduct
PAIS ———; s.a. College students—Ethics; Colleges and universities—Administration—Student participation

BPI EDUCATION; s.a. Students

SELF-INCRIMINATION. *Use* Confidential Communications; Witnesses

SELF-INSTRUCTION. *See* Adult Education; Correspondence Schools and Courses

SELF-INTEREST. *Use* Individualism

SELF-REALIZATION. *Use* Success

SELF-RELIANCE. *Use* Individualism; Success

SELLING. *See* Salesmen and Salesmanship

SEMANTICS
LC ———; s.a. Ambiguity; Definition (logic); Meaning (psychology); Phraseology; subds. *Semantics* and *Words—History* under names of languages, e.g., English language—Semantics; Latin language—Words—History; Vocabulary
SEARS ———; s.a. Language and languages; Words, New
RG ———; s.a. Association (psychology); Cognition
NYT PSYCHOLOGY AND PSYCHOLOGISTS; s.a. Language and languages
PAIS LANGUAGES; s.a. Thought and thinking
BPI PSYCHOLOGY; s.a. Thought and thinking

SEMINARIANS. *Use* Clergy; Theology

SEMI-PRECIOUS STONES. *See* Precious Stones

SENESCENCE. *See* Old Age

SENIOR CITIZENS. *See* Age; Old Age Assistance; Retirement

SENSES AND SENSATION
See also specific senses, e.g., Color sense; Hearing; Pain; Pleasure; Taste; Touch; Vision; etc.
LC ———; s.a. After-images; After-sensation; Intuition (psychology); Sense-organs; Sensory deprivation; Space perception; Time perception
SEARS ———; s.a. Gestalt psychology; Intellect
RG ———; s.a. Perception
NYT PSYCHOLOGY AND PSYCHOLOGISTS; s.a. Brain
PAIS PSYCHOLOGY; s.a. Knowledge, Theory of; Physiology
BPI ———; s.a. Psychology, Physiological

SENSITIVITY TRAINING. *See* Group Relations Training

SENSORY DEPRIVATION. *Use* Senses and Sensation

SENTENCES (Criminal procedure). *Use* Judgments; Punishment

SENTENCES, PRISON. *See* Prisons and Prisoners

SEPARATE MAINTENANCE. *Use* Alimony

SEPARATION (Law). *Use* Divorce; Marriage Law

SEPARATION OF POWERS
Scope: Works on the division of power between executive, legislative and judicial branches. Works on the separation of powers between central and local authorities are entered under Federal government.

LC ——; s.a. Constitutions; Delegated legislation; Executive impoundment of appropriated funds; Incompatibility of offices; Judicial power; Legislation; Political questions and judicial power

SEARS EXECUTIVE POWER; s.a. Constitutional law; Political science

RG ——; s.a. Constitutional law; Executive privilege (government information); Judicial review

NYT Subd. *Politics and government* under names of countries, e.g., Finland–Politics and government; s.a. U.S.–Constitution; World government

PAIS ——; s.a. Delegation of powers; Judicial review; Power (political science)

BPI ——; s.a. Executive power; War and emergency power

SEPARATIONS. *Use* Adultery; Alimony; Marriage Law

SERFDOM. *Use* Land Tenure; Slavery

SERIGRAPHY. *Use* Printing Industry

SERMONS. *Use* Preaching

SERVANTS. *Use* Household Employees

SERVICE AT COST (Public utilities). *Use* Municipal Ownership; Public Utilities

SERVICE CONTRACTS. *Use* Contracts

SERVICEMEN. *Use* Military Service as a Profession; Soldiers

SERVITUDE. *See* Slavery

SERVOMECHANISMS. *Use* Automation; Cybernetics

SET THEORY. *Use* Logic, Symbolic and Mathematical

SETTLEMENTS (Law). *Use* Marriage Law

SEWAGE DISPOSAL. *Use* Public Health; Refuse and Refuse Disposal; Sanitation; Water–Pollution

SEWAGE IRRIGATION. *Use* Fertilizers and Manures

SEWING
LC ——; s.a. Clothing and dress; Dressmaking; Embroidery; Needlework; Quilting; Tailoring
SEARS ——; s.a. Embroidery; Home economics
RG ——; s.a. Curtains and draperies; Dressmaking
NYT ——; s.a. Apparel; Embroidery
PAIS ——; s.a. Patterns (dress); Sewing by men; Sewing equipment
BPI ——; s.a. Dress patterns; Needlework materials

SEX
LC ——; s.a. Celibacy; Change of sex; Cunnilingus; Fellatio; Generative organs; Homosexuality; Hygiene, Sexual; Lesbianism; Masturbation; Orgasm; Promiscuity; Prostitution; Puberty; Reproduction; Sex and religion; Sex differences (psychology); Sex in advertising; Sex in art; Sex in marriage; Sex instruction; Sex role; Sex symbolism; Sexual cycle; Sexual disorders; Sexual perversion; Transvestism; Trials (rape)
SEARS ——; s.a. Birth control; Free love; Marriage; Reproduction; Man–Sexual behavior; Sex instruction; Sexual hygiene; Woman–Sexual behavior

RG ——; s.a. Frigidity (psychology); Generative organs; Gonorrhea; Impotence; Moving pictures in sex instruction; Oedipus complex; Orgasm; Reproduction; Sex (psychology); Sexual behavior; Sexual ethics; subd. *Sexual behavior* under groups of people, e.g., Students–Sexual behavior; Syphilis; Venereal diseases; Virginity

NYT ——; s.a. Birth control and planned parenthood; Ethics and morals; Psychology and psychologists; Reproduction (biological); Sex education; Venereal diseases

PAIS SEX EDUCATION; s.a. Homosexualism; Marriage; Sex and law; Sex crimes; Sexual ethics; Venereal diseases

BPI ——; s.a. Marriage; Reproduction; Sex (biology); Sex (psychology); Sex crimes; Sex instruction

SEX CRIMES. *Use* Prostitution; Vice

SEX CUSTOMS. *Use* Manners and Customs; Moral Conditions

SEX EDUCATION. *Use* Health Education; Hygiene; Venereal Diseases

SEX IN ART. *Use* Art, Immoral; Erotica; Nude in Art

SEXUAL CYCLE. *Use* Reproduction

SEXUAL DISORDERS. *Use* Sex

SEXUAL ETHICS. *Use* Adultery; Bigamy; Birth Control; Chastity; Dating (Social customs); Ethics; Homosexuality; Marriage; Prostitution; Sex; Social Ethics

SEXUAL HYGIENE. *Use* Birth Control; Hygiene; Sex; Venereal Diseases

SHAME. *Use* Emotions

SHAREHOLDERS. *See* Stock-exchange

SHEETS. *Use* Beds and Bedding

SHELTERED WORKSHOPS. *Use* Rehabilitation; Vocational Rehabilitation

SHERIFFS. *Use* Law Enforcement; Police

SHIELDING (Radiation). *Use* Radiation

SHIFT SYSTEMS. *Use* Night Work

SHINGLES. *Use* Roofs

SHIP SUBSIDIES. *Use* Merchant Marine

SHIPMASTERS. *Use* Maritime Law

SHIPMENT OF GOODS
LC ——; s.a. C.I.F. clause; C.O.D. shipments; Drop shipments; F.O.B. clause; Freight and freightage; Invoices; Physical distribution of goods; subd. *Transportation* under commodities, e.g., Explosives–Transportation
SEARS MATERIALS HANDLING; s.a. Commerce; Marketing; Packaging; Transportation; Trucks
RG ——; s.a. Forwarding companies; Freight handling
NYT FREIGHT FORWARDING (Domestic and foreign); s.a. Ships and shipping; Transportation; Trucks and trucking industry

SHIPMENTS OF GOODS, *cont.*
PAIS ——; s.a. Delivery of goods; Packing for shipment
BPI ——; s.a. Carriers; Delivery of goods

SHIPPING CONFERENCES. *Use* Monopolies

SHIPS AND SHIPPING. *Use* Boats and Boating; Cargo Handling; Containers; Foreign Trade; Freedom of the Seas; Freight and Freightage; Maritime Law; Merchant Marine; Naval Art and Science; Ocean Travel; Ports; Seamen; Sea-power; Shipment of Goods; Transportation; Voyages and Travels; Warships

SHIPWRECKS. *Use* Disasters; Ocean Travel; Voyages and Travels

SHOCK. *Use* Neuroses

SHOCK THERAPY. *Use* Psychiatry; Therapeutics

SHOCK WAVES. *Use* Jet Planes; Noise

SHOES AND SHOE INDUSTRY. *Use* Boots and Shoes; Leather Industry and Trade

SHOOTING. *Use* Firearms

SHOOTING (Sport). *Use* Hunting

SHOOTING, MILITARY. *Use* Ballistics; Gunnery

SHOP MANAGEMENT. *See* Factory Management

SHOP STEWARDS. *Use* Works Councils

SHOPLIFTING. *Use* Theft

SHOPPER'S GUIDES. *See* Consumer Education

SHOPPING AND SHOPPERS
LC SHOPPING; s.a. Automobile purchasing; Consumer education; Consumers; Marketing (home economics); Purchasing; Rationing, Consumer; Retail trade
SEARS SHOPPING; s.a. Buying; Consumers; Home economics
RG ——; s.a. Christmas shopping; Purchasing
NYT HOME ECONOMICS; s.a. Consumers and consumption; Credit; Discount selling; Retail stores and trade
PAIS ——; s.a. Consumers; Customer relations; Purchasing, Household
BPI MARKETING (Home economics); s.a. Consumer education; Consumers; Shopping

SHOPPING CENTERS. *Use* Department Stores

SHOPPING MALLS. *Use* Department Stores; Streets

SHORE PROTECTION. *Use* Beaches; Coasts; Ports; Reclamation of Land; Seashore

SHORT SELLING. *Use* Stock-exchange; Wall Street

SHORT STORIES. *Use* Fiction; Tales

SHORT TAKE OFF AND LANDING AIRCRAFT. *Use* Jet Planes

SHORTHAND. *Use* Abbreviations; Business Education; Writing

SHOT PUTTING. *Use* Track Athletics

SHOTGUNS. *Use* Firearms; Gunnery

SHOW WINDOWS. *Use* Merchandising; Sales Management

SHOWMEN. *See* Entertainers

SHOWROOMS. *Use* Merchandising

SHRINES. *Use* Miracles

SHRUBS. *Use* Plants

SICK
Scope: Works on aid for the sick.
LC ——; s.a. Chronically ill; Cookery for the sick; Diet in disease; First aid in illness and injury; Invalids; Nurse and patient; Sick—Psychology; Sick—Recreation
SEARS ——; s.a. Health resorts, spas, etc.; Home nursing; Hospitals
RG SICK, THE; s.a. Convalescence; Handicapped; Physicians and patients
NYT MEDICINE AND HEALTH; s.a. Mental health and disorders; Nursing homes
PAIS HOSPITALS—PATIENTS; s.a. Hospitals—Outpatient services; Mental institutions—Patients; Nurses and nursing
BPI SICKNESS; s.a. Insurance, Health; Sick leave

SICK LEAVE. *Use* Absenteeism (Labor); Vacation, Employee

SICKNESS. *Use* Communicable Diseases; Diseases; Invalids; Sick

SIDESHOWS. *Use* Amusement Parks; Festivals

SIDEWALKS. *Use* Streets

SIDING. *See* Walls

SIEGES. *Use* Battles

SIGHT. *Use* Eye; Optics

SIGN LANGUAGE. *Use* Deafness; Language and Languages; Signs and Symbols

SIGN PAINTING. *Use* Painting, Industrial

SIGNALS AND SIGNALING. *Use* Ciphers; Emblems; Naval Art and Science; Signs and Symbols

SIGNALS AND SIGNS. *Use* Traffic Safety

SIGNATURES (Writing). *Use* Writing

SIGNS. *Use* Acronyms; Billboards; Posters

SIGNS AND SYMBOLS
LC ——; s.a. Cipher and telegraph codes; Heraldry; Logography; Military symbols; Omens; Signs and symbols in literature; Symbolism
SEARS ——; s.a. Abbreviations; Christian art and symbolism; Cryptography; Electric signs; Signals and signaling
RG SYMBOLS; s.a. Cross and crosses; Emblems; Sign language; Symbolism in art; Symbolism in literature
NYT ——; s.a. Advertising—U.S.—Outdoor advertising; Codes (ciphers); Crosses and crucifixes; Traffic (vehicular and pedestrian) and parking
PAIS ——; s.a. Emblems; Flags; Signs and signboards
BPI SIGNS; s.a. Emblems, Automobile; Road signs; Symbols

SIKHS—RELIGION. *Use* Hinduism

SILENT FILMS. *See* Moving Pictures

SILK SCREEN PRINTING. *Use* Printing Industry

SILVERSMITHING. *Use* Jewelry

SIMPLEX METHOD. *Use* Linear Programming

SIMULATION METHODS. *Use* Management Games; Operations Research

SIMULATORS. *Use* Educational Technology

SIN
LC	——; s.a. Fall of man; Repentance; Sins; Temptation; Vices
SEARS	——; s.a. Atonement; Christian ethics; Free will and determination; Salvation
RG	——; s.a. Confession; Deadly sins; Good and evil
NYT	RELIGION AND CHURCHES; s.a. Bible; Prayers and prayer books
PAIS	RELIGION; s.a. Christianity and other religions
BPI	RELIGION

SINGERS. *Use* Musicians; Singing and Songs

SINGING AND SONGS
LC	SINGING; s.a. Ballads; Carols; Choruses; Lullabies; National music; Negro songs; Singing—Interpretation; Songs; Songs (American, British, etc.); subd. *Songs and music* under subject, e.g., Cowboys—Songs and music; Topical songs; Vocal music
SEARS	SINGING; s.a. Black songs; Choral music; Folk songs; School songbooks; Singing games; Songs (American, French, etc.); subd. *Songs and music* under subject, e.g., Politics—Songs and music; Vocal music
RG	SINGING; s.a. Choral groups and societies; Choral singing; National songs; Phonograph records—Songs; Phonograph records—Vocal music; Rock 'n roll singers; Sailors songs; Sea songs; Songs
NYT	MUSIC; s.a. Entertainment and amusements; names of choirs, songs, singers, songwriters, etc.; Opera
PAIS	SINGING; s.a. Music; Music festivals; Opera
BPI	MUSIC; s.a. Bands; Composers; Music, Popular (songs, etc.); Rock groups; Singers

SINGING SOCIETIES. *See* Choral Music

SINGLE PARENT FAMILY. *Use* Family; Fathers; Maternal and Infant Welfare; Mothers; Parent and Child

SINGLE PEOPLE. *Use* Celibacy; Dating (Social customs); Divorce

SINS. *Use* Sin

SISTERHOODS. *Use* Monastic and Religious Life of Women

SITUATION ETHICS. *Use* Existentialism

SKATING. *Use* Winter Sports

SKEPTICISM. *Use* Atheism; Belief and Doubt; Rationalism; Truth

SKETCHING. *See* Drawing

SKIING. *Use* Winter Sports

SKILLED LABOR. *Use* Labor and Laboring Classes; Labor Supply; Manual Labor; Work

SKIN. *Use* Allergy; Beauty, Personal; Color of Man

SKIN DIVING. *Use* Underwater Exploration

SKIN-GRAFTING. *Use* Surgery

SKY DIVING. *Use* Parachuting

SKYJACKING. *See* Abduction (Kidnapping); Offenses Against Public Safety

SKYLIGHTS. *Use* Lighting

SKYSCRAPERS. *Use* Apartment Houses; Office Buildings

SLANDER (Law). *See* Libel and Slander

SLANG. *Use* Americanisms; Language and Languages; Vocabulary

SLAUGHTERING. *Use* Jews—Rites and Ceremonies; Meat Industry and Trade

SLAVERY
See also Slavery in the U.S. and similar headings.
LC	——; s.a. Freedmen; Liberty; Reconstruction; Serfdom; Slave narratives; Slave records; Slave-trade; State rights; U.S.—History—Civil war; Villeinage
SEARS	——; s.a. Abolitionists; Contract labor; International law; Peonage; Southern states—History; Underground railway
RG	——; s.a. Abolitionists; Freedmen; Indentured servants; Labor, Compulsory
NYT	——; s.a. Agriculture and agricultural products—U.S.—Labor; Civil war (U.S.) (1861-65); Negroes (general); Negroes (in U.S.)—History
PAIS	——; s.a. Labor, Compulsory; Land tenure
BPI	——; s.a. Land tenure

SLEEP
LC	——; s.a. Children—Sleep; Hibernation; Sleep disorders; Sleeping customs; Sleeping sickness; Snoring; Somnambulism
SEARS	——; s.a. Mind and body; Rest; Subconsciousness
RG	——; s.a. Dreams; Insomnia; Narcolepsy
NYT	——; s.a. Hypnosis; Narcolepsy
PAIS	——; s.a. Insomnia; Sleep learning; Sleep therapy; Somnambulism
BPI	——; s.a. Insomnia

SLEEP-LEARNING. *Use* Learning, Psychology of

SLEEPLESSNESS. *See* Sleep

SLEIGHING. *Use* Winter Sports

SLIDE MACHINES. *Use* Machine Accounting

SLIDES (Photography). *Use* Photography

SLIP COVERS. *Use* Upholstery

SLOGANS, MOTTOES AND CATCH-PHRASES. *Use* Proverbs; Quotations; Terms and Phrases; Trade-marks

SLOPES (Soil mechanics). *Use* Soils

SLOW LEARNING CHILDREN. *Use* Child Study; Exceptional Children; Mentally Handicapped Children

SLUDGE. *Use* Refuse and Refuse Disposal

SLUMS. *Use* Cities and Towns; Housing; Poverty; Tenement-houses; Urban Renewal

SMALL ARMS. *See* Firearms

SMALL BUSINESS
Scope: Works on small independent enterprises as contrasted with "big business" in general and in the U.S. as a whole.
LC ——; s.a. Cottage industries; Entrepreneur; Franchises (retail trade); Industrial promotion; New business enterprises; Self-employed
SEARS ——; s.a. Black businessmen; Business; Retail trade
RG ——; s.a. Franchise system; Self-employed
NYT U.S.–ECONOMIC CONDITIONS AND TRENDS –SMALL BUSINESSES; s.a. Credit–U.S.–Small business; Retail stores and trade
PAIS ——; s.a. Corporations–Size; Franchises
BPI BUSINESS, SMALL; s.a. Black capitalism; Industries, Size of; Minority business enterprises

SMALL CLAIMS COURTS. *Use* Courts

SMALL GROUPS. *Use* Alienation (Social psychology); Leadership; Social Groups; Social Psychology

SMALL LOANS. *Use* Credit; Loans, Personal

SMALLPOX–PREVENTION. *Use* Vaccination

SMELTING. *Use* Metal Industries; Steel Industry and Trade

SMOG. *Use* Air–Pollution

SMOKE. *Use* Air–Pollution; Fuel

SMOKE SCREENS. *Use* Chemical Warfare

SMOKING
LC ——; s.a. Cigarette habit; Smoking–Physiological effect; Smoking–Psychological aspect; Tobacco habit
SEARS ——; s.a. Cigarettes; Tobacco habit
RG ——; s.a. Cigars; Tobacco pipes
NYT TOBACCO, TOBACCO PRODUCTS AND SMOKERS' ARTICLES
PAIS ——; s.a. Cigar industry; Cigarette industry
BPI ——; s.a. Television broadcasting–Smoking hazard coverage; Tobacco pipes

SMUGGLING. *Use* Crime and Criminals; Tariff

SNOBS AND SNOBBISHNESS. *Use* Aristocracy; Social Classes

SNORING. *Use* Sleep

SNOW AND ICE REMOVAL. *Use* Streets

SNOWMOBILES. *Use* Motor Vehicles; Winter Sports

SNOWSHOES AND SNOWSHOEING. *Use* Winter Sports

SNUFF. *Use* Tobacco

SOAP INDUSTRY. *Use* Cleaning Compounds

SOAP OPERAS. *See* Radio Broadcasting and Programs

SOCIAL ACCOUNTING. *See* National Income

SOCIAL ACTION. *Use* Religion and Sociology; Social Policy

SOCIAL ADJUSTMENT. *Use* Behavior (Psychology); Social Groups; Social Psychology

SOCIAL AND ECONOMIC SECURITY. *Use* Guaranteed Annual Income; Minimum Wage; Welfare Economics

SOCIAL CASEWORK. *Use* Counseling; Interviewing; Prisons and Prisoners; Social Service

SOCIAL CHANGE
LC ——; s.a. Agriculture–Social aspects; Cultural lag; Culture diffusion; Economic development–Social aspects; Industry–Social aspects; Progress; Revolution (theology); Social history; Social values; Subculture
SEARS ——; s.a. Anthropology; Evolution; Progress; Social conditions
RG ——; s.a. Educational sociology; Social revolution
NYT SOCIAL CONDITIONS AND WELFARE; s.a. Evolution; Sociology; U.S.–History
PAIS ——; s.a. Community development; Social life and customs
BPI ——; s.a. Social conditions; Sociology

SOCIAL CLASSES
LC ——; s.a. Caste; Elite (social sciences); Prestige; Social conflict; Social mobility; Speech and social status
SEARS ——; s.a. Aristocracy; Class conflict; Nobility; Success
RG ——; s.a. Middle classes; Snobs and snobbishness; Upper classes
NYT SOCIAL CONDITIONS AND WELFARE; s.a. Society; Sociology
PAIS SOCIAL STATUS; s.a. Equality; Middle classes; Students' socio-economic status
BPI ——; s.a. Clubs; Middle classes; Occupations; Social mobility

SOCIAL CONDITIONS. *Use* Moral Conditions; Social Change; Social Conflict; Social Ethics; Social Policy; Social Problems; Social Surveys; Sociology; Subculture; Violence; War and Society

SOCIAL CONFLICT
LC ——; s.a. Conflict of generations; Social control; Social psychology
SEARS ——; s.a. Conflict of generations; Revolutions; Social classes
RG ——; s.a. Generation gap; Parent-child relationship; Youth-adult relationship
NYT SOCIAL CONDITIONS AND WELFARE; s.a. Sociology
PAIS ——; s.a. Conflict of generations; Parent and child (law)
BPI SOCIAL PROBLEMS; s.a. Communism; Poverty; Social conditions; Socialism

SOCIAL CONFORMITY. *See* Behavior (Psychology)

SOCIAL CONTRACT. *Use* Liberty; Sovereignty

SOCIAL CONTROL. *Use* Lobbying; Social conflict; Sociology

SOCIAL DEMOCRACY. *See* Socialism

SOCIAL DESIRABILITY. *Use* Social Psychology

SOCIAL DISTANCE. *Use* Human Relations

SOCIAL DISTINCTION. *See* Elite (Social sciences)

SOCIAL ECOLOGY. *Use* Ecology; Human Ecology

SOCIAL EDUCATION. *Use* Behavior Therapy; Group Relations Training

SOCIAL EQUALITY. *See* Equality

SOCIAL ETHICS
LC	——; s.a. Altruism; Civics; Fellowship; Socialist ethics; Totalitarian ethics; Wealth, Ethics of
SEARS	——; s.a. Citizenship; Crime and criminals; Sexual ethics; Social problems
RG	——; s.a. Christian ethics; Church and race problems
NYT	ETHICS AND MORALS; s.a. Social conditions and welfare; Sociology
PAIS	——; s.a. Business ethics; Political ethics
BPI	ETHICS; s.a. Business ethics; Political ethics

SOCIAL EVOLUTION. *See* Social Change

SOCIAL GROUP WORK. *Use* Adult Education; Clubs; Social Service

SOCIAL GROUPS
LC	——; s.a. Acculturation; Coalition (social sciences); Elite (social sciences); Personality and culture; Reference groups; Small groups; Social participation; Subculture
SEARS	SOCIAL PSYCHOLOGY; s.a. Community life; Leadership; Social adjustment
RG	GROUPS (Sociology); s.a. Age groups; Social psychology
NYT	SOCIOLOGY; s.a. Society
PAIS	——; s.a. Assimilation (sociology); Group behavior; Neighborhoods
BPI	GROUPS (Sociology); s.a. Group relations training; Pressure groups

SOCIAL HISTORY
See also subds. *Social conditions* and *Social history* under names of places, e.g., Appalachia—Social conditions.
LC	——; s.a. Moral conditions; Rural conditions; Social change; Social mobility; Social movements; Social stability; Sociology; Technology and civilzation
SEARS	SOCIAL CONDITIONS; s.a. Cost and standard of living; Counter culture; Economic conditions; Social problems; Social surveys
RG	——; s.a. Urbanization
NYT	SOCIOLOGY; s.a. Civilization; Culture; U.S.—History
PAIS	SOCIAL CONDITIONS; s.a. Poor
BPI	SOCIAL CONDITIONS; s.a. Poverty

SOCIAL HYGIENE. *See* Hygiene; Public Health; Venereal Diseases

SOCIAL INSURANCE. *Use* Insurance, Social; Old Age Assistance; Pensions; Retirement

SOCIAL INTERACTION. *Use* Group Relations Training

SOCIAL ISOLATION. *Use* Alienation (Social psychology)

SOCIAL LIFE AND CUSTOMS. *Use* Celibacy; Culture; Manners and Customs; Social Change; Social History

SOCIAL LEGISLATION. *Use* Insurance, Social

SOCIAL MEDICINE. *Use* Medical Care

SOCIAL MOBILITY. *Use* Occupational Mobility; Social Classes

SOCIAL MOVEMENTS. *Use* Social History

SOCIAL NORM. *Use* Behavior (Psychology)

SOCIAL PARTICIPATION. *Use* Social Groups

SOCIAL PLANNING. *See* Social Policy

SOCIAL POLICY
See also subd. *Social policy* under names of places, e.g., South Africa—Social policy.
LC	——; s.a. Christian democracy; Economic security; Land reform; Social action; Social reformers; Welfare state
SEARS	——; s.a. Economic policy
RG	——; s.a. Economic policy; Social action
NYT	ECONOMICS; s.a. Labor; Social sciences
PAIS	——; s.a. Welfare economics
BPI	——; s.a. Social conditions

SOCIAL PRESSURE. *Use* Lobbying; Public Opinion

SOCIAL PROBLEMS
LC	——; s.a. Liquor problem; Migrant labor; Mutualism; Parasitism (social sciences); Public welfare; Race discrimination; Social conflict; Social reformers; Technology and civilization
SEARS	——; s.a. Community centers; Discrimination; Housing; Unemployed; Woman—Social conditions
RG	——; s.a. Poor; subd. *Social problems* under names of cities, e.g., Ithaca—Social problems
NYT	SOCIAL CONDITIONS AND WELFARE; s.a. Discrimination; Freedom and human rights
PAIS	——; s.a. Church and social problems; Cost and standard of living; Poverty
BPI	——; s.a. Crime and criminals; Race discrimination; Sociology

SOCIAL PROGRESS. *Use* Progress

SOCIAL PSYCHIATRY. *Use* Mental Hygiene; Psychiatry

SOCIAL PSYCHOLOGY
LC	——; s.a. Acculturation; Behavior (psychology); Community psychology; Ethnopsychology; Human ecology; Hysteria (social psychology); Morale; National characteristics; Propaganda; Social conflict; Social desirability; Social facilitation; Social groups; Stereotype (psychology)

SOCIAL PSYCHOLOGY, *cont.*
SEARS ——; s.a. Crowds; Human relations; National characteristics; Political psychology; Race psychology; Social adjustment; Sociometry
RG ——; s.a. Adjustment, Social; Human relations
NYT PSYCHOLOGY AND PSYCHOLOGISTS; s.a. Sociology
PAIS ——; s.a. Group relations training; Small groups
BPI ——; s.a. Alienation (social psychology); Interviews; Violence

SOCIAL REFORM. *See* Social Problems

SOCIAL REFORMERS. *Use* Social Policy; Social Problems

SOCIAL REVOLUTION. *Use* Social Change

SOCIAL SCIENCES
Scope: General and comprehensive works dealing with anthropology, sociology, political science and economics.
LC ——; s.a. Civics; Human behavior; Human ecology; Power (social sciences); Social sciences and state; Social scientists; Statics and dynamics (social sciences)
SEARS ——; s.a. Economics; Political science; Social change
RG ——; s.a. Behavioral sciences; Civilization; Forecasts (social sciences)
NYT ——; s.a. Economics; Politics and government; Sociology
PAIS ——; s.a. Behavioral sciences; Political science
BPI ——; s.a. Behavioral sciences; Human ecology

SOCIAL SECURITY. *See* Insurance, Social; Old Age Assistance; Welfare Economics

SOCIAL SERVICE
Scope: Works on methods of welfare work, public and private.
LC ——; s.a. Community organization; Counseling; Marriage counseling; Medical care; Medical social work; Parole; Public welfare; Social service, Medical
SEARS ——; s.a. Probation; Social case work; Social group work; Welfare work in industry
RG ——; s.a. Legal aid; Social work
NYT WELFARE WORK (U.S. only); s.a. Social conditions and welfare
PAIS ——; s.a. Community funds; School social work
BPI ——; s.a. Social workers

SOCIAL SETTLEMENTS. *Use* Community; Playgrounds

SOCIAL STABILITY. *Use* Sociology

SOCIAL STATUS. *Use* Aristocracy; Caste; Elite (Social sciences); Labor and Laboring Classes; Middle Classes; Social Classes; Upper Classes

SOCIAL STRATIFICATION. *See* Social Classes

SOCIAL STUDIES. *See* Social Sciences

SOCIAL SURVEYS
Scope: Works on methods of investigation and research dealing broadly with social and economic conditions of communities. For surveys of individual regions and cities see that particular geographical entity with subd. *Social conditions,* e.g., Washington, D.C.—Social conditions.
LC ——; s.a. Canvassing (Church work); Economic surveys; Family life surveys; Occupational surveys
SEARS ——; s.a. City planning; Educational surveys
RG ——
NYT Surveys and series of articles published in New York Times; s.a. Social conditions and welfare; U.S.—Economic conditions
PAIS ——; s.a. Community surveys; Economic surveys
BPI ——; s.a. Sociology

SOCIAL VALUES. *Use* Social Change; Social Ethics; Value

SOCIAL WELFARE. *See* Charities; Cost and Standard of Living; Public Welfare; Social Problems; Social Service

SOCIAL WORK. *Use* Charities; Social Service

SOCIALISM
LC ——; s.a. Collectivism; Democracy; Equality; Government ownership; Guild socialism; Individualism; Mutualism; National socialism; Nationalization; People's democracies; Social conflict; Social ethics
SEARS ——; s.a. Labor and laboring classes; Proletariat; Syndicalism; Utopias
RG ——; s.a. Collective settlements; Industrial democracy; Socialism, Christian
NYT ——; s.a. Communism
PAIS ——; s.a. Government ownership; Nationalism and socialism
BPI ——; s.a. Collective settlements

SOCIALIZATION. *Use* Acculturation

SOCIALIZED MEDICINE. *See* Insurance, Health; Medical Care

SOCIALLY HANDICAPPED. *Use* Handicapped

SOCIALLY HANDICAPPED CHILDREN. *Use* Child Study

SOCIETIES. *Use* Learning and Scholarship

SOCIETIES, SECRET. *Use* Secret Societies

SOCIETY. *Use* Aristocracy; Charities; Elite (Social sciences); Entertaining; Etiquette; Manners and Customs; Social Classes; Upper Classes

SOCIETY, PRIMITIVE
LC ——; s.a. Anthropology; Blood brotherhood; Economics, Primitive; Ethnology; Gipsies; Indians—Social life and customs; Industries, Primitive; Law, Primitive; Man, Primitive; Nomads; Taboo; Totemism; Tribal government; Tribes and tribal systems; Village communities; Wild men

SEARS   ——; s.a. Art, Primitive; Cannibalism; Clans and clan system; Indians of North America—Social life and customs; Music, Primitive; Religion, Primitive

RG   ——; s.a. Man, Prehistoric; Nomads; Religion, Primitive; Stone age; Stone implements and weapons

NYT   ARCHEOLOGY AND ANTHROPOLOGY; s.a. Civilization; Culture; Sociology

PAIS   ——; s.a. Government, Primitive; Tribes and tribal system

BPI   SOCIOLOGY; s.a. History

SOCIETY AND WAR. *See* War and Society

SOCIOLINGUISTICS. *Use* Language and Languages

SOCIOLOGICAL JURISPRUDENCE. *Use* Law

SOCIOLOGY

LC   ——; s.a. Acculturation; Historical sociology; Individualism; Industrial sociology; Mass society; Religion and sociology; Social control; Social groups; Social history; Social sciences; Social stability

SEARS   ——; s.a. Educational sociology; Social change; Social classes; Social conditions; Social problems; Social psychology

RG   ——; s.a. Power (social sciences); Social gospel; Sociology, Christian; Sociology, Rural

NYT   ——; s.a. Families; Leaders

PAIS   ——; s.a. Church and social problems; Community life; Political sociology; Sociology, Urban

BPI   ——; s.a. Family; Human ecology; Sociology, Industrial

SOCIOLOGY, MILITARY. *Use* Armed Forces; Militarism; War and Society

SOCIOLOGY, RELIGIOUS. *See* Religion and Sociology

SOCIOLOGY, RURAL. *Use* Community; Country Life; Migration, Internal; Peasantry; Rural Conditions; Villages

SOCIOLOGY, URBAN. *Use* Cities and Towns; Migration, Internal; Suburbs; Urbanization

SOCIOMETRY. *Use* Social Psychology

SODOMY. *Use* Homosexuality

SOFT DRINK INDUSTRY. *Use* Beverages

SOFTBALL. *Use* Baseball

SOIL. *Use* Soils

SOIL CONSERVATION. *Use* Conservation of Natural Resources; Erosion; Reclamation of Land; Soils

SOIL FERTILITY. *Use* Fertilizers and Manures; Soils

SOILS

LC   ——; s.a. Agricultural chemistry; Bacteriology, Agricultural; Fertilizers and manures; Forest soils; Frozen ground; Land; Mineralogy; Soil conservation; Soil inoculation; Watershed management

SEARS   ——; s.a. Erosion; Irrigation; Reclamation of land; Soil—Bacteriology; Soils (engineering)

RG   ——; s.a. Compost; Gardening—Soil preparation, Slopes (soil mechanics)

NYT   SOIL; s.a. Environment; Fertilizer; Nature

PAIS   ——; s.a. Agricultural chemicals; Fertilizer industry; Soil erosion; Soil surveys

BPI   ——; s.a. Conservation of resources; Soil mechanics; Soil pollution

SOLAR ACTIVITY. *Use* Sun

SOLAR ENERGY. *Use* Sun

SOLAR HEATING. *Use* Heating

SOLAR POWER. *Use* Sun

SOLAR RADIATION. *Use* Radiation; Sun

SOLAR SYSTEM. *Use* Astronomy; Earth; Sun

SOLDER AND SOLDERING

LC   ——; s.a. Alloys; Metal industries; Metal-work; Sealing (technology); Welding

SEARS   ——; s.a. Alloys; Plumbing; Welding

RG   ——; s.a. Alloys; Sealing (technology); Steel-welding; Welding

NYT   WELDING

PAID   WELDING; s.a. Metals

BPI   ——; s.a. Brazing; Sealing compounds; Underwater welding and cutting; Welding

SOLDIERS

LC   ——; s.a. Armed forces; Boys as soldiers; Generals; Jews as soldiers; Mercenary troops; Military art and science; Pensions, Military; Soldiers in art; subd. *Military life* under armies, e.g., U.S. Army—Military life; Veterans

SEARS   ——; s.a. Armies; Military biography; Military service as a profession; Scouts and scouting

RG   ——; s.a. Military life; Narcotics and servicemen; Women as soldiers

NYT   U.S. ARMAMENT AND DEFENSE—ARMY; s.a. Military art and science

PAIS   SERVICEMEN; s.a. Military service; Negroes as soldiers

BPI   ——; s.a. Military art and science; Veterans

SOLDIERS, DISABLED. *See* Invalids

SOLICITORS. *See* Lawyers

SOLVENTS. *Use* Cleaning Compounds

SOMATOLOGY. *Use* Anatomy, Human; Color of Man

SOMNAMBULISM. *Use* Dreams; Sleep

SONGS. *Use* Singing and Songs

SONIC BOOM. *Use* Jet Planes

SOPORIFICS. *See* Narcotics

SORCERY. *See* Occult Sciences

SOUL

LC   ——; s.a. Anatman; Atman; Immortality; Pre-existence; Reincarnation; Transmigration

SOUL, *cont.*
SEARS ——; s.a. Future life; Man (theology); Personality; Spiritual life
RG ——; s.a. Future life; Reincarnation; Spirit
NYT RELIGION AND CHURCHES; s.a. Philosophy
PAIS RELIGION; s.a. Man; Psychology
BPI RELIGION; s.a. Man; Philosophy

SOUL MUSIC. *See* Jazz Music

SOUND AND SOUND RECORDING
LC SOUND; s.a. Acoustic phenomena in nature; High-fidelity sound systems; Sounds (for sound effects); subd. *Sound effects* under subjects, e.g., Radio broadcasting—Sound effects; Vibration
SEARS SOUND; s.a. Phonetics; Sound—Recording and reproducing; Ultrasonics
RG SOUND; s.a. Acoustics, Architectural; Microphones; Phonograph records—Sounds; Sounds (for sound recording)
NYT SOUND; s.a. Acoustics; Noise
PAIS SOUND RECORDING; s.a. Hearing; Phonograph records
BPI SOUND; s.a. Hearing; Noise control

SOUND EFFECTS. *See* Sound and Sound Recording

SOUND MOTION PICTURES. *See* Moving Pictures

SOUND PRESSURE. *Use* Ultrasonics

SOUNDING AND SOUNDINGS. *Use* Oceanography

SOUNDPROOFING. *Use* Noise

SOUTH POLE. *Use* Antarctic Regions

SOUTHERN STATES. *Use* Confederate States of America; Slavery

SOUVENIRS. *Use* Tourist Trade

SOVEREIGNS. *See* Heads of State

SOVEREIGNTY
LC ——; s.a. Autonomy; Equality of states; Legitimacy of governments; Self-determination, National; Social contract; Sovereignty, Violence of; State rights
SEARS THE STATE; s.a. Constitutional law; International law
RG ——; s.a. Airspace (international law); State, The
NYT Subd. *Politics and government* under names of countries, e.g., Norway—Politics and government; s.a. International relations; World government
PAIS ——; s.a. Equality of states; State, The
BPI ——; s.a. Airspace (international law); Space law

SPACE AND UPPER ATMOSPHERE. *Use* Airspace (International law); Artificial Satellites; Astronautics; Astronomy; Astrophysics; Atmosphere, Upper; Outer Space; Space Flight

SPACE FLIGHT
LC ——; s.a. Extraterrestrial bases; Flight; Interplanetary voyages (imaginary); Lunar probes; Manned flights; Navigation (astronautics); Orbital transfer (space flights); Outer space explorations; Space flight to the moon; Space ships; Voyages and travel

SEARS ——; s.a. Astrodynamics; Astronauts; Lunar probes; Manned flights; Outer space—Exploration; Space probes
RG ——; s.a. Ground support systems (space flight); Life support systems (space environment); Lunar probes; Navigation; Voyages (imaginary)
NYT ASTRONAUTICS; s.a. Aerospace industries and sciences; Communications satellites; Space and upper atmosphere
PAIS ——; s.a. Astronautics; Astronauts; Lunar explorations; Satellites, Artificial; Space vehicles
BPI ——; s.a. Apollo project; Astronautics; Astronauts—Lunar surface activities; Lunar bases; Orbital rendezvous (space flight); Space flight—Manned flights; Space vehicles

SPACE LAW. *Use* Airspace (International law); Artificial Satellites; Sovereignty

SPACE MEDICINE. *Use* Aviation Medicine

SPACE PERCEPTION. *Use* Senses and Sensation

SPACE SHIPS. *Use* Rockets (Aeronautics); Space Flight

SPACE STATIONS. *Use* Artificial Satellites

SPACE TRAVEL. *See* Space Flight

SPACE VEHICLES. *Use* Artificial Satellites; Outer Space; Rockets (Aeronautics); Space Flight

SPASTIC PARALYSIS. *See* Cerebral Palsy

SPAWNING. *Use* Reproduction

SPEAKING. *See* Debates and Debating; Lectures and Lecturing; Oratory; Preaching; Voice

SPECIAL DAYS, WEEKS AND MONTHS
See also names of special days, e.g., Christmas; Flag Day; Halloween; Memorial Day; or months, e.g., Ramadan.
LC DAYS; s.a. Fasts and feasts; Holiday decorations; Leap year; Promotion of special events
SEARS BIRTHDAYS; s.a. Festivals; Holidays
RG ——; s.a. Fasts and feasts; Holidays; Vacations; Wedding anniversaries
NYT HOLIDAYS AND SPECIAL OCCASIONS; s.a. Festivals
PAIS SPECIAL DAYS AND WEEKS; s.a. Anniversaries; Christmas business; Holidays
BPI DAYS; s.a. Anniversaries; Holidays; Vacations

SPECIAL DISTRICTS. *Use* Local Government; Metropolitan Government

SPECIAL DRAWING RIGHTS. *Use* Finance; Foreign Exchange

SPECIAL FUNDS. *Use* Budget

SPECIAL SALES. *Use* Sales

SPECIALTY STORES. *Use* Department Stores

SPECIE. *See* Money

SPECIES. *Use* Evolution

SPECIFICATION WRITING. *Use* Technical Writing

SPECTATOR CONTROL. *Use* Mobs; Riots

SPECTRUM ANALYSIS. *Use* Optics; Sun

SPECULATION. *Use* Business Ethics; Commodity Exchanges; Gambling; Investments; Over-the-counter Markets; Risk; Stock-exchange; Wall Street

SPEECH
LC ———; s.a. Accents and accentuation; Communication; Communicative disorders; Diction; Extemporaneous speaking; Language arts; Oral communication; Oratory; Speech and social status
SEARS ———; s.a. Language and languages; Phonetics; Rhetoric; Speech disorders; Style, Literary
RG ———; s.a. Elocution; Singing—Diction; Stammering; Voice
NYT ———; s.a. Debating; Language and languages
PAIS ———; s.a. Languages; Public speaking; Speeches, addresses, etc.; Vocabulary
BPI ———; s.a. Language and languages; Public speaking; Voice

SPEECH—IDENTIFICATION. *Use* Voice

SPEECH, LIBERTY OF. *See* Liberty of Speech

SPEECH DISORDERS. *Use* Speech

SPEECH PATHOLOGY. *See* Speech

SPEECHES, ADDRESSES, ETC.
LC ———; s.a. Debates and debating; Introduction of speakers; Lectures and lecturing; Orations; Oratory; Parliamentary practice; Preaching; subd. *Addresses, essays, lectures* under subject, e.g., Geology—Addresses, essays, lectures
SEARS ———; s.a. After-dinner speeches; Orations; Toasts
RG ———; s.a. Baccalaureate addresses; Public speaking
NYT SPEECHES AND STATEMENTS (General), s.a. Debating; Speech
PAIS ———; s.a. Debating; Public speaking
BPI PUBLIC SPEAKING; s.a. Television public speaking

SPEED LIMITS. *Use* Traffic Safety

SPEED READING. *Use* Reading

SPELEOLOGY. *Use* Caves

SPERMATOGENESIS. *Use* Embryology

SPERMATOZOA. *Use* Reproduction

SPIES
LC ———; s.a. Agents provocateurs; Military art and science; Secret service; War (international law); Women as spies
SEARS ———; s.a. Secret service; Subversive activities; World War, 1939–1945—Underground movements
RG ———; s.a. Espionage; Trials (espionage)
NYT ESPIONAGE; s.a. International relations
PAIS ———; s.a. Aerial reconnaissance; Intelligence service
BPI ESPIONAGE; s.a. Industrial espionage; Secret service

SPINNING. *Use* Handicraft; Textile Industry and Fabrics

SPIRIT. *Use* Soul

SPIRITS, ALCOHOLIC. *See* Liquors

SPIRITUAL LIFE. *Use* Monastic and Religious Life of Women; Monasticism and Religious Orders; Religion; Soul

SPIRITUALISM. *Use* Future Life; Occult Sciences; Psychical Research

SPIRITUALS. *Use* Negro Music

SPOILS SYSTEM. *See* Corruption (Politics); Patronage, Political

SPONTANEOUS GENERATION. *Use* Life; Reproduction

SPORTS
See also names of particular sports, e.g., Baseball, Fencing, Water sports, Winter sports.
LC ———; s.a. Doping in sports; Exercise; Physical fitness; Self-defense; Sport clothes; Sport stories; Sports—Economic aspects; Sports—Philosophy; Sports—Social aspects; Sports and state; Stadiums
SEARS ———; s.a. Coaching (athletics); College sports; Outdoor life; Sports—Equipment and supplies
RG ———; s.a. Athletes; Physical education and training; Recreation
NYT ———; s.a. Athletics
PAIS ———; s.a. College athletics; School athletics
BPI ———; s.a. Athletics; Olympic games

SPORTS CARS. *Use* Automobiles

SPORTS IN RADIO. *See* Radio Broadcasting and Programs

SPRAYING AND DUSTING. *Use* Pests

SPRINGS. *Use* Water

SQUARE DANCING. *Use* Dancing

SQUATTERS. *Use* Public Lands

STABILIZATION IN INDUSTRY. *See* Business Cycles

STADIUMS. *Use* Sports

STAGE. *See* Acting; Drama; Theater

STAGE FRIGHT. *Use* Acting; Public Speaking

STAGGERED HOURS. *Use* Night Work

STAINS AND STAINING. *Use* Finishes and Finishing

STALACTITES AND STALAGMITES. *Use* Caves

STAMINA, PHYSICAL. *See* Physical Fitness

STAMMERING. *Use* Speech; Voice

STAMPS, POSTAGE. *See* Postage Stamps

STANDARD OF LIVING. *Use* Cost and Standard of Living

STANDARD OF VALUE. *See* Money; Value

STANDARD TIME. *See* Time

STANDARDS AND STANDARDIZATION. *Use* Production Standards; Quality Control

STANDARDS OF MASS. *Use* Weights and Measures

STARS. *Use* Astronomy; Astrophysics

STARVATION. *Use* Nutrition

STATE, THE
Scope: For specific activities of a state see such headings as, e.g., Education and state; Sports and state; etc.
LC ——; s.a. Boundaries; Communist state; Law and politics; Legitimacy of governments; National state; Nationalism; People (constitutional law); Public interest; Reason of state; States, New; Territory, National; Welfare state
SEARS THE STATE; s.a. International law; Political science; Sovereignty; States, New
RG ——; s.a. Corporate state; Individual and state; States, New
NYT POLITICS AND GOVERNMENT; s.a. Local government; World government
PAIS ——; s.a. Government liability; Nations, New; Sovereignty; State government; State succesion; Underdeveloped states
BPI POLITICAL SCIENCE; s.a. States, New

STATE AND ART. *See* Art and State

STATE AND EDUCATION. *See* Education and State

STATE AND INDUSTRY. *See* Industry and State

STATE AND MUNICIPAL RELATIONS. *Use* Municipal Government

STATE AND SCIENCE. *See* Science and State

STATE BOARDS OF EDUCATION. *Use* Educational Administration

STATE CONSTITUTIONS. *Use* Constitutions

STATE FARMS. *Use* Collective Farming; Farms and Farming

STATE FINANCE. *Use* Debts, Public; Finance, Public

STATE GOVERNMENTS
Scope: Works on state governments in general and in the U.S. See also subd. *Government and politics* under names of specific states.
LC ——; s.a. Exclusive and concurrent legislative powers; Interstate agreements; Interstate controversies; Statehood (American politics); Taxation, State
SEARS ——; s.a. Federal government; Political science
RG ——; s.a. Constitutions, State; Governors
NYT LOCAL GOVERNMENT; s.a. names of individual states; States (U.S.); U.S.—Politics and government—Local government
PAIS STATE GOVERNMENT; s.a. Federal and state relations
BPI ——; s.a. Governors

STATE INSTITUTIONS. *Use* Public Institutions

STATE LEGISLATURES. *Use* Legislative Bodies

STATE OF SIEGE. *Use* Battles; Revolutions; War

STATE PARKS. *See* Parks

STATE PLANNING. *See* Economic Policy; Regional Planning; Social Policy

STATE PUBLICATIONS. *Use* Government and the Press; Government Publications

STATE RIGHTS
LC ——; s.a. Federal government; Nullification; Secession; Sovereignty; Statehood (American politics)
SEARS ——; s.a. Political science; Slavery in the U.S.
RG ——; s.a. Federal and state relations; States (U.S.)
NYT LOCAL GOVERNMENT; s.a. Politics and government; States (U.S.); U.S.—Politics and government—Local government
PAIS ——; s.a. Federal and state relations; Secession
BPI ——; s.a. Federal government

STATE SONGS. *Use* National Songs

STATE SUCCESSION. *Use* State, The

STATE UNIVERSITIES AND COLLEGES. *Use* Colleges and Universities

STATEHOOD (American politics). *Use* State Governments; State Rights

STATELESSNESS. *Use* Aliens; Citizenship; Exiles

STATES, NEW. *Use* State, The; Underdeveloped Areas

STATES' RIGHTS. *See* State Rights

STATESMEN. *Use* Diplomacy; Heads of State

STATICS AND DYNAMICS (Social sciences). *Use* Economic Development; Social Sciences

STATION WAGONS. *Use* Automobiles

STATIONERY. *Use* Paper Making and Trade

STATISTICAL INFERENCE. *See* Probabilities

STATISTICAL SERVICES. *Use* Information Services

STATISTICS
LC ——; s.a. Biometry; Economics, Mathematical; Military statistics; Nonparametric statistics; Probabilities; Statistical decision; Statistics—Graphic methods; subd. *Statistical methods* and *Statistics* under specific subjects, e.g., Agriculture—Statistical methods
SEARS ——; s.a. Census; Probabilities; Sampling (statistics); Vital statistics
RG ——; s.a. Criminal statistics; Distribution (probability theory); Economic statistics; Statistical methods
NYT ——; s.a. Economics; Population and vital statistics
PAIS ——; s.a. Government statistics; Market statistics
BPI ——; s.a. Business statistics; Economic statistics

STATURE. *Use* Growth; Posture

STATUTES. *Use* Law; Ordinances, Municipal

STEALING. *Use* Burglary; Theft

STEAM HEATING. *Use* Heating

STEAM-FITTING. *See* Plumbing

STEAM-PIPES. *Use* Heating; Plumbing

STEAMSHIPS. *Use* Merchant Marine; Ocean Travel

STEEL INDUSTRY AND TRADE
LC ———; s.a. Blast furnaces; Iron and steel workers; Iron industry and trade; Metal trade; Metallurgy; Smelting; Steelwork
SEARS ———; s.a. Electrometallurgy; Iron industry and trade; Ironwork; Ore dressing; Smelting
RG STEEL INDUSTRY; s.a. Steel workers; Steel works
NYT STEEL AND IRON; s.a. Metals and minerals; U.S. armament and defense—Defense contracts and production
PAIS IRON AND STEEL INDUSTRY; s.a. Iron founding; Metal trades; Pipes, Steel; Scrap metal industry
BPI STEEL INDUSTRY; s.a. Rolling mills; Smelting works; Steel works

STEEL METALLURGY. *Use* Metal Industries

STEEL-WELDING. *Use* Solder and Soldering

STENOGRAPHERS AND TYPISTS. *Use* Business Education

STEP CHILDREN. *Use* Parent and Child

STEP PARENTS. *Use* Maternal Deprivation

STEPMOTHERS. *Use* Mothers

STEREOPHONIC SOUND SYSTEMS. *Use* High Fidelity Sound Systems

STEREOTYPE (Psychology). *Use* Social Psychology

STERILIZATION. *Use* Birth Control; Population; Reproduction

STEVEDORING. *Use* Cargo Handling; Ports

STIGMATIZATION. *Use* Miracles

STILLBIRTH. *Use* Labor (Obstetrics)

STIMULANTS (Drugs). *Use* Antidepressants; Drug Abuse; Liquors; Narcotics

STOCHASTIC PROGRAMMING. *Use* Linear Programming

STOCK AND STOCK BREEDING
LC ———; s.a. Animal industry; Breeding; Livestock breeding; Marketing of livestock; Pastures; Poultry breeding; Sheep breeding; Swine breeding
SEARS LIVESTOCK; s.a. Dairying; Domestic animals; Livestock judging
RG LIVESTOCK; s.a. Stock ranges
NYT LIVESTOCK
PAIS LIVESTOCK INDUSTRY; s.a. Cattle industry; Horses
BPI LIVESTOCK; s.a. Cattle industry; Meat industry

STOCK BROKERS. *Use* Over-the-counter Markets; Stock-exchange; Wall Street

STOCK CERTIFICATES. *Use* Stock-exchange

STOCK COMPANIES. *Use* Corporations; Partnership; Stock-exchange

STOCK CONTROL. *See* Inventories

STOCK MARKET. *Use* Stock-exchange; Wall Street

STOCK RANGES. *Use* Pastures; Stock and Stock Breeding

STOCK TRANSFERS. *Use* Stock-exchange; Transfer (Law)

STOCK-EXCHANGE
LC ———; s.a. Block trading; Capital stock; Capitalists and financiers; Finance; Foreign exchange; Investment banking; Margins (security trading); Minority stockholders; Option (contracts); Over-the-counter markets; Preferred stocks; Speculation; Stock price forecasting; Stocks—Prices; Tender offers (securities); Wall Street
SEARS ———; s.a. Bonds; Foreign exchange; Securities; Speculation; Stock companies; Stocks
RG ———; s.a. Bonds; Corporations—Finance; Employees as stockholders; Investor relations programs; Manipulation (securities); Put and call transactions; Securities; Stocks—Marketing; Stocks—Rights
NYT STOCKS AND BONDS; s.a. Company reports; Corporations; names of exchanges, e.g., Stock Exchange, New York (NYSE); Property and investments; Stocks and bonds
PAIS STOCK EXCHANGES; s.a. Investments; Jobbers (securities); Restricted stock options; Securities; Stock brokers; Stock certificates; Stock market; Stock option contracts; Stockholders; Stocks, Preferred
BPI STOCK EXCHANGES; s.a. Bonds; Brokers; Dividends; Money brokers; Proxies; Puts and calls; Short selling; Stock market; Stock purchase options; Stock purchase warrants; Stockholders; Stocks, Preferred

STOCKHOLDERS. *Use* Corporations; Stock-exchange

STOCKYARDS. *Use* Meat Industry and Trade

STOCKS. *Use* Annuities; Bonds; Corporations; Investments; Negotiable Instruments; Over-the-counter Markets; Risk; Stock-exchange; Transfer (Law); Trusts and Trustees

STOCKS—PRICE FORECASTING. *Use* Business Forecasting

STOMACH. *Use* Digestion

STOMATOLOGY. *See* Dentistry

STONE AGE. *Use* Archaeology; Society, Primitive

STONES, PRECIOUS. *See* Precious Stones

STORAGE AND MOVING TRADE
LC ———; s.a. Carriers; Transportation; Warehouses
SEARS TRANSPORTATION; s.a. Carriers and carts
RG MOVING; s.a. Airplanes in moving; Moving and storage companies
NYT MOVING INDUSTRY; s.a. Storage; Trucks and trucking industry

STORAGE AND MOVING TRADE, *cont.*
PAIS ———; s.a. Carriers; Moving, Household
BPI STORAGE; s.a. Moving; Warehouses

STORAGE IN THE HOME. *Use* Home Economics

STORE DETECTIVES. *Use* Department Stores; Police

STORE FIXTURES. *Use* Merchandising

STORE HOURS. *Use* Sabbath

STORES, CHAIN. *See* Chain Stores

STORES, DEPARTMENT. *See* Department Stores

STORES, RETAIL. *Use* Chain Stores; Department Stores

STORES SYSTEMS. *Use* Inventories; Materials Management

STORIES. *See* Fiction

STORMS. *Use* Disasters; Weather

STORY TELLING. *Use* Children's Literature

STOWAGE. *Use* Cargo Handling

STRAINS AND STRESSES. *Use* Strength of Materials

STRATEGIC MATERIALS. *Use* Raw Materials

STRATEGY. *Use* Battles; Military Art and Science; War

STRATOSPHERE. *Use* Atmosphere, Upper

STRAW VOTES. *See* Elections; Public Opinion

STREAM POLLUTION. *See* Water—Pollution

STREAMLINING. *See* Aerodynamics

STREET CARS. *Use* Local Transit

STREET CLEANING. *Use* Public Health; Refuse and Refuse Disposal; Sanitation; Streets

STREET FIGHTING (Military science). *Use* Military Art and Science; Riots

STREET LIGHTING. *Use* Lighting; Streets; Traffic Safety

STREET MUSICIANS. *Use* Musicians

STREET SIGNS. *Use* Signs and Symbols; Streets; Traffic Safety

STREETS
LC ———; s.a. Cycling paths; Driveways; Highway law; Lighting; Private roads; Roads; Shopping malls; Street-railroads; Street signs; Traffic noise; Traffic safety
SEARS ———; s.a. Cities and towns; City traffic; Street cleaning; Street lighting
RG ———; s.a. Gutters; Street trades
NYT ———; s.a. Roads; Traffic (vehicular and pedestrian) and parking
PAIS ———; s.a. Highways; Sidewalks
BPI ———; s.a. Pavements; Snow and ice removal

STRENGTH OF MATERIALS
LC ———; s.a. Elasticity; Strains and stresses; Structural design
SEARS ———; s.a. Materials; Strains and stresses

RG ———; s.a. Deformation (mechanics); Dispersion strengthening; Fracture of solids; Wind pressure
NYT BUILDING; s.a. Architecture and architects; names of building materials, e.g., Wood and wood products
PAIS MATERIALS; s.a. Building materials; Raw materials
BPI ———; s.a. Impact; Steel—Strength; Strains and stresses

STRIKES AND LOCKOUTS
LC ———; s.a. Collective bargaining; Direct action; Industrial relations; Labor laws and legislation; Rent strikes; Trade unions
SEARS ———; s.a. Arbitration, Industrial; Collective bargaining; Labor unions; Passive resistance; Syndicalism
RG STRIKES; s.a. Injunctions; Labor disputes; Sabotage; Trade agreements
NYT STRIKES; s.a. Labor—U.S.—Strikes; specific types of strikes, e.g., Hunger strikes
PAIS STRIKES; s.a. Labor disputes; Lockouts; Picketing; Wildcat strikes
BPI STRIKES; s.a. Boycott; Picketing

STRING QUARTETS. *Use* Chamber Music

STRIP MINING. *Use* Mines and Mineral Resources

STRUCTURAL ENGINEERING. *Use* Engineering Design; Strength of Materials

STUCCO. *Use* Plaster and Plastering

STUDENT ACHIEVEMENTS. *Use* Academic Achievement

STUDENT ACTIVITIES. *Use* Students

STUDENT AID. *Use* College Costs; Scholarship; Students

STUDENT ATTITUDES. *Use* Students

STUDENT CHEATING. *See* Cheating (Education)

STUDENT COOPERATIVES. *Use* Cooperative Societies

STUDENT COUNCILS. *See* Self-government (In education)

STUDENT COUNSELORS. *Use* Personnel Service in Education

STUDENT DEMONSTRATIONS. *Use* Demonstrations; Student Movements; Youth Movement

STUDENT EMPLOYMENT. *Use* Employment; Seasonal Industries

STUDENT GUIDANCE. *See* Personnel Service in Education

STUDENT LOANS. *Use* Loans, Personal; Scholarship

STUDENT MOBILITY. *Use* Migration, Internal

STUDENT MOVEMENTS
LC ———; s.a. Student strikes; Youth movement
SEARS COLLEGE STUDENTS—POLITICAL ACTIVITY; s.a. Politics, Practical; Students
RG ———; s.a. College students—Political activities; Vietnamese war, 1957- —Protests, demonstrations, etc. against

NYT COLLEGES AND UNIVERSITIES–U.S.–STU-DENT ACTIVITIES AND CONDUCT; s.a. Children and youth; Colleges and universities–U.S.–Campus administration

PAIS COLLEGE STUDENTS–POLITICAL ACTIV-ITIES; s.a. College students–Discipline; Students

BPI STUDENT DEMONSTRATIONS; s.a. Politics, Practical; Youth–Political activities

STUDENT OPINION. *Use* Public Opinion

STUDENT STRIKES. *Use* Student Movements

STUDENT TEACHING. *Use* Observation (Educational method); Teachers, Training of

STUDENT UNIONS. *Use* Students

STUDENT WITHDRAWALS. *Use* Dropouts; School Attendance

STUDENT-ADMINISTRATOR RELATIONSHIPS. *Use* Self-government (In education)

STUDENTS

LC ——; s.a. College costs; Degrees, Academic; Dropouts; Grading and marking; Greek letter societies; Self-government (in education); Student aid; Student attitudes; Student movements; Student strikes; Students' societies; subd. *Students* under names of universities, colleges, schools; Talented students; Universities and colleges–Graduate work

SEARS ——; s.a. College and school journalism; College students; Colleges and universities; Fraternities and sororities; Student activities; Student loan funds; Students, Foreign; Scholarships, fellowships, etc.

RG ——; s.a. College clubs and societies; College students–Political activity, names of types of students, e.g., Law students, Graduate students; Student unions

NYT COLLEGES AND UNIVERSITIES–U.S.–STUDENT ACTIVITIES AND CONDUCT; s.a. Education and schools–U.S.–Student activities and conduct; names of student societies, etc.; Scholarships and fellowships

PAIS ——; s.a. College fraternities; College students; Graduate students; High school students; Student activities; Student loans; Student organization and societies; Students–Political activities

BPI ——; s.a. College costs; Colleges and universities–Graduate work; High school students; Student loans; Students' societies; Youth market

STUDENTS, FOREIGN. *Use* Students; Visitors, Foreign

STUDENTS' SOCIETIES. *Use* Students

STUTTERING. *See* Speech

STYLE, LITERARY. *Use* Editing; Letter-writing; Oratory; Speech

STYLE IN DRESS. *See* Costume; Fashion

STYLE MANIKINS. *Use* Models, Fashion

SUBCONSCIOUSNESS. *Use* Dreams; Hypnotism; Psychical Research; Psychoanalysis; Sleep; Thought Transference

SUBCULTURE

LC ——; s.a. Culture; Social groups

SEARS COUNTER CULTURE; s.a. Bohemianism; Collective settlements

RG COUNTER CULTURE; s.a. Groups (sociology); Hippies; Social change

NYT CULTURE; s.a. Children and youth–Behavior and training; Hippies; Manners and customs; Social conditions and welfare

PAIS CULTURE; s.a. Communal settlements; Gangs; Social conditions

BPI CULTURE; s.a. Hippies; Social conditions

SUBJECT HEADINGS. *Use* Abstracting; Indexing; Libraries and Librarians

SUBJECTIVITY. *Use* Belief and Doubt; Knowledge, Theory of

SUBLIMINAL PERCEPTION. *Use* Mental Suggestion; Perception

SUBMARINE EXPLORATION. *See* Underwater Exploration

SUBMARINE GEOLOGY. *Use* Oceanography

SUBMARINE WARFARE. *Use* Naval Art and Science

SUBMARINES. *Use* Warships

SUBMERGED LANDS. *Use* Oceanography; Public Lands; Seashore; Territorial Waters

SUBPOENA. *Use* Witnesses

SUBROGATION. *Use* Suretyship and Guaranty

SUBSCRIPTION RADIO BROADCASTING. *Use* Radio Broadcasting and Programs

SUBSCRIPTION TELEVISION. *Use* Television Broadcasting

SUBSIDIES

Scope: Financial and other aid given without equivalent recompense, by government to private enterprise. For federal government aid to states see Grants-in-aid.

LC ——; s.a. Bounties; Economic policy; Export premiums; Foreign trade promotion; Priorities, Industrial; Rent subsidies; Research grants

SEARS ——; s.a. Commercial policy; Economic assistance (domestic); Industry and state

RG ——; s.a. subd. *Federal aid* under subjects, e.g., Housing–Federal aid; Tobacco subsidies

NYT Names of industries receiving subsidies, e.g., Railroads

PAIS ——; s.a. Housing subsidies; Railroad subsidies

BPI ——; s.a. Agricultural administration; Airlines–Subsidies

SUBSOIL RIGHTS. *See* Mines and Mineral Resources

SUBSTITUTE PRODUCTS

See also names of substitute products, e.g., Nylon; Saccharin.

SUBSTITUTE PRODUCTS, *cont.*
LC ———; s.a. Chemurgy; Commercial products; Nonwoven fabrics; Substitution (economics); Synthetic fabrics; Synthetic products; Tea substitutes; Waste products
SEARS COMMERCIAL PRODUCTS; s.a. Plastics; Rayons; Rubber, Artificial; Synthetic fabrics; Synthetic products
RG ———; s.a. Food substitutes; Leather substitutes; Sugar substitutes; Textile fabrics, Nonwoven
NYT Names of types of products, e.g., Fuel; Rubber; Textiles; Sweeteners, Artificial; s.a. Food and grocery trade
PAIS SYNTHETIC PRODUCTS; s.a. Food substitutes; Nonwoven fabrics; Plastics industry; Rubber, Synthetic; Textile fibers, Synthetic
BPI SUBSTITUTES; s.a. Food substitutes; Nonwoven fabrics; Paper textiles; Plastics; Synthetic products

SUBSTITUTE TEACHERS. *Use* Teachers

SUBSTITUTION (Economics). *Use* Consumption (Economics); Economics; Value

SUBTENANTS. *Use* Landlord and Tenant

SUBURBS
LC ———; s.a. Metropolitan government; Municipal powers and services beyond corporate limits; Suburban crime; Suburban homes; Suburban life; subd. *Suburbs and environs* under names of cities and towns; Urbanization
SEARS CITIES AND TOWNS; s.a. Architecture, Domestic; Metropolitan areas; Suburban life; subd. *Suburbs and environs* under names of cities
RG ———; s.a. City planning; Regional planning; Suburban life
NYT Names of cities, e.g., Chicago metropolitan area; s.a. Area planning and renewal; Housing; Zoning
PAIS ———; s.a. Country houses; Land subdivision; Suburban development
BPI ———s.a. Cities and towns; Community

SUBVENTIONS. *See* Subsidies

SUBVERSIVE ACTIVITIES
LC ———; s.a. Conspiracies; Insurgency; Political crimes and offenses; Treason
SEARS ———; s.a. Espionage; Political crimes and offenses; Sabotage
RG ———; s.a. Internal security; Terrorism
NYT U.S.–INTERNAL SECURITY; s.a. Espionage; Sabotage; subd. *Espionage and subversion* under names of places, e.g., Great Britian–Espionage and subversion
PAIS ———; s.a. Sabotage; Spies
BPI ESPIONAGE; s.a. Sabotage; Terrorism

SUBWAYS. *Use* Local Transit; Railroads

SUCCESS
LC ———; s.a. Applications for positions; Prediction of occupational success; Prediction of scholastic success; Self-realization; Success–Programmed instruction

SEARS ———; s.a. Ability; Business; Business ethics; Leadership; Saving and thrift; Wealth
RG ———; s.a. Failure (psychology); Self-reliance
NYT PSYCHOLOGY AND PSYCHOLOGISTS
PAIS ———; s.a. Ability; Academic achievement
BPI ———; s.a. Ability; Leadership

SUFFICIENT REASON. *Use* Logic

SUFFRAGE. *Use* Age (Law); Citizenship; Civil Rights; Democracy; Elections; Politics, Practical; Voters, Registration of; Voting

SUFFRAGETTES. *See* Woman–Rights of Women; Women's Liberation Movement

SUGAR INDUSTRY. *Use* Beets and Beet Sugar

SUGAR SUBSTITUTES. *Use* Substitute Products

SUGGESTION, MENTAL. *See* Mental Suggestion

SUGGESTION SYSTEMS. *Use* Rewards (Prizes, etc.)

SUICIDE. *Use* Death; Mortality

SUMMER EMPLOYMENT. *Use* Seasonal Industries

SUMMER HOMES. *Use* Home Ownership

SUMMER RESORTS
LC ———; s.a. Health resorts, watering places, etc.; Seaside resorts
SEARS ———; s.a. Health resorts, spas, etc.
RG ———; s.a. Seaside resorts
NYT TRAVEL AND RESORTS; s.a. Hotels, bars, motels, night clubs and restaurants; Vacations
PAIS RESORTS; s.a. Health resorts; Winter resorts
BPI ———; s.a. Hotels; Winter resorts

SUMMER SCHOOLS
LC ———; s.a. University extension; Vacation schools
SEARS VACATION SCHOOLS; s.a. Playgrounds; Public schools; Schools
RG ———; s.a. Educational workshops; School year
NYT EDUCATION AND SCHOOLS; s.a. Colleges and universities
PAIS ———; s.a. Extension education; Vacation schools
BPI SCHOOLS; s.a. Education

SUMMER THEATER. *Use* Theater

SUN
LC ———; s.a. Architecture and solar radiation; Eclipses, Solar; Solar activity; Solar system; Spectrum analysis; Sun (in religion, folk-lore, etc.); Sun worship
SEARS ———; s.a. Solar energy; Solar system; Sunspots
RG ———; s.a. Solar radiation; Sunspots
NYT SPACE AND UPPER ATMOSPHERE–SUN; s.a. Astronautics; Weather
PAIS ———; s.a. Astronomy; Solar power
BPI ———; s.a. Solar power; Solar radiation

SUNDAY LEGISLATION. *Use* Ecclesiastical Law; Religious Liberty; Sabbath

SUNDAY OBSERVANCE. *Use* Sabbath

SUNDAY SCHOOLS. *Use* Religious Education

SUNDIALS. *Use* Time

SUN-SPOTS. *Use* Magnetism, Terrestrial; Sun

SUPERMARKETS. *Use* Chain Stores; Food Industry and Trade

SUPERNATURAL. *Use* Miracles; Occult Sciences; Prophecies; Religion

SUPERPHOSPHATES. *See* Fertilizers and Manures

SUPERSONICS. *See* Ultrasonics

SUPERSTITIONS. *Use* Dreams; Folklore; Occult Sciences; Taboo

SUPERVISION OF EMPLOYEES
LC ———; s.a. Industrial relations; School supervision; State supervision of teaching; Supervision of social workers; Supervisors; Supervisors, Dismissal of
SEARS PERSONNEL MANAGEMENT; s.a. Factory management; Industrial management
RG SUPERVISORS; s.a. Business management and organization; Office management
NYT LABOR—U.S.—FOREMEN AND SUPERVISORS; s.a. business, commodity, company, industry and organization names; Executives; Management, Industrial and institutional
PAIS FOREMEN AND SUPERVISORS; s.a. Business organization and administration; Personnel management
BPI ———; s.a. Foremen; Human relations

SUPPLEMENTARY EMPLOYMENT. *Use* Employment

SUPPLY AND DEMAND
LC ———; s.a. Consumption (economics); Exchange; Free trade and protection; Overproduction; Production (economic theory); Value
SEARS CONSUMPTION (Economics); s.a. Competition; Economics; Industry; Prices
RG ———; s.a. Consumption (economics); Prices; Value (economic theory)
NYT ECONOMICS; s.a. Consumers and consumption; Credit
PAIS ———; s.a. Black markets; subd. *Supply and demand* under specific headings; e.g., Air pilots—Supply and demand
BPI ———; s.a. Consumption (economics); Production

SUPPORT (Domestic relations). *Use* Divorce; Family; Parent and Child

SUPREMACY OF LAW. *See* Rule of Law

SUPREME COURT (U.S.). *Use* Judges; Justice, Administration of; Law

SURETYSHIP AND GUARANTY
LC ———; s.a. Bail; Liability (law); Subrogation
SEARS COMMERCIAL LAW; s.a. Criminal law; Justice, Administration of
RG ———; s.a. Bail; Insurance, Surety and fidelity
NYT BONDING AND BONDSMEN; s.a. Banks and banking; Courts; Prisons and prisoners
PAIS INSURANCE, SURETY AND FIDELITY; s.a. Bail
BPI ———; s.a. Judicial bonds

SURGERY
LC ———; s.a. Amputation; Blood—Transfusion; Bone-grafting; Chemosurgery; Children—Surgery; Electrosurgery; Fractures; Lasers in surgery; Obstetrics—Surgery; Skin-grafting; Surgical nursing; Veterinary surgery
SEARS ———; s.a. Anesthetics; Antiseptics; Artificial organs; Cryo-surgery; Operations, Surgical; Orthopedia; Surgery, Plastic; Vivisection
RG ———; s.a. subd. *Surgery* under names of organs and regions of the body; Surgical instruments and apparatus; Transplantation of organs, tissues, etc.
NYT SURGERY AND SURGEONS; s.a. Anesthesia; Body, Human; Transplants
PAIS ———; s.a. Surgical instruments industry; Transplantation of organs, tissues, etc.
BPI ———; s.a. Eye—Surgery; Heart—Surgery

SURREALISM. *Use* Art, Modern—20th Century; Modernism (Art)

SURROGATES' COURTS. *See* Probate Law and Practice

SURVEILLANCE, ELECTRONIC. *See* Wire-tapping

SURVEYING. *Use* Aerial Photography; Cartography; Maps

SURVEYS. *Use* Research

SURVEYS, SOCIAL. *See* Social Surveys

SURVIVAL. *See* Food; Nutrition; Outdoor Life; Rescue Work

SURVIVOR'S BENEFITS
Scope: Works on benefits from any source, public or private.
LC ———; s.a. Civil service pensions; Insurance, Life; Old age pensions; Pensions, Military; Workmen's compensation
SEARS INSURANCE, LIFE; s.a. Annuities; Insurance, Social; Workmen's compensation
RG ———; s.a. Insurance, Social; Pensions
NYT LIFE INSURANCE; s.a. Casualty insurance; Pensions and retirement
PAIS ———; s.a. Pensions, Civil—Survivors benefits; Veterans—Survivors benefits
BPI INSURANCE, LIFE; s.a. Insurance, Group life; Insurance trusts

SWEARING. *Use* Oaths

SWINDLERS AND SWINDLING. *Use* Counterfeits and Counterfeiting; Crime and criminals; Fraud

SWING MUSIC. *See* Jazz Music

SWITCHING THEORY. *Use* Logic, Symbolic and Mathematical; Operations Research; System Analysis

SYLLOGISM. *Use* Logic

SYMBIOSIS. *Use* Parasites

SYMBOLIC AND MATHEMATICAL LOGIC. *See* Logic, Symbolic and Mathematical

SYMBOLISM. *Use* Emblems; Mythology; Signs and Symbols

SYMBOLISM (Psychology). *Use* Dreams; Psychoanalysis

SYMBOLS. *Use* Abbreviations; Acronyms; Ciphers; Signs and Symbols

SYMPATHY. *Use* Emotions; Human Relations

SYNAGOGUES. *Use* Jews

SYNAPSES. *Use* Nervous System

SYNDICALISM. *Use* Socialism; Trade unions

SYNDICATES (Finance). *Use* Banks and Banking

SYNONYMS. *Use* Language and Languages; Vocabulary

SYNTHETIC FABRICS. *Use* Textile Industry and Fabrics

SYNTHETIC PRODUCTS. *Use* Plastics Industry and Trade; Substitute Products

SYPHILIS. *Use* Sex; Venereal Disease

SYSTEM ANALYSIS
LC ——; s.a. Bond graphs; Discrete time systems; Electric networks; Graphic methods; Mathematical models; Nonlinear theories; Switching theory
SEARS OPERATION RESEARCH; s.a. Cybernetics; Management; Systems engineering
RG SYSTEMS ANALYSIS; s.a. Flow charts; U.S.—Defense, Department of—Systems analysis, Office of
NYT SYSTEMS ANALYSIS; s.a. Data processing (information processing) equipment and systems
PAIS ——; s.a. Information processing systems
BPI ——; s.a. Computer systems management; Flow charts

SYSTEM SIMULATION. *Use* Management Games

SYSTEMS ENGINEERING. *Use* Automation; Cybernetics; Design, Industrial; Operations Research; Plant Layout; System Analysis

SYSTEMS IN MANAGEMENT. *Use* Operations Research; System Analysis

T

TABLE
Scope: Works dealing with receptions at home.
LC ——; s.a. Caterers and catering; Grace at meals; Menus
SEARS DINNERS AND DINING; s.a. Carving (meat, etc.); Table etiquette
RG TABLE SETTING; s.a. Table decoration; Table linen
NYT COOKING; s.a. Tableware
PAIS COOKS; s.a. Restaurants; Tableware
BPI TABLE SETTING AND DECORATION; s.a. Tableware

TABLE ETIQUETTE. *Use* Etiquette

TABLE TALK. *Use* Wit and Humor

TABLES, MATHEMATICAL. *See* Mathematics

TABLEWARE. *Use* Table

TABOO
LC ——; s.a. Sacrilege; Taboo, Linguistic; Totemism
SEARS MANNERS AND CUSTOMS; s.a. Rites and ceremonies; Society, Primitive
RG ——; s.a. Religion, Primitive; Totemism
NYT RELIGION AND CHURCHES; s.a. Superstitions; Witchcraft
PAIS RELIGION; s.a. Society, Primitive
BPI RELIGION; s.a. Manners and customs

TABULATING MACHINES. *Use* Machine Accounting

TACTICS (Military). *See* Guerilla Warfare; Military Art and Science

TAILORING
Scope: Works on cutting and making of men's and women's clothing. See Dressmaking for works limited to constructing women's clothing.
LC ——; s.a. Garment cutting; Men's clothing; Uniforms, Military
SEARS ——; s.a. Clothing trade; Fashion
RG CLOTHING INDUSTRY; s.a. Garment factories; Tailors
NYT APPAREL; s.a. Sewing
PAIS CLOTHING INDUSTRY; s.a. Clothing and dress; Fashion industry
BPI TAILORS AND TAILORING; s.a. Clothing and dress—Men; Clothing industry

TALENTED CHILDREN. *See* Child Study; Talented Students

TALENTED STUDENTS
Scope: Students with above-average abilities at college and university level. See Gifted children for works on students of like abilities in Grades 1-12.
LC ——; s.a. Gifted children; Universities and colleges—Honors courses
SEARS SCHOLARSHIPS, FELLOWSHIPS, ETC; s.a. Gifted children; Musical ability
RG COLLEGE STUDENTS, MENTALLY SUPERIOR; s.a. Ability; Genius; Learning, Psychology of
NYT EDUCATION AND SCHOOLS—U.S.—GIFTED CHILDREN; s.a. Scholarships and fellowships
PAIS COLLEGE STUDENTS; s.a. Children, Gifted

BPI   STUDENTS; s.a. Colleges and universities; Schools

TALES
Scope: Stories in prose or verse, especially traditional and popular tales of uncertain origin.
LC   ——; s.a. Allegories; Fables; Homiletical illustrations; Parables; Short stories
SEARS FABLES; s.a. Fairy tales; Folklore; Legends
RG   FOLKLORE; s.a. Legends; Mythology
NYT   BOOKS AND LITERATURE
PAIS   LITERATURE
BPI   LITERATURE; s.a. Fiction

TALKIES. *See* Moving Pictures

TALKING BOOKS. *Use* Blind; Phonograph Records

TALMUD
LC   ——; s.a. Christianity in the Talmud; Rabbinical literature; Women in the Talmud
SEARS ——; s.a. Hebrew literature; Judaism
RG   ——; s.a. Jewish theology; Philosophy, Jewish; Tradition (Judaism)
NYT   ——; s.a. Jews
PAIS   RELIGIOUS LITERATURE; s.a. Jews
BPI   JEWISH LITERATURE; s.a. Jews

TANK CARS. *Use* Railroads

TANK SHIPS. *Use* Merchant Marine

TANKS, MILITARY. *Use* Armaments

TANNING. *Use* Leather Industry and Trade

TAP DANCING. *Use* Dancing

TAPE RECORDINGS. *Use* Phonograph Records; Sound and Sound Recordings

TAPE RECORDINGS (Data storage). *See* Data Tapes

TAPESTRY
LC   ——; s.a. Art, Decorative; Arts and crafts movement; Needlework; Wall paper
SEARS ——; s.a. Decoration and ornament; Design, Decorative; Textile industry and fabrics
RG   ——; s.a. Craftsmanship; Needlework; Tapestry weaving
NYT   TAPESTRIES; s.a. Handicrafts; Interior Decorating
PAIS   WEAVING (Handicrafts); s.a. Carpet industry; Handicrafts
BPI   ARTS AND CRAFTS; s.a. Handicraft

TARGET PRACTICE. *Use* Firearms; Gunnery

TARIFF
LC   ——; s.a. Commercial treaties; Customs unions; Economic policy; Free ports and zones; Reciprocity
SEARS ——; s.a. Commercial policy; Foreign policy; Taxation
RG   ——; s.a. Balance of trade; Free trade and protection
NYT   COMMERCE; s.a. Smuggling
PAIS   ——; s.a. Customs administration; Favored nation clause

BPI   ——; s.a. Duty free importation; Free trade and protection

TASTE (Aesthetics). *See* Aesthetics

TAVERNS. *Use* Bars and Barrooms; Hotels, Taverns, etc; Restaurants, Lunchrooms, etc.

TAX ACCOUNTING AND AUDITING
Scope: For works on the investigation of tax returns, see Tax auditing. For works on preparation of tax returns, see Tax accounting.
LC   TAX ACCOUNTING; s.a. Tax auditing; Tax deductions; Tax planning; subd. *Accounting* under individual taxes, e.g., Income tax—Accounting
SEARS ACCOUNTING; s.a. Auditing
RG   TAX AUDITING; s.a. Tax accounting
NYT   TAXATION; s.a. Accounting
PAIS   TAX ACCOUNTING; s.a. Tax auditing; Taxation
BPI   TAX AUDITING; s.a. Tax evasion and avoidance; Tax fraud; Tax planning

TAX CONSULTANTS. *Use* Accountants; Lawyers

TAX DEDUCTIONS. *Use* Charitable Uses, Trusts and Foundations; Tax Accounting and Auditing; Taxation, Exemption from

TAX EVASION AND AVOIDANCE. *Use* Passive Resistance; Tax Accounting and Auditing; Taxation, Exemption from

TAX PLANNING. *Use* Tax Accounting and Auditing

TAX RETURNS. *Use* Income Tax; Taxation

TAX SHARING. *See* Federal Government

TAXATION
See also names of specific taxes, e.g., Business tax; Income tax; Inheritance and transfer tax; Property tax; Sales tax; etc.; and subd. *Taxation* under appropriate subjects, e.g., Corporations—Taxation.
LC   ——; s.a. Absenteeism; Capital levy; Depreciation; Finance, Public; Licenses; Local taxation; Revenue; Single tax; Taxation, Exemption from; Taxing power
SEARS ——; s.a. Assessment; Internal revenue; Tariff
RG   ——; s.a. Intergovernmental tax relations; Tax administration and procedure; Value added tax
NYT   ——
PAIS   ——; s.a. Taxation of articles of consumption
BPI   ——; s.a. Corporate income tax; Municipal taxation; Value added tax

TAXATION, DOUBLE. *Use* Income Tax

TAXATION, EXEMPTION FROM
LC   ——; s.a. Corporations, Nonprofit—Taxation; Tax deduction; Tax evasion
SEARS TAXATION; s.a. Endowments—Laws and regulations; Estate planning
RG   ——; s.a. Foundations, Charitable and educational—Taxation; Securities, Tax exempt
NYT   TAXATION; s.a. Corporations; Foundations

TAXATION, EXEMPTION FROM, *cont.*
PAIS   TAXATION—EXEMPTION; s.a. Taxation and government property; Tax evasion and avoidance
BPI   ——; s.a. Foundations, Charitable and educational—Taxation; Institutions, Nonprofit—Taxation

TAXATION, LOCAL. *See* Local Government

TAXATION, PROGRESSIVE. *Use* Income Tax

TAXATION—REAL ESTATE. *Use* Real Property

TAXATION, STATE. *Use* State Governments

TAXATION OF BONDS, SECURITIES, ETC. *Use* Bonds

TAXES. *See* Taxation

TAXICABS. *Use* Local Transit; Motor Vehicles

TEA INDUSTRY. *Use* Beverages

TEACHER-PRINCIPAL RELATIONSHIP. *Use* Educational Administration; School Supervision

TEACHERS
See also names of types of teachers, e.g., College teachers; Music teachers.
LC   ——; s.a. Deans (in schools); Educators; Home and school; School employees; Teachers, Training of; Teaching
SEARS   ——; s.a. Educational associations; School superintendents and principals
RG   ——; s.a. Academic freedom; School and the home; Substitute teachers
NYT   TEACHERS AND SCHOOL EMPLOYEES; s.a. Colleges and universities—U.S.—Teachers; Education and schools
PAIS   ——; s.a. Academic freedom; Women as teachers
BPI   ——; s.a. Collective bargaining—Education; College professors and instructors

TEACHERS, TRAINING OF
Scope: History and methods of training teachers as opposed to works dealing with study of education as a science which are entered under Education—Study and teaching.
LC   ——; s.a. Student teaching; Teachers—In-service training; subd. *Teacher training* under specific subjects, e.g., Mathematics—Teacher training
SEARS   TEACHERS—TRAINING; s.a. Education—Study and teaching; Teachers' workshops
RG   TEACHERS—EDUCATION; s.a. Schools of education; Student teachers
NYT   TEACHERS AND SCHOOL EMPLOYEES; s.a. Education and schools
PAIS   TEACHERS—TRAINING; s.a. Teachers colleges
BPI   ——; s.a. Teachers; Teaching

TEACHERS AND PARENTS. *See* Home and School

TEACHERS AND SCHOOL BOARDS. *Use* Educational Administration

TEACHERS' COLLEGES. *Use* Accreditation (Education); Colleges and Universities; Teachers, Training of

TEACHERS' WORKSHOPS. *Use* Teachers, Training of

TEACHING
Scope: Works on art and method of teaching. See also specific methods, e.g., Montessori method of education; Project method in teaching; and subd. *Instruction and study* or *Study and teaching* under subjects, e.g., Architecture—Study and teaching.
LC   ——; s.a. Academic freedom; Examinations; Grading and marking (students); Lectures and lecturing; Lesson planning; Programmed instruction; Questioning; Remedial teaching; Teachers, Training of
SEARS   ——; s.a. Classroom management; Educational psychology; Reading—Remedial teaching; School supervision; Teaching teams
RG   ——; s.a. Individual instruction; Motivation (education); Psychology, Educational; subd. *Remedial teaching* under subjects
NYT   EDUCATION AND SCHOOLS; s.a. Colleges and universities
PAIS   TEACHERS; s.a. Education—Aids and devices; Teaching machines; Tutors and tutoring
BPI   ——; s.a. Audio-visual instruction; Child study; Instructional materials centers

TEACHING—AIDS AND DEVICES. *Use* Educational Technology; Moving Pictures in Education; Programmed Instruction; Radio in Education; Television in Education

TEACHING—EXPERIMENTAL METHODS. *See* Educational Planning and Innovations

TEACHING, FREEDOM OF. *Use* Academic Freedom

TEACHING DEMONSTRATIONS. *Use* Educational Planning and Innovations

TEACHING MACHINES. *Use* Audio-visual Education; Audio-visual Materials; Educational Technology; Programmed Instruction; Teaching

TEAM TEACHING. *See* Teaching

TEAROOMS. *See* Restaurants, Lunchrooms, etc.

TECHNICAL ASSISTANCE. *Use* Economic Assistance, Foreign; Economic Development; Industrialization; Underdeveloped Areas

TECHNICAL DRAWINGS. *See* Drawing

TECHNICAL EDUCATION
Scope: Works on education in technology. See Technology—Study and teaching for works dealing with methods of instruction in technology.
LC   ——; s.a. Employees, Training of; Manual training; Retraining, Occupational
SEARS   ——; s.a. Evening and continuation schools; Industrial arts education; Occupational training; Professional education
RG   ——; s.a. Industrial education; Trade schools; Vocational education
NYT   VOCATIONAL TRAINING, GUIDANCE AND AIMS; s.a. Commercial education; Labor—U.S.—Education and schools; Science and technology—Education and schools—U.S.
PAIS   ——; s.a. Apprenticeship; Employees—Training; Industrial arts; Vocational education

BPI ——; s.a. Employees, Training of; Occupational training

TECHNICAL LITERATURE. *Use* Technical Writing

TECHNICAL MANUALS. *Use* Handbooks

TECHNICAL REPORTS. *Use* Technical Writing

TECHNICAL WORKERS. *Use* Labor and Laboring Classes; Manual Labor

TECHNICAL WRITING
Scope: Guides to authorship in engineering, science and technology. See Technical reports for works on processing and use of scientific and technical reports.
LC ——; s.a. Science news; Specification writing; Technical reports
SEARS ——; s.a. Authorship; Technology—Language
RG ——; s.a. Publishers and publishing—Scientific literature; Scientific literature; Technical literature
NYT WRITING AND WRITERS; s.a. Books and literature; Science and technology
PAIS ——; s.a. Authorship; Technical literature
BPI ——; s.a. Booksellers and bookselling—Technical literature; Technical literature

TECHNOCRACY. *Use* Capitalism; Science and State; Technology

TECHNOLOGICAL INNOVATIONS
Scope: Fundamental technological improvements or changes in materials, processes, production methods, organization or management, which increase efficiency and production. See Inventions for works dealing with new inventions.
LC ——; s.a. Machinery in industry; Progress; subd. *Technological innovations* under subjects, e.g., Building—Technological innovations
SEARS MACHINERY IN INDUSTRY; s.a. Inventions; Patents
RG TECHNOLOGICAL CHANGE; s.a. Industrial research; Technology assessment; Technology transfer
NYT INVENTIONS AND INVENTORS; s.a. Machinery, industrial equipment and supplies; Science and technology
PAIS ——; s.a. Machinery in industry; Technology transfer
BPI TECHNOLOGICAL CHANGE; s.a. Automation; Diffusion of innovations

TECHNOLOGY
LC ——; s.a. Industrial arts; Science; Technocracy; Unemployment, Technological
SEARS ——; s.a. Technology and civilization
RG ——; s.a. Inventions; Space technology; Underdeveloped areas—Technology
NYT SCIENCE AND TECHNOLOGY; s.a. Automation; Engineering and engineers
PAIS ——; s.a. Automation; Inventions
BPI ——; s.a. Engineering; Forecasts (technology)

TECHNOLOGY AND CIVILIZATION. *Use* Progress; Social History; Social Problems

TECHNOLOGY TRANSFER. *Use* Industrial Research; Information Sciences; Inventions; Technological Innovations

TEEN-AGE MARRIAGE. *Use* Marriage; Youth

TEENAGERS. *See* Adolescence; Youth

TEETH AND DENTISTRY. *Use* Dentistry

TELECOMMUNICATION
LC ——; s.a. Communication and traffic; Information theory; Phototelegraphy; Radio facsimile; Television
SEARS ——; s.a. Artificial satellites in telecommunication; Cables, Submarine; Microwave communication systems; Telegraph
RG ——; s.a. Cipher and telegraph codes; Communications satellites; Emergency communication systems; Radio telegraph
NYT COMMUNICATIONS; s.a. Codes (cipher); Communications satellites; Data processing (information processing) equipment and systems; Facsimile systems; Telegraphy
PAIS COMMUNICATION SYSTEMS; s.a. Facsimile transmission; Police communication systems; Satellites, Artificial—Communication uses
BPI ——; s.a. Data transmission systems; Facsimile transmission

TELEGRAPH. *Use* Ciphers; Telecommunication

TELEPATHY. *Use* Thought Transference

TELEPHONE SELLING. *Use* Salesmen and Salesmanship

TELEPHONES (For picturephone and videovoice). *Use* Television

TELEPHOTOGRAPHY. *Use* Photography

TELESCOPES. *Use* Astronomy; Optical Trade

TELEVISION
Scope: Works including general technical works on television principles and equipment.
LC ——; s.a. Industrial television; Telecommunication; Television broadcasting; Television frequency allocation; Television—Production and direction
SEARS ——; s.a. Closed-circuit television; Color television; Community antenna television
RG ——; s.a. Communications satellites; Video recorders and recording
NYT TELEVISION AND RADIO; s.a. Communications; Telephones (for picturephone and videovoice)
PAIS ——; s.a. Video recording; Videotape
BPI ——; s.a. Microwave communication systems; Television stations; Underwater television

TELEVISION—CENSORSHIP. *Use* Freedom of Information

TELEVISION—PROGRAMS. *Use* Television Programs

TELEVISION ADVERTISING. *Use* Advertising; Television Broadcasting; Television Programs

TELEVISION ADVERTISING—NEGROES, APPEAL TO. *Use* Negroes and Business

TELEVISION AND CHILDREN. *Use* Moving Pictures and Children; Television Broadcasting

TELEVISION AND POLITICS. *Use* Advertising, Political; Public Relations

TELEVISION AND RADIO—COMMUNICATIONS SATELLITES. *Use* Artificial Satellites

TELEVISION AND RADIO—NONCOMMERCIAL TELEVISION AND RADIO. *Use* Audio-visual Education; Radio in Education; Television in Education

TELEVISION AND RADIO—PROGRAMS—NEWS PROGRAMS. *Use* Journalism

TELEVISION AUDIENCES. *Use* Television Broadcasting

TELEVISION AUTHORSHIP. *Use* Television Programs

TELEVISION BROADCASTING
Scope: Works on the art and practice of television transmission for public reception. For specific aspects see Television in education; Television in politics; Television in religion; etc.
LC ———; s.a. Mass media; Television audiences; Television industry; Television programs; Videotape recorders and recording
SEARS ———; s.a. Subscription television; Television advertising; Television and children
RG ———; s.a. Television programs; Television stations; Video recorders and recording
NYT TELEVISION AND RADIO; s.a. Communications; News and news media
PAIS TELEVISION; s.a. Video recording; Videotape
BPI ———; s.a. Mass media; Television public speaking

TELEVISION CAMERAS. *Use* Cameras

TELEVISION IN EDUCATION
LC ———; s.a. Closed circuit television; Educational broadcasting; Radio in education; Television in teacher training
SEARS AUDIO-VISUAL EDUCATION; s.a. Radio in Education; Teaching—Aids and devices
RG ———; s.a. Radio in education; Television stations, Educational
NYT TELEVISION AND RADIO—NONCOMMERCIAL TELEVISION AND RADIO; s.a. Education and schools—U.S.—Teaching aids
PAIS ———; s.a. Radio in education; Television stations, Noncommercial
BPI EDUCATION; s.a. Radio broadcasting; Television broadcasting

TELEVISION INDUSTRY. *Use* Television Broadcasting

TELEVISION PROGRAMS
LC ———; s.a. Quiz shows; Television adaptations; Television programs, Public service
SEARS TELEVISION BROADCASTING; s.a. Television advertising; Television plays; Television scripts
RG ———; s.a. Television authorship; Television programs—Biographical programs
NYT TELEVISION AND RADIO—PROGRAMS—(name of program, e.g., 60 Minutes); s.a. News and news media

PAIS TELEVISION—PROGRAMS; s.a. Television—Documentary programs
BPI TELEVISION BROADCASTING—PROGRAMS

TELEVISION STATIONS. *Use* Television; Television Broadcasting

TELEVISION STATIONS, EDUCATIONAL. *Use* Television in Education

TELEVISION STATIONS, NONCOMMERCIAL. *Use* Television in Education

TEMPERAMENT
LC ———; s.a. Character; Emotions; Individuality
SEARS ———; s.a. Mind and body; Psychology
RG ———; s.a. Man—Constitution; Typology (psychology)
NYT PSYCHOLOGY AND PSYCHOLOGISTS; s.a. Mental health and disorders; Mind
PAIS PSYCHOLOGY; s.a. Behavior (psychology)
BPI PERSONALITY; s.a. Behavior (psychology)

TEMPERANCE
Scope: General works including fiction on the question of temperance. See Alcoholism for works on drunkenness and medical aspects of the problem. See Liquor for works of technical and administrative nature.
LC ———; s.a. Alcoholics; Conduct of life; Prohibition; Temperance societies
SEARS ———; s.a. Alcohol—Physiological effect; Behavior; Liquor problem
RG ———; s.a. Alcohol and youth; Prohibition
NYT LIQUOR; s.a. Alcohol; Alcoholism
PAIS ———; s.a. Alcoholism; Prohibition
BPI ALCOHOL—PHYSIOLOGICAL EFFECT; s.a. Alcoholism; Personnel management—Liquor problem

TEMPERATURE
LC ———; s.a. Body temperature; Boiling points; Melting points; Thermal stress
SEARS ———; s.a. Heat; Low temperature; Thermometers and thermometry
RG ———; s.a. Atmospheric temperature; Climate
NYT HEAT; s.a. Freezing
PAIS CLIMATE; s.a. Weather
BPI ———; s.a. Thermocouples; Thermostats

TEMPORARY EMPLOYMENT. *Use* Employment; Seasonal Industries

TEMPTATION. *Use* Sin

TENANT. *See* Landlord and Tenant

TENDER OFFERS (Securities). *Use* Stock-exchange

TENEMENT-HOUSES
LC ———; s.a. Labor and laboring classes—Dwellings; Social problems; subd. *Poor* under names of cities, e.g., New York (City)—Poor
SEARS ———; s.a. City planning; Housing; Landlord and tenant
RG ———; s.a. Housing; Slums
NYT HOUSING; s.a. Urban Areas; U.S.—Economic conditions and trends—Antipoverty
PAIS ———; s.a. Redevelopment, Urban; Slums

BPI   SLUMS; s.a. City planning; Urban renewal

TENSION. *See* Anxiety

TENURE, ACADEMIC. *See* Academic Freedom

TENURE OF LAND. *See* Land Tenure

TENURE OF OFFICE. *See* Municipal Officials and Employees

TERMINAL CARE. *Use* Death; Nurses and Nursing

TERMS AND PHRASES
See also subd. *Terms and phrases* or *Terminology* under names of languages and subjects, e.g., English language—Terms and phrases; Botany—Terminology; etc.
LC   ——; s.a. Names; Slogans
SEARS PROVERBS; s.a. Epigrams; Quotations
RG   ——; s.a. Allusions; Quotations
NYT   QUOTATIONS AND PROVERBS; s.a. Language and languages; Slogans, mottoes and catch-phrases
PAIS   Subd. *Terminology* under specific subjects, e.g., Patent law—Terminology
BPI   TERMINOLOGY; s.a. Slogans; Words

TERRACES (Agriculture). *Use* Farms and Farming

TERRITORIAL WATERS
LC   ——; s.a. Coasts; Freedom of the seas; Jurisdiction, Territorial; Neutrality; Sealing; Territory, National
SEARS BOUNDARIES; s.a. Fisheries—Laws and regulations; International law
RG   ——; s.a. Fishery laws and legislation; Submerged lands
NYT   WATERS, TERRITORIAL; s.a. names of bodies of water, e.g., Black Sea; Ships—International incidents
PAIS   ——; s.a. Continental shelf; Maritime law
BPI   ——; s.a. Fishing laws and legislation; International law; Maritime law

TERRITORY, NATIONAL
LC   ——; s.a. Acquisition of territory; Conquest, Right of; Leased territories; Military occupation
SEARS BOUNDARIES; s.a. Geopolitics; Political science
RG   STATE, THE; s.a. International law; Jurisdiction, Territorial
NYT   GEOGRAPHY; s.a. International relations; Waters, Territorial
PAIS   ——; s.a. Boundaries, State; Geography, Political
BPI   BOUNDARIES; s.a. Boundaries, State; Territorial waters

TERRORISM
LC   ——; s.a. International offenses; Nihilism; Subversive activities
SEARS POLITICAL CRIMES AND OFFENSES; s.a. Anarchism and anarchists; Hijacking of airplanes; Revolutions; Violence
RG   ——; s.a. Bomb scares; Kidnapping
NYT   BOMBS AND BOMB PLOTS; s.a. Espionage; Sabotage; names of terrorist groups, e.g., Sinn Fein, Tupamaros, etc.

PAIS   ——; s.a. Anarchism; Sabotage
BPI   ——; s.a. Assassination; Kidnapping, Political

TESTIMONY. *See* Witnesses

TESTING APPARATUS. *Use* Scientific Apparatus and Instruments

TESTS, ABILITY. *Use* Ability—Testing; Occupational Aptitude Tests; Personality Tests; Tests, Mental

TESTS, EDUCATIONAL. *Use* Ability—Testing; Examinations; Grading and Marking (Students); Tests, Mental

TESTS, MENTAL
See also names of specific tests, e.g., Binet-Simon test; Rorschach test; Stanford-Binet test; etc.; and types of tests, e.g., Maze test; Vocabulary test; etc.
LC   MENTAL TESTS; s.a. Ability grouping in education; Character tests; Clinical psychology; Occupational aptitude tests; Personality tests; subd. *Testing* under special subjects, e.g., Attitude (psychology)—Testing; Musical ability—Testing
SEARS MENTAL TESTS; s.a. Ability testing; Educational tests and measurements; Psychology, Physiological
RG   INTELLIGENCE TESTS; s.a. Aptitude tests; Prediction of scholastic success; Questions and answers
NYT   MENTAL TESTS; s.a. Psychology and psychologists
PAIS   ——; s.a. Factor analysis; Tests, Ability; Tests, Educational
BPI   ABILITY TESTS; s.a. Psychometrics; Self evaluation

TETRAPLEGIA. *Use* Paralysis

TEXTBOOKS
Scope: Works about textbooks only. For textbooks on a subject, see name of subject with the subd. *Textbooks*, e.g., Physical geography—Textbooks.
LC   ——; s.a. Handbooks, vade-mecums, etc.
SEARS ——; s.a. subd. *Handbooks, manuals, etc.* under subject, e.g., Photography—Handbooks, manuals, etc.
RG   ——; s.a. Booksellers and bookselling—Textbooks; Hornbooks; Readers (books)
NYT   ——; s.a. Books and literature—Book trade; Books and literature—Censorship
PAIS   ——; s.a. Handbooks, vade-mecums, etc.
BPI   ——; s.a. Books; Education market

TEXTILE CHEMISTRY. *Use* Dyes and Dyeing; Textile Industry and Fabrics

TEXTILE DESIGN. *Use* Art and Industry; Commercial Art; Design; Textile Industry and Fabrics

TEXTILE INDUSTRY AND FABRICS
See also names of special fabrics, e.g., Linen; Metal cloth; Nylon; etc; and names of articles manufactured, e.g., Carpets; Hosiery; etc.
LC   ——; s.a. Dry-goods; Synthetic fabrics; Tapestry; Textile fibers, Synthetic; Textile mills

TEXTILES INDUSTRY AND FABRICS, *cont.*
SEARS ——; s.a. Bleaching; Textile chemistry; Textile design
RG TEXTILE INDUSTRY; s.a. Wool industry; Yarn
NYT TEXTILES
PAIS TEXTILE INDUSTRY; s.a. Batik industry; Cotton textile industry
BPI TEXTILE INDUSTRY; s.a. Spinning; Weaving

TEXTILE WORKERS
LC ——; s.a. Collective bargaining—Textile industry; Wages—Textile workers; Weavers
SEARS ——; s.a. Labor and laboring classes; Labor unions
RG ——; s.a. Cotton mills—Employees; Textile industry—Wages and hours
NYT TEXTILES—U.S.—LABOR; s.a. Labor; names of textile workers unions, e.g., Textile Workers Union of America (TWUA)
PAIS ——; s.a. Labor conditions—Textile industry; Trade unions—Textile workers
BPI ——; s.a. Knitting mills—Employees; Wages and salaries—Textile workers

THEATER
Scope: Works on drama as acted on the stage and works on historical, legal, moral and religious aspects of the theater. Works on drama from a literary point of view are entered under Drama. See also types of drama, e.g., American drama; Children's plays; Comedy; English drama; Mime; Puppets and puppet plays; etc.
LC ——; s.a. Acting; College theater; Experimental theater; Summer theater; Theater and society
SEARS ——; s.a. Actors and actresses; Amateur theatricals; Make-up, Theatrical; Performing arts; Shadow pantomimes and plays
RG ——; s.a. Church and the theater; Theater, Experimental
NYT ——; s.a. Entertainment and amusements; "Happenings"; Marionettes
PAIS ——; s.a. Actors; Opera
BPI ——; s.a. Actors and actresses; Theatrical production

THEATER AND STATE. *Use* Art and State

THEATERS
Scope: Works dealing only with theater buildings, architecture, construction, decoration, etc.
LC ——; s.a. Moving picture theaters; Music-halls (variety theaters, cabarets, etc.)
SEARS ——; s.a. Architecture; Centers for the performing arts; Theaters—Stage setting and scenery
RG THEATER BUILDINGS; s.a. Concert halls; Opera houses; Stage lighting
NYT THEATER
PAIS THEATER
BPI ——; s.a. Moving picture theaters

THEATRICAL AGENCIES. *Use* Acting

THEATRICAL COSTUME. *See* Costume

THEATRICAL PRODUCTION. *Use* Theater

THEFT
LC STEALING; s.a. Bank robbers; Larceny; Offenses against property; Pickpockets; Pillage; Thieves
SEARS CRIME AND CRIMINALS; s.a. Robbers and outlaws
RG THIEVES; s.a. Accomplices; Burglary and burglars; Cattle thieves; Robberies and assault; Securities, Theft of
NYT ROBBERIES AND THEFTS; s.a. Loot and looting; names of stolen goods, e.g., Art
PAIS ——; s.a. Automobile thieves; Receiving stolen goods; Shoplifting; subd. *Theft losses* under specific subjects, e.g., Railroads—Theft losses
BPI ——; s.a. Embezzlement; Retail trade—Theft losses

THEISM. *Use* Atheism; God; Religion

THEOCRACY. *Use* Nationalism and Religion

THEOLOGIANS. *Use* Clergy

THEOLOGICAL EDUCATION. *Use* Religious Education

THEOLOGY
LC ——; s.a. Disputations, Religious; Fate and fatalism; God; Rationalism; Religion and science; Secularism; Theology, Doctrinal
SEARS ——; s.a. Catechism; Creeds; Eschatology
RG ——; s.a. Heresy; Mysticism; Revelation; Secularism; Skepticism
NYT RELIGION AND CHURCHES; s.a. names of denominations, e.g., Episcopal; Protestant
PAIS RELIGION; s.a. Atheism; Christianity and other religions; Churches; Clergy
BPI RELIGION; s.a. Seminarians; Theological seminaries

THEOLOGY, PRACTICAL. *Use* Ecclesiastical Law; Preaching

THERAPEUTICS
LC ——; s.a. Bibliotherapy; Chiropractic; Diet in disease; Massage; Materia medica; Narcotics; Organotherapy; Shock therapy; Therapeutics, Physiological
SEARS ——; s.a. Chemistry, Medical; Hydrotherapy; Occupational therapy; Radiotherapy
RG ——; s.a. Acupuncture; Recreational therapy
NYT MEDICINE AND HEALTH; s.a. Drugs and drug trade; names of diseases, e.g., Multiple sclerosis
PAIS MEDICINE; s.a. Drugs; Physical therapy
BPI MEDICINE; s.a. Drugs; Nurses and nursing; Nutrition

THERAPEUTICS, SUGGESTIVE
LC ——; s.a. Mental healing; Mental suggestion; New thought; Pastoral psychology; Psychotherapy
SEARS ——; s.a. Faith cure; Hypnotism; Psychology, Pastoral
RG MEDICINE, MAGIC, MYSTIC, ETC.; s.a. Faith cure; Pastoral counseling

NYT   MENTAL HEALTH AND DISORDERS; s.a. Handicapped; Mental deficiency and defectives
PAIS PSYCHOTHERAPY; s.a. Mentally ill—Care and treatment; Occupational therapy
BPI   PSYCHOTHERAPY

THERMAL EQUILIBRIUM. *See* Heating

THERMAL STRESS. *Use* Temperature

THERMOMETERS AND THERMOMETRY. *Use* Temperature

THERMOSPHERE. *Use* Atmosphere, Upper

THERMOSTATS. *Use* Temperature

THERMOTHERAPY. *Use* Physical Therapy

THIEVES. *Use* Theft

THINGS (Law). *Use* Property

THINKING. *See* Thought and Thinking

THIRD WORLD. *See* States, New; Underdeveloped Areas

THOROUGHFARES. *See* Roads; Streets

THOUGHT AND THINKING
LC   ——; s.a. Association of ideas; Attitude change; Common sense; Comprehension; Ideology; Logic; Memory; Reasoning; Semantics; Thought transference; Wisdom
SEARS ——; s.a. Attention; Intellect; Judgement; Perception
RG   ——; s.a. Cognition; Judgement (logic); Meditation; Psychology, Educational; Self
NYT   BRAIN; s.a. Intelligence; Logic; Mind; Psychology and psychologists
PAIS ——; s.a. Knowledge, Theory of; Problem solving; Psychology
BPI   ——; s.a. Cognition; Learning, Psychology of; Logic; Problem solving

THOUGHT TRANSFERENCE
LC   ——; s.a. Clairvoyance; Mind-reading; Psychical research
SEARS ——; s.a. Hypnotism; Mental suggestion; Subconscious
RG   TELEPATHY; s.a. Clairvoyance; Extra-sensory perception
NYT   BRAIN; s.a. Mind; Psychic phenomena
PAIS EXTRASENSORY PERCEPTION; s.a. Hypnotism; Thought and thinking
BPI   EXTRASENSORY PERCEPTION; s.a. Psychological research; Thought and thinking

THREE-MILE LIMIT. *See* Territorial Waters

THRIFT. *Use* Saving and Savings

TIDES. *Use* Oceanography; Water

TILES. *Use* Bricks; Ceramics

TILES, ROOFING. *Use* Roofs

TILLAGE. *Use* Agriculture; Farms and Farming

TIMBER. *Use* Forests and Forestry; Trees

TIME
LC   ——; s.a. Astronomy, Spherical and practical; Chronology; Horology; Space and time; Time—Measurements
SEARS ——; s.a. Clocks and watches; Sundials
RG   ——; s.a. International date line; Periodicity; Space and time; Time systems and standards; Timing devices
NYT   ——; s.a. Relativity (physics); Watches and clocks
PAIS ——; s.a. Calendar; Clock and watch industry; Daylight saving
BPI   ——; s.a. Calendar; Clocks and watches

TIME, USE OF. *Use* Leisure; Recreation; Work

TIME AND MOTION STUDY. *Use* Factory Management; Job Analysis; Production Standards; Work Measurement

TIME PERCEPTION. *Use* Senses and Sensation

TIMIDITY. *Use* Emotions

TIMING DEVICES. *Use* Time

TIPPING. *Use* Etiquette; Non-wage Payments

TITHES. *Use* Ecclesiastical Law

TITLES (Personal). *Use* Etiquette

TITLES OF HONOR AND NOBILITY. *Use* Etiquette; Genealogy

TOASTS. *Use* Speeches, Addresses, etc.

TOBACCO
LC   ——; s.a. Cigarette manufacture and trade; Cigar manufacture and trade; Nicotine; Tobacco pipes; Tobacco workers
SEARS ——; s.a. Pipes, Tobacco; Tobacco habit
RG   ——; s.a. Cigarettes; Snuff
NYT   TOBACCO, TOBACCO PRODUCTS AND SMOKERS ARTICLES; s.a. Taxation
PAIS TOBACCO INDUSTRY; s.a. Cigar industry; Smoking
BPI   ——; s.a. Cigarette industry; Snuff; Tobacco industry

TOBACCO HABIT. *Use* Cigarettes; Smoking; Tobacco

TOBOGGANS AND TOBOGGANING. *Use* Winter Sports

TOILET
LC   ——; s.a. Costume; Hairdressing; Perfumes; Toilet preparations
SEARS BEAUTY, PERSONAL; s.a. Beauty shops; Hair; Hygiene
RG   ——; s.a. Baths; Deodorants; Manicuring
NYT   TOILETRIES AND COSMETICS; s.a. Cleansers; Shaving and shavers
PAIS COSMETIC INDUSTRY; s.a. Toilet goods industry
BPI   TOILET GOODS; s.a. Bath preparations; Cosmetics

TOLERANCE (Engineering). *Use* Engineering

TOLERATION
LC   ——; s.a. Discrimination; Indifferentism (religion); Liberty of conscience; Teaching, Freedom of
SEARS   ——; s.a. Academic freedom; Freedom of conscience; Human relations
RG   ——; s.a. Prejudice; Religious liberty
NYT   FREEDOM AND HUMAN RIGHTS; s.a. Discrimination; names of subjects of toleration or intoleration, e.g., Minorities, Religion
PAIS   ——; s.a. Discrimination; Religious liberty
BPI   RACE DISCRIMINATION; s.a. Human relations; Minorities

TOLL ROADS. *Use* Roads

TOOL AND DIE INDUSTRY. *Use* Machinery—Trade and Manufacture; Tools

TOOLS
See also names of specific tools, e.g., Saws.
LC   ——; s.a. Hardware; Implements, utensils, etc.; Industrial equipment; Machinery; Man, Prehistoric—Tools
SEARS   ——; s.a. Carpentry tools; Power tools
RG   ——; s.a. Electric tools; Machine tools; Stone implements and weapons
NYT   TOOLS AND IMPLEMENTS; s.a. Hardware; Machine tools
PAIS   TOOL INDUSTRY; s.a. Machine tool industry; Power tools
BPI   ——; s.a. Garden tools, equipment and supplies; Machine tools

TOPIARY WORK. *Use* Gardening

TOPOGRAPHY. *Use* Aerial Photography; Maps

TORTS. *Use* Liability (Law); Negligence; Obligations

TORTURE. *Use* Atrocities; Concentration Camps

TOTALITARIANISM
Scope: Works on highly centralized government systems permitting no rival loyalties or parties.
LC   ——; s.a. Collectivism; Despotism; Dictatorship of the proletariat; Totalitarian ethics
SEARS   ——; s.a. Dictators; National socialism
RG   ——; s.a. Dictatorship; Fascism; National socialism
NYT   ——; s.a. Communism; Politics and government
PAIS   ——; s.a. Authoritarianism; Communism
BPI   POLITICAL SCIENCE; s.a. Nationalism

TOTEMISM
LC   ——; s.a. Animal-worship; Society, Primitive; Taboo; Totems; Tribes and tribal system
SEARS   TOTEMS AND TOTEMISM; s.a. Ethnology; Indians of North America—Religion and mythology
RG   ——; s.a. Animals in religion, folklore, etc.; Religion, Primitive; Taboo
NYT   ARCHEOLOGY AND ANTHROPOLOGY; s.a. Myths; Religion and churches; Superstitions
PAIS   RELIGION
BPI   RELIGION

TOTEMS. *Use* Totemism

TOURISM. *See* Tourist Trade

TOURIST ACCOMODATION. *See* Hotels, Taverns, etc.

TOURIST TRADE
LC   ——; s.a. Sightseeing business; subd. *Tourist camps, hostels, etc.* under names of cities; Travel; Visitors, Foreign; Youth hostels
SEARS   ——; s.a. Camping; Health resorts, spas, etc.; Hotels, motels, etc; Voyages and travel
RG   ——; s.a. Camp sites, facilities, etc.; Hotels, taverns, etc.; Souvenirs; Travel—Economic aspects
NYT   TRAVEL AND RESORTS; s.a. Camps and camping; Vacations
PAIS   ——; s.a. Motels; Resorts; Travel
BPI   ——; s.a. Hotels; Motels; Tourist camps, hostels, etc.

TOWNS. *See* Cities and Towns

TOWNSHIP GOVERNMENT. *See* Local Government

TOXINS AND ANTITOXINS
LC   ——; s.a. Bacteriology; Immunity; Ptomaines; Serumtherapy; Toxic and inflammable goods, Labeling of
SEARS   IMMUNITY; s.a. Physiological chemistry; Poisons
RG   ——; s.a. Antigens and antibodies; Red tide
NYT   POISONING AND POISONS; s.a. Biology and biochemistry; Medicine and health
PAIS   MEDICINE, PREVENTIVE
BPI   TOXICOLOGY; s.a. Immunity; Vaccination

TOYS
LC   ——; s.a. Amusements; Electronic toys; Miniature objects
SEARS   ——; s.a. Dollhouses; Dolls; Electric toys
RG   ——; s.a. Booksellers and bookselling—Toy departments; Christmas gifts for children
NYT   TOYS AND PLAYTHINGS; s.a. Children and youth; Dolls
PAIS   TOY INDUSTRY
BPI   ——; s.a. Model kits, Plastic; Railroads—Models; Toy industry

TRACERS (Biology). *Use* Radiotherapy

TRACK ATHLETICS
LC   TRACK—ATHLETICS; s.a. Athletics; Cycling; Relay racing; Running
SEARS   ——; s.a. College sports; Walking
RG   ——; s.a. Decathlon; Shot putting; Vaulting (sport); Weight-throwing
NYT   TRACK AND FIELD; s.a. Athletics; Sports
PAIS   SPORTS; s.a. College athletics; Olympic games
BPI   ATHLETICS; s.a. Sports

TRACKING AND TRAILING. *Use* Hunting

TRACKING RADAR. *Use* Radar

TRADE. *See* Business; Foreign Trade

TRADE AGREEMENTS. *Use* Collective Bargaining; Foreign Trade; Strikes and Lockouts

TRADE AND PROFESSIONAL ASSOCIATIONS
Scope: Works on business and professional associations whose aim is protection or advancement of their interests without special regard to the relation of employer and employees. See also subd. *Trade associations* under names of trades and industries, e.g., Food industry—Trade associations; and names of associations, e.g., Small Manufacturers Council.
LC ———; s.a. Boards of trade; Guilds; Medical societies; subd. *Societies* under names of trades and industries, e.g., Wool and trade industry—Societies; Trade-unions
SEARS ———; s.a. Associations
RG ———; s.a. Associations, institutions, etc.
NYT ORGANIZATIONS, SOCIETIES AND CLUBS; s.a. names of associations, e.g., Society of Accountants
PAIS TRADE ASSOCIATIONS
BPI TRADE ASSOCIATIONS; s.a. Professional associations, etc.

TRADE BARRIERS. *See* Commercial Policy; Tariff

TRADE JOURNALISM. *See* Journalism

TRADE MARKS. *Use* Trade-marks

TRADE PRACTICES. *Use* Business Ethics; Industrial Laws and Legislation; Monopolies; Wealth, Ethics of

TRADE REGULATION. *Use* Advertising, Fraudulent; Business Law; Commercial Law; Copyright; Industrial Laws and Legislation; Interstate Commerce; Monopolies; Patent Laws and Legislation; Priorities, Industrial

TRADE ROUTES. *Use* Transportation

TRADE SCHOOLS. *Use* Apprentices; High Schools; Occupational Training; Technical Education

TRADE SECRETS. *Use* Business Ethics

TRADE WASTE DISPOSAL. *Use* Refuse and Refuse Disposal

TRADE-MARKS
LC ———; s.a. Abbreviations; Acronyms; Business names; Industrial laws and legislation; Marks of origin; Patent laws and legislation; Property; Slogans—Law and legislation; Union label; Water-marks; subd. *Trade-marks* under specific industries and products, e.g., Paper making and trade—Trade-marks; Perfumes—Trade-marks
SEARS ———; s.a. Commerce; Manufacturers; Patents
RG TRADE MARKS AND TRADE NAMES; s.a. Branded merchandise; Printers marks; Private brands
NYT TRADEMARKS AND TRADE NAMES; s.a. Labeling and labels
PAIS TRADE MARKS AND NAMES; s.a. Labels; Private brands
BPI ———; s.a. Brand name goods; Emblems, Automobile

TRADES. *See* Industrial Arts; Occupations

TRADE-UNIONS
LC ———; s.a. Boycott; Business agents (trade union); Company unions; Corporate state; Hiring halls; Independent unions; Industrial relations; International labor activities; Management rights; Picketing; Trade and professional associations
SEARS LABOR UNIONS; s.a. Arbitration, Industrial; Guilds; Strikes and lockouts; Syndicalism
RG ———; s.a. Gilds; Industrial relations; Injunctions
NYT LABOR; s.a. names of industries and unions, e.g., American Federation of labor—Congress of Industrial Organizations (AFL-CIO)
PAIS ———; s.a. Gild socialism; Labor; Strikes
BPI ———; s.a. Collective bargaining; Open and closed shop

TRADITIONS. *See* Folklore; Manners and Customs; Rites and Ceremonies; Special Days, Weeks and Months

TRAFFIC ACCIDENTS
LC ———; s.a. Drinking and traffic accidents; Hit-and-run drivers; School safety patrols
SEARS ———; s.a. Accidents; Traffic regulations
RG ———; s.a. Automobile driving; Insurance, Automobile
NYT TRAFFIC (Vehicular and Pedestrian) AND PARKING; s.a. Accidents and safety; Automobiles
PAIS ACCIDENTS, TRAFFIC; s.a. Drinking and traffic accidents; Hit and run drivers; Traffic safety
BPI ———; s.a. Automobile drivers—Liquor problem; Automobile industry

TRAFFIC CONTROL. *See* Traffic Safety

TRAFFIC COURTS. *Use* Courts

TRAFFIC ENGINEERING. *Use* City Planning; Traffic Safety

TRAFFIC NOISE. *Use* Noise; Streets

TRAFFIC REGULATIONS. *Use* Traffic Accidents; Traffic Safety

TRAFFIC SAFETY
LC ———; s.a. Automobile drivers' tests; Motor vehicles—Inspection; Road construction—Safety measures; Speed limits; Traffic accidents
SEARS AUTOMOBILES—LAWS AND REGULATIONS; s.a. City traffic; Express highways; Traffic engineering; Traffic regulations
RG ———; s.a. Automobile driving; Pedestrians; Roads—Safety devices and measures
NYT TRAFFIC (Vehicular and Pedestrian) AND PARKING; s.a. Accidents and safety; Signals and signs
PAIS ———; s.a. City planning—Traffic aspects; Motor vehicles—Safety measures; Street lighting; Traffic signs and signals
BPI ———; s.a. City traffic; Road signs; Roads—Safety measures; Traffic regulations

TRAGEDY. *Use* Drama

TRAILS. *Use* Backpacking; Roads; Walking

TRAINING, PHYSICAL. *See* Physical Fitness

TRAMPS. *Use* Begging; Vagrancy

TRANCE. *Use* Hypnotism

TRANQUILIZING DRUGS. *Use* Anesthesia and Anesthetics; Barbiturates

TRANSCENDENTALISM. *Use* Idealism

TRANSFER (Law)
LC ——; s.a. Acquisition of property; Assign-ments; Bulk sales
SEARS BUSINESS—LAWS AND REGULATIONS; s.a. Property; Stocks
RG PROPERTY; s.a. Land titles; Stocks
NYT STOCKS AND BONDS; s.a. Law and legislation; Legal profession; Property and investments
PAIS MONEY, TRANSFER OF; s.a. Land titles—Registration and transfer; Stocks—Transfer
BPI TRANSFER OF FUNDS; s.a. Conveyancing; Stock transfers

TRANSFER OF FUNDS. *Use* Checks (Banking); Negotiable Instruments; Transfer (Law)

TRANSFER OF TRAINING. *Use* Educational Psychology; Learning, Psychology of

TRANSFER TAX. *See* Inheritance and Succession

TRANSIENT LABOR. *See* Migrant Labor

TRANSIENTS, RELIEF OF. *Use* Public Welfare

TRANSISTOR RADIOS. *Use* Radio—Apparatus and Supplies

TRANSIT SYSTEMS. *Use* Local Transit; Transportation

TRANSLATING AND INTERPRETING
LC ——; s.a. Translating services; subd. *Translating* under subjects, e.g., Science—Translating
SEARS ——; s.a. Language and languages
RG TRANSLATIONS AND TRANSLATING; s.a. Machine translating; Publishers and publishing—Translations
NYT TRANSLATION; s.a. Books and literature; Language and languages
PAIS ——; s.a. Copyright—Translations; Translating services
BPI TRANSLATIONS; s.a. Language and languages; Translators

TRANSLITERATION. *Use* Alphabet

TRANSMIGRATION. *Use* Soul

TRANSMUTATION (Chemistry). *Use* Metal Industries; Nuclear Physics; Radiation

TRANSMUTATION OF PLANTS. *Use* Plants

TRANSPARENCIES. *Use* Audio-visual Materials; Photography

TRANSPLANTATION OF ORGANS, TISSUES, ETC. *Use* Artificial Organs; Operations, Surgical; Surgery

TRANSPLANTATION OF ORGANS, TISSUES, ETC.—MORAL AND RELIGIOUS ASPECTS. *Use* Medical Ethics

TRANSPORTATION
See also specific means of transport, e.g., Air transport; Automobiles; Ferries; Railroads; etc.
LC ——; s.a. Interstate commerce; Locomotion; Merchant marine; Shipment of goods; Storage and moving trade; subd. *Transportation* under special subjects, e.g., Petroleum—Transportation; Transportation and state; Waterways
SEARS ——; s.a. Freight and freightage; Trade routes
RG ——; s.a. Local transit—Federal aid; Rapid transit—Federal aid; Urban transportation
NYT ——; s.a. Ships and shipping; Transit systems
PAIS ——; s.a. Carriers; Transportation—Federal aid; Transportation—Finance
BPI ——; s.a. Communication and traffic; Local transit

TRANSPORTATION, AUTOMOTIVE. *Use* Motor Vehicles

TRANSSEXUALISM. *See* Change of Sex

TRANSVESTISM. *Use* Sex

TRAPPING. *Use* Hunting

TRASH. *See* Refuse and Refuse Disposal

TRAUMATISM. *Use* Neuroses

TRAVEL
Scope: Works on the enjoyment of travel, advice to travelers, etc. Descriptions of actual voyages are entered under Voyages and travel or under names of places with subd. *Description and travel*, e.g., U.S.—Description and travel.
LC ——; s.a. Admission of non-immigrants; Games for travelers; Hotels, taverns, etc.; International travel regulations; Luggage; Manners and customs; Summer resorts; Travel costs; Voyages and travels
SEARS ——; s.a. Automobiles—Touring; Health resorts, spas, etc.; Ocean travel; Travelers, American
RG ——; s.a. Passports; Student travel; Vacations
NYT TRAVEL AND RESORTS; s.a. Hotels, bars, motels, night clubs and restaurants; Ocean voyages; Vacations
PAIS ——; s.a. International travel regulations; Tourist trade; Visas
BPI ——; s.a. Automobile touring; Tourist trade; Travel regulations

TRAVELERS. *Use* Americans in Foreign Countries; Explorers; Visitors, Foreign

TRAVELERS CHECKS. *Use* Checks (Banking)

TRAWLS AND TRAWLING. *Use* Fisheries

TREASON
LC ——; s.a. Sabotage; Sedition; Subversive activities; Trials (treason)
SEARS ——; s.a. Crime and criminals; Political crimes and offenses
RG ——; s.a. Espionage; Internal security; Sub-versive activities

NYT ——; s.a. Espionage; Loyalty oaths and tests;
U. S.—Internal security
PAIS ——; s.a. Conspiracy; Turncoats
BPI ESPIONAGE; s.a. Industrial espionage; Loyalty

TREATIES
See also names of treaties, e.g., Versaillles, Treaty of,
1919 and subd. *Treaties* or *Foreign relations—
Treaties* under names of countries or tribes,
e.g., Mexico—Treaties; Iroquois Indians—
Treaties; etc.
LC ——; s.a. Concordats; Executive agreements;
International law; Peace treaties
SEARS ——; s.a. Arbitration, International; Congresses
and conventions; Diplomacy
RG ——; s.a. Alliances; Commercial treaties and
agreements; International cooperation
NYT Subjects of treaties, e.g., Space; Seabed; s.a.
International relations; United Nations
PAIS ——; s.a. Alliances; Commercial treaties and
agreements
BPI ——; s.a. Commercial treaties and agreements;
World politics

TREE OF LIFE. *Use* Immortality

TREES
See also names of trees, e.g., Oak; and types of trees,
e.g., Dwarf trees; Evergreens.
LC ——; s.a. Afforestation; Forests and forestry;
Reforestation; Timber
SEARS ——; s.a. Botany; Lumber and lumbering;
Plants; Pruning; Tree planting
RG ——; s.a. Forest ecology; Landscape gardening;
Roadside improvement; Timber line
NYT TREES AND SHRUBS; s.a. Forests and forestry;
Wood and wood products
PAIS ——; s.a. Afforestation; Christmas trees; Cities
and towns—Trees
BPI ——; s.a. Forests and forestry; Lumber; Timber;
Woodlots

TRESPASS. *Use* Real Property

TRIAL BY JURY. *See* Jury

TRIAL MARRIAGE. *See* Dating (Social customs)

TRIALS
LC ——; s.a. subd. by type of crime, e.g., Trials
(adultery), Trials (malpractice), Trials (murder),
Trials (treason), etc.; Civil procedure; Cross-
examination; Legal etiquette; Newspaper
court reporting; Trial practice
SEARS ——; s.a. Courts martial and courts of inquiry;
Crime and criminals; Criminal law; Jury; War
crime trials; Witnesses
RG ——; s.a. Conduct of court proceedings; Pre-
trial procedure; Procedure (law)
NYT COURTS; s.a. Legal profession
PAIS ——; s.a. Bail; Grand jury
BPI ——; s.a. Actions and defenses; Burden of
proof; Courts; Justice, Administration of;
Lawyers

TRIBES AND TRIBAL SYSTEM
LC ——; s.a. Clans and clan system; Consanguinity;
Detribalization; Gipsies; Totemism; Tribal
government

SEARS CLANS AND CLAN SYSTEM; s.a. Communism;
Ethnology; Family; Feudalism; Totems and
totemism
RG ——; s.a. Kinship; Society, Primitive
NYT ARCHEOLOGY AND ANTHROPOLOGY; s.a.
Civilization; Man
PAIS ——; s.a. Nomads; Society, Primitive
BPI TRIBES AND TRIBALISM; s.a. Political
science; Sociology

TRIBOLOGY. *Use* Bearings (Machinery)

TRICYCLES. *See* Bicycles and Bicycling

TRINITY. *Use* Jesus Christ

TROPICAL CROPS. *Use* Farm Produce

TROTTING RACES. *See* Horse-racing

TRUANCY (Schools). *See* School Attendance

TRUCK FARMING
LC ——; s.a. Horticulture; Vegetable gardening
SEARS VEGETABLE GARDENING; s.a. Gardening;
Vegetables
RG ——; s.a. Companion crops; Vegetable
gardening
NYT AGRICULTURE AND AGRICULTURAL
PRODUCTS; s.a. Food and grocery trade;
Markets
PAIS VEGETABLE INDUSTRY; s.a. Horticulture;
names of specific vegetable industries, e.g.,
Tomato industry
BPI FARM PRODUCE; s.a. Agriculture; Vegetables

TRUCKS AND TRUCKING INDUSTRY. *Use* Freight
and Freightage; Materials Handling; Motor
Vehicles; Shipment of Goods; Storage and
Moving Trade

TRUE-FALSE EXAMINATIONS. *Use* Examinations

TRUST COMPANIES
LC ——; s.a. Custodianship accounts; Safe-
deposit companies; Trusts and trustees
SEARS ——; s.a. Banks and banking; Clearing house;
Corporations
RG INVESTMENT TRUSTS; s.a. Custodianship
accounts; Real estate investment trusts; Trusts
and trusteeships
NYT BANKS AND BANKING; s.a. names of trust
companies, e.g., Trust Company of New Jersey;
Wills and estates
PAIS ——; s.a. Investment trusts; Trusts and trustees
BPI ——; s.a. Banks and banking—Trust depart-
ments; Custodianship accounts

TRUST FUNDS. *Use* Trusts and Trustees

TRUSTS, CHARITABLE. *See* Charitable Uses, Trusts
and Foundations

TRUSTS, INDUSTRIAL
LC ——; s.a. Big business; Business enterprises;
Competition; Consolidation and merger of
corporations; Partnership; Restraint of trade
SEARS ——; s.a. Capitalism; Conglomerate corpora-
tions; Corporations; Interstate commerce;
Railroads—Consolidations

TRUSTS, INDUSTRIAL, *cont.*
RG   ——; s.a. Business consolidation and mergers; Monopolies
NYT   CORPORATIONS; s.a. Banks and banking; Cartels; Finance
PAIS   ——; s.a. Cartels; Holding companies
BPI   ——; s.a. Monopolies; subd. *Antitrust cases* under various subjects, e.g., Retail trade—Antitrust cases

TRUSTS AND TRUSTEES
LC   ——; s.a. Executors and administrators; Guardian and ward; Public trustees
SEARS COMMERCIAL LAW; s.a. Estate planning; Inheritance and succession; Pensions; Trust companies
RG   ——; s.a. Custodianship accounts; Guardian and ward
NYT   TRUST FUNDS; s.a. Foundations; Stocks and bonds; Wills and estates
PAIS   ——; s.a. Employees' trusts; Investment trusts
BPI   ——; s.a. Employees trusts; Executors and administrators

TRUTH
LC   ——; s.a. Belief and doubt; Evidence; Skepticism
SEARS ——; s.a. Agnosticism; Pragmatism; Truthfulness and falsehood
RG   ——; s.a. Honesty; Lying; Reality
NYT   PHILOSOPHY; s.a. Logic; Psychology and Psychologists
PAIS   KNOWLEDGE, THEORY OF; s.a. Ethics
BPI   KNOWLEDGE, THEORY OF; s.a. Ethics; Philosophy

TRUTH IN ADVERTISING. *See* Advertising, Fraudulent

TRUTH SERUMS. *See* Narcoanalysis

TUITION. *See* College Costs

TUNNELS AND TUNNELING. *Use* Civil Engineering; Local Transit

TURBULENCE. *Use* Aerodynamics

TURKEY INDUSTRY. *Use* Poultry Industry

TURNCOATS. *Use* Loyalty; Treason

TURNOVER TAX. *Use* Business Tax

TUTORS AND TUTORING. *Use* Teaching

12-MILE LIMIT. *See* Territorial Waters

TWENTIETH CENTURY
Scope: Works covering progress and development during this period in one or several countries. See also Nineteenth century; etc.
LC   ——; s.a. Civilization, Modern—20th century; Twentieth century—Forecasts
SEARS ——; s.a. History, Modern—20th century; Twenty-first century
RG   ——; s.a. History, Modern; names of decades, e.g., Nineteen hundred and forties, etc.
NYT   Specific dates and subjects, e.g., World War II (1939–45); s.a. Civilization; History; Man
PAIS   CIVILIZATION; s.a. History
BPI   TWO THOUSAND (Year); s.a. History; Man

TYPE AND TYPE FOUNDING. *Use* Printing Industry

TYPESETTING. *Use* Printing Industry

TYPEWRITERS. *Use* Office Equipment and Supplies

TYPEWRITING. *Use* Business Education

TYPISTS. *Use* Office Employees

TYPOGRAPHY. *See* Printing Industry

TYPOLOGY (Psychology). *Use* Temperament

TYRANNY. *Use* Despotism

U

UHF RADIO. *See* Radio, Short Wave

ULTRAMONTANISM
LC   ——; s.a. Popes—Infallibility; Vatican Council, 1869–1870
SEARS CATHOLIC CHURCH; s.a. Popes—Infallibility
RG   CATHOLIC CHURCH—RELATIONS; s.a. Church—Authority; Popes—Primacy
NYT   ROMAN CATHOLIC CHURCH (General); s.a. Religion and churches; Roman Catholic Church—Popes
PAIS   ROMAN CATHOLIC CHURCH; s.a. Vatican
BPI   CATHOLIC CHURCH; s.a. Papacy

ULTRASONICS
Scope: Works on sounds inaudible to the human ear.
LC   ——; s.a. Sound pressure; Ultrasonic waves
SEARS ——; s.a. Ultrasonic waves
RG   ——; s.a. Sound; Ultrasonic waves
NYT   SOUND; s.a. Science and technology
PAIS   PHYSICS
BPI   ULTRASONIC WAVES; s.a. Ultrasonic testing

UNCERTAINTY (Information theory). *Use* Information Sciences; Probabilities

UNDERACHIEVERS. *Use* Academic Achievement

UNDERDEVELOPED AREAS

LC ——; s.a. Community development; Technical assistance

SEARS ——; s.a. Industrialization; States, New

RG ——; s.a. Economic assistance in underdeveloped areas; Investments, Foreign (in underdeveloped areas)

NYT ECONOMIC CONDITIONS AND TRENDS; s.a. Foreign aid (government and UN programs); United Nations (UN)

PAIS UNDERDEVELOPED STATES; s.a. Economic development; Industrial development

BPI ——; s.a. Economic assistance; Food relief

UNDERGROUND FACTORIES. *Use* Factories

UNDERGROUND NUCLEAR EXPLOSIONS. *Use* Atomic Energy

UNDERGROUND PRESS. *Use* Press

UNDERGROUND RAILWAY. *Use* Slavery

UNDERSTANDING. *See* Knowledge, Theory of

UNDERTAKERS AND UNDERTAKING. *Use* Burial; Funeral Rites and Ceremonies

UNDERWATER EXPLORATION

LC ——; s.a. Oceanographic research; Photography, Submarine; Underwater drilling; Underwater television

SEARS ——; s.a. Aquanauts; Manned undersea research stations

RG ——; s.a. Archaeology, Submarine; Skin diving

NYT OCEANS AND OCEANOGRAPHY; s.a. Divers and diving; Marine biology; Treasure, Sunken

PAIS OCEANOGRAPHY; s.a. Marine research; Ocean bottom

BPI OCEANOGRAPHY; s.a. Marine resources; Ocean bottom

UNDERWRITING. *See* Insurance

UNEMPLOYMENT. *Use* Employment; Guaranteed Annual Income; Labor and Laboring Classes; Labor Supply; Manpower; Migrant Labor; Poverty; Public Welfare; Right to Labor; Seasonal Industries; Social Problems; Vagrancy

UNEMPLOYMENT, TECHNOLOGICAL. *Use* Machinery in Industry; Technology

UNEMPLOYMENT INSURANCE. *Use* Insurance, Social; Work Relief

UNETHICAL TRADE PRACTICES. *Use* Business Ethics; Commercial Crimes

UNFAIR LABOR PRACTICES. *Use* Industrial Laws and Legislation; Industrial Relations; Labor Laws and Legislation; Management Rights

UNGRADED CLASSES. *Use* Nongraded Schools

UNIFIED OPERATIONS (Military science). *Use* Military Art and Science

UNION AGREEMENTS. *See* Collective Labor Agreements

UNION LABEL. *Use* Open and Closed Shop

UNION SHOP. *Use* Collective Bargaining; Open and Closed Shop

UNIONS, LABOR. *See* Trade-Unions

UNIT PRICING. *Use* Consumer Protection; Labels; Prices

UNITED NATIONS. *Use* Arbitration, International; International Cooperation; International Offenses; International Relations; Treaties; World Politics

UNITED NATIONS—ECONOMIC ASSISTANCE. *Use* Economic Assistance, Foreign; Industrialization

UNITED NATIONS—TRUSTEESHIP COUNCIL. *Use* Colonies; Native Races

U. S.—BUDGET. *See* Budget

U. S.—CONGRESS. *Use* Legislation; Legislative Bodies; Parliamentary Practice

U. S.—CONSTITUTION. *Use* Constitutions; Democracy; Equality; Executive Power; Justice, Administration of; Law; Legislation; Separation of Powers

UNITED STATES—DEFENSES

See also subd. *Defenses* under names of countries, e.g., France—Defenses.

LC ——; s.a. Defense contracts; Military assistance

SEARS INDUSTRIAL MOBILIZATION; s.a. Armaments; Atomic power; Ballistic missiles; Internal security; Military service, Compulsory; Military service as a profession; Munitions; Ordnance; Radar; U.S. Armed Forces; War—Economic aspects

RG NATIONAL DEFENSE; s.a. Air defenses; Atomic bomb shelters

NYT U. S. ARMAMENT AND DEFENSE; s.a. Arms control and limitation and disarmament; North Atlantic Treaty Organization

PAIS NATIONAL DEFENSE; s.a. Civil defense; War and emergency powers

BPI NATIONAL DEFENSE; s.a. Armed forces; Disarmament and arms control

U. S.—DEPARTMENTS AND AGENCIES. *Use* Federal Government; Public Administration

U. S.—ECONOMIC ASSISTANCE PROGRAMS. *Use* Economic Assistance, Foreign

U. S.—ECONOMIC CONDITIONS AND TRENDS. *Use* Big Business; Competition; Economic Assistance, Domestic; Employment; Gross National Product; Industry; Inflation (Finance); Interstate Commerce; Labor Supply; Monetary Policy; Monopolies; Poverty; Rural Conditions; Small Business

U. S.—FEDERAL RESERVE SYSTEM. *Use* National Banks (U. S.)

U. S.—FINANCES. *Use* Currency Question; Debts, Public

U. S.—POLITICS AND GOVERNMENT. *Use* Business and Politics; Civil Service; Corruption (In politics); Democracy; Electioneering; Elections; Federal Government; Government, Resistance to; Industry and State; Right and Left (Political science); Local Government; Politics, Practical; Riots; State Governments; State Rights; Wire-tapping

U. S.—PRESIDENT. *Use* Executive Power; Presidents; Veto

U. S.—SUPREME COURT. *Use* Constitutions; Law

UNITIZED CARGO SYSTEMS. *Use* Cargo Handling; Containers; Freight and Freightage

UNITS. *Use* Weights and Measures

UNIVERSAL MILITARY TRAINING. *See* Military Service, Compulsory

UNIVERSE. *Use* Astronomy; Astrophysics; Outer Space

UNIVERSITIES AND COLLEGES. *Use* Accreditation (Education); Coeducation; Colleges and Universities; Education; Education, Higher

UNIVERSITY DEGREES. *See* Degrees, Academic

UNIVERSITY EXTENSION
Scope: Works on special programs in higher education for those who could not otherwise pursue such education.
LC ——; s.a. Correspondence schools and courses; Education of adults; Summer schools
SEARS ——; s.a. Adult education; Education, Higher
RG ——; s.a. Adult education; Evening and continuation schools
NYT COLLEGES AND UNIVERSITIES; s.a. Commercial education; Correspondence courses; Education and schools—U. S.—Adult education
PAIS ——; s.a. Correspondence education; Summer schools
BPI COLLEGES AND UNIVERSITIES; s.a. Adult education; Correspondence schools and colleges

UNIVERSITY GRADUATES. *See* College Graduates

UNMARRIED MOTHERS. *Use* Illegitimacy; Maternal and Infant Welfare

UNORDERED MERCHANDISE. *Use* Mail-Order Business

UNSKILLED LABOR. *Use* Labor and Laboring Classes

UNTOUCHABLES. *Use* Caste

UPHOLSTERY
LC ——; s.a. Furniture; Interior decoration; Slip covers
SEARS ——; s.a. Drapery; Furniture
RG ——; s.a. Automobiles—Upholstery; Textile fabrics
NYT DRAPERY AND UPHOLSTERY; s.a. Furniture; Interior decoration; Textiles
PAIS INTERIOR DECORATION; s.a. Furniture industry; Household furnishings

BPI ——; s.a. Interior decoration; Office decoration

UPPER CLASSES
LC ——; s.a. Aristocracy; Social classes
SEARS ——; s.a. Aristocracy; Social classes
RG ——; s.a. Aristocracy; Elite (social sciences)
NYT SOCIAL SCIENCES; s.a. Nobility; Society; Sociology
PAIS ELITE (Social sciences); s.a. Class struggle; Social status
BPI ELITE (Social sciences); s.a. Social classes

URBAN AREAS. *Use* Cities and Towns; City Planning; Community; Housing; Local Government; Metropolitan Government; Migration, Internal; Municipal Government; Neighborhood; Regional Planning; Urban Renewal; Urbanization

URBAN DESIGN. *See* City Planning

URBAN DEVELOPMENT. *See* City Planning

URBAN GUERILLAS. *See* Guerilla Warfare

URBAN REDEVELOPMENT. *See* Urban Renewal

URBAN RENEWAL
Scope: General works and works limited to economic, sociological or political factors. See Cities and towns—Planning for works on architectural and engineering aspects.
LC ——; s.a. Cities and towns—Civic improvement; Community organization; Metropolitan areas
SEARS ——; s.a. Community life; Metropolitan areas
RG ——; s.a. Business districts; Community organization
NYT AREA PLANNING AND RENEWAL; s.a. Building; U.S.—Economic conditions—Anti-poverty; Urban areas
PAIS REDEVELOPMENT, URBAN; s.a. City planning; Slums
BPI ——; s.a. City Planning; Slums

URBAN TRANSPORTATION. *Use* Local Transit; Transportation

URBANIZATION
LC ——; s.a. Rural-urban migration; Social history
SEARS CITIES AND TOWNS; s.a. headings beginning with the word Municipal; Sociology, Urban
RG ——; s.a. Cities and towns—Growth; Metropolitan areas; Rural-urban migration
NYT URBAN AREAS; s.a. Area planning and renewal; Building; Housing
PAIS ——; s.a. Cities and towns; Sociology, Urban
BPI METROPOLITAN AREAS; s.a. Suburbs; names of central cities of metropolitan areas, e.g., Baltimore

USEFUL ARTS. *See* Industrial Arts; Technology

USURY LAW. *Use* Commercial Crimes; Interest and Usury; Loans

UTOPIAS. *Use* Communism; Socialism

V

VACATION HOUSES. *Use* Home Ownership

VACATION SCHOOLS. *Use* Summer Schools

VACATIONS. *Use* Backpacking; Recreation; Summer Resorts; Tourist Trade; Travel

VACATIONS, EMPLOYEE
LC   ——; s.a. Industrial recreation; Leave of absence; Sick leave
SEARS   HOURS OF LABOR; s.a. Holidays; Labor and laboring classes
RG   ——; s.a. Employees—Leaves of absence; Non-wage payments
NYT   VACATIONS; s.a. Labor—U.S.—Holidays and special occasions; Labor—U.S.—Vacations
PAIS   VACATIONS, EMPLOYEES'; s.a. Hours of labor; Leave of absence; Maternity leave
BPI   VACATIONS, EMPLOYEES; s.a. Leave of absence; Sabbaticals, Industrial; Vacations

VACCINATION
See also subd. *Vaccination* under names of diseases, e.g., Tetanus—Vaccination.
LC   ——; s.a. Immunity; Inoculation; Smallpox—Prevention; Toxins and antitoxins
SEARS ——; s.a. Communicable diseases; Public health
RG   ——; s.a. Antigens and antibodies; Immunity
NYT   VACCINATION AND VACCINES; s.a. disease names, e.g., Smallpox; Immunization and immunity; Medicine and health
PAIS   ——; s.a. Communicable diseases; Public health
BPI   ——; s.a. Immunity; Public health

VADE-MECUMS. *See* Handbooks

VAGABONDAGE. *See* Vagrancy

VAGRANCY
LC   ——; s.a. Children, Vagrant; Tramps; Wayfaring life
SEARS ROGUES AND VAGABONDS; s.a. Begging; Tramps; Unemployed
RG   ——; s.a. Gypsies; Homeless, The; Outdoor life
NYT   VAGRANCY AND VAGRANTS; s.a. Beggars and begging; Crime and criminals; Hippies
PAIS   ——; s.a. Beggars and begging; Transients, Relief of
BPI   CRIME AND CRIMINALS; s.a. Manners and customs; Poverty

VALUATION
See also subd. *Valuation* under specific kinds of property, e.g., Real estate—Valuation. See Assessment for works on valuation for taxing purposes.
LC   ——; s.a. Assessment; Customs appraisal; Depreciation
SEARS ——; s.a. Assessment

RG   ——; s.a. Cost; Depreciation
NYT   PROPERTY AND INVESTMENTS; s.a. Insurance; Property insurance; Real estate
PAIS   ——; s.a. Depreciation; Land values
BPI   ——; s.a. Assessment; Depreciation

VALUE
Scope: Works on theory of value in economics. Works on moral and aesthetic values are entered under Social values; Worth; and Aesthetics.
LC   ——; s.a. Austrian school of economists; Prices; Supply and demand
SEARS ECONOMICS; s.a. Prices
RG   VALUE (Economic theory); s.a. Cost; Inflation (finance)
NYT   ECONOMICS; s.a. Economic conditions and trends; Labor
PAIS   ——; s.a. Cost; Supply and demand
BPI   ——; s.a. Marginal utility; Substitution (economics); Value (psychology)

VALUE (Psychology). *Use* Attitude (Psychology); Value

VALUE ADDED TAX. *Use* Business Tax; Taxation

VALVES, AEROSOL. *Use* Packaging

VAN ALLEN RADIATION BELT. *Use* Radiation

VARIANCE ANALYSIS. *Use* Biometry; Sampling (Statistics)

VARIATION (Biology). *Use* Evolution; Genetics; Heredity

VARIETY STORES
LC   ——; s.a. Chain stores; Department stores; Dry goods; Five and ten cent stores
SEARS DEPARTMENT STORES; s.a. Retail trade; Shopping centers
RG   ——; s.a. Retail trade; Sixty-nine cents shops
NYT   RETAIL STORES AND TRADE; Discount selling
PAIS   ——; s.a. Department stores; Discount houses (retail trade)
BPI   ——; s.a. Department stores; Supermarkets

VARIETY THEATERS. *See* Vaudeville

VARNISH AND VARNISHING. *Use* Finishes and Finishing; Painting, Industrial

VASCULAR SYSTEM. *See* Cardiovascular System

VATICAN. *Use* Catholic Church; Papacy; Ultramontanism

VAUDEVILLE
LC   ——; s.a. Burlesque (theater); Music halls (variety theaters, cabarets, etc.)
SEARS ——; s.a. Amusements; Theater
RG   ——; s.a. Amusements; Music-halls (variety theaters, etc.)

VAUDEVILLE, *cont.*
NYT ———; s.a. Entertainment and amusements; Theater
PAIS THEATER; s.a. Amusement industry
BPI THEATER; s.a. Entertainers; Entertaining

VAULTING (Sport). *Use* Track Athletics

VAULTS. *Use* Roofs

VEGETABLE KINGDOM. *See* Plants

VEGETABLE OILS. *See* Oil Industries; Oils and Fats

VEGETABLES
See also names of vegetables, e.g., Celery.
LC ———; s.a. Food, Raw; Greens, Edible; Root-crops; Truck farming; Vegetables, Dried (Canned, Frozen, etc.)
SEARS ———; s.a. Cookery—Vegetables; Plants; Vegetable gardening
RG ———; s.a. Canning and preserving; Greens, Edible; Vegetarianism
NYT FRUIT AND VEGETABLES; s.a. Agriculture and agricultural products; Food and grocery trade
PAIS VEGETABLE INDUSTRY; s.a. names of specific vegetable industries, e.g., Potato industry
BPI ———; s.a. Crops; Vegetables, Frozen

VEGETARIANISM. *Use* Diet; Nutrition; Vegetables

VEGETATION AND CLIMATE. *Use* Crops; Natural History

VEHICLES. *Use* Automobiles; Bicycles and Bicycling; Motor Vehicles

VENDORS AND PURCHASERS. *Use* Commercial Law; Deeds; Real Property; Sales

VENEREAL DISEASES
See also names of venereal diseases, e.g., Syphilis.
LC ———; s.a. Hygiene, Sexual; Premarital examinations
SEARS ———; s.a. Prostitution; Sexual hygiene; Woman—Health and hygiene
RG ———; s.a. Public health
NYT ———; s.a. Medicine and health; Sex
PAIS ———; s.a. Prostitution; Sex education
BPI ———; s.a. Prostitution

VENTILATION
See also subd. *Ventilation* or *Heating and ventilation* or *Heating, cooking, etc.,* under specific subjects, e.g., Factories—Heating and ventilation; Tunnels—Ventilation; etc.
LC ———; s.a. Dampness in buildings; Heating; Sanitation
SEARS ———; s.a. Air conditioning; Chimneys; Sanitation, Household
RG ———; s.a. Air conditioning
NYT AIR CONDITIONING AND VENTILATING; s.a. fields of use, e.g., Automobiles; Heating; Office buildings and other commercial properties
PAIS HEATING AND VENTILATION; s.a. Air conditioning industry; Oil burners
BPI ———; s.a. Building—Heating and cooling aspects; Environmental engineering (building)

VERBAL BEHAVIOR
LC ———; s.a. Speech; Verbal learning
SEARS COMMUNICATION; s.a. Children—Language
RG ———; s.a. Learning, Psychology of; Speech
NYT SPEECH; s.a. Language and languages; Speeches and statements (general)
PAIS SPEECH; s.a. Communication; Languages
BPI SPEECH; s.a. Voice

VERMIN. *See* Pests

VERSIFICATION
LC ———; s.a. Accents and accentuation; Alliteration; Blank verse; subd. *Versification* under modern languages; e.g., English language—Versification; and subd. *Metrics and rhythmics* under ancient languages, e.g., Greek language—Metrics and rhythmics
SEARS ———; s.a. Poetry; Rhyme
RG ———; s.a. Poetics; Rime
NYT BOOKS AND LITERATURE—POETRY; s.a. Language and languages; Writing and writers
PAIS LITERATURE; s.a. Poets
BPI POETRY; s.a. Authorship

VERTEBRATES. *Use* Animals; Birds

VESTED RIGHTS. *Use* Property

VETERANS
See also appropriate subd., e.g., Veterans—Disabled; Veterans—Employment; Veterans—Loans.
LC ———; s.a. Bounties, Military; Negroes as soldiers; Soldiers—Civil status
SEARS ———; s.a. Military service as a profession; Pensions, Military; Seamen
RG ———; s.a. Negro veterans; U.S.—Veterans administration hospitals
NYT ———; s.a. Drug addiction, abuse and traffic; U.S. armament and defense
PAIS ———; s.a. American Legion; Retired military personnel
BPI ———; s.a. Hospitals, Military; Veterans, Disabled

VETERINARY MEDICINE. *Use* Domestic Animals

VETO
Scope: Works about the presidential veto in the U.S.
LC ———; s.a. Disallowance of legislation; Exclusion, Right of
SEARS EXECUTIVE POWER—U.S.; s.a. Constitutional law
RG ———; s.a. Parliamentary practice; Presidents—U.S.—Powers and duties
NYT U.S.—PRESIDENT, EXECUTIVE OFFICE OF THE
PAIS ———; s.a. U.S.—President—Powers and duties; U.S.—President—Veto
BPI EXECUTIVE POWER; s.a. Constitutional law; Presidents (U.S.)

VIBRATION. *Use* Mechanical Engineering; Sound and Sound Recording

VIBRATION (Therapeutics). *Use* Massage; Physical Therapy

VICE
See also types of vices, e.g., Gambling; Prostitution; etc.
LC ——; s.a. Art, Immoral; Degeneration; Literature, Immoral; Virtues
SEARS CRIME AND CRIMINALS; s.a. Ethics; Pornography; Sin; Virtue
RG ——; s.a. Conduct of life; Delinquents; Immoral literature and pictures
NYT ——; s.a. Prisons and prisoners; Sex crimes
PAIS CRIME AND CRIMINALS; s.a. Ethics
BPI MORAL CONDITIONS; s.a. Crime and criminals

VICTIMLESS CRIMES. *See* Crimes Without Victims

VICTIMS OF CRIME. *Use* Crime and Criminals

VIDEO RECORDERS AND RECORDING. *Use* Audio-visual Materials; Television

VIETNAM WAR
LC VIETNAMESE CONFLICT, 1961–; s.a. subds. e.g.,–Children;–Destruction and pillage;–Diplomatic history;–Economic aspects;–Social work; etc.
SEARS VIETNAMESE CONFLICT, 1961–; s.a. subds. e.g.,–Public opinion;–Refugees;–War work; etc.
RG VIETNAMESE WAR, 1957–; s.a. subds. e.g.,–Aerial operations;–American participation;–Atrocities;–Negroes;–Protests, demonstrations, etc.; etc.
NYT VIETNAM; s.a. U.S. armament and defense
PAIS VIETNAMESE CONFLICT, 1961–; s.a. subds. e.g.,–Aerial operations;–Atrocities;–Casualties;–Peace and mediation; etc.
BPI ——; s.a. subds. e.g.,–Atrocities;–Casualties;–Economic aspects;–Protest demonstrations; etc.

VIEW FINDERS. *Use* Cameras

VIEWS. *Use* Landscape Protection

VILLAGE COMMUNITIES. *Use* Peasantry; Society, Primitive; Villages

VILLAGE LIFE. *Use* Country Life; Rural Life

VILLAGES
LC ——; s.a. Rural conditions; Sociology, Rural; Village communities
SEARS ——; s.a. Cities and towns; Country life; Local government
RG ——; s.a. City and country; Village life
NYT RURAL AREAS; s.a. Community centers; names of specific villages
PAIS ——; s.a. Commons; Community life, Rural
BPI ——; s.a. Cities and towns; Rural conditions

VILLEINAGE. *Use* Slavery

VIOLENCE
LC ——; s.a. Fighting (psychology); Violent deaths
SEARS ——; s.a. Aggressiveness (psychology); Sabotage; Social psychology
RG ——; s.a. Assault and battery; Terrorism
NYT ——; s.a. Bombs and bomb plots; Children and youth–Behavior and training; Riots; Social conditions and welfare
PAIS ——; s.a. Massacres; Terrorism
BPI ——; s.a. Violence and television

VIOLENT DEATHS. *Use* Death; Mortality; Violence

VIRGIN BIRTH
LC ——; s.a. Immaculate conception; Jesus Christ–Nativity; Mary, Virgin–Virginity; Virgin birth–Mythology
SEARS MARY, VIRGIN; s.a. Mythology
RG MARY, VIRGIN; s.a. Christianity; Jesus Christ–Nativity
NYT RELIGION AND CHURCHES; s.a. denomination names, e.g., Protestant Episcopal Church; Jesus Christ
PAIS CHRISTIANITY AND OTHER RELIGIONS; s.a. Roman Catholic Church
BPI CATHOLIC CHURCH; s.a. Christianity

VIRGIN MARY. *See* Virgin Birth

VIRGINITY. *Use* Sex

VIRTUES
See also specific virtues, e.g., Charity; Kindness; Patience.
LC ——; s.a. Cardinal virtues; Character; Human acts; Vice
SEARS ETHICS; s.a. Behavior; Human relations
RG ——; s.a. Moral attitudes; Situation ethics
NYT ETHICS AND MORALS; s.a. Psychology and psychologists
PAIS ETHICS; s.a. Legal ethics; Social ethics
BPI ETHICS; s.a. Business ethics; Conduct of life

VIRUSES. *Use* Bacteria; Bacteriology; Communicable Diseases; Diseases

VISAS. *Use* Travel

VISION. *Use* Blind; Dreams; Eye; Miracles

VISITING HOUSEKEEPERS. *Use* Household Employees

VISITORS, FOREIGN
LC ——; s.a. Exchange of persons program; Students, Foreign
SEARS EXCHANGE OF PERSONS PROGRAMS; s.a. Cultural relations; International cooperation; Tourist trade
RG ——; s.a. Foreign students in (name of country); Travelers
NYT CULTURAL RELATIONS; s.a. People-to-People program; Travel and resorts
PAIS FOREIGN VISITORS IN [name of country]
BPI FOREIGN VISITORS; s.a. Foreign students in the U.S.; Tourist trade

VISUAL AIDS. *Use* Audio-visual Materials; Communication; Graphic Methods; Signs and Symbols

VISUAL EDUCATION. *Use* Audio-visual Education; Moving Pictures in Education

VITAL FORCE. *Use* Force and Energy

VITAL STATISTICS
LC ——; s.a. Biometry; Census; Death–Causes; Demography; Fertility, Human
SEARS ——; s.a. Population; Statistics
RG ——; s.a. Population–Statistics; Registers of birth, etc.

VITAL STATISTICS, *cont.*
NYT   POPULATION AND VITAL STATISTICS; s.a.
         Births
PAIS   ——; s.a. Births; Mortality
BPI   ——; s.a. Demography; Population—Statistics

VITAMINS
LC   ——; s.a. Deficiency diseases; Nutrition;
         Vitamin therapy
SEARS ——; s.a. Food; Physiological chemistry
RG   ——; s.a. Deficiency diseases in animals;
         Food, Enriched
NYT   ——; s.a. Food; Medicine and health
PAIS   ——; s.a. Diet; Nutrition
BPI   ——; s.a. Diet; Food, Enriched; Nutrition

VIVISECTION. *Use* Surgery

VOCABULARY
Scope: General works and works on English vocabulary.
         For works dealing with other languages, see
         subds. *Dictionaries, Glossaries,* or *Vocabulary*
         after names of languages, e.g., French language—
         Vocabulary.
LC   ——; s.a. English language—Word frequency;
         Homonyms; Synonyms; Word recognition
SEARS ——; s.a. Children—Language; Semantics;
         Speech; Words, New
RG   ——; s.a. Slang; Words
NYT   LANGUAGE AND LANGUAGES; s.a. Books
         and literature; Dictionaries
PAIS   DICTIONARIES; s.a. English language; subds.
         Dictionaries or *Terminology* under specific
         subject, e.g., Accounting—Dictionaries
BPI   WORDS; s.a. Dictionaries; English language

VOCAL CORDS. *Use* Voice

VOCAL MUSIC. *Use* Choral Music; Opera; Singing and
         Songs

VOCATIONAL EDUCATION
LC   ——; s.a. Agricultural education; Blind—
         Education; Deaf—Education; Manual training;
         Vocational rehabilitation
SEARS ——; s.a. Professional education; Technical
         education
RG   ——; s.a. Business education; Education,
         Cooperative
NYT   VOCATIONAL TRAINING, GUIDANCE AND
         AIMS; s.a. Commercial education; Education
         and schools
PAIS   ——; s.a. Employees—Training; Retraining,
         Occupational
BPI   ——; s.a. Employees, Training of; Occupational
         training

VOCATIONAL GUIDANCE
LC   ——; s.a. Languages and vocational opportuni-
         ties; Occupations and race; Personnel service in
         education; Professions; Youth—Employment
SEARS ——; s.a. Blind—Education; Deaf—Education
RG   ——; s.a. Counseling; Educational guidance;
         Occupations; Personnel service in education

NYT   VOCATIONAL TRAINING, GUIDANCE AND
         AIMS; s.a. Commercial education; Education
         and schools—U.S.; Labor—U.S.—Unemploy-
         ment and job market
PAIS   ——; s.a. Counseling; Occupations
BPI   ——; s.a. Occupations; Retraining, Occupational

VOCATIONAL REHABILITATION
LC   ——; s.a. Blind—Employment; Deaf—Employ-
         ment; Rehabilitation centers
SEARS HANDICAPPED; s.a. Occupational therapy;
         Physically handicapped; Vocational education
RG   ——; s.a. Handicapped—Employment; Rehabili-
         tation
NYT   HANDICAPPED; s.a. Vocational training,
         Guidance and aims
PAIS   ——; s.a. Employment—Disabled; Retraining,
         Occupational
BPI   ——; s.a. Prisoners—Rehabilitation; Retraining,
         Occupational

VOCATIONAL TRAINING. *Use* Occupational Training;
         Technical Education; Vocational Education

VOCATIONS. *See* Occupations; Professions

VOICE
LC   ——; s.a. Diction; Stammering; Vocal cords;
         Voice culture
SEARS ——; s.a. Oratory; Phonetics; Public speaking
RG   ——; s.a. Automatic speech recognition; Elocu-
         tion; Larynx; Speech
NYT   SPEECH; s.a. Speeches and statements (general);
         Voiceprints
PAIS   SPEECH; s.a. Singing; Speech—Identification
BPI   ——; s.a. Automatic speech recognition;
         Ventriloquism

VOTERS, REGISTRATION OF
LC   ——; s.a. subd. *Voting registers* under names
         of places; Voting
SEARS ELECTIONS; s.a. Suffrage
RG   ——; s.a. Election laws; Suffrage
NYT   ELECTIONS (U.S.)—VOTING REQUIRE-
         MENTS AND VOTERS—REGISTRATION OF
         VOTERS; s.a. Politics and government; subds.
         Elections or *Politics and government* under
         names of places, e.g., Chicago—Elections
PAIS   VOTING—REGISTRATION; s.a. Local elec-
         tions; Primaries
BPI   VOTING; s.a. Election law; Elections

VOTING
LC   ——; s.a. Ballot; Politics, Practical; Suffrage;
         Voters, Registration of
SEARS SUFFRAGE; s.a. Elections; Primaries; Represen-
         tative government and representation
RG   ——; s.a. Literacy tests (election law);
         Referendum
NYT   ELECTIONS (U.S.)—VOTING REQUIREMENTS
         AND VOTERS; s.a. Subds. *Elections* or
         Politics and government under names of places,
         e.g., Massachusetts—Elections
PAIS   ——; s.a. Elections; Referendum
BPI   ——; s.a. Elections; Majorities

VOWS. *Use* Oaths

VOYAGERS. *See* Explorers

VOYAGES AND TRAVELS
LC ———; s.a. Adventure and adventurers; Explorers; Scientific expeditions; Seafaring life; subd. *Description and travel* or *Discovery and exploration* under names of places

SEARS ———; s.a. Discoveries (in geography); Geography; Scientific expeditions; Seamen; Tourist trade
RG VOYAGES; s.a. Cruising; Ocean travel; Shipwrecks
NYT TRAVEL AND RESORTS; s.a. means of travel, e.g., Ships and shipping; Ocean voyages; Vacations
PAIS TRAVEL; s.a. Space flight
BPI ———; s.a. Travel

WAGE-PRICE POLICY. *Use* Inflation (Finance); Prices; Wages and Salaries

WAGERS. *Use* Gambling

WAGES, GUARANTEED. *See* Guaranteed Annual Income; Minimum Wage; Negative Income Tax

WAGES AND SALARIES
See also subd. *Salaries, allowances, etc.* or *Wages and salaries* under subjects, e.g., Accountants—Salaries, allowances, etc.
LC WAGES; s.a. appropriate subd. by occupation, industry, or special category of wage earners, e.g., Wages—Steel workers; Wages—Women; Cost and standard of living; Equal pay for equal work; Incentives in industry; Overtime; Piece work
SEARS WAGES; s.a. Guaranteed annual income; Profit sharing; Wage-price policy
RG WAGES; s.a. Labor cost; Non-wage payments; Salaries
NYT LABOR—U. S.—WAGES AND HOURS; s.a. Income; White collar workers
PAIS ———; s.a. Bonus system; Income
BPI ———; s.a. Deferred compensation; Non-wage payments; Payrolls; Wage differentials; Wage-price policy

WAITERS AND WAITRESSES. *Use* Caterers and Catering; Food Service; Restaurants, Lunchrooms, etc.

WALKING
LC ———; s.a. Athletics; Locomotion; Trails
SEARS ———; s.a. Backpacking; Hiking; Track athletics
RG ———; s.a. Hitchhiking; Pedestrians
NYT ———; s.a. Camps and camping; Hitchhiking; Jogging
PAIS HIKING; s.a. Camps and camping; Trails
BPI RECREATION; s.a. Camping; Leisure

WALL STREET
Scope: Works on the speculative activities of Wall Street, the financial district.
LC ———; s.a. Brokers; Speculation

SEARS ———; s.a. Speculation; Stock exchange
RG ———; s.a. Brokers; Stock exchange
NYT STOCKS AND BONDS; s.a. commodities and commodity exchanges and brokers; exchange names, e.g., Stock Exchange, American
PAIS ———; s.a. Investments; Stock exchange
BPI ———; s.a. American Stock Exchange; New York Stock Exchange; Short selling; Stock market

WALLS
LC ———; s.a. Brick walls; Concrete walls; Masonry; Retaining walls
SEARS ———; s.a. Foundations; Mural painting and decoration
RG ———; s.a. Paneling; Partitions
NYT BUILDING; s.a. Roofing and siding; Wallboard
PAIS WALLBOARD INDUSTRY; s.a. Building; Building materials
BPI ———; s.a. Foundations; Retaining walls

WAR
See also names of wars, e.g., U. S.—History—Queen Anne's War, 1702–1713; Russo-Japanese War, 1904–1905; European War, 1914–1918; World War II, 1939–1945; Vietnamese Conflict 1961–; etc.
LC ———; s.a. Battles; Civil war; Militarism; Military art and science; Naval art and science; War and society
SEARS ———; s.a. Armies; Chemical warfare; International law; Psychological warfare; Revolutions
RG ———; s.a. Atomic warfare; Guerrilla warfare
NYT WAR AND REVOLUTION; s.a. Arms control and limitation and disarmament; International relations; U. S. armament and defense
PAIS ———; s.a. Aerial warfare; Biological warfare; War (international law)
BPI ———; s.a. Disarmament and arms control; Strategy

WAR (International law)
LC ———; s.a. Aggression (international law); Belligerency; Crimes against peace; Neutrality; War victims

WAR (International Law), *cont.*
SEARS   INTERNATIONAL LAW; s.a. Spies; War crime trials; World War, 1939–1945—Atrocities
RG   WAR, LAWS OF; s.a. Intervention (international law); War crimes
NYT   WAR CRIMES AND CRIMINALS; s.a. International law; War and revolution; War claims and compensation
PAIS   ——; s.a. Armistices; War criminals
BPI   WAR; s.a. International law

WAR—CASUALTIES (Statistics, etc.). *Use* Mortality

WAR, COST OF. *Use* Debts, Public; Disarmament; War—Economic Aspects

WAR—ECONOMIC ASPECTS
Scope: Works on the economic causes of war and the effect of war on industrial and economic activity.
LC   ——; s.a. Armies, Cost of; Competition, International; Priorities, Industrial; Rationing, Consumer
SEARS   ——; s.a. Debts, Public; Industrial mobilization; Munitions
RG   ——; s.a. Profiteering; subd. *Cost* under names of wars; War finance; War profits
NYT   WAR AND REVOLUTION; s.a. Foreign aid; U. S. armament and defense; U. S. armament and defense—Budget
PAIS   ——; s.a. Industrial mobilization; Profiteering; Purchasing, Military and naval; War, Cost of
BPI   ——; s.a. Insurance, War risk; subd. *Economic aspects* under names of wars; U. S.—Armed forces—Procurement

WAR, MARITIME (International law). *Use* Freedom of the Seas

WAR—SONGS. *Use* National Songs

WAR AND CIVILIZATION. *Use* War and Society

WAR AND EMERGENCY POWERS. *Use* Constitutions; Executive Power; Priorities, Industrial; Separation of Powers; U. S.—Defenses

WAR AND MORALS. *Use* War and Religion; War and Society

WAR AND RELIGION
LC   ——; s.a. Conscientious objectors; Jihad; Nonviolence; War and morals
SEARS   ——; s.a. Pacifism; World War, 1939–1945—Religious aspects
RG   ——; s.a. Conscientious objectors; subd. *Moral and religious aspects* under names of wars
NYT   WAR AND REVOLUTION; s.a. Conscientious objectors; Religion and churches; U. S. armament and defense—Draft and recruitment, Military
PAIS   ——; s.a. Conscientious objectors; Pacifism
BPI   CONSCIENTIOUS OBJECTORS; s.a. Religion

WAR AND REVOLUTION. *Use* Government, Resistance to; Guerilla Warfare; Militarism; Revolutions; Right and Left (Political science); War

WAR AND SOCIETY
LC   ——; s.a. Atomic warfare and society; Sociology, Military; War and morals
SEARS   WAR AND CIVILIZATION; s.a. Civilization; Progress
RG   ——; s.a. Atomic warfare and society; War and morals
NYT   WAR AND REVOLUTION; s.a. Civilization; Culture; Social conditions and welfare
PAIS   ——; s.a. Civilization; Sociology, Military
BPI   WAR

WAR CLAIMS AND COMPENSATION. *Use* War (International law)

WAR CONTRACTS. *See* Defense Contracts

WAR CRIME TRIALS
LC   ——; s.a. Crimes against peace; International offenses; Trials (crimes against humanity); Trials (genocide)
SEARS   ——; s.a. World War, 1939–1945—Atrocities
RG   ——; s.a. Nuremberg trials; Vietnamese war, 1957- —Atrocities—My Lai massacre
NYT   WAR CRIMES AND CRIMINALS; s.a. Jews—Europe; Minorities—Nazi policies; subd. *War crimes and criminals* under names of wars, e.g., World War II—War crimes and criminals
PAIS   WAR CRIMINALS; s.a. Trials
BPI   WAR CRIMES; s.a. World War, 1939–1945—War criminals

WAR DEBTS. *See* Debts, Public

WAR FINANCE. *Use* War—Economic Aspects

WAR GAMES. *Use* Military Art and Science

WAR OF 1914. *See* European War, 1914–1918

WAR PENSIONS. *See* Pensions, Military

WAR PROFITS. *Use* Black Market; Priorities, Industrial; War—Economic Aspects

WAR VETERANS. *See* Veterans

WAR VICTIMS. *Use* Atrocities; War (International law)

WAREHOUSES. *Use* Inventories; Storage and Moving Trade

WARRANTY. *Use* Commercial Law; Liability (Law)

WARSHIPS
LC   ——; s.a. Armored vessels; Battleships; Cruisers (warships)
SEARS   ——; s.a. Aircraft carriers; Naval art and science; Sea power; Submarines
RG   ——; s.a. Aircraft carriers; Carriers
NYT   SHIPS AND SHIPPING; s.a. Shipbuilding, conversion and repair; U. S. armament and defense—Navy
PAIS   ——; s.a. Ships, Atomic-powered; Ships, Naval; Submarines, Atomic-powered
BPI   ——; s.a. Aircraft carriers; Ships

WASHING MACHINE INDUSTRY. *Use* Laundries and Laundering

WASTE LANDS. *Use* Reclamation of Land

WASTE MATERIALS AND DISPOSAL. *Use* Chemical Industries; Containers; Environmental Policy; Pollution; Refuse and Refuse Disposal; Sanitation; Waste Products; Water–Pollution

WASTE PAPER INDUSTRY. *Use* Paper Making and Trade

WASTE PRODUCTS
See also subd. *By-products* under specific industries, e.g., Gas manufacture and works–By-products.
LC ———; s.a. Factory and trade waste; Reactor fuel reprocessing; Scrap metals
SEARS ———; s.a. Refuse and refuse disposal; Salvage (waste, etc.); Substitute products
RG ———; s.a. Refuse, Utilization of; Scrap metal
NYT WASTE MATERIALS AND DISPOSAL; s.a. Sanitation; Water pollution
PAIS REFUSE DISPOSAL; s.a. Industrial waste; Salvage (waste, etc.)
BPI ———; s.a. Factory and trade waste

WATCHES AND CLOCKS. *Use* Time

WATCHMEN. *Use* Detectives; Police

WATER
LC ———; s.a. Drinking water; Hydrology; Irrigation water; Mineral waters; Sea water; Water resources development
SEARS ———; s.a. Hydraulic machinery; Lakes; Rain and rainfall; Rivers; Water power
RG ———; s.a. Hydrologic research; Springs; Tide power; Water supply–Fluoridation
NYT ———; s.a. Water pollution; Waterways
PAIS ———; s.a. Hydroelectric power; Saline water; Salt water; Tidal power
BPI ———; s.a. Dams; Steam; Water conservation

WATER–POLLUTION
LC ———; s.a. Eutrophication; Marine ecology; Pollution; Refuse and refuse disposal
SEARS ———; s.a. Ecology; Factory and trade waste; Man–Influence on nature; Water–Analysis
RG WATER POLLUTION; s.a. Detergent pollution of rivers, lakes, etc.; Fresh water ecology; Marine pollution; Sea water–Pollution
NYT WATER POLLUTION; s.a. Environment; Waste materials and disposal
PAIS WATER POLLUTION; s.a. Oil pollution of rivers, harbors, etc.; Waste disposal in the ocean
BPI WATER POLLUTION; s.a. Detergent pollution of water; Sewage disposal; Water purification

WATER–SUPPLY
Scope: Works on surveys of water resources of a region primarily with reference to the supply of water for domestic and manufacturing purposes, or for agriculture.
LC ———; s.a. subd. *Water–supply* under cities and specific subjects, e.g., Fire extinction–Water supply; Wells
SEARS ———; s.a. Aqueducts; Water conservation

RG ———; s.a. Arid regions; Irrigation water
PAIS ———; s.a. Irrigation; Reservoirs
BPI ———; s.a. Dams; Reservoirs

WATER CONSERVATION. *Use* Water–Supply

WATER DISTRICTS. *Use* Local Government

WATER POLLUTION. *Use* Water–Pollution

WATER POLLUTION–CONTROL. *Use* Environmental Policy

WATER PURIFICATION. *Use* Water Supply

WATER RESOURCES DEVELOPMENT
LC ———; s.a. Flood control; Irrigation
SEARS ———; s.a. Inland navigation; Water power
RG ———; s.a. Arid regions; Flood prevention and control
NYT WATER; s.a. Energy and power
PAIS ———; s.a. Flood control; Rivers–Regulation
BPI ———; s.a. Reservoirs; Water supply

WATER-MARKS. *Use* Trademarks

WATER-POWER ELECTRIC PLANTS. *Use* Electric Power Plants

WATERS, TERRITORIAL. *Use* Boundaries; Freedom of the Seas; Maritime Law; Territorial Waters; Territory, National

WATERSHED MANAGEMENT. *Use* Soils; Water Resources Development

WATERWAYS
Scope: Works on canals, lakes, rivers, straits, etc., as highways of transportation and commerce. See also names of waterways, e.g., St. Lawrence Seaway.
LC ———; s.a. Intracoastal waterways; Transportation
SEARS ———; s.a. Canals; Inland navigation
RG ———; s.a. Inland navigation; Inland water transportation
NYT WATERWAYS AND OTHER BODIES OF WATER; s.a. Bridges and tunnels; Ponds
PAIS ———; s.a. Lakes; Rivers
BPI ———; s.a. Barges; Canals

WAYFARING LIFE. *Use* Outdoor Life; Vagrancy

WEALTH
LC ———; s.a. Consumption (economics); Gross national product; Luxury; Property; Saving and investment
SEARS ———; s.a. Capitalists and financiers; Inheritance and succession; Millionaires; Success
RG ———; s.a. Prosperity; Rich, The
NYT PROPERTY AND INVESTMENTS; s.a. Income; Wills and estates
PAIS ———; s.a. Income; Money; Wealth, Ethics of
BPI ———; s.a. Capital; Poverty

WEALTH, ETHICS OF
LC ———; s.a. Avarice; Religion and economics
SEARS WEALTH; s.a. Business ethics; Honesty
RG SOCIAL ETHICS; s.a. Altruism; Business ethics

WEALTH, ETHICS OF, *cont.*
NYT ETHICS AND MORALS; s.a. Property and investments; U. S.—Economic conditions and trends
PAIS ——; s.a. Business ethics; Trade practices
BPI WEALTH; s.a. Business—Social aspects; Poverty

WEAPONS
LC WEAPONS SYSTEMS; s.a. Gunnery; Intercontinental ballistic missile bases; Ordnance
SEARS ARMS AND ARMOR; s.a. Firearms
RG WEAPONS SYSTEMS; s.a. Chemical and biological weapons; Guided missiles
NYT ——; s.a. Armament, defense and military forces; Atomic energy and weapons
PAIS ARMAMENTS; s.a. Atomic weapons; Guided missiles
BPI WEAPONS SYSTEMS; s.a. Atomic weapons; Munitions

WEATHER
See also weather phenomena, e.g., Cyclones; Drought; Hurricanes; Snowstorms; Storms; Tornadoes; Winds.
LC ——; s.a. Acclimatization; Climatology; Man—Influence of environment; Weather control; Weather—Mental and physiological effects
SEARS ——; s.a. Climate; Sun; Temperature; Weather forecasting
RG ——; s.a. Fog dispersal; Meteorology; Rain making
NYT ——; s.a. Seasons and months
PAIS ——; s.a. Weather—Business aspects; Weather—Military applications
BPI ——; s.a. Industry and weather; Meteorological services

WEATHER LORE. *Use* Folklore

WEATHERING. *Use* Erosion; Finishes and Finishing; Materials

WEAVING. *Use* Basket Making; Handicraft; Tapestry; Textile Industry and Fabrics

WEDDINGS. *Use* Etiquette; Marriage

WEEDS
LC ——; s.a. Aquatic weeds; Herbicides; Weed control
SEARS ——; s.a. Agricultural pests; Botany, Economic
RG ——; s.a. Gardening; Grasses
NYT ——; s.a. Plants; Seaweed
PAIS WEED CONTROL; s.a. Herbicides
BPI ——; s.a. Herbicides; Railroads—Weed removal; Weeds—Control

WEIGHT CONTROL
LC CORPULENCE; s.a. Fat; Reducing exercises; Weight reducing preparations
SEARS ——; s.a. Diet; Exercise
RG WEIGHT (Physiology); s.a. Exercise; Food habits
NYT WEIGHT; s.a. Exercise; Food—Diet and nutrition
PAIS REDUCING PREPARATIONS; s.a. Diet; Nutrition
BPI WEIGHT (Physiology); s.a. Diet; Reducing drugs

WEIGHTLESSNESS. *Use* Aviation Medicine; Man—Influence of Environment

WEIGHTS AND MEASURES
LC ——; s.a. Grain—Weights and measures; Mensuration; Standards of mass; Weighing machines
SEARS ——; s.a. Electric measurements; Measuring instruments
RG ——; s.a. Scales (weighing instruments); Units
NYT ——; s.a. Metric system
PAIS ——; s.a. Measurement; Metric system
BPI ——; s.a. Decimal system; Metric system

WEIGHT-THROWING. *Use* Track Athletics

WELDING. *Use* Metal Industries; Solder and Soldering

WELFARE. *See* Public Welfare; Welfare Economics

WELFARE ECONOMICS
LC ——; s.a. Economic policy; Economic security; Social policy
SEARS ECONOMIC POLICY; s.a. Public welfare; The State
RG SOCIAL AND ECONOMIC SECURITY; s.a. Old age pensions; Pensions, Industrial
NYT ECONOMICS; s.a. Economic conditions and trends (general); Income; Pensions and retirements
PAIS ——; s.a. Income—Guaranteed income; Insurance, Social
BPI ——; s.a. Family allowances; Public welfare

WELFARE FUNDS (Trade unions). *Use* Non-wage Payments; Old Age Assistance

WELFARE STATE. *Use* Public Welfare; Social Policy

WELFARE WORK. *Use* Charities; Counseling; Disaster Relief; Legal Aid; Medical Care; Public Welfare; Social Service; Work Relief

WELLS. *Use* Boring; Petroleum Industry and Trade; Water—Supply

WEST AND EAST. *See* East and West

WESTERN MUSIC. *See* Music

WETBACKS. *See* Aliens; Migrant Labor; Seasonal Industries

WETLANDS. *Use* Wildlife Conservation

WHALING. *Use* Fisheries; Hunting

WHARVES. *Use* Ports

WHIPPING. *See* Punishment

WHITE COLLAR CRIMES. *See* Commercial Crimes; Theft

WHITE COLLAR WORKERS. *Use* Civil Service; Clerks; Labor and Laboring Classes; Office Employees; Professions; Secretaries

WHITE-SLAVE TRAFFIC. *See* Prostitution

WHOLE AND PARTS (Psychology). *Use* Perception

WHOLESALE TRADE. *Use* Commerce; Marketing

WIDOWS. *Use* Single People; Survivor's Benefits; Woman; Woman—Rights of Women

WILD ANIMALS. *See* Predatory Animals

WILD LIFE. *Use* Animals; Predatory Animals

WILD MEN. *Use* Society, Primitive

WILDCAT STRIKES. *Use* Strikes and·Lockouts

WILDERNESS AREAS. *Use* Conservation of Natural Resources; Forest Reserves; National Parks and Reserves; Natural Resources; Parks; Public Lands; Wildlife Conservation

WILDERNESS SURVIVAL. *Use* Outdoor Life

WILDLIFE. *Use* Animals; Wildlife Conservation

WILDLIFE CONSERVATION
LC ———; s.a. Forest reserves; Game protection; National parks and reserves; Predatory animals; Wilderness areas
SEARS WILDLIFE—CONSERVATION; s.a. Forests and forestry; Natural history; Natural resources; Rare animals; Zoology, Economic
RG ———; s.a. Animals—Protection; Wetlands
NYT WILDLIFE SANCTUARIES; s.a. Birds
PAIS ———; s.a. Game laws; Game preserves
BPI WILDLIFE, CONSERVATION OF; s.a. Game and game birds; Parks

WILL
LC ———; s.a. Belief and doubt; Character tests; Desire; Impulses; Inhibition
SEARS ETHICS; s.a. Brainwashing; Mental suggestion
RG ———; s.a. Free will and determinism; Self
NYT PHILOSOPHY
PAIS PHILOSOPHY; s.a. Psychology
BPI PHILOSOPHY; s.a. Psychology

WILLS
LC ———, s.a. Charitable uses, trusts and foundations; Decedents' estates; Disinheritance; Legacies
SEARS ———; s.a. Genealogy; Inheritance and succession; Property; Trust companies; Trusts and trustees
RG ———; s.a. Estate planning; Executors and administrators; Inheritance
NYT WILLS AND ESTATES; s.a. Deaths; Taxation—Federal—Inheritance and estate taxes
PAIS ———; s.a. Election (wills); Probate courts
BPI ———; s.a. Estates (law); Probate law

WIND EROSION. *Use* Erosion

WIND POWER. *Use* Natural Resources

WIND TUNNELS. *Use* Aerodynamics

WINDOW GARDENING. *Use* Gardening

WINDS. *Use* Atmosphere; Weather

WINE INDUSTRY. *Use* Liquors

WINTER RESORTS. *Use* Summer Resorts; Tourist Trade; Winter Sports

WINTER SPORTS
LC ———; s.a. Iceboats; Olympic games (winter); Sleighing; Snowmobiles
SEARS ———; s.a. Hockey; Snowshoes and snowshoeing
RG ———; s.a. Skating; Toboggans and tobogganing

NYT SPORTS; s.a. Physical education and training; Skiing
PAIS ———; s.a. Sports; Winter resorts
BPI ———; s.a. Skis and skiing; Sports

WIRE-TAPPING
LC ———; s.a. Eavesdropping; Evidence (law); Telephone—Laws and regulations
SEARS WIRE TAPPING; s.a. Eavesdropping; Criminal investigation; Privacy, Right of
RG WIRE TAPPING; s.a. Electronics in criminal investigation, espionage, etc.; Espionage
NYT WIRETAPPING AND OTHER EAVESDROPPING DEVICES AND METHODS; s.a. Crime and criminals; Telephones—U. S.; U. S.—Politics and government
PAIS WIRE TAPPING; s.a. Eavesdropping; Electronics in criminal investigation, espionage, etc.
BPI WIRE TAPPING; s.a. Criminal investigation; Politics, Corruption in

WISDOM
LC ———; s.a. Experience; Intellect; Judgment; Learning and scholarship
SEARS REASON; s.a. Intellect; Thought and thinking
RG ———; s.a. Genius; Judgment
NYT PSYCHOLOGY AND PSYCHOLOGISTS; s.a. Intelligence; Mind
PAIS INTELLIGENCE; s.a. Learning and scholarship; Thought and thinking
BPI JUDGMENT; s.a. Common sense; Intelligence

WIT AND HUMOR
See also American wit and humor; English wit and humor; College wit and humor; and subd. *Anecdotes, facetiae, satire, etc.* under subjects, e.g., Music—Anecdotes, facetiae, satire, etc.
LC ———; s.a. Comedy; Humorists; Irony; Political satire; Practical jokes; Table talk
SEARS ———; s.a. Anecdotes; Nonsense verse; Parody; Satire
RG HUMOR; s.a. Caricatures and cartoons; Humorists; Laughter; Puns and punning; Satire
NYT HUMOR AND WIT; s.a. Books and literature
PAIS LITERATURE; s.a. Caricatures and cartoons; Theater
BPI HUMOR; s.a. Entertainers; Literature; Satire

WIT AND HUMOR, PICTORAL. *Use* Caricatures and Cartoons

WITCHCRAFT. *Use* Occult Sciences; Taboo

WITNESSES
Scope: Works on witnesses in legal procedure.
LC ———; s.a. Cross-examinations; Evidence (law); Examination of witnesses; False testimony; Perjury
SEARS ———; s.a. Courts martial and courts of inquiry; Trials
RG ———; s.a. Evidence, Hearsay; Subpoenas; Trials (perjury)
NYT TRIALS; s.a. Courts; Law and legislation; Oaths; Perjury
PAIS ———; s.a. Criminal law; Informers (law); Self-incrimination
BPI ———; s.a. Courts; Depositions; Subpoena

WIVES. *Use* Family; Marriage Law; Woman

WOMAN
See also Women as authors; Women in literature; etc., for works on women's achievement; and names of professions with division *Women* for material on work conditions, e.g., Artists, Women; Authors, Women; etc.

LC   ——; s.a. Family; Femininity (psychology); Girls; Husband and wife; specific groups, e.g., Diplomats' wives, Navy wives, etc.; Widows; Women, Negro

SEARS   ——; s.a. Blacks; Women in the U. S.; Young women

RG   ——; s.a. Housewives; Ladies; Negro women; Single women

NYT   WOMEN; s.a. Families and family life; Housework; Negroes (in U. S.)

PAIS   WOMEN; s.a. Mothers; Wives; Women's liberation movement

BPI   WOMEN; s.a. Advertising—Women, Appeal to; Brides; Executives' wives

WOMAN—CIVIL RIGHTS. *Use* Woman—Rights of Women; Women's Liberation Movement

WOMAN—EMPLOYMENT
See note under Woman.

LC   ——; s.a. Equal pay for equal work; Manpower; Wages—Women

SEARS   ——; s.a. Discrimination in employment; Hours of labor; Labor supply

RG   ——; s.a. Business and professional women; Household employees; Married women—Employment

NYT   LABOR—U. S.—WOMEN; s.a. Day care centers; Labor—U. S.—Youth, Employment of; Women

PAIS   EMPLOYMENT—WOMEN; s.a. Business and professional women; Women in industry

BPI   WOMEN—EMPLOYMENT; s.a. Maternity benefits; Mothers—Employment

WOMAN—EQUAL RIGHTS. *Use* Equal Pay for Equal Work; Woman—Rights of Women; Women's Liberation Movement

WOMAN—HEALTH AND HYGIENE

LC   ——; s.a. Clothing and dress—Hygienic aspects; Exercise for women

SEARS   ——; s.a. Menopause; Woman—Diseases

RG   ——; s.a. Beauty, Personal; Menstruation

NYT   MEDICINE AND HEALTH—U. S.—WOMEN; s.a. Mental health and disorders; Venereal disease

PAIS   WOMEN; s.a. Health

BPI   WOMEN—HEALTH AND HYGIENE; s.a. Hygiene; Medical care

WOMAN—RIGHTS OF WOMEN

LC   ——; s.a. Married women; Widows; Woman—Legal status, laws, etc.

SEARS   WOMAN—CIVIL RIGHTS; s.a. Woman—Suffrage; Women's liberation movement

RG   WOMAN—EQUAL RIGHTS; s.a. Woman—Employment; Women's liberation movement

NYT   WOMEN—U. S.; s.a. Freedom and human rights; Labor—U. S.—Discrimination; Labor—U. S.—Women

PAIS   WOMEN—EQUAL RIGHTS; s.a. Women, Status of; Women's liberation movement

BPI   ——; s.a. Women—Employment; Women's liberation movement

WOMAN SUFFRAGE. *Use* Women's Liberation Movement

WOMAN'S VOTE. *See* Women's Liberation Movement

WOMEN. *Use* Civil Rights; Coeducation; Daughters; Education of Women; Equality; Homosexuality; Monastic and Religious Life of Women; Mothers; Woman; Woman—Health and Hygiene; Woman—Rights of Women; Women's Liberation Movement

WOMEN IN ART. *Use* Artists; Nude in Art

WOMEN IN INDUSTRY. *Use* Woman—Employment

WOMEN'S LIBERATION MOVEMENT

LC   ——; s.a. Abortion; Civil Rights; Equal pay for equal work; Equality; Femininity (psychology); Woman; Woman—History and condition of women; Woman—Social and moral questions

SEARS   ——; s.a. Woman; Woman—Civil rights; Woman—Social conditions

RG   ——; s.a. Woman—Equal rights; Woman suffrage

NYT   WOMEN; s.a. Minorities (ethnic, racial, religious); names of women's groups, e.g., Women, National organization for (NOW)

PAIS   ——; s.a. Women—Equal rights; Women, Status of

BPI   ——; s.a. Women—Employment; Women—Rights of women

WOOD AND WOOD PRODUCTS. *Use* Forests and Forestry; Paper Making and Trade; Trees

WOODWORKING. *Use* Furniture

WOOL INDUSTRY. *Use* Textile Industry and Fabrics

WORDS. *Use* Americanisms; Language and Languages; Quotations; Semantics; Terms and Phrases; Vocabulary

WORK

LC   ——; s.a. Fatigue, Mental; Industrial sociology; Manual labor; Production standards; Skilled labor; Work, Method of

SEARS   ——; s.a. Hours of work; Labor and laboring classes; Proletariat

RG   ——; s.a. Labor and laboring classes; Right to labor

NYT   LABOR; s.a. Domestic service; Service industries; White collar workers

PAIS   ——; s.a. Right to work; Technical workers

BPI   ——; s.a. Job satisfaction; Labor and laboring classes

WORK, RIGHT TO. *See* Right to Labor

WORK, THERAPEUTIC EFFECT OF. *See* Occupational Therapy

WORK COUNCILS. *Use* Works Councils

WORK DESIGN. *Use* Job Analysis

WORK EXPERIENCE. *See* Apprentices; Education, Cooperative

WORK MEASUREMENT
LC ——; s.a. Efficiency, Industrial; Production standards
SEARS JOB ANALYSIS; s.a. Motion study; Time study
RG ——; s.a. Efficiency, Industrial; Labor productivity
NYT LABOR—U. S.—PRODUCTIVITY; s.a. Management, Industrial and institutional
PAIS ——; s.a. Labor productivity; Time and motion study
BPI ——; s.a. Performance; Work sampling

WORK RELIEF
Scope: Works on public efforts to relieve unemployment.
LC ——; s.a. Cooperative societies; Economic assistance, Domestic; Full employment policies; Relief (aid)
SEARS PUBLIC WELFARE; s.a. Labor and laboring classes; Labor supply; Retraining, Occupational
RG ECONOMIC ASSISTANCE, DOMESTIC; s.a. Hard-core unemployed; Unemployment—Relief measures
NYT WELFARE WORK; s.a. Labor—U. S.—Unemployment and job market; Unemployment insurance
PAIS ——; s.a. Government business enterprises; Public works
BPI PUBLIC WORKS; s.a. Government business enterprises; Public works—Federal aid

WORK RULES. *Use* Labor Laws and Legislation

WORK STANDARDS. *See* Production Standards; Work Measurement

WORK STOPPAGES. *See* Strikes and Lockouts

WORKING CLASSES. *See* Labor and Laboring Classes; Proletariat

WORKING DAY. *See* Night Work

WORKING LIFE, LENGTH OF. *Use* Age and Employment

WORKING WOMEN. *See* Woman—Employment

WORKING-MEN'S ASSOCIATIONS. *See* Trade-unions

WORKMEN'S COMPENSATION
LC ——; s.a. Employers' liability; Insurance, Employers' liability; Liability (law); Negligence; Survivors' benefits
SEARS ——; s.a. Insurance, Social; Labor law and legislation; Occupational diseases; Occupations, Dangerous; Personal injuries
RG INSURANCE, WORKMEN'S COMPENSATION; s.a. Employers liability; Insurance, Health
NYT WORKMEN'S COMPENSATION INSURANCE; s.a. company and industry names, e.g., Eastman Kodak; Disability insurance (for sickness benefits)
PAIS ——; s.a. Insurance, Liability

BPI INSURANCE, WORKMEN'S COMPENSATION; s.a. Insurance, Accident; Insurance, Liability

WORKS COUNCILS
Scope: Works on committees of workers formed by an employer for the discussion of problems of industrial relations.
LC ——; s.a. Industrial councils; Industrial organization; Labor laws and legislation; Shop stewards
SEARS INDUSTRIAL MANAGEMENT; s.a. Collective bargaining; Employee's representation in management
RG EMPLOYEES REPRESENTATION IN MANAGEMENT; s.a. Industrial democracy; Industrial relations
NYT LABOR; s.a. Collective bargaining
PAIS ——; s.a. Employees' representation in management; Industrial relations
BPI ——; s.a. Collective bargaining; Employees representation in management; Shop stewards

WORKSHOPS. *Use* Factories; Plant Layout

WORKSHOPS FOR THE HANDICAPPED. *See* Vocational Rehabilitation

WORK-STUDY PLAN. *See* Education, Cooperative

WORLD. *See* Earth

WORLD ECONOMICS. *See* Commercial Policy; Economic Policy

WORLD GOVERNMENT. *Use* Sovereignty; State, The; World Politics

WORLD HISTORY. *Use* Current Events; History

WORLD LANGUAGE. *See* Language and Languages

WORLD MAPS. *Use* Maps

WORLD POLITICS
Scope: Historical accounts of international intercourse. Theoretical works are entered under International relations. Works dealing with bilateral relations between states are entered under the name of state with subd. *Foreign relations*, e.g., U. S.—Foreign relations—Japan.
LC ——; s.a. Eastern question; Geography, Political; Peaceful change (international relations)
SEARS ——; s.a. International organization; Political science
RG ——; s.a. Current events; Great powers
NYT INTERNATIONAL RELATIONS; s.a. United Nations; World government
PAIS ——; s.a. Geopolitics; International relations
BPI ——; s.a. Communism and democracy; Isolationism

WORLD POLITICS—1945-1965. *Use* Cold War

WORLD WAR, 1914-1918. *See* European War, 1914-1918

WORLD WAR, 1939-1945—ATROCITIES. *Use* War (International law); War Crime Trials

WORLD WAR, 1939-1945—NEGROES. *Use* Negroes as Soldiers

WORLD WAR, 1939-1945—RATIONING. *Use* Priorities, Industrial

WORLD WAR, 1939–1945—RELIGIOUS ASPECTS. *Use* War and Religion

WORLD WAR, 1939–1945 – UNDERGROUND MOVEMENTS. *Use* Guerilla Warfare; Secret Service; Spies

WORLD WAR I (1914–1918). *Use* European War, 1914–1918

WORMS, INTESTINAL AND PARASITIC. *Use* Parasites

WORRY. *Use* Anxiety; Emotions; Mental Hygiene

WORSHIP
Scope: Works on religious worship.
LC ——; s.a. Cult; Fetishism; Idols and images—Worship; Liturgies; Nature worship; Worship (religious education)
SEARS ——; s.a. Ancestor worship; Devotional exercises; Public worship; Sacrifice; Theology
RG ——; s.a. Church attendance; Prayer
NYT RELIGION AND CHURCHES; s.a. Prayers and prayer books
PAIS CHURCH ATTENDANCE; s.a. Churches; Religion
BPI RELIGION

WORTH. *Use* Value

WRAPPING MACHINES. *Use* Packaging

WRAPPING MATERIALS. *Use* Packaging

WRECKS. *See* Disasters; Maritime Law; Rescue Work

WRESTLING. *Use* Self-defense

WRITING
Scope: Works on the art and history of writing in general. See Authorship, Penmanship and Report writing for practical manuals.
LC ——; s.a. Alphabet; Autographs; Cave drawings; Ciphers; Mirror writing; Petroglyphs
SEARS ——; s.a. Cuneiform inscriptions; Hieroglyphics; Picture writing; Shorthand
RG ——; s.a. Calligraphy; Manuscripts (papyri); Paleography; Picture writing; Signatures (writing)
NYT HANDWRITING; s.a. Alphabets; Archeology and anthropology
PAIS CRYPTOGRAPHY; s.a. Archeology; Shorthand reporting
BPI ——; s.a. Archeology; Graphology

WRITING AND WRITERS. *Use* Anonyms and Pseudonyms; Biography (As a literary form); Books; Censorship; Copyright; Editing; Fiction; Letter Writing; Literature; Plots (Drama, novel, etc.); Publishers and Publishing; Report Writing; Technical Writing; Versification

WRITING-MATERIALS. *See* Office Equipment and Supplies

X

XEROGRAPHY. *Use* Photography—Printing Processes

X-RAYS. *Use* Radiotherapy

Y

YACHTS AND YACHTING. *Use* Boats and Boating; Ocean Travel

YARN. *Use* Handicraft; Textile Industry and Fabrics

YEARBOOKS. *Use* Handbooks

YELLOW DOG CONTRACT. *Use* Open and Closed Shop

YIDDISH LITERATURE. *Use* Jewish Literature

YOGA
LC ——; s.a. Fakirs; Meditation (Hinduism); Yoga, Bhakti; Yoga, Hatha
SEARS ——; s.a. Hinduism; Philosophy, Hindu; Theosophy

RG ——; s.a. Hinduism; Mysticism—Hinduism
NYT ——; s.a. Hinduism; Mystics and mysticism
PAIS HINDUISM; s.a. Hindus
BPI HINDUISM; s.a. Philosophy; Religion

YOUTH
LC ——; s.a. Adolescent boys; Adolescent girls; Age; Age (law); Teen-age marriage; Youth movement
SEARS ——; s.a. Adolescence; Blacks; Dropouts; Juvenile delinquency; Negro children; Young men; Young women
RG ——; s.a. Boys; Girls; Hippies; Negro youth
NYT CHILDREN AND YOUTH; s.a. Education and schools; Hippies; Negroes (in U.S.)

PAIS ——; s.a. Children; Negro youth; Rural youth; Young adults

BPI ——; s.a. Students; Youth market

YOUTH, BLACK. *See* Youth

YOUTH—EMPLOYMENT. *Use* Age (Law); Child Labor; Vocational Guidance

YOUTH—POLITICAL ACTIVITIES. *Use* Student Movements; Youth Movement

YOUTH AND BUSINESS. *Use* Recruiting of Employees

YOUTH AND LAW. *Use* Age (Law); Juvenile Delinquency

YOUTH HOSTELS. *Use* Tourist Trade

YOUTH MOVEMENT

LC ——; s.a. Student movements; Youth—Political activity

SEARS ——; s.a. Demonstrations; Students—Political activity

RG ——; s.a. Counter culture; Student movement

NYT CHILDREN AND YOUTH—BEHAVIOR AND TRAINING; s.a. Colleges and universities—U.S.—Student activities and conduct; Hippies

PAIS ——; s.a. Students—Political activities; Youth—Political activities

BPI YOUTH—POLITICAL DEMONSTRATIONS; s.a. Student demonstrations; Students; Youth

YOUTH-ADULT RELATIONSHIP. *Use* Conflict of Generations; Social Conflict

Z

ZEN (Sect)

LC ——; s.a. Buddhist sects; Monastic and religious life (Zen Buddhism); Temples, Zen

SEARS ZEN BUDDHISM; s.a. Buddha and Buddhism; Meditations; Spiritual life

RG ZEN BUDDHISM; s.a. Buddha and Buddhism; Diet

NYT BUDDHISM; s.a. Religion and churches

PAIS BUDDHISM

BPI RELIGION; s.a. Philosophy

ZERO POPULATION GROWTH. *Use* Population

ZIONISM

Scope: Works on the movement looking toward the creation and maintenance of a Jewish state or "national home" in Palestine.

LC ——; s.a. Balfour declaration; Israel and the Diaspora; Jews—Political and social conditions; Labor Zionism; Nationalism—Jews; Religious Zionism

SEARS ——; s.a. Jewish question; Jews—Restoration

RG ——; s.a. Jerusalem; Jewish-Arab relations

NYT IMMIGRATION AND EMIGRATION—ISRAEL; s.a. Israel; Middle East

PAIS ——; s.a. Palestine; Revisionist Zionism

BPI ISRAEL; s.a. Immigration and emigration—Israel; Investments, American—Israel

ZODIAC. *Use* Astronomy

ZONING. *Use* City Planning; Factories; Land; Ordnances, Municipal; Real Property; Regional Planning; Suburbs

ZONING MAPS. *Use* Maps

ZOO ANIMALS. *Use* Animals

ZOOLOGICAL GARDENS. *Use* Parks

ZOOLOGY, ECONOMIC

Scope: General and comprehensive works on animals injurious and beneficial to man and on the extermination of wild animals, venemous snakes, etc.

LC ——; s.a. Birds, Injurious and beneficial; Insects, Injurious and beneficial; Pests; Predatory animals

SEARS ——; s.a. Agricultural pests; Domestic animals

RG ——; s.a. Pest control; Predation (zoology)

NYT ANIMALS; s.a. names and kinds of animals; Pests and pesticides

PAIS ANIMALS; s.a. Ecology; Pesticides

BPI ANIMALS; s.a. Ecology; Pest control; Wildlife, Conservation of

ZOOS. *Use* Animals; Parks